Confronting the Yugoslav Controversies

Central European Studies

Charles W. Ingrao, senior editor
Gary B. Cohen, editor

Confronting the Yugoslav Controversies

A Scholars' Initiative

Edited by Charles Ingrao and Thomas A. Emmert

UNITED STATES INSTITUTE OF PEACE PRESS
WASHINGTON, D.C.

Purdue University Press
West Lafayette, Indiana

Printed in the United States of America. First revision.

Library of Congress Cataloging-in-Publication Data

Confronting the Yugoslav Controversies: A Scholars' Initiative / edited by Charles Ingrao and Thomas A. Emmert.
   p. cm.
 ISBN 978-1-55753-533-7
 1. Yugoslavia--History--1992-2003. 2. Former Yugoslav republics--History. 3. Yugoslavia--Ethnic relations--History--20th century. 4. Former Yugoslav republics--Ethnic relations--History--20th century. 5. Ethnic conflict--Yugoslavia--History--20th century. 6. Ethnic conflict--Former Yugoslav republics--History--20th century. 7. Yugoslav War, 1991-1995. 8. Kosovo War, 1998-1999. 9. Kosovo (Republic)--History--1980-2008. I. Ingrao, Charles W. II. Emmert, Thomas Allan, 1945-
 DR1316.C66 2009
 949.703--dc22
                       2008050130

Contents

Acknowledgments

Given the multilateral nature of this project, it is impossible to acknowledge fully all of those who contributed materially to its completion. We begin, therefore, with an apology to the many scholars, program officers, editors, journalists, and public officials who advanced the project's agenda, but whose names do not appear below.

The Scholars' Initiative began modestly enough in 1997 when our colleague Dušan Bataković expressed an interest in beginning a dialogue between Serbian and Western historians to help rebuild the professional relationships that had been destroyed by the recent wars of Yugoslav succession. It assumed a much broader scope, thanks in large part to the encouragement and financial support from a series of institutional donors. An initial grant from the U.S. Institute of Peace (USIP) and the sustained support of Daniel Serwer transformed a modest historians' dialogue into a regionwide initiative that committed a broad range of scholarly disciplines to a sustained program of public engagement. Paul McCarthy and the staff of the National Endowment for Democracy (NED) provided funds for research by successor state scholars, much as Ivan Vejvoda and the German Marshall Fund's Balkan Trust permitted us to employ a stable of ten journalists as media liaisons in every republic capital, plus Banja Luka, Novi Sad and Priština. Deans Margaret Rowe, Toby Parcel and John Contreni of Purdue University's College of Liberal Arts (CLA) filled in gaps in the funding chain, most notably by paying for roughly a quarter of the 37 trans-Atlantic trips made during the project's career; CLA donors Fred and Ruth Graf provided unrestricted funds from the college's Peace Studies program that defrayed communications costs, including maintenance of the project website. The Institute for Historical Justice and Reconciliation (IHJR) advanced modest, but essential grants as needed to fund researchers, liaisons and conference meetings during the three-year period (2005-2007) during which the SI operated under the IHJR's auspices. Finally, recent grants from the National Council for Eurasian and East European Research (NCEEER) and a second Balkan Trust grant have assured that the project will continue through the end of 2009. In addition to these donors, a number of individuals and institutions hosted a series of SI conferences and satellite meetings (see Appendix), most notably Fuada Stanković (rector, University of Novi Sad), Ambassador Jacques-Paul Klein (mission chief, UNMiBH-Sarajevo), Jason Vuic (director, Ohio State University's Center for Slavic & East European Studies),

Franz Szabo (director, University of Alberta's Canadian Centre for Austrian and Central European Studies), and Rüdiger Malli (rector, Andrássy University).

Several publishers have provided a platform for SI-commissioned publications, most notably Purdue University Press Director Thomas Bacher, and editors Steve Sabol of *Nationalities Papers* and Marie-Janine Calic of *Südosteuropa*. We also acknowledge the pre-publication receipt of Carla del Ponte's *Madame Prosecutor* through the good offices of co-author Chuck Sudetić and Other Press publisher Judith Gurewich.

Readers can consult the team mastheads and histories at the beginning of each chapter, as well as the plenary roster in the appendix for a comprehensive list of scholars (in **boldface**) who not only had unrestricted access to the process, but contributed materially to it. Nonetheless, the contributions of several team leaders, authors, and other participants bear special mention for the energy and dedication that they brought to the enterprise. In addition to her work as a team leader, Sabrina Ramet stood out in a group of scholars that included Eric Gordy, Marko Hoare, James Lyon, Dunja Melčić, James Sadkovich, and Mark Wheeler who provided detailed commentaries for most of the team chapters; in 2004, she also traveled at her own considerable expense to Sweden's Hinseberg Prison to interview ICTY inmate Biljana Plavšić. Matjaž Klemenčič undertook multiple trans-Atlantic flights in discharging his obligations, including a trip to Houston, Texas for the sole purpose of interviewing former U.S. Secretary of State James Baker. He was also one of several scholars, including Horst Haselsteiner, Dubravko Lovrenović, Gojko Mišković, Boban Petrovski, and Drago Roksandić who actively recruited scholars in their respective corners of the region. We acknowledge the special effort of those scholars who accepted the extraordinary burden of assuming leadership of a research team in mid-stream, including Marie-Janine Calic, Georg Kastner, Andrew Wachtel and Advisory Board member Gale Stokes, who readily volunteered to fill the void left by the sudden, tragic death of Dennison Rusinow.

In addition, several team leaders demonstrated considerable political courage in the face of personal attacks from nationalist colleagues in their midst. None has been more courageous than Darko Gavrilović, who undertook crucial interviews and helped observe the tenth anniversary of the July 1995 Srebrenica massacre by co-chairing public presentations in Washington, London, Novi Sad and Banja Luka, despite being labeled an "Ustasha" and CIA spy by his colleagues at the University of Banja Luka -- seven of whom petitioned to have him removed from the faculty. Nor did Dušan Janjić ever waver in refuting predictions that an ethnic Serb could never present a balanced narrative of Kosovo's decade under the Milošević regime. Chapter 7: The War in Croatia benefited from the extremely close collaboration of Serbian military historian Mile Bjelajac and Croatian sociologist Ozren Žunec. The son of a Yugoslav army general, Bjelajac had never met Ozren Žunec, who had directed Croatian military counter-intelligence during the Great Homeland War. Although it took some weeks to persuade them to establish telephone contact, they soon forged a close bond that held firm in December 2005 when three junior Croatian scholars chose to resign from their team rather than partake in the process of revising an early draft that Bjelajac had written. In a meeting in his Zagreb office, Žunec responded to the litany of personal attacks on Bjelajac by exclaiming that, having been wounded five times fighting for his country, he was determined not to witness another war. His determination was echoed hours later by Croatian President Stipe Mesić, who exclaimed that the multilateral effort that Žunec and Bjelajac personified was "exactly what we need" for building bridges between the two countries.

Whereas it is always a pleasure to acknowledge the contributions and sacrifices of friends and colleagues, we are saddened to note the passing of five of our colleagues. We initially resolved to dedicate this volume to the memory of our beloved colleague and team leader Dennison Rusinow following his death in January 2004 at the hands of an inattentive truck driver. What we could not imagine was the untimely passing of four other key project participants in the space of less than two years. Although he had only recently received his doctorate, Brian Hodson had already begun to make his mark in the field and had contributed critiques of several team drafts before dying of heart failure at age 38. Sociologist Lazar Vrkatić, who had co-organized the project's initial organizational meeting in Morović was killed a few months later at age 47 in a car crash on the Belgrade-Niš *autoput*. Belgrade law professor and human rights advocate Olga Popović-Obradović had been preparing an article on the 1974 Yugoslav constitution for the SI's special issue of *Nationalities Papers* when she was diagnosed with cancer, to which she succumbed at age 53. Branislava Stankov researched and wrote the bulk of chapter 4's treatment of crimes against women prior to her death from cancer at age 40. We hope that this volume contributes to their memory.

In Memorium

Brian Hodson
Olga Popović-Obradović
Dennison Rusinow
Branislava Stankov
Lazar Vrkatić

INTRODUCTION

❖ Charles Ingrao ❖

It was the kind of scene most people would never forget. On 10 March 1988 a car carrying two British army corporals inadvertently encountered a large funeral procession that had gathered outside a Belfast cemetery to bury three slain IRA gunmen. The crowd quickly converged on the men, who were dragged from the vehicle, beaten, stripped, and then hoisted over a wall just out of sight of security cameras, where they were summarily executed. Surely the horrific news footage that flashed on the television screen that evening was not that unusual for British or Irish viewers. But it left this American observer searching for answers. Later that evening I wrote to a dear friend and colleague at the University of Cambridge, who had just arranged for me to spend the following spring there as a visiting fellow. In the letter I advised him that, upon my arrival in Cambridge, I would ask him how the nightmare that had gripped Northern Ireland could be resolved. That moment came ten months later, as we and our wives sat comfortably around the fireplace in his living room. "Okay, Tim, what *is* the solution in Northern Ireland?" Alas, my expectations were dashed by a response that was quick, laconic, and anticlimactic: "That's just it, Charlie. There *is* no solution!"

Perhaps my friend attributed my optimism to the naïveté that often springs so readily from ignorance. After all, I was a central European historian whose focus on sectarian conflict centers on the Habsburg and Ottoman Empires rather than on a country that takes pride in its historic and cultural exceptionalism. He may have even attributed my search for answers to the maddening syndrome that afflicts so many Americans who believe that there is a solution to *every* problem for those who are willing to invest the time, energy, and resources necessary to achieve it. Indeed, native New Yorkers like me tend not only to demand answers but also to ask plaintively why the problem hasn't already been diagnosed, addressed, and resolved.

Certainly these were considerations that came to mind during that Cambridge spring and the rest of 1989 as the iron curtain came down, thereby freeing the lands and peoples of central Europe to resurrect the very nationalistic agendas

1

that had earlier helped bring down the Habsburgs and Ottomans. Whereas the ultimate dissolution of Czechoslovakia and Yugoslavia may have been inevitable, it was at least possible to discern a cause for the divisions that have promoted the creation of ethnically homogenous states—and the erection of divisions that inure their people against future political or cultural reintegration. Simply put, the peoples of former multinational polities like the Habsburg and Ottoman Empires are divided by a common history. With independence, elites across central Europe have legitimated newly created nation-states by crafting mutually exclusive, proprietary historical accounts that justify their separate existence. Inevitably, each narrative employs a different array of "truths," many of which are either distorted or blatantly untrue, while carefully excising "inconvenient facts" that promote the utility of multiethnic coexistence and justify the dissonant narrative or political agenda of other national groups. The resulting divergent recitations of history not only unite each new republic's constituent "state-forming" nationality but also sow mistrust, resentment, and even hatred between them and other peoples with whom they had previously coexisted. This has become true between Serbs and their former wartime adversaries in Bosnia, Croatia, Slovenia, and Kosovo.

Yet whereas this volume focuses on competing narratives and memory of the recent Yugoslav conflicts, it is important for us to appreciate the sheer geographic breadth of the problem. Certainly it pervades Habsburg central Europe, dividing Czechs from Germans, Poles from Ukrainians and Jews, and Hungarians from virtually all of their neighbors; it is equally evident at the other end of the multiethnic Ottoman world, pitting Turks against Armenians, Israelis against Palestinians, and Cypriots against each other. But it is also a salient issue worldwide. Seven decades of historical reflection have not bridged the chasm between the Japanese and their Chinese and Korean neighbors' memory of the rape of Nanjing and thousands of "comfort women." Nor has a half-century of independence resolved historical disputes between Indians and Pakistanis over why and how their subcontinent was partitioned.

In reality, these disputes have more in common than the immediate trauma inflicted by warfare and crimes against humanity. Aside from the Chinese–Japanese conflict, they also reflect the consequences of nation-state building in a multiethnic world, including the construction of rival narratives designed to justify the process and efficacy of separation. Moreover, all are exacerbated by the difficulty of confronting myths and inconvenient truths in an age of mass politics—particularly in democratic societies. Notwithstanding the many positive attributes of democracy and the almost universal faith that it inspires as an instrument of societal justice and stability, the greater accountability of popularly elected leaders mortgages their ability to confront and reconcile competing narratives. This is not to say that fascist and other authoritarian leaders have not also fastened on divisive nationalist discourse to strengthen their hold on power, only that they enjoy much greater leeway in suppressing, modifying, or discrediting it altogether. Thus the relative ease with which successive Soviet leaders unmasked the cult of Stalin and the insufficiency of Marxist economics, much as their Chinese counterparts could acknowledge the excesses of Mao's Cultural Revolution and, someday, the thousands of demonstrators killed in Tiananmen Square. Changing six postwar decades of Japanese schoolbooks has proven far more difficult.[1]

Thus, we present this volume on the Yugoslav tragedy with the understanding that the events of the 1990s fit within a much broader, two-century-long continuum of mass politics and media. The proprietary national narratives that have emerged have created or intensified tensions between nations and ethnic groups through the insertion of myths and the exclusion of inconvenient facts. Scholars have certainly played a significant role in this process, especially during the initial stages of state creation, to be used by successive generations of elected politicians, whether to ensure their electoral survival or expand their appeal and power. Their contribution is clearly visible in the volume's opening chapter, where proprietary nationalist narratives provided politicians with the wedge they needed to split Yugoslavia into pieces. The ensuing decade of conflict has erected further obstacles through the creation of wartime narratives that have shifted blame to other protagonists. The international community has been particularly critical of the failure of Serbia's newly democratic leaders and free media to acknowledge the substantial record of war crimes perpetrated by its military, police, and paramilitary forces. The assertion of some Serbian nationalist politicians that "all sides sinned equally" has done little to mollify either Serbia's critics in the West or its former adversaries. Yet the same can be said of the Bosnian, Croatian, and Kosovo-Albanian media, political leadership, and publics at large, who are reluctant to concede even the smallest point of their narratives of victimization to the Serbian enemy—including the admittedly far less extensive war crimes committed by their own commanders. Nor has a lengthy string of indictments for war crimes and even genocide significantly reduced the public adulation of their wartime military and political leaders—including an unsavory assortment of common criminals.[2] So long as politicians retain a de facto monopoly over public memory, perception, and interpretation, they will continue to discredit and marginalize the few independent voices that challenge them. Indeed, there exist many among the region's political and media elite who privately concede the corruption of their vocal majority's historical accounts but who nonetheless lack the courage to challenge them.

The Scholars' Initiative represents an attempt by historians and social scientists to challenge the tendentious nationalistic narratives that have succeeded so well in dividing the peoples of central Europe by exposing and discrediting each belligerent's myths about the Yugoslav conflicts while simultaneously inserting indisputable but inconvenient facts known to their former adversaries. Its work is embodied in the research of eleven teams of historians and social scientists, each of which was commissioned to focus on the most contentious issues that impede mutual understanding between the Serbs and their wartime adversaries across the new territorial and cultural frontiers of former Yugoslavia.

That said, this volume does not pretend to be all things to all people. Although the research teams have benefited from the enormous amount of extant documentary evidence and secondary sources, it is impossible to prepare a definitive account only a decade after the end of the Yugoslav wars; at the very least, that must await the release of additional memoirs, trial transcripts, and above all, official state documents currently under seal. Nor does the book pretend to resolve all of the major controversies that divide the former adversaries and their advocates, especially in the continued absence of definitive evidence. Instead, each team has indicated points of agreement, while highlighting the existence of two or more contradictory explanations or interpretations that require further research. Far from presenting the final word on the Yugoslav conflicts, we view this contribution as a first step, an initial installment in a discovery process that we hope will continue for decades as more evidence is uncovered.

Given limited financial resources and the need to minimize the volume's size and cost, we do not pretend to present a comprehensive narrative of all the key events, personalities, or other developments that one would expect in a truly comprehensive account. Rather our goal here is to focus on the targeted controversies, presented in a positivist narrative that is readily accessible to scholars and laypeople alike. Readers in search of more lengthy analysis may wish to consult the project Web site,[3] which contains rather fuller treatments drafted by the research teams prior to their abridgement for inclusion in this volume. Limited space, financial and human resources have also obliged us to bypass or minimize coverage of some controversies. We have, for example, foregone any attempt to focus on the Yugoslav conflicts' pre-Milošević origins, which surely go back to World War II, and could be traced to 1389 or even to the medieval or ancient pedigree of the region's peoples. We have also given only brief coverage to the Bosniak–Croat war, having judged—rightly or wrongly—that its legacy presents less formidable obstacles to reconciliation between those two groups than their respective conflicts with the Serbs. We have also wholly avoided interethnic tensions within Macedonia, partly because international engagement and mediation have limited their domestic impact but also because they are less vested in competing historical narratives. Finally, the incremental emergence of evidence of crimes committed against Kosovo's residual Serb minority since 1999 (particularly in March 2004), including such "late-breaking stories" as ICTY Prosecutor Carla del Ponte's allegations of KLA kidnappings and organ theft deserve to be studied more thoroughly and judiciously than has proven possible under present financial and time constraints.[4] We do, however, hope to turn to these matters in the future, much as we invite other scholars to devote their attention to them by applying some of the methodologies that we have employed here.

One controversy that does not lend itself to abridgement is the dissolution of the Socialist Federation of Yugoslavia (SFRY), which has generated far more scholarship over the past two decades than can be handled definitively in a standard book chapter. Hence, at the suggestion of political scientist Lenard Cohen, the project commissioned a special, freestanding volume dedicated exclusively to the subject that could serve as a resource in the chapter's preparation and to which the team authors can refer readers for more detailed information and analysis.[5] In addition, the same team subsequently generated three articles by historian and political scientist Sabrina Ramet that appeared in two special issues of the journals *Nationalities Papers*[6] and *Südosteuropa*,[7] which bundled a dozen case studies and reports by project participants from several teams.

Whereas we have been obliged to be selective in the choice and length of coverage, other aspects of the project have demanded that we place a premium on inclusivity. The number of controversies embraced by each research team reflects a commitment to examining all of those controversies that, in our view, preempt constructive discourse between the former belligerents. The commitment to inclusivity has also extended to project participants. Throughout its course, the project has routinely welcomed any academics, including graduate students, whose curricula vitae presented the semblance of expertise. In the end not a single successor state scholar who has sought to join the project has either been denied admission or been removed. We have, however, felt obliged to make some exceptions to the project's "open enrollment" policy. As a *scholars'* initiative, we have admitted virtually none of the many accomplished Western investigative journalists who have published significant accounts. Given the greater overlap between the two professions within some of the successor states, we have permitted the participation of some journalists from the region who hold advanced academic degrees or university faculty positions. We have also welcomed the heads of research institutes and repositories who, in some cases, do not have a doctorate in history, law, or a social science. The need to avoid real or apparent conflicts of interest has also prevented us from allowing the active participation of successor state scholars who hold high-level government positions. During the course of our work, no fewer than a dozen scholars either entered politics or were named to high-level judicial, diplomatic or foreign policy-making positions, including three scholars who had already contributed significantly to one of the team reports. Although most stayed on board and continued to enjoy access to project correspondence, all were recused from playing an active role in the preparation or criticism of the team reports after they had been nominated for government positions.

Perhaps our single greatest concern throughout the project has been to sustain a universal commitment to scholarly methodologies, most notably the impartial weighing and representation of evidence with maximum transparency. Toward this end, a detailed prospectus was drafted shortly after the project's initial organizational meeting in Morović, Serbia, in September 2001 that clearly enumerated principles, policies, and procedures for posting on the project Web site. Thereafter, key decisions were routinely disseminated to all project participants via e-mail. The research teams first convened in Sarajevo in July 2002 to draft a research agenda. The team leaders reconvened in Edmonton in September 2003 to present the first of what would become multiple drafts of the team reports. Throughout this process individual contributions and successive drafts of reports were routinely discussed at the team level before being passed on to all project participants, each of whom had the right to make detailed comments that ranged from fulsome praise to withering criticism. At the conclusion of each round of criticism, all comments were bundled together and sent in a single e-mail to every project participant so that s/he could check succeeding drafts for mandated revisions. Once a report had finally passed muster, it was immediately distributed to the media and an assortment of regional NGOs, government supporters in Washington, the EU, and the successor states to promote public awareness and discussion.

The pursuit of inclusivity, impartiality and transparency necessitated the aggressive recruitment of scholars from all eight Yugoslav entities, including a large number of scholars from Serbia, which reflects both its higher population and the existence of a distinctly Serbian narrative for all eleven controversies. Moreover, from the beginning, every research team has been codirected by *two* scholars, one of whom was invariably an ethnic Serb. This preponderance is evident in the comprehensive list of scholars that appears in the appendix, which has been organized by country to document the project's multilateral posture. We have done so, however, with the foreknowledge that our project participants cannot be easily pigeonholed by nationality, particularly the large number who are fervently antinationalist and highly critical of their regime's actions during the Yugoslav wars—including more than a few American and western European scholars! Moreover, several participants hold dual nationality, whereas others are natives of one country and citizens of another while living and working in a third. Nonetheless, we hope that, by articulating project membership by nationality, we can answer one of the most frequently asked questions that has been posed to us by laypeople, journalists, government officials, and academics in each of the successor states.

Nationality is hardly the only attribute that bears on the claim of impartiality. Funding sources have already been held up to scrutiny and interpreted—or at least represented—by some within the successor states as evidence of bias. Of course, most scholars are aware that public foundations generally give money to proposals they like but never interfere with the compilation of research or the conclusions derived from it. This was certainly the case with our donors. Nonetheless, the long list of acknowledgements includes the names of institutions that will raise eyebrows within the successor states, most notably the Serbian Ministry of Science, the provincial government of Vojvodina, the U.S. Institute of Peace (USIP), and the National Endowment for Democracy (NED).[8] If certain donors have subjected the project to guilt by association, the lack of adequate funding has posed a problem by limiting the array of languages available for publication and for posting on the project Web site. Although translations are offered online in Bosnian-Croatian-Serbian (BCS), its evolution into a trinity of three distinct languages has made it impossible to obscure the nationality of the individual translator, in most instances a Serb whose antinationalist credentials have been insufficient to prevent a priori accusations of bias by some Bosnian, Croatian, and Albanian readers. Finally, in representing place names in the text, the editors have taken refuge in the prevailing practice of employing prewar nomenclature (Kosovo rather than Kosova or Kosovo-Metohija; Priština, not Prishtinë; Foča, not Srbinje or other postwar innovations employed in *Republika Srpska*).

The commitment to transparency extends to the presentation of the team reports, which appear here in chapter format and are prefaced by a roster of all team members who enjoyed access to every step of the research and writing process. Because there was a wide variation in levels of participation, the names of those who actively contributed to the process of shaping the chapter are listed in boldface; additionally, the chapter masthead is accompanied by a brief team history that identifies personnel developments, satellite meetings, the apportionment of research stipends, and specific contributions by individual team members. The plenary roster of all project participants posted in the appendix likewise distinguishes between access and activity, while listing the years during which each scholar joined and, in some cases, left the project.

Finally, we should define the meaning of membership because it does not necessarily represent active contributions by each individual listed on the plenary roster or unanimous agreement by all project participants. Rather, it represents the names of all those scholars who enjoyed open access to the process, with the right to see and comment on every draft once it left the team and was posted to the project at large for additional comment and criticism. In reality, many of the scholars listed on the plenary roster were content to observe (and, in some cases, ignore) the intensive discussion of team drafts, even though they did not necessarily agree with everything within them. For sake of greater clarity, we have endeavored to identify as best we can those scholars who did contribute materially, whether by commenting, participating in a team or plenary meeting, conducting interviews or other research, or making a written contribution to any of the successive drafts or collateral SI publications.

By contrast, team membership represented a closer affiliation with the chapters that appear in this volume, if only because members had the right to insist on the inclusion of relevant publications, documentation, or arguments as they inspected every draft. With one exception, the team leaders and principal authors worked hard to accommodate team members' requests, whether by integrating their contributions or by mentioning the lack of unanimity on some issues and listing alternative views. In one instance, a principal author who had successfully pressed for changes in several of the other team drafts withdrew from the project rather than address criticisms and incorporate contributions by fellow team members. As a rule, however, the numerous face-to-face meetings between scholars have been attended by a high degree of mutual respect and collegiality, during which participants have generally achieved a consensus on the evidence that governs most major controversies. This is not to say that individual participants have not sometimes felt uncomfortable about the resolution of one controversy or another that reflected poorly on their country or national group. Although team members had the right to insist that the final report address their concerns by representing their position, perhaps a half dozen chose instead to resign from their team (and, on occasion, from the project) in order to express either their dissatisfaction with an interim draft or their apprehension over the consequences that its eventual publication might have on their career prospects.

The selection of team leaders also requires some explanation. From the very beginning we have recognized and appreciated the role that Western scholars could play in this project, whether in facilitating the interactions between their colleagues from the successor states or in codirecting some of the research teams. On the surface at least, their greater distance from the horrors of the Yugoslav wars suggested that it might be easier for them to withstand both the pull of national loyalties and the pressure of institutional politics. Yet the project has always been committed to maximizing interaction between successor state scholars and to securing public acceptance of the SI's findings within their countries, which would be best served by promoting a greater sense of ownership in the process. Hence, our hope to enlist as many successor state scholars as possible to the point of affording them right of first refusal.

This was not that easy. At the time there were few successor state scholars with established reputations about a war that had just ended; many who had were already invested in nationalist discourse that would be hard to revise or repudiate and, in several cases, committed to careers in government and politics that wholly foreclosed their participation. We were, however, pleased to discover that there were many Serbian scholars eager to strike out on a fresh path in conjunction with their colleagues across the successor states, western Europe, and the Atlantic.

Nor was it particularly difficult finding Croatian and Slovenian scholars, whose countries had emerged triumphant from the wars and had somewhat greater access to institutional financial support. Actively engaging Bosnian and Kosovo Albanian scholars proved much more difficult. One reason was that foreign governments, international organizations, and NGOs had established literally hundreds of missions in the postwar Bosnian Federation and Kosovo that offered alternative income sources for well-educated professionals who were conversant in English and other western European languages. The SI could not compete with them with the modest sums at its disposal, with the result that several scholars in the Federation and Kosovo politely declined our invitations to become team leaders or research stipendiaries. Another problem was the devastating human toll that ethnic cleansing had exacted there. From the beginning there was somewhat less enthusiasm for engaging with Serbian scholars, a reluctance among Kosovo Albanians that was abetted by the desire to achieve independence from Belgrade. Hence, whereas we were ultimately able to engage ethnic Serb scholars to codirect each research team, the final roster of team leaders included prominent scholars from Albania, Croatia, and Slovenia, together with eight from the U.S., Germany, Great Britain, and New Zealand—but none from the Federation or Kosovo. It is difficult to overstate the effort that they have expended and the contribution that they have made in producing this volume. The process of revising and expanding the initial drafts at the Edmonton meeting lasted four years until the approval of the last of the team reports in the fall of 2007, after which some teams undertook additional changes in response to comments by four outside referees. Most reports went through eight to ten drafts before successfully passing through the highly public and sometimes humbling projectwide review that came to be known as the Gauntlet. Four reports needed to be totally rewritten, including one that went through three wholly new drafts, each written by a different team member until it finally passed muster. A fifth needed to be replaced after the principal author declined to incorporate contributions by some team members or carry out changes mandated by the outside referees.

This is not to say that we are as yet wholly satisfied with the product published here. As stated earlier, we present this volume as a first installment in a process that will surely benefit from further research, pending access to additional funding and the appearance of new sources. At this point we invite the reader to examine what the teams have concluded based on evidence that we have judged valid. Although we seek a consensus, we also expect criticism, which we regard as an integral part of this process. We only ask that the criticism be backed by evidence and logic, not by "patriotic" appeals or special pleading that has no place in scholarly discourse. We also invite criticism of the project's design and implementation, which was actually the most challenging task we faced in bringing so many scholars together to work toward a common goal.

Nor should other scholars who have not heretofore participated feel that their only recourse is to criticize either the project or its results from a distance. Rather, they should feel free to join the process, not only through constructive criticism but through active participation in the project's subsequent public outreach—whether by engaging in future public presentations or by joining in the research and writing of later updates, whether on the Web or in later published editions. In return we ask only that their engagement adhere to the same level of collegiality that has characterized our activities to date. This invitation applies especially to scholars from the successor states—and, above all, to those from Bosnia and Kosovo—who we hope will ultimately assume full ownership of every phase of this enterprise. Admittedly, few Western societies have suffered so severely from the tyranny of mythmaking and selective memory that cultural elites have imposed on the public and their elected representatives. Yet we should all feel an obligation to confront it.

Notes

1   Charles Ingrao, "Weapons of Mass Instruction: Schoolbooks and Democratization in Central Europe," *Contexts: The Journal of Educational Media, Memory and Society* 1, no. 1 (Spring 2009), 199–200.

2   Tihomir Loža, "Honoring the Dead," *Transitions Online,* 10 July 2007, www.tol.cz *(accessed 18 July 2007).*

3   www.cla.purdue.edu/si.

4   Carla del Ponte and Chuck Sudetic, *Madame Prosecutor* (New York: Other Press, 2009), 273-303.

5   Lenard Cohen and Jasna Dragović-Soso, eds., *State Collapse in South-Eastern Europe: New Perspectives on Yugoslavia's Disintegration* (West Lafayette, IN: Purdue University Press, 2008).

6   Sabrina Ramet, "Explaining the Yugoslav Meltdown, 1: 'For a Charm of Pow'rful Trouble, Like a Hell-broth Boil and Bubble': Theories about the Roots of the Yugoslav Troubles," and "Explaining the Yugoslav Meltdown, 2: A Theory about the Causes of the Yugoslav Meltdown: The Serbian National Awakening as a 'Revitalization Movement,'" in Thomas Emmert and Charles Ingrao, eds., "Resolving the Yugoslav Controversies: A Scholars' Initiative," special issue, *Nationalities Papers* 32, no. 4 (2004), 731–779, republished as *Conflict in Southeastern Europe at the End of the Twentieth Century: A Scholars' Initiative* (New York and London: Routledge, 2006).

7   Sabrina Ramet, "The Dissolution of Yugoslavia: Competing Narratives of Resentment and Blame," *Südosteuropa* 55 (2007), 26–69.

8   Thus a column suggesting that the SI and its USIP and NED were tools of the U.S. State Department, the Pentagon, Richard Holbrooke, and Wesley Clark. Miroslav Lazanski, "Gnjilane u Virdžiniji," *Politika,* 17 February 2007 (for translation by BBC Monitoring European, see "Serbian Commentary Slams Scholars' Project on 'Rewriting' Balkan History," 20 February 2007, *www.cla.purdue.edu/SI/Politika_Article_17.Feb.07).*

1

Latinka Perović, team leader
Andrew Wachtel, team leader

Christopher Bennett	Tvrtko Jakovina	Davorka Matić
Mark Biondich	Goran Jovanović	Louis Sell
Audrey Helfant Budding	**Dejan Jović**	Predrag Simić
Cathie Carmichael	**Matjaž Klemenčič**	Arnold Suppan
Dušan Djordjevich	**Todor Kuljić**	Ljubinka Trgovčević
Danica Fink-Hafner	Tomaz Mastnak	Frances Trix
Eric Gordy		**Mitja Žagar**

This chapter rests substantially on scholarship commissioned by the Scholars' Initiative, most notably Lenard Cohen and Jasna Dragović-Soso, eds., *State Collapse in South-Eastern Europe: New Perspectives on Yugoslavia's Disintegration* (West Lafayette, IN: Purdue University Press, 2008), and on a series of articles by Sabrina P. Ramet that appeared in special issues of *Südosteuropa* 55 (2007), and *Nationalities Papers* 32/4 (December 2004), which was subsequently republished in Thomas Emmert and Charles Ingrao, eds., *Conflict in Southeastern Europe at the End of the Twentieth Century: A Scholars' Initiative* (New York & London: Routledge, 2006). The National Endowment for Democracy provided funds for individual research conducted by Dejan Jović. In writing the final draft Andrew Wachtel focused on the preconditions and causes of Yugoslavia's dissolution, Christopher Bennett on the complex chronology of the breakup.

The team benefited from the earlier leadership of Lenard Cohen and Jasna Dragović-Soso (2001-2004), and Sabrina Ramet (2004-2008), as well as from extensive comment and criticism during project-wide reviews in March-April 2004 and January 2005, from the four anonymous outside referees engaged by the publishers in 2007-2008, and by several team members who assisted in addressing their concerns in the final draft published here.

The Dissolution of Yugoslavia

◆ Andrew Wachtel and Christopher Bennett ◆

The violent breakup of Yugoslavia in the early 1990s occasioned a great deal of writing, both popular and scholarly. By now, at least in the academic community, there is substantial agreement as to the causes and chronology of the dissolution, though this has not necessarily trickled down to the popular level (particularly in the independent states that emerged from the carnage). This chapter is not meant to add significantly to the scholarship on this topic. Rather, it sums up much research that has been done by other scholars and represents, we believe, a broad consensus within the profession. Insofar as it can claim originality, it is solely in the metaphor we will use to describe the process.

There is certainly no denying that Yugoslavia always faced multiple threats to its stability and longevity. Explaining its demise is, therefore, no simple task. A metaphor drawn from medicine will be helpful to understand our overall understanding of the issue. When a human being dies it is sometimes the case that a single cause of death can be established: heart failure, a stroke, for example. In other cases, however, multiple organ systems fail more or less simultaneously in a cascading series of disasters. Death, when it occurs, cannot be ascribed to loss of liver or kidney function but to the combination of interlinked failures whose origins can often be seen to stretch back relatively far into the past, well before the final crisis began. The collapse of Yugoslavia in the early 1990s is analogous to a case of multiple organ failure. The patient had been in delicate health for some time. Although its ailments were not necessarily terminal, its survival required constant attention and careful treatment by a devoted staff of caregivers.

Looking back, the historian can easily find chronic weakness in the Yugoslav body politic's political, economic, and cultural systems. That it survived without serious threat for its first four decades was due largely to the adeptness of Marshal Tito and the men who succeeded him. Their work was undone during the period 1985–1990 by a particular concatenation of circumstances that pushed the patient from a chronic to an acute stage of disease, leading eventually and seemingly inevitably to the equivalent of multiple organ failure and death.

Nevertheless, history is not teleology; death was not necessarily inevitable, for at various points interventions that could have been undertaken might have averted the eventual catastrophe, though there is of course no guarantee.

Admittedly there are those historians who believe in teleology (at least implicitly) and believe whatever aspect of history they study is the ultimate driver of events. This can lead to two problems that we will try to avoid here. First, working back from a particular moment (in this case the collapse of Yugoslavia, but we could equally be discussing the outbreak of World War I or the French Revolution), historians tend to show why that outcome was inevitable, ignoring the paths not taken and opportunities missed that potentially could have led to other scenarios. Second, like medical subspecialists, historians tend to give pride of place to their own objects of study. So although political historians may well recognize that many factors were involved in the demise of Yugoslavia, they will tend to conclude that, in the end, it was political failure that drove the state to its death, just as a cardiologist might tend to think that while multiple organs were affected, in the end it was the heart that stopped. In this chapter we will write like a pathologist, attempting on the basis of the research of a wide variety of "single organ specialists" to reconstruct the complex sequence of events that led to the death of the patient called Yugoslavia while simultaneously pointing out moments when other interventions could have been tried.

Our reconstruction will focus on three spheres whose long-term problems put the Yugoslav state in a vulnerable position entering the late 1980s: these can be called broadly the political (the perceived illegitimacy or at least ineffectiveness of the central state and rise of competing power centers within the country), the economic (the inability of Communist states in general and the Yugoslav state in particular to generate wealth and provide sufficient economic opportunity and prosperity for its citizens), and cultural (the inability or unwillingness of the Yugoslav state to create a sufficiently large group of citizens with a shared national identity and the existence and growth of separate national narratives that directly competed with, and eventually overwhelmed, the Yugoslav narrative). We also recognize that a series of endogenous and exogenous shocks in the late 1980s and very early 1990s drove the patient from a chronic to an acute and ultimately incurable state of disease. Among the latter we will point to a new geopolitical climate created by the weakening of the USSR and especially the strengthening of the EU, which spurred the ambitions and actions of leading local political and cultural actors.

In the case of state collapse, as in our analogy of death, there is always a tendency to try to understand the outcome by delving deep into the past, into the genetics of the state, as it were. One could, in principle, start from the murky moment when separate groups of Slavic invaders entered the Balkans in the sixth and seventh centuries AD. Although few writers have chosen to go that far back, many commentators, particularly in the popular press, did try to explain the destruction of Yugoslavia through recourse to some variation of the "ancient hatreds" argument—Yugoslavia fell apart because its constituent peoples had from time immemorial disliked each other and had only been waiting for an opportunity to get at each other's throats within the "artificial" creation of Yugoslavia. This explanation has generally been rejected by serious historians for two separate reasons. First, it is possible to find evidence of earlier animosity between or among a variety of groups within many existing states, yet these animosities do not inevitably lead to conflict in the present—think of the bloody battles between German-speaking Protestants and Catholics, for example, or the North and the South in the United States as recently as the 1860s. Second, at least in the case of Yugoslavia, it is difficult to find examples of sustained interethnic conflict before the modern period.

Although the "hatred" that drove Yugoslavia to its death may not have been ancient, this does not mean that its roots are to be discovered only in the very recent past. There is a good deal of scholarly consensus that the experience of the first Yugoslav state, which came into existence at the end of World War I, is relevant to understanding the prehistory of the disease that killed the patient in the early 1990s. Although the new state was born with high optimism, serious political problems surfaced quickly, particularly a tension between the Serbs' vision of a tightly centralized, unitary state and the federal model sought by Croats and, to a lesser extent, by Slovenes.[1] These political problems, which plagued the state almost throughout its entire existence and which ultimately proved insoluble in the interwar period, were documented extensively by Ivo Banac in his classic study *The National Question in Yugoslavia*.[2] Of course, if South Slav unitarism irritated some Croats and Slovenes, nonconstituent peoples in the first Yugoslavia (like the Albanians, Muslim Slavs, Macedonians, Hungarians, and Germans) had even less reason to be satisfied with their lot. The political weakness of the interwar Yugoslav state certainly made its destruction at the hands of the Axis powers easier in 1941, and the distrust and hatred among ethnic groups within Yugoslavia was exploited by the occupying powers between 1941 and 1945.[3]

Important as the interwar period was to creating the background conditions for the formation of the post-World War II Communist state, the development of that state itself is far more crucial to understanding the bases for Yugoslav collapse in the 1990s. The Communist-led government that came to power in the aftermath of World War II was well aware of the savage intertribal fighting that had claimed at least one half of the total casualties sustained among Yugoslavs. They believed, and probably correctly, that the roots of this fighting lay in the failure of interwar Yugoslavia, particularly the constant conflict between Serbs and non-Serbs, which had been its most characteristic and tragic feature. In the political arena, there had certainly been ample cause for resentment, as the

Belgrade government had undoubtedly—sometimes with malice aforethought, sometimes not—slighted Yugoslavia's non-Serbian citizens. In the cultural arena, the situation had been far less dire, but there remained a deeply held suspicion on the part of many non-Serbs that Yugoslav nation building, particularly state-sanctioned Yugoslav nation building, had in fact been nothing more than an attempt to Serbianize the country.

Tito and his followers were not about to repeat the mistakes of the royal administration, but neither were they prepared to give up control over the country as a whole. Their political solution was the paper creation of a federal system (as enshrined in the 1946 constitution) in which equal rights were vested in six national republics (Croatia, Slovenia, Montenegro, Macedonia, Bosnia-Hercegovina, and Serbia, with the latter including the autonomous province of Vojvodina and the autonomous region of Kosovo-Metohija). At the same time, central control was assured by reserving true political power in the country for the fully centralized Communist Party. Thus, as one historian put it succinctly: "A study of the formal constitutional provisions does not convey the reality of Yugoslav society in the early post-war years. Just as the autonomy of the republics and the communes was severely circumscribed by the centralised nature of the administrative hierarchy, so the structure of government was controlled by the Communist Party."[4]

Regarding the "national question" the new government trod a fine line. Before the war, the Communist Party of Yugoslavia had been a strong supporter of unitarist Yugoslavism, even before such a policy had officially been embraced by the government.[5] And although the Communists' attitudes toward unitarism wavered during the thirties, they never really abandoned it.[6] However, the Yugoslavism envisioned by the Communists was, at least theoretically, quite different from that proposed by most other interwar unitarists. Interwar unitarism had been based fundamentally on a racial principle: the three constituent Yugoslav peoples were seen as one, and differences between them were ultimately inessential. The goal of the majority of the unitarists, therefore, was to effect a synthesis of the separate national cultures into a new Yugoslav culture, thereby recreating a unified Yugoslav people and nation. The Communists, on the other hand, "maintained that the creation of a new supranational 'universal' culture was fully compatible with the flourishing of individual 'national cultures' in a particular multiethnic country."[7] Such a supranational culture went beyond the national to the ideological, and it would overarch and connect the national cultures rather than eliminate them. As such it was potentially sympathetic to a variety of supranational strategies that had arisen during the interwar years as a challenge to the vision of a unified multicultural Yugoslavia.

During World War II, of course, rather little could be done to establish a supranational organization. Although the central committee of the Yugoslav Communist Party continued to function during the war, the partisan groups that did the bulk of the fighting were organized on the local, rather than the national level. This policy was dictated by the conditions of German, Italian, Bulgarian, and Hungarian occupation, which made reliable communications with any center difficult and at times impossible. It was also an effective strategy to rally members of the various nationalities, many of whom were suspicious of integrationist tendencies.[8] Nevertheless, the Communists always envisioned the creation of a single postwar state rather than a collection of independent Yugoslav nations. Their slogan during and after the war embodied this dualism; they fought for "the brotherhood and unity of the peoples of Yugoslavia."

This locution was clearly meant to be a replacement of the concept of the "three-named people" that had dominated the royal government's attitude toward the national question, and it had a number of advantages. First of all, it could be interpreted as being more inclusive because the "peoples of Yugoslavia" were clearly a more diverse group than the Slovenes, Serbs, and Croats who had been the only recognized source for Yugoslavs in the interwar period. Certainly, the national idea had now expanded to include Montenegrins and Macedonians (officially recognized for the first time as a separate South Slavic people), and by the early 1960s it had expanded further with the recognition of the Bosnian Muslims as a national group. Even non-Slavic groups were theoretically included, although the retention of the country's name called this into question.[9] Second, the plural *peoples* rather than the singular *people* implied a recognition of and tolerance for diversity. No longer was the goal of the country to be the recreation of a unified ethnos. Rather, any unity would have to be created on some other basis, at least theoretically.

Examined closely, however, "brotherhood and unity" was no less problematic a formula than the Trinitarian one it superseded. After all, unless brotherhood and unity are understood to refer to separate things, the slogan is an oxymoron. Unity, if it could be achieved, would result in full agreement and synthesis, whereas brotherhood, although it certainly emphasizes closeness, implies difference and potential disagreements of all kinds. In addition, and in this respect there was little difference between the interwar and postwar formulations, the citizens of the country were still viewed primarily as members of a given people. The state was understood to be constituted by agreements among the peoples rather than as an aggregate of individuals each one of which had, in theory, a direct contractual relation to the state. In this context, personal and cultural realization was conceived as possible only within a national envelope. To be sure, the envelopes were more numerous than before, but the country was still oriented toward communitarian rather than individual values. This would prove a major problem in the 1960s, when federal structures weakened.

Throughout most of the 1950s, the authorities tried to make it appear that the centripetal force of brotherhood and the centrifugal force of unity were in equilibrium, but this balance was more apparent than real. Particularly in the years after the split with Stalin when Yugoslavia felt itself to be entirely surrounded by hostile states, unity was the far more important element, and the central government tended to control all significant activities. What is more, even in the cultural sphere the expectation was that some kind of homogenization would eventually occur, even if it was not being forced and even if it did not require the elimination of the national cultures.[10] Indeed, such an outcome was in keeping with the general principles of Tito and the men surrounding him who had from the very beginning "felt that Yugoslavia would be unified, solid, that one needed to respect languages, cultural differences, and all specificities which exist, but that they are not essential, and that they can't undermine the whole and the vitality of the country."[11] Nevertheless, and this is crucial, the maintenance of central control was made a great deal easier by the presence of an attractive new national formula that helped convince Yugoslavia's citizens that the government was not merely replaying prewar unitarism.

Any discussion of the basic conditions leading to Yugoslavia's breakup must truly begin from the moment when the balance of power began to shift from unity to brotherhood. Depending on a given scholar's set of interests and point of view, the effects of this change can be felt in the political, economic, and cultural spheres. They can also be seen to have released previously suppressed (or repressed, depending on one's point of view) underlying visions of the Yugoslav state and its premises that were held by the various national groups within the state. Let us start with cultural issues and then move on to political and economic ones.

States experience economic and/or political collapse, but they do not always fission into their various constituent parts. Yugoslavia did so. In great measure this occurred because sufficient numbers of people holding Yugoslav citizenship stopped thinking of themselves as Yugoslavs (if they ever had done so) and saw themselves instead as Croats, Serbs, Slovenes, Macedonians, and so forth. To be sure, even the most seemingly homogeneous states, when examined closely, turn out to have significant potential differences, be they regional, dialectical, confessional, class, or other. But when crisis comes, a sufficient number of citizens (never all, to be sure) decide that "we are all in this together" and choose to overlook those differences in favor of the nation as a whole. There are two main reasons why this did not happen in the 1980s in Yugoslavia—historical (members of the various sub-Yugoslav groups had held competing national identities for long periods of time) and educational/cultural (the Yugoslav state had always been ambivalent about the project of creating a Yugoslav national identity and by the 1960s had pretty much abandoned the project, hoping that ideological and economic integration would break down particularist identities over time).

Scholars have offered a number of additional insights about why the expected class-based solidarity envisioned by theoreticians of Communism was eventually trumped by particularist nationalism. In the specific case of Yugoslavia, part of the problem was in the initial design of the country, which, as Audrey Helfant Budding points out, was organized in contradictory ways: "no single criterion guided the Partisans' decisions either in creating federal units or in drawing their borders. Considerations of historical precedent, ethnonational demarcation, economic development and political reliability all played their parts."[12] Even so, most of the Yugoslav republics and provinces were in fact constituted around an ethnic majority (Bosnia-Hercegovina, with its mixed population of Muslims, Serbs, and Croats, was the great exception). As long as the state was governed by a centralized Communist Party, these decisions were not particularly important, but a series of power struggles in the course of the 1960s saw centralists (as represented by Aleksandar Ranković and others) lose out to decentralizers (led by Slovene Edvard Kardelj). In discussing the constitutional changes that provided the legislative structure for the decentralization, Helfant Budding notes: "Yugoslavia's constitutional decentralization occurred on the *territorial* level. Republics and provinces, not nations, gained greater independence in their own actions and greater control over decisions taken at the federal center. The process was legitimated, however, with reference to *national* rights and *national* equality."[13]

The political fragmentation of the country was mirrored in its economy, where republicanization took place rapidly from the late 1960s on. As John Allcock put it: "The steady republicanization of the economy, however, meant that the commitment of liberals to widening the scope of market forces came increasingly to be posed in terms of a conflict of interests between the federation and the republics. As republics were readily conceptualized in national terms, the dispute over economic modernization came to be represented (certainly in popular and journalistic discourse) as a matter of the adverse effects of the power of 'Belgrade,' working together with the 'backward South' (Bosnia-Hercegovina, Macedonia, Montenegro), upon the economic development of the 'advanced' North (Croatia and Slovenia). Economic modernization thereby came to be linked generally to the forces of nationalism which the Tito regime had worked so hard since 1945 to defeat."[14]

Dejan Jović has done important work to explain why the decentralizers eventually won the day. He focuses on the need for the Yugoslav state to distinguish itself on the one hand from the USSR and on the other from the interwar "bourgeois" Yugoslav state. "Kardelj's main argument linked the ideology of antistatism with identity and sovereignty of Yugoslavia. He argued that Yugoslavia would not be different from the two antipodes (inter-war Yugoslavia and Soviet socialism) unless it was further decentralized. The main goal of socialism was that everyone decided upon the results of their labour. This principle applied to nations as well."[15] Kardelj's victory, however, as enshrined in the Yugoslav Constitution of 1974, was pyrrhic. In Jović's view, then, the Yugoslav state "withered away" to be replaced by republican governments, which became increasingly in thrall to nationalist sentiment. The central state was so weakened that it became unable to compete with the much stronger Republican governments, particularly after the death of the great centralizer Tito in 1980.

It is important to recognize that these processes (political and economic) of fragmentation along republican lines took place in the context of a state that had never been economically self-sustaining. As Michael Palairet points out: "Ever since 1945, the economic ambitions of the Yugoslav regime had consistently outrun the resources that its socialized sector could generate. Therefore, this sector had to draw on resources external to it, mainly resources external to Yugoslavia."[16] As long as ready sources of external cash were available (which took the form of foreign aid, borrowing, and/or remittances from Yugoslavs working abroad) to help float the economy, economic problems could remain under the radar screen. By the mid-1970s, however, international credit tightened, remittances declined as the European economies faltered, and real economic strains began to become apparent.

Thus, by the middle to late 1970s, Yugoslavia had changed from a country marked by brotherhood and unity with the emphasis on the latter, to a society with very little unity and with brotherhood more in principle than in fact. Indeed, as Sabrina Ramet showed in her important book *Nationalism and Federalism in Yugoslavia*, from the 1970s forward, the separate Yugoslav republics behaved in great measure as if they were independent entities whose priority was to maximize the well-being of their inhabitants, regardless of the effect that this might have on the country as a whole.

In this environment, the various peoples of Yugoslavia began to remember (or were encouraged to recall) a series of grievances that they interpreted in national terms. For although the call to rebuild the country in the spirit of socialist cooperation had succeeded for a few decades in convincing people to ignore their differences, it could not completely overcome the fact that the various peoples of Yugoslavia held varied and often incompatible stories about the state and their involvement in it. The absence of a federal education system after 1948 and the fact that important topics relating to history and culture could be and were taught quite differently in the different republics meant that these various national points of view were never harmonized in a coherent way during the existence of Communist Yugoslavia.[17]

In the case of the Serbs, the national narrative centered around the "sacrifices" they had made in creating Yugoslavia after World War I and about their supposedly disadvantaged position in the Communist state. These concerns fed into a longer-term Serb narrative that focused on Serbian suffering and heroism, which in some quarters was traced all the way back to the fateful Battle of Kosovo in 1389.[18] Drawing on folk poetry in which the loss of this battle was depicted as an apocalyptic choice of the Kingdom of Heaven over the Kingdom of Earth, Serbian thinkers and writers created the image of Serbia as a martyr nation that was constantly being asked to spill its blood for the sake of others without receiving the benefits that should accrue for such heroism.

The popular novel *Knjiga o Milutinu* (*A Book about Milutin*, 1985) by Danko Popović provides an excellent example of this sort of thinking.[19] The majority of the novel consists of a monologue by the title character. Imprisoned after World War II as a kulak, although merely the owner of a small farm, he tells his life story in a thick peasant dialect. He recounts the deaths of his father and brothers in the Balkan Wars, his experiences as a soldier during World War I, the hard lot of his life as a farmer in interwar Yugoslavia, and his efforts to save his son, who is eventually killed during World War II. The novel ends with a short section in which a prison comrade describes Milutin's death.

A Book about Milutin is, however, little more than a pretext on which to string a litany of complaints and questions, most of which have to do with Serbia's alleged tendencies to sacrifice its own interests for the sake of others, and the ungratefulness of those for whose sake the sacrifices were made. Milutin's suspicions about the wisdom of the Yugoslav idea date from before the beginning of World War I, but his common-sense opposition to unification is shown to be opposed by intellectuals—in this case, the village teacher. After hearing about the "heroic" assassination of Franz Ferdinand, our hero says: "It just don't seem right to me. I don't like this empty heroing of them Bosnians, killing off princes and their wives, and afterwards hiding their asses so our peasants have to pay the piper, ain't that it? . . . But the teacher just went on. There, he goes, in Bosnia and the other places where our brothers, the Southern Slavs live the uprising has all but burst into flames up. 'From your mouth to god's ears, teach'—and I go out into the fields, but I don't believe in no Slavs. . . . I hear, our brothers, but my brother already died for some 'our brother.'"[20]

Milutin's rambling monologue provides plenty of fictional ammunition for the standard Serbian anti-Yugoslav claim: that the other South Slavic nations are happy to allow the Serbs to do their fighting for them, something that the naive and idealistic Serbs have continually done to their own detriment.[21] Furthermore, it brings to the surface an even more inflammatory issue: the behavior of the Croatian Ustaša during World War II. "Well in those days, my boys, refugees came to our village. . . . I remember that one day Lazar and Vasilij came. They had taken in refugees and had heard what was happening to the Serbs in Croatia.

They told me, but I didn't want to hear. Don't you guys tell me this, I say. Pašić and Prince Aleksandar, Colonel Garašanin and Mladen should hear this. It's they built this big country."[22]

By the mid-1980s, however, the dissatisfaction of Serb intellectuals and political figures with the state of affairs in Yugoslavia revolved ever more frequently around the issue of Kosovo. The population of this territory, the incorporation of which had been Serbia's national obsession in the nineteenth century, had become increasingly Albanian in the course of the existence of the Communist state. Although there were a number of reasons for this demographic shift, many Serbs tended to believe in a variety of conspiracy theories and to focus on a few incidents of mistreatment of Serbs in the region. The most notorious expression of these theories was the draft memorandum written by a number of members of the Serbian Academy of Arts and Sciences (SANU). Never officially published, the text was leaked to the press in 1986 and became a cause célèbre. Although the memorandum was ostensibly written to find a way to preserve the integrity of Yugoslavia, its authors spent most of the document proving that Tito's Yugoslavia had discriminated against Serbs in a variety of ways, supposedly permitting Serbia's economic subjugation to Croatia and Slovenia as well as the "genocide" perpetrated by the Albanians against the Serbs of Kosovo.[23]

By contrast, Croatian discourse tended to reject or minimize Serb suffering, substituting its own narrative of victimization. Although the list of grievances stretched as far back as the unwelcome Serb colonization of Croatia's Krajina frontier in early modern times, they crystallized around the charge that Yugoslavia had been merely a mask for Serbian hegemony. From the adoption of the first Vidovdan Constitution in 1921 to the abrupt cancellation of the constitutional compromise of 1939, Serbia had employed every means to impose its hegemony over the interwar kingdom. Still, Croatians had not been disloyal to that state; rather they had insisted that it live up to its promises to be equitable to all its citizens (or at least all of its South Slav citizens). Whereas Serbs focused their discussion of World War II around the massacres of Serbs by the Croatian fascist state (NDH), Croatians tended to minimize the extent of wartime persecutions of Serbs in Croatia (and sometimes even hinted that the NDH, while not a paragon of virtue, was a not completely unreasonable response to Serb bullying in the interwar period), to point out that the Serbs had their own collaborationist state, albeit not an "independent" one, and to note that the Serbian Chetniks were hardly free of guilt for the intercommunal massacres that took place during the war.[24] Turning to the Communist period, Croats cited the overrepresentation of Serbs and Montenegrins in the police and military hierarchy, as well as the flow of federal taxes from Croatia (and Slovenia) to support failed development projects planned in Belgrade.[25]

In the Communist period, one of the most significant cultural attempts to foster Croatian national feeling, and one of the first public signs of the so-called Croatian Spring movement, was the publication of the "Declaration Concerning the Name and the Position of the Croatian Literary Language" in March 1967. This document was a direct repudiation of the 1954 Novi Sad agreement on the Serbo-Croatian language that had been signed by leading Serbian and Croatian intellectuals, and it illustrates how far the country had moved from the "unity" of the initial postwar period; equally important, in demanding recognition of the Croatian literary language as an independent entity, it undermined the only remaining historical connection to the original Yugoslav movements of the nineteenth century (as far back as the Illyrian movement of the 1830s and 40s). For however relations between Serbs and Croats may have fluctuated in the ensuing years, the goal of an integrated literary language had remained intact (with the notable exception of the World War II period). By opening the door to full linguistic separation, the Croatian cultural nationalists thus called all other types of Serbian/Croatian cooperation into question.

In the literary arena, leading Croatian publications did everything possible to stress the autochthonous nature of Croatian culture: "The emphasis was on things Croatian and on the revival of Croatian national consciousness."[26] It was no coincidence that the cultural society *Matica hrvatska* began its ambitious publication of a series of books titled Five Centuries of Croatian Literature at this time. Thus, it is no exaggeration to say that the Croatian revival was spearheaded by cultural figures rather than Croatian politicians, who until early 1970 were divided on this issue.[27]

Few Croatian intellectuals hid their support of separatist ethnic national feelings at this time. A particularly strident presentation of Croatian intellectual opinion can be seen in the proceedings of a conference that was held in Zagreb in 1970.[28] Attended by most of Croatia's leading intellectuals, the conference amounted to a full-scale attack on the previous school program for the teaching of literature and a call to arms to use literature and culture to create specifically Croatian citizens. "The duty of Croatian schools is to make available to the Croatian student, the future Croatian intellectual, the basic works of value of Croatian literary culture and of Croatian culture in general."[29] This required the separation of Croatian literature from the "literatures of the Yugoslav nations," a sharp reduction in the number of Serbian writers being taught (in this respect, Croatian intellectuals hoped to bring their education program in line with that of the Slovenians, who were admired for basically all but ignoring the literatures of the other Yugoslav peoples), as well as the elimination of any attempt at demonstrating that such a concept as a unified Yugoslav literature had ever existed.

The suppression of the liberal Croatian Spring movement in 1971 was taken by many Croats as evidence that the Communist state was no more willing to tolerate Croatian desires for more autonomy than the interwar state had been, even though the 1974 Yugoslav Constitution incorporated much of what had been demanded by Croatians. As Jill Irvine puts it: "The end of the Croatian Spring ushered in a period of bitter quiescence in which Croatia was often described as the 'sullen republic.' But the significance of the Croatian Spring was much wider than simply its effect on Croatia. It signified, in important ways, the beginning of the end for Yugoslavia."[30] Irvine points to three important outcomes that helped to pave the way to dissolution. First, the 1974 constitution, the promulgation of which was meant to prevent outbursts like the Croatian Spring movement, enshrined a weakened federal center and devolved ever more power to the republics. Second, the sidelining of popular leaders in both Croatia and Serbia in response to the events of 1968–1971 provided an opening for renewed political power on the part of religious institutions, particularly the Catholic Church in Croatia. And finally the suppression of the Croatian Spring helped to deligitimize the Partisan legacy on which the postwar Yugoslav state was based.

Slovenes' concerns about Communist Yugoslavia were similar to those of Croats. Though undoubtedly less rancorous in their views, they nevertheless felt economically exploited by a system that they believed used the surpluses generated by their labor to support development projects in other parts of the country. Furthermore, even more than their Croatian counterparts, Slovene intellectuals feared creeping denationalization. They resented the fact that their children were forced to learn Serbo-Croatian while no one else was required to learn Slovene. These tensions came to a head during discussions of a core curriculum program that was proposed in the early 1980s as a way to ensure that all Yugoslav school children possessed at least some common cultural knowledge despite the lack of a national system of education. Even though the core was to constitute at most 50 percent of the literature curriculum with the rest being left to the discretion of republic-level authorities, Slovene intellectuals protested stridently. In August 1983, the Slovene writer Ciril Zlobec wrote an emotionally loaded critique of the core curriculum in the official Slovene newspaper *Delo*. He claimed that "the proposal offers a state education instead of the conscious knowledge of one's own national and personal essence . . . It is an anti-cultural, anti-pedagogic, anti-educational and anti-ethical document." And he wondered what would happen to the spiritual, cultural, and historic identity of Slovene children after their twelve-year "journey through the desert of spirit" that was embodied in this document.[31] Another Slovene writer, Janez Menart, calculated that according to the core proposal a Serbo-Croatian speaking primary school pupil would read only three Slovene poems, whereas a Slovene-speaking pupil would read more than thirty-five Serbo-Croatian poems. "What a bad trade!" he concluded.[32]

Defenders of the core noted that it was to cover only half of the literature curriculum. The rest was to be at the discretion of republics and provinces, thereby allowing ample room to present individual national traditions.[33] Nevertheless, at a public meeting in Ljubljana organized by the Slovene Writers Union on 19 September, leading Slovene writers (Ciril Zlobec, Rudi Šeligo, Janez Rotar, Bojan Štih) rejected the proposed common core out of hand. By this point they were not so much concerned with the raw numbers of writers or texts included or even the language in which they were presented but rather the entire idea of whether a national core curriculum was necessary. A Belgrade newspaper summarized the basic attitude of all the speakers in one sentence: "We Slovenes will alone decide about our schools, and nobody should dictate to us."[34]

Although less important for the weakening of the Yugoslav body politic in the period before the dissolution of Yugoslavia, the unofficial narratives of other groups in the state, including Bosnian Muslims and Kosovar Albanians, also contributed to the sense that Yugoslavia was a country in which centrifugal forces were becoming ever more powerful.

Because the Bosnian Muslims (Bosniaks) are Slavic speakers whose ancestors converted to Islam during the long period of Ottoman rule, they were always a bone of contention between Serbian and Croatian nationalists, who tended to think of them as "really" Serbs or Croats respectively. A separate Bosnian Muslim identity was slow to develop. In the period before the creation of the first Yugoslavia, as Xavier Bougarel notes, "The Muslim secular intelligentsia was divided into pro-Croat and pro-Serb factions, which both equally rejected the name 'Muslims,' preferring to declare themselves Croats or Serbs 'of Islamic faith.'"[35] According to Bougarel, the founding of the Movement for the Autonomy of Bosnia-Hercegovina "constituted the first organized manifestation of a nascent Muslim nationalism."[36]

In the immediate post-World War II period, the Yugoslav Communists, in keeping with their antireligious ideology, abolished many traditional Muslim organizations. Nevertheless, they made serious efforts to balance the various ethnoreligious groups in the newly created Republic of Bosnia-Hercegovina. If Serbs were overrepresented in the 1950s, by the mid-1960s a fairly strict "affirmative action" program ensured representation more or less equal to the population of the republic. Although no Bosniak category was available on census forms in the 1950s, the category of Muslims in an ethnic sense was added in 1961, and they were officially recognized as a national group in 1974.

Nevertheless, there were still areas of friction between at least some members of the Bosnian Muslim population and the state. In 1983, thirteen Bosnian Muslims, including Alija Izetbegović (who would later become the first president of an independent Bosnia-Hercegovina) were imprisoned for "endangering the fraternity and unity of the Yugoslav nations" through their publication of an Islamic declaration that, the prosecution insisted, called for the creation of an "ethnically pure" Bosnia-Hercegovina.[37]

The extent to which the concerns of even nonreligious Bosnians tended to be ignored in Yugoslavia can perhaps best be felt in an exchange between a school teacher named Mubera Mujagić and a number of leading Yugoslav academics and journalists in 1984. At a public meeting sponsored by the Writers' Organization of Sarajevo to discuss proposed revisions to the nationwide core, Mujagić hinted at what had hitherto been a taboo topic: the anti-Ottoman and anti-Muslim messages in Petar Petrović Njegoš's *The Mountain Wreath* (*Gorski vijenac*) as well as Ivan Mažuranić's *The Death of Smail-Aga Ćengić* (*Smrt Smail Age Čengića*). She suggested that these canonical works be excluded from the Yugoslav primary school core curriculum because they might "evoke national intolerance." This led to a series of responses and counterresponses in the Belgrade biweekly *Intervju*.[38] Although not disputing Njegoš's position as a great writer and thinker, Mujagić, who publicly identified herself as a Yugoslav, asked: "What kind of spirit can these works offer us? Can they evoke catharsis in the reader, a feeling of unity, Yugoslavism, accord, solidarity, toleration, and cosmopolitanism, or do they create bile, poison, and hatred towards anyone who belongs to another belief or nation?" Mujagić's critics responded to her allegations in a couple of ways. Some defended Njegoš as a great thinker and writer whose thought soars above all petty local differences and forms an indelible part of the national legacy that should not be censored just because it might offend someone in the present (Miroslav Egerić). Others insisted that the characters and times described in Njegoš's work had nothing to do with the nations of contemporary Yugoslavia (Milorad Vučelić). All agreed that only poor teaching could possibly allow any student to come away from the text with an incorrect impression. No one responded directly to Mujagić's claims, which were backed up by a teacher named Jakov Ivaštović, who, like Mujagić, reported that students did indeed interpret *The Mountain Wreath* in a nationalist vein.

Kosovar Albanians had always had issues about their inclusion in an avowedly South Slavic state. Although rarely stated in terms of a wish for a Greater Albania, there was nevertheless a strong feeling that the inclusion of a large number of Albanian speakers in both the first and second Yugoslavias was somehow illegitimate.[39] Despite the Serbs' tendency especially after 1985 to focus on purported Albanian attempts to seize demographic control over the province, Albanians tended to point out that at a variety of times (particularly during the interwar period as well as between 1946 and 1966) there had been heavy-handed attempts by the authorities to colonize the region with Serbs and that Albanians had been noticeably underrepresented in political bodies during these periods. Although things had clearly been significantly better for the Albanian population between 1974 and 1986, Albanians still felt marginalized and underrepresented. Riots in 1981, which were brutally suppressed by the Yugoslav authorities, were a hint that despite Kosovo's greater autonomy, tensions between the Albanian majority and the Yugoslav state had not been eliminated. Further, the abrogation of Kosovo's autonomy by the Milošević regime in 1989 led to a virtual state of war between the Serbian authorities and the population at large (though at this point and through 1995, largely under the influence of Ibrahim Rugova, the Kosovar Albanians employed a strategy of passive resistance rather than military action to oppose the Yugoslav state.[40]

At the same time, in parallel to these various nationalist narratives, there always existed and continued to exist up until and even beyond the collapse of Yugoslavia a variety of supranational or nonnational discourses that Sabrina Ramet has helpfully labeled "cosmopolitan":

> In the Yugoslav and post-Yugoslav context, cosmopolitan narratives have included liberal, feminist, social democratic, and socialist/Communist narratives, each having its own view of the past, its own understanding of the challenges which history has thrown up. In none of the cosmopolitan narratives is history cast as the struggle of one's own nation against hostile neighboring nations. In the Yugoslav context, "Yugoslavism" (or sometimes, "Yugoslav socialist patriotism") was seen as signifying the subscription to precisely such a cosmopolitan narrative.[41]

It is difficult to gauge the level of support for narratives such as these at various points in Yugoslavia's existence, particularly because a number of surveys undertaken in the late 1960s and early 1970s revealed that many Yugoslav citizens expressed both national and supranational identities.

Nevertheless, by the middle of the 1980s, Yugoslavia was in serious straits. In the economic and political spheres there was an ever-increasing tendency toward republicanization, which was linked with particularist nationalism. Simultaneously, the opinion leaders of the various constituent peoples were increasingly telling themselves and their conationals incompatible stories about the past and present of the country. Despite these serious danger signs, the country might well have limped along from crisis to crisis had not two important exogenous factors coincided with the appearance on the political stage of a number of ambitious figures who had a vested interest in the country's breakup.

The two exogenous factors were the weakening of the USSR and the expansion of the EU. While neither of these two processes was undertaken with an eye toward destabilizing Yugoslavia, both had that effect. The belief that a large state was a necessary precondition for military and economic security had been an important factor in holding Yugoslavia together from the beginning. Indeed, one of the reasons that Croatians and Slovenes had been willing to join the Kingdom of the Serbs, Croats, and Slovenes in the first place was the realization that failure to do so would have meant the incorporation of significant portions of their territory into Italy, which had been promised most of Dalmatia and Istria by the allies for its assistance during the Great War. The willingness of Hungary, Italy, and Bulgaria to effectively annex portions of the country during World War II certainly worked to reinforce the idea that Yugoslav unity was necessary to fend off rapacious neighbors. After the Tito–Stalin split of 1948, fear of the USSR had been an important unifying factor for Yugoslavia. Yugoslav military planning was focused primarily on repelling a Soviet attack, which, given the Soviet invasions of Hungary in 1956 and Czechoslovakia in 1968, did not seem at all far-fetched. However, the unwillingness (or inability) of the USSR to intervene directly in Poland to stop the growth of the Solidarity movement in the early 1980s was an early sign that the danger of external military invasion was waning (fear of an invasion from the capitalist West had already dissipated by the 1960s). Mikhail Gorbachev's elevation to the position of general secretary of the Communist Party and his almost immediate announcement of the need for glasnost and perestroika was a strong sign that the USSR was confronting a major crisis of its own. By the end of the 1980s it had become clear that the USSR would not intervene to prevent democratization in its East European satellites, and the pressure for an end to monopolistic Communist Party rule became ever stronger.

As the need for a large Yugoslavia to provide for defense lessened in the course of the 1980s, the parallel (though unrelated) process of European expansion began to make it more imaginable that a large state was no longer necessary for economic security and prosperity. The slow expansion of the EU to include Ireland (1973), Greece (1981), and Portugal (1986) was an indication that smaller countries with per capita incomes and economic prospects not significantly better than those of at least some areas of Yugoslavia could be economically viable independent states as members of a larger block.

The final death knell for Yugoslavia occurred when the new possibilities engendered by a changing external world combined with on-going republican-ization and nationalization of the country opened the door inside Yugoslavia for a generation of political leaders able and willing to exploit the situation for their own purposes. To be sure, certainly since the death of Tito in 1980, real power in Yugoslavia had been held by republican-level politicians. They had, however, managed recruitment and advancement through the undemocratic structures of the Communist Party. As pressures for democratization grew in the course of the 1980s, canny political figures came to recognize that public support would be necessary to retain power. The obvious basis of support for all such politicians was nationalism, and in each of the republics the most powerful political parties to emerge were formed on the basis of ethnic affiliation. In some cases their foundations were laid by the former Communist elites, in others by those who had been sidelined earlier for nationalist tendencies.

Even before this process had achieved its final form, its basic attributes had been worked out by the Serbian Slobodan Milošević, who came to power after ousting his erstwhile mentor Ivan Stambolić in 1987. Although an enormous amount of scholarship has focused on Milošević's role in the destruction of Yugoslavia, there is little evidence to indicate that he came to power with a developed plan to destroy the country. Unquestionably, he recognized that in a democratizing situation in a country organized as Yugoslavia was, an appeal to Serbian interests would be necessary to garner the support he needed to control Serbian politics. Specifically, Milošević appealed to Serb worries over the emotional issue of the status of Kosovo. Nevertheless, initially at least, it appears that his goal was not the destruction of Yugoslavia but rather the recentralization of the country under his own leadership. Only after it became clear that no such project was realistic did Milošević recalibrate and turn to a policy of uniting all Serbs in a single state, which could only be achieved by changing the republican borders of Croatia and Bosnia.

Nevertheless, whether his actions were entirely deliberate or simply opportunistic, Milošević must shoulder a great deal of blame for the final destruction of Yugoslavia. There will, of course, always be historians who say that the country was in dire straits and that had there been no Milošević another equivalent figure would have come along to deliver the coup de grace. Perhaps this is so, but the historical record shows that it was Milošević and no one else whose actions pushed the country over the brink. It was Milošević who purged, recentralized, and revamped Serbia's Communist Party with nationalism; it was also Milošević who systematically overturned the Titoist settlement in such a way that bred fear among Yugoslavia's non-Serbs; and it was Milošević, more than anyone else, who undermined the eleventh-hour attempts of Yugoslavia's last prime minister, Ante Marković, to reform Yugoslavia and thereby to find a way out of the crisis into which the country had descended.

That Milošević was able to have so great an impact was in large part a result of the structures for social control built into Communist societies in general, the so-called nomenklatura system that he inherited in 1986 when he became president of Serbia's League of Communists. By controlling patronage in the League of Communists, Milošević was able to stamp his authority on Serbian society, moving apparatchiks, whose primary qualifications were personal loyalty, into key posts and edging out independent thinkers until he was powerful enough to move against his mentor. Indeed, the decisive battle in Yugoslavia's disintegration was, in many ways, fought not in 1991 but in 1987. The struggle was not between Serbs and non-Serbs but between two wings of the Serbian League of Communists, between advocates of Yugoslavia's restructuring in such a way that Serbs would reassert themselves at the expense of the country's other peoples and those who clung to Tito's concept of a multinational state. The principal protagonists were Milošević himself, on the one hand, and Dragiša Pavlović, president of Belgrade's League of Communists, representing the Stambolić wing, on the other. The battlegrounds were the Serbian League of Communists and the Serbian media.

The danger to Yugoslavia's stability presented by any attempt to reconstruct the country on the basis of Serb domination was obvious in terms of demographics. Although Serbs were the most numerous people in Yugoslavia, with 4.9 million living in inner Serbia, 1.3 million in Kosovo and Vojvodina, and close to 2 million outside Serbia, they formed only 36 percent of the population according to the 1981 census, and that proportion was declining. Serbs therefore formed a sufficiently great proportion of the population to destabilize Yugoslavia but not to dominate it.

During 1987, Milošević and Pavlović slugged it out within the media organs that each man controlled. However, the odds were stacked against Pavlović and, by extension, Stambolić, because of Milošević's control of the Communist apparatus. Indeed, Milošević was able to ratchet up the pressure on Pavlović and by extension Stambolić with mass protest rallies attended on occasions by more than 100,000 people. The rallies, or meetings as they were called, were carefully stage-managed and reinforced the message that was coming from the Milošević-controlled media, namely that Serbia had been the victim of a historical injustice that needed to be put right.

The power struggle within Serbia's League of Communists came to a head at the eighth plenum in September 1987 when Milošević called for Pavlović's expulsion. Milošević had prepared the ground well and came to the plenum with the backing of senior Communists for a return to strict party discipline before launching his final offensive. Like his meetings, the plenum was stage-managed, and Milošević was inundated with telegrams and messages of support from Serb Communists the length and breadth of Serbia, Kosovo, and Vojvodina. At the end of September the battle was won and Pavlović expelled. Three months later, Stambolić resigned as president of Serbia, and Milošević replaced him with one of his allies. In a book published a year later in Zagreb (because no Serbian publisher was prepared to touch it), Pavlović wrote prophetically: "If a nation adopts the right to be angry, how can it deny the same right to another? A confrontation of two nations leads to a war."[42]

With Pavlović out of the way, Milošević further purged Serbia's League of Communists and media to silence all remaining dissenting voices. The purges were part of the so-called antibureaucratic revolution that was supposed to weed out corruption in the League of Communists but, in practice, served to root out all potential opposition. Meanwhile, the campaign against Yugoslavia's prevailing structure went into overdrive in the media and at Milošević's rallies. Rabble-rousing tactics that had started in Kosovo were extended throughout Serbia and beyond. Momentum was sustained by paying unemployed young men to go around the country from meeting to meeting while Serbs from all over Yugoslavia, including Bosnia-Hercegovina and Croatia, were encouraged to attend. Demonstrators carried pictures of Milošević, waved nationalist flags, sang nationalist songs, and habitually called for the execution of Kosovo's Albanian leadership at the meetings that the Serbian media hailed as the "third Serb uprising." (The first two uprisings had occurred at the beginning of the nineteenth century against Ottoman rule).[43]

In the course of 1988, the rallies spread first to Vojvodina and then to Montenegro. Steadily, Milošević ratcheted up the pressure on the leaderships of both Vojvodina and Montenegro, which were already unpopular, until toward the end of the year tens and even hundreds of thousands of demonstrators regularly surrounded the parliaments, demanding the resignations of the governments. In the absence of any support from the federal authorities, both governments caved in, Vojvodina in October 1988 and Montenegro in January 1989. As soon as the governments resigned, they were replaced with Milošević supporters who proceeded to carry out a thorough purge of society, the party, and the media.

While Milošević was dismantling Tito's Yugoslavia piecemeal, the federal authorities were at a loss how to react. At the height of the assault on Vojvodina, federal President Raif Dizdarević warned that he might have to impose a state of emergency, but backed down rather than risk open conflict as more than 350,000 people rallied in Belgrade. Quite simply, Yugoslavia's federal government was not equipped to deal with so determined an assault on its authority. This was partly the fault of the Titoist system because the center lacked sufficient authority to bring Serbia into line, but it was also the result of a malaise in the rest of the country. Montenegro, Macedonia, and Kosovo were bankrupt. Bosnia-Hercegovina's leadership was embroiled in the Agrokomerc scandal, the collapse of Yugoslavia's twenty-ninth largest company with debts of $900 million. And Croatia was still governed by the generation of conservatives whom Tito had installed in the early 1970s in the wake of the Croatian Spring.

As Milošević moved against Kosovo, an increasingly forlorn federal League of Communists of Yugoslavia decided that its best tactic was to sacrifice the recalcitrant province. Non-Serbian Communists were concerned by the upsurge of nationalism in Serbia but convinced themselves that by sacrificing Kosovo they might satisfy Milošević's ambitions while simultaneously hoping that Kosovo might yet prove his undoing. In this way, Kosovo's Albanian leadership was dismissed in November 1988 and replaced with Milošević appointees. The dismissals provoked demonstrations among the province's Albanians, and by February 1989 the demonstrations had escalated into a general strike as well as an underground hunger strike by 1,300 miners from the Trepča lead and zinc mines. When Kosovo's new, pro-Milošević leadership resigned on 28 February it appeared that the strikers had won the day; victory, however, was short-lived.

In Belgrade, Milošević organized fresh and even larger rallies at which he promised that the organizers of Kosovo's general strike would be punished. Once again, the federal authorities acquiesced. The resignations were withdrawn, a partial state of emergency imposed, and the military moved in. On 23 March, Kosovo's assembly was coerced into accepting a new constitution returning authority to Serbia. Five days later, the Serbian parliament incorporated the constitutional changes to the status of Kosovo and Vojvodina into the Serbian constitution and introduced a new interpretation of the concept of sovereignty, that is sovereignty within the nation. Whereas republican leaders hitherto had represented all people living in their republic irrespective of their ethnic identities, Milošević claimed the right to represent all Serbs throughout Yugoslavia. Because large Serb communities lived in six of Yugoslavia's eight federal units, this direct appeal to them above the heads of their republican leaderships was an extremely powerful weapon that he set about using to undermine authority in the governments of Bosnia-Hercegovina and Croatia. In response to the changes, Albanians took to the streets to defend the old constitution; demonstrators clashed with police and twenty-eight people were killed.[44]

The balance of power within Yugoslavia had shifted decisively toward Milošević following his victory in Kosovo. By this time, he controlled four of Yugoslavia's eight federal units and was strong enough to ignore federal opposition. Indeed, he was now able to use his own newly acquired federal muscle to extend his power base further. Thus far, the League of Communists of Yugoslavia had remained united and had acquiesced in the face of Milošević's onslaught. That changed in the aftermath of the Kosovo clampdown when, under pressure from their domestic public, Slovenia's Communists broke ranks.

The Slovene Communist leadership was aware of the perception of many Slovenes that their separate cultural and linguistic identity was threatened by Yugoslavia's Serbo-Croat–speaking majority and pandered to it. At the federal level, Slovenia's Communists worked to retain as much autonomy as possible, whereas at home they attempted to promote a sense of Slovene national pride, including a publicity drive around the theme "Slovenia My Homeland" in the mid-1980s. In addition to promoting pride in Slovenia, the Slovene Communists used Slovene media to articulate their own vision of Yugoslavia's future, and as the Yugoslav economy disintegrated in the 1980s, they became increasingly prepared to use the media to blame other republics and the federal government in Belgrade for the country's economic ills, making it clear that they were tired of subsidizing poorer federal units when living standards were also declining at home.

Despite obvious attempts by Slovenia's Communists to court popularity at home, in the long run the growth of opposition to the Communist state was a more significant factor in the evolution of Slovene nationalism. Traditionally, Slovenia's Communists had tolerated a far broader spectrum of views with many more dissenting voices than any other part of Yugoslavia. But in the 1980s, as the failings of the Communist system became too great to conceal, a new generation of activists began to mold a political opposition around specific issues and via alternative art forms.

The issue that galvanized Slovene public opinion was the court martial of Janez Janša, a senior *Mladina* writer on military affairs (and candidate for president of Slovenia's Youth Organization), and three others. On 31 May 1988, Janša was arrested on suspicion of betraying military secrets. Soon after, two other *Mladina* journalists and a noncommissioned officer were also charged with offenses relating to the disclosure of military secrets after classified documents were found at *Mladina*'s offices. The documents in question were believed to be plans for a military takeover of Slovenia. The arrests followed shortly after a series of articles had embarrassed the federal defense minister, Branko Mamula, into an early resignation. The population at large considered the arrests and trial nothing short of an attack on Slovenes and Slovenia. Almost immediately, *Mladina* journalists founded a Committee for the Protection of Human Rights to monitor the trial, and Slovenes took to wearing *Janez Janša* badges to demonstrate solidarity with the accused.

Whether or not the four defendants had committed an offense had ceased to matter as far as most Slovenes were concerned. The four were widely viewed as martyrs who had been framed by a military that *Mladina*'s investigative reporting had already discredited. Meanwhile, the *Jugoslovenska narodna armija* (JNA, Yugoslav People's Army) further incensed Slovene public opinion by insisting that the trial be held in Serbo-Croat. The result was a remarkable homogenization of Slovene society and national mobilization behind the accused. When all four were found guilty and sentenced to terms of between five months and four years, more than 50,000 people surrounded the courthouse in the center of Ljubljana, a remarkable number in a city of only 300,000.

In the aftermath of the Janša trial, relations between the JNA and Slovenia continued to deteriorate amid persistent rumors of a military coup d'état. Although Slovenia's Communist leadership still hoped to appease Milošević, the republic's increasingly vociferous opposition made it clear that its sympathies lay with the Kosovo Albanians. When the Albanian miners began their underground hunger strike, the Committee for the Protection of Human Rights began collecting money for them and their families. When the federal presidency sent the military into Kosovo, more than 1 million Slovenes—half the total population—signed a petition against the state of emergency, 450,000 in one day. On 27 February Slovenia's opposition organized a rally at Cankarjev Dom, Ljubljana's cultural center, to demonstrate solidarity with Kosovo's Albanians. In the face of intense public pressure, the republic's Communist leadership decided belatedly to join the protest. In this way, leading Communists, including President Milan Kučan, shared the platform with the non-Communist opposition. The rally was broadcast live on television and radio, and for the first time, Slovenia's Communists openly defied the federal League of Communists of Yugoslavia. Soon after the Cankarjev Dom meeting, Slovenia withdrew its police contingent from Kosovo.[45]

The decision to break ranks was not taken lightly. At the time, Milošević's star was in the ascendant. He controlled Serbia, Vojvodina, and Montenegro and was in the process of cementing his control over Kosovo. Moreover, he had already begun to extend the same rabble-rousing tactics to the Serb communities of Bosnia-Hercegovina and Croatia. Kučan was aware of the risks involved in both standing up to Milošević and in doing nothing. To be sure, Slovenes generally looked upon Kosovo's Albanians in a condescending fashion as a result of the gulf in development between Kosovo and Slovenia. However, the bloodshed in Kosovo, which had a population comparable to Slovenia's, had shocked Slovenes and made them fear for their own security. At the same time, like Communists throughout Eastern Europe, Slovenia's Communists were unpopular, and the opposition was growing increasingly confident. For Kučan, Kosovo was as much an opportunity as a threat. By taking a firm stance, he calculated that he would be able to rejuvenate the Slovene League of Communists and boost his own popularity at home even if that meant a head-on collision with Milošević.

In the wake of Slovenia's volte-face, Milošević attempted to pressure Slovenia into submission. The Serbian media turned on Slovenia; Serbia, Vojvodina, and Kosovo began to boycott Slovenian products and nationalize the assets of Slovenian companies; and a meeting to "present the truth" about Kosovo to the Slovene public was scheduled for 1 December 1989. Faced with the prospect of several hundred thousand Serbs descending on Ljubljana for the "Meeting of Truth," as it was called in Serbia, Kučan banned the rally. The "truth" about Kosovo had already been displayed on 28 June 1989, the six-hundredth anniversary of the battle of Kosovo Polje, when more than a million Serbs descended on Kosovo to hear Milošević tell them: "Six centuries [after the battle of Kosovo Polje], we are again engaged in battles and quarrels. These are not armed battles, but the latter cannot be ruled out yet."

Developments in Slovenia had hitherto been broadly in line with the rest of Eastern Europe, where Communism was rapidly disintegrating. Slovenia's Communists decided that they could not stem the democratic tide and opted for a multiparty system. However, any move toward Western-style democracy in Slovenia would be scuppered if Milošević succeeded in recentralizing Yugoslavia. As a result, Kučan began to espouse a confederal arrangement in which each republic could choose its own form of government. According to Kučan's vision of Yugoslavia, republics desiring to remain Communist could do so, whereas those wishing to evolve into multiparty democracies would also be free to abandon Communism. On 27 September 1989, Slovenia's parliament passed fifty-four amendments to the constitution formally renouncing the League of Communists' monopoly on political power and including the explicit right to self-determination, that is secession from Yugoslavia.[46]

Despite the disintegration of Communist rule elsewhere, Milošević still hoped to use the League of Communists to extend his political influence throughout Yugoslavia and called an extraordinary fourteenth congress of the LCY for January 1990 toward this end.[47] The congress was billed as the clash of alternative visions of Yugoslavia's future development. Milošević intended to use it to impose on the federal party his model of a Serbian League of Communists, regenerated through unity, discipline, and the exclusion of dissenting voices. Kučan hoped to expand local autonomy within Yugoslavia by turning the LCY into a loose association of separate Communist Parties. In the event, Kučan was shouted down by Milošević's supporters and unable even to present his proposals, let alone discuss the future shape of Yugoslavia. As it became clear there would be no discussions, the Slovenian delegation walked out. In the absence of the Slovenes, Milošević attempted to resume the congress, but when the Croatian delegation walked out as well, the Bosnian and Macedonian Communists were no longer prepared to continue, and the meeting was suspended.

For almost forty-five years, Communism had been the glue holding Yugoslav society together. In its absence, Yugoslavia remained intact, though the country Tito had built was no more. In a climate of goodwill it likely would have been possible to erect a third Yugoslavia out of the ruins of the Titoist state because it is difficult for any country actually to fall apart. In effect, the demise of Communism had merely reopened the debate that had preoccupied Yugoslav politicians during the 1920s as to the best form of government for their common state. As Sabrina Ramet has observed,

> Certainly, the years of relative internal peace in socialist Yugoslavia, 1945–1985, were sufficient time in which the country could, with a more wisely developed political formula, have constructed a system capable of overcoming such economic and political storms as would come its way. Among many citizens of the SFRY there was a genuine commitment to building a common life—but the minimal demands which Yugoslavs had included the chance for a better life, fairness, respect for human rights, and a legitimate state. Had these things been achieved, collapse and war could most certainly been avoided. This means, of course, that democratization would have had to be undertaken *before* the country's crisis of legitimation became overwhelming.[48]

And there were still forces at work to save the patient. In March 1989, Ante Marković, Yugoslavia's last prime minister, came into office and, having formed a government of technocrats, began addressing Yugoslavia's economic ills. Marković reasoned that because the political crisis that had brought the country to the brink of disintegration was rooted in the economic downturn of the 1980s, the solution, too, would be found in the economy. Moreover, despite the ongoing trade war between Slovenia and Serbia, the Marković reforms, which involved both a wage freeze and price liberalization, generated impressive results, slashing inflation from more than 2,000 percent at the end of 1989 to below 10 percent in just two months and overseeing a doubling in the country's foreign currency reserves.

Marković aimed to capitalize on his economic successes by founding his own non-Communist political party, with which he hoped to contest as yet unscheduled federal elections. He reasoned that if he could organize nationwide elections he might just be able to give the federal government a democratic mandate and legitimacy that the republics, all still governed by Communists, lacked. For the initiative to have any chance of succeeding, Marković needed to hold federal elections before any of the republics went to the polls. But because Slovenia's Communists had already committed themselves to multiparty elections in April 1990, he needed to persuade them to delay their poll, something they were unwilling to do.

As far as Slovenia's Communists were concerned, any move aimed at increasing the authority of Yugoslavia's federal center was a potential threat, and they were not prepared to commit Slovenia's future to the outcome of elections that had not yet been organized and that might evolve into another vehicle for Serb nationalism. Indeed, the atmosphere of fear that Milošević had created through mass rallies, hysterical media reporting, and police rule in Kosovo was driving events. Because Slovenia's population was overwhelmingly Slovene, the choice of electoral system was not especially controversial. Nonetheless, by holding multiparty elections at a republican as opposed to a federal level, Slovenia's Communists were setting a precedent the consequences of which would be felt elsewhere.[49]

In Croatia, where elections took place two weeks after Slovenia, the choice of electoral system was extremely important, given that some 25 percent of the population was not Croat, that nearly 12 percent of the population was Serb, and that Serb political representation had been a prominent feature of the Communist system. In retrospect, therefore, the system that was selected, namely a majoritarian, first-past-the-posts system, was not best suited to the republic. It was, however, deliberately chosen by the Communists, now calling themselves the Party of Democratic Change, in the mistaken belief that they would be its beneficiaries. In the event, although the former Communists polled well, the system worked against them and handed an ethnically based party, the *Hrvatska demokratska zajednica* (HDZ, Croat Democratic Union), led by Franjo Tudjman, a Partisan and Titoist general turned nationalist dissident, an absolute majority in parliament on a minority poll.[50]

Whether or not different electoral results in Croatia based on a more appropriate electoral system would have made any difference in the evolution of Yugoslavia's disintegration is debatable. What is clear is that the advent of democracy as represented by multiparty elections transformed the relationship between Croats and Serbs in Croatia. Whereas the Communist system had for good reason bent over backward to make Serbs feel secure in Croatia, political power had now been transferred to a political party that represented exclusively Croat interests, had won most votes by promising to stand up to Milošević's brand of Serb nationalism, and would rapidly alter the republic's constitution to change the status of Croatia's Serbs from one of the republic's nations to that of a minority. [51] The issue of Serb rights in a democratic Croatia was real, even if Belgrade's actions ostensibly on behalf of Croatia's Serbs were anything but constructive and only exacerbated the situation.

As Communism was defeated in multiparty elections in Slovenia, Croatia, and then Bosnia-Hercegovina, the *Jugoslovenska narodna armija* (JNA, Yugoslav National Army), which was constitutionally committed both to preserving the "gains of the revolution" and to a unitary state, attempted to disarm the territorial armies of each republic in turn and was largely successful with the partial exception of Slovenia. The JNA then formed a Serbian alliance by default because only Milošević appeared faithful to Communism and eager to maintain a unitary state. Indeed, in the run-up to the December 1990 election in Serbia, which Milošević could not avoid, hard-line Communists including Milošević's wife, Mira Marković, and senior JNA officers created a new Communist Party, *Savez Komunista—pokret za Jugoslaviju* (SKPJ, League of Communists—Movement for Yugoslavia), and endorsed Milošević's newly renamed Socialists as the only party to vote for.[52]

Milošević's Socialists held on to power in a contest in which the main opposition, Vuk Drašković's *Srpski pokret obnove* (SPO, Serb Renewal Movement), appeared, if anything, even more nationalist. Milošević succeeded where other former Communist leaders failed by maintaining tight control of the media, using a first-past-the-posts electoral system (requiring only a relative majority of votes for an absolute majority of seats), and by a healthy electoral bribe in the form of massive wage and pension increases on the eve of the elections. This was achieved through an illegal loan from Serbia's main bank to the Serbian government. The bank printed whatever money Milošević felt he needed to get elected, effectively stealing 18 billion dinars, or $1.7 billion at prevailing exchange rates, from the rest of the country. This move ended the Marković reform program and triggered a return to inflation as soon as the size of the "loan" became clear. Although the vote was not overtly rigged, the opposition felt cheated, alleged fraud, and organized street protests against the biased reporting of state television. These culminated in a Belgrade rally attended by more than 150,000 people on 9 March 1991, that degenerated into street fighting, required the deployment of the JNA to restore order, and cost the lives of two people, one protestor and one policeman.

The events of 9 March 1991 were significant on several levels. Firstly, they revealed how determined Milošević was to hang on to power. Secondly, they led to renewed attempts by Milošević to create crises elsewhere in the Yugoslav federation and especially in Croatia to divert attention from the situation within Serbia and paint the opposition as unpatriotic. And thirdly, they confirmed to Slovene minds the need to extricate Slovenia as quickly as possible from the quagmire into which the rest of Yugoslavia was headed.

Dejan Jović makes clear that attitudes toward secession in both Slovenia and Croatia were divided and evolving in response to events elsewhere in Yugoslavia. In addition, he shows that although the two republics presented a joint confederal proposal to the rest of the country on 2 October 1990, they were actually watching each other's moves. Slovenia wished to distance itself from the conflicts brewing in Croatia and elsewhere in order to be in a position to negotiate directly with Serbia. Croatia did not wish to be left behind in a rump Yugoslavia. However, both republics remained cautious because neither wished to be blamed by the outside world for the breakup of Yugoslavia. The confederal proposal itself was, according to Jović, "a genuine attempt to achieve first a *de facto* and then a *de jure* independence without violence." Indeed, it would later form the basis of internationally brokered attempts to hold Yugoslavia together in some form, but only after the outbreak of hostilities. At the time it was presented, the confederal proposal was rejected by all other republics and federal units.[53]

On the same day that Milošević's Socialists were elected, 23 December 1990, Slovenes went to the polls in a referendum in which 88.2 percent of the electorate backed independence, although the actual question included an option that once independent Slovenia could enter into an association of Yugoslav states, should they wish to form a confederation. Three days later the Slovene parliament declared its intent to secede from Yugoslavia in six months' time. The intervening period was to be used to negotiate models of independence. The JNA's 1989 intervention in Kosovo and the ongoing suppression of the province's Albanian majority had a huge impact on Slovene attitudes toward the rest of the Yugoslav federation, stoking fears of a similar scenario within Slovenia itself. Moreover, events in Croatia, where a Serb revolt began in the immediate aftermath of the April 1990 election, appeared increasingly to be heading in a similar direction.

To be sure, the advent of multiparty democracy and the possibility of the fragmentation of Yugoslavia opened genuine questions about how to regulate relations between communities and develop appropriate mechanisms for autonomy and cultural rights that needed to be addressed. However, the way in which Milošević set about resolving these questions on behalf of the Serb communities in Croatia and Bosnia-Hercegovina could only exacerbate the situation, alienate the country's other peoples, and be detrimental to the longer-term interests of the very people he claimed to represent.

Having been orally abused and physically threatened in the Zagreb parliament to which they had been elected, MPs from the *Srpska demokratska stranka* (SDS, Serb Democratic Party) in Croatia formed the Union of Communes of Lika and Northern Dalmatia out of the constituencies they had won in the election; the union had its own parliament, the Serb National Council, in Knin. The Knin parliament's first move was to proclaim the sovereignty and independence of the Serb nation. It then permanently severed relations with Zagreb and announced a Serb referendum on autonomy to be held over a two-week period in August and September 1990. Croatian government attempts to intervene and halt the referendum were blocked by the JNA.

The majority of Croatia's Serbs and especially the urban population had largely ignored Milošević's propaganda offensive, which had started in the 1980s with ceremonies commemorating Serb war dead at sites of *Ustashe* atrocities during World War II, and voted for the reformed Communists in the 1990 election. They were acutely aware of their vulnerability in the event of conflict with the Croat majority and would have preferred not to have to choose camps. In the event, however, they had little choice because of a tit-for-tat escalation in hostilities and an increasingly intense media war over which they had minimal influence. The Serb revolt was at first confined to shooting at trains and harassing foreign tourists in the region around Knin. But each month it intensified, non-Serbs moved out, shooting incidents became more frequent, and bombs began going off elsewhere in Croatia. By autumn 1990, Croatia was locked in a spiral of violence that was pushing the republic steadily toward bloodshed. The first victim would be a Serb in the Croatian police killed by Serb militants on 23 November for being on the wrong side.

As the security situation in Croatia deteriorated, Milošević tried repeatedly together with Borisav Jović, the federal president and head of the country's armed forces during the critical year between 15 May 1990 and 15 May 1991, to have a state of emergency imposed on the entire country. Following the 9 March demonstrations in Belgrade, Jović called a meeting of the federal presidency that was also attended by military leaders for this purpose. Representatives of the four federal units controlled by Milošević voted for the imposition of a state of emergency but needed one more vote to put it into effect. They anticipated that the vote would come from the Bosnian member of the presidency, Bogić Bogićević, who happened to be a Serb. However, Bogićević refused to succumb to their intense pressure.[54]

On 15 March in the wake of his failure to impose a state of emergency, Jović resigned together with the representatives of Montenegro and Vojvodina, claiming that the balance of power within the presidency was leading to the breakup of the country but actually inducing the constitutional crisis himself. Jović returned to the presidency a few days later without any explanation. The night of the resignations, Milošević went on Belgrade television to state that Serbia would no longer obey the federal presidency and was mobilizing police reservists to avert rebellion in Kosovo and the Sandžak. He also urged Serbs to unite behind him to defend themselves. The next day, the Serb National Council in Knin proclaimed the secession of the heavily Serb-populated Krajina from Croatia, and Serbia's prime minister informed his assembly that Bosnian and Croatian forces were preparing an offensive against Serb-populated towns.

As important as what was actually happening in Yugoslavia during 1990 and the first half of 1991 were perceptions of what was taking place. These perceptions depended not on real events but on the atmosphere created by political rhetoric and rival media because a climate for war existed months and possibly years before anyone was killed. The first showdown took place in Pakrac, a Serb-majority town in western Slavonia, where on 2 March armed Croats and Serbs faced each other with the JNA in the wings. This was the culmination of several weeks' struggle over control of the police station. Media were also there in force, and though shots were fired, both militias backed down, and the day passed without casualties. Nevertheless, Radio Belgrade reported that six Serbs had been killed.[55]

In Pakrac, both the Serb and Croat militias were made up of people from the town itself. Many had lived their entire lives there and knew their adversaries personally. A sense of community persisted, and neither side could demonize the other to the level necessary for fighting to break out. Indeed, had territorial disputes been left to the locals, they probably could have been worked out because all sides had too much to lose in the event of war. But outsiders who did not have the same sense of community or of the potential losses involved increasingly dictated the pace of events.

In the next showdown on 31 March a Croatian policeman and a Serb rebel died as the Krajina militia clashed with Croatian police over control of the Plitvice national park. After a day's fighting, the Croatian police had the upper hand and had captured twenty-nine Serb fighters. That night, the federal presidency met in emergency session and, at Jović's insistence, ordered the JNA to take control of the situation and to prevent further bloodshed. It was the beginning of a pattern that was to last until autumn, when the JNA gave up all pretence of neutrality.[56]

Three days before the Plitvice clashes, Yugoslavia's six republican presidents began a series of monthly summits aimed at resolving the crisis. Though Bosnia-Hercegovina and Macedonia were eager to agree to anything that might hold Yugoslavia together and their presidents presented a compromise model for

Yugoslavia to their peers on 3 June the gulf between the Serbian position and that of Slovenia and Croatia was too great to be bridged. Meanwhile, the situation on the ground in Croatia continued to deteriorate as the pattern of Serb provocation and Croat reprisal acquired a self-sustaining momentum. On 2 May twelve Croatian policemen were killed in Borovo Selo, a Serb village just outside Vukovar in eastern Slavonia, and several of their bodies were mutilated by paramilitary forces loyal to Serbian Radical Party leader Vojislav Šešelj in the first atrocity to be committed in the conflict. That night, after another emergency session of the presidency, JNA units were again deployed to separate factions. The next day, Tudjman went on television to announce that war had begun.

Borovo Selo was the last occasion when Jović could use his position as president to direct federal policy. His mandate ran out on 15 May, when he was due to hand over power to Croatia's representative on the presidency, Stjepan Mesić. The handover should have been a formality because every year on that date a new president was appointed, with the office rotating among the federal units. However, though it was Croatia's turn to head the presidency, the Serbian bloc rejected Mesić's appointment. The presidency was divided; Mesić was not elected; and the body that was Yugoslavia's head of state and commander in chief of its armed forces left in limbo.

The toxic combination of escalating violence in Croatia and political deadlock added to the resolve of Slovenia's leaders to distance themselves from the rest of the country and spurred their preparations for independence. Fearful of being left behind, Croatia's leaders decided to follow Slovenia and hastily organized an independence referendum on 19 May, which they formally presented as a choice between a federation and a confederation. In the poll, 84 percent of the Croatian electorate voted, of whom 93 percent, that is 78.1 percent of those eligible, supported the proposal "that the Republic of Croatia, as a sovereign and independent state, which guarantees cultural autonomy and all civic rights to Serbs and members of other nationalities in Croatia, can enter into a union of sovereign states with other republics." Because the Serbs of *Krajina* had organized their own plebiscite two months earlier and voted unanimously to remain part of Yugoslavia, Tudjman was aware that an independence declaration appeared to play into Milošević's hands. However, he viewed it as the least of many evils, deciding that the risk of remaining part of a rump state without Slovenia was greater than that of declaring independence. The date set for the formal declaration was 29 June, three days after Slovenia's proposed date, which would give Tudjman time to see how Serbia and the JNA reacted to it.[57] In the intervening month, Croatia joined Slovenia in intensive lobbying of international opinion.

Hitherto, the international community had played no direct role in the Yugoslav drama and had no intention of becoming involved. Although the major powers were aware that the country was disintegrating, they could see no easy solutions and felt no obligation to try to resolve the internal problems of another country. When the Cold War ended, Yugoslavia lost its strategic importance as a buffer state between East and West. Moreover, other regions of the world had superseded Yugoslavia in the pecking order of international importance. Eastern Europe's emerging democracies became the focus of diplomatic activity and foreign investment in the region while events in the Middle East, Iraq's invasion of Kuwait, and the Gulf War, eclipsed all others.

Nevertheless, international opinion mattered greatly. Yugoslavs looked abroad, and especially to the European Community, for help in the transition from Communism. The European Community may or may not have been in a position to help. However, one of the European Community's requirements for assistance was that Yugoslavia stay together. The European Community was loath to see Yugoslavia fragment into ministates because fragmentation was likely to be messy and risked setting a precedent for the USSR, which at the time also appeared to be on the verge of disintegration. Although the European Community expected a resolution of Yugoslavia's internal conflict without recourse to violence, its insistence on something akin to the status quo may have inadvertently contributed to the deadlock in the country's constitutional talks. By insisting on a single entity and refusing to concede even the possibility of a transition to a looser association of republics, the European Community appeared to be backing Serbia and the JNA.

While Slovenia and Croatia sought to internationalize Yugoslavia's internal conflict to improve their position vis-à-vis that of Serbia, what international intervention there was only undermined their position. Diplomatic efforts focused on pressuring Slovenia and Croatia into abandoning their independence declaration. Though well-intentioned, such moves bolstered the resolve of the JNA and risked legitimizing their use of force. Indeed, it may not have been the declarations themselves but the eleventh-hour intervention by U.S. Secretary of State James Baker, designed to head off Slovenia and Croatia's independence declarations, that pushed Yugoslavia over the edge into war. Five days before Slovenia was due to declare independence, Baker, who was on an official visit to Albania, made an unscheduled stopover in Belgrade to make the U.S. position on Yugoslav matters clear. During his one-day visit he met with Yugoslavia's republican leaders and military chiefs and, before flying out, declared that the United States would not recognize Slovenia or Croatia "under any circumstances."[58]

In spite of Baker's and others' warnings, the leaders of Slovenia and Croatia determined to press ahead with independence declarations. Indeed, as they got wind of JNA plans, both republics brought forward the date for their independence declarations to 25 June. Just over a day later in the early hours of 27 June the JNA dispatched tanks to secure Slovenia's border crossings and Ljubljana airport but making them crisscross the republic in such as way as to exert maximum pressure on the authorities. It was the formal beginning of the wars of Yugoslavia's dissolution. Fearful of the consequences of remaining in a truncated Serb-dominated state, non-Serb political leaders in Bosnia-Hercegovina and Macedonia now took the first steps that would lead to their secession the following year even though they would have preferred the preservation of Yugoslavia and had hitherto not seriously contemplated secession. In recalling the security that all of the republics had enjoyed before 1986, Bosniak playwright Abdulah Sidran spoke for many non-Serbs across Yugoslavia in stating: "With [former Serbian League of Communists President] Nikezić I'd enter into a federation. With Stambolić I'd enter into a confederation. But with Milošević, I wouldn't even enter into a bus."

In the end, despite Marković's efforts to stabilize the Yugoslav and the international community's reluctance to accept the prospect of disintegration, the patient had become too ill to save. Yes, there were many factors at work in the death of Yugoslavia, none of which by itself would have been sufficient to prove fatal. Many were of long duration, whereas others dated from the 1980s and early 1990s. But it can also be said that the final blow was self-inflicted.

Notes

1   On the optimism of the immediate post-World War I period, see Andrew Wachtel, "Yugoslavie, 1918–1921," in *Sortir de la grande guerre*, eds. Christophe Prochasson and Stéphane Audoin-Rouzeau (Paris: Editions Tallandier, 2008). For a balanced discussion of the entire interwar period, see Ferdo Ćulinović, *Jugoslavija između dva rata*, 2 vols. (Zagreb: Historijski institut Jugoslavenske Akademiji Znanosti i Umjetnosti u Zagrebu, 1961).

2   The importance of these preconditions has also been emphasized by a number of team members and other SI scholars including Mark Biondich and Stevan K. Pavlowitch. As Biondich puts it: "Whether or not one believes that the interwar state was a political failure, what is perhaps far more significant is the widespread *perception* of failure. . . . Communist and national historiographies alike agreed that the interwar political experiment was an abysmal failure. As such, Communist and nationalist presentations of the interwar period were responsible for the widespread sense that no positive lessons could be learned from the interwar period." "The Historical Legacy: The Evolution of Interwar Yugoslav Politics, 1918–1941," in Lenard Cohen and Jasna Dragović-Soso, *State Collapse in South-Eastern Europe: New Perspectives on Yugoslavia's Disintegration* (West Lafayette, IN: Purdue University Press, 2008), 65. As a result, this legacy could not be drawn upon when the Communist version of Yugoslavia failed in its turn.

3   For important discussions of Yugoslavia during World War II, see Fikreta Jelić-Butić, *Četnici u Hrvatskoj 1941–1945* (Zagreb: Globus, 1986); Fikreta Jelić-Butić, *Ustaše i NDH* (Zagreb: S. N. Liber & Školska knjiga, 1977); and Matteo J. Milazzo, *The Chetnik Movement and the Yugoslav Resistance* (Baltimore and London: Johns Hopkins University Press, 1975).

4   Singleton, Fred, *A Short History of the Yugoslav Peoples* (Cambridge: Cambridge University Press, 1985), 211.

5   "In the early 1920s, unitarist Yugoslavism was not official policy, even though the country was being governed in a centralist way. Unitarist Yugoslavism was to be in-

troduced only after the establishment of the royal dictatorship in 1929. Communists, however, were unitarists from the very foundation of Yugoslavia." Aleksa Djilas, *The Contested Country: Yugoslav Unity and Communist Revolution, 1919–1953* (Cambridge, MA: Harvard University Press, 1991), 61. The basis for their belief in unitarism was, of course, Marxist theory, which predicted that nations would eventually disappear, their place taken by international working class solidarity. Hence, anything that could be done to hasten the disappearance of nationalism was to the good.

6   The waverings were the result of the Stalinist revision of Marx's views of nationalism. Stalin recognized that national cultures were still quite important, and in his typically pragmatic fashion decreed that this was not a problem for the Soviet Union (and, by extension, for Yugoslavia) as long as culture was "national in form, socialist in content."

7   Lenard J. Cohen, *Broken Bonds: Yugoslavia's Disintegration and Balkan Politics in Transition*, 2nd ed. (Boulder, CO: Westview Press, 1995), 25.

8   Ivo Banac goes so far as to assert that the success of the Communists was due solely to their embracing the "clear identity of the constituent parts." He says, "They did not win the war under the banner of Yugoslav unitarism; they won under the banner of the national liberation of Slovenia, Croatia, Serbia, Macedonia, and so on." "An Interview with Ivo Banac," in *Why Bosnia?* ed. Rabia Ali and Lawrence Lifshultz (Stony Creek, CT: Pamphleteer's Press, 1993), 141.

9   The treatment of non-Slavic minorities in post-World War II Yugoslavia varied. Germans, for example, who had been one of the largest prewar minority populations, were almost all expelled after the war. Many Italians were expelled as well, though those Italians who declared themselves Communists were generally allowed to stay. On the issue of Italians in postwar Yugoslavia, see Pamela Ballinger, *History in Exile: Memory and Identity at the Borders of the Balkans* (Princeton: Princeton University Press, 2003). Albanians, most of whom lived in Kosovo, were by far the largest remaining non-Slavic minority in Communist-era Yugoslavia. The fluctuations of relations with that minority group are discussed later in this chapter.

10   "During the 1950s, 'Yugoslav' was touted sometimes as an ethnic/national category in its own right, sometimes as a supranational category. This Yugoslavism (*jugoslovenstvo*) campaign reached its culmination at the seventh congress of the LCY in 1958. Although the party program adopted on that occasion denied the intention of assimilating the composite groups into a homogeneous Yugoslav nation, the concept of 'Yugoslav culture' endorsed by the congress implied an expectation of homogenization." Sabrina Ramet, *Nationalism and Federalism in Yugoslavia, 1962–1991* (Bloomington: Indiana University Press, 1992), 50.

11   Milovan Djilas, "Novi tok istorije," *Socijalizam* 33, nos. 1–4 (1990), 37, quoted in Cohen, 24.

12   Audrey Helfant Budding, "Nation/People/Republic: Self-Determination in Socialist Yugoslavia," in Cohen and Dragović-Soso, *State Collapse*, 98.

13   Ibid., 103.

14   John Allcock, *Explaining Yugoslavia* (New York: Columbia University Press, 2000), 90.

15   Dejan Jović, "Yugoslavism and Yugoslav Communism: From Tito to Kardelj," in *Yugoslavism: Histories of a Failed Idea, 1918–1992*, ed. Dejan Djokić (London: Hurst & Company, 2003), 174.

16   Michael Palairet, "The Inter-Regional Struggle for Resources and the Fall of Yugoslavia," in Cohen and Dragović-Soso, *State Collapse*, 222.

17   For a discussion of the variety of ways in which historical and literary topics were covered in Yugoslav schools, see Andrew Wachtel, *Making a Nation, Breaking a Na-*

tion: Literature and Cultural Politics in Yugoslavia (Palo Alto, CA: Stanford University Press, 1998), 179–181, and Andrew Wachtel and Predrag Marković, "A Last Attempt at Educational Integration: The Failure of Common Educational Cores in Yugoslavia in the Early 1980s," in Cohen and Dragović-Soso, *State Collapse*, 203–219.

18   For more on the Serbian victimization narrative, see Sabrina Ramet, "The Dissolution of Yugoslavia: Competing Narratives of Resentment and Blame," *Südosteuropa* 55 (2007), 30–40.

19   Popović's novel won the coveted Isidora Sekulić prize in 1985 and went through at least nine editions in the first year after its publication.

20   Danko Popović, *Knjiga o Milutinu* (Belgrade: Biblioteka Književne novine, 1986), 6–7.

21   See, for example, Milutin's complaints about the Macedonians (41) and about the Croats and Slovenes (43).

22   Ibid., 79.

23   See *Memorandum Srpske akademije nauka i umetnosti*. Nick Miller points to the importance of the Kosovo issue and the SANU Memorandum in changing the tenor of Serbian intellectual discourse in Yugoslavia. "One can argue that until 1986, the Serbian intellectual movement might have retained the purity of its origins as a return to engagement and advocacy of democratic reform, had the issue of Kosovo not emerged. Nevertheless, and with great force, Kosovo did come to subsume virtually every other principled issue . . . from about 1985 onward. . . . unfortunately, Serbian intellectual arguments regarding Serbian suffering became spiritual, and they ultimately focused much more on the alleged desire of Tito and his heirs to crush the Serbian nation as such, with Kosovo as Tito's proving ground, than they did with actual conditions in Kosovo or relatively more banal (and certainly less emotional) issues like respect for intellectual engagement. . . . The Serbian intellectual opposition accomplished one critical task: it painted a picture of a divided and degraded Serbia, victimized by Bolshevism as it had earlier been victimized by other foreign notions and demands; it developed what became a 'deeply embedded cognitive blueprint' that framed the actions of politicians, intellectuals, and ordinary Serbs thereafter." Nick Miller, "Return Engagement: Intellectuals and Nationalism in Tito's Yugoslavia," in Cohen and Dragović-Soso, *State Collapse*, 186–187.

24   During the existence of Yugoslavia, such narratives circulated publicly primarily in the Croatian émigré community. As Mark Biondich puts it: "It is hardly surprising that, among politically active Croats outside Yugoslavia after 1945, the Second World War would be commemorated through Bleiburg and not Jasenovac. . . . Insofar as Croat responsibility for any crimes was acknowledged, it was in the context of political errors committed by a criminal element within the regime or relative to the crimes perpetrated by the Serb royalist Chetniks or Tito's Communist partisans, both of which were seen as ideological variations of the Great Serbian theme." "'We Were Defending the State': Nationalism, Myth, and Memory in Twentieth-Century Croatia," in *Ideologies and National Identities: The Case of Twentieth-Century Southeastern Europe*, ed. John R. Lampe and Mark Mazower (Budapest: CEU Press, 2004), 68.

25   Ramet, "Competing Narratives," 41-50.

26   Bogdan Raditsa, "Nationalism in Croatia since 1964," in *Nationalism in the USSR and Eastern Europe in the Era of Brezhnev and Kosygin*, ed. George W. Simmonds (Detroit: University of Detroit Press, 1977), 464.

27   See Ramet, *Nationalism and Federalism*, 109.

28   The conference proceedings were published as *Mjesto i položaj hrvatske književnosti u nastavnim programima za škole drugog stupnja i za gimnazije*. (Rijeka: Matica hrvatska, 1971).

29   Ibid., 31; from a speech by Ivo Frangeš.

30   Jill Irvine, "The Croatian Spring and the Dissolution of Yugoslavia," in Cohen and Dragović-Soso, *State Collapse*, 168.

31   Ciril Zlobec, "Jezgra nisu kraj posla," *Politika*, June 30, 1983, 5, and "Smišljena podvajanja," *Borba*, August 23, 1983, 15.

32   Janez Menart, "Ogledalo pesnika Janeza Menarta," *Borba*, September 10–11, 1983, 11.

33   R. Lazarević, "Strah od 'tuđih' pisaca," *Politika*, 18 September 1983, 7.

34   Aleksandra Plavevski, "Sami ćemo odlučivati," *Politika Ekspres*, September 21, 1983, 7.

35   Xavier Bougarel, "Bosnian Muslims and the Yugoslav Idea," in Djokić, 101–102.

36   Ibid., 104.

37   For more on this event, see Mitja Velikonja, *Religious Separation and Political Intolerance in Bosnia-Herzegovina* (College Station: Texas A&M Press, 2003), 227–228.

38   The series of articles began with an attack on Mujagić by Miroslav Egerić, a professor from the Philosophy at Novi Sad on November 23, 1984 (5) and continued with a long and sometimes rambling response by Mujagić on January 4, 1985 (16–18). It was followed a week later by another attack on Mujagić by Milorad Vučelić (36) and concluded with a group of four letters to the editor on January 18 (4). The quotations here are from Mujagić's response of January 4, p. 18. Thanks to Dejan Jović for bringing this material to our attention.

39   As Hugh Poulton puts it: "in the first Yugoslavia, the Kosovo Albanians were seen essentially as alien interlopers living in Serbia's heartland. Similarly the attitude of the Albanians to the state and this blatant Serbian repression was unremittingly hostile." "Macedonians and Albanians as Yugoslavs," in Djokić, 127. On the relative absence of overt calls for Greater Albania, nevertheless, see Robert C. Austin, "Greater Albania: The Albanian State and the Question of Kosovo, 1912–2001" in Lampe and Mazower, 235–247.

40   On the evolution of Kosovar resistance in the 1980s and into the 1990s see Henry H. Perritt Jr., *Kosovo Liberation Army: The Inside Story of an Insurgency* (Champaign: University of Illinois Press, 2008).

41   Ramet, "Competing Narratives," 60. For more on supranational cultural narratives of Yugoslavism, see Andrew Wachtel, *Making a Nation, Breaking a Nation*.

42   Dragiša Pavlović, *Olako obećana brzina* (Zagreb: Globus, 1988).

43   Ibid.; Bogdan Bogdanović, *Mrtvouzice* (Zagreb: BST/Cesarec, 1988); interviews with Željko Simić (Serbia's minister of information and close Milošević confident in 1987), Ljubinka Trgovćević, Bogdan Bogdanović, Kosta Čavoški, Vesna Pešić, and Dragan Veselinov by Christopher Bennett, January–February 1992).

44   Miranda Vickers, *Between Serb and Albanian: A History of Kosovo* (London: Hurst & Co, 1998), 236.

45   James Gow, *Legitimacy and the Military: The Yugoslav Crisis* (London: Pinter, 1992), 90–94.

46   Interviews with Jože Mencinger, Janez Janša, Dimitrij Rupel, Jelko Kacin, Rastko Močnik, and Anton Bebler by Christopher Bennett, June–December 1991.

47   Mitja Žagar, "Yugoslavia, What Went Wrong? Constitutional Development and Collapse of a Multiethnic State," in *Reconcilable Differences: Turning Points in Ethno-Po-*

litical Conflict, eds., Sean Byrne and Cynthis L. Irvin, (West Hartford, CT: Komarian Press, 2000), 142.

48 Sabrina Ramet, "Explaining the Yugoslav Meltdown, 1: 'For a Charm of Pow'rful Trouble, Like a Hell-broth Boil and Bubble': Theories about the Roots of the Yugoslav Troubles," in Thomas Emmert and Charles Ingrao, eds., *Conflict in South-Eastern Europe at the End of the Twentieth Century: A 'Scholars' Initiative' Assesses Some of the Controversies* (London: Routledge, 2006), 28.

49 Although Kučan was reelected president, a coalition of six opposition parties called Demos defeated his now reformed Communists in the April parliamentary election, which took place before Marković was able to form a party. For more, see Matjaž Klemenčič and Mitja Žagar, *The Former Yugoslavia's Diverse Peoples* (Santa Barbara: ABC-Clio, 2004), 226–228.

50 Marcus Tanner, *Croatia: A Nation Forged in War* (New Haven: Yale University Press, 1997) 228.

51 In *Blueprints for a House Divided: The Constitutional Logic of the Yugoslav Conflicts* (Ann Arbor: Michigan University Press, 1999), Robert Hayden examines the constitutional nationalism at the heart of Yugoslavia's dissolution and the incompatibility of ethnic rule with multiethnic territories.

52 Slavoljub Djukić, *Milošević and Marković: A Lust for Power* (Montreal: McGill-Queen's University Press, 2001), 34.

53 Dejan Jović, "The Slovenian-Croatian Confederal Proposal," in Cohen and Dragović-Soso, *State Collapse*, 249–280.

54 Laura Silber and Allan Little, *Yugoslavia: Death of a Nation* (New York: Penguin Books, 1997).

55 Radio Belgrade had sent a reporter from Belgrade to cover the standoff rather than allow the Zagreb correspondent to report on it as would have been the case under normal circumstances. Interview with Radio Belgrade's Zagreb correspondent Vesna Knežević, September 1991.

56 Interviews with Ivan Zvonimir Čičak, Mate Granić, Branko Horvat, Vesna Knežević, Mario Nobilo, Janko Pleterski, Žarko Puhovski, Milorad Pupovac, Jovan Rašković, and Stipe Šuvar, by Christopher Bennett, 1991–1992.

57 Christopher Bennett, *Yugoslavia's Bloody Collapse* (London: Hurst & Co, 1995), 152.

58 For a full discussion of international involvement in the dissolution crisis, see chapter 5.

2

Melissa Bokovoy, team leader
Momčilo Pavlović, team leader

Milan Andrejevich   **Thomas Emmert**   **Dušan Janjić**
Marina Blagojević   **Bernd Fischer**   **Predrag Marković**
Ferit Duka   **Ranka Gašić**   **Besnik Pula**
Valentina Duka   **Nebojša Vladisavljević**

Melissa Bokovoy and Nebojša Vladisavljević contributed substantial portions of the text presented here by Momčilo Pavlović. Dr. Vladisavljević's entry ("Controversy Four") is based in part on his "Grassroots Groups, Milošević or Dissident Intellectuals? A Controversy over the Origins and Dynamics of Mobilization of Kosovo Serbs in the 1980s" that appeared in *Nationalities Papers* 32/4 (December 2004), which was subsequently republished in Thomas Emmert and Charles Ingrao, eds., *Conflict in Southeastern Europe at the End of the Twentieth Century: A Scholars' Initiative* (New York & London: Routledge, 2006).

The National Endowment for Democracy funded coordinated research by six team members. The current draft also benefited considerably from comment and criticism from members of Research Teams 2 and 8, most notably participants in two satellite meetings on 15–16 October 2004, hosted by Ohio State University's Center for Slavic and East European Studies in Columbus, Ohio (Melissa Bokovoy, Thomas Emmert, Bernd Fischer, Charles Ingrao, Momčilo Pavlović, Besnik Pula, Jason Vuić, and Frances Trix), and on 16–17 December 2004, at the Center for Interethnic Tolerance and Refugees, Skopje, Macedonia (Ferit and Valentina Duka, Ylber Hysa, Charles Ingrao, Dušan Janjić, Linda Karadaku-Ndou, Leon Malazogu, Gojko Mišković, and Momčilo Pavlović). The final draft was approved after project-wide review in February 2005.

KOSOVO UNDER AUTONOMY, 1974–1990

◆ Momčilo Pavlović ◆

Introduction

Ethnic relations are the crucial issue in Kosovo, especially between the Albanians and the Serbs. These groups have not managed to find a suitable and long-lasting political solution to administering Kosovo together. From the time the territory of Kosovo became a part of Serbia and then of Yugoslavia in the early decades of the twentieth century, the Kosovo problem has been seen by some as a problem of continual "status reversal." Whenever the Serbs administered Kosovo, as they did in the interwar period and from the end of World War II until lately, Kosovo Albanians[1] were discriminated against in political, economic, social, and cultural spheres and then were forced or intimidated into leaving.[2] On the other hand, when Albanians were in a position to dominate, usually with the help of foreign troops—Ottoman, Austro-Hungarian, Italian, German, Bulgarian, and NATO—the Serbs suffered discrimination and often had to flee from Kosovo (such was the case in both World Wars, as well as today). This idea of status reversal must, however, be examined carefully. Throughout the twentieth century, the period of Albanian ascendancy in Kosovo is very short. Veljko Vujačić observed in 1996:

> The turbulent twentieth century has witnessed many reversals of ethnic fortune in the Balkans, with power shifting from one to another group, not the least between Serbs and Albanians in Kosovo. On both sides, painful historical memories were reinforced by a constant process of power and status-reversal and conflict over a shared territory. This never-ending cycle of status-reversal can be briefly summarized as follows: Moslem (not Catholic or Orthodox) Albanians were the privileged group under the Ottoman empire (at least relative to Orthodox Serbs); Serbs "came out on top" after the Balkan wars (1912–1913) and the formation of Yugoslavia (1918); the status/power relationship changed in World War Two when a large part of Kosovo became a part of "greater Albania" under the sponsorship of Mussolini's Italy; in

1945, the Serbs "took over," albeit under the auspices of communist Yugo-slavia and in the name of "brotherhood and unity"; after Kosovo became a fully autonomous province (1974), high Albanian birth rates and the gradual "Albanianization" of the local Communist party once more raised the painful specter of status-reversal (for Serbs); with the advent of Milošević to power, Serbs emerged as the dominant status group for the third time in this century. In each of these cases, the process of status-reversal was accompanied by a revival of unpleasant memories as well as actual instances of persecution which further reinforced them.[3]

The real problem with such an interpretation is that the Kosovo Albanians never held sole state power, nor did Albanians ever have the monopoly on vio-lence.

It has been proven over the course of the last 150 years that symbolically Kosovo has meant different things to Kosovo Albanians and Serbs. It is not that these groups did not want to live together, for there is evidence of peaceful coex-istence; rather, the adjoining nation-states of Albania and Serbia sought expan-sion into this province in their efforts to create a larger, that is "greater," Albania and Serbia.[4] Such nationalist ideologies and platforms often destabilized rela-tionships because of the threat of armed conflict, either by guerrilla, police, or military action.

Each national group, Serbs and Albanians, based its claims on very contro-versial arguments and policies. Some Serbs argued that the continuing Albanian drive for an independent Kosovo, more or less intensive at different times, was evident in Albanian disloyalty to the state: rebellions, demonstrations, robbery, and attacks on the Serbs and their property. At the same time, Albanians continu-ously tried to present their problem as an international one; that is, they tried to make the international community see them as an oppressed minority in Serbia and Yugoslavia. Albanians were quick to point out that in periods of Serb domi-nation the authorities put evident pressure on the Albanians by arresting and ha-rassing them, by making plans for the colonization of Kosovo after World War I, and by changing Kosovo's ethnic structure to the benefit of the Serbs.

Although living on the same territory and often in the same towns and vil-lages, the Kosovo Serbs and Albanians lived in a sort of apartheid. Notwithstand-ing some better moments in their relations and examples of cooperation (above all, in the economic sphere), there was no incentive to create a multiethnic society with stable and lasting institutions. However, there was evidence that relations between Serbs and Albanians between 1974 and 1981 were tolerably improving as a result of the ideology and policies of the League of Communists, the per-sonal authority of Tito until his death in 1980, the state's monopoly of violence, the international position of Yugoslavia, a broad autonomy granted to Kosovo by the 1974 constitution, and the improving socioeconomic and cultural conditions of the ethnic Albanian population. Nevertheless, these policies were neither successful nor perceived as balanced. A year after Tito's death the Albanian–Serb conflict erupted, and during the 1980s, the largest numbers of political prisoners in the Socialist Federal Republic of Yugoslavia (SFRY) were Kosovo Albanians. Within a decade the country disintegrated through violent conflict.

The focus of this research centers on the policies of the Serbs in Kosovo, on the dramatis personae, goals, methods, and results of that policy. These policies were, clearly enough, part of the general processes in the Yugoslav federation after Tito's death in 1980. By the end of the 1980s, the disintegration processes accelerated even further, influenced by events abroad, especially in Eastern Europe. We emphasize the political processes in Serbia, which have always had a direct impact on Serb–Albanian relations in Kosovo, especially on the Kosovo Serbs, and on the degree of Kosovo Serb influence on the policies emanating from Belgrade. We also attempt to distinguish facts from interpretation and propaganda and to offer differing opinions on the same events. A reconstruction of events and an analysis of this period will be presented only in general in order to concentrate on the following four major controversies concerning Serb–Albanian relations:

1. The dramatic demographic changes in Kosovo between 1961 and 1981 and the reasons for an increase in the Albanian population from 67.08 percent of the population in 1961 to 77.4 percent of the population in 1981.[5]

2. The demands of the Kosovo Albanians for political and economic equality in the SFRY, the League of Communists of Yugoslavia's (LCY's) response—greater autonomy, constitutional changes, but denial of republican status—and a specific Serbian response based upon what some Serbs perceived to be an ever escalating scale of Albanian demands—a separate republic, secession, and unification with Albania.

3. The reasons and causes of Serbian migration from Kosovo, ranging from economic and familial to escalating violence and intimidation of Serbs by Albanians.

4. The relationship between Kosovo Serbs and Serb nationalist intellectuals and officials of the Milošević regime. As the Kosovo Serbs became more discontented with the changing ethnic composition of Kosovo and the post-1966 twist in interethnic politics, what role did grassroots efforts play in the political struggles in late socialist Yugoslavia?

Controversy 1: Demographic Changes in Kosovo, 1974–1981

The territory of Kosovo comprised 4.26 percent of the whole territory of Yugoslavia; 7 percent of the Yugoslav population lived there in 1981. In the early 1970s there were 916,168 ethnic Albanians, 228,264 Serbs, 31,555 Montenegrins, and 12,244 ethnic Turks in Kosovo. The Albanians made up 73.7 percent of the population of the region, the Serbs 18.4 percent, the Montenegrins 2.5 percent, and the Turks 1 percent. From 1945 to 1961, the proportion of Serbs in the province remained about 25 percent of the population. Beginning in 1961, the proportion of Serbs in the province fell. During the decades 1961–1971 and 1971–1981 the proportion fell at the same rate of about 5 percent per decade.

The demographic development in Kosovo is one of the most topical and at the same time one of the most delicate questions that researchers are currently facing. The problem lies in the lack of real information about population. The Albanians boycotted the last population census in Serbia of 31 March 1991. Because of that, their number is based on statistical estimates.[6] The previous two censuses in Kosovo (1971 and 1981) are suspect. (Federal Secretariat of Information, 1998). According to new analyses, the 1961 census, implemented under the supervision of federal and republican bodies, is the last one that may be considered objective. This census registered 646,805 Albanians and 227,016 Serbs (Table 1).[7]

Table 1. Kosovo's population by nationality.

	1948		1953		1961		1971		1981	
	Number	Percent	Number	Percent	Number	Percent	Number	Percent	Number	Percent
Albanians	498,242	68.5	524,559	64.9	646,805	67.2	916,168	73.7	1,226,736	77.4
Serbs	171,911	23.6	189,869	23.5	227,016	23.6	228,264	18.4	209,498	13.2
Montenegrins	28,050	3.9	31,343	3.9	37,588	3.9	31,555	2.5	27,028	1.7
Moslems	9,679	1.3	6,241	.8	8,026	.8	26,357	2.1	58,562	3.7
Romanies	11,230	1.5	11,904	1.5	3,202	.3	14,593	1.2	34,126	2.2
Turks	1,315	.2	34,583	4.3	25,784	2.7	12,244	1	12,513	.8
Croats	5,290	.7	6,203	.8	7,251	.8	8,264	.7	8,717	.6
Yugoslavs	—	—	—	—	5,206	.5	920	.1	2,676	.2
Others	2,103	.3	3,541	.3	3,110	.2	5,328	.3	4,584	.2
Total	727,820		808,141		963,988		1,243,693		1,584,441	

Source: Data from *Statistički Bilten*, no. 727, 1972, 11. Cited in Ruža Petrović and Marina Blagojević, *The Migrations of Serbs and Montenegrins from Kosovo and Metohija: Results of the Survey Conducted in 1985–1986* (Belgrade: Serbian Academy of Sciences and Arts, 1992), 78.

The censuses of 1971 and 1981 were implemented under the supervision of the authorities in Kosovo. In the 1981 census, the cooperation of the republic organs was explicitly rejected with the excuse that the statistical organs of the republic were not competent to undertake the census in Kosovo. Separatist demonstrations took place during the census.

Why did the proportion of Serbs decline in Kosovo? Numerous reasons for this decrease have been cited. Two of the most prevalent are: (1) the birthrate of the Albanian community of Kosovo, 35 per 1,000; and (2) the migration of the Serbs from the region. As Table 1 demonstrates there was a numerical decrease of Serbs as well as a proportional decrease between 1971 and 1981. Controversies arose over the increase in Albanian birthrates and the cultural norms ascribed to these increases; there was also controversy concerning the reasons for the Serb exodus from Kosovo. We will first turn our attention to the Albanian community's birthrates and consider the reasons for Serbian migration in another section below.

In 1979, Kosovo had the highest birthrate in Yugoslavia and in Europe, 26.1 per 100 people, compared to 8.6 for the national Yugoslav average.[8] During the 1980s, the discourse in the media in Serbia concerning the birthrates among Albanian women took on racial overtones. As Julie Mertus and others have noted, the study of higher Albanian birthrates has often been presented as a conscious decision on the part of Albanians to reproduce rapidly in order to change the demographic picture of Kosovo. In this regard, Albanian women are portrayed as baby factories. In fact, the difference can be ascribed to patterns of rural and urban communities, cultural and societal norms and expectations. It must be noted that Albanians are a larger percentage of the rural population in Kosovo. Mertus points out that urban Albanian women and other urban women in Yugoslavia had nearly identical birthrates.[9]

The discussion about birthrates must be framed within a larger discussion about the region's economic position vis-à-vis the other regions of the former Yugoslavia. Kosovo was the poorest and least developed region in Yugoslavia. The more developed republics of Yugoslavia and the region of Vojvodina gave 3 percent of their income for the development of the underdeveloped republics of Macedonia, Montenegro, Bosnia-Hercegovina, and the region of Kosovo. In 1971, Kosovo secured a special status through a mechanism by which its share was increased in the so-called Federation Fund for Inducing a Faster Development of the Underdeveloped Republics and Region of Kosovo. Kosovo received a share of 33.25 percent of this fund from 1971 to 1975, 37.1 percent from 1976 to 1980, and 43.5 percent from 1981 to 1985. The rest went to the other underdeveloped republics. The Republic of Serbia not only contributed to this federation fund but also provided other extra means for inducing the faster development of Kosovo.[10]

Within the party organizations of Yugoslavia and Serbia, Kosovo was seen as a development problem. According to Michael Palairet, "the development gap between Kosovo and the Yugoslav average has widened persistently and significantly. In 1952, Kosovo's per capita social product was 44 percent of that of Yugoslavia, but by 1988 it was down to 27 percent."[11] This decline was partly due to the high birthrates, which meant that absolute increase in the province's income still translated into per capita declines. Palairet noted that much of the early investment in Kosovo went to extracting Kosovo's mineral resources and ignoring investment in manufacturing and other sectors of the economy. After 1966, the federal government began to pour in resources for job creation in industry. Palairet pointed out that the return on the investment noted above was "abnormally low." "The official statistics indicate that between 1971 and 1988 each unit of investment generated only 65 percent of the incremental income achieved in Yugoslavia as a whole. Frustration reigned as the money disappeared or appeared in large building projects. Slovenia went so far as to announce well before it declared itself independent that it was cutting its contribution by half."[12] Kosovo's poor economic performance is one of the reasons why Serbs chose to migrate to other parts of Yugoslavia.

This poor economic performance translated into high rates of unemployment: 29.1 percent, two and one-half times higher than the official rates in the rest of Yugoslavia. Seventy percent of the unemployed were young people between the ages of 20 and 25. The number of unemployed Albanians and Serbians reflects their proportion of the population. Between 1970 and 1982, the percentage of unemployed Kosovo Albanians rose from 76 percent to 77.6 percent, whereas that of Kosovo Serbs fell from 17.6 percent to 15.1 percent. The fact that Kosovo Albanians had gained greater political clout in Kosovo under the 1974 constitution did not necessarily translate into an advantage in employment in state-run enterprises. Indeed, Serbs and Montenegrins held 30 percent of the jobs in this sector.[13]

Controversy 2: Issues Surrounding the Kosovo Albanians and Their Political and Economic Status

During the Communist period, Albanians and Serbs made contact through politics, that is through the Communist Party and its affiliated organizations, such as the Youth Association, syndicate organizations, the Socialist Association of the Working People, and the Union of Combatant Associations. The slogan "brotherhood and unity" allowed politicians an unlimited space for action and suppression of any sign of nationalism. The Kosovo constitution included the statement that all nations and ethnic groups in Yugoslavia fought against the fascists and formed an inseparable "brotherhood and unity" during the war. The fictive idea of brotherhood and unity was the unifying principle of the League of Communists of Yugoslavia. However, because there were more Serbs and Montenegrins both among Communists before 1941 and among resistance fighters afterward, Kosovo Albanians sometimes equated Communist Party domination with the domination of Serbian Communist officials and Serbian policy.

The period between 1948 and the mid-1960s can be characterized as a time when the Serbian minority in Kosovo dominated the province, symbolized by Aleksandar Ranković's security police's vigorous and at times brutal suppression of Albanian nationalism. During these years a substantial number of Albanians left the province. According to Nurcan Özgür Baklacioglu, "after 1958 the migrations of Albanians between Kosovo and Macedonia were the most significant amongst all other migrations occurring inside ex-Yugoslavia. The difference in minority policies and their applications, as well as the different economic and political conjectures prevailing in Macedonia and Kosovo after 1946, caused continuous Albanian movement between these two territories."[14]

Shifting political alliances, together with demographic and social factors, altered the landscape by the end of the 1960s. Changes in the political status of Kosovo within Communist Yugoslavia began in the 1940s, and over the course of the next thirty years, the Autonomous Kosovo–Metohija Region (1947) became the Autonomous Province of Kosovo and Metohija (1963) and then the Socialist Autonomous Province of Kosovo (1969).

In 1966, Tito and the League of Communists removed Ranković, limited the Serb-dominated UDBA and its anti-Albanian policies in the province, and subsequently sanctioned decentralization by granting more decision-making powers to the republics. What followed was Tito's and the LCY's attempts to reverse the severe discrimination against Albanians in the political, social, and economic life in Kosovo. Nevertheless, the LCY eventually discovered that the Albanians, especially students and intellectuals, were not satisfied with limited gains and wanted to push for greater autonomy; that is, an Albanian language university and recognition by the LCY that Albanians in Communist Yugoslavia should have the same political status as the South Slavs. As we will see, for some this meant the creation of a seventh republic in Kosovo. Ensuing crises in Kosovo, especially in 1968 and 1981, were the result of the LCY's "inability or unwillingness to grant the Albanian population symbolic [or political] equality with the Slav nationalities,"[15] that is republic status.

During both crises, Kosovo was moving closer to becoming a specific polity as a result of changes to the constitution of 1963 and then the adoption of a new constitution in 1974 that granted both Kosovo and Vojvodina status as "autonomous provinces" of Serbia. This meant that the provincial elites could forge direct links with federal (*federativna*) authorities and bypass republican authorities. In effect, the federal constitution of 1974 gave Kosovo de facto republican status, but not de jure status. As Albanian political leader Azem Vllasi observed, "Kosovo functioned as a republic in the federal state of Yugoslavia; we were not [a republic] only in name."[16] This de facto equality increased the desire of ethnic Albanians to fight for all forms of political, economic, social, and cultural equality in Kosovo.

Immediately after 1974, political relations between Kosovo's Serbs and Albanians seemed stable, at least on the surface. However, vivid social and cultural contrasts between the rich and the poor, between tradition and modernity, between new trends and the way of life from the previous century were evident. Party institutions dominated political discourse full of slogans and ideology. In reality, these ethnic communities lived apart but in peace, although there were, of course, some minor incidents. The parallel lives of the Serbs and the Albanians in Kosovo, which had lasted for centuries, continued during the Communist period as a result of the LCY's policy of creating and maintaining separate institutions on the basis of ethnicity due to fears that the Serbs would dominate. For example, the lectures at the university were held separately in Serbian and in Albanian.

Controversy revolves around the issue of whether or not the desired goal of the Kosovo Albanians was in fact republican status or secession. Kosovo Serbs and Belgrade believed that Kosovo Albanians would continue to seek greater and greater concessions. Many argued that after 1968, the Albanians in Kosovo were not only striving for some significant improvement of their status, but also for secession of Kosovo from Yugoslavia. Vladimir Matić in a December 2003 report for the Public International Law and Policy Group titled "Unbreakable Bond: Serbs and Kosovo" noted the development of a unified and well-connected Albanian elite as a result of the establishment of the University of Priština. This elite pushed for republican status for Kosovo, "part of which was the right to secede. [This desire was portrayed] as separatist in Belgrade and was met by a re-awakening of Serbian nationalism."[17]

The Constitution of 1974 and Some Political Results

The process of reorganizing the Yugoslav federation, which started in the late 1960s, reached its climax in the 1974 constitution. For the first time, republics and even the autonomous provinces of Vojvodina and Kosovo had their own constitutions. Many authors believe that the 1974 constitution gave to the republics and provinces prerogatives of the federal state and thus endangered that state. Some even want to trace the destruction of the country and the savage civil war to the crises that resulted from the constitutional changes.[18] In the 1974 constitution there are no articles concerning autonomous provinces per se (save Articles 1 and 4), but nevertheless the position of a province had always been treated in practice as equal to that of the republics. By this constitution, the provinces did in fact become independent of Serbia, whereas the republic of Serbia was at the same time dependent on its provinces. Serbia was a kind of federation within a federation.

Thus the Socialist Autonomous Province of Kosovo (SAP Kosovo), until 1968 known as Kosovo and Metohija, obtained a constitution in 1974 for the first time, according to which it had a right to regulate independently its social and economic affairs and its political bodies. The constitution defined the Kosovo Assembly as the highest institution of self-management and the highest authority of the province. The assembly was constituted by the Council of Associated Labor (ninety delegates), Council of Municipalities (fifty delegates), and the Socio-Political Council (fifty delegates).

According to the constitution, the Assembly of SAP Kosovo had the power to change the constitution of SAP Kosovo, had a vote in the event of changes to the federal constitution or to the constitution of Serbia, and had the power to decide on other crucial questions regarding the political, social, and cultural development of the region.[19] It also had the power to issue laws and budgets, to appoint and recall the president and the members of the executive council of the SAP Kosovo Assembly, the judges of the Constitutional Court of Kosovo, the judges of the Supreme Court of Kosovo, secretaries of the region, and other officials in Kosovo institutions. It controlled the executive council and other administration bodies of the province.

The nine-member presidency of SAP Kosovo was another important institution of the region, constituted in 1974. The presidency was a representative of the province, and it had "a right and obligation to initiate debate on important questions for the social and political life of the province" in the SAP Kosovo Assembly and in other institutions. These important questions included, above all, those related to the "equality of the nations and national groups." The presidency had to perform special tasks in the sphere of "national defense," and in the event of war, it had to lead the "people's resistance" in the region. Other institutions of the region (executive council of the SAP Kosovo Assembly, Constitutional Court, Supreme Court, and other judicial bodies) basically performed the same functions as their counterparts in Serbia and the Yugoslav federation.

The autonomous provinces had a special status in the Republic of Serbia. They had the right to independently issue laws and constitutions within their jurisdiction, provided they were not in opposition to the federal constitution and federal laws. On the other hand, the Republic of Serbia could only issue a constitution with the approval of provincial assemblies, and any laws it passed were only valid for the territory of Serbia outside the provinces. This territory was not defined either by the constitution or by the laws, although the term itself had been used since World War II. The provinces were represented in the federal institutions as equals, and their representatives often voted differently from those

of the Republic of Serbia. Besides, it often happened that the representatives of
Slovenia and Croatia seconded the position of their colleagues from the autonomous provinces.[20] However, when the votes of the provinces were in accordance
with those of Serbia, other republics objected to what amounted to Serbia's having three votes in federal institutions. Some politicians from Serbia responded
by stressing that they had nothing against other republics' forming autonomous
provinces on their own territory in order to obtain more votes. Therefore, from
1974 onward, Kosovo had almost all the prerogatives of other federal units.

Until the early 1990s, the Kosovo Albanians participated in the institutions
of the federation and the Republic of Serbia. From 1978 until 1988 they held, as
representatives of SAP Kosovo, the following posts in federal institutions:

1978	Sinan Hasani, vice president of the SFRJ assembly
1979	Fadilj Hoxha, vice president of the presidency of the SFRJ
1983	Aslan Fazlija, president of the federal council of the SFRJ assembly
1984	Ali Shukrija, president of the CK SKJ presidency
1985	Ilijaz Kurteshi, president of the SFRJ assembly
1985	Sinan Hasani, vice president of the SFRJ presidency
1986	Sinan Hasani, president of the SFRJ presidency
1986	Hashim Redxepi, president of the presidium of the Union of Yugoslav Socialist Youth
1988	Kazazi Abaz, president of the council of republics and provinces of the SFRJ assembly

Moreover, ethnic Albanians have represented Yugoslavia in fifteen countries
as ambassadors. Three of them held the post of the assistant federal secretary for
foreign affairs; three of them were general consuls; one of them was a director
of a culture information center; and seven of them were heads of administration
bodies and counselors in the federal foreign office. Moreover, they held important posts in defense: four of them were generals of the Yugoslav army; one of
them was assistant federal secretary for defense; and two of them were commanders of the territorial defense of SAP Kosovo. They were also represented in

the institutions of Serbia, Macedonia, and Montenegro, whereas in Kosovo they held the majority of posts.

In summary, from 1974 to 1988, we find ethnic Albanians holding a number of leadership positions in the federation, some republics, and SAP Kosovo (Table 2). For the first two decades after the war, Communists of Serbian and Montenegrin ethnic origin prevailed in party leadership and in other institutions, in large measure because they had fought for the Communist resistance. By the late 1960s ethnic Albanians, already predominant in numbers, were steadily increasing their role in the politics and social life of the province but still not in direct proportion to their share of the population. Of the 47,791 Communists in Kosovo in 1973, 29,507 (61.7 percent) were ethnic Albanians, whereas 12,515 (26.2 percent) were Serbs and 3,824 (8.0 percent) Montenegrins. Ethnic Albanians still felt that they were being treated unequally because their representation in the League of Communists had not yet reached the percentage of Albanians in the total Kosovo population (73 percent in the 1971 census), whereas the Serbs constituted 26.2 percent of the League of Communists despite comprising only 18.3 percent of the total population.

Table 2. Number of ethnic Albanians in leadership positions.

Institutions	November 1974	November 1988
Federal	41	38
Republic of Serbia	17	20
Republic of Macedonia	21	18
Republic of Montenegro	10	11
SAP Kosovo	99	171

By the logic of Yugoslavia's ideology of brotherhood and unity, higher rates of Albanian participation in the political institutions of the 1970s federation would suggest that ethnic Albanians accepted the political system and that they enjoyed rights similar to those of other nations and national groups in Yugoslavia. This argument, however, ignores other factors like equality of employment, economic status, and the viability of cultural institutions. It also masks a crucial political factor: the will of the Albanians to form a republic of their own—a republic that might include the Albanian regions of Montenegro and Macedonia. To some within the Serbian Communist Party, the federal government had neither the will nor the means to begin a dialogue for this eventuality.[21] Therefore, the Serbian Communist Party stepped into this vacuum and suggested an alternative to the 1974 de facto status of Kosovo.

An Attempt to Change the Constitutional Position of Serbia in 1977

On 16 January 1975, less than a year after the constitution was issued, the presidency of Serbia demanded its revision, explaining that it had brought disunity to the Republic of Serbia and that it was Serbia alone, among all other federal units, that had not obtained its "historic right to a national state within the Yugoslav federation." This demand was aimed at recovering and reinforcing Serbia's power over its autonomous provinces. It was formulated by a group of legal experts who were engaged for this task by the presidency of Serbia. Two years later, these experts published their analysis in a so-called blue book, a top-secret document on the malfunction of relations between Serbia and its provinces (appointment of officials, defense, planning, administration of justice, security, etc.). This publication caused a clash within the state and party leaderships of Serbia. The party leadership thought it unacceptable and censured it as "a centralist document." The conflict was solved by the supreme arbiter, Tito, at a meeting with the representatives of the Central Committee of Serbia (T. Vlaškalić), Regional Committee of Vojvodina (D. Alimpić), and Regional Committee of Kosovo (M. Bakalli) held on 27 July 1977. Tito insisted on keeping the constitution intact regarding the position of the provinces, thus being consistent with his principle of ethnic balance and suppressing the power of the largest federal unit and its supposed aspiration for centralism and unitarism. Tito's influence ended this dispute, but the problem, for both the Albanians and the Serbs, remained unsolved.

1981 Demonstrations in Kosovo

In March 1981, a little less than a year after Tito's death, demonstrations broke out in Kosovo. These demonstrations came as a surprise to the political leadership and to the public in general. Later, party and federal authorities blamed the Albanian leadership for not being strict enough in fighting nationalism and, then, for covering it up and not realizing the true causes of the problem. Yugoslav—especially Serbian—politicians and public opinion after 1981 always pointed out the continuity of "Albanian counterrevolution." At the time, terms such as *counterrevolution* and *irredentism* were in common use. By branding them counterrevolutionaries, the Yugoslav leadership was in denial about the real problems facing Kosovo: its unequal political status, the socioeconomic crises that resulted in deeply divided national communities, and the nationalist sentiments that grew out of the events of 1981.

Disagreements and controversies surround any discussion of the intentions and motivations of the demonstrators. The initial riot began in the cafeteria at the University of Priština, whose students were expressing frustration at and concern over a number of issues of some immediacy to them: unemployment and the inability of the federal state to recognize the demographic boom in higher education in Kosovo. These dissatisfactions were symbolized by inedible food and the squalid living conditions at the overcrowded and underfunded university. Kosovo's ratio of students was 274.7 per 1,000 inhabitants, the highest in the SFRY, compared to the national average of 194.9.[22] Initially, Serbian students at the university joined in the protests. Extrapolating from their experiences, these youthful protesters fixed on the broader theme of the inequities for all students in the province and for Albanians in particular. The demonstrations grew into mass protests all across Kosovo, and the main goal appeared to be the creation of a republic and not secession or unification with Albania, even though some support for the latter could be found.[23]

After the 1981 demonstrations the Kosovo question became the country's critical political problem. Everyone agreed that the whole country should exert itself in searching for a solution. Many protesters were arrested. Mahmut Bakalli was recalled from the post of president of the provincial committee of Kosovo, and Veli Deva was appointed in his place (he was previously himself recalled by Bakalli in 1971). The rector of Priština University was also recalled.

It is important to point out that until 1990 the Kosovo question was treated on the federal level, with significant differences of opinion.[24] The most important tasks were undertaken by federal institutions, not by Serbian ones. On November 17, 1981, the League of Communists of Yugoslavia agreed on a document titled "Political Platform for Action of the Yugoslav League of Communists in the Development of Socialist Self-Management, Brotherhood and Unity and Spirit of Community." In this document demonstrations were called "aggressive, ruthless, brutal and devastating actions with the scope of forming the Republic of Kosovo, which would secede from Serbia and Yugoslavia."

What is interesting is how the Yugoslav central authorities, as well as the international community (which also wanted nothing to do with the complex national issues being raised with the 1981 events), reacted to the events. Lacking any hard evidence of outside agitators, the LCY turned to the Kosovo Albanian leadership, who were accused of not waging an effective campaign against "greater Albanian nationalism and irredentism." The term *irredenta* in the hands of LCY officials meant "not only organized anti-Yugoslav activities for the purpose of uniting Kosovo with Albania, but almost any kind of Albanian national feelings or popular resentment."[25] The LCY really feared the rise of a mass-based separatist movement, which would constitute a major threat to the territorial integrity of Yugoslavia. The vagaries of the causes of the demonstrations and their organizers did not prevent the LCY from pursuing the arrest, prosecution, and imprisonment of 226 workers for "organized activity" as well as "verbal crimes."[26] From this time forward, Kosovo Albanians would make up the highest percentage of political prisoners in the SFRY. Amnesty International and others noted that by the mid-1980s plainclothesmen and military checkpoints proliferated across the province.[27]

Despite the delusions of the party leadership, most of the organizations advocating some type of Albanian nationalism were formed *after* the riots. According to Aleksandar Tijanić, "it is impossible that militant chauvinists and separatists have branches in every little village, enterprise, school, or sports association where inter-ethnic incidents are occurring."[28] Analyzing the incidents, Tijanić argued that Yugoslavia's central authorities "grossly underestimated to what extent the idea of a Kosovo republic seems natural to most Albanians." He urged his readers to understand what was happening in Kosovo in the early 1980s by considering the nationalist movements of the south Slavs in the nineteenth century.

Despite Tijanić's appeal for understanding the demonstrations as part of a larger historical example of ethnicity and nationalism in the Balkans, the federal authorities branded the events of 1981 counterrevolutionary, and the Serbian party leadership characterized them as an ethnic threat that gave rise to a Serbian nationalist reaction. Serbian migration from Kosovo became the symbol of Serbian victimization by Kosovo Albanians.

Controversy 3: Reasons and Causes of Serbian Migration from Kosovo

Serbian migration from Kosovo was a permanent process since the early 1960s. The reasons for migrations were manifold, but public opinion believed them to be fear, pressure, inequality, and the failure of legislation to protect people and their possessions. This public opinion was shaped by Yugoslav and, especially, Serbian press reports about harassment of, violence (especially rape) against, and general mistreatment of Kosovo's Serbs. The press reported violations against private and state property, such as sabotage, fires, disturbances of rail communications, explosions, and attacks on police and provincial authorities.[29] In addition, the Serbian population in Kosovo, especially after the political changes in the 1960s, considered themselves to be discriminated against in the labor market and before the provincial courts and police. Although little investigation was ever done to verify many of these reports,[30] a controversy broke out concerning the reasons for this continuous emigration of Serbs and Montenegrins from Kosovo. The 1981 Yugoslav census listed approximately 110,000 Serbs from Kosovo living in other parts of Yugoslavia, 85,000 of whom had left the province between 1961 and 1981. Emigration continued into the 1980s. As a result, nearly a third of Kosovo Serbs had moved out of the autonomous province since 1961.[31]

The 1960s mix of politics, demographic decline, and steady migration out of Kosovo resulted in mounting grievances among Kosovo Serbs. The idea that Serbian emigration from Kosovo was a problem was brought out for the first time by Dobrica Ćosić in 1968, but this was censored by the Communist authorities. In the early 1970s, a number of Kosovo Serb officials raised the issue in Kosovo's party organs of the province's growing Albanization and the problems this posed for the non-Albanian population. Miloš Sekulović and Jovo Šotra pointed to growing pressure on Serbs, especially those living in the countryside, to emigrate from the province as well as their inadequate protection by the law enforcement agencies, their problems in education, and their obstacles to finding employment.[32] Kadri Reufi, an ethnic Turk, demanded that the leadership investigate the causes of the deteriorating position of this minority and claimed that the number of Turks in Kosovo was significantly reduced in the 1971 census because they were labelled Albanians. All three individuals were removed from the Provincial Committee and public life, the effect of which was to silence other non-Albanian politicians. The appeals of party members and ordinary people to local authorities and the provincial leadership were either ignored or rejected and the appellants harassed.

The major consequence of the 1981 events in Kosovo was the aggravation of already fragile ethnic relations. During the early 1980s, the majority of Yugoslav citizens who were arrested under Article 136 of the federal criminal code for "association for purposes of hostile activity" were Albanians. Modest improvements in Albanian access to state jobs and managerial positions during the 1970s and the outbreak of the demonstrations in 1981 led to complaints by Serbs in the region about "Albanianization." Despite the perceived reversal of fortunes, Serbs still held 52 percent of managerial positions and 20 percent of jobs in state positions. But perceptions are believed to have played a role in intensifying the migration of Serbs and Montenegrins from Kosovo.

Although the migration of the Serbs from Kosovo had been fairly constant since the end of World War II, it was only after 1981 that it was discussed in public. The leadership was driven to action by public opinion. The issue was discusssed at the eleventh conference of the Central Committee of the Yugoslav League of Communists, held on 20 December 1983. Beginning in 1985, Serbs and Montenegrins from Kosovo organized protests in the form of petitions and visits to party and state officials in Belgrade. In addition, Serbian intellectuals fixed upon this question and believed that Kosovo Albanians were winning the demographic battle. Although a 1986 memorandum by leading intellectuals of the Serbian National Academy of Arts and Sciences alleged systematic discrimination against Serbs and Serbia in the SFRY, it argued that the most egregious acts were taking place in Kosovo, where the Serbs of Kosovo were being subjected to "physical, political, legal, and cultural genocide."[33] Reflecting on the centuries-long struggle for independence by Serbia, the memorandum argued that all of Serbia's sacrifices had been ignored and its independence usurped by the legal dismemberment of Serbia under the 1974 constitution. It stated:

> A nation [Serbia] that has regained statehood after a long and bloody struggle, that has achieved civil democracy, and that lost two and a half million kinsmen in two world wars underwent the experience of having a bureaucratically constructed party commission determine that after four decades in the new Yugoslavia it alone was condemned to be without its own state. A more bitter historic defeat in peacetime cannot be imagined.[34]

The defeat was not only a legal and political one but also a demographic one.

According to the memorandum Kosovo Albanians were not only intimidating and driving out Serbs from Kosovo but they were outpacing Serbs in their birthrates. Thus, the memorandum proclaimed, "The expulsion of the Serbian nation from Kosovo bears spectacular witness to its historic defeat." By pointing out the declining birthrates among Serbs and suggesting that the Serbian nation in Kosovo faced "biological extinction," two highly charged sexual and gendered images came to represent the viewpoint of the Serbian intellectuals. Serbian women in this nationalist project had to resume their natural roles as mothers and bearers of the national citizens. Serbian men also had to be rejuvenated and protect the nation and Serbian women from a virile Albanian movement and its men. In the mid-1980s, rumors and unfounded accusations circulated that Albanian men were preying upon and raping Serbian women in Kosovo. Such rumors soon became embedded in Serbian popular culture with the production of both a play and a movie that featured the rapes of Serbian women by Albanian men.[35]

Many of the sentiments expressed in the memorandum and public discussions about Kosovo in Serbia were the backdrop for a 1985–1986 survey of Serbs who had left Kosovo titled "The Migration of Serbs and Montenegrins from Kosovo." This study was commissioned by the Serbian Academy of Arts and Sciences and conducted by Ruža Petrović and Marina Blagojević in the highly politicized environment of the 1980s. The authors' findings indicate that more than three quarters of the emigration originated from noneconomic factors, mainly verbal pressure, damage to property, or seizure of crops and land, violence (assaults, fights, stoning, attacks on children and women, serious injury, attempted and committed rape), trouble at work, and inequities in the public sector. What also emerged from the survey was that there was a clear territorial pattern of emigration largely resulting from the level of pressure and inequalities. The latter was inversely related to the proportion of Serbs in a settlement, and the critical point for a major increase in the pressure was if their numbers dropped below 20–30 percent. This finding was compatible with evidence from the official census that there was a strong trend toward emigration of Serbs from settlements where they accounted for less than 30 percent of the population.[36] Therefore, the decreasing proportion of Serbs in a settlement led to a sharp increase in pressure and inequities, which in turn resulted in emigration.

Petrović and Blagojević analyzed the migrations based on two different interpretations of why the migrations occurred. The first thesis was that the Serbian migrations were "normal migrations" motivated by "economic reasons" and that other ethnic groups in Kosovo migrated out as well during the same period. The migrations were ascribed to the process of "overall economic growth" and the "relative lag in economic development." The lack of economic opportunities also prompted a large number of Kosovo Albanians to migrate to other parts of Yugoslavia and to western Europe, with 45,000 Albanians leaving the province between 1971 and 1981. The second interpretation was that the Kosovo Serbs were being driven out by Albanian separatists and by the policies of the Albanian authorities who ruled Kosovo when it achieved de facto republic status. Petrović and Blagojević concluded that the "pull factors" for migration were "mostly of a non-economic nature, not the kind of contemporary migrations prompted by the desire to improve one's economic and social position."[37]

They concluded further that although some left for economic reasons most emigrated out of the Kosovo province due to noneconomic reasons, such as threats to personal safety or property, ethnic discrimination, institutionalized discrimination by Albanian authorities, and a policy of "ethnic homogenization" by Albanian nationalists-separatists. According to some experts, "this study must be treated with some caution, not only because the Serbian Academy was at the forefront of national mobilization at the time, but also because of the survey's timing."[38] Analyzing the results, Helfant Budding notes that about two-fifths of the 500 families interviewed had emigrated before 1975.[39] Given the time lag, the intensity of news reports about intimidation and violence in Kosovo, and heightened Serb-Albanian tensions at the time of the survey, there may well have been some retrospective bias among the respondents. Nevertheless, interethnic tensions, especially among those Serbs whose presence in a community dropped below 30 percent, played a role in many emigration decisions according to the conclusions of the report.

Controversy 4: Kosovo Serbs, Serbian Nationalist Intellectuals, and Officials of the Milošević Regime

After the Albanian demonstrations of 1981, the mobilization of Kosovo Serbs began and developed largely in response to changes in the political context and within a political environment that was not totally unfavorable to the action of grassroots groups from this ethnonational group. This mobilization of the Kosovo Serbs played an important part in the political struggles in late socialist Yugoslavia. The controversy and debate revolve around the contention by many specialists that througout the 1980s Kosovo Serbs were little more than the passive recipients of the actions and attitudes of elites and counterelites. The specialists claim that the mobilization of various groups within this community was inspired, organized, and coordinated by the officials of Milošević's regime or by Serb nationalist intellectuals, or both. In fact, this was a grassroots mobilization.[41]

The mobilization of Kosovo Serbs, rooted in their discontent with the changing ethnic composition of Kosovo and the post-1966 change in interethnic politics, was initiated and spread principally by various grassroots groups within this community. The grievances of Kosovo Serbs could not translate into collective action in a political system that opposed any reference to their concerns, but they accumulated over time and eventually resulted in a high level of politicization of Kosovo's Serbs. As a local observer put it, "in the southern socialist autonomous province each and every head of a Serb household who takes himself seriously keeps a library of petitions, appeals, pamphlets and newspaper clippings."[42] The political change ultimately opened space for the collective action of various groups of Kosovo Serbs. In 1981, protests of Kosovo Albanians swept the autonomous province. As we have seen, a student protest over socioeconomic issues turned into large-scale demonstrations with some calling for a republic of Kosovo, even union with Albania. The government declared a state of emergency, deployed tanks and security forces, closed schools and factories, and suppressed demonstrations. The scale of the protests apparently surprised the federal leadership and raised fears of a major separatist movement. Officials now increasingly paid attention to the complaints alleging inequalities facing the non-Albanian population in terms of the use of language, access to jobs in the state-controlled part of the economy, allocation of public housing, and inadequate protection of their rights and property by the courts and law enforcement agencies. Kosovo's officials came under much closer scrutiny by the federal leadership, and Albanian-Serb relations in Kosovo ceased to be their exclusive domain. The prevention of Serb emigration and redress of the Serbs' other concerns now became part of the party's policy.

The political change raised the expectations of Kosovo Serbs that the authorities would fully address their concerns. Soon, however, many from the community felt that the new policy did not begin to address all of their concerns, and emigration continued. Some believed that high officials in Yugoslavia and Serbia were not aware of the scope of the problem; therefore, they arranged a number of private meetings, sometimes involving large delegations, with officials and other people they thought to be influential. They met, for example, with Nikola Ljubičić, president of Serbia's state presidency (1982–1984); with party officials in Montenegro; with Svetozar Vukmanović-Tempo, a retired member of Tito's old guard; with Branko Pešić, a Belgrade mayor; and many others.[43] In most cases the delegations were given a sympathetic hearing and assurances that the party's policies, including initiatives aimed at halting the emigration of Serbs, would be implemented.

Simultaneously, a growing number of ordinary people, mainly in predominantly Serb settlements, attended local meetings of official political organizations, mostly those of the Socialist Alliance of the Working People (SAWP, formerly the People's Front), to raise their concerns. In Kosovo Polje, a suburb of Priština with a dominant Serb population, roughly thirty political outsiders regularly debated various issues and forwarded the meetings' minutes to officials at all levels, from Priština and Kosovo to Serbia and the federation. Although remaining within the boundaries of officially permitted dissent, they increasingly laid blame for any inequalities on Kosovo's officials, both Albanians and Serbs. Early on the core members of this group, namely Kosta Bulatović, Boško Budimirović, and Miroslav Šolević, jointly prepared the meetings and gradually shifted the agenda from local problems to the issues of broader political significance.[44] Parallel developments unfolded in other predominantly Serb settlements.

Although Priština's and Kosovo's officials periodically attended the meetings in Kosovo Polje, the debaters felt that the authorities would not take their problems seriously unless they gained broader support among Kosovo's Serbs. Bulatović, Budimirović and Šolević, therefore, extended their activities beyond the official organizations and started mobilizing support at the grass roots. In 1985, they extended the core group to include informal advisors Zoran Grujić, a university professor, and Dušan Ristić, a former chief Kosovo official. They agreed that the post-1981 party's policy aimed at ending the politics of inequality and emigration of Serbs was adequate and that they should simply press the authorities to implement the policy.[45] In late October 1985, the Kosovo Polje group sent a petition to officials in Yugoslavia and Serbia. They protested against discrimination against Kosovo Serbs and asked for the protection of their rights and the establishment of law and order. They pointed out that Kosovo was becoming increasingly "ethnically clean" of Serbs, accused Kosovo's officials of the tacit approval of forced migration of Serbs out of the region, and demanded that Yugoslavia's and Serbia's authorities bring that trend to a halt.[46] About 2,000 people signed the petition within ten days, and by April 1986, the number of signatories had multiplied several times.

In 1986, prominent activists initiated several highly visible protests and a series of small-scale local protest events. In late February, early April, and early November, they sent large delegations to the capital to meet officials of Yugoslavia and Serbia. The protest events also included a very visible protest march of several hundred people that unfolded under the label of collective emigration just before the party congress in May, as well as a number of large public meetings in Kosovo Polje, including one before Serbia's party leader Ivan Stambolić.[47] There were also a series of small-scale protests across the autonomous province, mostly in the form of public meetings or outdoor public gatherings, organized in response to specific cases of nationalist-related violence. As people became aware of the advantages of noninstitutional action, they started petitioning local authorities, and sometimes managers of large state enterprises, to protest against discrimination at work.[48]

The main consequence of various post-1981 initiatives was the incipient and unconnected networks of activists and supporters in towns and villages inhabited by Serbs. Throughout 1986 the Kosovo Polje group, including the newly arrived Bogdan Kecman, worked to link the emerging local networks into a more powerful political force. Each of them took responsibility for a specific area of Kosovo and worked to strengthen links between the existing activists in the area, recruit new ones, and inform potential supporters about their initiatives. Before long the Kosovo Polje group could mobilize small groups of activists for protest events in and outside Kosovo within a few hours.[49] The activists' demands, which initially focused on the lack of protection by the law enforcement agencies and courts and inequalities in the public sector, gradually evolved toward constitutional issues. The protesters asserted that if the provincial officials were unable to guarantee protection to Serbs then Kosovo should be brought back under the jurisdiction of Serbia's authorities.[50]

Officials tolerated the mobilization for several reasons. Firstly, the highly decentralized political structure of socialist Yugoslavia, based partly on national rights and identities, encouraged groups to mobilize along national lines. After 1981 officials had already acknowledged the grievances of Kosovo Serbs and put emphasis on forestalling their emigration. Unlike Kosovo Albanian protesters in 1981, who had aimed at important constitutional change, Kosovo Serbs demanded little more than implementation of the existing party policy, which was much less likely to trigger repression. Serbs, though a minority group in Kosovo, constituted a majority in Serbia as a whole and a plurality in Yugoslavia, which rendered their concerns more urgent for Yugoslavia's political class. Other political changes also mattered. The change of political generations in the first half of the 1980s brought younger politicians into the highest regional offices, and many of them felt that repression against ordinary people would go against the values of their generation. Growing elite disunity, rooted in the decentralized political structure and intensified during leadership succession, had already resulted in deadlock at the federal level and now thwarted attempts to reach a common position on the grassroots protest.

Secondly, the modest scale of mobilization and its limited potential for expansion, which sharply distinguished it from the 1981 mobilization of Kosovo Albanians, were also important. The movement of a minority group in a peripheral region hardly posed a threat to the regime. Officials were mainly concerned about the potential implications for political stability at the center because protesters' demands were potentially highly resonant with Serbs outside Kosovo. Major protests of Kosovo Serbs that centered on the capital, such as the the May 1986 march, were therefore prevented. Officials often issued public threats to prominent activists, especially after the October 1985 petition, and Bulatović was briefly jailed in early April 1986.

Thirdly, activists opted for moderate protest strategies and repeatedly stressed that their protest was not antisystemic. The protests often unfolded under the auspices of the SAWP partly because officials rarely tolerated openly noninstitutional initiatives and partly because the minority constituency of the movement ruled out large-scale discontent. The highly decentralized political structure of socialist Yugoslavia—including complex relationships between organs of Yugoslavia, Serbia, and Kosovo; a high level of local autonomy; and a large number of official organizations—provided space for the activists to organize, recruit new supporters and appeal for support.

From the early 1980s various groups of Kosovo Serbs sought contacts with influential people. Activists kept in touch with some earlier Kosovo Serb migrants, such as the managers of state enterprises and middle-rank officials in the capital and reporters for the Belgrade media based in the province. The confidants helped by identifying targets for appeal outside Kosovo because the activists knew little about institutional structure and informal political alliances, and they commented on protest strategies. Activists also established contact with dissident intellectuals, including Dobrica Ćosić, a well-known dissident novelist who had been purged from the party over the policy on Kosovo in 1968. Ćosić supported their cause and suggested that they make use of all legal channels. Other contacts from the Belgrade dissident circles urged radical action early on and claimed that protests of Kosovo Serbs in the capital would trigger demonstrations by hundreds of thousands.[51] Ćosić claims that he initiated the October 1985 petition at a meeting with a number of Kosovo Serbs but that a Belgrade journalist, an earlier Serb migrant from Kosovo, actually wrote the first draft.[52] This is probably true. Although Kosta Bulatović claimed that he initiated and drafted the petition, other prominent activists suspected that the Belgrade journalist, a friend of Bulatović, wrote the text.[53]

In January 1986, some 200 Belgrade-based intellectuals signed a petition supporting the cause of Kosovo Serbs, and the writers' union subsequently held a number of protest meetings. A number of dissident intellectuals had already initiated a debate on Kosovo a year before, partly from the perspective of a revisionist history of Serb-Albanian relations and partly focusing on the current grievances of Kosovo Serbs.[54] Without doubt the dissident intellectuals' actions alerted the general public in central Serbia to the concerns of Kosovo Serbs and made a strong impression on officials throughout Yugoslavia and Serbia. However, this was only a part of the intellectuals' sweeping critique of the Communist regime and had little to do with either the creation or consolidation of the local protest networks. There was little difference between a few meetings of activists with Ćosić and their contacts with other potential allies, insofar as the activists initiated nearly all of them. The significance of the October 1985 petition, drafted by the intellectuals, did not lie in its content; the same demands had featured prominently in the activists' discussions in the official organizations. The Kosovo Polje group had even drafted a similar petition two years before but collected only around seventy signatures.[55] The 1985 petition became important because nearly 2,000 Kosovo Serbs signed the text within ten days and thus demonstrated strong commitment to their cause despite a widespread fear of job loss or imprisonment.

Nor were the dissident intellectuals the only group that helped publicize the cause of the emerging movement. Kosovo Serb war veterans occasionally supported some activists' demands and demanded resignations of various Kosovo officials, both Albanians and Serbs. Before initiating any major protest event, prominent activists tested their ideas with at least some of their confidants to find out whether the chosen targets and timing were appropriate. While seeking contact with, and advice from, various quarters, the protest organizers made decisions on protest strategies on their own. They firmly believed that people at the grassroots level understood their problems best and could make appropriate decisions. More importantly, they were painfully aware that they, and not their confidants, would have to suffer the consequences of any wrong moves.[56]

Before 1988, political alliances in Kosovo's leadership had rarely followed ethnonational cleavage, and the views of most Albanian and Serb officials shifted over time with changes in the party's policy. This was reflected in the demands of Kosovo Serb activists for the resignations of some Albanian and Serb officials and their occasional support for other officials, both Serbs and Albanians. The activists had generally been cautious about Serbs in Kosovo's political establishment, feeling that their loyalty lay with the party's policy of the day.[57] After 1981, a number of Serb high officials, originally from Kosovo, who had occupied posts in federal organs were sent back to influential positions in Kosovo's leadership. The so-called weekend or traveling politicians, whose families stayed in Belgrade, had little connection with Kosovo Serb realities and were generally despised by ordinary people. The activists therefore continually sought allies among the leadership of Serbia but with little success.

Many authors consider 24 April 1987, the date of Milošević's visit to Kosovo, to be the moment when the Kosovo Serbs started to follow his policy. His visit to Kosovo Polje was not originally planned. Kosovo's officials designed Milošević's itinerary in such a way that he would not visit predominantly Serb settlements and thus would not have to face protesters. The Kosovo Polje group then staged a protest over a fake incident to attract the attention of Serbia's leadership. On 17 April the activists spread the word that Zoran Grujić, a university professor and coconspirator, had decided to emigrate from Kosovo. Apparently Grujić had been repeatedly interrogated by the police because of his links with the Kosovo Polje group. He claimed to have experienced problems at the University of Priština because of his Serb background. Within hours, around three hundred people gathered outside his house in protest. Of course, Grujić did not leave the province, but the activists exploited the case to invite Milošević to drop by on his Kosovo tour. Three days later Milošević, accompanied by Azem Vllasi, Kosovo's party leader, came to deliver a speech before three thousand Kosovo Serbs outside a local primary school. At the end, the activists insisted that he come again, this time not just to talk but also to listen to their complaints. Milošević accepted the invitation and approved their request to choose their own representatives for the meeting.

Milošević and Vllasi arrived in Kosovo Polje for this meeting in the afternoon of 24 April. When cars with the politicians approached the building, a crowd of several thousand protesters was already waiting. They passionately chanted: "We want freedom, we want freedom!" Police literally carried Milošević into the building while the protesters struggled to enter as well. It turned out that local party officials had drafted their own list of speakers, and when the police tried to stop others from entering the building, the chaos began. The police responded by beating protesters with truncheons, while the protestors threw stones at policemen and the building. Milošević was then asked to speak to the protesters and try to calm them down. Milošević asked the protesters to choose their own representatives, ordered the police not to beat people, and asked the protesters to maintain order themselves. The latter accepted this with ovations, and the meeting continued until early morning. The representatives, in most cases farmers, skilled workers, and teachers, spoke emotionally about inequalities and the lack of protection for Serbs from Kosovo's authorities. At the end, Milošević delivered a speech in which he made his position clear—namely his public disapproval of the use of force by the police.[58]

Milošević subsequently pulled all the strings to call a session of the Central Committee of Yugoslavia and demanded that specific targets be set for the performance of party and state organs in relation to the Kosovo problem. Milošević also demanded that a number of Kosovo's former chief officials, including Fadilj Hoxha, a retired member of Tito's old guard and an undisputed authority among Kosovo Albanians, be held accountable before the party for their alleged tacit approval of the so-called counterrevolution. Hoxha had already retired, and his removal from the party would not have important immediate consequences for the personal composition and policies of Kosovo's leadership. However, by calling into question Hoxha's credibility Milošević implicitly questioned the policy of federal leadership from the late 1960s and Kosovo's highly autonomous status, which had been achieved under Hoxha's leadership. As the intervention of Milošević related largely to the implementation of previously jointly approved policies and remained firmly on the Titoist course, Milošević gained support from officials from other republics without difficulty. However, the developments initiated clashes in the leadership of Serbia. Minor disagreements over policy details on Kosovo were exaggerated in the heat of the power struggle between the factions based on the personal networks of Milošević and those of his former protector Ivan Stambolić. These unfolded according to the rules of the game in socialist party-states, with little influence from society.[59]

Since the 1967–1974 constitutional reforms, the main concern of officials from Serbia had been the fragmented political structure of Serbia.[60] In the aftermath of the 1981 protests of Kosovo Albanians, Draža Marković and Petar Stambolić claimed that the eruption of protests had resulted from the unconstitutional extension of the autonomy of Serbia's provinces, but they had little success in persuading officials from other republics to help strengthen Serbia's central organs. Following the change of political generations, Ivan Stambolić reaffirmed the need for greater coordination between the central government of Serbia and its autonomous provinces and emphasized economic issues and the concerns of Kosovo Serbs. The rise of Milošević in 1987 changed little in this respect, and Milošević reiterated the demands of his predecessors. The change in leadership, however, turned the fortunes of the growing social movement. Whereas Stambolić had kept pressure on Kosovo's officials to address the problems of Kosovo Serbs and ignored the protest networks, Milošević aimed to establish control over the mobilization by co-opting prominent activists. The change partly originated from the spread of mobilization so that it now had to be dealt with either through suppression or co-optation. Also, Milošević exploited the mobilization for his own ends and often provoked activists to publicly denounce his opponents. The activists did not object because they now felt a degree of protection from federal and provincial officials and their protests achieved greater visibility. Prominent activists were in turn under strong pressure to channel their initiatives toward official organizations and employ their influence over local networks to halt noninstitutional action.[61]

The growing influence of Milošević on prominent activists often failed to be transformed into action on the ground partly because the activists intended to proceed with protests until their demands had been fully addressed and partly because of the highly decentralized character of their protest networks. Although influential, the Kosovo Polje group by no means presided over the networks, and other activists at times fully ignored its advice. Around thirty to forty prominent activists from various parts of Kosovo gathered occasionally and commanded sufficient influence to prevent any initiatives of which they disapproved or to start new ones. In the summer of 1988 the activists formed a protest committee that quickly became another important decision-making center. None of the three main circles of power within the social movement, however, could control a group of radical activists who at times would not listen to anybody's advice and proceeded with action, often getting support from one or two hundred supporters. The local networks, therefore, proceeded with protests across Kosovo. To placate Milošević they now staged all protests, even large outdoor gatherings, in the form of meetings of official organizations. In a growing number of cases officials who attended the meetings were booed at or prevented from speaking; in other cases the audience left the meetings altogether.

In the spring of 1988 prominent activists became increasingly skeptical about the claims of Milošević that a constitutional change aimed at empowering the central government of Serbia would occur in the near future. Convinced that pressure from the grass roots was essential to political change, they launched a petition in May 1988, before the federal party conference—the so-called small party congress—and soon presented it to officials of Yugoslavia and Serbia with nearly 50,600 signatures. The reason that nearly a quarter of Kosovo Serbs found themselves as signatories to the petition was that many activists signed up their whole families. Despite this wild exaggeration, the petition was a sort of plebiscite of Kosovo Serbs. The petitioners demanded that the federal organs temporarily establish direct rule in the province in order to establish security for the Serbs or, alternatively, recognize their right to self-defence. They also threatened that they might collectively emigrate from the province as a last resort.[62] Aware of the limits to the protest groups' organizational resources, officials in Yugoslavia and Serbia were nonetheless concerned that any activities under the label of collective emigration might trigger public unrest on a large scale. Milošević resolutely demanded a halt to such activities.[63]

Having to drop an important protest strategy and fearing a decline in participation by dispirited supporters, prominent activists found an alternative target—a protest in Novi Sad, the largest city in Vojvodina. After the unexpected success of the protest, the protest organizers and their nonelite allies outside Kosovo launched a series of protests in Vojvodina and Montenegro during the summer.[64] The protests coincided with a spiraling conflict among the elites of both republics and provinces over the amendments to the constitutions of Yugoslavia and Serbia, partly regarding the relations between Serbia's central government and its autonomous provinces. In September Kosovo Serbs began to protest all over the province. The activists now engaged in cooperation with Kosovo Serb intellectuals because they needed well-educated people to deliver speeches at a growing number of protests.[65] Although the local Serb intellectuals had timidly signaled their discontent with the position of Serbs in Kosovo, few of them took part in protest activities prior to late summer 1988.

The consolidation of support for the social movement among Kosovo Serbs and the efforts of Milošević to break the resistance of Kosovo's officials to the constitutional reform gradually affected political alliances in the provincial leadership, which had rarely followed ethnonational cleavage. The first signs of rising tensions occurred in early 1988 when several Serb officials from the Priština Committee openly supported prominent activists. The September protest campaign coincided with a break between Kosovo Albanian and Serb members of the Provincial Committee. Serbs now supported Milošević's demand for chief officials in Kosovo to resign because of their alleged obstruction of the party's policy; Albanians defended their leaders and objected to the significant constitutional changes. In the aftermath of the purges of Kosovo Albanian officials and the abrogation of Kosovo's autonomy in 1989, Milošević filled key political and public-sector positions with low-ranking Kosovo Serb officials, mainly those who had little connection with the grassroots mobilization. Because the constitutional changes and the greater involvement of the government of Serbia in the affairs of Kosovo met many important demands of the Kosovo Serbs, the movement swiftly disintegrated.

Conclusion

Without doubt, the support of dissident intellectuals and Milošević boosted the Kosovo Serb activists' prospects of success in terms of publicizing their cause and bringing urgency to their demands from chief officials. That support, nonetheless, mattered little in the creation and consolidation of the local protest networks. Although activists engaged in contacts with a range of influential people and opted for specific protest strategies with an eye on the broader political context, they remained an autonomous political factor and largely made decisions on their own. The mobilization originated from their discontent with the post-1966 change in the politics of inequality and a demographic decline of Kosovo Serbs, part of which resulted from their steady migration out of Kosovo. The changing political context strongly shaped the timing, forms, and dynamics of the mobilization. The changes in the party's policy on Kosovo after 1981 resulted in a softer approach by officials in Yugoslavia while at the same time excluding them from the authority of Kosovo's leadership. These developments opened the door for various groups to lobby officials outside the province and to initiate debates about their concerns in official organizations at the local level.

The slow response of the authorities to growing complaints shifted the efforts of some of the debaters to noninstitutional action and encouraged local protest networks. The relatively small scale and grassroots character of the protests and their moderate strategies, including mobilization partly within official organizations, shielded the activists from repression. Despite cooperation with Milošević, who put their demands firmly on the party's agenda, Kosovo Serb activists proceeded with noninstitutional action. The abrogation of Kosovo's autonomy, which met an important demand of Kosovo Serbs—the purge of Kosovo's leaders by Milošević and their replacement by Kosovo Serb party apparatchiks—effectively closed the space for autonomous political efforts by Kosovo Serbs. The dynamics of the mobilization of Kosovo Serbs differed little from the patterns of mobilization of other groups in socialist Yugoslavia, especially the protests of Kosovo Albanians in 1968 and 1981, because all unfolded in the aftermath of growing expectations and the relaxation of repression centered on those groups.[66] The case of the mobilization of Kosovo Serbs in the 1980s reveals that an exclusive focus on elites and their politics in the literature on conflicts surrounding the disintegration of Yugoslavia is misleading. Due to the gradual relaxation of repressive policies and practices, nonelite actors played an important political role even in the unlikely context of a socialist party-state.

Notes

1   Throughout this chapter the terms *Kosovo Serbs* and *Kosovo Albanians* are used to denote those Serbs and Albanians who lived in Kosovo during the period under discussion. Although one of our readers noted that the adjective form is *Kosovo*, we have decided to maintain the common usage of *Kosovo Serb* or *Kosovo Albanian* because in recent years the term *Kosovar* has been used almost exclusively for Kosovo Albanians and has a political, not simply a geographical dimension.

2   After World War II Yugoslav—not just Serb—Communist leaders made the most important decisions on Kosovo. The pressures on Kosovo Albanians after 1948 had a lot to do with security considerations—the reaction of the Yugoslav leadership to the support of their counterparts from Albania for Stalin and the Soviet bloc—and were not simply a result of an attempt of Serbs in the leadership to discriminate against Albanians. This is not to deny that the result was to disadvantage members of this community and that Serbs within this period had an upper hand over Albanians in Kosovo. However, much of the security situation in Kosovo during the 1950s and early 1960s was designed and implemented by the Serbian head of Yugoslav security services (UDBA), Aleksandar Ranković.

Between 1967 and 1971, constitutional amendments were introduced that began to alter the relationship of Vojvodina and Kosovo vis-à-vis Serbia and began to have a decisive impact on Serb-Albanian relations. Secondly, major political change in Kosovo occurred after 1966, following the demise of Ranković and the centralist faction in the Yugoslav leadership. The power shift led swiftly to changes in the ethnonational composition of the political elite in Kosovo.

3   Veljko Vujačić, "Historical Legacies, Nationalist Mobilization, and Political Outcomes in Russia and Serbia: A Weberian View," *Theory and Society* 25, no. 6 (December 1996), 769.

4   While much has been made about goals and aims of a "greater" Albania or Serbia, the historical origin of the "greater" designation begins in the early nineteenth century when nationalist leaders from countries throughout Europe sought to maximize state borders to include all members of their nation or territories allegedly theirs.

5   Albanian speakers were an absolute majority of Kosovo's inhabitants by the mid-nineteenth century, and the percentage of the majority increased over the twentieth and twenty-first centuries. For a discussion of this issue see Noel Malcolm, *Kosovo: A Short History* (London: Macmillan, 1998), 193–194.

6   Živorad Igić, *Kosovo i Metohija* (1981–1991): *Uvod u jugoslovensku krizu* (Priština, Podgorica: Jedinstvo, Oktoih, 1995).

7   *Statistički Bilten*, no. 727, 1972, 11. Cited in Ruža Petrović and Marina Blagojević, *The Migrations of Serbs and Montenegrins from Kosovo and Metohija: Results of the Survey Conducted in 1985–1986* (Belgrade: Serbian Academy of Sciences and Arts, 1992), 78.

8   *Statisktički Bilten*, no. 727, 1972, 11, cited in Miranda Vickers, *Between Serb and Albanian* (New York: Columbia University Press, 1998), 171; and Arshi Pipa and Sami Repishti, *Studies on Kosova* (Boulder: East European Monographs), 1984, 127.

9   Julie Mertus, *Kosovo: How Myths and Truths Started a War* (Berkeley: University of California Press, 1999), 8.

10   These extra monies may have benefited the Serbian population more than the Albanian population of Kosovo as reflected in the Serbian unemployment rate's falling and the Albanian unemployment rate's increasing in the period between 1970 and 1982. See discussion below and P. Prifiti, "Kosova's Economy," in Repishti, *Studies on Kosova*, 134–137.

11   Michael Palairet, "Ramiz Sadiku: A Case Study in the Industrialization of Kosovo," *Soviet Studies* 44, no. 5 (1992), 897–912.

12   Ibid., 899.

13   Prifiti, 134–137.

14   Nurcan Özgür Baklacioglu, "Albanian Migrations and the Problem of Security in the Balkans," *Turkish Review of Balkan Studies* 6 (2001), 75–121.

15   Paul Shoup, "The Government and Constitutional Status of Kosova: Some Brief Remarks," in *Studies on Kosova*, ed. Arshi Pipa and Sami Repishti (Boulder, CO: East European Monographs, 1984), 71.

16   Interview with Azem Vllasi, Priština, April 1995, in *Kosmet ili Kosova*, ed. Bahri Cani and Cvijetan Milovojević (Belgrade: NEA, 1996), 93, cited in Julie Mertus, *Kosovo: How Myths and Truths Started a War* (Berkeley: University of California Press, 1999), 19.

17   Vladimir Matić, "Unbreakable Bond: Serbs and Kosovo," report prepared for the Public International Law and Policy Group, December 2003. http://www.publicinternationallaw.org/publications/reports/UnbreakableBondSerbsandKosovo1203.pdf (accessed: 3 June 2004).

18   It may be misleading to focus on the 1974 Yugoslav constitution, which changed little in the constitutional structure of Yugoslavia (it made mostly symbolic changes). Most important were constitutional amendments introduced between 1967 and 1971 that had a decisive impact on Serb-Albanian relations. Also, although autonomous provinces were strongly empowered in the long process of constitutional reform, Serbia was still officially designated as a unitary state like other Yugoslav republics. Other constitutional provisions also left much space for contrasting interpretations simply because Yugoslav leaders could not agree on the more specific and precise text. Therefore, the empowerment of autonomous provinces was only partly due to the constitutional provisions. Draža Marković said that Serbia's high officials believed that it was not the constitution itself but its extreme interpretation resulting from informal power relations in the federation at the time that strongly disadvantaged Serbia's central institutions.

19   Beginning in 1989, the Serbian assembly prepared amendments to Serbia's constitution that would eradicate Kosovo's autonomy. To do so, however, required the provincial assembly of Kosovo to vote and accept these amendments. Police intimidation and cohesion of Kosovo's deputies on the eve of the vote resulted in the provincial assembly's acceptance of the amendments. Sabrina Ramet, *The Three Yugoslavias: State Building and Legitimation, 1918–2005* (Bloomington: Indiana University Press, 2006), 353.

20   Voting differently was, it seems, much more frequent. Although no one has, as far as we know, looked into the voting records, our impression on the basis of interviews with high officials of Serbia (those in office before the rise of Milošević) is that provincial high officials voted differently not only because their interests at times diverged with those of Serbia but often because they wanted to demonstrate publicly their newly acquired power. If this is true (answers from Serbia's high officials from different factions, generations, and institutional interests were very consistent in this respect), it is hardly a surprise that they came into conflict early, many years before the rise of Milošević.

21   The assumption behind this idea is that symmetric relationships between territorial units in a decentralized state are the only possible way to fairly and successfully regulate ethnonational conflict. This may be misleading. Research on ethnonational conflict regulation provides ample evidence that there is a variety of strategies to deal with the problem: recognition of identity of relevant groups, various levels of collective rights, territorial and nonterritorial autonomy, and so forth. Asymmetric relationships between ethnonationally based territorial units in decentralized states are often stressed as highly successful (e.g., post-Franco Spain, Canada, Russia in the 1990s). It is clear that Kosovo Albanians had obtained a recognition of their identity, very high level of collective rights, and extensive territorial autonomy but not the official right to self-determination, which was granted only to republics and constituent nations. That Kosovo did not become a republic was not simply a consequence of Yugoslavia's ideology of brotherhood and unity but perhaps had at least something to do with the comparative experience of dealing with similar phenomena. There is no reason to look at socialist Yugoslavia and its successor states as a special case—the comparative approach always brings a broader perspective on things.

22   Vickers, Between Serb and Albanian 197, cited in *Studies on Kosova*, 144.

23   For a more extensive discussion see Julie Mertus *Kosovo.*

24   There was in fact a considerable difference of opinions on the policy toward Kosovo. Serbia's leadership, often supported by high officials of Montenegro and Macedonia, often came into conflict with high officials of other republics as well as those of Vojvodina and Kosovo. This was especially the case in the 1980s. These disagreements, even conflicts, however, occurred within the narrow leadership circle, masked by a united

front that regional leaderships presented to society. This is hardly surprising given the authoritarian nature of the regime.

25 Kjell Magnusson, "The Serbian Reaction: Kosovo and Ethnic Mobilization among the Serbs," *Nordic Journal of Soviet and East European Studies* 4, no. 3 (1987), 10. According to one of our team leaders, the cited author confuses the alleged suppression of the expression of national feelings of Kosovo Albanians with the real or perceived fear of secessionism, widespread in the Yugoslav multinational leadership (not only among the Serbs). The leadership did not act principally against expressions of national feelings by Albanians. Kosovo's institutions, political and cultural, remained intact, and previous high officials were replaced by Kosovo Albanians, not Serbs; expressions of nationalism outside institutions by members of Yugoslavia's other ethnonational groups were also sanctioned, though less harshly than in post-1981 Kosovo. One should not confuse the rhetoric of the leadership (e.g., Albanian nationalism as counterrevolution, which was fully in line with the CPY ideology) with what they really feared—the rise of a mass-based separatist movement, that is, a major threat to the territorial integrity of Yugoslavia. This fear may have been irrational (this can certainly be discussed further) but it did produce tangible political consequences.

26 "More than 300 Persons Were Sentenced," *New York Times*, 19 October 1981, A4, cited in Mertus, 43.

27 *Yugoslavia: Prisoners of Conscience* (London: Amnesty International Publications, 1985), cited in Vickers, 224.

28 Aleksander Tijanić, "Koliko je oraha u kesi?" Duga, 18–31 October 1986, 28–31, cited in Magnusson, 11.

29 *Nin*, 2 November 1986, 23, cited in Magnusson, 8.

30 Ivan Janković, "Krivično pravno represije politički nenasilnih ponašanja na Kosovu: 1979–1988," in *Kosovski čvor: Drešiti ili seći?* 63, cited in Vesna Pešić, *Serbian Nationalism and the Origins of the Yugoslav* Crisis (Washington, DC: United States Institute of Peace, 1996).

31 Srdjan Bogosavljević, "A Statistical Picture of Serbian–Albanian Relations," in *Conflict or Dialogue: Serbian-Albanian Relations and the Integration of the Balkans*, ed. Dušan Janjić and Shkelzen Maliqi (Subotica: Open University, European Civic Centre for Conflict Resolution, 1994), 17–29.

32 Miloš Sekulović, interview by N. Vladisavljević, Belgrade, 18 August 2000. For details see Zejnel Zejneli, *Ko je izdao revoluciju* (Priština: Jedinstvo, 1988), 74–105.

33 Memorandum (1986), Serbian Academy of Arts and Sciences (SANU), cited in Gale Stokes, *From Stalinism to Pluralism* (Oxford: Oxford University Press, 1996).

34 Ibid.

35 Wendy Bracewell, "Rape in Kosovo: Masculinity and Serbian Nationalism," *Nations and Nationalism* 6, no. 4, 563–590. Bracewell gives an excellent summary of these issues, as does Julie Mertus in her chapter about the alleged rape of a Kosovo Serbian by Albanians in the late 1980s. See Julie Mertus, *Kosovo: How Myths and Truths Started a War* (Berkeley, CA: University of California Press, 1999), especially the chapter "'Impaled with a Bottle': The Martinovic Case, 1985."

36 See Srdjan Bogosavljević, "A Statistical Picture of Serbian-Albanian Relations," in Janjić and Shkelzen Maliqi, *Conflict or Dialogue*, 23, and Ruža Petrović and Marina Blagojević, *The Migrations of Serbs and Montenegrins from Kosovo and Metohija: Results of the Survey Conducted in 1985–1986* (Belgrade: SANU, 1992), 82–92, 100–104, 111–173.

37 Petrović and Blagojević, 82–92, 100–104, 111–173.

38   Audrey Budding, "Serbian Nationalism in the Twentieth Century," Expert Report Submitted to the International Criminal Tribunal for the Former Yugoslavia, 29 May 2002, 52. http://hague.bard.edu/reports/hr_budding-pt4.pdf (accessed 15 September 2007).

39   Ibid.

40   This section is a condensed version of Nebojša Vladisavljević's research and articles on the mobilization of the Kosovo Serbs, especially, "Grassroots Groups, Milošević, or Dissident Intellectuals? A Controversy over the Origins and Dynamics of Mobilization of Kosovo Serbs in the 1980s," *Nationalities Papers* 32, no. 4 (2004), 781–796; "Institutional Power and the Rise of Milošević," *Nationalities Papers* 32, no. 1 (2004), 183–205, and *Serbia's Antibureaucratic Revolution: Milošević, the Fall of Communism, and Nationalist Mobilization* (Basingstoke: Palgrave Macmillan, 2008).

41   See for example Laura Silber and Allan Little, *The Death of Yugoslavia* (London: Penguin, BBC, 1996), 34–47, 58–59; Tim Judah, *Kosovo: War and Revenge* (New Haven, CT: Yale University Press, 2000), 47–55; Noel Malcolm, *Kosovo: A Short History* (New York: New York University Press, 1998), 339–343; and Mertus, chapter 2.

42   Aleksandar Tijanić, *Šta će biti s nama* (Zagreb: Globus, 1988), 130–131.

43   For an account of one of the meetings see excerpts from the diary of Draza Marković in Mirko Djekić, *Upotreba Srbije: optužbe i priznanja Draže Markovića* (Belgrade: Besede, 1990), 209–210.

44   Boško Budimirović and Miroslav Šolević, interviews by N. Vladisavljevic, 15 and 17 July 2001, respectively.

45   Boško Budimirović and Miroslav Šolević, interviews, and Dušan Ristić in Miloš Antić, "Srbija nema rešenje za Kosovo," *Borba*, 11 February 1993.

46   "Zahtevi 2016 stanovnika Kosova," *Književne novine*, 15 December 1985.

47   For details see Vladisavljević, "Nationalism, Social Movement Theory, and the Grass Roots Movement of Kosovo Serbs," 772–773.

48   See, for example, "Šta je ko rekao u Kosovu Polju: stenografske beleške razgovora u noći 24. i 25. IV 1987," *Borba*, 8, 9–10, and 11 April 1987.

49   Boško Budimirović, Miroslav Šolević, and Bogdan Kecman, interviews by Vladisavljević, 29 August 2000.

50   See "Šta su Kosovci rekli u Skupštini," NIN, 23 and 30 March, and 6 and 13 April 1986, and "Šta je ko rekao u Kosovu Polju."

51   Miroslav Šolević and Boško Budimirović, interviews. See also Dobrica Ćosić, *Piščevi zapisi, 1981–1991* (Belgrade: Filip Višnjić, 2002), 169–170, 186–188.

52   Ćosić, *Piščevi zapisi*, 169–170.

53   Boško Budimirović and Miroslav Šolević, interviews.

54   For details on the views and actions of the intellectuals in relation to Kosovo see Jasna Dragović-Soso, *"Saviours of the Nation": Serbia's Intellectual Opposition and the Revival of Nationalism*, chapter 3 (London: Hurst, 2002). For the text of the intellectuals' petition see "Zahtev za pravnim poretkom na Kosovu," in Aleksa Djilas, ed., *Srpsko pitanje* (Belgrade: Politika, 1991), 260–261.

55   Šolević, interview.

56   Šolević, interview.

57   Budimirović, interview.

58   Based on detailed eyewitness accounts of the events in *Nedeljna Borba*, 25–26 April 1987, 9; *Borba*, 19 January 1993, 15; *Borba*, 20 January 1993, 15; and interviews of Budimirović, Šolević, and Kecman by Vladisavljević. For all seventy-eight speeches see the full transcript from the meeting published in *Borba*, 8, 9–10, and 11 May 1987.

59   Nebojša Vladisavljević, "Institutional Power and the Rise of Milošević."
60   Draža Marković, interview by Nebojša Vladisavljević, 16 August 2000.
61   Budimirović, Šolević, and Kecman, interviews, and Dušan Ristić cited in Antić, "Srbija nema rešenje za Kosovo."
62   Copy of the petition in Vladisavljević's possession. See excerpts in "Iz peticije 50.000 potpisnika," *Danas*, 5 July 1988.
63   Budimirović and Šolević, interviews, and Mićo Šparavalo, a prominent activist, cited in ENRfu Sava Kerčov, Jovo Radoš, and Aleksandar Raič, *Mitinzi u Vojvodini 1988. godine: rađanje političkog pluralizma* (Novi Sad: Dnevnik, 1990), 243–244.
64   Darko Hudelist, *Kosovo: bitka bez iluzija* (Zagreb: Centar za informacije i publicitet, 1989).
65   Stevan Marinković and Migo Samardžić, prominent activists, cited in Kerčov, Radoš, and Raič, *Mitinzi u Vojvodini*, 229–230, 241.
66   It has been noted in a review of this draft that in the late 1980s it was only the Kosovo Serbs who were marching to Belgrade to complain of their status and it was only the Serbs who were organizing protest meetings against the SFRY constitution. However, this observation does not take away from the argument that such mobilization was not unique for Socialist Yugoslavia. What differed, of course, was that this mobilization took place against the backdrop of the 1980s.

3

Drago Roksandić, team leader
Gale Stokes, team leader

Florian Bieber   **Dejan Jović**   **Toni Petković**
Silvano Bolčić   **Husnija Kamberović**   **Boban Petrovski**
Sumantra Bose   **Aleksandar Kasaš**   Milan Podunavac
Boro Bronza   **Matjaž Klemenčič**   **Dennison Rusinow†**
Bejtullah Destani   Miran Komac   **Mary Rusinow**
Mirjana Domini   **Ranko Končar**   **Bogoljub Savin**
Robert Donia   **Kristof Kozak**   Predrag Simić
Francine Friedman   Reneo Lukić   Ludwig Steindorff
Dejan Guzina   Alexander Mirescu   **Edin Veladžić**
Vesna Ivanović   Asim Mujkić   **Mark Wheeler**
Egidio Ivetić   **Zoran Oklopčić**   Jernej Zupančić
                         Srdja Pavlović

The National Endowment for Democracy funded individual research by Vesna Ivanović, Matjaž Klemenčič, and Drago Roksandić, as well as a satellite team meeting that Profs. Roksandić and Rusinow organized in Zagreb on 30 August 2003. Team co-leader Dennison Rusinow edited an initial draft that included textual contributions by Silvano Bolčić, Dejan Jović, Francine Friedman, Dejan Guzina, Egidio Ivetić, Zoran Oklopčić, Drago Roksandić and Mark Wheeler, which was then submitted for project-wide review in October-November, 2003. Following Prof. Rusinow's tragic death in January 2004, Prof. Stokes succeeded him as co-leader and assumed primary responsibility for rethinking and recasting the chapter. The final draft was approved following project-wide review in March 2005, during which it benefited from additional comment and criticism, particularly extensive, careful, and very useful editorial suggestions by Sabrina Ramet and team member Mark Wheeler.

Professor Stokes authored an earlier version of the chapter, "From Nation to Minority: Serbs in Croatia and Bosnia at the Outbreak of the Yugoslav Wars," *Problems of Post-Communism*, 56, no. 6 (November–December 2005), 3–20.

INDEPENDENCE AND THE FATE OF MINORITIES, 1991-1992

◆ Gale Stokes ◆

The question of what status minorities might have in the successor states to social-ist Yugoslavia was one of the central issues that informed the Wars of Yugoslav Succession, especially for many Serbs.[1] This chapter does not lay out a narrative of the early years of that conflict, nor is it a general discussion of minority rights throughout the 1990s and in all of the Yugoslav republics. It confines itself to the period 1991–1992 and assumes that readers will have a reasonably good grasp of the fundamental narrative. Instead the chapter focuses on why the minority issue was so important, asks how real the threat was to certain minorities, analyzes the impact of Alija Izetbegović's commitment to Islam, discusses the question of leadership, and evaluates the significance of the Badinter Commission's rulings.

Socialist Yugoslavia dealt with minority issues in an original way but was never completely successful in fulfilling the promise of removing nationalism from politics, which had been an important part of the Partisan movement's ap-peal during World War II. Communists in Tito's Yugoslavia (the Socialist Federal Republic of Yugoslavia, SFRY) did not accept the notion that majorities and mi-norities could be determining factors in political decision-making.[2] Accordingly, the Yugoslav Communist regime did not recognize the concept of ethnic or reli-gious minorities either. Instead, it considered the country to have six recognized Yugoslav nations (*narodi*): Serbs, Croats, Slovenes, Macedonians, Montenegrins, and since 1968, Muslims (as an ethnic category/nation, now calling themselves Bosniaks). These six nations were in principle equal, so that the Serbs, consti-tuting between 35 and 40 percent of the country's population, were considered formally equal to the Montenegrins, at less than 3 percent. All six nations were considered constitutive peoples, that is, peoples with their own republic, even if they happened to live outside of that republic. With minor exceptions, Yu-goslavia's numerous other peoples were classified as nationalities (*narodnosti*), although they enjoyed specific rights associated elsewhere with minority rights.[3]

The originality of the Yugoslav socialist framework was that no one in Yugoslavia was a minority, regardless of the actual size of a population or territory. Indeed, the concept of minority lost its neutral meaning and acquired negative—and occasionally insulting—connotations. Careful wording of Yugoslav constitutions and of constitutions in the republics and provinces made sure that the word disappeared from public usage, even when alternatives could not replace it in any meaningful sense.

Dejan Jović describes Yugoslav Communism as a "vision-driven project in which the elite did not primarily represent reality . . . but the desired future."[4] Thus the party condemned prewar Yugoslavia for its unitarism, centralism, statism, and bureaucratism, and dismissed the underlying principles of parliamentary government on which it had been founded. In its place the Communists offered a decentralized system of workers' self-management that offered dignity to all peoples, both narodi and narodnosti, under an overarching banner of socialism. Tito believed that ethnic groups could take pride in their identity and cultivate their culture more effectively in the Yugoslav socialist system than under either "bourgeois" democracy (i.e., prewar Yugoslavia) or Soviet-style Communism. Even more important than the cohesion this rejection of the past achieved was the contrast Yugoslav Communists drew between self-managing socialism and Soviet-style Communism. Yugoslav Communists were convinced, as were people in many parts of the world, that there was no going back from socialism to previous socio/economic systems—the direction of history was forward, and socialists were progressives who were in tune with that world-historical direction. But there were different types of socialism. The Yugoslavs saw worker self-management as significantly superior to the state socialism they associated with Stalin and his conservative successors. Because they considered the ethnic and national tensions lurking under the surface of Yugoslav society as obsolete throwbacks to a discredited past to which their own followers were too often prone, they dared not assign the level of importance to these tensions that events later proved they deserved. Instead Yugoslav Communist theorists overemphasized the threat from bureaucratic centralism, which they associated with the contrasting Soviet "Other." Once the Soviet system collapsed, therefore, both their view of socialism as a progressive force and their decision to define themselves in terms of contrast with the Soviet Union lost their justifications. The Yugoslav Communists were left with no levers of legitimacy. As Jović puts it, "the Yugoslav elite was totally unprepared and surprised when the Soviet system collapsed and liberalism, contrary to their expectations, entered the Yugoslav identity-making arena and emerged victorious."[5]

When Communism went under, the carefully constructed Yugoslav political vocabulary disintegrated. Previously "incorrect" concepts now became favored by new (anti-Communist) elites, while verbal markers of socialism, including narodnosti in its old sense, became obsolete. Whereas the size of a population had lost its importance under socialism, under nationalist democracy it became of decisive importance. Now it really mattered whether ethnic Albanians constituted 20 or 30 or 40 percent of Macedonia's total population. Now it mattered whether the Bosniak birthrate would increase or stagnate. At least some members of almost every ethnic group in the former Yugoslavia suddenly became frightened that they would be permanently relegated to the status of minority, outvoted in elections, pushed out of jobs, and otherwise discriminated against. Indeed, at least one scholar argues that fear was "the greatest determinant of ethnic nationalism throughout the region."[6] The fearful reactions had some basis in fact, but were intensified by nationalizing leaders in Serbia and Croatia and fanned by political parties in the other new states.

The lack of moderating leadership certainly made the minority situation much more difficult than it might have been, but the underlying problem lay in the contradiction at the heart of nationalism. The idea of nation is not possible unless there are those who are not part of the nation. There must be an "other," or the idea of nation makes no sense. Given the mixed populations of Eastern Europe, the creation of nation-states there in the 1870s and at the end of World War I simultaneously created minorities. Thus the question of minority status was not a side issue but grew out of the fundamental structure of the nation-state system into which the former republics of Yugoslavia suddenly, without much preparation, emerged as newly independent states. Minority issues arose in the former Yugoslavia not because of Balkan peculiarities, therefore, but as part of the continuation of a long European process of redrawing state borders along ethnic lines.[7] Just as the collapse of the multinational Austro-Hungarian Empire created a volatile situation for both new nations and new minorities in post-World War I Eastern Europe, so the collapse of the multinational Yugoslavia created a difficult situation for its peoples in the 1990s.

When the Yugoslav republics suddenly transformed themselves into sovereign, independent states, members of the formerly constituent peoples (narodi) who did not live in their home entity became instant minorities. Deprived of their status as constituent peoples, they all considered their new condition a demotion in status and rights. The leaders of both Serbia and Croatia specifically defined their own people as the rightful owners of "their" states, while classifying other peoples living within their borders as simply citizens of that state. The narodnosti lost their status too, but with the exception of Kosovor Albanians, the change was considerably less violent and disruptive than the change among the formerly constituent peoples.

The three most difficult minority issues raised when Yugoslavia disintegrated concerned the mixed populations of Bosnia-Hercegovina, the sizeable Serb minority in Croatia, and the Albanian population in Kosovo, which was part of Serbia.[8] The last of these constitutes a special case in its own right. Even before the republics of socialist Yugoslavia restructured themselves into independent nation states, the Albanian Kosovars had agreed that they could not continue to live as a minority in Serbia but had to form their own independent state. This complex issue is discussed in detail in chapter 8 of this volume. The issue of Croatian minorities was a smaller but still significant aspect of the overall problem. It too is not a primary concern of this chapter. Tens of thousands of Croats in Eastern Slavonia, Vojvodina, and parts of Bosnia suffered greatly and ended up having to flee for their lives. Despite these tragic events, in Northern Bosnia and in Sarajevo, where Croats constituted 7 percent of the population, they "tended to support a unified Bosnian state and a strong alliance with the Muslims as the best guarantee for their communities' survival."[9] Other Croats, living in compact Croat communities in Hercegovina, disagreed. But these Croats were not so much concerned about becoming a minority as they were in attaching themselves to Croatia proper or, at the very least, creating their own autonomous region. With the support of Franjo Tudjman, president of Croatia, they attempted this latter solution by proclaiming the Croat Union of Herceg-Bosna in July 1992. The brutal warfare that ensued between Herceg-Bosna and Muslim forces lasted until the Washington Agreement of 1994.

It was primarily Serbs who justified their aggressive policies by refusing to accept minority status. As the Bosnian Serb Nikola Koljević put it early in 1992, "I can understand the Muslim need or fear, if you wish, of Serbian or Croatian domination, . . . But you cannot make up for that by placing Serbs in the position of a minority."[10] Not all Serbs felt that way, of course. In the election of 1990, for example, Croatian Serbs cast the majority of their votes for the coalition that came closest to standing for the principles of civil democracy. More than half of the Serbs living in Croatia lived in the developed urban parts of the country, and according to Drago Roksandić, many of them had become culturally "Croatized." Roksandić argues that even if war might not have been preventable, at least it would have been significantly shortened "had it been possible in some way to create a working Croato-Serbian coalition to defend the territorial integrity and sovereignty of the republic of Croatia."[11] But this would have required both time and a cadre of Serbian and Croatian politicians willing to work together outside of the nexus of national homogenization. Neither of these requirements was at hand in 1990–1991. Thus, even before Croatia and Slovenia declared their independence in 1991, disaffected Serbs from the less developed and more conservative rural areas of Croatia announced their unwillingness to lose their status as a constituent people. In the Krajina area of Croatia, as well as in Eastern Slavonia, militant Serbs, threatened by what they took to be a recrudescence of an anti-Serb government they compared to the fascist regime of World War II and supported by a nationalizing leadership in Serbia itself, established their own autonomous regions. In Bosnia, similarly militant Serbs, expressing fear that they were about to be submerged in an Islamic state and with arms supplied by the collapsing Yugoslav National Army, also rose in revolt. Four years of vicious warfare led to widespread ethnic cleansing, massacres, and massive movements of refugees. Eventually in 1995, international intervention and a successful Croatian offensive in Krajina and northwest Bosnia stopped the fighting.[12]

One of the most consistent claims Serbs in Bosnia used to justify their fears was that the Muslim leader Alija Izetbegović was a religious fundamentalist who sought to establish an Islamic dictatorship over Bosnia. All outside observers agree that this was a false charge, but because it had a good deal of resonance among Serbs, a closer look at Izetbegović's views is warranted.[13]

Only two years after Izetbegović's birth in 1925, he and his family moved to Sarajevo, which remained his home until his death in 2003. Izetbegović attended the best gymnasium in Sarajevo and as a teenager during World War II joined a group called Young Muslims. As an expression of the desire to claim a political future for Bosnian Muslims as a national group, this organization of youthful enthusiasts could be compared to the Serbian Omladina of the nineteenth century or to Mazzini's Young Italy, both of which used the term *young* to mean that their nation was still at a formative stage but had a bright future. The group's primary interest was the regeneration of Islam, and for this reason its members were strongly anti-Communist. Izetbegović himself had been interested briefly in Marxism as a teenager, but he could not accept Communism's atheism. "A universe without God seemed to me unthinkable," he said in his memoirs.[14] When the activities of the Young Muslims sparked a modest interest among young anti-Communist Bosniaks at the end of the war, the Communists imprisoned Izetbegović and many others. After his release, he studied agronomy for a while, but eventually he took a degree in law and worked for several years on construction projects in Montenegro.

The primary document on which Bosnian Serbs based their fears of Izetbegović was his *Islamic Declaration*, a programmatic statement about the regeneration of Islam that began to circulate among Bosnian Muslims in 1970. The declaration, well within the tradition of liberal Islamic writing, sought a way for Muslims to recover from both the sterility into which Izetbegović felt Islamic education had fallen and the stagnation that he saw throughout the Islamic world. In the way of many religious reformers of all faiths, Izetbegović saw the purity of Islam sullied by "its discrepancy between word and deed; with its debauchery, filth, injustice and cowardice; with its monumental but empty mosques; with its large white turbans without ideals and courage; with a hypocritical Islamic phrase and religious pose; with this faith without faith."[15] One of the reasons for this state of affairs, Izetbegović thought, was that progressives in Islamic states—Turkey, for example—had adopted many of the superficial ways of the developed world without understanding the essence of Western success. What was that essence? Not fashionable styles of living in a consumer society, but work: "diligence, persistence, knowledge, and responsibility."[16] "The survival, strength, or weakness of Islamic societies is subject to the same laws of work and struggle as are other communities. . . . Miracles do not exist, except those created by work and knowledge."[17] But work and knowledge would not be enough if they were not informed by Islam, Izetbegović argued. Only a moral regeneration through a return to the basic insights of Islam would restore dignity to Muslims. Despite his criticism of the Muslim progressives who copied from Europe, Izetbegović's notion of dignity put him squarely in the twentieth-century world, where the notion of honor, growing out of the hierarchical medieval standards, had been replaced by the notion of dignity, which emphasizes the worth of every individual.[18] His critics often called Izetbegović a fundamentalist, and in a sense he was. He wished to return to the sources of Islam, although he rarely actually quotes a text from the Koran.[19] But he was also a modernist who criticized authoritarian regimes, sought improvements in education, and advocated protection for the rights of minorities. Whatever else he sought, Izetbegović wanted his people, Bosnian Muslims, to be able to hold their heads high in a contemporary world into which they had not yet entered in an authentic way.

The declaration was very much a document of its time, both in Islamic and European thought. In the declaration, and indeed in his entire oeuvre, Izetbegović was following a common strand of modern Islamic thought, namely, how to reconcile the precepts of Islam with the challenges actual life presented in the modern world. In the 1950s, stung by the Israeli successes, many Muslim authors sought similar answers. For example, in Egypt Qustantin Zurayq wrote, "A progressive, dynamic mentality will never be stopped by a primitive, static mentality."[20] Izetbegović's thinking also parallels that of Shaykh Abd al-Karim Mufti, who formed the Harakat movement in Morocco in 1969.[21] His writing, therefore, was consistent with the efforts of Muslims elsewhere to come to grips with modernity.

His work was also embedded in the milieu that produced antipoliticians elsewhere in Eastern Europe. In his moral and ethical precepts, Izetbegović was trying to think his way to an authentic reaction to the bureaucratized regime under which Bosnians and Yugoslavs lived. Despite the originality of its nationalities policies, the Yugoslav Communist regime was an authoritarian system that defended its power from criticism. In his belief that this kind of regime actually deprived human beings of their true nature, Izetbegović agreed with the *Praxis* philosophers. In the mid-1980s, he observed, "To reduce a man to the function of a producer and a consumer, even if every man is given his place in production and consumption, does not signal humanism but dehumanization. . . . To drill people to produce correct and disciplined citizens is likewise inhuman."[22] Writing within an entirely different discourse, the *Praxis* author Mihailo Marković said this in the mid-1970s: "The basic purpose of critical inquiry is the discovery of those specific social institutions and structures which cripple human beings, arrest their development, and impose on them patterns of simple, easily predictable, dull, stereotyped behavior."[23] Like the antipoliticians of the 1970s and 1980s in Czechoslovakia, Poland, and elsewhere, Izetbegović sought hope in internalizing an ethical and moral life. He did not seek to found a political movement that would seize power to implement its goals, thereby creating its own Bastille, as Adam Michnik put it. "Our prime means are personal example, books and words," Izetbegović wrote.[24] Václav Havel argued that the power of the powerless lay in living in truth. Izetbegović agreed, albeit in the context of Islam. "Every form of power in the world begins as a moral truth. . . . That is why a movement, which has Islamic order for its main goal, must before all be a moral movement."[25]

Clearly Izetbegović sought an ethical and moral change in Islam. But did this imply domination over others? At first glance, yes. Much in the same way that many Christians believe that they have a moral duty to Christianize others, so Izetbegović believed that a harmonious world was possible only under Islam. But this did not mean imposing that faith on others or rejecting the best of Western inventions, especially science and the kind of cooperative interaction that created the European Economic Community. Nationalism, he believed as early as 1970, had "become a luxury, a thing too expensive for small and even medium-sized nations." Instead, "the creation of the European Economic Community . . . constitutes the most constructive event in 20th century European history. And the establishment of this supranational structure was the first real victory of the European peoples over nationalism."[26]

In 1984 Izetbegović published a more thoughtful work, *Islam between East and West*, although because of the hostility of the Communist regime it had to be published initially in North America.[27] This later book was not a pamphlet designed to be spread underground to encourage believers but an extended set of comments he had already begun as early as 1946. The book was divided into two parts. Part 1 dealt with secular issues indicated by chapter titles such as "Creation and Evolution," "Culture and Civilization," "The Phenomenon of Art," and "Morality." Part 2 concerned religion, especially how Islam mediated between the materialist view of the world and the religious view. Izetbegović argued that there are three basic kinds of world views: the religious, the materialistic, and Islam. The materialist asks how do I live, the answer to which evolves through history, whereas the religious point of view asks why do I live, the answer to which is eternal and does not evolve. That is, the religious truths of Judaism, Christianity, and Islam are as appropriate for human beings today as they were when they were created. In the West there is a separation between the religious and the secular. The strength of Islam, Izetbegović believed, is that it "is a synthesis, a 'third road' between the two poles that mark all that is human."[28] In 1983, partially because of this manuscript, and as part of a campaign against "clerico-nationalism and Pan Islam in Bosnia-Hercegovina," Izetbegović was arrested again and sentenced to fourteen years of prison. He was released in 1988 after serving, as he puts it, two thousand and seventy-five days.

During the more than five years Izetbegović spent in jail in the 1980s, he managed to write more than 3,500 aphorisms, comments, and observations, which were later published as *Notes from Prison* (the original title in Bosnian was *Moj bijeg u slobodu*). These comments, written fifteen years after the *Islamic Declaration,* show how much continuity his thought retained. Even though he speaks often in these notes about religion, about his book *Islam between East and West*, and about Islam, overwhelmingly the sources of his comments are Western authors, not only the classics, such as Rousseau, Nietzsche, and the like, but even such relatively obscure observers as Bruno Bettleheim and Alvin Toffler. His remarks reveal a highly intellectualized mind and reinforce his strong interest in ethics, morality, and good sense. He is tolerant ("God forgive me if I am wrong, but I respect a good Christian more than a bad Muslim") and continues to admire the work ethic to which he ascribes the success of capitalism ("At the foundation of all the progress and power of the West in the last five centuries is the cult of work"). He again cites the EC as the model of cooperation for the Islamic world and, presumably, for Yugoslavia, and he reiterates his distrust of nationalism ("The true patriot is not the one who puts his homeland above others, but the one who acts so that it would be worthy of that praise. More than glory, he cares about the dignity of his homeland."). In important ways Izetbegović was a conservative, opposed to abortion and in favor of limiting women to the home and the family. And he was Muslim, but as the body of work accumulated over his adult life demonstrates, he was not a fundamentalist in the way we have come to think of them today. Indeed, he opposes ideological solutions: "The perfect man is not our aim, the perfect society even less. All we want are normal people and normal society. God, save us from any 'perfection.'"[29]

In 1994, when a German reporter characterized Izetbegović as a "Muslim in the European tradition of tolerance, open to the entire world," he replied, "My tolerance is not European but Islamic in origin. If I am tolerant, I am that first as a Muslim, and only then as a European. . . . I value Europe, but I think that it has far too high an opinion of itself." But it was not his intention to create an Islamic Republic. As he put it early in 1994 in a speech to the board of the political party he headed, "To be quite clear, I don't want an Islamic Republic, but I want Islam to survive in this part of the world, whether anybody likes it or not [*pa kome pravo kome krivo*]. . . . [W]e don't want to be assimilated. . . . We want to stay what we are, and we can say that with pride. We illustrate a European Islam here, a modern Islam. . . . Just maybe it is our mission to show Islam in a new and genuine light." In the Bosnia he hoped for, therefore, "no one will be persecuted for their religion, nationality or political conviction. That will be our fundamental law."[30]

After Izetbegović became president of Bosnia in 1990, this body of work, especially the *Islamic Declaration*, became fodder for the Serbian propaganda mills. In the political struggles that preceded the outbreak of actual fighting in Bosnia, Bosnian Serbs in particular repeatedly used claims that Izetbegović was a fundamentalist Muslim bent on placing Serbs under Islamic jurisdiction. Serbian writers plucked sentences and phrases from the *Islamic Declaration* to "demonstrate" that Izetbegović was "Ayatollah Khomeyni's right hand man," and even, not too logically, that the declaration was his *Mein Kampf*.[31] This campaign, however, smacked more of political mudslinging than of accuracy. Not that Izetbegović distanced himself from his Islamic views. Of the several factions that existed in the party he founded, the Party of Democratic Action (SDA), Izetbegović led the more religiously oriented wing. This led one of the early members of the SDA, Adil Zulfikarpašić, rather quickly to form his own, more secular party.[32] Also, Izetbegović did some foolish things that played directly into the hands of his Serbian opponents, such as visiting Turkey in July 1991, where he asked that Bosnia join the Organization of Islamic Countries.[33] Izetbegović often spoke of creating a civil society in Bosnia, but when he spoke to Muslim audiences abroad, he liked to stress "the need for the Muslim nation in Bosnia to have its own state," which is just what the Serbian nationalists accused him of trying to do.[34] In 1993 he received the King Faisal Foundation award for services to Islam, and in the next year he visited Mecca.[35] On the other hand, it was Izetbegović, along with Kiro Gligorov of Macedonia, who led an effort to create a reorganized Yugoslavia along the lines of a civil state. This effort to counter Slobodan Milošević's drive to Serbianize Yugoslavia failed, but it did provide a marked contrast to the intense nationalism of both Serbian and Croatian leaders in 1990 and 1991.

A telling argument against the view that Izetbegović sought to create an Islamic republic is that when such an opportunity presented itself, he did not take it. As Steven L. Burg and Paul Shoup point out, the most critical prewar moments came in the year 1990, when the Croatian and Slovenian republican governments took the position that Yugoslavia should be a confederal union of sovereign states, in other words, when those two states presented an option that only independence would satisfy. This put Bosnia on the spot with what appeared to be two choices: either let those two countries go and stay in a Yugoslavia that would be dominated by Serbia or create an independent state consisting of three increasingly divided ethnic groups. Izetbegović characterized this choice as one between leukemia and a brain tumor.[36] The first option was unacceptable to much of the non-Serbian population of Bosnia but not to some Bosnian leaders. In June 1991, Adil Zulfikarpašić and Muhamed Filipović negotiated an agreement with Radovan Karadžić and other Bosnian Serb leaders to keep Bosnia a sovereign and undivided state encompassing three constituent peoples. For this to happen, Bosnia would have to stay in a newly federated Yugoslavia. According to Zulfikarpašić, Milošević agreed to this plan, which also would have given Bosnia 60 percent of Sandžak and autonomy to the rest of that region.[37] Such a federal arrangement might have had significant long-term value for Yugoslav Muslims. Even though a newly federated Yugoslavia might be dominated by Serbs, it would nevertheless include in its various regions essentially all the Muslims living in Yugoslavia, encompassing those in Kosovo, Macedonia, Sandžak, and Montenegro, as well as in Bosnia. "Eventually," as Burg and Shoup put it, "the Muslims would have become a political force to be reckoned with in the new Yugoslavia."[38] This would have been especially true if Izetbegović had seen himself in a similar way as the Serb and Croat leaders saw themselves, as a charismatic or populist leader of Yugoslav Muslims. But this is not how he thought of himself. Izetbegović was a Bosnian and did not consider seriously the possibility of creating a larger Muslim entity. He feared that becoming a part of a Yugoslavia in which Milošević was the strongman would leave Bosnians second-class citizens and worried that the Croatian portions of Hercegovina, which had been part of the Croatian regional government (*banovina*) created by the royal Yugoslav government in 1939, would secede from Bosnia and join Croatia. The Croats confirmed this suspicion by reacting vigorously against Zulfikarpašić's proposal, which they argued constituted a secret deal of two peoples, the Serbs and Muslims, against a third, the Croats. Izetbegović refused to consider the possibility of a Bosnia without Croats. Contributing to his lack of interest in a project that would have the prospect of creating a Muslim entity in a rump Yugoslavia may have been his contacts with Albanian nationalists in prison. The Kosovars he met there proved to be entirely secular. "Religion has been superseded and is unnecessary for our people and its struggle for freedom," one of their leaders told him. Izetbegović found this lack of interest in Islam unacceptable, although, as he puts it, "we remained good friends."[39] In any event, Izetbegović insisted on maintaining Bosnia as a multinational state, even though he recognized that this meant Bosnia might have to declare its independence, which could well mean war. All the evidence suggests that he did not even consider the possibility of creating a powerful Muslim entity in a restructured Yugoslavia.[40]

One of the comments often made about Izetbegović's political leadership was that he was indecisive, ready to be swayed by whomever provided the most recent argument. *Notes from Prison* suggests that the reason for this may well be that he was too thoughtful to be a dynamic leader. This is not something that can be said about his main antagonists, Radovan Karadžić, Slobodan Milošević, and Franjo Tudjman. In the Bosnian elections of 1990, won by the three parties that most strongly represented the three main national groups, Karadžić, a

Sarajevo psychiatrist and sometime poet, emerged as the leader of the Bosnian Serbs. As former American ambassador to Yugoslavia Warren Zimmerman put it, Karadžić was "the polar opposite to Izetbegović."[41] Whereas Zimmerman considered Izetbegović a moderate and even charitable man, he characterizes Karadžić as a confrontational individual whose "single-mindedness in pursuit of the most radical Serbian agenda was matched by his deep-seated hostility, amounting to racism, toward Muslims, Croats, and any other non-Serbian ethnic group in his neighborhood."[42] Although he had not been particularly well known as a nationalist up until the late 1980s, he apparently had always tended toward violent ideas. In a 1992 film, for example, he "recounted how more than two decades ago he had written a poem beginning: I can hear disaster walking, The city is burning. . . . Every thing I saw in terms of a fight, in terms of war, in army terms."[43] "Today [Serbs] cannot live with other nations," Karadžić told Warren Zimmerman in 1992 as the war in Bosnia was beginning. "They must have their own separate existence. They are a warrior race and they can trust only themselves to take by force what is their due."[44] In contrast to Gligorov's and Izetbegović's efforts to find a solution, Karadžić and his party began to undermine the fragile structure of the Bosnian state. During 1991 they created three "Serb Autonomous Regions," began arming themselves by Serbianizing elements of the Yugoslav Peoples Army (JNA) in Bosnia, particularly the locally based territorial defense units, and created their own legislature.

Scholars' Initiative regional liaison Gojko Mišković testifies how thoroughly Karadžić's hostile approach had penetrated the discourse in Bosnia by mid-1991. In August of that year, Mišković participated in a meeting of representatives of twenty political parties from around Yugoslavia. The meeting was organized by his party, the Democratic Party [of Serbia], and took place in the Hotel Ilidža near Sarajevo. He describes the meeting:

> The entire atmosphere of the meeting was electric, like before a major storm on the open sea. . . . [After the meeting came to order about thirty minutes late], Velibor Ostojić, head of the delegation of the Serbian Democratic Party of Bosnia and Hercegovina (SDS), was the first to speak. Even the delay in the opening of the meeting drew his vehement and contentious rhetoric. Probably unnerved by the fact that he had to make a presentation, he made it clear in a raised voice that the SDS and the Serb people would not accept any concessions or compromises, because they were on their own turf (*svoji na svome*). As the strongest and the most prepared they were in a position to thwart plans for the independence of Bosnia and Hercegovina. While he was speaking, the delegations of the Serbian Socialist Party . . . and the Communist Union of Montenegro showed their support by nodding their heads. Immediately Ostojić's "dearest enemies" [the representatives of the Croatian Democratic Union of Bosnia and Hercegovina—HDZ BiH—and of the Muslim Party of Democratic Action—SDA] responded in the same contentious

way, after which [others] refined and supplemented the argument. The news
we heard the next morning from a tearful Dr. Gordana Hajduković (SDP-
Hrvatske) that the JNA and Serbian territorial troops had shelled her native
Osijek dealt the final blow to efforts to conduct calm discussions. The next
round of talks three weekends later was a complete fiasco and total failure.[45]

"The main reason that predetermined the failure of the discussions,"
Mišković believes today, "was the hostile and contentious tone of the representatives of the SDS, which had the character of a war cry from Serbian heroic
epics: either get out, or submit (*ili' se skloni, il' mi se pokloni*)." Surely not by
coincidence, a telephone conversation between Milošević and Karadžić taped at
about the same time as the party meeting in Sarajevo confirms that the Serbs had
already decided to use force in Bosnia. "You'll get everything, don't worry. We
are the strongest, " Milošević tells Karadžić. "Don't worry. As long as we have
the army, nobody can do anything to us."[46] Some in the West originally believed
that Karadžić, as well as the other Serb leaders in Serbia and Bosnia, were "rational people with whom one could argue, negotiate, compromise, and agree.
In fact, they respected only force or an unambiguous and credible threat to use
it."[47] As Edward P. Joseph put it, "No degree of assurance to the Serb minority in
either Croatia or Bosnia could likely have deterred Milošević from deploying the
arsenal of Yugoslavia for his aims."[48]

Franjo Tudjman, although on some occasions more willing to listen to ad-
monitions and advice from the Western powers than Karadžić, was almost the
equal of Karadžić in his nationalism, but of course on behalf of Croats. "He has
one purpose in life," remarked Lord Owen, "to control all the territory that he believes historically belongs to Croatia—and to that end he will use any means."[49]
At the first meeting of the Croatian Democratic Union (HDZ), Tudjman said ominously, "The NDH [Independent State of Croatia during World War II] was not
simply a quisling creation and a fascist crime; it was also an expression of the
historical aspirations of the Croatian people."[50] In the months from the time of
that statement until the election of 1990 brought Tudjman to power, one of the
most notable features of public life in Croatia was the vitriolic nature of Tudjman's campaign.[51] Susan Woodward notes that this was important not because it
was unique—Milošević achieved his power by similar outbursts against Kosovo
Albanians—but because it played a role in defining how far in the direction of
inflammatory prejudice it was permissible to go. Shortly after his election, Tudjman moved to rehabilitate those who served the fascist regime of the Independent
State of Croatia; streets and squares were renamed in honor of supporters of that
regime; and purges of Serbs from Croatian police forces spread even to the dismissal of Serbs in commercial ventures. Larger questions of how to approach the
transition that Croatia was undergoing in its social, economic, or ethnic dimensions never became the focus of his regime. Neither did Tudjman see coopera-

tion with educated urban Serbs who might have stood as a counterweight to the Krajina Serbs as worthy of interest, thus leaving moderate Croatian Serbs in a no-man's land between Milošević's nationalism and Tudjman's narrow vision of Croatia's future.

The contrast of these moves with Izetbegović's efforts to mediate is almost as great as the contrast between Izetbegović and Karadžić. Indeed, Tudjman never really accepted Bosnia as a state. Instead he believed it should be divided with Serbia, with at best a small Muslim enclave around Sarajevo. In other words, Tudjman's nationalist agenda seemed to consist of two goals typical of a nationalizing regime: first, to replace Serbs in positions of authority or of economic power with Croats, and second, to expand the borders of Croatia if possible. He succeeded in the first but at the expense of alienating even moderate Serbs in Croatia, and he failed in the second, although he and Milošević had discussions that Tudjman hoped would lead to the partition of Bosnia. Beyond his national goals, Tudjman had ambitions to be recognized as a European leader. But his nationalist policies, as well as his bombastic style and love of pomp and circumstance, gave the impression to many of a comic-opera ruler rather than a leader of substance. This reputation and appearance did not prevent him from providing hard-edged leadership for the Croats during the 1990s.

Surely the most complex of the main players in the Wars of Yugoslav Succession was Slobodan Milošević. Subtler in his political sensibilities than Karadžić, better prepared for negotiations and discussions than Tudjman, willing to turn on a dime when maintaining his political position required betraying a friend or an ally, and personally charming when he chose, Milošević was not known in his early career for any special advocacy of nationalism, as Tudjman had been over the course of his career. But in the spring of 1987 he realized that he could mobilize broad and enthusiastic support by stressing Serbian victimhood, especially in Kosovo. From the time he seized power later that year, he perfected a vigorous nationalist agenda that served what many believe was his main goal: to achieve and maintain himself in power. His ability to generate massive public displays of support for his policy of consolidating Serbian control over Kosovo, Vojvodina, and Montenegro by brutal tactics led him to think that perhaps he could achieve control over all of Yugoslavia. When that failed, he turned to a policy of uniting all Serbs in the former Yugoslavia, such as those in Bosnia and Krajina, under his control. In this process he demonstrated far more political horse sense than any other political figure. He knew how to coerce, how to generate public outcry suitable to his plans, and how to present bald-faced lies with a straight face. At the same time he knew how to negotiate, how to promise while simultaneously taking away, and how to keep his antagonists guessing.[52]

Milošević reached the peak of his power in Serbia just as socialism was collapsing elsewhere in Europe. As socialism weakened and Milošević, excited by his discovery of the power of Serbian nationalism, strengthened, other republics in the SFRY became increasingly unwilling to play second fiddle to Serb interests. It is not clear whether Milošević understood clearly what was going to happen, but by 1990 he had mobilized Serbian society in such a way that it was not willing to countenance cooperation with the other republics in a state based on mutual accommodation. He achieved this in part by extending his control over Serbian media. Whereas smaller independent voices, such as the news magazine *Vreme*, the TV station Studio-B, and the radio station B-92, survived in Belgrade, by 1991 the Milošević-controlled RTV Belgrade had become the primary source of political information not only in Serbia but also in those areas of Croatia and Bosnia controlled by Serbian forces. In fact, one of the first things that Serbian forces did when they seized a territory was to remove the television responders linked to Sarajevo or Zagreb and replace them with ones that could only receive RTV Belgrade. During the time of the most heated conflicts, over 60 percent of the population of Serbia watched the principal news program from RTV Belgrade, whereas only 2 percent were reading newspapers.[53] In 1989, when Franjo Tudjman, by profession a historian, published a book titled *Wastelands of Historical Reality* that provided significantly lower estimates of both Serb losses in World War II and Croatian atrocities than those accepted in Belgrade, the Belgrade media launched into what it called a "demystification of history."[54] Graves of World War II victims were opened and their remains shown, including explicit descriptions and pictures of mutilations and atrocities. Tudjman was referred to as "genocidal," "fascistoid," "heir of Ustasha leader Ante Pavelić," and "neo-Ustasha Croatian viceroy." Milošević, on the other hand, was "wise," "decisive," "unwavering," and the "man restoring the national dignity of the Serbian people." Of course, the Croatian media, controlled in Zagreb by Tudjman's people, reacted accordingly, characterizing Milošević as "Stalin's bastard" and "a bank robber," whereas Tudjman was "dignified" and "a wise statesman."[55] When war broke out in Bosnia in 1992, the Muslim forces became "jihad fanatics," "Muhaddjedin," and "terrorists." All sides used these destabilizing tactics, but as Mark Thompson, the historian of the media wars that forged the actual wars, put it, "Serbia set the pace."[56]

Given the misrepresentation of Izetbegović's views and the despicable media campaigns conducted by Serbian television (matched in Croatia), it would be easy to argue that the fears felt by Serbs in Croatia and Bosnia were manufactured out of whole cloth. However, this would not be entirely correct. During the socialist period, the consciousness of national differences appears to have declined, but a good deal of awareness of difference continued to exist under the surface. One ethnic relationship in particular had never dimmed, and that was the hostility between Serbs and Muslims, in particular between Serbs and the Albanians of Kosovo. This hostility had a long history that the ease of self-identification through religion, language, names, and dress exacerbated.[57] In Belgrade, for example, the traditional occupations held by Albanians—nighttime street washers and deliverers of coal to basement bins—clearly suggested that even more highly educated urban Serbs held Kosovars in low esteem.[58] This explains in part why Milošević was able to rouse Serbs over the question of Kosovo. His tactics tapped a deep-seated racial chord in the minds of many Serbs. This same sense also helped Karadžić in Bosnia to make Serbs there believe the worst about Izetbegović and the Muslims. Antagonism between Serbs and Croats, while not as deep seated as that between Serbs and Muslims, also had a long history, but it had decreased in saliency in socialist Yugoslavia. Nevertheless, there remained a sufficient residue of distrust that it could be prodded back to life by political leaders for their own purposes with relative ease. For this, Milošević, Tudjman, and Karadžić bear a heavy burden of responsibility.

The international community, distracted in part by the East European revolutions of 1989, the unification of Germany in the fall of 1990, and the war against Iraq in the spring of 1991, did not provide the aggressive attention toward the former Yugoslavia that a worsening situation there might normally have called for.[59] On the other hand, precisely these events had encouraged the Europeans to feel themselves well positioned to assume responsibility for maintaining stability in the Balkans. As one European diplomat put it, "This is the Hour of Europe, not of America."[60] The United States, already beginning to look forward to a presidential election in 1992, agreed. It had no intention of getting involved in a messy situation in the Balkans where the costs were likely to be high and the payoff for American interests low. The Bush administration was perfectly willing to let the Europeans confront the worsening situation in Yugoslavia on their own.

Today, in part because of events of the 1990s, the position of the European Union toward possible new members is summed up in the United Nation's post-1999 policy toward Kosovo: "standards before status." That is, in order to be eligible for treatment as a sovereign entity or possibly as an entrant into the European Union, a country must not only be democratic and have a market economy, but it must also demonstrate its willingness to support human rights and some 40,000 other rules and regulations that constitute the EU's standards (*acquis communautaire*).[61] Given the obvious desirability of joining the European Union, holding out on recalcitrant countries until they comply with these standards has proven to be a powerful tool in reshaping the new states of East Central Europe into democracies. As the events of 1990 through 1992 developed in the collapsing Yugoslavia, however, the European Community and NATO had little experience they deemed relevant in dealing with militant and recalcitrant nationalists. The general feeling, ill informed by widespread ignorance of Balkan affairs at the highest levels and the fact that NATO considered the Balkans "out of area" for military measures, was that the European Community imagined it could simply direct the unruly contestants to calm down and accept reasonable solutions.[62] Thus, when Serbian forces began to attack Croatian targets late in 1990 and when the violence escalated in 1991, the European Community equivocated. The first concerted action was the meeting that took place on Brioni shortly after Croatia and Slovenia declared "dissociation" from Yugoslavia. At this meeting it became clear that the head of the European delegation, Dutch Foreign Minister Hans Van den Broek, had little idea of the issues at stake. When Prime Minister of Yugoslavia Ante Marković sought to present proposals for keeping Yugoslavia together, for example, Van den Broek simply ignored him and "stormed out of the room muttering, in English, according to Slovenian president Milan Kučan, 'What a people! What a country!'"[63] Without actually making a considered decision on the matter, the European negotiators from the first implicitly accepted the nationalists' view that Yugoslavia was breaking up, thereby tacitly withdrawing support from the many Yugoslavs who wanted to keep the country together. The best the European negotiators could do at Brioni was to get Slovenia and Croatia to accept a ninety-day moratorium on their declarations of independence. The Slovenian case proved relatively unproblematic because Slovenia lacked a significant Serb minority. Accordingly, Kučan was able to reach an agreement with Slobodan Milošević fairly quickly that permitted Slovenia to go its way. In fact, as Sabrina Ramet reports, as early as January 1991, "in exchange for Milošević's assurances that Belgrade had no territorial pretensions vis-à-vis Slovenia, [Kučan] assured Milošević of his 'understanding' for Milošević's interest in uniting all Serbs in a greater Serbia."[64] Nevertheless, the Europeans took credit for the quick end of the hostilities in Slovenia, thus increasing their confidence in their ability to deal with the situation, although in fact European diplomacy had little to do with it.

Early in September 1991, as conditions deteriorated following the Brioni meeting, the EC convened a conference on Yugoslavia and appointed Peter Lord Carrington as its chief negotiator. Despite constant meetings, occasional agreements, and many proposals, as the fall wore on Lord Carrington found it difficult if not impossible to bring the negotiations to closure. A key moment came in October, when five of the six Yugoslav republics accepted, in principle at least, a plan that would reconstitute Yugoslavia as a federation or alliance of "sovereign and independent republics with international personality for those that wish it; a free association of the republics with an international personality, and comprehensive arrangements . . . for the protection of human rights and special status for certain groups and areas."[65] The republic that did not accept this proposal was Serbia. Invoking the principles that had been the norm in socialist Yugoslavia, Milošević argued that such an agreement would turn Serbs living in non-Serbian republics from a "nation" into a "national minority."[66] He insisted that instead of national minorities, Serbs should be considered "sovereign" in those republics. Of course, he was not willing to grant the same sovereign status to the Albanians living in the province of Kosovo. Serb leaders saw nothing wrong with this illogical position. As Radovan Karadžić put it, "Serbs have a right to territory not only where they're now living but also where they're buried, since the earth they lie in was taken unjustly from them." When asked if that meant Kosovars or Bosniaks should have the same right, he replied, "Of course not, because Croats are fascists and Muslims are Islamic fanatics."[67] The EC Conference gave the Serbs until 5 November to accept the plans for federation, which included "the principles of no unilateral change of borders, protection of human rights and the rights of ethnic and national groups." These "constitute universal, objective standards," the conference claimed, "which leave no room for compromise." If that did not occur, the declaration continued, "the Conference will proceed with the cooperative republics to obtain a political solution, in the perspective of recognition of the independence of those republics wishing it . . . ."[68] In other words, Serbia was informed that unless it gave up its demand for Serbs in Bosnia and Croatia to be "sovereign" and accepted their minority status, it could expect the European powers to recognize the independence of the other Yugoslav republics without further attention to Serbian concerns.

This is a key moment in the process leading to all-out war and shows how fundamental the issue of minority status was to the Serbs. For their part, the members of the EC felt that it would be possible to protect the rights of minorities, even substantial ones, if the new countries of Croatia and Bosnia accepted the European norms on minority rights. These norms began to emerge as aspects of international law after World War II in a number of international accords on human rights, not least of which was the charter of the United Nations, which declared that its signatories were determined "to reaffirm faith in fundamental human rights, in the dignity and worth of the human person, [and] in the equal rights of men and women of nations large and small." The signatories agreed to promote "respect for human rights and fundamental freedoms for all without distinction as to race, sex, language, or religion."[69] Between 1948 and the collapse of Communism at least seven international conventions prohibited a variety of violations of human rights, such as genocide, discrimination against women, torture, and other cruel, inhumane, or degrading treatment, while at the same time protecting various civil, political, economic, social, and cultural rights. Two institutions in particular, the Council of Europe and the Conference on Security and Cooperation in Europe (later the Organization for Security and Cooperation in Europe—OSCE), were responsible for tending to these rights, but neither of these entities had the ability to intervene in a sovereign country to protect the rights of minorities. Thus, even though Europeans felt that the rights of Serbs in Croatia and Bosnia *should* be protected, no mechanisms were in place to ensure that they *would* be.

If we discount the rhetoric and Milošević's willingness to resort to ethnic cleansing to establish the hegemony of Serbs, did the Serbian position have a reasonable basis? To some extent it did. For some Serbs, a proposal that made Serbs a minority rather than sovereign in Croatia—and might do the same later in Bosnia—simply perpetuated what they considered the injustices of borders established after 1945 by the Communists. Why, Serbian historian Dušan Bataković asks, was Kosovo, whose Albanian population constituted only 8.5 percent of the total population of the Serbian republic, made an autonomous region in Serbia while the Serbian population of the so-called Krajina was not, even though Serbs constituted 14.5 percent of the population of Croatia? And why was the Vojvodina given autonomous status in part for historical reasons, while the even better established historical identity of Dalmatia was not recognized?[70] These were legitimate questions. The thing that almost all outside observers found illegitimate, besides the unwillingness of Serbs to make the same concessions to Kosovar Albanians that they were asking for Serbs in Croatia and Bosnia, were the steps that Milošević took to respond to these grievances. Rather than insisting that the international community enforce minority rights in Croatia or Bosnia, he chose a war of ethnic cleansing to establish Serbian rights.[71] The international community believed minority issues would be answered when Croatia and other recognized states adhered to human rights standards and when they provided special status for places like Krajina. The Serbs did not think this likely.

The European Community faced several legalistic issues in working through their decision to move forward with recognition.[72] The first was how to consider the breakup of Yugoslavia. Serbia claimed that Croatia and Slovenia had seceded and therefore had no right to any assets formerly belonging to the SFRY.[73] On the other hand, Slovenia and Croatia claimed that Yugoslavia had simply disintegrated, and therefore they were entitled to a share of those assets. The Conference on Yugoslavia had created an arbitration commission of five constitutional judges headed by the president of the French Constitutional Council, Robert Badinter, to provide it with advisory opinions.[74] Near the end of November 1991, the commission reported and the conference accepted the Croatian position that "the SFRY is in the process of dissolution."[75] The commission based its judgment on the observation that the central government did not effectively exercise control over parts of the country. This raised the intriguing question of whether it would be possible for any entity in a federal state to bring about the dissolution of that state by simply ceasing to participate in it, surely not a principle that other federal states, such as the United States, would find congenial.[76] Indeed, the implication of this ruling was that unitary states such as the Serbs were demanding are more desirable than federations or confederations because they are less susceptible to secession, certainly not an appropriate principle in the age of the European Union. Another aspect of the decision was that the republics of the former Yugoslavia that did not dissociate themselves, namely Serbia and Montenegro, also lost their legal standing. Because the SFRY had "dissolved" rather than suffered the secession of several republics, technically it no longer existed, and in fact Serbia and Montenegro had to regain recognition in the year that followed.

How then should the members of the community proceed, especially given Serbia's rejection of the confederation plan of November and the EC's threat to move forward with recognition? Individual members of the community had their views. In Germany, the Bundestag had already voted to recognize Croatia and Slovenia in the summer of 1991, although the German government had not yet followed through. Germany's foreign minister, supported by a significant portion of the German population, kept suggesting that Germany was about to recognize both countries. Others argued that formal recognition would only exacerbate the situation. Lord Carrington, Cyrus Vance, and Javier Perez de Cuellar, the secretary-general of the United Nations, all believed strongly that the recognition of independence should "only be envisaged in the framework of an overall settlement."[77] Nevertheless, in order to paper over their differences and find a common way to proceed, a special meeting of EC foreign ministers decided on 16 December 1991 to ask those Yugoslav republics wishing to be recognized to petition for such recognition within one week, stating in their petitions that they accepted certain conditions, including the rights of minorities, the inviolability of frontiers, and other standard aspects of European political life.[78] Four republics responded, and in due course the Badinter Commission reported that only two of the applicants, Macedonia and Slovenia, had satisfied "the tests in the Guidelines on the Recognition of New States in Eastern Europe and the Soviet Union."[79] Neither Croatia nor Bosnia was deemed to have met the standards. In the case of Croatia the commission found that the Croatian government had not adequately addressed the special status provisions of the draft convention of 4 November.[80] Special status meant that an ethnic group forming a majority in a region (Serbs in Krajina, for example) could have an autonomous status, including the right to show national emblems and to have their own educational system, administration, and police force. Given that armed Serb units had occupied about one-third of Croatia by this time and had already established their own regimes in Eastern Slavonia and Krajina by force, it came as no surprise that the Croats were not willing to accept a provision they believed rewarded their attackers.

While the Badinter Commission was receiving responses from the republics and formulating its advice, Germany simply recognized Croatia on its own on 23 December to become effective on 15 January 1992. Foreign Minister Hans Dietrich Genscher took this action despite the pleas of UN General-Secretary Perez de Cuellar, who wrote Genscher noting previous agreements that recognition could "only be envisaged in the framework of an overall settlement" and warning "that early selective recognitions could result in a widening of the present conflict."[81] Susan Woodward argues that Genscher's actions had little to do with Balkan politics and a great deal to do with German internal politics and the foreign minister's personality.[82] Nevertheless, the decision forced the hand of the rest of the EC. On 15 January 1992, following in Germany's path and disregarding the Badinter Commission's report on Croatia, the European powers agreed to recognize formally the independence of both Croatia and Slovenia. Despite all the hopes for a common foreign policy contained in the documents creating the European Union, which were signed in Maastricht during this very period, Germany's ability to bring the rest of the community along killed Lord Carrington's efforts to achieve a comprehensive solution.[83]

The Badinter Commission had one more decision to make, namely, should the borders of the new states be the same as the republican borders of the former Yugoslavia? In arguing that they should, the commission based its decision on the principle of *uti possidetis.* This principle arose in the nineteenth century when newly independent countries were emerging from the declining Spanish Empire in Latin America. It held that when colonial states become independent they must do so within their colonial borders. New states may not legally change these borders by force. In 1986, in a case involving Burkina Faso and Mali, the International Court of Justice ruled that this principle was linked not solely to the decolonization process but also to the "phenomenon of the obtaining of independence wherever it occurs."[84] The purpose of *uti possidetis,* of course, is to prevent the opposing principle of self-determination from leading to chaotic minisecessions of every possible national or religious entity. The Badinter Commission, in a decision promulgated at the same time as the advisories regarding recognition, declared that this principle applied to the disintegrating Yugoslavia: "Whatever the circumstances, the right to self-determination must not involve changes to existing frontiers at the time of independence (*uti possidetis juris*)."[85] This decision essentially extended the Helsinki accords to the Yugoslav successor states. Those accords had confirmed the long-standing standard of the European state system that borders could be legally changed only by the mutual consent of the states involved. Each country that applied for recognition, therefore, had to agree specifically that changing borders by force was illegitimate.

In considering these questions, it is important to note first that the Badinter Commission was an arbitration committee of the ad hoc Conference on Yugoslavia, and therefore not competent to recast international law. Second, the actual policies of the various nations making up the European Community were not decided in the conference but by the individual states and the appropriate organs of the European Community. Thus, despite the rulings of the Badinter Commission that Macedonia met the established standards and Croatia did not, the European Community recognized Croatia and not Macedonia. And third, despite the enormous significance of the events in Yugoslavia to the people living there, Europe's primary attention in 1991 and 1992 was focused on the strains of the sea change in European affairs occasioned by the concurrent breakup of the Soviet Union and the negotiations that led to the creation of the European Union.

Given the context in which the discussions took place, could it be said that the Badinter Commission's decisions were appropriate? One could argue that the Badinter opinions were not consistent with international law, which "provides no right of secession, in the name of self-determination, to minorities."[86] Technically, the Badinter decisions were not based on self-determination but on the right of secession contained in the Yugoslav constitution of 1974 and other similar documents. Nevertheless, Yugoslavia was clearly disintegrating. The commission had to make the best of a volatile situation and to do it in a very short time frame. The short-term results seem clear: the Badinter decisions intensified the process of Yugoslavia's dissolution and did not slow the slide toward violence in Bosnia. They did not assist the European negotiators in finding a comprehensive solution for the Yugoslav situation, but they did provide a quasi-legal basis for the breakup and the entrance of the new countries into the international system of states.

In the long run, one of the unintended positive consequences of the commission's work was to bring the contradiction between the right of self-determination and the necessity to maintain state borders into clearer focus. During the decade of the 1990s, the European Union, the OSCE, and the Council of Europe devoted considerable effort to defining ways in which that contradiction could be resolved. When Woodrow Wilson spoke of the self-determination of peoples, he meant the creation of new states, particularly out of the Austro-Hungarian Empire. By the year 2000 or so, in significant measure because of efforts to understand and deal with problems in Yugoslavia and some regions of the former Soviet Union, Europeans had reached a new understanding of self-determination. In a world where changing borders was deemed illegitimate, self-determination could only mean self-determination *within* an established state—internal self-determination, as Antonio Cassese terms it.[87] People did have a right to their own language, their own schools, even perhaps their own administration—they had the right to self-determination in these senses, but not in the sense of creating a breakaway state. The 1990s saw a considerable expansion of this resolution of the contradiction between the principles of fixed borders and self-determination. For example, the Conference on Security and Cooperation in Europe (CSCE) created a high commissioner on national minorities in 1993, and in 1998 the Framework Convention for the Protection of National Minorities and the European Charter for Regional or Minority Languages came into effect. The European Court on Human Rights was restructured and by 2001 was handling almost 14,000 individual complaints a year.[88] The Badinter reports were an important part of a larger process that has led to reconciling the contradictory concepts of self-determination and *uti possidetis* by means of an international commitment to minority rights.

The strangest of the Badinter Commission's decisions was its suggestion that Bosnia conduct a referendum on the question of independence. In 1990, while Bosnia was still part of Yugoslavia, it had held its first open election since the imposition of Communism. A poll conducted by the newspaper *Danas* in May had 74 percent of the population supporting "the decision of the Bosnian leadership to forbid the formation of nationalist parties."[89] But the main party that sought to continue Yugoslavia by means of a negotiated settlement was the renamed Communist Party. The overwhelming mood of the electorate was that after fifty years the Communists had to go, no matter what the renovated party might advocate. During the campaign, the nationalist parties, which were in fact permitted, spoke of a harmonious relationship among the Bosnian people, but when these parties scored overwhelming victories in the winner-take-all election, purges fairly quickly left control of the Bosnian administration in the hands of three narrowly conceived parties. With no experience in democratic politics or statecraft, party leaders had neither the skills nor the will that would have been needed to implement a negotiated settlement. This was particularly true of Karadžić's Serbian Democratic Party (SDS), which, with psychological and material help from Serbia, consistently opposed Serbian inclusion in an independent Bosnia. When the war in Croatia began in earnest in the late summer of 1991, Serbian enclaves in Bosnia began to declare themselves autonomous entities and called on the JNA to protect them. Milošević responded by increasingly turning over control of the JNA forces in Bosnia to Bosnian Serbs, so that by the time a ceasefire between Croatia and Serbia had been achieved in January 1992 the Serbian elements in Bosnia were well armed and in effective possession of large parts of the territory they would claim as theirs. The Bosnian state, on the other hand, had been deprived of its ability to use force to maintain its integrity.[90]

It was under these conditions that the commission noted that the "Serbian people of Bosnia-Hercegovina" had moved from a position in November of simply staying in Yugoslavia to a vote in December to form a separate Serbian republic in Bosnia as part of a federal Yugoslav state and finally, in January 1992, to proclaiming the full independence of a Serbian republic. It concluded the obvious: it could not be established that all the people of Bosnia were united in their desire for an independent Bosnian state. The commission went on to suggest that "This assessment could be reviewed if appropriate guarantees were provided, possibly by means of a referendum of all the citizens."[91] This was a curiously technical finding, given the situation on the ground in Bosnia. One wonders how the commissioners, who had just admitted the intransigence of the Serbs, thought a referendum might stabilize the situation. In fact, what the commission had done was to agree that the Serbian population of Bosnia had the right to prevent the creation of a unified and independent Bosnia, a ruling consistent with the earlier ruling that a part of a federal state could delegitimize that state by not participating in its affairs. In essence, the commission, albeit probably unintentionally, accepted the Serbian position that the Serbs should not become a minority in a united Bosnia.

Despite serious misgivings about holding a referendum, Izetbegović agreed to do so. The vote, taken on 28 February and 1 March 1992, achieved a high turnout of 63.4 percent of the eligible voters, of whom almost 100 percent voted in favor of independence. That is, an absolute majority of the citizens of Bosnia voted for independence. Unfortunately, the overwhelming majority of those who had voted were Bosniaks and Croats. As could easily have been predicted, most Serbs, who constituted about one-third of the population of all of Bosnia, boycotted the elections.[92] Nevertheless, only two days later, Izetbegović declared the independence of Bosnia-Hercegovina. The international community, noting the intransigence of the Serbs, now backed away from its earlier belief that Bosnia could be a unified country. At a meeting held in Lisbon two weeks following the declaration of Bosnian independence, the EC brokered an agreement to divide the country into ten ethnically determined cantons. The Serbs and Croats accepted this idea, but Izetbegović did not, fearing that the Bosnian Muslims would be left an easy prey to more powerful Serbian and Croatian neighbors. By early April the "cleansing" of the Drina Valley was under way, and within weeks Serb forces had occupied about 60 percent of the country.

Almost all observers agree that the international community handled the breakup of Yugoslavia poorly. John Gillingham, for example, has called it "a running diplomatic fiasco."[93] The Europeans had difficulty dealing with the situation, first because they were divided among themselves not only in their ability to coordinate national foreign policies but also in the overlapping and sometimes conflicting international organizations that became involved. The United States, NATO, the United Nations, the CSCE, the European Union, and many NGOs all played their parts, not always in a coordinated way. The Badinter Commission, consisting of constitutional experts whose job was to deal with legal and technical issues in a volatile and rapidly developing situation, provided the rationales that supported a de facto policy of accepting the breakup of Yugoslavia, especially by conceding the right of Serbs in Bosnia to define themselves as a constituent people rather than a minority. The West also was unwilling to use force where it might have been effective. In October 1991, when Serbian and Montenegrin forces began shelling Dubrovnik, a strike by NATO forces on the Serbian artillery positions and a rag-tag supporting fleet in the Adriatic would have sent a clear message that aggression would be met by force. The failure to do so only confirmed the conclusion already reached by the Serbian military, on the basis of its study of the First Gulf War, that overt Western, particularly American and NATO, military intervention in Yugoslavia was highly unlikely.[94] When a military intervention did occur with the arrival of a United Nations Protection Force

(UNPROFOR), it did not come to prevent aggression or conquest but rather to enforce a ceasefire between the Serbs and Croats, a ceasefire that temporarily left 30 percent of Croatia in Serbian hands and freed up Serb forces in Bosnia. In short, the Europeans proved inexperienced in dealing with committed, intransigent parties in an area they considered less civilized than themselves. But at least the Europeans became involved. The United States, whose participation would prove essential in the end, stayed on the sidelines. By dithering and lack of firmness, the international community ended up by exacerbating the tensions that lay at the root of the conflict.

It is vital to recognize, however, that Europe did not create those tensions and was not responsible for the acts of those who instigated or carried out the wars or for the ethnic cleansings, atrocities, and mutilations that characterized them. For a while, it was a pastime of those involved to find the ultimate blame. Not surprisingly, each ethnic group blamed one or more of the others. Of the main leaders, it seems clear that Slobodan Milošević, Radovan Karadžić, and those around them bear the largest measure of responsibility for turning a difficult situation into a bloody and destructive war. In this they were abetted by Franjo Tudjman's nationalism and lust for territory, the ineptitude of the European governments, and the passivity of the United States. And yet, one should not overlook the larger context in which these events took place. Most of the countries that are now members of the European Union themselves went through bloody and violent upheavals before the map of imperial Europe as it stood in about 1850 was fully redrawn into a map of more or less ethnically homogeneous states. The Yugoslavs were left behind in this process. The historian Holm Sundhaussen has called the short twentieth century from 1914 to 1989 "the lost century" for the Balkans.[95] While the rest of Europe was fighting a great civil war (1914–1945) that eventually cleared the decks for an entirely new and original structure of international interaction, the Balkan states were enmeshed in the difficult problems of establishing new states. After World War II they found themselves suffocated within the Soviet sphere or, in the case of Yugoslavia, under a dictatorship that seemed liberal only in comparison to the Soviet model. Consequently, when Communism collapsed, none of the Yugoslav peoples had been through the difficult and complex process of negotiation and change that created the European Union. Instead, leaders such as Milošević and Tudjman, as well as their followers, retained ideas of national security and dignity that were at least two, and probably more, generations out of date. Milošević in particular believed he could use the issue of minority rights in a way that was consistent with the manner in which it had been used for aggressive purposes by Germany during the interwar years.[96] But Europe had changed. Power based primarily on the seizure of territory was now considered illegitimate.

Clearly the kind of leadership that the Serbs and Croats received made a difficult situation not only worse, but much worse. The unwillingness of Europe and the United States to take forceful action early also played an important role in permitting a dangerous situation to career out of control at least until 1995. On the other hand, considering that the international system grants its legitimacy and authenticity primarily to nation-states, and given that human and minority rights have become a central tenet of that system, it is difficult to see how any leadership could have saved socialist Yugoslavia or reconstituted its republics into new states without serious conflict.

Notes

1   For convenience, the terms *Serb* and *Croat* are used throughout. It must be kept in mind, however, as Drago Roksandić correctly points out, that these Yugoslav ethnic groups were not monolithic political blocks, especially before the outbreak of war.

2   The following is based on Dejan Jović, "Fear of Becoming a Minority as a Motivator of Conflict in the Former Yugoslavia," *Balkanologie* 5, no. 1–2 (December 2001), 21–26, and Dejan Jović, "Communist Yugoslavia and Its 'Others,'" in *Ideologies and National Identities: The Case of Twentieth-Century Southeastern Europe,* ed. John R. Lampe and Mark Mazower (Budapest and New York: CEU Press, 2004), 277–302, as well as other input. Silvano Bolčić also contributed to this section.

3   The glossary to the 1974 constitution of the SFRY defined *narodnosti* as "members of nations whose native countries border on Yugoslavia."

4   Jović, "Communist Yugoslavia and Its 'Others,'" 278.

5   Jović, "Communist Yugoslavia and Its 'Others,'" 290.

6   Alina Mungiu-Pippidi, "Nationalism after Communism: Lessons Learned," event summary of a talk given at the East European Studies program of the Woodrow Wilson International Center for Scholars, 8 September 2004, available on its Web site. http://www.wilsoncenter.org/index.cfm?topic_id=1422&fuseaction=topics.publications&doc_id=106116&group_id=7427.

7   For elaborations of this point see Gale Stokes, "Containing Nationalism: Solutions in the Balkans," *Problems of Post-Communism* 46, no. 4 (July–August, 1999), 3–10, and Gale Stokes, "Can Money Buy Stability in the Western Balkans? Lessons from the Recent Past," *Newsnet* 44, no. 1 (January 2004), 1–5.

8   There were, of course, many other issues, such as the future of the Jewish minority in Sarajevo, the case of Istria, or the condition of the Roma. For a study of one of these issues, see Matjaž Klemenčić and Jernej Župančić, "The Effects of the Dissolution of Yugoslavia on the Minority Rights of Hungarian and Italian Minorities in the Post-Yugoslav States," *Nationalities Papers* 32, no. 4 (December 2004), 853–896. Egidio Ivetić proposed a contribution for this project titled "The Istrian Case, between Yugoslavia and Post-Yugoslavia." Silvano Bolčić also proposed a contribution titled "'Yugoslavs' as a New Minority Post-1990," and Francine Friedman outlined a possible section on the Jews of Sarajevo.

9   Marcus Tanner, *Croatia: A Nation Forged in War*, 2nd ed. (New Haven, CT: Yale University Press, 2001), 285.

10   Quoted in Steven L. Burg and Paul Shoup, *The War in Bosnia-Herzegovina: Ethnic Conflict and International Intervention* (Armonk, NY: M. E. Sharpe, 2000), 126.

11 Drago Roksandić, "Comments Related to Serbs in Croatia," unpublished manuscript, 8.

12 For a more extended discussion of the wars in Croatia see chapter 7 of this volume.

13 There are perhaps a score of biographies of Slobodan Milošević, but I am not aware of a single full-scale biography of Izetbegović.

14 Alija Izetbegović, *Sjećanja: autobiografski zapis* (Sarajevo: TKD Šahinpašić, 2001), 23.

15 Alija Izetbegović, *Islamic Declaration*, 15. The copy I used is an English translation obtained from the Yale University library. It contains no publication data. Readers can access another translation at www.balkan-archive.org.yu/politics/papers/Islamic_Declaration_1990_reprint_English.pdf (accessed July 2004).

16 Izetbegović, *Declaration*, 7.

17 Izetbegović, *Declaration*, 36

18 On modernism conceived as the replacement of honor by dignity see Charles Taylor, *Multiculturalism*, ed. and intro. Amy Gutmann (Princeton, NJ: Princeton University Press, 1994).

19 " I have been attacked as a fundamentalist," he said, "and in a certain sense I was—demanding a return to the sources" (Izetbegović, *Sjećanja*, 35).

20 As quoted in Albert Hourani, *Arabic Thought in the Liberal Age, 1798–1939* (London: Oxford University Press, 1962), 354.

21 I would like to thank David Cook of Rice University for this reference.

22 Alija Izetbegović, *Islam between East and West* (Indianapolis: American Trust Publications, 1984), 38.

23 Mihailo Marković quoted in Gale Stokes, ed., *From Stalinism to Pluralism: A Documentary History of Eastern Europe since 1945*, 2nd ed. (New York: Oxford University Press, 1996), 120. Marković later became a supporter of Milošević and even appeared at The Hague as a witness for Milošević's defense.

24 Izetbegović, *Declaration*, 45.

25 Izetbegović, *Declaration*, 43.

26 Izetbegović, *Declaration*, 53.

27 Izetbegović, *Islam between East and West*.

28 Alija Izetbegović, *Izetbegović of Bosnia and Herzegovina: Notes from Prison, 1983–1988* (Westport, CT, and London: Praeger, 2002), 106, describing his earlier ideas in *Islam between East and West*.

29 During his stay in prison, Izetbegović numbered his notes consecutively, but in the published book he divided them into subjects for individual chapters so that the numbering is no longer consecutive. Therefore, I give citations for the above quotes, in the order in which they appear, with the page number followed by the item number on that page. Izetbegović, *Notes from Prison*, 32/1040; 71/1203; 203/2293; 79/1631; 195/712; 194/241; and 201/2013.

30 Alija Izetbegović, *Izetbegović: Odabrani govori, pisma, izjave, intervjui* (Zagreb: Prvo Muslimansko Dioničko Društvo Zagreb, 1995), 170, 39, and 89.

31 These charges are taken from a current Serbian Web site: http://www.srpska-mreza.com/librar/facts/alija.html, last revised 15 July 2003 (accessed 29 October 2004).

32 In fact, "Bosnian Moslems [sic] typically report not considering religious affiliation a significant part of personal or collective identity." Scott Atran, "Genesis of Suicide Terrorism," in *The Best American Science and Nature Writing, 2004*, ed. Steven Pinker (Boston, New York: Houghton Mifflin Company, 2004), 9.

33 Laura Silber and Allan Little, *Yugoslavia: Death of a Nation* (New York: Penguin, 1997), 213. Silber and Little are probably referring to the Organization of the Islamic

Conference, of which Bosnia-Hercegovina became an observer (i.e., not a full member) in 1994.

34   Burg and Shoup, *The War in Bosnia-Herzegovina*, 67.

35   Alija Izetbegović, *Odobrani govori, pisma, izjave, intervjui* (Zagreb: Prvo muslimankso dioničko društvo, 1995), 101. Thanks to Husnija Kamberović for comments at this point.

36   As reported by Jasminka Udovički and Ejub Štitkovac, "Bosnia and Hercegovina: The Second War," *Burn This House: The Making and Unmaking of Yugoslavia,* ed. Jasminka Udovički and James Ridgeway (Durham, NC, and London: Duke University Press, 2000), 175–176. This book is a revised and expanded edition of *Yugoslavia's Ethnic Nightmare* (1995), by the same editors.

37   Udovički and Štitkovac, "Bosnia and Hercegovina," 204n6.

38   Burg and Shoup, *The War in Bosnia-Herzegovina*, 72.

39   Izetbegović, *Sjećanja*, 58.

40   Izetbegović, *Sjećanja*, 96–100.

41   Warren Zimmerman, *Origins of a Catastrophe* (New York: Times Books, 1999), 174.

42   Zimmerman, *Origins of a Catastrophe*, 175. "In his fanaticism," Zimmerman wrote, "he invites comparison with a monster from another generation, Heinrich Himmler" (175).

43   Tim Judah, *The Serbs* (New Haven and London: Yale University Press, 2000), 43.

44   Zimmerman, *Origins of a Catastrophe,* 203.

45   Mišković e-mail to Stokes, 30 November 2004.

46   Dusko Doder and Louise Branson, *Milošević: Portrait of a Tyrant* (New York: Free Press, 1999), 96.

47   Richard Holbrooke, *To End a War,* rev. ed. (New York: Modern Library, 1999), 152.

48   Edward P. Joseph, "Back to the Balkans," *Foreign Affairs* 84, no. 1 (January/February 2005), 118. Joseph continues: "It is hard to overestimate how essential the minority-treatment principle is for the Balkans."

49   David Owen, *Balkan Odyssey* (London: Victor Gollanz, 1995), 74.

50   Quoted in Ejub Štitkovac, "Croatia: The First War," in Udovički and Ridgeway, *Burn This House,* 156.

51   Susan Woodward characterizes Tudjman's campaign as full of "anti-Semitic and anti-Serb vitriol." Susan Woodward, *Balkan Tragedy: Chaos and Dissolution after the Cold War* (Washington: Bookings Institution, 1995), 133.

52   For an excellent discussion of the personality of Milošević and his family, especially of Mira Marković, the wife who had such an influence on him, see Louis Sell, *Slobodan Milošević and the Destruction of Yugoslavia* (Durham, NC, and London: Duke University Press, 1992), 169–194. Sell believes Milošević was a "malignant narcissist," that is, an emotionally frigid individual who was so strongly self-centered that he believed his own wants and visions to be the truth, whatever the facts. See also Slavoljub Djukić, *Milošević and Marković: A Lust for Power* (Montreal: McGill-Queen's University Press, 2001).

53   Slightly modified from Eric D. Gordy, *The Culture of Power in Serbia: Nationalism and the Destruction of Alternatives* (University Park: Pennsylvania State University Press, 1999), 33.

54   A revised and updated English version appeared in 1996: Franjo Tudjman, *Horrors of War: Historical Reality and Philosophy* (New York: M. Evans, 1996).

55   Milan Milošević, "The Media Wars," in Udovički and Ridgeway, *Burn This House,* 113.

56 Mark Thompson, *Forging War: The Media in Serbia, Croatia, Bosnia, and Hercegovina* (Luton, UK: University of Luton Press, 1999), substantially revised from its initial publication in 1994. "Serbia Sets the Pace" is the title of chapter 4. See also, David Bruce MacDonald, *Balkan Holocausts? Serbian and Croatian Victim-Centered Propaganda and the War in Yugoslavia* (Manchester and New York: Manchester University Press, 2002).

57 Bojan Aleksov argues, for example, that Serbian historiography has consistently mythologized the emergence of Islam in the Balkans as being a result of the devşirme and of coercion rather than a complex and genuine phenomenon. In the 1990s, he writes, this tradition produced "a flood of press articles spreading hatred depic[ting] Muslims as an imminent danger" ("Perceptions of Islamisation in the Serbian National Discourse," paper presented at the Conference on Nationalism, Society, and Culture in Post-Ottoman South East Europe, St. Peter's College, Oxford, 29–30 May 2004, 12).

58 A survey conducted in 2001 showed that Serbs ranked Kosovar Albanians lowest in trust among eleven ethnic groups and Bosnia Muslims next lowest. Both were ranked lower than Roma. Alina Mungiu-Pippidi, "Milošević's Voters: Explaining Grassroots Nationalism in Postcommunist Europe," in *Nationalism after Communism: Lessons Learned,* ed. Alina Mungiu-Pippidi and Ivan Krastev (Budapest: Central European University Press, 2004), 53.

59 For a detailed discussion of the international reaction to the dissolution of the SFRY, see chapter 5 of this volume, "The International Community and the FRY/Belligerents" whose primary author is Matjaž Klemenčić, who also made significant contributions to this chapter.

60 Quoted by John Gillingham, *European Integration, 1950–2003: Superstate or New Market Economy* (Cambridge: Cambridge University Press, 2003), 282. James Gow, *Triumph of the Lack of Will: International Diplomacy and the Yugoslav War* (New York: Columbia University Press, 1997), characterizes this statement as "much derided" (48).

61 The so-called Copenhagen criteria for an associated country to move to membership, adopted in 1993, are "1) stability of institutions guaranteeing democracy, the rule of law, human rights, and respect for minorities; 2) the existence of a functioning market economy; 3) capacity to cope with competitive pressures and market forces within the Union; and 4) the ability to take on the obligations of membership."

62 Woodward, *Balkan Tragedy,* 150.

63 Silber and Little, *Death of a Nation,* 164–165; Woodward, *Balkan Tragedy,* 169.

64 Milan Kučan, interview by Sabrina Ramet, 6 September 1999.

65 "Peace Conference on Yugoslavia: Arrangements for General Settlement," (often referred to as the Carrington draft convention), The Hague, 18 October 1991, in *Yugoslavia through Documents: From Its Creation to Its Dissolution,* ed. Snežana Trifunovska (Dordrecht: Martinus Nijhoff Publishers, 1994), 357.

66 Note that according to the Constitution of Bosnia-Hercegovina adopted in December 1995 as part of the Dayton Accords, Bosniaks, Croats, and Serbs are all considered "constituent peoples (along with Others)" of the new state.

67 Zimmerman, *Origins of a Catastrophe,* 175.

68 European Community, "Declaration on the Situation in Yugoslavia," Brussels, 28 October 1991, in Trifunovska, *Yugoslavia through Documents,* 368–369.

69 Paul Gordon Lauren, *The Evolution of International Human Rights: Visions Seen,* 2nd ed. (Philadelphia: University of Pennsylvania Press, 2003), 188.

70 The percentages are as cited by Dušan Bataković, *Yougoslavie: Nations, Religions, Idéologies* (Lausanne, Switzerland: L'Age D'hommes, 1994), 242–243. According to

the figures cited by Tim Judah, the percentage of the Albanian population of Serbia as a whole in 1991 was 16.6 percent, and the percentage of Serbs living in Croatia as a whole was 12.2 percent. Actually, of course, most Croatian Serbs did not live in Krajina but in Zagreb and other urban areas. Tim Judah, *The Serbs: History, Myth, and the Destruction of Yugoslavia* (New Haven, CT: Yale University Press, 2000), 343–344.

71   James Gow argues, in fact, that "the committing of war crimes was the essence of Serbian strategy in the war." James Gow, *The Serbian Project and its Adversaries: A Strategy of War Crimes* (London: Hurst, 2003), 2.

72   For thorough discussions of the legal issues surrounding recognition, see Marc Weller, "The International Response to the Dissolution of the Socialist Federal Republic of Yugoslavia," *The American Journal of International Law* 86, no. 3 (July 1992), 569–607, and Roland Rich, "Recognition of States: The Collapse of Yugoslavia and the Soviet Union," *European Journal of International Law* 4 (1993), 36–65.

73   Daniele Conversi has argued that in fact it was not Croatia and Slovenia that were seceding but instead Serbia. By setting such aggressively irredentist conditions for maintenance of Yugoslavia, Serbia purposely undermined the relatively balanced structure of the state and ensured its breakup. See his "Central Secession: Towards a New Analytical Concept? The Case of Former Yugoslavia," *Journal of Ethnic and Migration Studies* 26, no. 2 (2000), 333–356, and "The Dissolution of Yugoslavia: Secession by the Centre?" in *The Territorial Management of Ethnic Conflicts,* ed. John Coakley (London: Frank Cass, 2003), 264–292.

74   Comments by Zoran Oklopčić have informed the discussion of the Badinter Commission.

75   "Opinion No. 1 of the Arbitration Commission of the Peace Conference on Yugoslavia," 29 November 1991, in Trifunovska, *Yugoslavia through Documents,* 417. The Badinter Commission reports, as well as a number of other documents, also can be found on the CD that accompanies Owen, *Balkan Odyssey.*

76   See Hurst Hannum, "Self-Determination, Yugoslavia, and Europe: Old Wine in New Bottles?" *Transnational Law and Contemporary Problems* 3 (Spring 1993), 64.

77   "Letter from the Secretary-General of the United Nations Addressed to the Minister for Foreign Affairs of the Netherlands," 10 December 1991, in Trifunovska, *Yugoslavia through Documents,* 428. The letter was to be transmitted to all twelve participants in the Conference on Yugoslavia, including (and especially) Germany.

78   The principles in the guidelines were directed to the emerging states of the former Soviet Union as well. By the Alma Ata Declaration of 16 December 1991, all but one of the twelve remaining unrecognized states of the former USSR agreed with the principles. The Baltic states had already been recognized, and Georgia did not sign.

79   "Opinion No. 6" and "Opinion No. 7," in Trifunovska, *Yugoslavia through Documents,* 495 and 500.

80   This draft convention can be found on the CD accompanying Owen, *Balkan Odyssey.*

81   Javier Perez de Cuellar to Hans-Dietrich Genscher, 14 December 1991, on CD accompanying Owen, *Balkan Odyssey.*

82   For a spirited defense of Germany's position see Daniele Conversi, "German-Bashing and the Breakup of Yugoslavia," *The Donald W. Treadgold Papers,* 16 (March 1998). For an excellent discussion of German policy, see Sabrina P. Ramet and Letty Coffin, "German Foreign Policy toward the Yugoslav Successor States, 1991–1999," *Problems of Post-Communism* 48, no. 1 (January–February 2001), 48–64.

83   The recognition of Croatia, and later Bosnia-Hercegovina, was not consistent with the Badinter Commission's decision on the dissolution of the SFRY because neither of those countries exercised effective control over their entire territory. Thus their recogni-

tion was a declaratory political act rather than a decision consistent with international law. See Thomas D. Musgrave, *Self-Determination and National Minorities* (Oxford: Clarendon Press, 1997), 200–207.

84   Rich, "Recognition of States," 58. Antonio Cassese holds that "it is beyond dispute that at present *uti possidetis* constitutes a general rule of international law." Antonio Cassese, *Self-Determination of Peoples: A Legal Reappraisal* (Cambridge: Cambridge University Press, 1995), 192.

85   "Opinion No. 2," in Trifunovska, *Yugoslavia through Documents*, 474. The relationship between this principle and the right of self-determination is far from clear. See, for example, J. Klabbers and R. Lefeber, "Africa: Lost between Self-Determination and *Uti Possidetis*," in *Peoples and Minorities in International Law*, ed. Catherine Brölmann, René Lefeber, and Marjoleine Zieck (Dordrecht: Martinus Nijhoff, 1993), 37–76.

86   R. Higgins, "Postmodern Tribalism and the Right to Secession: Comments," in Brölmann et al., *Peoples and Minorities*, 33.

87   Cassese, *Self-Determination of Peoples*.

88   "Historical Background," Section B, from the Web site of the European Court of Human Rights, www.echr.coe.int/Eng/EDocs/HistoricalBackground.htm (accessed 23 November 2004).

89   V. P. Gagnon Jr., *The Myth of Ethnic War: Serbia and Croatia in the 1990s* (Ithaca and London: Cornell University Press, 2004), 49.

90   For an excellent, detailed account of the formation of military forces in Bosnia, see Marko Attila Hoare, *How Bosnia Armed* (London: Saqi Books, in association with the Bosnian Institute, 2004).

91   "Opinion No. 4," 11 January 1992, in Trifunovska, *Yugoslavia through Documents*, 488.

92   See, among others, Sabrina Petra Ramet, *Balkan Babel: The Disintegration of Yugoslavia from the Death of Tito to the Fall of Milošević*, 4th ed. (Boulder, CO: Westview Press, 2002), 206.

93   Gillingham, *European Integration*, 281.

94   Gow, *The Serbian Project*, 102–113.

95   Holm Sundhaussen, "Das zwanzigste Jahrhundert als verlorenes Jahrhundert: Der Balkan und Europa," *Jahrbücher für Geschichte und Kultur Südosteuropas*, 3 (2001), 11–26.

96   This statement will raise a red flag with many readers who will accuse the author of comparing Milošević to Hitler. Milošević was several rungs below Hitler in his impact, his racism, and his cold brutality. However, even in the 1920s, German governments justified their aggressive policies toward East Central Europe by claiming that they were protecting German minorities. "[B]etween 1926 and 1933, Germany [was] . . . the foremost champion of minority rights." Carole Fink, *Defending the Rights of Others: The Great Powers, the Jews, and International Minority Protection, 1878–1938* (New York: Cambridge University Press, 2004), 295. These arguments, as well as the ones used by the Nazis in the Sudetenland and Danzig, are functionally equivalent to those made by Serbia regarding Croatia and Bosnia in the early 1990s.

4

Marie-Janine Calic, team leader
Momčilo Mitrović, team leader

Milan Andrejevich	**Elissa Helms**	**Lana Obradović**
Elazar Barkan	Dušan Janjić	**Tatjana Perić**
Alfred Bing	**Georg Kastner**	Ernest Plivac
Cathie Carmichael	Paul Leifer	**Šerbo Rastoder**
Judit Deli	**James Lyon**	**Jacques Semelin**
Marta Fazekas	David MacDonald	**Branislava Stankov†**
Horst Haselsteiner	Josef Marko	**Mirsad Tokača**
	Norman Naimark	

Principal author Marie-Janine Calic's text integrates significant data compiled by the late Branislava Stankov, Mirsad Tokača's Research & Documentation Center, and Momčilo Mitrović's Institute for Contemporary History in Belgrade. The chapter also incorporates material from a series of publications provided by Smail Čekić, director of the Institute for the Research of Crimes against Humanity & International Law. It reflects extensive input collected from several project-wide reviews.

Research stipends from the National Endowment for Democracy assisted the staff of team member Mirsad Tokača's Research & Documentation Center, and Branislava Stankov's investigation of sexual crimes against women conducted at Medica Zenica and the BiH Ministry of Human Rights and Refugees. As team leader, Marie-Janine Calic succeeeded Horst Haselsteiner (2001-2003) and Georg Kastner (2003-2005), each of whom authored drafts submitted for project-wide review in October 2003 and January 2004 respectively. A satellite meeting hosted by Andrássy University, Budapest, took place in December 2004. The final draft underwent extensive project-wide review in January-February 2006 and was subsequently adopted following the completion of additional revisions.

ETHNIC CLEANSING AND WAR CRIMES, 1991-1995

◆ Marie-Janine Calic ◆

Public perception has associated the Yugoslav wars of succession with all forms of ethnically inspired violence, from murder, rape, and torture to mass expulsion. Many of these systematic violations of international humanitarian law occurred in the context of ethnic cleansing—a purposeful policy that "means rendering an area ethnically homogenous by using force or intimidation to remove from a given area persons from another ethnic or religious group."[1] The violent breakup of the Socialist Federal Republic of Yugoslavia resulted in the largest refugee crisis in Europe since World War II. In 1991, half a million people were displaced in Croatia. Between 1992 and 1995, over half of Bosnia-Hercegovina's 4.4 million people were uprooted, including an estimated 1.3 million who were internally displaced, 500,000 who were refugees in neighboring countries, and 700,000 who had fled to Western European countries.[2] As a result, many municipalities in that country have changed their ethnic structure substantially and, perhaps, permanently.

This chapter aims at describing causes, features, and consequences of ethnic cleansing as a policy in Bosnia-Hercegovina during the war, which has posed substantial challenges to our research team. No other subject is so heavily charged with emotion, selective perception, and partiality as mass crimes and the phenomenon of ethnic cleansing. Conflicting perspectives and controversies concern both the quality and quantity of violence, and there is an obvious tendency of politicization. For instance, the number of victims on either side continues to be a controversial subject; figures presented often appear inflated. Interpretations constantly evolve in light of the quickly expanding body of primary evidence and secondary literature about the Yugoslav wars of succession. It is therefore important to keep some key concerns in mind.

First, the attempt to conceptualize ethnic cleansing as a policy involves nearly all of the crucial, controversial issues that have been debated since the breakup of Yugoslavia, such as the causes of the war and the roles and intentions of political leaders. These issues have been dealt with in depth by other teams' chapters in this project, and it appeared neither justified nor feasible to include differing accounts and competing interpretations of all these important aspects of the subject.

Second, systematic analysis of ethnic cleansing requires a certain selectivity of facts because the chapter aims at recounting main developments in an exemplary and systematic way. Space limitations simply do not permit a comprehensive narrative either of events or of all the atrocities committed during the war.

Third, the reliability of sources has been crucial. Given the limited resources at our disposal, it has been impossible to conduct primary research into mass crimes. We have, therefore, relied heavily on investigations of the International Criminal Tribunal for the former Yugoslavia (ICTY), international institutions, and the rather finite research conducted by individual scholars, most of whom are closely associated with a particular viewpoint. Although partisans of one side or another have questioned the impartiality of the ICTY, its investigative teams have conducted an enormous amount of research that meets high scholarly standards. Unfortunately, much of its work has not yet been made available to the community of scholars. We stress, therefore, that this chapter is part of a much longer *process* that cannot be deemed "final" in the absence of conclusive evidence.

Fourth, comparability and interpretation of events have given rise to dramatically different interpretations. There is still no consensus with regard to terminology, categorization, and interpretation of the phenomenon of ethnic cleansing.[3] For instance, the question of whether ethnic cleansing should per se be equated with genocide is highly controversial. There is little understanding that, although diverse acts of violence may share the same features, such as mass expulsion and large-scale atrocities, the underlying motivation and intention of major actors may be totally diverse in each single case. This chapter aims at providing careful analytical distinction, assuming that each set of events in which mass crimes occurred needs to be analyzed separately but without precluding any possible interpretation from the outset.

Fifth, there has been an inherent, although often unintended, tendency to "measure" guilt and attribute it collectively to the parties involved. At the same time, all parties to the conflict perceive themselves as the real victims of the war and believe that injustices continue to go unaddressed. Ethnic cleansing and other crimes were evidently perpetrated by all parties in the conflict, and there were victims on all sides, although the gravity and dimension differed markedly, as the UN Commission of Experts has clearly stated.

At the beginning of the war, most of the violations were committed by Serb forces against Bosniaks and, to a lesser extent, Croats, as the result of a highly developed policy of ethnic cleansing. Also, Croat forces conducted ethnic cleansing campaigns against Serbs in eastern and western Slavonia and in the Krajina region of Croatia, as well as against Bosniaks in Mostar and central Bosnia. Bosniak forces have victimized Serbs in Bosnia-Hercegovina, but in lesser numbers, with forceful population removal occurring only in limited areas.[4] Later, there were more massive campaigns against Serbs as well, especially in 1995, when a large number of the Croatian Serbs fled their home territory. During 1992–1995, Roma were also subjected to ethnic cleansing by Serb, Croat, and Bosnian Muslim forces.

Against this background, there are also conflicting positions concerning "moral equivalence": do all parties to the conflict really bear equal responsibility? Did all sides suffer equally in the war, and is there a (perceived) hierarchy among the victims? The community of analysts is divided among those who take an explicit moralist attitude and those who do not. This has resulted in unscholarly polemics against alternative approaches. Hopefully, the ICTY's work of creating an objective record of events and establishing individual blame instead of collective guilt will effect a consensus in the interpretation of events in the future. Until then, this chapter will avoid making summary judgments about individual perpetrators or the belligerents themselves in the absence of conclusive evidence. Instead, it will try to conceptualize the phenomenon of ethnic cleansing as a policy by analyzing its aims, mechanisms, and consequences, while recapitulating the main controversies surrounding it.

In light of the aforementioned challenges, this chapter undertakes the following. First, it discusses meaning and content of the term *ethnic cleansing*. Second, it gives a narrative of key events and analyzes main features of ethnic cleansing as a policy. Third, it presents two of the most contentious issues: the number of victims and possible distinctions between the terms *ethnic cleansing* and *genocide*.

The analysis is based on various sources: (a) a review of the literature and recent studies on the phenomenon of ethnic cleansing; (b) analysis of case material produced by the ICTY and other international institutions; (c) specific research by team members, in particular the Research and Documentation Center in Sarajevo[5] and witness statements collected by the Institute for Recent History of Serbia in Belgrade.

I. The Term *Ethnic Cleansing*

The term *ethnic cleansing* entered the vocabulary of international relations during the early phases of the war in Bosnia-Hercegovina, describing a set of grave human rights and humanitarian law violations.[6] Although there is widespread use of this term, both its origin and exact meaning are unclear.[7] Ethnic cleansing is a literal translation of the Serbo-Croatian/Croato-Serbian idiom *etničko čišćenje*, *čist* meaning "clean" or "without any contamination." Petrović assumes that it originates from military vocabulary because there is an expression "to clean the territory" of the enemy, which is "used mostly in the final phase of combat in order to take total control of the conquered territory."[8] The adjective *ethnic* may have been added because the enemies were considered to belong to separate ethnic communities. Although the term *ethnic cleansing* has become common during the war in Bosnia-Hercegovina, there is some evidence that it may date back to World War II and, perhaps, even earlier.[9]

Historical Background

Ethnic cleansing as a practice has occurred throughout history in various regional contexts and has assumed many forms, including forced migration, population exchange, deportation, expulsion, and genocide.[10] Following the creation of the modern Balkan states (starting with the Serbian uprisings of 1804–1813 and 1815 and the Greek War of Independence of 1821–1829) up to 1920, an estimated 5 to 10 million people, mostly Muslims, were expelled from their home territory, and up to 1.5 million were killed.[11] During the Balkan Wars of 1912–1913, when Serbia, Bulgaria, Montenegro, Greece, and Romania fought for the remaining areas of Ottoman control in the southern Balkans, this region saw massive ethnic cleansing operations and unspeakable atrocities in general.[12]

During World War II, large-scale operations occurred in various parts of then dismembered Yugoslavia. In the so-called Independent State of Croatia, the fascist Ustasha adopted racist policies against Serbs, Roma, and Jews, including expulsion, detention, extermination, and enforced conversion of non-Croat communities. On the Serb side, the nationalist Chetnik movement was striving for the creation of a Greater Serbia that would include territories of Croatia and Bosnia-Hercegovina and Macedonia and believed that desired territories had to be cleansed of non-Serb populations. In both cases the aim of ethnic homogenization was directly linked with the creation of nation states.[13]

Rough estimates assume that up to five million people of different ethnic, national, and religious origin were displaced during and after the wars of succession in the 1990s throughout the territory of the former Yugoslavia. Between 1992 and 1995, over half the 4.4 million inhabitants of Bosnia-Hercegovina were internally displaced or became refugees in neighboring countries. Against this background, events in the 1990s appear as a "third wave" of massive ethnic cleansing during state formation.[14]

In either case, such a policy was of a long-term nature because it aimed at creating conditions that would make it impossible for the expelled to return to their places of origin and its ultimate goal was to achieve ethnic homogeneity and exclusivity. The purpose of such a policy of ethnic homogenization may, nevertheless, have varied in different contexts:

- In a collapsing state ethnic cleansing often appears as the side effect of military conflagration over succession in an ethnically mixed setting. As long as the ethnically distinct population is identified with the enemy, or at least as a potential source of resistance, it appears logical to remove such population from strategic areas in order to establish effective control over that territory. The more homogeneous a region, the more easily power can be exerted. In this sense, ethnic cleansing appeared, in Clausewitz's terms, as a rational means to a specific end.

- Ethnic cleansing may occur as a more general policy when ethnic communities are identified with territories and the main aim is to establish a coincidence between borders and nations. In areas with mixed populations, the irreversible change of the demographic composition is instrumental in justifying territorial aspirations. It may also help to assure a certain bargaining position in ensuing political negotiations aiming at ethnic partition.

- Under certain circumstances, the aim might have been the physical extermination of an ethnic or religious group, including the elimination of all cultural traces of their presence. In this case, ethnic cleansing may be interpreted as genocide (further elaboration below).[15]

Definitions

Various definitions of ethnic cleansing have been put forward. According to a narrower definition by Bell-Fialkoff, "population cleansing is a planned, deliberate removal from a certain territory of an undesirable population distinguished by one or more characteristics such as ethnicity, religion, race, class, or sexual preference. These characteristics must serve as the basis for removal for it to qualify as cleansing."[16] Jacques Semelin on the other hand argues that ethnic cleansing is not necessarily a result of intent but may well appear as a by-product of violent conflagrations.[17]

Dražen Petrović gives a broader definition of ethnic cleansing, namely a "well-defined policy of a particular group of persons to systematically eliminate another group from a given territory on the basis of religious, ethnic or national origin. Such a policy involves violence and is very often connected with military operations. It is to be achieved by all possible means, from discrimination to extermination, and entails violations of human rights and international humanitarian law."[18]

Because ethnic cleansing usually involves physical abuse and mass killing, actual understanding tends to merge the meaning of the terms *ethnic cleansing* and *genocide*. The broadest approach in this regard has been presented by Michael Mann, who interprets genocide as a subcategory within the broader concept of ethnic cleansing. He puts particular emphasis on "the extent to which a group is eliminated (cleansed) from a community and the extent to which violence is used to achieve it." Consequently, he distinguishes between partial and total types of cleansing, encompassing forms of suppression, pogroms, politicide, and genocide.[19]

Most definitions by scholars insist, however, on an analytical distinction between the two terms, arguing against a tendency to confound and obfuscate them.[20] For instance, Norman Naimark maintains that "ethnic cleansing and genocide are two different activities, and the differences between them are important. As in the case of determining first-degree murder, intentionality is the critical distinction."[21] He underlines that ethnic cleansing forms a wider continuum, ranging from pressure to emigrate to population transfer and mass expulsion and eventually to genocide. By the same token, Jacques Semelin argues that

> Genocide comes within the same destructivity continuum as ethnic cleansing but is essentially distinguishable from it. Their respective dynamics are indeed both aimed at eradication. However, in the case of ethnic cleansing, the departure or flight of the targeted population is still possible, while in that of genocide, all ways out are barred. I would therefore define genocide as this specific civilian destruction process that is directed at the total eradication of a community.[22]

Várdy and Tooley suggest starting with a definition of genocide as "the planned, directed, and systematic extermination of a national or ethnic group," while insisting that ethnic cleansing is more focused on the process of removing people from a given territory."[23]

It goes without saying that the definition of ethnic cleansing will certainly undergo further examining and refining as scholars analyze this phenomenon in light of new evidence and continuing debate. At this stage, however, most scholarly definitions agree on (1) the *systematic character* of such a practice, (2) the identification of *specific target groups* by ethnic, national, or religious characteristics, (3) the *deliberate use of violence*, and (4) the implicit assumption of the intent of the *authorities either to support such a practice or to refrain from prevention.*

II. The Policy of Ethnic Cleansing in Croatia and Bosnia-Hercegovina

Ethnic cleansing and other violations of international humanitarian law happened within the wider context of political and military developments and structures during the Yugoslav wars of succession and, in particular, against a background of diverging interests and goals of the constituent people of the countries concerned with regard to the political future of their state.

The Disintegration of the SFRY and the War in Croatia, 1991–1992

For political, constitutional, and socioeconomic reasons, the SFRY started to dissolve in the late 1980s.[24] By the middle of 1990, Slovenia and Croatia were prepared to declare their independence. Serbia and Montenegro, together with many Serbs living in Croatia and Bosnia-Hercegovina, claimed that they wished to preserve Yugoslavia. In the spring of 1991, limited violent clashes between Croatian Serbs and Croatian police forces occurred in places like Plitvice and Borovo Selo. It was, however, not before Slovenia's and Croatia's declarations of independence on 25 June 1991 that larger armed conflicts erupted between armed forces of the breakaway republics, on the one hand, and the federal army, the Yugoslav Peoples Army (JNA), and Serb armed forces on the other hand (see chapter 7, "The War in Croatia").

The first mass killing of Croatian civilians and soldiers by local Serb units happened in Kozibrod on 26 July 1991. Atrocities were also committed in villages in Slavonia, Banija, and Dalmatia and in the town of Vukovar (on 19 November 1991). Mass crimes committed by Croats were reported to have occurred in Karlovac, Gospić, and western Slavonia.[25] On 14 September 1991, the Croatian leadership decided to blockade JNA bases, after which a general offensive against Croatia was launched, starting in western Slavonia. The JNA and local Serb forces expelled non-Serbs from the areas over which they took control. On 19 December 1991, the local Serb authorities declared independence from Croatia and proclaimed the para-state of Republika Srpska Krajina (RSK) with its own military force.

A UN-brokered truce in January 1992 brought a measure of normalcy. By February, an international United Nations Protection Force (UNPROFOR) was deploying in those areas in Croatia where Serbs constituted the majority or a substantial minority of the population, with the aim of preparing for a political solution to this conflict. The number of internally displaced people (IDPs) and refugees in Croatia, which had reached 550,000 by the end of 1991, dropped to 260,000 during the following year as many refugees returned to their homes. Nonetheless, as late as 1993–1994, the prewar ethnic Croat population had fallen from 50 percent to 4 percent in eastern Slavonia, from 20–30 percent to 2 percent in the Banija and Kordun, and from 20–25 percent to 5 percent in the Lika region; overall, the number of Croats living within the RSK had fallen from 353,595 to 18,200.[26] Serbs were also subject to discrimination in other parts of Croatia, particularly in towns and areas close to the front line. Some tens of thousands fled the country.[27] By mid-October 1991, 78,555 refugees from Croatia had arrived in Serbia.[28]

The Early Phase of the War in Bosnia-Hercegovina, 1992–1993

In light of these events, the general situation of neighboring Bosnia-Hercegovina began to deteriorate. According to the 1991 census, Bosnia-Hercegovina's population of 4,355,000 was composed of 43.7 percent Muslims, 31.2 percent Serbs, 17.3 percent Croats, and 5.5 percent Yugoslavs. Many parts of the republic were ethnically mixed, especially in urban areas. In the first multiparty elections of November 1990 in Bosnia-Hercegovina, the three major national parties (the Muslim dominated Party of Democratic Action, SDA; the Serb dominated Serbian Democratic Party, SDS; and the Croat dominated Croatian Democratic Union, HDZ) had won the majority of the seats in the bicameral National Assembly. The election results more or less reflected the ethnic composition of Bosnia's population. The three parties agreed to form a coalition government and to share power, but they became deadlocked over the future constitutional structure of Bosnia-Hercegovina and its political status.

The Serb and Croat leaderships, having in mind the unification of their nationals with their mother countries, supported plans for the "cantonization" of the republic of Bosnia-Hercegovina into three or more ethnically defined regions, each of which would be dominated by either the Bosniaks, Serbs, or Croats. The Bosniak leadership, on the other hand, sought to preserve Bosnia-Hercegovina as a unified, multiethnic, and unitary state. The Bosniak population was scattered across nearly the whole of Bosnia, with a large proportion concentrated in towns. The Serbs and Croats were more compactly settled in certain areas of Bosnia. It would have been difficult for Bosniaks to have carved out an ethnically defined federal state, which was being proposed by the Serb and Croat leaderships.

The dissolution of Yugoslavia forced Bosnia to confront the question of independence. The SDS spoke for most Serbs in wanting Bosnia-Hercegovina to remain in Yugoslavia because that would keep all of Bosnia's Serbs—and those Croatian Serbs living in the wholly contiguous RSK—together in a common state. By the summer of 1991, the SDA and HDZ began to favor independence, although many Croats envisioned this as an interim step toward eventual union with Croatia. The Bosnian Serb leadership had taken steps toward forming regional autonomous areas with quasi-state powers, which they declared in September 1991 as Serbian autonomous areas. The crisis came to a head on 14 October 1991, when the Croat and Bosniak members of the parliament declared Bosnia's sovereignty and independence, whereas the Serb representatives voiced their opposition to independence.

On 24 October 1991 the SDS deputies, who had left the Bosnian parliament, held a constituent meeting of an Assembly of the Serbian People in Bosnia-Hercegovina, and made the "decision for the Serbian People in Bosnia-Hercegovina to remain in the joint state of Yugoslavia." The SDS then held a plebiscite (9–10 November) in which Bosnian Serbs overwhelmingly voted in favor of remaining in Yugoslavia. Eleven days later, the assembly duly proclaimed as part of the territory of the federal Yugoslav state all municipalities, local communities, and populated places in which over 50 percent of the people of Serbian nationality had voted to remain in that state during the plebiscite, as well as those places where citizens of other nationalities had expressed themselves in favor of remaining in Yugoslavia. On 9 January 1992, the assembly proclaimed the Republic of the Serbian People of Bosnia-Hercegovina (SRBH), which formally declared its independence three months later (7 April). By August the name had been changed to Republika Srpska (RS), and it was declared a part of the federal state of Yugoslavia.

Whereas the SDS had been content to coexist with Bosniaks and Croats within a Yugoslav state that united all Serbs, they were now prepared to implement contingency plans for separation by force. And in this they could count on support from Belgrade. A number of key political and military leaders—including Serbia's member of the federal presidency, Borisav Jović, and JNA Admiral Branko Mamula—have acknowledged that plans were already in place in summer 1991 for fashioning new western and northern frontiers that encompassed Croatia's and Bosnia's Serb populations.[29] Indeed, by February 1992, the SDS already enjoyed effective control over roughly 60 percent of Bosnia, emboldening Karadžić to proclaim that it had "developed a reasonable program for full control" over those areas that they intended to keep within Yugoslavia. On 28 March the Bosnian Serb Assembly meeting in Sarajevo's Holiday Inn was presented with an ethnic map of Bosnia that suggested that the Bosnian Serb leadership had a clear vision of the future.[30]

The position of Bosnian Croats was a bit more complex. Whereas many Croats living in scattered communities across central Bosnia accepted the territorial integrity of the Republic of Bosnia-Hercegovina, both their leadership and the homogeneous Croat population concentrations along the Bosnian-Croatian frontier did not. On 12 November 1991 the Croatian Community of the Bosnian

Sava Valley was established in Bosanski Brod. The same day, representatives of the Hercegovinian and the Central Bosnian HDZ concluded a working meeting with the decision to direct their efforts toward the unification of the Croat people and to prepare for military actions. Six days later Croat leaders of various municipalities met in the western Hercegovinian town of Grude, where they founded the Croat Community of Herceg-Bosna (HZ-HB), which was defined as a political, cultural, economic, and regional entity. On 3 July 1992 the Croat state of Herceg-Bosna was officially proclaimed. Thus, while the Bosnian Croat leadership was ostensibly committed to assisting the Bosnian government in defending the republic's territorial integrity, there were many among them who anticipated the republic's partition and union with Croatia if the opportunity arose.

Whereas the SDS had a single objective and the HDZ enjoyed two options, the SDA had no agenda aside from preserving a single Bosnia. Indeed, the subsequent charge by Serb propaganda that the Bosniaks planned to commit genocide against them was refuted by the SDA's failure to prepare for an armed conflict until the eleventh hour.[31]

Against the background of irreconcilable views and complementary contingency plans among political leaders about the future constitutional setup of Bosnia-Hercegovina, tensions increased constantly throughout the winter of 1991–1992. They reached a peak after the 29 February and 1 March 1992 referendum on the republic's independence, which was held at the EU's request. Despite the boycott of the Serb SDS, 66 percent of the Bosnian citizens, mostly Muslims and Croats, voted in the referendum, 99 percent of whom supported an independent and sovereign Bosnia-Hercegovina. The independence of the Republic of Bosnia-Hercegovina was recognized on 6 April 1992 by the European Community, and on the following day it was recognized by the United States and Croatia.

In early March 1992, both SDS and SDA members erected barricades and checkpoints in Sarajevo. Forces loyal to the presidency seized strategic buildings and military equipment, while the SDS gradually took control of much of the city's western and northern suburbs. Following the international recognition of Bosnia-Hercegovina as a sovereign state on 6 April 1992, there was extensive gunfire, and both sides were shelling military and civilian targets within Sarajevo. Snipers deliberately targeted civilians. On 27 May 1992 Bosnian Serb mortar shells killed more than twenty civilians and injured more than one hundred others standing in a Sarajevo breadline (see chapter 6, "Safe Areas").[32] By September 1992, UNPROFOR had confirmed that the Bosnian Serb Army had created "siege conditions" in the Bosnian capital.[33]

Violent outbreaks also occurred in many other parts of Bosnia-Hercegovina in early April 1992 and quickly escalated into a major armed conflict. Serb armed forces undertook massive ethnic cleansing operations in order to consolidate territorial gains. Within a couple of months, hundreds of thousands of people were on the move, and several tens of thousands were killed; a clear majority of the dead and displaced were Bosniaks.[34]

Violent incidents had erupted even earlier in the ethnically mixed town of Bijeljina in northeast Bosnia. On 31 March 1992, local Serbs provoked armed clashes with the Bosnian Muslim Patriotic League and police and by 4 April had taken full control of the town, which was key to the Serb proclaimed Semberija and Majevica Autonomous Region.[35] On 4 April, President Alija Izetbegović issued the order for general mobilization of the Territorial Defense and declared a "state of imminent war danger" on 8 April 1992.

Between April and May 1992, Bosnian Serb forces and JNA attacked Bosnian towns such as Prijedor and other villages in the Kozarac region of northwest Bosnia-Hercegovina and Zvornik in northeast Bosnia-Hercegovina. Countless attacks occurred in towns and villages along the Drina and Sava Rivers, after which Serbian forces took control over a number of strategically important locations along the two corridors in northern and eastern Bosnia, such as Bosanski Brod (27 March), Bijeljina (4 April), Kupres (4 April), Foča (8 April), Zvornik (8 April), Višegrad (13 April), Brčko (30 April), and Prijedor (30 April). Areas that were captured and subsequently cleansed constitute an arc extending from Goražde in the southeast and along the Drina River through Zvornik, Banja Luka, and Prijedor before continuing along the Sava and Korenica Rivers, which form the boundaries with the Serb Krajina area in Croatia.

Some of the largest battles of the Bosnian war occurred during 1992 in the Posavina Corridor, which was of high strategic importance because it linked the western with the eastern part of the nascent Serb Republic and, at the same with the Serb para-state in Croatia, and rump Yugoslavia. The Bosnian Serb Army carried out ethnic cleansing operations in order to break military resistance by the Bosniak population and secure what they called the vital "corridor of life."

CIA analysts conclude that the scope, scale, and programming of crimes committed against Bosniaks and Croats in the Prijedor–Sanski Most–Ključ areas during May–July 1992 "would have been impossible had they not been conducted as military operations by units of the Bosnian Serb Army's 1st Krajina Corps."[36] From July to November 1992, the Army of the Serb Republic (VRS) assaulted Jajce and the Bihać pocket—the latter being able to resist Serb forces. Brutal fighting and atrocities occurred in the Drina Valley between April and December 1992, around Zvornik–Srebrenica and Foča–Goražde–Višegrad, where Bosnian Serb forces met stalwart Bosniak resistance.

A UN commission of experts discerned a specific pattern of military conquest and ethnic cleansing in Bosnia-Hercegovina. Bosnian Serbs took control over key municipalities that retained Bosniak or Croat-controlled units. Bosniaks and Croats were ordered to turn in their weapons, claiming that this was necessary to eliminate the threat from opposing forces.[37] Towns and surrounding villages were encircled and shelled, including Kozarac, Sanski Most, and Ključ in May 1992. VRS troops rounded up the entire population, separated the males of military age and interned them in camps—primarily Omarska, Keraterm, and Manjača. Women and children were expelled to Bosniak-held enclaves.[38] Non-Serb residents were often fired from their jobs, and their property was confiscated.[39]

In Resolution 771 (13 August 1992), the UN Security Council expressed grave alarm at continuing reports of widespread violations of international humanitarian law occurring in Bosnia-Hercegovina. The resolution referred to reports of forcible mass expulsion and deportation of civilians, imprisonment and abuse of civilians in detention centers, deliberate attacks on noncombatants, and wanton devastation and destruction of property. On 9 February 1993, the UN secretary-general submitted an interim report of the Commission of Experts (S/25274) that documented willful killing, practices of ethnic cleansing, mass killings, torture, rape, pillage and destruction of civilian property, destruction of cultural and religious property, and arbitrary arrests. All kinds of atrocities, including killings, sexual assaults, and rapes, were committed in order to implement the policy of ethnic cleansing.

Approximately 70 percent of the expulsions already had occurred between April and August 1992, during which time Serb armed forces attacked 37 municipalities, most notably Zvornik, Bratunac, Vlasenica, Višegrad, Prijedor, Sanski Most, Ključ, and municipalities along the Sava River Valley. In total, approximately 850 Bosniak- and Croat-occupied villages were physically destroyed and no longer exist, with entire families disappearing.[40] Roma and Romani communities were also affected throughout the years 1992–1995, particularly in Prijedor and the surrounding villages of Kozarac, Hambarine, Tukovi, and Rizvanovići. Particular atrocities happened in Vlasenica, Rogatica, and Zvornik and surrounding villages. Up to 30,000 Roma were expelled.[41]

In only a few months, many areas totally changed their ethnic structure. For example, in the eastern Bosnian municipality of Foča, Bosniaks and Croats comprised 51 percent of the population in 1991, whereas at the end of 1992, most of the non-Serb population had already been expelled. By 1997, the Bosniak and Croat population numbered only 434 persons, or 3.8 percent of the total population of the municipality. The situation was similar in other municipalities, such as Zvornik, where there were 31,000 Bosniaks and Croats in 1991 and fewer than 1,000 in 1997. In Bratunac the non-Serb community of 16,000 persons in 1991 was reduced to only hundreds by 1997.[42] Similar ethnic cleansing campaigns happened in Ključ, Prijedor, and Sanski Most. As a result, in thirty-seven municipalities the share of non-Serbs fell from 726,960 (53.97 percent) in 1991 to 235,015 (36.39 percent) in 1997, whereas the number of non-Serbs in the territory of the "federation" in Bosnia-Hercegovina, had increased by 41.18 percent. Altogether, the number of non-Serbs in the areas that now form the Republika Srpska had fallen by 81.74 percent.[43]

The "Second War" between Bosniaks and Croats, 1993–1994: New Violations against Serbs

In the early stages of the war, during most of 1992, Bosniaks and Croats fought together against the Bosnian Serbs. Their armed forces concluded a formal alliance and established joint command structures.

Nevertheless, as early as May 1992, the first confrontations among these allies occurred over control of barracks and munitions production facilities in joint Bosniak-Croat held territory.[44] From July onward, separate BH government and Croat military and civilian structures were established in many regions of Croat-Bosniak cohabitation. Following the creation of the Herceg-Bosna para-state, on 8 April 1992, the Croatian Defense Council (HVO) was formed as the supreme defense body. From their inception the Herceg-Bosna leadership and the HVO had very close relations with the Croatian government and the Croatian Army (HV).

Relations between the Bosnia-Hercegovina government and the HVO deteriorated in the autumn of 1992. In late October 1992, Croat-Bosniak violence escalated and developed into outright fighting (in Novi Travnik on 19 October and Vitez the following day), but conflagrations still could be contained. By January 1993 this was no longer possible because the Bosniak and Croatian leadership began fighting each other. In April 1993, Bosnian Croats launched an offensive in the Lašva Valley in Central Bosnia. Throughout 1993 and early 1994, fighting in central and southern BH intensified. In an attempt to secure control of the Lašva Valley, the HVO attempted to eject the non-Croat population. On 16 April 1993, the HVO systematically destroyed the village of Ahmići. Investigations by the UN and others indicate that the attack was preplanned. It resulted in a "deliberate massacre of unarmed, unwarned civilians: the Bosnian Croats systematically set out to find and execute the entire population."[45]

Serious violations of international humanitarian law were also committed against Bosnian Muslims in the cities, towns, villages, and hamlets of the municipalities of Vitez, Busovača, Kiseljak, Vareš, Žepče, Zenica, Duvno, Stolac, Mostar, Jablanica, Prozor, Čaplijna, Gornji Vakuf, Novi Travnik, Travnik, Kreševo, and Fojnica, all in the territory of the Republic of Bosnia-Hercegovina. According to the ICTY,

> The HVO intimidated, coerced or forcibly transferred Bosnian Muslim civilians in different ways: terrorizing them or ordering them under threat of

physical harm to leave their villages to the territory not occupied or controlled by the HVO; detaining and transferring them to detention sites and thereafter taking them to HVO checkpoints to then walk to Bosnian Muslim territory; and detaining them at HVO detention centres and using them in prisoner exchanges. [46]

The persecution of Bosniak civilians, as alleged above, was on such a large-scale and widespread basis that it significantly reduced the Bosniak civilian population from those areas of the municipalities of Vitez, Busovača, and Kiseljak where the HVO seized control.[47] Conversely, Bosnian armed forces committed massacres against Croats at Uzdol and Stupni Do.[48] It has even been argued that the Bosnian side committed crimes against the Croats on a much larger scale and that Croats acted only out of self-defense.[49]

Serbs also faced new persecutions. According to the ICTY, the region of Srebrenica was the scene of humanitarian law violations against Serbs. In 1993, local Bosniak armed forces captured the village of Kravica and surrounding areas, committing massacres, looting, and destroying houses. The prosecutor charged that Bosniak armed units engaged in various military operations against Bosnian Serb forces during the period from May 1992 to February 1993, in the course of which "Bosniak armed units in the Municipalities of Bratunac, Srebrenica and Skelani, burnt and otherwise destroyed a minimum of fifty predominantly Serb villages and hamlets. As a result, thousands of Serb individuals fled the area."[50] Commander Naser Orić was found guilty because he failed to take necessary measures to prevent murder and cruel treatment in a number of instances.[51] Last but not least, there is evidence that Serbs were also victimized on a larger scale in the territories held by Bosniak and Croat forces.[52] According to the Office of the United Nations High Commissioner for Refugees (UNHCR) estimates, the Serb population fell between 1991 and mid-1994 from 43,595 to 5,000 in Western Hercegovina; from 79,355 to 20,000 in the Zenica region; from 82,235 to 23,000 in the Tuzla area; and from 29,398 to 1,609 in the Bihać region.[53]

Srebrenica, 1995

As ethnic cleansing produced waves of refugees and humanitarian plight, the UN Security Council declared Srebrenica, Sarajevo, Tuzla, Žepa, Goražde, and Bihać to be safe areas and deployed a "light option" of 7,500 UN peacekeepers. In July 1995, the Bosnian Serb army overran the Srebrenica and Žepa safe areas, forcing over 30,000 people to flee and massacring an additional 6,500–8,800 male Srebrenica detainees in a couple of days. These mass killings represent the worst atrocity to have taken place on European soil since World War II. Witness testimony has revealed that Serb troops detained Bosniak men who had fled to the UNPROFOR compound at Potočari, while capturing others hiding in the woods, often telling them they would be treated in accordance with the Geneva conventions. Instead, thousands of prisoners were gathered together in detention sites across the area, many of them in the small town of Bratunac. There is abundant evidence that most of the mass executions followed a well-established pattern: "the men were first taken to empty schools or warehouses. After being detained there for some hours, they were loaded onto buses or trucks and taken to another site for execution."[54] Mass killings following the military conquest of the then UN-protected safe area of Srebrenica count as the first legally recognized genocide in Europe since World War II (see chapter 6, "Safe Areas").

Operations Flash and Storm in Croatia, 1995

One of the largest ethnic cleansing operations happened on the territory of Croatia. Zagreb launched two major military operations to destroy the Serb para-state: Operation Flash in western Slavonia in May 1995 and Operation Storm in August 1995. Between 4 August 1995 and 15 November 1995, a large part of the Serb population in Croatia either fled or was expelled (see chapter 7, "The War in Croatia").

According to the ICTY's office of the prosecutor (OTP), the higher Croatian authorities

> planned, instigated, ordered, committed or otherwise aided and abetted in the planning, preparation, or execution of persecutions of the Krajina Serb population in the southern portion of the Krajina region. Croatian forces directed violent and intimidating acts against Krajina Serbs, including the plunder and destruction of their property, thereby forcing them to flee the southern portion of the Krajina region. These acts were intended to discourage or prevent those who had already fled the area, either immediately before or during Operation Storm in anticipation of an armed conflict, from returning to their homes. The effect of these violent and intimidating acts was the deportation and/or displacement of tens of thousands of Krajina Serbs to Bosnia and Hercegovina and Serbia.[55]

According to witness statements and Serbian refugee organizations, expulsion also took place in those areas where no military operations occurred—a clear indication that ethnic cleansing was not a mere by-product of the war. Displaced persons and refugees from Croatia report the same discriminatory practices that were known in Bosnia-Hercegovina (and directed against the non-Serb population there), including threats, restriction of the freedom of movement, isolation at the workplace and layoffs, detention, liquidation, and other terrorizing measures.[56] The exact number of Serbs who fled their homes has yet to be settled. The figure ranges from 150,000 to 300,000, depending on the source. The Hague Tribunal's indictment of Ante Gotovina cites 150,000–200,000 refugees. According to the Croatian Helsinki Committee for Human Rights, more than 400 Serb civilians were killed and over 22,000 homes burned during and after Operation Storm. Serbian sources speak about 405,000 Serb refugees from Croatia.[57]

III. Features of Ethnic Cleansing as a Policy

Crime of the State and Other Authorities

There is abundant evidence that ethnic cleansing appeared as a campaign, pattern, or systematic policy, which is based on the very idea of ethnic purification as an organizing principle of state and society. In the words of the UN commission of experts, "the patterns of conduct, the manner in which these acts were carried out, the length of time over which they took place and the areas in which they occurred combine to reveal a purpose, systematicity and some planning and co-ordination from higher authorities."[58] The special rapporteur of the UN, Tadeusz Mazowiecki, has made it clear "that the principal objective of the military conflict in Bosnia-Hercegovina is the establishment of ethnically homogeneous regions. Ethnic cleansing does not appear to be a consequence of the war but rather its goal."[59]

The question of whether there existed a long-term plan to cleanse territories of unwanted population is a matter of controversy that relates directly to the countless debates about the causes of Yugoslavia's disintegration, the very nature of the wars of succession, and the question of Serbian and Croatian war aims in Bosnia-Hercegovina.

Many authors believe that Serbian war aims embraced the creation of a greater Serbian state, which implied the expulsion of non-Serbs from territories taken under control.[60] James Gow maintains that the commission of war crimes was even an essential part of the Serbian expansionist project.[61] Others have emphasized an alleged conspiracy between Tudjman and Milošević to carve up Bosnia,[62] which in Smail Čekić's interpretation included a joint genocidal intent.[63]

The ICTY office of the prosecutor maintains that early measures to prepare ethnic cleansing operations by Serb armed forces in Bosnia-Hercegovina can be traced back as early as the second half of 1991. The sentencing judgment against Republika Srpska's wartime presidency comember Biljana Plavšić states that already in October 1991 and in the following months the leading Serb party, SDS, "intensified efforts to ensure that the objective of ethnic separation by force would be achieved if a negotiated solution did not occur. These efforts included the arming of parts of the Bosnian Serb population in collaboration with the Yugoslav National Army (JNA), the Ministry of Internal Affairs (MUP) of Serbia and Serbian paramilitaries."[64]

As early as November 1991, Radovan Karadžić asserted in a much quoted public speech: "Let us separate as many things as possible. Like in the days of the Turks. One Serbian town center, one Turkish town center, Serbian affairs, Turkish affairs, Serbian cafes, theaters, schools and everything else. This is the only solution."[65] Also, the constitution of the Republika Srpska made it clear that it should be a state exclusively for Serbs. On 21 November 1991, the assembly proclaimed as part of the territory of the federal Yugoslav state all municipalities, local communities, and populated places in which over 50 percent of the Serbian population had voted to remain in that state during the plebiscite. This means that numerous municipalities with a mixed population were included in the territory of this para-state. Yet, Article I.1 of the constitution declared that the Republika Srpska was "the state of the Serb people," without mentioning citizens of other nationalities. This article suggests the conclusion that the strategic aim of the Republika Srpska was to create a purely Serbian state and that the crimes committed during the armed takeover and cleansing of ethnically mixed areas were directly connected with this goal.

Frequently, crimes in connection with ethnic cleansing were carried out by paramilitary forces. These irregular troops were supported, equipped, and supplied by the governments they served, and they usually acted in agreement with local authorities or higher military commanders. In 1994, the UN Commission of Experts identified more than eighty different paramilitary groups. Many of them joined in the armed conflict, operating with the regular armies and under regular army officers' command. Others operated independently in certain geographic areas from which the personnel in these units came. Hence the commission's judgment that "the outcome of such a structure and the strategies and tactics employed help to blur the chain of command and conceal responsibility. This concealment may well be intended by some of the parties to provide a shield of plausible deniability."[66]

There is evidence that the Yugoslav army supported the VRS after its official withdrawal from Bosnia-Hercegovina in May 1992 by arming, supplying, and reinforcing it periodically and by paying the salaries of some of its officers. The degree of influence that this gave the FRY over the Bosnian Serbs is harder to assess. The International Court of Justice (ICJ) established that "the FRY was in a position of influence over the Bosnian Serbs who devised and implemented the genocide in Srebrenica, unlike that of any of the other States [and that] links, . . . though somewhat weaker than in the preceding period, remained very close."[67] The charges focus on the JNA's command responsibility "in the planning, preparation, facilitation and execution of the forcible removal of the majority of non-Serbs," support to the political leadership and armed forces of the Bosnian Serbs, participation in planning and execution of ethnic cleansing operations, and support for irregular forces and manipulation of the media.

The same charge of command responsibility has been leveled against Belgrade's political leadership. Former president of Serbia and of the Federal Republic of Yugoslavia Slobodan Milošević was charged with genocide, crimes against humanity, grave breaches of the Geneva conventions, and violations of the laws or customs of war.[68] Together with officials of the Bosnian Serb leadership, he was accused of having participated in a "joint criminal enterprise," the purpose of which was "the forcible and permanent removal of the majority of non-Serbs, principally Bosnian Muslims and Bosnian Croats, from large areas of the Republic of Bosnia-Hercegovina."[69] Charges of genocide and complicity to commit genocide include the mass killings in Srebrenica and the murder or mistreatment of Bosnian Muslims in detention facilities. The ICTY notes, "The detention of thousands of Bosnian Muslims in detention facilities within Bosnia-Hercegovina, including those situated within the territories listed above, under conditions of life calculated to bring about the partial physical destruction of those groups, namely through starvation, contaminated water, forced labor, inadequate medical care and constant physical and psychological assault".[70] Milošević's death brought a sudden end to his trial and left open the question of whether he was guilty of the charge of genocide.

The OTP has also charged that the Croatian leadership intended to forcibly remove the Krajina Serbs from their home territory. The indictments avoid the term *ethnic cleansing*, although the charges fall fully within the parameters of the definition of the practice. Prominent General Ante Gotovina is accused together with others—including President Franjo Tudjman—of having

> participated in a joint criminal enterprise, the common purpose of which was the forcible and permanent removal of the Serb population from the Krajina region, including by the plunder, damage or outright destruction of the property of the Serb population, so as to discourage or prevent members of that population from returning to their homes and resuming habitation.[71]

Whether and to what extent ethnic cleansing was planned, supported, and executed with the help of authorities in Belgrade and Zagreb will need much more research in primary sources, including those compiled by the ICTY and other institutions.

Deliberate Use of Violence

The ultimate goal of ethnic cleansing operations was to remove the target population from a given territory. All kinds of violent means were used as instruments to achieve this goal by instilling fear among the victims. Methods used included administrative measures (such as dismissal from work, discrimination, refusal of hospital treatment) and intimidation, as well as repression and terrorizing acts, such as beatings, torture, shooting, or using explosives against homes, summary executions, and similar acts.[72]

Following the outbreak of military confrontation in March–April 1992, the campaign of "persecution" deliberately used the following methods:

- Killings during attacks on towns and villages

- Cruel and inhumane treatment during and after the attacks

- Forced transfer and deportation

- Unlawful detention and killing, forced labor, and use of human shields

- Cruel and inhumane treatment and inhumane conditions in detention facilities

- Destruction of cultural and sacred objects

- Plunder and wanton destruction

The authors of a research project among Bosnian refugees concluded that the extent and the features of violence used in the context of ethnic cleansing operations were highly dependent on the specific conditions prevailing in the area, such as ethnic composition, the distance to the line of confrontation, and the political affiliations of the regional elite. The general characteristics were as follows:

- Extreme violence was used by the perpetrators if the percentage of the ethnic group to be evicted from a certain area was high.

- Ethnic cleansing was particularly brutally designed if the (defending) political and military authority in the area concerned was poorly organized.

- The outcome of ethnic cleansing depended on the level of political organization and military supply of the attacking forces.

Measures usually went far beyond the degree of violence (physical and non-physical) necessary to establish control over the public order, and they potentially involved two distinct targets: those who were physically exposed to deliberate coercion and violence, and those who observed the violence and whose fear the perpetrator wanted to increase. Because the latter group identified with the victims, they perceived themselves as potential future victims and thus despaired or complied.

The forced expulsions were consistently implemented by lightning attacks and shelling followed by mechanized units entering the villages. Frequently, the women were separated from the men and taken to detention facilities or were expelled to other areas. Also, there was systematic burning of homes in rural areas, which had particularly devastating psychological effects on people. Building a new house was a life project for which families worked for years. A house often symbolized the social worth of a family; it was the proof of hard work and commitment to its future well-being.[73] Burning of houses was a particularly effective tool to prevent the unwanted population from returning to its place of origin.

Mirsad Tokača's research has determined that in 1992 alone at least 50,000 persons were killed in Bosnia-Hercegovina, and the overwhelming majority of them were Bosniak civilians. Eighty percent of the killings occurred in May, June, July, and August 1992, thereby illustrating a direct correlation between ethnic cleansing and killings. Major mass killings happened, for instance, in Foča, Sanski Most, Prijedor, and Bratunac and other places. In fact, there have been 1,100 recorded cases of mass killings and 320 potential sites where the bodies of individuals can be found.[74]

There were about four hundred detention facilities in thirty-four municipalities. These facilities included prisons, police stations, schools, barracks, factories, and community centers, where people were detained by force and exposed to serious physical and mental abuse. Living conditions in these facilities were "disastrous . . . inhuman and really brutal"; the concept of sanitation did not exist. The temperature inside was low; the inmates slept on the concrete floor; and they relieved themselves in the compound or in a bucket placed by the door at night. There was not enough water, and any water that became available was contaminated."[75] There were killings in thirty-eight detention facilities in twenty-one municipalities. Most victims were killed while in detention; others were killed while performing forced labor or while being used as human shields during combat operations. Over 1,600 detainees are listed as having been killed in nineteen detention facilities, and the number killed in the remainder of the facilities is not specified. The killings occurred between May and December 1992.

Grave violations of international humanitarian law also happened during the Croatian attack on the Krajina in 1995. Charges include the following: persecution of Serbs in the municipalities of Benkovac, Donji Lapac, Drniš, Gospić, Gračac, Knin, Korenica, Obrovac, Šibenik, Sinj, and Zadar; systematic plunder of public or private property by Croatian forces, including homes, outbuildings, barns, and livestock; deportation; murder of at least 150 Krajina Serbs; and other inhumane acts, including humiliation and degradation by Croatian forces. Furthermore, Croatian forces have been charged because they systematically set fire to or otherwise destroyed villages, homes, outbuildings, and barns belonging to

Krajina Serbs and because they killed their livestock and spoiled their wells. Thousands of dwellings were destroyed.[76]

Destruction of Identity

As stated above, ethnic cleansing is directed against a population that can be identified by ethnic, national, or religious characteristics. The wider aim of such a policy, besides the physical removal from a territory, is to offend the collective identity of the targeted population, including its language, history, culture, and family relations. Towns, sacred sites, and city centers were continuously shelled and razed to the ground in order to cut off local communication lines, thus making impossible the normal functioning of social life among the target community.

Cultural vandalism reveals the inherent aim of ethnic cleansing to destroy buildings and monuments as the most prominent symbols of the political power, historical identity, and national consciousness of the unwanted group. The systematic destruction of religious and cultural symbols suggests that the intention is to eliminate any vestige of the opponent's presence in the respective areas. Throughout Bosnia-Hercegovina, as well as in parts of Croatia (and, later, Kosovo), sacred sites and other symbols of cultural heritage were systematically damaged, for the most part, in the absence of military activity. Aside from mosques and churches, other religious and cultural objects such as cemeteries and monasteries were targeted.[77]

The destruction of cultural heritage was most comprehensive in areas under Serb control. In Croatia, the religious monuments, parochial archives, and other cultural objects of the non-Serb communities (Croat Roman Catholic churches, but also Protestant congregations of Slavonia's Hungarian minority) suffered systematic and widespread destruction. Virtually no Catholic churches were left intact within the confines of the Republika Srpska Krajina.[78] In Bosnia-Hercegovina virtually every Muslim house of worship (some 1,000 mosques, as well as dervish lodges, saints' shrines, and other sacred sites), as well as 75 percent of all Catholic churches were destroyed or severely damaged in areas that came under Serb control. Those located in town centers were not only burned or blown up, but the buildings were razed and the rubble carted away to remove all traces.[79] In addition, even the names of towns were changed to minimize the earlier presence of non-Serb populations.

Serbian Orthodox heritage also suffered, primarily at the hands of Croatian forces. Within Croatia, Croat forces perpetrated attacks against Orthodox churches and other sacred sites both in the early phases of the war and during the final offensives in 1995. But whereas many Orthodox churches and sacred sites were damaged, the majority of Serbian Orthodox churches in Croatia survived the war intact.[80] In Hercegovina, following the April–June 1992 JNA siege of Mostar, Croat extremists blew up the Serbian Orthodox cathedral and the Serbian Orthodox monastery at Žitomislić just south of the city. There were also attacks on Orthodox churches in Hercegovina, as well as in the Posavina region in northeastern Bosnia, which was the scene of bitter fighting between Serb and Croat militias. During the "war within a war" between Bosnian-Croat forces and the mainly Muslim Bosnian army, Croat forces destroyed some 80 mosques and damaged about 120 more. Muslim militias and civilians in turn destroyed 8 Catholic churches and damaged about 70 more. For the most part, however, both Roman Catholic and Serbian Orthodox churches in towns that remained or came under the control of the Sarajevo government survived intact.[81]

Humiliation and Sexual Abuse

Crimes conducted in the framework of ethnic cleansing were often accompanied and reinforced by the massive humiliation of the victims, aiming at intimidating the opponent's population and forcing it to give up its resistance. Generally, aggression combined with humiliation is successful in creating a state of instability and confusion among the targeted population and their leaders, for they show that they, obviously, are not capable of protecting their own ethnic community. This behavior is "rational" in the sense that it intends to provoke fear and instability in order to break resistance or to deter the opposing side from taking combat action.

A particularly efficient method is sexual abuse, most notably rape.[82] It was committed systematically against women of all ages, frequently in front of the victims' relatives or in women's camps.[83] Such assaults are especially effective in intimidating and demoralizing the opposing side, including men who play the role of warriors, defenders, husbands, and fathers. Indeed, sexual abuse is not only an instrument to intimidate and humiliate the victims and their families but also an assault on social values, family structures, and ethnic identity. In patriarchal societies women are mainly seen as responsible for the biological reproduction and cultural preservation of their ethnic community. Hence, rape not only stigmatizes individuals and families, but it also offends ethnic identities and the entire social system, especially if the role and status of men are associated with their sexuality and the women are seen as the men's possessions. In a conflict situation, rape usually does not have a sexual function but offers satisfaction to the perpetrator through humiliation and degradation of the victim by producing a feeling of power, supremacy, and dominance. The Yugoslav war of dissolution is not the only case in which gender-specific violence was applied on a large scale and systematic raping appeared as a war tool.[84] Rape of women belonging to enemies defeated in war has been a tool in various historical contexts because these women were valued for their reproductive power. Thus the opinion of the OTP that

> like torture, rape is used for such purposes as intimidation, degradation, hu-
> miliation, discrimination, punishment, control or destruction of a person.
> Like torture, rape is a violation of personal dignity, and rape in fact consti-
> tutes torture when inflicted by or at the instigation of or with the consent or
> acquiescence of a public official or other person acting in an official capac-
> ity.[85]

The ICTY has meanwhile defined the status of rape as a crime under cus-
tomary international law.[86]

It is difficult to establish the exact number of systematic rapes committed
during the war. Women usually do not speak about such crimes because they are
ashamed and fear social stigmatization. Figures widely differ, with initial estimates by women's and human rights groups ranging as high as 50,000 victims.
Although this number is no longer regarded as credible, it is still not possible to
identify reliable data regarding rape and sexual assault. According to the International Human Rights Law Institute at DePaul University in Chicago there were
approximately 1,100 reported cases of rape and sexual assault, and there were
162 detention sites where people were sexually assaulted.[87] The Association of
Camp Inmates, on the other hand, claims that between 1992 and 1995 there were
more than 650 camps with more than 200,000 civilians imprisoned and about
30,000 killed or missing. The association has evidence that more than 25,000
women in camps survived torture, sexual abuse, and rape.[88]

IV. Controversies

Discussions of the total number of victims in Bosnia-Hercegovina started during
the war and are still ongoing. Estimates are sometimes not transparent; numbers appear highly inflated; and they frequently bear implications for political
debates.[89] How many people were displaced or died in the war in Bosnia-Hercegovina between 1992 and 1995?

Counting the Victims

According to UNHCR, more than two million people had been uprooted by
the end of the war in 1995. Approximately half of them fled abroad, whereas
the other half was internally displaced. There was a total of 1,097,900 IDPs in
Bosnia-Hercegovina in 1995. However, exact figures on displacement by ethnic
affiliation are not available for the war period. UNHCR in mid-1994 presented
rough population estimates but underlined that these estimates were derived from

various sources and were only indicative. By then, population structures had already changed substantially due to forced migration.[90]

A more precise ethnic breakdown is available for the post-Dayton period: the Norwegian Refugee Council reports a total of 386,110 displaced persons in Bosnia-Hercegovina in mid-2003. The national structure is as follows: Serbs, 207,955; Bosniaks, 147,611; Croats, 29,489; and others, 1,055.[91]

In April 1993, 585,000 refugees from Slovenia, Croatia, and Bosnia-Hercegovina were registered in Serbia and Montenegro. Following the operations of the Croatian Army in the Krajina, an additional 189,000 people fled to Serbia and Montenegro.[92]

Following the transfer of territories between the two entities under the Dayton Accords, over 60,000 people were displaced between 1996 and 1999.[93] In 1997, the number of internally displaced was already significantly lower: 450,000 displaced persons were registered in the federation, and 366,000 in the Republika Srpska.[94]

Estimates range from about 25,000 to 329,000 deaths—many of them were "biased by the historical knowledge, political views, and individual war experience of the authors."[95] Local estimates have mostly relied on data collected by the governmental Institute for Public Health (IPH) in Sarajevo, such as those of I. Bošnjović, V. Žerjavić, and M. Prašo.[96] Sead Hadžović, for instance, mentions 230,000 dead (71 percent Bosniaks, 9.5 percent Serbs, 9.5 percent Croats).[97] A common problem presented by such tabulations is the duplication of names and the difficulty of culling names of survivors who had been initially listed as dead or missing. In recent years, the nongovernmental Research and Documentation Center (IDC) in Sarajevo has undertaken to establish an accurate account that presently constitutes "the largest single source of primary source materials relating to wartime atrocities and violations of international humanitarian law in Bosnia-Hercegovina."[98] After painstakingly examining and comparing the lists of dead and missing, it has challenged the previously accepted estimate of 200,000–250,000 dead, presenting a much lower figure that is unlikely to grow far beyond 100,000.

As of June 2007, team member Mirsad Tokača's Documentation Center has proven a total number of 92,207 killed and missing persons in the three-and-one-half-year war (with a projected final tally at just over 100,000). The ethnic breakdown is as follows: 64,036 Bosniaks, 24,905 Serbs, 7,788 Croats, 478 others or unknown.[99] The government-related Institute for the Research of Crimes against Humanity (Smail Čekić), however, questions Tokača's research methodology. Indeed, even Tokača admits that his positivist methodology will inevitably overlook some victims who left no surviving family members to report their disappearance. Nonetheless, it seems unlikely that such unaccounted victims would

comprise more than a small fraction of the difference between the center's confirmed dead and the earlier 200,000–250,000 figure.

Indeed, a recent study by the Demographic Unit of the ICTY substantially
agrees with Tokača's finding, estimating a total of 102,622 war-related deaths
from Bosnia-Hercegovina from 1992 to 1995. This analysis has used military records of fallen soldiers of the BH government army, Republika Srpska army, and
the Croatian Defense Council. In addition, it has drawn on ICRC lists of missing
persons and the Federal Institute for Statistics Mortality Database and other quan-
titative data.[100] One thing on which both groups of authors agree is that their data
may still be incomplete and should be understood as work in progress.

War Crimes, Crimes against Humanity, Genocide

There has been considerable controversy over whether or not actions that are
committed in the framework of ethnic cleansing constitute war crimes, crimes
against humanity, or genocide. From the outset, there has been a broad public
perception that the atrocities committed by Serbian forces on the territory of the
former Yugoslavia constitute genocide.[101] Both Bosnian government officials and
scholars insist that the Bosniaks were victims of a genocide that was planned and
executed by Serbs.[102] Smail Čekić charges both Serbia and Croatia with genocide,
referring to a "joint criminal undertaking" in Zagreb and Belgrade to establish
"the Greater Serbia and the Greater Croatia states. The goal of this ideology,
politics and practice was a war to conquer territories, a 'habitat,' to take another
people's country (Bosnia-Hercegovina)."[103] He equates "Serb and Croat projects"
and their "goal to conquer, divide and liquidate the Republic of Bosnia-Hercegovina, and exterminate the Bosniaks or reduce their number to a meaningless
ethnic group."[104]

In 1993, the Bosnian government filed a case against the government of
Serbia and Montenegro before the ICJ in The Hague, arguing that Yugoslavia
had "planned, prepared, conspired, promoted, encouraged, aided and abetted and
committed" genocide against its population. Belgrade filed a counter suit accusing Bosnia-Hercegovina of committing genocide against the Bosnian Serb population (that suit was dropped in 2000). Hearings of the case against Serbia began
in February 2006. It explicitly charged the systematic practice of ethnic cleansing of the citizens and sovereign territory of Bosnia-Hercegovina and claimed
that the responsibility lay with an entire state and not simply individuals. On 26
February 2007, the ICJ cleared Serbia of genocide charges, ruling that "Serbia
has not committed genocide through its organs or persons," nor was Serbia "complicit in genocide." But the court found that Belgrade did not use its influence to
prevent genocide and that it failed to punish those who carried out massacres.[105]

Moreover, the ICJ rendered its judgment without examining evidence that the Serbian government had provided the ICTY case against Slobodan Milošević. One individual who did see these documents was ICTY prosecutor Carla del Ponte, who writes that

> The Supreme Defense Council's minutes and other secret personnel files provide compelling evidence of Serbia's control and direction of the Serb war effort in BiH. They detail how Belgrade financed and supplied the Serbs' war effort. They show how the VRS . . . was an appendage of the Yugoslav army. . . . that Serbian forces, including secret police, played a role in the takeover of Srebrenica and in the preparation of the massacre there.[106]

The issue of whether or not Serbian actions in Bosnia-Hercegovina constitute genocide divides the communities of scholars, analysts, and politicians. It has been rightly noted that there is a correlation between methodology and conclusions.[107] Authors who apply definitions of genocide based on political or social scientific considerations tend to equate ethnic cleansing with genocide. For instance, Norman Cigar argues that Serbian political, cultural, and ecclesiastical elites prepared a climate conducive to the execution of genocide during the war and that Serbian forces committed genocide against Bosniaks.[108] Also, Michael A. Sells supports the interpretation that Serbian forces intended to destroy Bosnia's Muslims as a people.[109] By the same token, some Western and Bosnian scholars maintain that the term *ethnic cleansing* was only used as a euphemism in order to conceal the hidden agenda of genocide.[110] Serb officials and scholars have countered by charging the other side with genocide, recently claiming that "perhaps a greater genocide was committed against the Serbs in Sarajevo than against Bosniaks in Srebrenica."[111] Nevertheless, they have yet to provide sufficient data to support their claims, which the ICTY has not supported with a charge of genocide.

A more differentiated assessment appears if a legal definition is applied. In strictly legal terms, several of the instruments of ethnic cleansing employed in former Yugoslavia merit prosecution under the statutory provisions of the ICTY[112]:

> • *Grave breaches of the Geneva Conventions of 1949* (including willful killing; torture or inhuman treatment, including biological experiments; willfully causing great suffering or serious injury to body or health; extensive destruction and appropriation of property, not justified by military necessity and carried out unlawfully and wantonly; compelling a prisoner of war or a civilian to serve in the forces of a hostile power; willfully depriving a prisoner of war or a civilian of the rights of fair and regular trial; unlawful deportation or transfer or unlawful confinement of a civilian; taking civilians as hostages)

- *Violations of the laws or customs of war* (employment of poisonous weapons or other weapons calculated to cause unnecessary suffering; wanton destruction of cities, towns or villages, or devastation not justified by military necessity; attack, or bombardment, by whatever means, of undefended towns, villages, dwellings, or buildings; seizure of, destruction or willful damage done to institutions dedicated to religion, charity and education, the arts and sciences, historic monuments and works of art and science; plunder of public or private property)

- *Genocide* (acts committed with intent to destroy, in whole or in part, a national, ethnical, racial or religious group)

- *Crimes against humanity* (directed against any civilian population—murder; extermination; enslavement; deportation; imprisonment; torture; rape; persecutions on political, racial and religious grounds; other inhumane acts)

Although various definitions of genocide have been put forward, many scholars have implicitly or explicitly accepted the definition proposed by the UN Genocide Convention of 9 December 1948 (Art. 2), which defines genocide as the intentional destruction of a group, in whole or in part[113]:

genocide means any of the following acts committed with intent to destroy, in whole or in part, a national, ethnical, racial or religious group, as such:

(a) Killing members of the group;

(b) Causing serious bodily or mental harm to members of the group;

(c) Deliberately inflicting on the group conditions of life calculated to bring about its physical destruction in whole or in part;

(d) Imposing measures intended to prevent births within the group;

(e) Forcibly transferring children of the group to another group.

To date, the OTP has characterized only a few of the most extreme examples of ethnic cleansing committed by Serb forces in Bosnia-Hercegovina as acts of genocide. Beside the indictment against Slobodan Milošević, those against Republika Srpska President Radovan Karadžić and VRS Commander Ratko Mladić conclude that they should be charged with genocide on the grounds of internment of civilians in detention facilities and inhumane treatment therein. It also claims that those plans of the political and military leadership contained elements that would lead to the destruction of the non-Serb groups. Thus "the project of an ethnically homogenous State formulated against a backdrop of mixed populations necessarily envisages the exclusion of any group not identified with the Serbian one."[114]

Mass killings following the military conquest of the then UN-protected safe area of Srebrenica in July 1995 count as the first legally recognized genocide in Europe since World War II. Although the government of Republika Srpska has acknowledged the crimes committed in Srebrenica in mid-1995 in a report published in 2004, the entity's war veterans association still denies that such crimes ever happened, pointing instead to the victims on the Serb side.[115] Nonetheless, as discussed in chapter 6, "Safe Areas," the ICTY has compiled massive proof of the "vast amount of planning and high-level coordination that had to be invested in killing thousands of men in a few days."[116] The Tribunal has also provided overwhelming evidence of a massive effort by the VRS to exhume as many corpses as possible from mass graves and disperse them in remote areas—measures that would not have been undertaken had the majority of the bodies been combat victims. Also, there is forensic evidence that most of the victims were indeed killed in cold blood. One question that does remain is whether Serb authorities intended from the outset to exterminate Srebrenica's male population or Ratko Mladić made that decision only after learning that ARBiH units had escaped to Tuzla.

A two-hour video tape in which members of the paramilitary unit Scorpions execute young men suggests at the very least Belgrade's involvement in the massacre. The ICTY prosecution claims that the Serbian interior ministry in Belgrade that controlled the Scorpions must have given consent for the latter to operate on Bosnian territory and has indicted JNA army chief Momčilo Perišić for providing assistance to the VRS and not preventing or punishing crimes committed in the Sarajevo and Srebrenica safe areas.[117]

The judgment against former JNA Lieutenant Colonel Radislav Krstić, who commanded the Drina Corps from 13 July 1995 through the end of the war, discusses extensively the question of whether events in Srebrenica fall under the parameters of genocide. It concludes that the intent to kill all the Bosnian Muslim men of military age in Srebrenica constitutes an intent to destroy in part the Bosniak group and, therefore, must be qualified as a genocide. This view was supported by the Appeals Chamber. The killing was engineered and supervised by some members of the main staff of the Serb armed forces—which constitutes the requisite proof of specific intent. In the OTP's view:

> By seeking to eliminate a part of the Bosnian Muslims, the Bosnian Serb forces committed genocide. They targeted for extinction the forty thousand Bosnian Muslims living in Srebrenica, a group which was emblematic of the Bosnian Muslims in general. They stripped all the male Muslim prisoners, military and civilian, elderly and young, of their personal belongings and identification, and deliberately and methodically killed them solely on the

basis of their identity. The Bosnian Serb forces were aware, when they embarked on this genocidal venture, that the harm they caused would continue to plague the Bosnian Muslims. The Appeals Chamber states unequivocally that the law condemns, in appropriate terms, the deep and lasting injury inflicted, and calls the massacre at Srebrenica by its proper name: genocide. Those responsible will bear this stigma, and it will serve as a warning to those who may in future contemplate the commission of such a heinous act.[118]

The judges made clear, however, that "forcible transfer does not constitute in and of itself a genocidal act."[119] Such a decision only encourages scholars to continue to debate the conceptual dimensions of genocide. Helen Fine has suggested a paradigm for the detection of genocide; it includes these conditions:

- There was a sustained attack or continuity of attacks by the perpetrator to physically destroy group members;

- The perpetrator was a collective or organized actor (usually the state) or commander of organized actors;

- The victims were selected because they were members of the collectivity;

- The victims were defenseless or were killed regardless of whether they surrendered or resisted; and

- The destruction of group members undertaken to with intent to kill and murder was sanctioned by the perpetrator.[120]

It has been pointed out, on the other hand, that not every single crime should and could be viewed as genocide, which is characterized by the particular intent to destroy a group "as such." Some continue to argue that genocide, the "ultimate crime," should not be diluted by too broad an interpretation but should be reserved only for acts of exceptional gravity and magnitude.[121] In any event, debates over terminology should not divert us from recognizing and concurring with the overwhelming body of evidence of the crimes themselves.

Conclusion

The phenomenon of ethnic cleansing belongs to the most emotional and controversial issues surrounding the breakup of Yugoslavia. Beside the unspeakable cruelty with which the war was conducted, it was the very idea of ethnic purification as an organizing principle of state and society that came as a shock to the world public. Ethnic cleansing designates a systematic policy of forced population transfer based on the identification of target groups by ethnic, national, and religious characteristics. This policy intended the physical removal of the unwanted population from a territory, including the elimination of all cultural and social traces of their presence. Offending the collective identity of the victims' group, including its language, family relations, and cultural heritage, was aimed at creating conditions that would make it impossible for the expelled to return to their places of origin.

The method of ethnic cleansing comprises a broad variety of techniques, and its purposes have varied in different historical and geographical contexts. It formed a continuum, ranging from pressure to emigrate, to population transfer and mass expulsion, and eventually to genocide. Whereas in some cases ethnic cleansing was aimed at the physical destruction of an ethnic community (for instance, in Srebrenica), in other cases the objective was limited to the conquest of a strategically or economically important region through expulsion of the unwanted population but without a clear intent to exterminate that community in whole or in part. In conclusion, ethnic cleansing should not per se be identified with genocide. Politically charged debates over the term and its definition cannot, however, call into question the extent and horror of the crimes committed and recounted in this chapter.

Notes

1   United Nations Security Council. *Final Report of the United Nations Commission of Experts Established Pursuant to SCR 780 (1992)*, S/1994/674, 27 May 1994; *Annex IV: The Policy of Ethnic Cleansing*, S/1994/674/Add. 2 (Vol. I), 28 December 1994, 5. Available at: http://www.law.depaul.edu/institutes_centers/ihrli/_downloads/_Annex_IV.pdf (accessed 10 October 2008).

2   Norwegian Refugee Council/Global IDP Project, *Profile of Internal Displacement: Bosnia and Herzegovina*. Compilation of the information available in the Global IDP Database of the Norwegian Refugee Council, 13. Available at: http://www.internal-displacement.org/8025708F004BE3B1/(httpInfoFiles)/D59391E740546796802570BA0 0561848/$file/Bosnia%20and%20Herzegovina%20-March%202005.pdf (accessed 10 October 2008).

3   Andrew Bell-Fialkoff, *Ethnic Cleansing* (New York: Palgrave Macmillan, 1996); Norman M. Naimark, *Fires of Hatred: Ethnic Cleansing in Twentieth Century Europe* (Cambridge: Harvard University Press, 2001); Dražen Petrović, "Ethnic Cleansing: An Attempt at Methodology," *European Journal of International Law*, 5, no. 3 (1994), 1–19; Cathie Carmichael, *Ethnic Cleansing in the Balkans: Nationalism and the Destruction of Tradition* (London and New York: Routledge, 2002); Philipp Ther, "A Century of Forced Migration: The Origins and Consequences of 'Ethnic Cleansing,'" in *Redrawing Nations. Ethnic Cleansing in East-Central Europe, 1944–1948*, ed. Philipp Ther and Ana Siljak (Lanham, Boulder, New York, and Oxford: Rowman & Littlefield, 2001), 43–72; Anna Simons, "Making Sense of Ethnic Cleansing," *Studies in Conflict and Terrorism* 22, no. 1 (January–March 1999), 1–20.

4   *Final Report of the UN Commission of Experts, Annex IV*, 5, 21.

5   The RDC is a nongovernmental organization registered on the state level in BiH, formed in April 2004. It is the successor organization to the State Commission for Gathering Facts about War Crimes, which was established by the presidency of BiH in April 1992.

6   See the *Periodic Reports on the Situation of Human Rights in the Territory of the Former Yugoslavia Submitted by Mr Tadeusz Mazowiecki,* special rapporteur of the Commission on Human Rights, to the UN Security Council and the General Assembly. Available at http://www.haverford.edu/relg/sells/reports/mazowiecki.html (accessed 10 October 2008).

7   Dražen Petrović, "Ethnic Cleansing: An Attempt at Methodology," *European Journal of International Law* 5, no. 3 (1994), 1–19.

8   Ibid., 2.

9   Noel Malcolm mentions that the term *čišćenje* was used in 1942 by Stevan Moljević, an advisor to Četnik-leader Draža Mihailović, who advocated a Greater Serbia from which undesirable elements such as Muslims and Albanians would have to be "cleansed." Noel Malcolm, *Kosovo: A Short History* (London: Macmillan, 1998), 298.

10   Andrew Bell-Fialkoff, "A Brief History of Ethnic Cleansing," in *Foreign Affairs* 72, no. 3 (1993), 110–121, and Bell-Fialkoff, *Ethnic Cleansing.*

11   Justin McCarthy, *Death and Exile: The Ethnic Cleansing of Ottoman Muslims, 1821–1922* (Princeton, N.J.: Darwin Press, 1995).

12   Carnegie Endowment for International Peace, *Report of the International Commission to Inquire into the Causes and Conduct of the Balkan Wars* (Washington, DC: The Endowment, 1914, reprint under the title *The Other Balkan Wars* (Washington, DC: Carnegie Endowment for International Peace, 1993; Dimitrije Djordjević, "Migrations during the 1912–1913 Balkan Wars and World War I," in *Migrations in Balkan History,* ed. Ivan Ninić (Belgrade: Serbian Academy of Sciences and Arts, Institute for Balkan Studies, 1989), 115–129.

13   Jozo Tomasevich, *War and Revolution in Yugoslavia, 1941–1945: Occupation and Collaboration* (Stanford: Stanford University Press, 2001).

14   Robert M. Hayden, "Schindler's Fate: Genocide, Ethnic Cleansing, and Population Transfers," in *Slavic Review* 55, no. 4 (1996), 728–748.

15   Norman M. Naimark, *Fires of Hatred: Ethnic Cleansing in Twentieth Century Europe* (Cambridge: Harvard University Press, 2001), 3.

16   Bell-Fialkoff, *Ethnic Cleansing,* 3–4.

17   Jacques Semelin, "Analysis of a Mass-Crime: Ethnic Cleansing in the Former Yugoslavia, 1991–1999," *The Specter of Genocide: Mass Murder in Historical Perspective,* ed. Robert Gellately and Ben Kiernan (Cambridge: Cambridge University Press, 2003), 353–370.

18   Petrović, "Ethnic Cleansing," 11.

19   Michael Mann, *The Dark Side of Democracy: Explaining Ethnic Cleansing* (Cambridge: Cambridge University Press, 2004), 11–12.

20   Naimark, *Fires of Hatred*; Bell-Fialkoff, *Ethnic Cleansing,* 1–4.

21   Naimark, *Fires of Hatred,* 3.

22   Jacques Semelin, "What is Genocide?" *European Review of History* 12, no. 1 (March 2005), 81–89.

23   Steven Béla Várdy and T. Hunt Tooley, eds., *Ethnic Cleansing in Twentieth-Century Europe* (New York: Columbia University Press, 2003), 3.

24   For extensive discussion of controversies over the breakup of Yugoslavia see Sabrina P. Ramet, *Thinking about Yugoslavia: Scholarly Debates about the Yugoslav Breakup and the Wars in Bosnia and Kosovo* (Cambridge: Cambridge University Press, 2005).

25   Ivo Goldstein, *Croatia: A History*, 2nd ed. (London: Hurst & Company, 2001), 229.
26   According to Ozren Žunec (forthcoming), figures are based on Milan Babić's testimony at the ICTY.
27   Goldstein, *Croatia*, 233.
28   Momčilo Mitrović, "Etničko čišćenje kao strategija država na prostoru bivše SFRJ" (Ethnic Cleansing as a Strategy of States on the Territory of the Former SFRY), *Tokovi istorije* 1–2 (2005), 187.
29   Smail Čekić, *Aggression against the Republic of Bosnia and Herzegovina* (Sarajevo: Institut za istraživanje zločina protiv čovječnosti i medjunarodnog prava, 2005), 363, 420, 446, and 552, also cites the Serbian daily *Vreme* and Croatia's Federal President Stjepan Mesić and Prime Minister Ante Marković. Čekić also refers to Borisav Jović, *Poslednji Dani SFRJ* (The Last Days of SFRJ), 2nd ed. (Kragujevac: Prizma, 1996), 152, 159–62, 367.
30   Čekić, *Aggression against Bosnia*, 562, 629–631.
31   Marko Attila Hoare, *How Bosnia Armed* (London: Saqi Books, 2004), 47. For RS media claims, see *Final Report of the UN Commission of Experts, Annex V: The Prijedor Report*, S/1994/674/Add. 2 (Vol. I), 28. December 1994, 9, para. 13; Christopher Bennett, *Yugoslavia's Bloody Collapse: Causes, Course, and Consequences* (New York: New York University Press, 1995), 184; Roy Gutman, *A Witness to Genocide* (New York: Lisa Drew Books, 1993), ix–x; David Bruce MacDonald, *Balkan Holocausts? Serbian and Croatian Victim-Centred Propaganda and the War in Yugoslavia* (Manchester and New York: Manchester University Press, 2002), 237.
32   Benjamin Rusek and Charles Ingrao, "The Mortar Massacres: A Controversy Revisited," *Nationalities Papers* 32, no. 4 (2004), 830, 836–837, 846.
33   International Tribunal for the Prosecution of Persons Responsible for Serious Violations of International Humanitarian Law Committed in the Territory of Former Yugoslavia since 1991, *Case No. IT–98–29–T*, 5 December 2003, Prosecutor v. Stanislav Galić, *Judgement and Opinion*, para. 185–205. Available at http://www.un.org/icty/galic/trialc/judgement/index.htm (accessed 10 October 2008). On the siege of Sarajevo see Central Intelligence Agency, Office of Russian and European Analysis, *Balkan Battlegrounds: A Military History of the Yugoslav Conflict, 1990–1995*, vol. 1, (Washington, DC: Central Intelligence Agency, 2002), 152–154.
34   United Nations, *Report of the Secretary-General Pursuant to General Assembly Resolution 53/55 (1998), The Fall of Srebrenica*, para. 6. Available at www.un.org/peace/srebrenica.pdf (accessed 10 October 2008) and at http://www.xs4all.nl/~adampost/Archive/SR/sr_002.htm (accessed 10 October 2008).
35   CIA, *Balkan Battlegrounds*, vol. 1, 135.
36   Ibid., 145.
37   CIA, *Balkan Battlegrounds*, vol. 2, 304.
38   Ibid., 305.
39   *Final Report of the UN Commission of Experts, Annex IV*, 9, para. 28.
40   ICTY, *Case No. IT–00–39&40/1-S*, 27 February 2003, Prosecutor v. Biljana Plavšić, *Sentencing Judgement*. Available at http://www.un.org/icty/ plavsic/trialc/judgement/index.htm (accessed 10 October 2008).
41   ERRC Country Report, *The Non-Constituents: Rights Deprivation of Roma in Post-Genocide Bosnia and Herzegovina*. Available at http://www.errc.org/cikk.php?cikk=112 (accessed 13 October 2008).
42   International Tribunal, *Case No. IT–00–39&40/1–S*, para. 37.

43   Ibid., para. 36.
44   CIA, *Balkan Battlegrounds*, vol. 1, 158.
45   Ibid., 192.
46   ICTY, *Case No. IT–95–14, "Lasva Valley,"* 25 April 1997, the Prosecutor of the Tribunal against Tihomir Blaškić, *Second Amended Indictment*. Available at http://www. un.org/icty/indictment/english/bla-2ai970425e.htm (accessed 10 October 2008).
47   Ibid.
48   CIA, *Balkan Battlegrounds*, vol. 1, 203–206.
49   Charles R. Shrader, *The Muslim-Croat Civil War in Central Bosnia: A Military History, 1992–1994* (College Station: Texas A&M University Press, 2003), denies that the HVO committed crimes against Muslims, alleging that the "HVO was forced to react" and that it "adopted a classic 'active defense.'" Further, "the HVO, surrounded and heavily outnumbered, had neither the means nor the opportunity to engage in a planned program to attack, dispossess, and expel Muslims from the areas in which they lived" (160). Instead, ARBiH leaders were "accusing the HVO of the very crimes they themselves were committing" (161).
50   ICTY, *Case No. IT-03-68 P,* 30 June 2005, the Prosecutor of the Tribunal against Naser Orić, *Third Amended Indictment*. Available at http://www.un.org/icty/indictment/english/ori-3ai050630e.htm (accessed 10 October 2008).
51   ICTY, *Case No. IT–03–68–T*, 30 June 2006, Prosecutor v. Naser Orić, *Judgement*. Available at http://www.un.org/icty/oric/trialc/judgement/ori-jud060630e.pdf (accessed 10 October 2008).
52   Momčilo Mitrović, *Muslimanski logor Visoko* (The Muslim Camp Visoko) (Beograd: Military Historical Institute, 1995); Momčilo Mitrović, *Sarajevska raskršća* (Sarajevo Crossroads) (Beograd: Military Historical Institute, 1996); Momčilo Mitrović, *Zatvori i logori za Srbe u Hrvatskoj i BiH* (Prisons and Camps for Serbs in Croatia and BiH) (Beograd: Military Historical Institute, 1997).
53   UNHCR, *Information Notes of Former Yugoslavia* (September 1994) 9.
54   ICTY, *Case No. IT–98–33–A*, 19 April 2004, Appeals Chamber, Prosecutor v. Radislav Krstić, *Judgement*. Available at http://www.un.org/icty/krstic/Appeal/judgement/index. htm (accessed 10 October 2008).
55   ICTY, *Case No. IT–01–45*, 19 February 2004, Prosecutor v. Ante Gotovina, *Amended Indictment*. Available at http://www.un.org/icty/indictment/english/got-ai040224e.htm (accessed 10 October 2008).
56   Ibid., 2–8.
57   Momčilo Mitrović, "Etničko čišćenje Srba iz Zagreba 1992–1994.—po oralnoj istoriji" (Ethnic Cleansing of Serbs from Zagreb, 1992–1994, According to Oral History), *Tokovi istorije*, nos. 3–4 (2003), 89–98.
58   *Final Report of the Commission of Experts*, S/1994/674, 27 May 1994, 35, para. 140.
59   [Second] *Mazowiecki Report*, E/CN.4/1992/S-1/10, 27 October 1992, point 6. Available at http://www.haverford.edu/relg/sells/reports/mazowiecki27Oct92.htm (accessed 10 October 2008).
60   See for instance, Laura Silber and Allan Little, *The Death of Yugoslavia* (London: Penguin Books, 1995); James Gow, *The Serbian Project and Its Adversaries: A Strategy of War Crimes* (London: Hurst, 2003); Norman Cigar, *Genocide in Bosnia: The Policy of Ethnic Cleansing* (College Station: Texas A&M University Press, 1995); Tilman Zülch, *Etničko čišćenje: genocid za Veliku Srbiju* (Ethnic Cleansing: Genocide for Greater Serbia) (Sarajevo: Vijeće Kongresa Bošnjačkih Intelektualaca, 1996).

61 Gow, *Serbian Project*.

62 Silber and Little, *Death of Yugoslavia*, 325.

63 Čekić, *Aggression against Bosnia*.

64 ICTY, *Case No. IT–00–39&40/1–S*, para. 12.

65 ICTY, *Case No. IT–95–5–R61/IT–95–18–R61*, 11 July 1996, Prosecutor v. Radovan Karadžić/Ratko Mladić, *Review of the Indictments Pursuant to Rule 61 of the Rules of Procedure and Evidence*, p. 20. Available at http://www.un.org/icty/karadzic&mladic/trialc/rev-ii960716-e.pdf (accessed 10 October 2008).

66 *Final Report of the Commission of Experts*, S/1994/674, 27 May 1994, 32, para. 124.

67 Case concerning the application of the convention on the prevention and punishment of the crime of genocide (Bosnia and Herzegovina v. Serbia and Montenegro): Judgment, 26 February 2007, ICJ Web site, 156. www.icj.cij.org/icjwww/idocket/ibhy/ibhyjudgment/ibhy_ijudgment_20070226_frame.htm (accessed 10 October 2008).

68 ICTY, *Case No. IT–02–54–T*, 21 April 2004, the Prosecutor of the Tribunal against Slobodan Milošević, *Amended Indictment*. Available at http://www.un.org/icty/indictment/english/mil-ai040421-e.htm (accessed 10 October 2008).

69 Other individuals mentioned in the indictment are: Radovan Karadžić, Momčilo Krajišnik, Biljana Plavšić, General Ratko Mladić, Borisav Jović, Branko Kostić, Veljko Kadijević, Blagoje Adžić, Milan Martić, Jovica Stanišić, Franko Simatović (also known as Frenki), Radovan Stojićić (also known as Badža), Vojislav Šešelj, Željko Ražnatović (also known as Arkan), and other known and unknown participants.

70 ICTY, *Case No. IT–02–54–T*.

71 ICTY, *Case No. IT–01–45*, 24 February 2004, the Prosecutor v. Ante Gotovina, *Amended Indictment*. Available at http://www.un.org/icty/indictment/english/got-ai040224e.htm (accessed 10 October 2008).

72 Mirsad Tokača, *Violation of Norms of International Humanitarian Law during the War in Bosnia and Herzegovina* (Sarajevo: 2005).

73 Tone Bringa, *Being Moslem the Bosnian Way: Identity and Community in a Central Bosnian Village* (Princeton, NJ: Princeton University Press, 1995), 86.

74 ICTY, *Case No. IT–00–39&40/1–S*, para. 42.

75 Ibid., para. 47.

76 ICTY, *Case No. IT–01–45*.

77 ICTY, *Case No. IT–95–5–R61/IT–95–18–R61*.

78 For damage to Catholic churches, see Ilija Živković, ed., *The Wounded Church in Croatia: The Destruction of the Sacral Heritage of Croatia, 1991–1995* (Zagreb: The Croatian Conference of Bishops, 1996).

79 András Riedlmayer, *Destruction of Cultural Heritage in Bosnia-Hercegovina, 1992–1996: A Post-War Survey of Selected Municipalities*, expert report commissioned by the International Criminal Tribunal for the Former Yugoslavia (The Hague: ICTY, 2002) and expert testimony before the International Court of Justice in the case Bosnia-Hercegovina v. Serbia-Montenegro, 17 March 2006.

80 Slobodan Mileusnić, *Duhovni genocid: pregled porušenih, oštećenih i obesvećenih crkava, manastira i drugih crkvenih objekata u ratu 1991–1995* (Spiritual Genocide: A Survey of Destroyed, Damaged, and Desecrated Churches, Monasteries, and Other Church Buildings during the War, 1991–1995), 3rd ed. (Belgrade: Muzej Srpske Pravoslavne Crkve, 1997).

81 On the destruction of Catholic churches in Bosnia, see Ilija Živković, ed., *Raspeta crkava u Bosni i Hercegovini: uništavanje katoličkih sakralnih objekata u Bosni i Her-*

cegovini (1991–1996) (Banja Luka, Mostar, Sarajevo: Hrvatski Informativni Centar, 1997). On the cultural destruction in Bosnia in general, see András Riedlmayer, "From the Ashes: The Past and Future of Bosnia's Cultural Heritage," in *Islam and Bosnia: Conflict Resolution and Foreign Policy in Multi-Ethnic States*, ed. Maya Shatzmiller (Montreal: McGill-Queen's University Press, 2002), 98–135; Riedlmayer, "Convivencia under Fire: Genocide and Book-Burning in Bosnia," in *The Holocaust and the Book: Destruction and Preservation*, ed. Jonathan Rose (Amherst: University of Massachusetts Press, 2001), 266–291.

82   *Second Interim Report of the Commission of Experts*, UN Doc. S/26545, 6 October 1993, para. 68–69.

83   Beverly Allen, *Rape Warfare: The Hidden Genocide in Bosnia-Herzegovina and Croatia* (Minneapolis: University of Minnesota Press, 1996).

84   Cheryl Benard and Edit Schlaffer, *Vor unseren Augen. Der Krieg in Bosnien—und die Welt schaut weg* (München: Heyne, 1993).

85   ICTY, *Case No. IT–95–17/1–T*, 10 December 1998, Prosecutor v. Anto Furundzija, *Judgement*, 69. Available at http://www.un.org/icty/furundzija/trialc2/judgement/furtj981210e.pdf (accessed 10 October 2008).

86   ICTY, *Case No. IT–96–23&IT–96–23/1–A, "Foča,"* 12 June 2002, Appeals Chamber, Prosecutor v. Dragoljub Kunarac, Radomir Kovač, and Zoran Vuković, *Judgement*. Available at http://www.un.org/icty/kunarac/appeal/judgement/index.htm (accessed 10 October 2008).

87   *Final Report of the United Nations Commission of Experts, Annex IX: Rape and Sexual Assault*, S/1994/674/Add.2 (Vol. V), 28 December 1994, p. 7, para. 4, available at http://www.law.depaul.edu/institutes_centers/ihrli/_downloads/ANNEX_IX.pdf (accessed 10 October 2008).

88   Savez Logoraša, ed., *Upoznajmo Savez Logoraša Bosne i Hercegovine* (Get to Know the Union of Camp Inmates of BiH) (Sarajevo: Savez Logoraša Bosne i Hercegovine, Centar za istraživanje i dokumentaciju, 2003), 1–2.

89   Mirna Skrbić, "Counting the Dead," *Transitions Online* 4 (April 2006). http://www.tol.cz/look/TOL/article.tpl?IdLanguage=1&IdPublication=4&NrIssue=161&NrSection=1&NrArticle=16246&search=search&SearchKeywords=skrbic&SearchMode=on&SearchLevel=0 (accessed 19 October 2008).

90   United Nations High Commission for Refugees (UNHCR), *Information Notes of former Yugoslavia* (September 1994).

91   Norwegian Refugee Council/Global IDP Project, *Profile of Internal Displacement: Bosnia and Herzegovina*, 37.

92   Mitrović, "Etničko čišćenje kao strategija," 188.

93   Norwegian Refugee Council/Global IDP Project: *Profile of Internal Displacement*, 7.

94   Ibid., 8.

95   Ewa Tabeau and Jakub Bijak, "War-Related Deaths in the 1992–1995 Armed Conflicts in Bosnia and Herzegovina: A Critique of Previous Estimates and Recent Results," *European Journal of Population* 21, no. 2–3 (June 2005), 192.

96   Ibid., 194.

97   Sead Hadžović, "Sastavni dio ciljeva rata protiv BiH—genocid i etničko čišćenje" (Integral Part of War Aims against BiH—Genocide and Ethnic Cleansing), in *Ratovi u Jugoslaviji 1991–1999.—zbornik diskusija i saopštenja sa okruglog stola (novembar 2001)* (Wars in Yugoslavia, 1991–1999: Presentations and Declarations at a Round Table Discussion in November 2001), ed. Radoslav Ratković (Beograd: Društvo za

istinu o antifašističkoj narodnooslobodilačkoj borbi u Jugoslaviji 1941–1945, 2002), 265–273.

98   Lara J. Nettelfield, "Presentation for Reintegrating Bosnia: Ten Years after the Dayton Peace Agreement," University of Michigan, Ann Arbor, 29 October 2005.
99   http://www.idc.org.ba/presentation/research_results.htm (accessed 10 October 2008).
100 Tabeau and Bijak, "War-Related Deaths."
101 Roy Gutman, *A Witness to Genocide: The 1993 Pulitzer Prize-Winning Dispatches on the Ethnic Cleansing of Bosnia* (New York: Macmillan, 1993); Smail Čekić, *Agresija na Bosnu i genocid nad Bošnjacima 1991–1993.* (Aggression against Bosnia and Genocide against Bosniaks) (Sarajevo: NIPP Ljiljan, 1994); Smail Čekić, ed., *Genocid u BiH 1991–1995* (Genocide in Bosnia and Herzegovina 1991–1995) (Sarajevo: Institut za Istraživanje Zločina protiv Čovječnosti i Međunarodnog Prava, 1997); Cigar, *Genocide in Bosnia*, 60; Thomas Cushman and Stjepan G. Mestrović, eds., *This Time We Knew: Western Responses to Genocide in Bosnia* (New York: New York University Press, 1996); Michael Anthony Sells, *The Bridge Betrayed: Religion and Genocide in Bosnia* (Berkeley: University of California Press, 1996); Damir Mirković, "Ethnic Conflict and Genocide: Reflections on Ethnic Cleansing in the Former Yugoslavia," *Annals of the American Academy of Political and Social Science* 548 (November 1996), 191–199.
102 See Tokača, *Violation of Norms of International Humanitarian Law.*
103 Čekić, *Aggression against Bosnia*, 1249.
104 Ibid., 1250.
105 Merdijana Sadović, "Serbia Acquitted of Genocide," IWPR, *Tribunal Update*, no. 490, 26 February 2007. Available at http://www.iwpr.net/?p=tri&s=f&o=333556&apc_state=henitri200702 (accessed 10 October 2008).
106 Carla del Ponte and Chuck Sudetić, *Madame Prosecutor* (New York: Other Press, 2009), 356–358.
107 Ramet, *Thinking about Yugoslavia*, 15.
108 Cigar, *Genocide in Bosnia.*
109 Sells, *Bridge Betrayed.*
110 Čekić, *Genocid u BiH 1991–1995*; Bennett, *Yugoslavia's Bloody Collapse.*
111 Quoted from Aldijana Osmeragić, "Nad Srbima u Sarajevu počinjen genocid veći nego u Srebrenici" (Genocide against Serbs in Sarajevo Was Larger than in Srebrenica), *Oslobodjenje*, 26 March 2005.
112 *Statute of the International Criminal Tribunal for the Former Yugoslavia.* Available at http://www.un.org/icty/legaldoc-e/index.htm (accessed 10 October 2008).
113 http://www.preventgenocide.org/law/convention/text.htm#II (accessed 19 October 2008).
114 ICTY, *Case No. IT–95–5–R61/IT–95–18–R61*, 53.
115 Nerma Jelačić and Mirna Mekić, "Serbs Subvert Srebrenica Commemoration," IWPR, *Balkan Crisis Report*, no. 563, 30 June 2005. Available at http://iwpr.net/?p=bcr&s=f&o=242035&apc_state=henibcr89187b7f19b1ed1462caae0587a75ad8 (accessed 10 October 2008).
116 Ibid.
117 Del Ponte and Sudetić, *Madame Prosecutor*, 317.
118 ICTY, *Case No. IT–98–33–A*, para. 37.
119 Ibid., para. 33.

120 Quoted in George J. Andreopoulus, "Introduction: The Calculus of Genocide," in *Genocide: Conceptual and Historical Dimensions*, ed. George J. Andreopoulus (Philadelphia: University of Pennsylvania Press, 1997), 5.

121 ICTY, *Case No. IT 95–18–R61/Case No. IT–95-5–R61, 27 June 1996, Prosecutor of the Tribunal v. Radovan Karadžić, Ratko Mladić, Rule 61 Hearing, Opening Statement* by Mr Eric Ostberg, Senior Trial Attorney, provisional transcript, 18–28, esp. 25. Available at http://www.un.org/icty/transe5&18/960627it.htm (accessed 10 October 2008).

5

Dušan Janjić, team leader
Matjaž Klemenčič, team leader

Vlado Azinović	**John Fine**	**Emil Kerenji**
Alfred Bing	**Zlatko Hadžidedić**	**Vladimir Klemenčič**
Sumantra Bose	**Marko Attila Hoare**	Miloš Ković
Daniele Conversi	**Charles Ingrao**	Vladimir Petrović
Dušan Djordjevich	Constantin Iordachi	**Nikola Samardžić**
Keith Doubt	**A. Ross Johnson**	Brendan Simms

Principal author Matjaž Klemenčič acknowledges the extensive input by team members, including several pages of text contributed by Marko Attila Hoare, Charles Ingrao and Alfred Bing. Funding from the National Endowment for Democracy and the Slovenian Research Council facilitated Prof. Klemenčič's research, including numerous interviews with Slovenian government officials and former U.S. Secretary of State James Baker.

Profs. Klemenčič and Dušan Janjić assumed team leadership from John A. Fine (2001-2003) in order to streamline the team's internet communication. An initial draft was submitted for project-wide review in November 2003, which mandated considerable expansion in the chapter's length and research base. Although the text was adopted following project-wide review in April 2005, further revisions were undertaken in 2008 to address concerns raised by two of the four outside referees.

The chapter cites several confidential interviews conducted by SI scholars with several current and former officials from the U.S. State Department and IFOR military; in each case their identities will be recorded and stored in the Purdue University archives for later release, upon request, consistent with terms negotiated with each individual.

THE INTERNATIONAL COMMUNITY AND THE FRY/BELLIGERENTS, 1989-1997

◆ Matjaž Klemenčič ◆

For almost four decades after World War II, the international community supported socialist nonaligned Yugoslavia as a symbolic and even strategic crossroads between the polar world of the cold war. Billions of dollars of aid flooded the country in the belief that it was important to support Tito's Yugoslav experiment.[1] When the crises leading to Yugoslavia's dissolution mounted in the last years of the 1980s, both the United States and the Soviet Union/Russian Federation tried to maintain the status quo and hold together a Yugoslavia that had become an empty shell. Instead of seeking to facilitate a peaceful transformation of the country's dissolution, the international community attempted to support a unified Yugoslavia and thus arguably bears some responsibility for the violence and insecurity that followed. Both the United States and Russia, along with other states, ignored the basic truth that no state, whatever its origins, can expect to survive without the support and at least the passive allegiance of most of its citizenry.[2]

What role did the international community play in the Yugoslav crisis in the first half of the 1990s? Could the bloody demise of Yugoslavia have been prevented if the international community had reacted sooner? Scholars disagree in their assessments of the real intentions of the world powers toward Yugoslavia. According to most Western authors, in the late 1980s political leaders from most of Europe and also the U.S. desperately wanted to preserve the territorial integrity of Yugoslavia. In contrast, others (and also almost all the pro-Milošević Serb politicians) suggest that the breakup of Yugoslavia was the ultimate goal of the West.[3] Slobodan Milošević started his defense in The Hague by blaming foreigners for the breakup.[4] Some authors, such as Russian historian Elena Guskova and Polish political scientist Marek Waldenberg, blame the West not only for the dissolution but also for the violent nature of the breakup.[5] One can argue that the dissolution was unavoidable, but one can also contend that the process might have been more peaceful if the international community had acted differently.

The U.S. was closely involved in the international diplomacy related to the dissolution of Yugoslavia, although its policy toward Yugoslavia was inconsistent from the very beginning. Three phases characterize U.S. policy: (1) an initial reluctance to interfere in a primarily European problem, (2) an attempt at diplomacy, and finally, (3) armed intervention.[6] Its policy was in part determined by domestic public opinion polls and the actions of the U.S. Congress. Interestingly, the ethnic background of members of Congress and their constituencies played a role, as did activities in the United States of the leaders of different immigrant ethnic groups from the territories of the former Yugoslavia.

How aware were U.S. politicians of the situation in Yugoslavia? The CIA predicted in an October 1990 report that Yugoslavia would cease to function within one year and would probably dissolve within two years. According to its report, economic reform would not prevent the breakup. The agency predicted that Serbia would block Slovenian and Croatian attempts to secede from the Yugoslav confederation, that there would be a protracted armed uprising by the Albanians in Kosovo, and that Serbia would foment uprisings by Serbian minorities in Croatia and Bosnia. It noted the possible danger of ethnic violence becoming an organized civil war between republics but considered that unlikely. It concluded that there was nothing the United States or its European allies could do to preserve unity and that Yugoslavs would see any such efforts as antithetical to the principles of democracy and self-determination.

The CIA discussion on historical background and the economy, as well as the maps and tables that followed in the report are accurate. As then U.S. Ambassador to Belgrade Warren Zimmermann wrote in his memoirs, this prescient analysis erred only on Kosovo, which remained tense but quiet, and on the timetable for civil war, which unfolded even faster than predicted. In its main elements, the estimate proved deadly accurate.[7] From an historian's point of view, this report is a relatively good analysis of the situation in Yugoslavia at that time.[8]

In spite of CIA warnings, it became clear that the United States did not want to get intensively involved in the Yugoslav crisis and that it would let the European states, especially the EC, try to solve it. The Bush administration was too busy resolving the crisis in Iraq and did not want to be involved in another regional crisis. Until 1992 this administration tried to avoid playing any important role in solving the Yugoslav crisis. Because Bush was afraid that any action by his administration would influence the outcome of the U.S. presidential election in November, the U.S. opposed recognition of new states as the country collapsed. Moreover, the U.S. was afraid that the Yugoslav crisis would influence the very complicated internal political situation in the Soviet Union.

The key personalities of this period were U.S. Ambassador to Belgrade Warren Zimmermann; Undersecretary of State Lawrence Eagleburger, who had also served as U.S. ambassador to Yugoslavia in the late 1970s; and National Security Adviser Brent Scowcroft, who had served as military attaché in Belgrade in the early 1960s. They represented the "pro-Serbian lobby" in the Bush administration, which was also connected to Yugoslavia through political and economic interests (e.g., the Yugo-America Company, in which Henry Kissinger, former U.S. secretary of state, took part).[9] From the beginning and not very effectively, these administration members supported the territorial integrity of Yugoslavia and the economic reform policy of Ante Marković. These views were shared by U.S. Secretary of State James Baker, who at the same time was known to have often said: "We don't have a dog in this fight."[10]

On 18 June 1991 at the Berlin Aspen Institute, Baker demanded that members of the Organization for Security and Cooperation in Europe (OSCE) do everything they could to preserve the unity of the states of Eastern Europe.[11] Three days later he visited Belgrade and demonstrated that he did not have a plan and that he had few ideas to offer on Yugoslavia except to suggest that the United States wanted a united Yugoslavia that was also democratic. He told the leaders of Yugoslavia's republics that they should continue to negotiate. He called for the devolution of additional authority, responsibility, and sovereignty to the republics.[12] At the same time he expressed continued U.S. support for a united Yugoslavia by promising Milošević that the United States would not recognize the independence of either Slovenia or Croatia.[13]

In his memoirs Baker distinguished between the independence proclamations of Slovenia and Croatia, on the one hand, and Bosnia-Hercegovina and Macedonia, on the other. He was of the same opinion in February 2005 when he gave an interview to this author.[14] Lawrence Eagleburger would later comment: "How could we recognize Croatia and Slovenia, which had pursued independence unilaterally and in violation of the Helsinki principles, and not recognize Skopje and Sarajevo, which had done so in a peaceful and democratic manner?" Moreover, not recognizing Bosnia-Hercegovina and Macedonia, he noted, "could create real instability, which less than mature players in Serbia and Greece might decide to exploit."[15]

Although interpretations of Baker's visit have varied, Zdravko Tomac probably spoke for many Croats when he wrote that, "James Baker . . . actively encouraged the federal government, Serbia and the Yugoslav Federal [sic] Army. By insisting on the territorial integrity of Yugoslavia, he agreed with Milošević's policy and endorsed the JNA's [Yugoslav National Army's] threat to Slovenia."[16] Then Slovenian Prime Minister Lojze Peterle emphasized in his memoirs that Baker insisted that Yugoslavia ought to stay together but not at any price; he implied that it should be democratic.[17] Slovene politicians tried to tell Baker that it was far too late to call off the transition to independence, but Baker did not want to listen.[18]

Many U.S. politicians were so naive (ignoring the power of the national/ethnic movements and national/ethnic problems in general that could not be solved by economic measures) that they believed the market-oriented economic reforms of Ante Marković, along with financial aid from the West, especially the U.S., could stop nationalist and separatist tendencies. Thus the U.S. let the EU take the lead.[19]

In spite of the reluctance of the U.S. administration, the U.S. Congress did at times try to influence the situation in Yugoslavia. The Yugoslav crisis—especially the crisis in Kosovo—brought quite a few debates in both chambers of Congress. Representatives and senators were active in introducing amendments to foreign aid bills and special resolutions regarding the critical conditions in Yugoslavia. In the years 1985–1995, Representative Helen Delich-Bentley (R-MD), of Serb descent, made an important contribution to lobbying for the "Serb Truth,"[20] with support of other members of Congress from districts where large numbers of the electorate were of Serb descent. Those Congress members were almost always in a bind, however, because their constituencies usually included not only Serb Americans, but Croat Americans, Slovene Americans, and Albanian Americans as well.[21]

Germany's role during the dissolution is another controversy. Some authors consider that from the very beginning of the Yugoslav crisis, Germany together with Austria, Hungary, and Denmark at least covertly supported and encouraged Slovene and Croatian strivings for independence.[22] Scholars on the team agree that Germany, Austria, Denmark, and Hungary were certainly sympathetic to the Croatian and Slovenian causes, but we conclude that they did not actually encourage independence.

This position is supported by Michael Libal, the former head of the South-Eastern European Section of the German Foreign Ministry. He claims that although German parliamentarians demanded from the German government recognition of Slovenia and Croatia in June of 1991, the German government tried to use the threat of recognition only as a method of pressure on the Serbs of Croatia and the Yugoslav government to end the military fighting. Already on 24 August 1991, German Foreign Minister Hans Dietrich Genscher called the Yugoslav ambassador in Bonn, Boris Frlec,[23] to make clear the attitude of the German government not only to him but also, via an appropriate press release, to the public at large. The core of Genscher's démarche was a threat of recognition: "If the bloodshed continues and the policy of faits accomplis by force supported by the Yugoslav army is not halted immediately, the Federal Government [of

Germany] must seriously examine the recognition of Croatia and Slovenia in their given frontiers."[24]

Whereas Germany reluctantly supported the independence of Slovenia and Croatia, the Soviet Union wanted Yugoslavia to be preserved at all costs. Already during the first period of the Yugoslav crisis, the Soviet Union itself had experienced independence movements and declarations of independence by some of its Soviet republics. Soviet Foreign Minister Alexander Bessmertnych had stated already in April 1991 that keeping the territorial integrity of Yugoslavia was "one of the preconditions for stability in Europe."[25] It is important to note, however, that the Soviet political leadership decided to help Yugoslavia only politically through international institutions and not militarily.

The Yugoslav crisis presented a profound shock for many members of the nonaligned movement because Yugoslavia was a founding member. A large gap in understanding the Yugoslav crisis developed between some nonaligned countries that supported the unity of Yugoslavia at all costs and some Muslim countries that were most concerned about supporting Yugoslavia's Muslim population. Support from the nonaligned countries (which then represented almost two-thirds of the member states of the UN) would be very important for Serb policy, and thus the position of some Muslim countries was a great disappointment for Serb politicians.[26]

Hungary did not support the breakup of Yugoslavia out of concern for the large Hungarian minority in Vojvodina (Serbia). As Foreign Minister Géza Jeszenszky stated publicly and not particularly diplomatically, Hungary aimed to establish "friendly" relations with Croatia and a "correct" one with Serbia.[27] Borisav Jović rejects any suggestion that Hungary supported the preservation of Yugoslavia. In his diary he writes that in December 1990 the U.S. "asked Hungary with American help to use all of its forces to destroy the socialist system in Yugoslavia and the unity of Yugoslavia and to take particular measures against Serbia."[28] Jović supported this by citing the illegal importation of weapons by Croatia from Hungary (20,000 tommy guns) in 1990, which Croatia undertook, from his point of view, to form its own army.

Italy, by contrast, remained in an ambivalent position. The Italian foreign minister, Gianni De Michelis, strongly supported a united Yugoslavia. In the spring of 1991 he said to his Slovene counterparts, "In Europe there is no place for new states, and I am sure that you do not want to immigrate to another continent."[29] He also opposed the changing of Yugoslavia's internal borders. He expressed this position very clearly at a conference of foreign ministers on 10 July 1991, where he also advocated a system of minority protection that would be based on international law, similar to the protection existing in German South Tyrol.

France also fought for the further existence of a united Yugoslavia, influenced perhaps by old traditions of French friendship with the Serbs. Keeping together the Yugoslav federation would, in the French view, avoid the spreading of separatist and nationalist tendencies to other European regions. It would also thwart plans for establishing a new *Mitteleuropa* under German leadership. French policy also took the position that the rights and interests of the Serb minority in Croatia were threatened after Croatia declared its independence.[30] It should be remembered, of course, that France had its own minority problems, especially with the Basques and the separatists in Corsica.[31]

Great Britain tried to keep a low profile on the Yugoslav crisis, especially because the U.S., its most important ally, was doing the same. Although Great Britain had a history of intensive contacts with Serbia, this did not appear to play an important role at the time.

The position of the Netherlands toward the Yugoslav crisis was influenced especially by the fact that it presided over the EC in the second half of 1991.[32] At the beginning of the conflict, Prime Minister Ruud Lubbers and Foreign Minister Hans van den Broek led the policy of supporting a unified Yugoslavia and not recognizing Slovenia and Croatia. In the second half of 1991, van den Broek was the greatest opponent of the German initiative for the recognition of Slovenia and Croatia.[33]

The Austrian government's statements about Yugoslavia had to be in accord with those of the EC because the Austrian government was then concerned about not disturbing Austria's application for EC membership. The Austrian position toward the Yugoslav crisis was influenced also by the fact that Slovenes and Croats live in Austria as indigenous minorities and that many *Gastarbeiter* from Yugoslavia worked in Austria. Moreover, the Austrian economy was affected by the crisis. Austria was especially afraid of a great influx of refugees. There was debate within the Austrian government because Austrian Chancellor Franz Vranitzky followed the path of his fellow Socialists in support of a united Yugoslavia, whereas his foreign minister, Alois Mock (Austrian People's Party), was a leading advocate for the recognition of Slovenia and Croatia. Despite the debate, Austria gave Slovenia loans so that it could continue its imports and exports in June and July 1991.[34]

On 9 July 1991 Chancellor Vranitzky invited representatives of Western social-democratic parties to Vienna in order to exchange views on the Yugoslav crisis. The leader of the German Socialists, Bjoern Engholm, demanded recognition of Slovenia and Croatia as a result "of the end of the negotiations and not at the beginning of negotiations." The leader of the Italian Socialists, Betino Craxi, was afraid of a "chain reaction," but he still demanded a new order on the territory of Yugoslavia and the recognition of the new states. The president of PASOK (Greek Socialists), Carolos Papoulias, warned "against threatening the security of the Mediterranean."[35] This was in line with the Greeks' support for the preservation of the unity of Yugoslavia at all costs. Greece was the only country with a prevailing Orthodox Christian population in the EC/EU. Orthodoxy was a bond that connected them with the Serbs. The Greeks were also upset because of the international recognition of Macedonia.[36]

International organizations and their working bodies, like the OSCE, the EC, the European Parliament, NATO, and the UN also tried to deal with the Yugoslav crisis. The positions of individual members of these bodies differed. Often they mirrored the official policy of their states or their homeland political parties; at other times individual members represented their own opinions. Until the beginning of military clashes in Yugoslavia, however, the consensus of these international organizations and their working bodies was that Yugoslavia should keep its territorial integrity and that it should become a democracy.

On 18 December 1990 the EC foreign ministers demanded respect for human rights and democratic principles in Yugoslavia, along with the territorial integrity and unity of Yugoslavia and respect for the interests of the republics. Already on 14 February 1991, Slovene Prime Minister Peterle met with European Parliament President Enrique Baron and European Commission member Abel Juan Matutes and acquainted them with Slovenia's attempts to achieve independence and its desire to become a full member of the EC.[37]

At their 9 April 1991 meeting, presidents and prime ministers of EC member states again demanded that the territorial integrity of Yugoslavia be preserved. This was the EC position for the next few months. In addition to promises about associate membership once Yugoslavia had solved its internal problems,[38] the EC also tried to preserve Yugoslav territorial integrity by offering credits. In May 1991, on the occasion of his visit to Belgrade, EC Commission President Jacques Delors promised to request $4.5 billion in aid from the EC in support of the Yugoslav commitment to political reform.[39] A day before Slovenia and Croatia declared independence, on 24 June 1991, a third financial protocol was approved with which the EC gave Yugoslavia 1.5 billion German marks in loans. At the same time the European Investment Bank also assured Yugoslavia that it would provide another loan of 1.5 billion German marks.[40] Twelve EC foreign ministers declared that they did not support Slovenian and Croatian independence endeavors.

The West tried to resolve the Yugoslav crisis with economic and political pressure, whereas the Soviet Union only provided Marković's government with oil and weapons. The West did not oppose the decision of the Soviet Union to sell arms to the JNA, which included twenty MiG-29 airplanes, rocket weapons, radar equipment, and other equipment.[41] The Soviet Union's Mikhail Gorbachev and the Soviet generals were also determined to keep Yugoslavia united.[42]

The OSCE also got actively involved in the Yugoslav crisis. Only a few days before the Slovene and Croatian declarations of independence, at a meeting of foreign ministers of the OSCE on 19–20 June in Berlin, the foreign ministers accepted "mechanisms of quick interventions" in case critical circumstances developed that would endanger the common security.[43] Yugoslav Foreign Minister Budimir Lončar warned members of the conference that the dissolution of Yugoslavia would also destabilize other parts of Europe.[44] All participants in the conference expressed their interest in keeping Yugoslavia united as a democratic and federated state.[45] The foreign ministers of Germany (Genscher), the United States (Baker), the Soviet Union (Bessmertnych), and Yugoslavia (Lončar) declared in separate statements that it was up to the nations of Yugoslavia to decide on its future. Importantly, Genscher also mentioned that the right of secession, included in the Yugoslav constitution of 1974, should be respected.[46]

During these early months before war, NATO and the UN did not give special attention to the crisis in Yugoslavia. Both organizations limited their reactions to following the situation in Yugoslavia and issuing statements that warned that the crisis could destabilize the region. It can be argued that the decision to use the UN to organize the military coalition for Desert Storm had significant negative consequences for the Yugoslav conflict. With Yugoslavia's long history of participation in the UN, strong ties with Third World countries, and nonmembership in the EC or in NATO, the UN was the one international organization that perhaps could have mounted an external intervention that all parties in Yugoslavia would most likely have accepted as neutral and legitimate.

The European Parliament devoted much of its time to the Yugoslav crisis. Already in March 1991 it passed a resolution declaring "that the constituent republics and autonomous provinces of Yugoslavia must have the right freely to determine their own future in a peaceful and democratic manner and on the basis of recognized international and internal borders." Otto von Habsburg played quite an important role in passing this and all the subsequent resolutions in the European Parliament that supported the principle of self-determination[47] for Slovenes, Croats, Kosovo Albanians, and the other nations of Yugoslavia. In the second half of 1991, Habsburg finished most of his speeches in the European Parliament by saying: "*Ceterum autem censeo Croatiam et Sloveniam esse reconoscendam*" (Otherwise, I think that Croatia and Slovenia ought to be recognized).[48] The Greens in the European Parliament sharply criticized the situation in Yugoslavia and expressed their criticisms in a letter to van den Broek and Delors.[49]

At the beginning of July 1991, under the leadership of Belgian Prime Minister Wilfried Martens, a meeting of the presidency of the European People's Party took place. At this meeting they passed a resolution on the situation in Yugoslavia, condemned the attack of the JNA on Slovenia, and stated "that Slovenes and Croats . . . when they declared the independence of their states acted in accordance with their right of self-determination as well as with the wishes of their nation." At the same time they demanded that the international community recognize Slovenia and Croatia as independent states if there was not a peaceful solution to the crisis within three months.[50]

In December 1990 more then 88 percent of all eligible voters of Slovenia and in May 1991 more than 80 percent of eligible voters of Croatia voted for independence. Slovene politicians negotiated with the federal government for a peaceful separation from the rest of the Yugoslav republics but without success. On 25 June 1991, Croatia and Slovenia carried through with their intent to declare independence. This triggered an attack by the JNA on Slovenia, with the goal of overthrowing the Slovene proindependence government and gaining control over the territory, with special concern for the borders with Austria and Italy.

During the Slovenian Ten-Day War, the JNA lost the international public relations campaign. German Foreign Minister Genscher accused the JNA of "running amok" in Slovenia. Evidence of how much Germans were interested in solving the conflict was the visit of Genscher to Slovenia on the invitation of Slovene Foreign Minister Dimitrij Rupel. He landed in nearby Carinthia, Austria, on 2 July with the intention of driving into Slovenia, but because of the fighting he could not enter Slovenia. Instead Slovene President Milan Kučan and Rupel discussed the issues with Genscher in Carinthia. The result was the continuing support of Genscher for the Slovene cause throughout the conflict.[51]

Others joined the fray. British Foreign Secretary Douglas Hurd told the British parliament that the JNA had hastened the disintegration of Yugoslavia. Italy said it would "act in solidarity" with Croatia and Slovenia unless the JNA respected a cease-fire. In the U.S. the chairman of the Senate Foreign Relations Committee, Claiborne Pell (D–RI), urged President Bush to support Slovene and Croatian independence if Yugoslavia's "renegade army does not cease its wanton aggression."[52] In spite of these calls, the Bush administration limited itself only to criticizing the JNA's actions. As the world's sole remaining superpower, the U.S. frowned on secessionism as a threat to the hard-won status quo. Its leaders also retained that Wilsonian preference for following Balkan violence from as far a distance as possible. Hence, whereas there were discussions among different desks of the Departments of State and Defense, as there had been during the Wilson administration concerning different options for the region,[53] the conventional wisdom was that the EC should lead attempts to resolve the Yugoslav crisis.

The EC, which tried for a long time to play a role more significant and independent than that of the United States in foreign policy in general, accepted the opportunity to mediate in the Yugoslav crisis.[54] Already on 27 June Genscher asked the OSCE to start procedures that its member states had accepted a week before in Berlin. In accordance with the mechanisms designed for "extraordinary circumstances," on Genscher's demand the OSCE Committee of Senior Officials met on 3 and 4 July 1991 and asked the belligerents in Yugoslavia to stop the fighting and offered to send a group of observers.[55] In July 1991, the EC sent the foreign ministers of the sitting EC troika (representing the states holding the presidency, his predecessor, and his successor) as mediators to Yugoslavia. The troika made three visits to Yugoslavia, which resulted in a cease-fire between the Slovene Territorial Defense Force and the JNA; by 7 and 8 July, they had convened a conference at Brioni for the purpose of resolving the crisis.

The EC-sponsored Brioni Accord prevented further air raids or other military activity by the JNA against Slovenia. Mediators from the EC quickly negotiated an agreement between Slovenia and the JNA because the EC did not want war on its borders. They also still hoped that Slovenia might act as a democratizing force in Yugoslavia.[56] After its defeat, the JNA decided to retreat from Slovenia with all its equipment and machinery. The Brioni Accord, in effect, recognized the Slovene military victory and also made Slovenia and Croatia subject, de facto, to international law and cleared the way for the eventual recognition of their statehood.[57] With a mandate from the CSCE to deploy thirty to fifty observers, the EC began its first-ever effort at peacekeeping.[58] Parallel to the withdrawal of the Yugoslav army from Slovenia, the armed conflict in Croatia widened.

Although Croatia and Slovenia had declared their independence, most of the world did not support their declarations and still wanted to preserve Yugoslavia. All of the great powers—the U.S., the Soviet Union, China, Britain, and France—remained united in their support for the idea of a united Yugoslavia, as did EU members Sweden, Denmark, Italy, and Greece and former Communist bloc states Romania, Poland, and Hungary. The governments of neighboring Austria as well as Germany expressed their sympathy with Croatia and Slovenia; however, they did not recognize their independence.

In German parliamentary debates on the situation in Yugoslavia in September 1991, Chancellor Helmut Kohl argued that if the Yugoslavs could no longer live in peace, Germany would have to consider the question of recognizing those republics that no longer wanted to be part of Yugoslavia.[59] Genscher was even more explicit: "If those peoples of Yugoslavia who desire independence cannot realize it through negotiations, we will recognize their unilateral declarations of independence."[60] Addressing the JNA, he said: "With every shot of your cannons and tanks, the hour of recognition moves closer. We shall not be able to disregard this further."[61] This view was soon adopted as well by Lord Peter Carrington, the former British foreign secretary and former secretary-general of NATO. And at a press conference on 12 September 1991, French President François Mitterrand stated that "after the events of the last months, in the future it is possible to think about independence for Slovenia and Croatia."[62] As the fighting continued through the autumn of 1991 and after a long struggle in the EU, Germany prevailed and the EU announced on December 1991 that it would recognize Slovenia and Croatia as independent states. Numerous states opposed this action. With the support of Great Britain and France, the U.S. at the beginning of December 1991 even suggested a special resolution of the UN Security Council (UNSC) that would demand that Germany stop asking for the recognition of Slovenia and Croatia by the international community. Genscher eventually succeeded in changing the perspective of his French colleague, Roland Dumas, and thus France no longer supported the U.S. position.[63] At the same time Genscher warned the U.S. not to use the UN to "torpedo" European actions for peace.[64]

The role of Yugoslavia's neighbors also caused controversy. Hungary and Albania were, of course, interested in the destiny of their ethnic minorities in Yugoslavia. Both countries took precautions to defend their airspace,[65] and Albania placed its army in a state of alert.[66] Under the pressure of public opinion, the policies of Austria and Italy toward Slovenia and Croatia also started to change in the summer of 1991,[67] and Bulgaria, always conscious of its historical ties with Macedonia,[68] hinted that it was prepared to recognize an independent Macedonian state. It finally did so on 15 January 1992.

Nevertheless, in the second half of 1991 there were still voices calling for the preservation of a democratic Yugoslavia.[69] The large socialist faction of the European Parliament was one of the main opponents to diplomatic recognition of Croatia and Slovenia. In October 1991, Jannis Sakellarion, the Greek press representative of this faction, declared that if Croatia were recognized as an independent state, then the Serbs of Croatia should also have the right to self-determination because Serbs in some parts of Croatia represented a majority of the population. Motives for such positions by European socialists might be explained by their sympathies for Yugoslav self-management as a "third way" between capitalism and communism. These pro-Yugoslav views of the European Left were eventually transformed in the course of events to pro-Serbian positions. The views of this socialist faction played a decisive role in the decision of the European Parliament not to support a proposal by the Christian-Democrats that advocated recognition of Slovenia and Croatia if the Serbs violated the cease-fire and if the UN was forced to intervene militarily.[70]

In the second half of 1991 NATO also started to deal with the Yugoslav conflict.[71] Already on 7 June 1991, the foreign ministers of NATO declared that the security of the NATO states depended on the security of all other states in Europe.[72] Member states of NATO on 4 June 1992 accepted in the Oslo Declaration that NATO, on demand of the OSCE or UN, could intervene militarily outside of its member states.[73]

From the beginning of the crisis, the UN had called for noninterference in Yugoslavia's internal affairs. Therefore, until Slovenia and Croatia were internationally recognized, the organization could not send peace-keeping missions into Yugoslavia until all the involved parties agreed. UN Secretary-General Pérez de

Cuéllar opposed the recognition of Slovenia and Croatia and condemned the German intention to recognize their independence as an "insane step." Because the Germans did not react to his statements, de Cuéllar on 12 December 1991 sent a letter to the presiding minister of the EC Council of Foreign Ministers, van den Broek, and asked him to send the letter to other EC member states. Genscher answered de Cuéllar the next day and said that de Cuéllar was, with this letter to van den Broek, "encouraging those forces in Yugoslavia which were already fighting against a successful conclusion of peace efforts in Yugoslavia."[74]

De Cuéllar then wrote to Genscher and expressed his concern over the "untimely recognition for which there had not been a vote."[75] De Cuéllar also informed Genscher that the presidents of Bosnia-Hercegovina and Macedonia asked him not to act in favor of the recognition of Slovenia and Croatia and that if they were recognized, there would be danger of war spreading into their republics as well. De Cuéllar's letter started new discussions. U.S. President George Bush again criticized the plans for the recognition of Slovenia and Croatia and instructed U.S. Ambassador to the UN, Thomas Pickering, to ask the German government to reconsider its position on recognition.[76]

While the international community dealt with the question of what to do with Slovenia and Croatia, armed conflict in Croatia started to spread dangerously. The EC on 7 September called a peace conference in The Hague that, on Genscher's advice, was presided over by Lord Carrington.[77] Although some members of the international community had already started to change their positions concerning the independence of Slovenia and Croatia and in spite of the fact that the Yugoslav federation had practically ceased to exist, the Hague conference still tried to find a solution within the framework of preserving Yugoslavia. Carrington picked up where the failed Izetbegović–Gligorov Plan had left off. He recognized six republics as the constituent units of the former federal state and produced a plan that would give each of them as much sovereignty as it wanted.[78]

Efforts to solve the crisis were supported also by the UN Security Council (UNSC). Invoking Chapter 7 of the UN charter and declaring that the Yugoslav conflict had became a "direct threat to international peace and security," the UNSC on 25 September 1991 passed the first of sixty-seven resolutions that would be adopted by January 1995. This first resolution, number 713, imposed a general and complete embargo on all deliveries of weapons and military equipment to Yugoslavia.[79] This resolution still dealt with the conflicts in Yugoslavia as if they were the internal affair of a UN member state. The resolution did not have any serious consequences for the JNA, which had stocks of weaponry in its arsenals, but it had serious consequences for the Croatian side.[80] The weapons embargo on Yugoslav republics made it possible for Milošević to strengthen his own power in rump Yugoslavia and to strengthen the offensive against Croatia.

On 8 October 1991, on the day the three-month moratorium enacted under the Brioni Accord ended, UN Secretary-General de Cuéllar decided to send Cyrus Vance, former U.S. secretary of state, to the Balkans as his personal envoy. In de Cuéllar's view the EC could not be neutral in imposing a just peace.[81] In cooperation with Lord Carrington, Vance was authorized to start a negotiating process that they hoped would be fruitful under the auspices of the EC and the UN.[82]

On 15 October 1991 Mikhail Gorbachev invited Tudjman and Milošević to Moscow. Gorbachev was sure that the events in Yugoslavia only "mirrored the horrors" that could be possible in the Soviet Union. Both leaders pleaded that they would, in the course of November and with the assistance of the Soviet Union, the U.S., and the EC, find an honest solution to end the fighting.[83] Very soon the international community discovered that these promises would not be kept.

The EC's Hague conference issued a draft general settlement on 24 October 1991. It called for the demilitarization of all ethnic enclaves, a guaranteed autonomy for Kosovo and Vojvodina, and new relations among the republics. As an answer to the Carrington plan, the Serbs boycotted the conference in The Hague. Therefore on 4 November the EC prepared a new version of the plan that did not mention Vojvodina and Kosovo any more; it talked only in general about territories with special status.[84] This proposal did not fulfill the goals of the Serbian leadership either. They still wanted a Yugoslav federation that would remain the only heir of the SFRY and that would unite "all those republics and peoples" that wished to remain in the federation.[85]

The basis for a new settlement was certainly offered by the legal opinion of the Arbitration (Badinter) Commission that argued that since 8 October, Yugoslavia had been a "state in the process of dissolution." Nonetheless, on 8 November the EC proceeded with its strategy of imposing trade sanctions on and threatening the isolation of Yugoslavia in order to press Serbia into accepting its plan and to get both Croatia and Serbia to sign a cease-fire.[86] In this framework the EC also discussed compensatory measures for parties such as Bosnia-Hercegovina and Macedonia, "which do cooperate in a peaceful way towards a comprehensive political solution on the basis of the EC proposals."[87]

Finally, on 23 November in Geneva, Milošević accepted a cease-fire under the auspices of the UN and welcomed the Vance proposal to station UN blue helmet units on occupied Croatian territories. The Croatian government also agreed to this because it was aware that its armed forces would not be able to fight the Serbs on occupied territories while at the same time defending its compatriots in Bosnia-Hercegovina. The Croatian government demanded, however, that the UN troops be stationed at the border with Serbia (the ex-republican border between Croatia and Serbia) and not at the front line, as Milošević demanded.[88]

While the EC member states got actively involved in the crises, the UN continued to remain passive. German Foreign Minister Genscher talked about that in a speech he gave on the occasion of a German–Italian meeting in Venice on 22 and 23 November 1991. He stated that what was going on in Yugoslavia was not a civil war but "an attack on Croatia and therefore it does not concern only the EC and OSCE, but it should be above all the business of the UN Security Council to deal with the problem."[89]

On the demand of the SFRY government, the Security Council finally discussed the situation in Yugoslavia on 27 November 1991. The UNSC unanimously adopted Resolution 721, proposed by the UK, France, and Belgium, empowering Vance to prepare the diplomatic terrain for UN peacekeeping forces on the territory where the fighting had occurred and asking all parties to the conflict to observe a cease-fire and to fulfill UNSC Resolution 713 of 25 September 1991.[90] This resolution sent an additional message: the Soviet Union had unified its views on the use of UN peacekeeping forces with those of the Western powers, and the EC accepted defeat in its attempts to solve the Yugoslav crisis.[91]

The EC defeat convinced the Germans that they should meddle directly in the Yugoslav crisis. On 27 November in an address to the *Bundestag*, German Chancellor Kohl set 24 December 1991 as the date for German recognition of Slovenia and Croatia.[92] This provoked many opposing views within the international community. At a joint press conference in Bonn between Kohl and Mitterand on 15 November 1991, Mitterrand emphasized that this question could not be solved under time pressure and without due caution. He believed that it was first of all a question of guaranteeing minority rights as well as a question of borders.[93]

The EC peace plan accepted the French position that recognition should only come after arrangements for human rights and common relations had been settled. The JNA had begun its withdrawal from Croatia on 28 November. On 2 December 1991 Genscher demanded that the UNSC meet and discuss a possible UN peacekeeping operation in Yugoslavia. On 15 December 1991 the UNSC met again and adopted UNSC Resolution 724 to send a group of observers to Yugoslavia to prepare the terrain for a peacekeeping mission and report on how UNSC Resolution 713 was being fulfilled. All UNSC member states were asked to establish a body to ensure that the weapons embargo would be fulfilled.[94] President Izetbegović made an emotional appeal to Genscher in early December not to recognize Croatia prematurely, for it would mean war in his republic.

Despite all this, at an all-night EC meeting of foreign ministers in Brussels on 15–16 December, Chancellor Kohl refused to budge. Although accused of locking the door and using bullying tactics, Kohl in fact obtained the agreement of Britain, France, and Spain for a compromise on Yugoslavia that would preserve unity among the twelve EC members. In this compromise all six republics of Yugoslavia were eligible for recognition. They required that the republics request recognition formally by 23 December and meet the criteria established by the Badinter Commission, including commitments to continue working toward an overall settlement by 15 January 1992 and to meet UN, EC, and OSCE criteria on the rule of law, democracy, human rights, disarmament, nuclear nonproliferation, regional security, the inviolability of frontiers, and guarantees for the rights of ethnic and nationality groups and minorities.[95] According to Carrington's letter to van den Broek, Germany's success in its campaign for the recognition of Croatia and Slovenia was the death knell to peace negotiations. This is a major unresolved controversy. Some scholars, like team member Marko Hoare, argue:

> In fact, it was precisely the "even-handed" approach of the European powers, their unwillingness to take sides or to intervene in force, that had encouraged the apparently stronger side—Serbia and the JNA—to exploit this vacillation and attack. There were many faults on the Croatian side—above all the demotion of the status of Serbs in Croatia from "nation" to "minority," but ultimately this war involved an attack by one side against the other. Withholding recognition from Croatia, the side that was attacked, "as a reward for a peaceful settlement" could not have worked because it was not Croatia that was blocking a peaceful settlement. . . . Both Norman Cigar and Martin Špegelj have written about how the JNA was on the verge of military collapse in Croatia by late 1991. It was the cease-fire resulting from the diplomatic efforts of Vance and others that allowed the JNA to survive the war in Croatia, technically undefeated, and to regroup to attack Bosnia.

The EC decision in December to recognize Croatia (and Slovenia) was criticized from some quarters for not going sufficiently far in protecting the rights of the Serbs in Croatia, and it left open the question of what would become of the other four republics. The internationalization of the crisis also affected Milošević's calculations. He became convinced that Serbia should look for help from the UN, where the idea of Yugoslavia was still alive. Therefore the federal government of Yugoslavia on 25 December 1991 demanded intervention by the UN blue helmets on occupied Croatian territories and asked de Cuéllar to personally intervene in favor of the peace process "because the EC is acting in favor of secessionists and violates international law."[96]

The Vance plan differed on many issues from the EC plans, which tried in vain to keep Yugoslavia intact. It foresaw a cease-fire on all territories in question, 10,000 blue helmets, and the creation of United Nations Protected Areas (UNPA) in those territories where the Serbs lived in Croatia and that were until then occupied by JNA. Meanwhile, the JNA would withdraw from Croatia.[97] Tudjman proclaimed the entrance of blue helmets into Croatian territory as an important victory for Croatia. He was ready to fulfill the Vance plan to please the international community, which demanded this in order to recognize Croatia as an independent state.[98] Milošević acted similarly and accepted blue helmets in Croatia. We presume that he believed that it represented the first step toward a plebiscite to enable the annexation of ethnically Serb parts of Croatia to Serbia.[99] The other possibility is that he thought that the introduction of UN troops would freeze existing lines of confrontation, which would, in time, transform themselves naturally into new, de facto international borders.[100]

Remarkably, the Belgrade regime acted against the leadership of the Serbs of Krajina. Milošević and his collaborators believed that Vance and the new UN secretary-general, Boutros Boutros-Ghali from Egypt, were "realists," that is, pro-Serb. Vance and Boutros-Ghali still treated the Yugoslav wars as a civil war and not as an international war that could threaten international peace. UN Resolution 727 of 8 January 1992 also reflected this approach and authorized the sending of fifty military liaison officers to promote the maintenance of the cease-fire, as if this were a fight between two armed factions.[101] From the beginning of the conflict, Slovenes and Croats considered the actions of the Yugoslav army and Serb insurgents as acts of aggression on the newly established states of Slovenia and Croatia.[102]

These first days of January 1992 were quite interesting in the reactions of the international community toward the Yugoslav crisis. They were also important because Milošević's regime also declared its (war) aims. Milošević wanted to create a rump Yugoslavia that would also be the only lawful successor of the former SFRY, in which all those who wanted to keep their Yugoslav citizenship would live. Actually it was an open call to arms to create Great Serbia and to introduce new wars.

On 13 January 1992, the Vatican recognized Slovenia and Croatia, and the next day the Badinter Commission submitted its expected evaluation of the candidates for recognition. The commission recommended immediate recognition of Slovenia and Macedonia; recognition of Croatia conditioned on certain assurances concerning democratic principles, national minorities, and border protections; and a referendum for Bosnia-Hercegovina, which, crucially, was to be valid only if all three communities (Serb, Croat, and Muslim) participated in significant numbers. (The application from Kosovo was considered invalid because it did not come from a recognized republic.)[103]

Realistically, the commission's opinion did not have much influence on the decisions of those EC states that had demanded it. When they recognized Croatia and Slovenia on 15 January 1992, those states demanded that Croatia incorporate the necessary assurances into its constitution. Croatia gave them only a written promise to comply, and such compliance did not happen until a change of regime in Croatia in the year 2000.

In April 1992 the United States finally recognized Slovenia, Croatia, and Bosnia-Hercegovina within its current borders. Serbia (with autonomous regions Kosovo and Vojvodina) and Montenegro formed a new entity, the Federal Republic of Yugoslavia (FRY), which Milošević hoped would encompass also the ethnically Serb territories in neighboring Croatia and Bosnia-Hercegovina.

Macedonia had to wait for international recognition because the Greeks opposed it on the grounds that the international community should not recognize a state that had irredentist objectives. Ironically, the EC had asked the Montenegrin government to request recognition, and the Badinter commission had excluded any connection between the name of Macedonia and irredentist demands toward neighbors.[104] Greece believed that the name was its exclusive property and that the very use of this name by the former Yugoslav republic showed the irredentist plans of that state toward Aegean Macedonia. Because both states were not able to solve these problems, Greece in 1992 introduced economic sanctions against Macedonia and hindered the formation of EU policy toward Macedonia.[105] Eventually, the UN intervened, and the foreign ministers of Greece and Macedonia met in New York and signed an agreement (on 13 September 1992) by which Greece rescinded its economic sanctions, but Macedonia was required to change its state flag because it contained Greek symbols. By 1993 they were able to solve some disagreements on the name of the new state. Greece accepted a temporary name for Macedonia—the Former Yugoslav Republic of Macedonia—and Macedonia became a member of the UN in April 1993 under this name.[106]

There were also quite a few unsolved questions regarding the new Macedonian state's relationship with the FRY, especially concerning the border. At the request of the Macedonian government and Macedonian émigré organizations in the United States and Canada,[107] NATO peacekeeping forces of 1,000 American soldiers were stationed at the border of Macedonia with the FRY to prevent war from spreading to Macedonia (UNSC Resolution 795, 9 December 1992).[108]

Eventually the UN introduced economic sanctions against the FRY with Security Council Resolution 757/1992, which isolated the FRY from the rest of the world.[109] This "third Yugoslavia" soon got new political leadership. The first president of the FRY was the "spiritual father of the Serbs," Dobrica Ćosić, while an American businessman of Serb descent, Milan Panić, became the new Yugoslav prime minister. Panić was a surprise for everyone. Milošević chose him because he thought that Panić would be the right man to help fight the international isolation of the FRY, whereas the U.S. government counted on Panić to help the international community find a solution to the crisis in the former Yugoslavia. Thus the State Department gave permission for Panić, an American citizen, to head the government of the FRY.[110] Panić supported the attempts of the international community to find a peaceful solution to the Yugoslav crisis, especially at the 1992 conference in London, but Panić only remained in office until he lost the election for president of the Republic of Serbia on 20 December 1992. A few days after the election he had to resign.

The main problem for the international community was Bosnia-Hercegovina, the only republic of the former Yugoslavia in which none of the Yugoslav ethno-nations had an absolute majority in the population. The constitutive nations of Bosnia-Hercegovina in 1991 were the Bosniaks (i.e., Bosnian Muslims, 43.7 percent), Serbs (31.4 percent), and Croats (17.3 percent).[111] The Muslims had a majority in central Bosnia, in northeastern Bosnia (south of Tuzla), in Cazinska krajina (northwestern corner of Bosnia), and in northern Hercegovina. They were a relative majority of the cities of these regions. The Serbs had a majority in Bosanska krajina, Semberija, and eastern Hercegovina. Croats were a majority in western and central Hercegovina, in parts of Posavina (northern Bosnia), and in some parts of central Bosnia.

Although the Serbs, Croats, and Muslims traditionally lived together, the demands by nationalistic politicians that Bosnia-Hercegovina be reorganized into homogeneous national territories inevitably required the division of ethnically mixed territories into their Serb, Croat, and Muslim parts. Due to estranged interethnic relations, the president of the presidency of Bosnia-Hercegovina, Alija Izetbegović, had already in July 1991 demanded that UN peacekeepers be stationed in Bosnia-Hercegovina. Because of the philosophy of the UN, which did not want to intervene to prevent the start of violence but only to "stop" it once it broke out, Izetbegović's proposal did not succeed. Also, demands by some Western diplomats for an international protectorate over Bosnia-Hercegovina remained unanswered.

International peacemakers called a conference on Bosnia in the beginning of February 1992 to find a comprehensive political settlement under the auspices of the EC troika and its chair, José Cutileiro from Portugal. Cutileiro's plan did not advocate the division of Bosnia-Hercegovina into three entities but only into "spheres of interest" of the three ethnic groups. In principle, this plan was approved by Croats and Muslims as well as by the Serbs. Thus, instead of establishing a constitution for Bosnia-Hercegovina, or a constituent assembly to write one, the EC negotiators accepted the view that the internal conflict was ethnically based and that the power-sharing arrangement of the coalition should translate into a triune state in which the three main ethnic parties (Party for Democratic Action, *Stranka demokratske akcije* [SDA]; Serbian Democratic Party, *Srpska demokratska stranka* [SDS]; and Croatian Democratic Union, *Hrvatska demokratska zajednica* [HDZ]) divided territorial control among themselves. By the time of the Lisbon conference all three parties expected ethnic cantonization of the republic into three parts.

At a meeting in Lisbon on 23 February, EC Chair Cutileiro showed a map that divided Bosnia-Hercegovina in a way that Croats and Muslims controlled about 56 percent of the territory and Serbs 44 percent. No one was happy with this plan. Serbs wanted a larger percentage of the territory; Croats did not achieve what they wanted (because of their low numbers); and Muslims would be affected badly by any territorial division.[112] Therefore, at the meeting convened by Cutileiro in Sarajevo on 27 February, Izetbegović again talked about a united multiethnic Bosnia to be comprised of citizens and not nations. As a result, the agreement on a confederated Bosnia-Hercegovina—which representatives of the Bosnian Serbs made a precondition for Bosnian-Serb participation in a referendum on independence for Bosnia-Hercegovina—was not signed.

In spite of this, Bosniaks, in cooperation with Bosnian Croats, issued writs for a referendum, which took place on 29 February and 1 March. Bosnian Serbs boycotted the referendum, and thus the turnout was 63.04 percent. In spite of the fact that more than 99 percent of those who participated voted for the independence of Bosnia-Hercegovina, this percentage was still too small to cement a new state community.[113] When the government of Bosnia-Hercegovina declared the results of the referendum and, on its basis, the independence of Bosnia-Hercegovina (on 3 March), the first armed clashes occurred in Sarajevo. The Lisbon talks were forgotten. An overwhelming majority of the Serbs were sure that they wanted to stay in Yugoslavia, whereas a similarly overwhelming majority of the Croats and Muslims were sure that they wanted to leave.

During this period of complicated interethnic relations in Bosnia-Hercegovina, the international community, especially the United States, had to deal with the problem of the international recognition of Bosnia-Hercegovina and Macedonia. After a great deal of discussion, the foreign ministers of the EC countries and the U.S. resolved that the EC countries would recognize Bosnia-Hercegovina on 6 April and that the United States would recognize Slovenia and Croatia as well.[114]

At the same time, Lord Carrington and Cutileiro continued to try to find a peaceful solution to the crisis in Bosnia-Hercegovina. In spite of an outbreak of armed clashes, the international community still thought that the Bosnian crisis could be solved by peaceful means. This can be confirmed by the fact that on 13 March Sarajevo became the headquarters of the general staff of UNPROFOR under the leadership of Canadian General Lewis MacKenzie.[115] The leaders of all sides, Muslim Alija Izetbegović, Serb Radovan Karadžić, and Croat Mate Boban even succeeded in accepting a "declaration on constitutional principles for a republic" in Lisbon on 18 March 1992. According to the declaration, Bosnia-Hercegovina would be comprised of three "constitutive entities which should be based on ethnic principles; the constitution of its geographic territories should also be based on economic, physical-geographical and other criteria."[116]

Emboldened by the growing U.S. pressure on Europe for immediate recognition of Bosnian sovereignty and, perhaps, by promises of support from Middle Eastern leaders (or by the negative implications of the accord for Bosnia and the Muslim nation), President Izetbegović reneged on his commitment to the document within a week.[117] He was followed by the Croat leader Mate Boban, who saw the opportunity to gain more territory in a new round of negotiations. Izetbegović rejected Cutileiro's plan because it would neglect Bosniaks' interests, demanding cantonization of Bosnia-Hercegovina as *conditio sine qua non* for its international recognition.[118]

Some scholars claim that Izetbegović changed his approval of this plan under the influence of U.S. Ambassador Zimmermann, who encouraged him to resist Serbian and European pressures.[119] In an interview published in 1994 in the Belgrade weekly *Vreme,* Zimmermann denied this but said that "he asked Izetbegović why he signed something that he did not agree to."[120] The conversations of Zimmermann with Izetbegović were one of the first signs that the U.S. would become more involved in the Yugoslav drama. This was partially the result of criticism that it had not been providing leadership of the Western world and partly the result of intensive lobbying in Washington by Bosnian representatives.[121]

When the representatives of all three constituent nations of Bosnia-Hercegovina met again in Brussels on 30 March, it was clear that war could not be avoided because the Serbian side was unwilling to talk any more. Under these circumstances, the EC recognized the independence of Bosnia-Hercegovina on 6 April 1992. The U.S. followed the next day. The Assembly of the Serb Nation in Bosnia-Hercegovina soon declared the independence of the Serb Republic of Bosnia-Hercegovina (later renamed *Republika Srpska*, Serb Republic).

In the spring of 1992, Europe's bloodiest conflict since World War II began in ethnically mixed Bosnia-Hercegovina. From the very beginning of the war, the international community tried to stop the fighting and to find a peaceful solution to all questions. All the peace plans suggested by the UN and the EC/EU were based on the condition that Bosniaks would not be forced to leave their homes in those territories where they were a majority before the war. By May–June 1992, the issue of national sovereignty was beginning to confront Western governments with a dilemma: strategically Bosnia-Hercegovina was perhaps not terribly significant, but there was a growing humanitarian crisis for all the world to see.

The so-called CNN effect influenced acceptance of many decisions in attempts to reach peace. One such event, which shocked viewers all over the world, happened on 27 May in Sarajevo, where sixteen people were killed and dozens more were wounded by a grenade on Vasa Miskin Street.[122] Serb media tried to convince the world that Muslims had targeted their own people in order to invoke the sympathy of the West.[123] By the next day, the EC and the United States had reacted by imposing sanctions against the FRY. The UNSC confirmed the economic sanctions the next day. Resolution 757 outlawed Serbia from the international community until the attacks stopped. This resolution also asked NATO to organize supervision over the flow of traffic on the Adriatic Sea to ensure respect for the economic sanctions against the FRY and for the arms embargo on weapons for all of the regions of the former Yugoslavia.[124]

At the same time, conditions in Sarajevo under siege worsened. UNPRO-FOR could do nothing, in spite of the fact that catastrophe was anticipated. Some blame this on the UN secretary-general himself, who looked upon the war in the former Yugoslavia as "the war of the rich."[125] However, many in the West agitated for doing something as soon as possible. The Islamic world also reacted sharply to the persecution of its fellow believers in Bosnia-Hercegovina. Forty-seven member states of the Islamic Conference Organization cut diplomatic ties with the FRY. Saudi King Fahd asked President Bush in a special letter to do something for Bosnian Muslims.[126]

To calm down public opinion, the officers of UNPROFOR who remained in Sarajevo wanted to convince the Bosniak government and the Bosnian Serbs to agree on security for the airport in Sarajevo so that humanitarian aid could be delivered. Bosnian Serbs promised to withdraw their troops. This victory convinced UN Secretary-General Boutros-Ghali to suggest to the UNSC on 6 June that it widen the UNPROFOR mandate in Bosnia-Hercegovina and strengthen the forces of the UN with one battalion. Thus Resolution 759 was passed, in which the UNSC noted the agreement of all parties to the reopening of the Sarajevo airport for humanitarian purposes under the executive authority of the UN and demanded that all parties and others concerned immediately create the necessary conditions for the unimpeded delivery of humanitarian supplies to Sarajevo and other destinations in Bosnia-Hercegovina.

Meanwhile, the attacks of Serb forces convinced U.S. Secretary of State James Baker to consider military intervention. He constructed "Game Plan: New Steps in Connection with Bosnia." This would enable humanitarian aid to reach Sarajevo "with all possible means." President Bush supported Baker in this effort, whereas U.S. Secretary of Defense Richard Cheney and General Colin Powell, chairman of the Joint Chiefs of Staff, were against the plan. Although Bush theoretically had the last word, "bureaucratic-military obstruction" made it impossible for a feasibility study of this plan. This was Baker's last attempt to influence events in the Balkans. Later he was named leader of the campaign for the reelection of George Bush, and Lawrence Eagleburger replaced him.[127]

The Serb army attacks and Baker's proposals made it possible for European leaders to sharpen their views. In concurrence with a German proposal they demanded the opening of the Sarajevo airport and declared that they would still try to resolve the crisis peacefully. Nevertheless, they did not eliminate the possibility of the use of military means if the Serbs continued to block the flow of humanitarian aid.[128] French President Mitterrand annulled this decision. Without consulting either his European or American partners, he flew into Sarajevo to support his understanding that the conflict in Bosnia should be viewed not as aggression but as civil war.[129]

The international community had to deal with the question, were the wars in Croatia and Bosnia civil wars or international conflicts (for which the FRY would be guilty of the charge of aggression)? Academic and popular literature on the war in Bosnia still remains deeply divided on this basic issue. Supporters of the external aggression thesis were strong proponents of preserving and developing Bosnia-Hercegovina as a single, united state, whereas those who believed the 1992–1995 conflict was primarily a civil war demonstrated a range of attitudes from cautious neutrality to active hostility in their analysis of the post-1992 state.[130]

Certainly to the outside world the war appeared as a conflict among neighbors, sometimes in the same village or town, and presented the ugly traits usually associated with such a war. Most researchers, however, believe that this should not distract attention from the fact that the rebellion of the Croatian and Bosnian Serbs could not have taken place, and above all could not have been successful in the beginning, without the decisive involvement of the Serbian-led Yugoslav army. Among the EC member states, Germany was adamant that this was blatant aggression by one Yugoslav republic and one Yugoslav nation against another and should not be tolerated by the international community. This, however, did not reflect a naive and one-sided good-versus-evil view that demonized the Serbs, as some critics of German policy like to pretend when trying to evade a discussion of the objective foundations of Germany's views on the conflict.

Certainly international recognition of Slovenia and Croatia in January 1992, followed by the recognition of Bosnia-Hercegovina in April 1992 and the recognition of Macedonia in April 1993, was very important because from then on one could talk only about international conflict and not civil war in the former Yugoslavia. Nevertheless, in the summer of 1992 it appeared that most Western diplomats still considered it as a civil war. From the Serb point of view, of course, it was a civil war. Few were surprised, therefore, when French President Mitterrand flew into Sarajevo on 28 June 1992 to observe what was going on in Bosnia-Hercegovina and to conclude that it was a civil war that could only be solved with negotiations and not with force.

The international media supported Mitterrand's bravery in traveling to Sarajevo; however, diplomats did not. English Foreign Minister Douglas Hurd remarked that this was the "brave gesture of a president who is getting old."[131] The reactions in Belgrade and in the Bosnian Republika Srpska were more positive. Five months later, General Momir Talić, commander of the First Corps of the Serbian Bosnian army, in an interview for Paris's *Le Monde*, declared that Karadžić successfully used Mitterrand's *coup de theater* to the Bosnian Serbs' own advantage. Serb troops withdrew from the airport, as UNSC Resolution No.

761 of 29 June demanded. International public opinion seemed convinced that military intervention was not necessary.[132] Already on that day the first plane with humanitarian aid landed at Sarajevo airport.[133] The airlift soon played the role—as one Bosniak journalist observed—of morphine with which the West provided aid to the victims of war. At the same time, the West prolonged the war by giving Bosniaks the possibility of surviving but not of defending themselves.[134]

In the summer of 1992 greater alarm all over the world was provoked by *Newsday* correspondent Roy Gutman, who publicized his discovery of Serb concentration camps in northern and western Bosnia.[135] Gutman's articles on Muslim and Croatian Bosnian prisoners in concentration camps and his photographs of living skeletons in a concentration camp in Omarska (north of Banja Luka) forced the international community to demand action at once. One day before Gutman's article was published, the U.S. Department of State admitted knowing about the described horrors, but in a special statement it also said that there was nothing the U.S. could do to prevent them.

Once television stations from all over the world started to transmit photographs from the concentration camps (there were 94 of them with 400,000 prisoners[136]), President George Bush called a press conference at Patterson Air Force Base in Colorado to condemn ethnic cleansing.[137] The Balkan question also became a burning question in the U.S. presidential campaign because it gave Bill Clinton many opportunities to criticize Bush and to condemn the persecution and killing of people because of their ethnicity.[138]

Already in the summer of 1992 the UNSC accepted Resolution 770, which demanded that unimpeded and continuous access to all camps, prisons, and detention centers be granted immediately to the International Red Cross and that all detainees receive humane treatment. In addition, the UNSC also asked the member states and regional institutions to use all necessary means to enable the flow of humanitarian aid to Bosnia-Hercegovina.[139] Thus, the UNSC indirectly allowed for the use of force. The same day, the UNSC also passed Resolution 771, which "strongly condemns violations of international humanitarian law, including those involved in the process of ethnic cleansing.[140]

At a London conference on Yugoslavia that started on 26 August, UN Secretary-General Boutros-Ghali and British Prime Minister John Major offered a strong condemnation of the FRY. It soon became clear, however, that the Western powers wanted to continue a policy of noninterference and that they did not plan to revoke the arms embargo on the territory of the former Yugoslavia. The conference ended on 27 August, when all the participants accepted a statement of principles. But these principles contained all the contradictions and equivocation on the problem of national self-determination and the collapse of a state that had characterized Western action during the previous fourteen months.[141]

After this conference did not produce the desired results, the international community started to coordinate its efforts. Cyrus Vance, as representative of the UN secretary-general, and David Owen, former UK foreign secretary, became cochairs of the new International Conference on the Former Yugoslavia (ICFY). ICFY thus joined the other international organizations that were operating to find a solution to the Yugoslav crisis.

In mid-September Lord Owen and Cyrus Vance visited Sarajevo, Zagreb, and Belgrade and, in consultation with political leaders there, agreed to new negotiations, which started in Geneva at the end of September. Izetbegović continued to defend a unified and centralized Bosnia-Hercegovina, which Western diplomats looked on as an irrational option. Soon afterward the military alliance between the Bosnian government and Croatia began to break down, and it officially ended on 24 October. The consequences of this were clear by November, when fighting erupted between Bosnian Croat forces and the Bosnian government. Unfortunately, this new outbreak of violence in Bosnia-Hercegovina confirmed the thesis of those diplomats who believed that the Bosnian War was the result of irrational tribal conflict.[142]

On 6 October 1992 the UNSC unanimously passed Resolution 780, which requested the secretary-general to establish, as a matter of urgency, an impartial commission of experts with a view to providing him with its conclusions on the evidence of grave breaches of the Geneva conventions and other violations of humanitarian law committed in the territory of the former Yugoslavia.[143] With Resolution 781, which was passed 9 October, the Security Council decided to establish a ban on military flights in the airspace of Bosnia-Hercegovina, to examine without delay all the information brought to its attention concerning the implementation of the ban, and in the case of violations, to consider urgently further measures necessary to enforce it. This resolution, as well as Resolution 786 (adopted on 10 November, which reconfirmed prohibition against the use of aircraft and helicopters), did not have any special effect, however, because Boutros-Ghali and UNPROFOR commanders did not want to provoke the Serbs; it was thus accepted only as a warning.[144]

The Bosnian Serb army did not pay attention to all of these resolutions. Because of numerous infringements, from 10 October onward NATO started to use airborne warning and control system (AWACS) airplanes. This support of the UNSC began NATO's active involvement in the war in Bosnia-Hercegovina. During this period, Owen, Vance, and their collaborators tried to find a diplomatic solution to the land dispute that would be acceptable to all sides in the conflict. They tried to prevent the division of Bosnia-Hercegovina into three parts and, in accordance with the directives of the London conference, tried to keep intact its ethnic structure.

Because of the dangers of a widening conflict, U.S. President Bush changed his views toward the Yugoslav crisis. The fact that he lost the November 1992 election to Clinton also played a role. Bush, who stayed in office until 20 January 2003, called an ICFY meeting in Geneva. Lawrence Eagleburger surprised everyone by his condemnation of Serb war crimes and his demand for the establishment of an international court for war crimes on the territory of the former Yugoslavia, where Milošević, Šešelj, Karadžić, General Ratko Mladić, Željko Ražnatović (widely known as Arkan), and others could be tried.[145]

Already on 2 January 1993, a new meeting of the ICFY was called. Vance and Owen showed their peace plan for Bosnia-Hercegovina. The territory of the republic would be divided into ten provinces (three for every ethnic group plus the neutral region of Sarajevo) drawn on the basis of geographic and historical criteria as well as the ethnic mix of the local population. The constitution established a power-sharing agreement among the nations of local and central governments, and a weak, decentralized state. Nonetheless, the negotiators' mandate was still to obtain a cease-fire as rapidly as possible.[146]

Only the Croats agreed to the plan because it promised them 25 percent of the territory of Bosnia-Hercegovina. The Serbs were disappointed because the plan promised them only 42 percent of the Bosnia-Hercegovina territory. They would have to give up 24 percent of already occupied land. The Vance-Owen plan was criticized also by the Bosniaks, who thought that its fulfillment would sooner or later mean a division of Bosnia-Hercegovina between the Serbs and Croats, while it would at the same time encircle the Bosniaks in a ghetto where only traces of religious and cultural autonomy would be maintained.[147]

Vance and Owen renewed negotiations in Geneva on 10 January 1993. This time they changed tactics and bet everything on Milošević. They did not care much about Eagleburger's statement of 16 December 1992 that Milošević ought to be held accountable before a military court tribunal for crimes against humanity. Milošević at first did not want to cooperate, but in the end he came to Geneva.[148] He was forced to cooperate out of fear of NATO intervention, which seemed more and more likely, but also to save the FRY from international isolation. During that time, the Bush administration sent the aircraft carrier *J. F. Kennedy* with accompanying ships of the Sixth U.S. Fleet to the Adriatic.[149] Under the above-mentioned threats and due to the worsened economic situation in which the FRY found itself, Milošević was forced to fundamentally change his foreign policy and tried to convince Karadžić to sign at least the constitutional part of the Vance-Owen plan.[150]

During the course of negotiations in Geneva, newly elected U.S. President Bill Clinton replaced George Bush on 20 January 1993. The sympathies toward the Bosniaks expressed by the new president and his advisers during the presidential campaign were confirmed after he entered the White House. Until the Dayton agreement was reached, however, there was debate within Clinton's administration. Vice President Albert Gore; Anthony Lake; Gore's national security advisor, Leon Fuerth; and U.S. Ambassador to the UN Madeleine Albright pushed for the "lift and strike" approach, which meant sending arms shipments to Sarajevo's Bosniak government while threatening air strikes. The rest of the administration, especially Secretary of State Warren Christopher, Secretary of Defense Leslie Aspin Jr., and Chairman of the Joint Chiefs of Staff Colin Powell opposed this approach.[151] The new administration at first criticized the talks in Geneva because there the attackers were put on an equal footing with those whom they attacked. The Clinton administration also emphasized that the fulfillment of the Vance-Owen plan would mean that the world community for the first time in the twentieth century was rewarding a policy of aggression.[152]

Those who prevailed among the policymakers in the White House were the ones who thought that the U.S. should take the initiative and solve the Bosnian question based on moral values.[153] Therefore, the United States started to search for a possible solution that would include lifting the weapons embargo for the Muslims and having NATO airplanes enforce no-fly zones over Bosnia-Hercegovina. If this could be done, the Serbs would lose at least some of their military superiority.[154] This plan was met by great resistance from the European allies, the Pentagon, and even the Russian government. Critics of the Russian government from nationalistic circles accused President Boris Yeltsin and Russian Foreign Minister Andrei Kozyrev of "treason against their Slavic brothers."[155]

In numerous diplomatic actions and in the U.S. Congress, President Clinton pleaded for the stationing of U.S. troops in Bosnia. At the same time, he was under pressure from military leaders in the Pentagon, who doubted that the bombing of Bosnian Serb positions would be successful. Clinton was actually on the verge of not executing the lift and strike option.[156] The U.S. position was indeed complicated. To explain the outcome of the Dayton agreement it is necessary to trace the triangular interplay among the three sides to Western policy: the British and French (broadly pro-Belgrade), the U.S. Congress (broadly pro-Bosnian), and the Clinton administration (vacillating between the two).

In spite of diplomatic efforts, the fighting and ethnic cleansing in Bosnia-Hercegovina continued. To protect its credibility and to ease the pressure from international public opinion, the UNSC tried to convince the Bosniaks to accept the Vance-Owen plan. However, it also promised that crimes against humanity committed by Serbs and Croats against Bosniaks would not remain unpunished. Thus the UNSC, on a proposal by France, passed UNSC Resolution 808 on 22 February establishing the International Criminal Tribunal for the Former Yugoslavia (ICTY) at The Hague. The next day, after clearing it with UN Secretary-

General Boutros-Ghali, President Clinton proclaimed that the West would airlift supplies to the Bosniaks, who were cut off from their supply lines.[157]

By the end of February 1993 Russia had asked all sides involved to agree to a cease-fire, emphasized its support for the Vance-Owen plan, and expressed its support for a formation of military forces of the UN, in which Russian forces and NATO would cooperate. Negotiations over the Vance-Owen plan continued during March, April, and May 1993, but they stalled repeatedly over the same problem as in Lisbon: the lines of the map. After breaking the plan down into its parts—the constitutional principles, a peace agreement to cease hostilities, the delineation of provincial boundaries, and an interim constitution—the cochairmen obtained signatures from all three parties on only the constitutional principles. The other parts obtained no more than two signatures, in shifting combinations over the course of three months.[158]

Nevertheless, by 25 March, the Bosnian government and Bosnian Croats had signed all four documents, while the Bosnian Serbs refused to sign those provisions related to the provincial boundaries and the interim constitution. The solution was to put pressure on the Bosnian Serbs by turning again to President Milošević. If Bosnian Serbs did not sign by 26 April, sanctions on the FRY would be substantially extended and tightened.[159] Because the Bosnian Serbs resisted, on 31 March the UNSC accepted Resolution 816, which strengthened its enforcement of a no-fly zone over Bosnia-Hercegovina. NATO planes began overflights—Operation Deny Flight—on 12 April.[160]

Karadžić reacted to this with threats of new violence. Only fifteen minutes after the operation began, Bosnian Serbs answered with a new attack on Srebrenica, which caused the passage of UNSC Resolution 819 on 16 April.[161] Because of the new eruption of violence, the UN decided to punish the FRY with economic sanctions.[162] New sanctions meant a real economic catastrophe for the FRY. Milošević realized that he could not fight against the whole world; therefore, he pushed for a compromise in Bosnia-Hercegovina. Milošević was also aware of new debates in the White House, where the president and his advisers were seriously discussing an end to the arms embargo for the Bosniaks and the bombing of Serb military targets.[163]

The possibility of military intervention increased so dramatically that the international community started to discuss a postwar scenario.[164] This convinced Milošević to put pressure on the Bosnian Serbs to accept the Vance-Owen plan. With the assistance of Greek Prime Minister Konstantin Mitsotakis, Milošević convened a meeting at Vouliagmeni, near Athens, on 1–2 May of the cochairmen and Yugoslav, Croatian, and Bosnian leaders: Ćosić, Bulatović, Tudjman, Izetbegović, and Karadžić. After heated discussions the meeting ended with the promise of Karadžić to support the Vance-Owen plan if it were accepted also by the parliament of Republika Srpska.[165]

This parliament met on 5 May and decided on holding a referendum to let the people decide whether to accept the Vance-Owen plan.[166] On 15 and 16 May 1993, 96 percent of all Bosnian Serbs who voted rejected the plan. After this political defeat, Milošević introduced economic sanctions against the Bosnian Serbs and at least on paper closed the border on the Drina River. In reality, FRY resources continued to pour into the Republika Srpska.

The Bosnian Serb refusal of the Vance-Owen agreement surprised the Clinton administration. A meeting of the UNSC was called. The Bosnian Serb actions were condemned even in Moscow,[167] and on 6 May, UNSC Resolution 824 declared that Sarajevo, Tuzla, Žepa, Goražde, Bihać, and Srebrenica should be treated as safe areas[168] (next chapter).

Because of political and military changes that occurred in the spring of 1993 in Bosnia-Hercegovina and in the Federal Republic of Yugoslavia (e.g., the outbreak of fights between Bosniaks and Croatians and the defeat of Milan Panić in the Serbian election) as well as in the international community (Cyrus Vance's resignation), the EC foreign ministers decided to start a new cycle of peace negotiations among the warring Bosnian sides. Between June and September 1993 a new peace plan was formulated. Called the Owen-Stoltenberg plan, after the cochairmen, it returned to the ethnic principles of Lisbon and divided Bosnia into a confederation of three ethnic states.[169] In spite of the fact that a solution on division into three parts was in place, many questions were left unsolved. The most burning of these concerned how much territory Bosniaks would get because they controlled only 10 percent of Bosnia-Hercegovina but demanded 40–45 percent of its territory.[170] In a radio broadcast on 31 July Izetbegović announced that the Muslims would now have to fight for territory to ensure their survival as a nation.[171] In this unsettled climate, on 18 August in Geneva, Owen and Stoltenberg presented their plan for the future of Bosnia-Hercegovina. It included maps according to which Serbs would control 52 percent of the territory; Croats, 19 percent; and Bosniaks, 30 percent.

On 20 August the Bosnian government rejected the plan and brought negotiations to a standstill. At the same time it appeared that there were efforts by some Muslim politicians to create a Muslim state. Non-Muslims were expelled from villages and towns; Muslim schools sprang up to give children religious training (financed by Arab Muslim states); and circles within the government demonstrated increasing radicalism.

In the autumn of 1993 the war intensified. The violence reached one of its peaks on 9 November 1993, when Croats continued their merciless siege of Mostar, willfully destroying its sixteenth-century bridge, a symbol of Bosnian unity and culture.[172] This action shocked the world and began to have an immediate impact on the policies of the international community.

Under increasing pressure from front-line states, particularly Hungary, to relieve the costs of the sanctions to their economies and political stability, the EC began to discuss terms under which sanctions on the FRY might be gradually lifted.

The first sign of change was an increased interest by the Clinton administration in the Bosnian war. One reason for this was the success of the nationalist opposition in the Russian elections. Their leader, Vladimir Zhirinovsky, attacked the foreign policy of Yeltsin and Kozyrev and at the same time promised "Serb brothers, traditional allies of Russia" all the help they needed.[173] The Clinton administration was aware of the fact that the Bosnian question was a salient issue in Russian internal politics, and it had to consider how to prevent tensions between Russia and the U.S. because of the Balkan crisis. With the help of the Vatican and Bonn, the United States started to plan an intervention that would lead to peace between the Croats and the Bosniaks, isolate the Serbs, and strengthen Macedonian independence.[174]

One of the main reasons for the failure of international policy in Bosnia-Hercegovina was the effort of many to view all sides as equally responsible, which some criticized as fruitless passivity.[175] By opposing air strikes on Serbian targets, Boutros-Ghali was in reality supporting the Bosnian Serbs, who were happy with his policy. At an international conference in Kuala Lumpur, Izetbegović said that among thirty UNSC resolutions on Bosnia-Hercegovina, only the one that prohibited the Bosniaks to be armed was implemented.[176] Boutros-Ghali tried to find excuses for his policy by saying that NATO's attacks would be more dangerous for UN troops on the ground than for the Serbs. As a former Egyptian foreign minister during the Tito period, he seemed to suffer from "Yugo-nostalgia."[177]

The unease over the ineffectiveness of the international community showed also in Brussels at a NATO summit on 10–11 January 1994, which U.S. President Bill Clinton attended.[178] At the end of the meeting a communiqué for the public was issued in which NATO threatened the Bosnian Serbs again with air strikes if they did not stop the siege of Sarajevo, permit a rotation of UN troops (from Canadian to Dutch) in Srebrenica that the Bosnian Serb Army was blocking, and permit the use of the Tuzla airport for UN humanitarian aid.[179] The NATO summit did not decide when these air strikes would occur if the Serbs did not fulfill their demands. The French response (in reverse of their previous position) was to mobilize Boutros-Ghali, persuading him to reverse his position of mid-January and agree to start air strikes by 26 January if those demands were not met. The French did that under the pressure of public opinion in their own land.[180] In spite of this French viewpoint, Clinton still doubted the readiness of the European allies to act. At the end of the summit, he told them not to threaten air strikes if they did not think they could fulfill the threat. He said: "At stake is not only the security of the Sarajevo townspeople and the possibility to end this horrible war, but also the credibility of the [NATO] alliance."[181]

This new ICFY tactic yielded an area of wide cease-fire among all three parties in Bosnia-Hercegovina and also between the Croatian government and Krajina Serbs—a Christmas truce from 23 December 1993 to 15 January 1994. In January, a new UNPROFOR commander for Bosnia-Hercegovina, British Lieutenant General Michael Rose, committed himself to building on the diplomatic progress of his predecessor in Sarajevo, Belgian Lieutenant General Francis Briquemont, with a "robust" approach to implementing its mandate.

And then the tragedy of 6 February 1994 took place. A 120-millimeter mortar fired into the Markale market in Sarajevo killed at least 68 people and wounded 197, providing the psychological shock necessary to mobilize diplomatic efforts from many sides. Aided by a NATO ultimatum to the Bosnian Serb army issued on 9 February to "end the siege of Sarajevo" by withdrawing or regrouping under UNPROFOR control, all heavy weapons from an exclusion zone around Sarajevo of twenty kilometers had to be removed within ten days or be subjected immediately to air strikes. The first of three negotiated cease-fires over the next six weeks appeared to create momentum for peace "from the bottom up."[182] NATO's ultimatum to the Bosnian Serbs was one of the decisive factors in the quest for a solution to the Bosnian crisis because the West turned from peacekeeping to peacemaking.[183]

Once NATO had addressed this ultimatum to the Bosnian Serbs—without informing Moscow about it—Zhirinovsky announced that air strikes on Serb positions in Bosnia-Hercegovina would mean a "declaration of war with Russia . . . and the beginning of World War III."[184] Russian foreign minister Kozyrev also wrote in a letter to Boutros-Ghali that "any type of air raids . . . could provoke the worst consequences."[185]

In the meantime, part of the international community worked toward an agreement between the Croats and Bosniaks to be negotiated and implemented as soon as possible.[186] The impulse for agreement was initiated by Pope John Paul II, the Croatian Catholic Church, and Bosnian Franciscans. It was supported also by Turkish, German, and especially U.S. diplomats.[187] President Clinton's special representative, Charles Redman, and U.S. Ambassador to Croatia Peter W. Galbraith presented Croatian President Franjo Tudjman with plans for a Muslim-Croatian federation in Bosnia-Hercegovina. With various threats (e.g., economic sanctions) they convinced Tudjman to give up, at least temporarily, the idea of a division of Bosnia-Hercegovina and persuaded the warring Bosnian Croats and Bosniaks to stop fighting each other.[188]

For perhaps the first time, the U.S. and other members of the international community appeared to mean business. With the help of Russian diplomats and threats of air strikes, they convinced the Bosnian Serbs to withdraw some of their heavy weaponry from the hills surrounding Sarajevo.[189] In the first armed action ever by NATO, two F-16 fighter jets shot down four Yugoslav planes that had violated the no-fly zone over Bosnia-Hercegovina. This time, even the Russians thought that the action was justified.[190]

The actions of the international community brought results. On 2 March 1994 the international mediators practically forced the Muslims and Bosnian Croats to sign the Washington framework agreement, which unified the territories under their control into the Federation of Bosnia-Hercegovina. After some days of Croat-Bosniak negotiations in Vienna, they formally signed the so-called Washington agreement in the U.S. capital on 16 March 1994; in addition to Tudjman and Izetbegović, President Clinton also attended.[191] Because of the federation, the Bosnian Croats would permit supplies to flow again to the Bosnian government (including weapons and materiel for the army) along routes they controlled, and joint operations could be encouraged between the Croatian Defense Council (*Hrvatsko vjeće odbrane,* HVO) and government forces.[192]

While providing a welcome cease-fire and the revival of commerce through the opening of routes in areas controlled by the federation, the Washington agreement also encouraged an intensification of the Bosnian government military offensive during the spring, confirmed General Mladić's interpretation of the discussion of August 1993 that Serbs were at war with NATO, and returned negotiations on a peace agreement to the situation that existed before May 1993. Now the Bosnian Croats and the Bosnian government favored peace, whereas the Bosnian Serbs were again in the opposition. To ward off what appeared to be a death blow to ICFY from U.S. initiatives and to avoid the fate of the Hague conference in December 1991 and the Lisbon negotiations in March 1992, the cochairmen proposed to set up a negotiating group of the major powers. This contact group, composed of representatives from the United States, Great Britain, France, Germany, and Russia, was to work out the missing ingredient to a general peace—an agreement between the new Bosnian–Croat federation and the Bosnian Serbs. The EU and the UN were excluded from the negotiating process in hopes of making it easier to negotiate.[193]

In the summer of 1994, the group emerged with its peace plan, which recognized the existing borders of Bosnia-Hercegovina as a whole but more importantly allocated 51 percent of the territory to the Muslim-Croat federation and 49 percent to the Bosnian Serbs, effectively reducing the latter's previous gains by one-third. The plan was issued to all sides with a fortnight's deadline to reply.[194] After the Bosnian Serbs rejected the contact group plan, the UNSC adopted two resolutions in September.

Resolution 942 introduced economic sanctions against the Bosnian Serbs and prohibited any diplomatic contacts with their leaders. Resolution 943 suspended the restrictions on travel and sports imposed by earlier resolutions on the

FRY for an initial period of 100 days from the receipt by the council of a report from the secretary-general that the authorities of the FRY had effectively closed its international border with the Republic of Bosnia-Hercegovina with respect to all goods except foodstuffs, medical supplies, and clothing for essential humanitarian needs.[195]

In the United States, new attacks by Serbs on Bihać triggered yet another assault on the administration's policy and sharp criticism of the Europeans, particularly the British. The attack on Clinton administration policy was led by incoming Senate Majority Leader Bob Dole and by Newt Gingrich, the incoming House majority leader. Both demanded UN withdrawal, U.S. air strikes, and the arming and training of the army of the Sarajevo government. In order to stave off Congressional demands for more concrete action, the U.S. administration unilaterally withdrew from policing the arms embargo in mid-November 1994.[196]

Despite seventy-seven cease-fires from March 1992 until May 1994 and numerous diplomatic missions, in particular by Richard Holbrooke, U.S. assistant secretary of state for European and Canadian affairs, ethnic cleansing continued in Bosnia-Hercegovina. However, the sequence of events that was to change fundamentally the dynamic of the conflict and immensely enhance the prospects for peace began with the fall of western Slavonia in Croatia. On 1–2 May 1995, Croatian armed forces mounted a surprise attack known as Operation Flash, which successfully reclaimed for the Croatian government control of UN Sector West (western Slavonia), which was part of the Serb-controlled Krajina.[197]

The fall of western Slavonia showed that all the fanfare about a union between the Serbs in Bosnia and Croatia was a hollow boast. But the Croatian Serb authorities ignored the lesson. After four years of rejecting any compromise and expunging all traces of Croat history in their domain, they would not alter course. The EU, the U.S., and Russia did not ignore the lesson. Keen to forestall another Croat incursion, the diplomatic representatives of the U.S., UK, EU, and UN stationed in Zagreb pressed a special peace plan for Croatia that was intended to rectify the loopholes in the Vance plan. First conceived in late 1994, the so-called Z4 plan attempted to reconcile Croatia's insistence on preserving the integrity of its frontiers with Serb insistence on self-determination.[198] Tudjman agreed gingerly, though only as a starting point for discussions; Milošević supported the agreement. But Croatian Serb leaders, Milan Martić and Milan Babić, rejected it outright.

After the Serbs in Slavonia were defeated, Bosnian Serbs captured Žepa and Srebrenica. The diffidence of the international community manifested itself once again as the Srebrenica "safe" area's 300-man Dutch "protection force" allowed the Bosnian Serb victors to round up and massacre almost 8,000 Bosnian Muslim men and boys.[199] International outrage forced a new resolve that quickly led to the resolution of the Croatian and Bosnian conflicts and, following a second Markale marketplace attack, a NATO air campaign against the Serb positions that brought the Serbs back to the peace table. By then, Milošević's dream of Greater Serbia had been crushed in Croatia. On 4 August 1995, Croat formations estimated at 150,000 men launched a coordinated series of around thirty attacks into the former UN Sectors North and South along a 300-kilometer front.[200]

This operation, known as Operation Storm, lasted only five days. Knin, the capital of the Krajina, fell on the second day. With Operation Storm, the Croatian army regained control over most of the territories of the RSK.[201] Croatia was again unified, with the exception of Baranja and eastern Slavonia (Croatian *Podunavlje*). An offensive of united Croat-Bosniak forces against the Bosnian Serbs continued in Bosnia-Hercegovina.

On 8 September 1995, the foreign ministers of Bosnia-Hercegovina, Croatia, and the FRY, meeting in Geneva, agreed that Bosnia-Hercegovina would remain a country divided into two entities—a Croatian-Muslim entity and a Serbian one. In October of the same year a cease-fire started. On 1 November 1995 peace negotiations began at an American air force base near Dayton, Ohio, ending with the signing of a peace agreement in December 1995 in Paris.[202] The signatories of this agreement were Izetbegović of Bosnia-Hercegovina, Milošević of Serbia, and Tudjman of Croatia.

The reactions to the signing of the Dayton agreement were the most euphoric in Belgrade, where the people honored Milošević as a visionary, and in Zagreb, where Tudjman evaluated it as a "victory of Croatian diplomacy" because the Croats lost the least of all the belligerents in the conflict. In Bosnia-Hercegovina there were many who had doubts about the peace.[203] Dayton did not hold the warring parties accountable for the return of refugees and apprehension of war criminals. Nor was either the explicit responsibility of the 60,000 NATO-led troops that had been charged with maintaining order and protecting Bosnia-Hercegovina's internationally recognized frontiers. In accordance with a special agreement between NATO and Russia, 2,000 Russian soldiers would be stationed in Tuzla. Having averted another human catastrophe like Srebrenica, the great powers were once again unwilling to get too deeply involved in affairs in which they had no compelling national interest.

Their diffidence was most evident in the decision not to enforce the Dayton articles that mandated the apprehension and transfer of individuals who had been indicted by the ICTY. The first signs surfaced right after the initialing of the draft agreement at Dayton, when officials of the U.S. Department of Defense inserted language in the final text that relieved the multinational "Implementation

Force" (IFOR) of responsibility for apprehending indictees, except when they encountered them "during the normal course of their duties." The wording came as a surprise to the U.S. negotiating team headed by Ambassador Richard Holbrooke, which had anticipated that indictees like Bosnian Serb President Radovan Karadžić and commanding General Ratko Mladić would be detained within a month or two.[204] Instead, the high priority that the Pentagon attached to "force preservation" prevailed in the ensuing confrontation with an increasingly frustrated State Department as President Clinton weighed the political consequences that U.S. casualties would have on the broad but shallow popular support for U.S. participation in the military occupation of Bosnia.

The gap between the promise of Dayton and the tactical avoidance of ICTY fugitives by U.S. and other IFOR military units became evident as the U.S., Britain, and France led sixty thousand troops into Bosnia during the winter of 1995–1996. Whereas White House Press Spokesman Mike McCurry announced that pictures of all of the indictees were being distributed at IFOR checkpoints, the photographs were posted only at the headquarters compounds far removed from the checkpoints and, presumably, from the fugitives themselves. When a Bosnian-Croat fugitive, Miroslav Bralo, turned up at a checkpoint in Vitez and offered to surrender, Dutch IFOR units merely took down his name and address, then returned to their base to look for his picture. It soon became apparent that U.S. military commanders were actively forestalling efforts by the Dutch, Danish, and other IFOR contingents to apprehend fugitives, a charge confirmed by military and civilian officials from several NATO countries and former Swedish Prime Minister Carl Bildt, then serving as the international community's high representative for Bosnia.[205]

Even the war's most wanted indictees were effectively immune from arrest. Between late February and early July 1996, a specially designated U.S. Army reconnaissance team observed Ratko Mladić himself on at least twenty occasions, closely tailing him roughly a dozen times as he commuted between his command post inside Mount Žep, the nearby compound of the VRS Sixty-Fifth Protective Regiment, and other locations in the vicinity of Han Pijesak. Its commanding officer alleges that on several other occasions the unit delivered U.S. Colonel (later Major General) John Batiste and an MP escort to the Mount Žep and VRS regimental headquarters purportedly for face-to-face meetings with Mladić, allegedly to negotiate terms for Mladić's surrender; the platoon even rehearsed the protocol for his "permissive detention"—though never any procedure for forcibly arresting him. The close surveillance and furtive meetings came to an abrupt end on 6 July 1996 when a large crowd of demobilized soldiers from the Sixty-Fifth accosted the reconnaissance unit outside the Mount Žep facility immediately following Batiste's last meeting with Mladić.[206]

Such deferential treatment extended to Radovan Karadžić, who regularly commuted between his Pale home and office in full view of the town's International Police Task Force (IPTF) headquarters manned by Austrian, Swedish, and Ukrainian officers who neglected to report the encounters to their Sarajevo headquarters.[207] The U.S. military's refusal to apprehend him exacerbated tensions with the State Department, which regarded his total removal from politics as indispensable to stabilizing postwar Bosnia.[208] The task of securing Karadžić's withdrawal fell to Richard Holbrooke who, in turn, sought the assistance of Slobodan Milošević. Milošević readily accepted the challenge, given his immediate strategic interest in retaining American and western support, including the removal of sanctions. Karadžić agreed to leave, but only on condition that he be left alone. Holbrooke accepted Karadžić's terms, knowing fully well that the U.S., French and British military had no intention of arresting any ICTY indictees, but declined to put such a promise in writing. Instead, he instructed his close associate Christopher Hill to draft a memorandum to be signed by Karadžić in which he agreed to give up power and retire to private life. The agreement almost came to grief when Holbrooke vigorously refused Karadžić's demand—and Hill's appeal—that he also affix his signature to it. Securing Karadžić's signature required a late night helicopter flight to Pale by Milošević's state security chief Jovica Stanišić, who overcame Karadžić's resistance after several hours of intensive discussions.[209] Whereas Holbrooke, High Representative Carl Bildt, and Karadžić himself have readily confirmed that the Bosnian Serb leader pledged to step down, Holbrooke and other U.S. officials have consistently claimed that there was no quid pro quo; by contrast, Karadžić has insisted since his July 2008 arrest that he was promised immunity from *prosecution* in exchange for his withdrawal.[210] What we know from three senior State Department officials with intimate knowledge of Holbrooke's activities is that the ambassador explicitly assured Karadžić that he would not be *arrested*, a concession that is common knowledge among several others at the State Department who have heretofore remained silent.[211]

Indeed, the U.S. prohibition was so proscriptive that not a single one of more than fifty indictees was apprehended by IFOR during the first eighteen months of its deployment in Bosnia. In desperation, ICTY prosecutor Louise Arbour appealed to Ambassador Jacques-Paul Klein, who headed the UN Transitional Administration in Eastern Slavonia (UNTAES). On 27 June 1997, Klein broke the ice by orchestrating the capture and rendition of Croatian-Serb indictee Slavko Dokmanović, which Arbour used to goad IFOR's U.S. commanders into action.

That summer, British IFOR personnel initiated the process of capturing ICTY fugitives, many of whom had lived openly, often in the presence of IFOR soldiers engaged in "the normal course of their duties."[212]

The breakup of multinational empires in Europe by the end of World War I resulted in a proliferation of sovereign states. The breakup of Yugoslavia in the early 1990s resulted in a further proliferation of states. The international community should have tried much sooner to foster a peaceful dissolution of Yugoslavia with the encouragement of and support for new democratic states that protected the rights of all the people who lived within their borders. All this may well have failed, but it would have been the "right thing to do." Although the actions and inactions of the international community were not the primary causes for the violent dissolution of Yugoslavia, they at least helped to foster a climate that only encouraged increasing instability in the region.

The major powers definitely wanted to see a political solution to the conflict but were from the start unwilling to place either the region's immediate interests or the timeless universal values of the UN Charter ahead of their own national agenda. The EU was divided in its views on the Yugoslav crisis, and the U.S. hesitated while long and exhausting discussions were held among the principals in the U.S. government. Chairman of the Joint Chiefs of Staff Colin Powell and others continued to defend their ultimately discredited view that military intervention would be too costly.[213]

Thus Great Britain, France, and particularly the United States worked for three years to avoid direct military intervention that threatened to incur considerable costs both in treasure and the lives of their own citizen soldiers. Instead, they pursued the Vance-Owen plan and the Dayton Accords, which tacitly accepted territorial changes brought about by war crimes enumerated in the previous chapter. Even when they felt compelled to intervene militarily in 1995 (and again in 1998–1999) to forestall an even greater humanitarian catastrophe, the Big Three were content to assume a passive stance once that cataclysm had been successfully averted.

Bill Clinton eventually agreed with Richard Holbrooke, who described the Bosnian situation as "the greatest collective security failure of the West since the 1930s." In his book *To End a War*, Holbrooke ascribes the failure to five factors: (1) a misreading of Balkan history that viewed ethnic strife as too ancient and ingrained to be prevented by outsiders, (2) the apparent loss of Yugoslavia's strategic importance after the end of the cold war, (3) the triumph of nationalism over democracy as the dominant ideology of post-Communist Yugoslavia, (4) the reluctance of the Bush administration to undertake another military commitment so soon after the 1991 Iraq war, and (5) the decision of the United States to turn the issue over to Europe instead of NATO and the confused and passive European response. To Holbrooke's list Bill Clinton added a sixth factor: some European leaders were not eager to have a Muslim state in the heart of the Balkans, fearing it might become a base for exporting extremism. [214]

The failure of the international community to deal effectively with first the crisis and then the tragedy of Yugoslavia's dissolution will continue to be a subject of intense scrutiny and analysis among scholars. Perhaps the continuing nightmare in Darfur only reminds us of the relevance of such analysis.

Notes

1   Lorraine M. Lees, *Keeping Tito Afloat: The United States, Yugoslavia, and the Cold War* (University Park: Pennsylvania State University Press, 1997).

2   A. Ross Johnson, "Security and Insecurity in the Balkans," in *Integrating Regional and Global Security Cooperation*, ed. Klaus Lange and Leonid L. Fituni (Munich: Hanns Seidel Stiftung, 2002), 113–118.

3   Marek Waldenberg, *Rozbicie Jugoslawii: od separacji Slowenii do wojny kosowskiej* (Warszawa: Scholar, 2003); Jelena Guskova, *Istorija jugoslovenske krize 1990–2000* (History of the Yugoslav Crisis, 1990–2000), 2 vols. (Beograd: Izdavački grafički atelje "M," 2003).

4   "Milošević launches his defense," *Radio Free Europe/Radio Liberty Balkan Report* 8, no. 32, 3 September 2004.

5   Waldenberg, *Rozbicie Jugoslawii*; Guskova, *Istorija jugoslovenske krize.*

6   Paul Shoup, "The Disintegration of Yugoslavia and Western Foreign Policy in the 1980s," unpublished paper at International Conference on Rethinking the Dissolution of Yugoslavia, Centre for South-East European Studies, School of Slavonic and East European Studies/University College London, 18–19 June 2004; Jože Pirjevec, *Jugoslovanske vojne 1991–2001* (Ljubljana: Cankarjeva založba, 2003); James Gow, *Triumph of the Lack of Will: International Diplomacy and the Yugoslav War* (New York: Columbia University Press; London: Hurst, 1997); Michael Libal, *Limits of Persuasion: Germany and the Yugoslav Crisis, 1991–1992* (Westport and London: Praeger, 1997). Klaus Peter Zeitler, *Deutschlands Rolle bei der völkerrechtlichen Anerkennung der Republik Kroatien unter besonderer Berücksichtigung des deutschen Außenministers Genscher* (Marburg: Tectum Verlag, 2000).

7   Warren Zimmermann, *Origins of a Catastrophe: Yugoslavia and Its Destroyers— America's Last Ambassador Tells What Happened and Why* (New York: Times Books, 1996), 84.

8   Yugoslavia transformed, National Intelligence Estimate, 1 October 1990. Declassified on 29 September 1999, code F-1995-00796. http://www.foia.cia.gov/browse_ docs.asp?doc_no=0000254259&title=%28EST+PUB+DATE%29++YUGOSLAV IA+TRANSFORMED&abstract=NATIONAL+INTELLIGENCE+ESTIMATE&n o_pages=0023&pub_date=10%2F1%2F1990&release_date=9%2F29%2F1999&key words=YUGOSLAVIA%7CINTELLIGENCE+ESTIMATE%7CSERBIA%7CTRAN SFORMED%7CKOSOVO&case_no=F%2D1995%2D00796&copyright=08release_d

ec=RIPPUB&classifiaction=U&showPage=0011 (accessed 27 November 2005). First mentioned in David Binder, "Yugoslavia Seen as Breaking Up Soon," *New York Times*, 28 November 1990, A7.

9   Ben Cohen and George Stamkovski, eds., *With No Peace to Keep: United Nations Peacekeeping and the War in the Former Yugoslavia* (London: Grainpress Ltd., 1995), 149; Jane M. O. Sharp, *Anglo-American Relations and Crisis in Yugoslavia* (Paris: Serie transatlantique, 1999), 16; compare "Enttäuschung über Ablehnungsfront," *Frankfurter Allgemeine Zeitung*, 17 December 1991.

10 Laura Silber and Allan Little, *Yugoslavia: A Death of a Nation* (London: Penguin Books, 1997), 201.

11 Thomas L. Friedman, "Soviet Aid Plans Outlined by Baker," *New York Times*, 19 June 1991, A13.

12 Robert L. Hutchings, *American Diplomacy and the End of the Cold War: An Insider's Account of U.S. Policy in Europe, 1989–1992* (Baltimore: Johns Hopkins University Press, 1997), 311.

13 Thomas L. Friedman, "Baker Urges End to Yugoslav Rift," *New York Times*, 22 June 1991, A1, A4.

14 James Baker, "Nekdanji državni sekretar: intervju," *Mladina*, no. 14 (2005), 36–40.

15 James A. Baker III, *The Politics of Diplomacy: Revolution, War, and Peace, 1989–1992* (New York: G. Putnam's Sons, 1995), 640.

16 Zdravko Tomac, *The Struggle for the Croatian State: Through Hell to Diplomacy* (Zagreb: Profikon, 1993), 126.

17 Lojze Peterle, *Z nasmehom zgodovine* (Celje, Celovec, Gorica: Mohorjeva družba, 2004), 167.

18 Kučan, in interview with Sabrina Ramet, Ljubljana, 6 September 1999, quoted in Sabrina Ramet, *The Three Yugoslavias: State-Building and Legitimation, 1918–2004* (Washington: Woodrow Wilson Center Press; Bloomington and Indianapolis: Indiana University Press, 2006), 23.

19 Louis Sell, *Slobodan Milošević and the Destruction of Yugoslavia* (Durham, NC, and London: Duke University Press, 2002).

20 Even James Baker remembered her numerous resolutions in the House of Representatives on behalf of the Serbs in an interview with Matjaž Klemenčič on 2 February 2005.

21 Paul Hockenos, *Homeland Calling: Exile Patriotism and the Balkan Wars* (Ithaca and London: Cornell University Press, 2003), 145–146.

22 Ibid, 159.

23 Boris Frlec was since 1989 ambassador of SFRY in Bonn. Although a Slovene, he continued to represent Yugoslavia in accordance with the Brioni Agreement.

24 Libal, *Limits of Persuasion*, 39.

25 Quoted in Peter Radan, "Secessionist Self-Determination: The Cases of Slovenia and Croatia," *Australian Journal of International Affairs* 48, no. 2 (November 1994), 187; Guskova, *Istorija jugoslovenske krize.*

26 Ibid., 447–466.

27 Imre Szilágyi, "Hungary and the Disintegration of Yugoslavia," unpublished manuscript.

28 Borisav Jović, *Zadnji dnevi SFRJ—odlomki iz dnevnika* (Last days of the SFRY— Excerpts from the Diary), (Ljubljana: Slovenska knjiga, 1996), 237.

29   Jens Reuter, "Jugoslawien: Versagen der internationalen Gemeinschaft?" *Südosteur-opa* 42, no. 6 (1993), 333.

30   Zeitler, *Deutschlands Rolle*, 93–94.

31   Zeitler, *Deutschlands Rolle*, 96–97.

32   Norbert Both, *From Indifference to Entrapment: The Netherlands and the Yugoslav Crisis, 1990–1995* (Amsterdam: Amsterdam University Press, 2000).

33   Zeitler, *Deutschlands Rolle*, 100; compare also Joachim Bläsing, et al., eds., *Die Niederlande und Deutschland. Nachbarn in Europa* (Hannover: Niedersächsische Landeszentrale für politische Bildung, 1992).

34   Zeitler, *Deutschlands Rolle*, 109. See also Matjaž Klemenčič and Vladimir Klemenčič, *The Endeavors of Carinthian Slovenes for Their Ethnic Survival with/against Austrian Governments after World War II* (Klagenfurt/Celovec: Mohorjeva zalozba, 2008).

35   Ibid.

36   Michas Takis, *Unholy Alliance: Greece and Milošević's Serbia,* Eastern European Studies, no. 15 (College Station: Texas A&M University Press, 2002).

37   "Slowenien will in die EG," *Frankfurter Allgemeine Zeitung*, 15 February 1991; Zeitler, *Deutschlands Rolle*, 124.

38   Archiv der Gegenwart (Zeitschrift), 1 July 1991, 35795; Zeitler, *Deutschlands Rolle*, 124.

39   Judy Dempsey, "Yugoslavia Seeks $4.5bn to Help Its Economic Reforms," *Financial Times*, 23 May 1991, 1.

40   "EG will Jugoslawien helfen," *Frankfurter Allgemeine Zeitung*, 15 April 1991; Zeitler, *Deutschlands Rolle*, 125.

41   Hans-Joachim Hoppe, "Moscow and the Conflict in Former Yugoslavia," *Aussenpolitik* 43, no. 3 (1997), 269.

42   Tomac, *The Struggle for the Croatian State*, 449.

43   Zeitler, *Deutschlands Rolle*, 116.

44   Nenad Ivanković, *Bonn. Die zweite kroatische Front* (Gießen: Justus-Liebig-Universitätsverlag, 1996), 33.

45   Hans-Dietrich Genscher, *Erinnerungen* (Berlin: Siedler Verlag, 1995), 934.

46   Ibid., 934–935.

47   Otto von Habsburg, *Zurück zur Mitte* (Wien und München: Amalthea, 1991), 70.

48   Stephan Baier and Eva Demmerle, *Otto von Habsburg. Die Biografie* (Wien: Amalthea, 2002), 473.

49   Zeitler, *Deutschlands Rolle*, 150.

50   Ibid.

51   Genscher, *Erinnerungen*, 939; Dimitrij Rupel, *Skrivnost države: Spomini na domače in zunanje zadeve 1989–1992* (Ljubljana: Cankarjeva založba, 1992), 154–155.

52   Silber and Little, *Yugoslavia: A Death of a Nation*, 164.

53   Uroš Lipušček in his book *Ave Wilson: ZDA in prekrajanje Slovenije v Versaillesu 1919–1920* (Ljubljana: Sophia, 2003), successfully proved that there was an option for smaller states in the region of former Yugoslavia on the table of U.S. Department of State analysts after World War I.

54   Rosalyn Higgins, "The New United Nations and Former Yugoslavia," *International Affairs* 63, no. 3 (July 1993), 473.

55   Archiv der Gegenwart (Zeitschrift), 18 July 1991, 35855.

56   Rupel, *Skrivnost države*, 158–182.

57 Matjaž Klemenčič, "Slovenia at the Crossroads of the Nineties: From the First Multi-party Elections and the Declaration of Independence to Membership in the Council of Europe," *Slovene Studies* 14, no. 1 (1992 [published in 1994]), 11.

58 Susan L. Woodward, *Balkan Tragedy: Chaos and Dissolution after the Cold War* (Washington, DC: The Brookings Institution, 1995), 168.

59 Michael Libal, *Limits of Persuasion: Germany and the Yugoslav Crisis, 1991–1992* (Westport, CT: Greenwood, 1997), 44.

60 Ibid., 45.

61 Ibid.

62 "Le Conférence de Presse Du President dela République 'La géopolitique de l'Europe a grand besoin d'une théorie des ensembles,'" *Le Monde*, 13 September 1991, 2.

63 Hans Dietrich Genscher, *Rebuilding a House Divided: A Memoir by the Architect of Germany's Reunification* (New York: Broadway Books, 1998), 512–513.

64 Klaus Peter Zeitler, *Deutschlands Rolle bei der völkerrechtichen Anerkennung der Republik Kroatien unter besonderer Berücksichtigung des deutschen Außenministers Genscher* (Marburg: Tectum Verlag, 2000), 168.

65 MTI (Budapest), 28 August 1991, in FBIS, *Daily Report* (Eastern Europe), 29 August 1991, 9.

66 AFP (Paris), 5 July 1991, in FBIS, *Daily Report* (Eastern Europe), 5 July 1991, 1.

67 *Parlamentarisch-Politischer Pressedienst* 42, no. 77 (10 July 1991), 1; Zeitler, *Deutschlands Rolle*, 111.

68 Matjaž Klemenčič, "Pregled zgodovine Makedonije in Makedoncev od naselitve Slovanov v 6. stoletju do samostojne države s spornim imenom v 21. stoletju," in *Zbornik Janka Pleterskega*, ed. Oto Luthar and Jurij Perovšek (Ljubljana: Založba ZRC, ZRC SAZU, 2003), 91–105.

69 Sell, *Slobodan Miloševic and the Destruction of Yugoslavia*, 44.

70 Compare Gemeinsamer Entschließungsantag zur Lage in Jugoslawien vom 09. Oktober 1991, Europäisches Parlament, DOC-DE/RC/116975.

71 "Die Deutschen wollen keine Verbände aus der NATO lösen," *Die Welt*, 2/3 November 1991.

72 Zeitler, *Deutschlands Rolle*, 155–157.

73 Osloer Erklärung des Ministerrates des Nordatlantikrats der NATO vom 04. Juni 1992, Bulletin No. 64, 12 June 1992, 613.

74 Wortlautauszüge des Briefes von Genscher an Pérez de Cuéllar, DPA, 15 December 1991.

75 Wortlautauszüge aus dem Briefe des UNO-Generalsekretärs an Genscher, DPA, 15 December 1991.

76 "Die Krieg geht unterdessen weiter," *Frankfurter Allgemeine Zeitung*, 16 December 1991.

77 John Newhouse, "Bonn, der Westen und die Auflösing Jugoslawiens: der Versagen der Diplomatie. Chronik eines Skandals," *Blätter für deutsche und internationale Politik 1992*, no. 10, 1195.

78 Silber and Little, *Yugoslavia: The Death of a Nation*, 190.

79 UN Security Council Resolution 713/1991. *Europa Archiv* 21/1991, S. D 550.

80 Reneo Lukic, "Yugoslavie: Chronique d'une fin annoncée," *Politique internationale* 53 (Fall 1991), 138.

81 Zeitler, *Deutschlands Rolle*, 166–167.

82 Baker, *Politics of Diplomacy*, 638.

83   Gow, *Triumph of the Lack of Will*, 186, 193.
84   "Treaty Provisions for the Convention," *Review of International Affairs* 42, nos. 995–997 (1991), 33.
85   Carsten Giersch and Daniel Eisermann, "Die westliche Politik und der Kroatien-Krieg 1991–1992," *Südosteuropa* 43, in general nos. 3–4 (1994), 110.
86   Woodward, *Balkan Tragedy*, 181.
87   Robert Mauthner and Laura Silber, "EC Puts Sanctions on Yugoslavia," *Financial Times*, 9–10 November 1991, 24.
88   Elisabeth Roberts, "Next Balkan Flashpoint?" *The World Today* 54, no. 4 (1999), 402.
89   Der Bundesminister des Auswärtigen, Mitteilung für die Presse No. 1248/91, 22 November 1991.
90   UN Security Council Resolution 721/1991. Archiv der Gegenwart, 23 December 1991, 36347.
91   Pirjevec, *Jugoslovanske vojne 1991–2001*, 98–99.
92   Genscher, *Erinnerungen*, 958.
93   Many observers have seen positions expressed by the German government at this press conference as a sign of indulgence—that is, the German government should have changed its plan expressed in Rome a week before that it would recognize Slovenia and Croatia already in 1991. Zeitler, *Deutschlands Rolle*, 96.
94   UN Security Council Resolution 724/1991. Archiv der Gegenwart, 23 December 1991, 36349.
95   Genscher, *Erinnerungen*, 961.
96   Gustav Gustenau, "Die 'Neuordnung Jugoslawiens,'" *Österreichische Milit. Zeitschrift*, no. 2 (1992), 106.
97   Roberto Bendini and Jakkie Potgieter, *Analysis Report: Former Yugoslavia, Disarmament and Conflict Resolution Project. Managing Arms in Peace Processes—Croatia and Bosnia-Herzegovina* (New York and Geneva: United Nations, 1996), 21, 26, 195.
98   Branka Magaš and Ivo Žanić, eds., *Rat u Hrvatskoj i Bosni i Hercegovini, 1991–1995* (Zagreb: Jesenski i Turk; Sarajevo: Dani, 1999), 89.
99   Pirjevec, *Jugoslovanske vojne 1991–2001*, 109–110.
100   Silber and Little, *Yugoslavia: Death of a Nation*, 198.
101   Boutros Boutros-Ghali, *Unvanquished: A U.S.–UN Saga* (London and New York: I. B. Taurus Publishers, 1999), 38.
102   This problem was treated also in discussion at a June 2004 conference on dissolution of former Yugoslavia in London, where Paul Shoup criticized the U.S. Government for not doing everything it could to ensure the territorial integrity of Croatia after it was recognized by the U.S.
103   Leo Tindemans et al., *Unfinished Peace: Report of the International Commission on the Balkans* (Washington, DC: Carnegie Endowment for International Peace; Berlin: Aspen Institute, 1996), 39.
104   Peter Carrington, "Turmoil in the Balkans: Developments and Prospects," *RUSI Journal* 137, no. 5 (1992), 4.
105   Loring M. Danforth, *The Macedonian Conflict: Ethnic Nationalism in a Transnational World* (Princeton: Princeton University Press, 1995).
106   Ibid., 30–32.
107   Matjaž Klemenčič, "Delovanje makedonskih izseljencev iz ZDA in Kanade za neodvisnost in mednarodno priznanaje Makedonije," *Studia Historica Slovenica* 5, no. 13 (2005), 585–605.

108 John B. Allcock, "Macedonia," in *The States of Eastern Europe*, vol. 2, *South-Eastern Europe*, ed. David Turnock and Francis W. Carter (Aldershot, UK: Ashgate, 1999), 141–166.

109 Paul Lewis, "U.N. Votes 13–0 for Embargo on Trade with Yugoslavia, Air Travel and Oil Curbed," *New York Times,* 31 May 1992, 1; Paul Lewis, "U.N. Is Said to Be Ready on Yugoslav Sanctions," *New York Times,* 30 May 1992, 3.

110 Chuck Sudetich, "American Takes Helm in Belgrade," *New York Times,* 15 July 1992, A6.

111 Milena Spasovski, Dragica Živković, and Milomir Stepić, "The Ethnic Structure of the Population in Bosnia and Hercegovina," in *The Serbian Question in the Balkans,* ed. Duška Hadži-Jovanović (Beograd: Faculty of Geography, University of Belgrade, 1995), 283.

112 Pirjevec, *Jugoslovanske vojne 1991–2001,* 124.

113 Mladen Mirosavljević, "Referendum uspješno proveden, čeka se me|unarodna reakcija," *Vjesnik,* 4 March 1992, 1; Magaš and Žanić, *Rat u Hrvatskoj i Bosni i Hercegovini,* 385.

114 Baker, *Politics of Diplomacy,* 639–640.

115 Lewis MacKenzie, *Peacekeeper: The Road to Sarajevo* (Vancouver, Toronto: Douglas and McIntyre, 1993), 106–107.

116 Tindemans et al., *Unfinished Peace,* 48; Carrington, "Turmoil in the Balkans," 2.

117 David Binder, "U.S. Policymakers on Bosnia Admit Errors in Opposing Partition in 1992," *New York Times,* 29 August 1993, A10.

118 Jasminka Udovički and James Ridgeway, eds., *Burn this House: The Making and Unmaking of Yugoslavia* (Durham, NC, and London: Duke University Press, 1997), 206.

119 Pirjevec, *Jugoslovanske vojne 1991–2001,* 131.

120 "Moja uloga u Bosni," *Vreme International* 5, no. 191 (1994), 18.

121 Gow, *Triumph of the Lack of Will,* 88.

122 Benjamin Rusek and Charles Ingrao, "The 'Mortar Massacres': A Controversy Revisited," in *Conflict in South-Eastern Europe at the End of the Twentieth Century: A 'Scholars Initiative' Assesses Some of the Controversies,* ed. Thomas Emmert and Charles Ingrao (London and New York: Routledge, 2006), 104.

123 MacKenzie, *Peacekeeper,* 194.

124 Dick A. Leurdijk, *The United Nations and NATO in the Former Yugoslavia: Limits to Diplomacy and Force* (The Hague: Netherlands Atlantic Commission and the Netherlands Institute of International Relations "Clingendael," 1996), 24.

125 Richard H. Ullman, ed., *The World and Yugoslavia's Wars* (New York: Council on Foreign Relations, 1996), 100.

126 Tom Gallagher, "Bosnian Brotherhood," *Transition* 1, no. 3 (1995), 23.

127 Baker, *Politics of Diplomacy,* 648–650.

128 Leurdijk, *United Nations and NATO,* 23.

129 Martin Rosefeldt, "Deutschlands und Frankreichs Jugoslawien-politik in Rahmen der Europaischen Gemeinschaft (1991–1993)," *Sudosteuropa* 42, no. 11–12 (1993), 648–649.

130 Sumantra Bose, *Bosnia after Dayton: Nationalist Partition and International Intervention* (London: Hurst and Company, 2002), 18.

131 John Newhouse, "Bonn, der Westen und die Auflösung Jugoslawiens: der Versagen der Diplomatie. Chronik eines Skandals," *Blätter für deutsche und internationale Politik 1992,* no. 10, 1203.

132 Cohen and Stamkovski, *With no Peace to Keep*, 55, 183.

133 Ibid., 23, 83.

134 Pirjevec, *Jugoslovanske vojne 1991–2001*, 169.

135 Roy Gutman, *A Witness to Genocide: The First Inside Account of the Horrors of "Ethnic Cleansing" in Bosnia* (Shaftesbury: Element Books, 1993), xii.

136 Lila Radonjić, *Naš slučaj*, part 2 (Beograd: Vreme knjige, 1996), 140.

137 Pirjevec, *Jugoslovanske vojne 1991–2001*, 174.

138 Gwen Ifill, "Clinton Seeking Forceful Image as a Leader in Foreign Affairs," *New York Times*, 28 June 1992, A1, A16, A17; Andrew Rosenthal, "Clinton Attacked on Foreign Policy," *New York Times*, 28 July 1992, A1, A10; Gwen Ifill, "Clinton Counters on Foreign Policy," *New York Times*, 29 July 1992, A1; Lawrence Freedman, "Why the West Failed," *Foreign Policy*, no. 97 (Winter 1994–95), 61–62.

139 Paul Lewis, "U.N. Council Votes to Support Force in Assisting Bosnia," New York Times, 14 August 1992, 1; "Nova resolucija VS OZN", *Delo,* 20 August 1992, 1.

140 Cohen and Stamkovski, *With no Peace to Keep*, 111; Daniel Bethlehem and Marc Weller, eds., *The "Yugoslav" Crisis in International Law: General Issues* (Cambridge: Cambridge University Press, 1997), xxxvii; Rosefeldt, "Deutschlands und Frankreichs Jugoslawienpolitik," 638.

141 Gustenau, "Die 'Neuordnung Jugoslawiens,'" 490; Brendan Simms, *Unfinest Hour: Britain and the Destruction of Bosnia* (London: Penguin Books, 2002), 21.

142 Pirjevec, *Jugoslovanske vojne 1991–2001*, 194–198.

143 Cohen and Stamkovski, *With No Peace to Keep*, 107, 152.

144 Francine Boidevaix, *Une diplomatie informelle pour l'Europe: Le Groupe de Contact Bosnie* (Paris: Fondation pour les Etudes de Défense, Librarie de la Documentation française, 1997), 34; Woodward, *Balkan Tragedy*, 296.

145 Cohen and Stamkovski, *With No Peace to Keep*, 152.

146 Ibid.; Pirjevec, *Jugoslovanske vojne 1991–2001*, 210–214.

147 Ejup Ganić, *Bosanska otrovna jabuka* (Sarajevo: Bosanska knjiga, 1995), 263; Owen, *Balkan Odyssey*, 91–94.

148 "Izetbegović bittet islamische Staaten um Hilfe für Bosnier," *Frankfurter Allgemeine Zeitung*, 12 January 1993, 1; "Gespräche über die Aufteilung Bosnien Hercegovinas auf Antrag der Regierung in Sarajevo zurückgestellt," *Frankfurter Allgemeine Zeitung*, 12 January 1993, 1; "Vermittler verlangen die Annahme des Friedenplanes durch Serbien," *Frankfurter Allgemeine Zeitung*, 16 January 1993, 1; Duško Doder and Louise Branson, *Milošević: Portrait of a Tyrant* (New York: The Free Press, 1999), 179; Commission on Security and Cooperation in Europe, 103rd Cong., 1st sess., *Crisis in Bosnia-Herzegovina*, hearing, 4 February 1993 (Washington, DC: U.S. Government Printing Office, 1993), 24.

149 Ed Vulliamy, *Seasons in Hell: Understanding Bosnia's War* (New York and London: Simon and Schuster, 1994), 251.

150 Radonjić, *Naš slučaj*, part 2, 290–292.

151 Madeleine Albright, *Madam Secretary* (New York: Maramax Books, 2003), 181.

152 Ali Rabia and Lawrence Lifschultz, eds., *Writings on the Balkan War: Why Bosnia?* (New York: Pamphleteers Press, 1993), 389.

153 Commission on Security and Cooperation in Europe, 23.

154 Cohen and Stamkovski, *With No Peace to Keep*, 81.

155 David Owen, *Balkan Odyssey* (London: Victor Gollancz, 1995), 116.

156 Pirjevec, *Jugoslovanske vojne 1991–2001*, 225.

157 "Serbischer Minister spricht von internationaler Hysterie wegen Bosnien-Hercego-vina," *Frankfurter Allgemeine Zeitung*, 24 February 1993, 1; "Vermittler verlangen die Annahme des Friedenplanes durch Serbien," *Frankfurter Allgemeine Zeitung*, 24 February 1993, 1; "Serben Hauptschuldige," *Frankfurter Allgemeine Zeitung*, 24 February 1993, 2; "Pirjevec," *Jugoslovanske vojne 1991–2001*, 227–228.

158 Woodward, *Balkan Tragedy*, 307.

159 Gustenau, "Die 'Neuordnung Jugoslawiens,'" 233.

160 Cohen and Stamkovski, *With No Peace to Keep*, 152.

161 Bendini and Potgieter, *Analysis Report: Former Yugoslavia*, 122–123.

162 Freedman, "Why the West Failed," 66.

163 Gow, *Triumph of the Lack of Will*, 246.

164 Boutros-Ghali, *Unvanquished: A U.S.–UN Saga*, 84.

165 Gow, *Triumph of the Lack of Will*, 247.

166 Ivo H. Daalder, *Getting Dayton: The Making of America's Bosnia Policy* (Washington, DC: Brookings Institution Press, 2000), 114.

167 Freedman, "Why the West Failed," 66; "Clinton fordert entschiedene Schrite gegen bosnische Serben," *Frankfurter Allgemeine Zeitung*, 7 May 1993, 1.

168 Leslie Benson: *Yugoslavia: A Concise History* (New York: Palgrave, 2001), 167; Woodward, *Balkan Tragedy*, 312.

169 Nimet Beriker Atiyras, "Mediating Regional Conflicts and Negotiation Flexibility: Peace Efforts in Bosnia-Herzegovina," *Annals of the American Academy of Political and Social Sciences* 542 (November 1995), 195.

170 "Pirjevec," *Jugoslovanske vojne 1991–2001*, 270.

171 Woodward, *Balkan Tragedy*, 310–311.

172 Ibid., 312.

173 Lenard J. Cohen, "Russia and the Balkans: Pan-Slavism, Partnership, and Power," *International Journal, Canadian Institute of International Affairs* 4, no. 49 (Fall 1994), 835.

174 Hans Koschnik, "Ethnisch gesäubert!?—Bosnien Herzegowina, Kroatien und Serbien nach dem Dayton Abkommen," *Zeitgeschichte* 25 (March–April 1998), 114.

175 Božo Mašanović, "Diplomatski vrvež med vikendom v Parizu," *Delo*, 24 January 1994.

176 Gow, *Triumph of the Lack of Will*, 139–140.

177 Lewis MacKenzie, *Peacekeeper*, 217–274.

178 "Clinton bekräftigt in Brussel das amerikanische Engagement für Europa," *Frankfurter Allgemeine Zeitung*, 10 January 1994, 1; "Pirjevec," *Jugoslovanske vojne 1991–2001*, 301.

179 Commission on Security and Cooperation in Europe, 103rd Congress, 1st sess., *Bosnia's Second Winter under Siege*, hearing, 8 February 1994 (Washington, DC: U.S. Government Printing Office, 1994).

180 Commission on Security and Cooperation in Europe, 103rd Congress, 1st sess., *Bosnia's Second Winter under Siege*, hearing, 4 February 1993 (Washington, DC: U.S. Government Printing Office, 1994); Boidevaix, *Une diplomatie informelle pour l'Europe*, 59.

181 Leurdijk, *United Nations and NATO*, 50.

182 "In zehn Tagen," *Frankfurter Allgemeine Zeitung*, 11 February 1994, 1.

183 "Eine Atempause für Sarajevo, Blauhelm-Soldaten überwachen die Waffenruhe," *Frankfurter Allgemeine Zeitung*, 11 February 1994, 1; Leurdijk, *United Nations and NATO*, 54.

184 Gregory L. Schulte, "Bringing Peace to Bosnia and Change to the Alliance," *NATO Review* 45, no. 2 (March 1997), 24.

185 Andrej Kozirev, *Preobraženije* (Moskva: Medžunarodnije otnošenija, 1995), 123.

186 Zdravko Tomac, *Zločin bez kazne* (Zagreb: Matrix Croatica, 1999), 365–367.

187 "Croatians and the War in Bosnia," *Strategic Comments of International Institute for Strategic Studies* 17 (January 1995), 1–4.

188 Gustenau, "Die 'Neuordnung Jugoslawiens,'" 278, 280.

189 Bendini and Potgieter, *Analysis Report: Former Yugoslavia*, 143; Owen, *Balkan Odyssey*, 358.

190 Gow, *Triumph of the Lack of Will*, 180.

191 Daalder, *Getting to Dayton*, 27.

192 Woodward, *Balkan Tragedy*, 315.

193 Helen Leigh-Phippard, "The Contact Group on (and in) Bosnia: An Exercise in Conflict Mediation?" *International Journal* 53, no. 2 (Spring 1998), 307.

194 Aleksandar Ćirić, "Podela Bosne 51:49," *Vreme International* 5, no. 191 (June 1994), 8–10.

195 Hans Stark, "Embargo mit begrenzter Wirkung: Die Sanktionen gegen Serbien und Montenegro," *Internationale Politik* 43, no. 7 (August 1997), 44.

196 Ramet, *Three Yugoslavias*, 124.

197 "Pad zapadne Slavonije," *Vreme International* 6, no. 237 (May 1995), 8–11

198 Peter W. Galbraith, ed., *The United States and Croatia: A Documentary History, 1992–1997* (Washington: U.S. Government Printing Office, 1998), 142–180.

199 Stojan Žitko, "Padec Srebrenice odmeva," *Delo,* 13 July 1995; "Od izbruha vojne do Daytona," *Delo,* 23 November 1995. See chapter 6 of this volume.

200 Zoran Kusovac, "Hronika Oluje," *Vreme International* 6, no. 251 (August 1995), 6–8.

201 Marcus Tanner, *Croatia: A Nation Forged in War* (New Haven and London: Yale University Press, 1997), 296–298.

202 Richard Holbrooke, *To End a War* (New York: Modern Library, 1998), 79–288.

203 Peter Potočnik, "Hrvati so dosegli največ!" *Delo,* 23 November 1995, 5.

204 Interview with senior State Department official #1 by Charles Ingrao.

205 Interviews with IFOR officials #1, #2; #3, #4. John Pomfret and Lee Hockstader, "In Bosnia, a War Crimes Impasse," *Washington Post Foreign Service*, 9 December 1997, A1. Carl Bildt, *Peace Journey: The Struggle for Peace in Bosnia* (London: Weidenfeld and Nicolson, 1998), 237. U.S. Ambassador William Montgomery would later claim that "senior officials of the uniformed and civilian sides of the United States Department of Defense absolutely refused to have anything to do with the apprehension of war criminals in Bosnia," and Bildt has described "a truly massive reluctance throughout the NATO chain of command—the senior commanders on all levels of relevance being American—to address [this] issue." Quoted in John Berlin, "Karadzic and Mladic Will Never Really 'Do Time,'" *UN Observer and International Report*, 11 August 2007. www.globalpolicy.org/intljustice/wanted/2007/0811neverdotime.htm (accessed 5 April 2008).

206 Interviews with U.S. IFOR official #3; typically a twelve-man unit drove directly behind from one to three VRS jeeps, within as little as fifty feet of Mladić. The 6 July altercation resulted in several minor injuries, plus the possible death of one VRS soldier

who was severely beaten by members of the reconnaissance unit. For contemporary media reports of varying accuracy, see "Yugoslavia: Close Encounter, " AP broadcast, 13:50, 11 June 1996; IFOR press briefing, Sarajevo, 6 July 1996; Ian Fisher, "Bosnian Serbs End Standoff by Allowing an Inspection," AP, 13 August 1996.

207   Anthony Lewis, "Winking at Karadzic," *New York Times*, 28 October 1996; interviews with IPTF Deputy Commissioner Robert Wasserman, IPTF-Pale staff, and Press Spokesman Alex Ivanko by Charles Ingrao.

208   Interviews with senior State Department official #1 and Intelligence and Research—Europe Director Daniel Serwer by Charles Ingrao.

209   The agreement, which was drafted under Hill's supervision, has been authenticated by Karadžić's legal team and a State Department source, bears the signatures of Aleksa Buha, Momčilo Krajišnik, Slobodan Milošević, Milan Milutinović, and Biljana Plavšić. Senior State Department official #2. Hill and Holbrooke have denied the assertions of both senior State Department officials #2 and #3.

210   "Bildt confidently predicts that Karadzic will leave gov't.," CourtTVNews, 5 April 1996; Bildt, *Peace Journey*, 237; www.courttv.com/archive/casefiles/warcrimes/reports/week3.html (accessed 5 April 2008); "Radovan Karadzic Finally Steps Aside," by James Hill, *Phoenix Gazette*, 23 July 1996. www.balkan-archive.org.yu/kosta/autori/hill.james/karadzic.steps.aside.html (accessed 5 April 2008); "Irregularities Linked to My Arrival before the Tribunal," pretrial statement by Radovan Karadžić, IT-95-5/18-I D11337-D11344, 1 August 2008.

211   Interviews with senior State Department officials #2, #3 and #4, and former Bosnian Foreign Minister Muhamed Sačirbey.

212   Interview with Ambassador Jacques-Paul Klein by Charles Ingrao; "Louise Arbour: Farewell Interview," IWPR, 30 August-5 September 1999 http://www.iwpr.net/ (accessed 5 November 2008). The British initiative likely reflected the replacement just one month earlier of Prime Minister John Major by Tony Blair.

213   Albright, *Madam Secretary*, 181–182; Colin Powell, *My American Journey* (New York: Random House, 1995), 576–577.

214   Holbrooke, *To End a War*, 22–31; Bill Clinton, *My Life* (New York: Knopf, 2004), 512–513.

6

Darko Gavrilović, team leader
Charles Ingrao, team leader

Vlado Azinović	Mark Etherington	**Lara Nettelfield**
Victor Bezruchenko	**Jan Willem Honig**	**Toni Petković**
Nejra Čengić	**Selma Leydesdorff**	**Benjamin Rusek**
Robert Donia	**Dubravko Lovrenović**	**Mirsad Tokača**
Robert DeGraaff	**Dunja Melčić**	Tatjana Tubić
Raphael Draschtak		**Cees Wiebes**

This chapter incorporates numerous interviews conducted by team co-leader Darko Gavrilović and individual research contributed by Robert Donia, Benjamin Rusek, and Cees Wiebes for Sarajevo and Tuzla, Victor Bezruchenko for Žepa, and Robert DeGraaf for Srebrenica. Victor Bezruchenko was recused from further team work after accepting a position with the ICTY. Text regarding mortar attacks in Sarajevo and Tuzla was based in part on Benjamin Rusek and Charles Ingrao, "The 'Mortar Massacres' Revisited" that appeared in *Nationalities Papers* 32/4 (December 2004), which was subsequently republished in Thomas Emmert and Charles Ingrao, eds., *Conflict in Southeastern Europe at the End of the Twentieth Century: A Scholars' Initiative* (New York & London: Routledge, 2006).

Dubravko Lovrenović worked tirelessly to recruit Bosnian scholars during his tenure as team co-leader (2001-2003). The National Endowment for Democracy funded individual research by Darko Gavrilović, Toni Petković, and Mirsad Tokača's Research & Documentation Center. The team also benefited from counsel and research material data provided by Directors Dr. Paul Richard Blum and the Nederlands Instituut voor Oorlogsdocumentatie (NIOD), Dr. Smail Čekić and the Institute for the Research of Crimes against Humanity & International Law, and Dr. Kathryne Bomberger and the International Commission for Missing Persons (ICMP). We are also grateful to former Republika Srpska President Dragan Čavić for making available to Dr. Gavrilović documentary evidence previously furnished to the ICTY. The report was adopted following project-wide review in January-February 2004.

SAFE AREAS

◆ Charles Ingrao ◆

The battle lines between the Bosnian Serbs and their opponents have not changed much since the creation of the six "safe areas" in the spring of 1993. The controversy over the wartime events in and around Bihać, Goražde, Sarajevo, Srebrenica, Tuzla, and Žepa still divides the Bosnian Serbs and their supporters from those of the Bosnian government and the bulk of the international community—except, perhaps, that it is the Bosnian Serbs who are on the defensive, whether in the accounts of scholars and journalists or in testimony given at The Hague Tribunal. Then as now, the prevailing discourse represents the safe areas' civilian populations as victims of the international community's lack of political will as they were subjected to a succession of barbaric acts that culminated in the July 1995 Srebrenica massacres. For their part, the Bosnian Serb military (VRS) and its apologists have generally denied the worst and most politically pivotal atrocities while claiming that their legitimate military operations not only were resisted by the Bosnian military (ARBiH) but were handicapped by one-sided UN resolutions, NATO interventions, and media scrutiny. Moreover, a number of UN officials have accused Bosnian government garrisons of deliberately provoking counterfire from VRS besiegers onto civilian targets in Sarajevo.[1]

The VRS saw its offensives as a justified response to the general security problems in their rear caused by the significant ARBiH presence in the safe areas. It is in this vein that this report will endeavor to be sensitive to the tactical dilemmas that the international community's actions presented to the Serb forces, even as it identifies crimes that they committed, oftentimes out of all proportion to the initial provocation and in disregard of the rules of war. At the same time, the evidence suggests that UN Security Council unilateralism—however ineffective it may have been in protecting the safe areas—was dictated by fear of a repetition of massive human rights violations like those committed by Serb forces during ethnic cleansing operations in Croatia (1991) and Bosnia (1992) but not by a serious attempt to impose a comprehensive program that would require a sustained investment of UN-mandated military resources.

I. Origins

The safe areas were created in 1993 in response to a humanitarian crisis that attended the siege of each city as its indigenous population was multiplied by thousands of refugees who had fled or been expelled by advancing VRS and other Serb forces. International observers within the besieged cities feared massive civilian casualties from hostile fire, starvation, and disease. They were no less apprehensive at the prospect that the fall of one or more cities would repeat on an even larger scale the resort to ethnic cleansing that had attended Serb advances elsewhere in Bosnia. Under the intense glare of media publicity, there prevailed a widespread feeling among foreign leaders and their UN representatives that the international community needed to at least appear to "do something" to ward off the impending human catastrophe. By the spring of 1993 Lord David Owen was not alone in contemplating the advantage of "leveling the playing field" somewhat by bombing VRS forces into relaxing or lifting the sieges.[2] A less intrusive solution surfaced in March 1993, following UN General Philippe Morillon's visit to Srebrenica. In an attempt to reassure the mass of residents and refugees who had blocked his departure from the city, he first pledged not to leave the city until humanitarian aid had been delivered, then negotiated a cease-fire with VRS commander Ratko Mladić.[3] As an additional guarantee to the city's estimated 35,000 residents and refugees, he announced that he was placing them under UN protection, an unauthorized pledge; surprised UN officials reluctantly endeavored to fulfill the pledge by sending a small detachment of Canadian troops to Srebrenica.

Morillon's démarche seconded efforts by the ICRC's Cornelio Sommaruga to persuade the UN to create a series of protected zones in default of any international sentiment to offer Bosnia's refugees sanctuary abroad.[4] The concept received an additional boost from several nonaligned UN member states, most notably Austrian Foreign Minister Alois Mock and Venezuela's Security Council representative, Diego Arria, who visited Srebrenica a few weeks later. By 16 April, with the town's fall seemingly imminent, UNSC Resolution 819 affirmed Srebrenica's status as a UN-protected safe area, which it based on the 1948 Convention against Genocide. Indeed, the text dwelt at length on a string of violations of International Humanitarian Law (IHL) by Serb paramilitaries, which it accused of attacking and forcibly expelling "innocent civilian populations" while harassing and interdicting UN humanitarian relief efforts. Three weeks later UNSC Resolution 824 (6 May 1993) extended UN protection to Bihać, Goražde, Sarajevo, Tuzla, and Žepa while demanding that the aforementioned paramilitaries cease hostilities and withdraw to a point at which they no longer constituted a menace to civilians.[5]

The establishment of the six Bosnian safe areas coincided with other initiatives advocated in the spring of 1993 by Britain, France, Russia, Spain, and the U.S., whose Joint Action Program led to the creation of the International Criminal Tribunal for the Former Yugoslavia, or ICTY (25 May) and the passage of UNSC Resolution 836 (4 June) authorizing the use of armed force to protect the safe areas. Significantly, the resolution characterized Bosnian Serb military attacks as a violation of Bosnia's sovereignty, thereby implying that this was not a domestic conflict or civil war being waged solely by indigenous paramilitaries but an international one that afforded greater protection, both to UN member Bosnia against foreign attack (whether from rump Yugoslavia or Croatia) and to its civilian population, who would now be covered by the broader umbrella of the 1977 Additional Protocol I for International Humanitarian Law (IHL); less clear was the authorization for UNPROFOR to "deter" and "respond" to attacks on the safe areas, which was left open to various interpretations that reflected the political courage of the interpreters.[6]

From the beginning, the five-power Joint Action Program and the UNSC resolutions manifested a lack of political will that seriously degraded the safe areas as an effective instrument for the protection of Bosnia's civilian population. Despite President George H. W. Bush's appeal to a New World Order and President Clinton's own rhetoric of universalism, the fact remained that at least four of the Security Council's permanent members were primarily motivated by their perception of what best served their national interest. Russia and its people were openly sympathetic to the militarily ascendant Bosnian Serbs and worked behind the scenes to limit UN intervention, whereas the other European powers had little interest in Bosnia aside from concern for the safety of their soldiers serving with UNPROFOR.[7] Despite its strident rhetoric in support of Bosnia's civilian population and its repeated calls for robust military countermeasures—preferably delivered from 35,000 feet (most notably "lift and strike")—the U.S. was unwilling to put a single U.S. soldier in harm's way. In the words of one senior U.S. diplomat, Washington's policy throughout the Yugoslav conflicts was to "do the least, and hope for the best."[8] Venezuela's Diego Arria put it best by concluding that "we see that one country can indeed abuse another so long as it is careful not to threaten or jeopardize the strategic interests of the international community."[9] Indeed, it was no coincidence that the nonaligned, nonpermanent members of the Security Council pushed the hardest to guarantee that the besieged cities would truly become protected areas and were critical of the safe area resolutions because they did not go far enough to guarantee a solution to the unfolding humanitarian crisis and would, at best, confirm the fait accompli of ethnic cleansing.[10] After all, countries like Cape Verde, Djibouti, Morocco, New Zealand, Pakistan, and Venezuela had nothing at stake in Bosnia, which afforded them the luxury of basing their positions primarily on humanitarian considerations.

The weaknesses in the UNSC Resolutions were readily apparent even before they were drafted. In their haste to do something while limiting the scope of their obligations, the framers had made no provision for defining the territorial limits of each safe area. But at least this was something that could be addressed at a later date. More problematic was the resolutions' failure to disarm the Bosnian forces operating within them. Indeed, existing international law assumed not only the prior agreement by the belligerents but the complete demilitarization of such safety zones.[11] By contrast, neither UNSCR 819 nor 824 provided for disarming BiH forces or, for that matter, required so much as Bosnian compliance with their terms.[12] Nor did the UN wring from the VRS permission to inspect the disposition of its besieging forces, even in those instances when they were obligated to withdraw to a preset distance from the existing lines of confrontation. As a result UN monitors were regularly fired upon whenever they attempted to verify VRS compliance.

To his credit, Morillon had concluded a tentative disarmament accord with Mladić and Commander Naser Orić on 18 April,[13] by which the town's newly installed Canadian peacekeepers would oversee the demilitarization of the town itself within seventy-two hours of their arrival. But the newly arrived 150-man Canadian battalion (CanBat) was too weak either to carry out its mission or to persuade Orić that it could protect Srebrenica in the event that the ARBiH defenders laid down all of their weapons. As a result, CanBat satisfied itself with disarming ARBiH units within the town while tacitly permitting them to keep the great majority of their weapons in the rest of the pocket. This was hardly acceptable to Mladić, whose chief of staff, Major General Manojlo Milovanović, characterized the 18 April disarmament as "just a farce."[14] Nor was a second disarmament agreement concluded on 8 May for the entire Srebrenica and Žepa pockets any more successful. ARBiH Commander-in-Chief Sefer Halilović instructed Orić to surrender only unusable equipment, having judged that CanBat was too weak to defend the safe area. Not surprisingly, Mladić reciprocated by disregarding a commitment to withdraw his forces 1.5 kilometers from battle lines. As a result, the fighting continued. During one two-week period in June 1993, CanBat reported no fewer than 1,200 violations with small caliber weapons, mortars, tanks, and artillery, including attacks on CanBat that killed one of its soldiers.[15]

It is certainly possible to understand the rationale behind both sides' unwillingness to execute the disarmament agreements. But although there was an understandable lack of trust between warring parties, both also regarded the UN itself to be untrustworthy. Although the UNPROFOR brass opposed creating safe areas without demilitarization, then Secretary for Peacekeeping Operations Kofi Annan explained that several UN members were reluctant to employ UNPROFOR in "disarming the victims because they recognized the unlikelihood that either side would voluntarily cease hostilities."[16] Of course, this does not mean that simply disarming Bosnian government forces would resolve all of the problems inherent in the safe area provisions. Whereas Lord Owen suggests that Bosnian Serb Field Commander Mladić did not intend to seize them, having seen the high cost of taking Vukovar, demilitarizing the safe areas would have simultaneously removed not only the justification for attacking them but the deterrence against occupying them.[17] Clearly, demilitarization could only work if UNPROFOR or some other armed force held Mladić and his troops at bay.

UN members were, however, unwilling either to abandon the safe areas' civilian populations or to provide sufficient military muscle to deter the Bosnian Serbs, even with Bosnian government troops in place to help them turn back an attack. Instead, the UN proved at least initially evenhanded insofar as it was unwilling to prevent both Bosnian government sorties and the inevitable—and far more deadly—VRS retaliatory strikes. Rather than deploy the 35,000 troops recommended by the U.S. military, or the 15,000 mandated by its own commanders, the UN chose the politically realistic "light option" of 7,500 favored by France. Yet, for all its gesticulating about the need for a much stronger UNPROFOR deterrent, the U.S. blocked Russian attempts to force a Security Council debate on force levels, lest it be embarrassed by its determination not to commit any troops of its own. Meanwhile, the Security Council turned a deaf ear to appeals from Venezuela, Djibouti, and others to intern VRS artillery capable of devastating the safe areas. To cover its own pusillanimity, a new UNSC Resolution 836 (4 June 1993) authorized the use of force against Bosnian Serb attacks even though it had no intention of backing them up. In his memoirs, Lord Owen describes the empty threat posed by UNSCR 836 as "the most irresponsible taken during" his tenure, having reputedly predicted at the time that Bosnian government sorties would drag the undermanned UNPROFOR units into the fighting.[18] Actually, UNPROFOR enjoyed the luxury of choosing whether it would be dragged in or simply look away as the belligerents continued the fight in and around all six safe areas. British forces in Goražde and the Scandinavian NordBat in Tuzla distinguished themselves by fighting hard to hold their ground against VRS attacks. Yet, given the higher priority that European contributors to UNPROFOR placed on the safety of their soldiers, it was much more likely that they would literally take the path of least resistance.

No less serious was the UN's failure to secure formal Bosnian Serb acceptance of the safe areas regime, thereby leaving both sides free to interpret the other's obligations. Certainly many Security Council members, UN officials, and the Bosnian government itself interpreted the resolutions as totally prohibiting any hostile action whatsoever against the safe areas, even if Bosnian government garrisons retained their weapons. Nor did any UNSC Resolution ever allude to either "safety and neutralized zones" (Articles 14 and 15 of the Geneva Convention) or "demilitarized zones" (Article 60 of Humanitarian Law). Yet by not engaging the Bosnian Serb political leadership in the process, the UN left the besieging forces free to predicate their observance on the total disarmament of their ARBiH garrisons and to justify continued military operations. Thus the 16 March 1994 report of the UN secretary-general lamenting that the safe areas were being used by the ARBiH "as locations, in which the troops could rest, train and equip themselves as well as fire at Serb positions, thereby provoking Serb retaliation." The report emphasized that for the safe-area concept to be sustained, there would have to be "full demilitarization by both sides on agreed conditions, assured freedom of movement, the impounding or withdrawal of heavy weapons and extensive UNPROFOR deployment." As a result, "UNPROFOR [had been placed] in a position of thwarting the military objectives of one party and therefore compromising its impartiality, which remains the key in its effectiveness in fulfilling its humanitarian responsibilities."[19]

II. The Safe Areas

A. Sarajevo

It is no secret that UN policy toward the safe areas was little more than a fig leaf to hide the great powers' naked self-interest, a stark truth that the international media did its utmost to expose through daily news releases that included sometimes graphic film footage of the human consequences. It is difficult to criticize the vital—and ultimately decisive—role that the media played as the self-appointed conscience of an otherwise oblivious world. At the same time, scholars must be sensitive to the media's shortcomings as a source of information and analysis. Few among the army of journalists were knowledgeable about the latitude that international law affords military commanders in warfare, let alone in siege operations, including finer points (such as the distinction between international and domestic conflict) that are still subject to debate by legal scholars. At the same time, they had a rather better developed sensitivity for human suffering, which inevitably turned most into advocates for the safe areas' civilian populations and, by extension, for the Bosnian government. But even here, the dynamics of the modern media ensured that the besieged populations would not receive equal attention. As the only safe area that was not fully encircled, Tuzla never attracted the kind of coverage afforded to the other five cities where the stakes seemed so much higher. Even the single bloodiest artillery salvo of the entire war, which killed seventy-one at a gathering of Tuzla high school students, received so little attention that the Bosnian Serbs never felt impelled to issue the usual denial of responsibility. After all, risks of an overarching humanitarian catastrophe and the potential political consequences simply did not exist in Tuzla.

Sarajevo was different. As the largest city and capital claimed by both sides, as well as the home of the 1984 Winter Olympics, it became the focus of media attention. As a result it also became the media battleground for validating the appeals and accusations of both sides. It is hardly surprising that each would commit war crimes in such an unconventional conflict that certainly had the trappings and, perhaps, the legal standing of a civil war. Apologists for the Bosnian Serbs invariably point to Bosnian government soldiers who ambushed a JNA column on 2 May 1992 as it attempted to evacuate Sarajevo despite having been granted safe passage by President Alija Izetbegović. Although he was genuinely shocked and outraged by their treachery, Izetbegović never attempted to apprehend or punish those responsible, doubtless because the city's undermanned garrison needed every available defender. The same logic may have persuaded government officials who successfully resisted the president's objections to entrusting Bosniak criminal gangs with defending Sarajevo during the first year of the war, even after they had singled out ethnic Serbs for punishment. Izetbegović was only able to neutralize the two most notorious gang leaders, Ramiz "Čelo" Delalić and Mušan Caco Topalović, in the summer of 1993, after they had begun preying on the general population. By then, however, the gangs may have accounted for a majority of all murders of Serb and Muslim civilians committed by Sarajevo's ARBiH defenders.[20]

Because none of the UNSC Resolutions ever charged the Bosnian defenders with any responsibility aside from not harassing UNPROFOR units, it is hardly surprising that they regularly launched attacks against the besieging Bosnian Serbs. On one occasion, French UNPROFOR units were compelled to attack them after they had occupied the demilitarized zone on Mount Igman.[21] Top UN officials have also contended that the ARBiH units sometimes positioned themselves near protected sites, such as Koševo Hospital, in order to draw return fire.[22] As a rule, however, it was the outraged VRS that responded both here and in the other safe areas, almost invariably with disproportionate force that included massive shelling. Although it is possible militarily to justify these retaliatory strikes as attempts at deterrence, the evidence suggests that they were motivated principally by the baser urge to inflict as much suffering as possible on the largely civilian population that lay in their sights. Indeed, successive VRS commanders Stanislav Galić (1992–1994) and Dragomir Milošević (1994–1995) were convicted by the ICTY of command responsibility for sniper attacks against noncombatants (including women and children) and indiscriminate artillery shelling against public buildings "of no military significance" with the principal intention of "spreading terror among the civilian population."[23] The intentional targeting of civilians comprises the strongest element in the long list of war crime charges that have been leveled against the besieging VRS forces. The case against the VRS can be divided into three categories. The first involves the besiegers' attempts to deprive the five encircled safe areas of basic services, including humanitarian shipments of food, medicine, and other supplies deemed essential for the survival of the civilian population. In May 1993 General Mladić informed the Bosnian Serb assembly of his intention to cut off the city's water and power supplies, while attributing the cutoffs to errant Bosnian government fire.[24] Whatever his plan, the UN Security Council placed responsibility squarely on his shoulders on 23 July 1993 by condemning the VRS blockade of Sarajevo. But were his actions illegal under IHL? Although it was obvious that the Bosnian Serb leadership was bent on a clearly illegal policy of ethnic cleansing, the rules governing siege warfare offered them considerable latitude. For example, Additional Protocol I governing *international* conflicts did not prohibit the use of starvation and deprivation of essential articles to force civilian evacuation when there was no way to prevent besieged soldiers from utilizing them. But the Bosnian Serbs did not even have to meet this condition if they were justified in their claim that the war was a *domestic* conflict. In any event, they ultimately permitted at least sporadic shipments of humanitarian supplies in all five of the encircled safe areas and ceded operation of Sarajevo's airport to UNPROFOR, which oversaw the distribution of an estimated 10,000 planeloads of essential supplies.[25] Less ambiguous is the prohibition of attacks on medical facilities, which Minister of Health of the Serbian Republic Dragan Kalinić had advocated destroying at the aforementioned meeting of the Bosnian Serb Assembly.[26] Kalinić's appeal came a month after the Koševo Hospital had been subjected to the first of several artillery attacks, in which even UNPROFOR forces were shot at while attempting to rescue patients from the facility.

Koševo Hospital was only one of several prominent civilian structures that were explicitly protected by IHL but came under deliberate artillery bombardment during the three-year siege. On 24 August 1992 the former special rapporteur of the UN Commission on Human Rights, Tadeusz Mazowiecki, reported deliberate attacks on cultural centers. The Polish diplomat was likely alluding to Sarajevo's Oriental Institute, which had been shelled and burned on 17 May, destroying the Ottoman-era provincial archive and Bosnia's largest collection of Islamic manuscripts, including over five thousand codices in Arabic, Persian, Ottoman, and Turkish. Yet the evening after his report, several VRS artillery positions opened fire on the National Library with incendiary shells in a barrage so focused that no other building in the area was hit. The famous Habsburg-era structure's interior, including virtually all of its 1.5 million volumes of Islamic literature, were consumed by the flames that evening and the following morning when a second barrage reignited the ebbing flames. Over the years, Bosnian Serb authorities have repeatedly denied responsibility, claiming that the fire was set from the inside, either to discredit the besiegers or to destroy its collection of five thousand Serbian language manuscripts. Although one VRS officer later privately admitted responsibility, his claim that it was an accident is contradicted by numerous eyewitnesses, some of whom were subject to a barrage of machinegun fire while attempting to save a small number of the collection's most valuable holdings, and by videotape footage that captured the flight of the phosphorous shells from the VRS artillery emplacements toward the library's glass roof.[27] One month later, Bosnian Serb artillery targeted the National Museum.[28] Despite losing all three hundred of its windows, the sturdily built National Library survived the bombardment; however, its director, Dr. Rizo Sijarić, was killed a year later when an incoming round exploded while he was working to cover shell holes with plastic sheeting recently provided by the UN.

The most egregious violations of IHL involved indiscriminate attacks, which are banned in international conflicts, and those that were explicitly directed against individual civilians, which are universally prohibited. Whereas the ICTY never disputed the VRS commanders' right to conduct siege operations against Sarajevo's 40,000-strong ARBiH garrison, there is little question that they employed tactics that were "deliberate, indiscriminate, excessive and disproportionate in relation to the anticipated concrete and direct military advantage."[29] Media video footage and extensive eyewitness testimony before the ICTY documented incessant sniper attacks during the siege of Sarajevo that targeted civilians of all ages and both sexes. One favorite target was the S curve near the city's landmark Holiday Inn, at which trams were obliged to slow down.[30] Attacks on ambulances merited special mention in UNSC Resolution 771's litany of blatant violations on IHL, even under the relaxed standards that Additional Protocol II applied to domestic conflicts. Mazowiecki's report went so far as to suggest that sniper activity and continuous shelling was "a deliberate attempt to spread terror among the population," a tactic explicitly banned by Protocol II, which was echoed in the ICTY indictments against the successive VRS commanders.[31] The intensity and indiscriminate nature of some of the attacks, including the firing of 3,777 rounds within a sixteen-hour period in July 1993 certainly gave some credence to this charge. So did General Milošević's repeated employment of "highly inaccurate" modified air bombs against civilian areas, which his own orders predicted would inflict "the greatest possible casualties."[32]

But the most heated accusations—and denials of responsibility—involve three mortar massacres that claimed the largest number of civilian casualties during the siege of the Bosnian capital, not so much because of the aggregate human loss but because of the role that they played in mobilizing international support for military intervention against the besieging Bosnian Serbs. The 27 May 1992 "breadline massacre" which killed 18 civilians and injured 160, had prompted the UN Security Council to impose sanctions against rump Yugoslavia. The first of two attacks on the Markale marketplace on 5 February 1994 killed 68 people and wounded 197. Following as it did heavy shelling that had claimed civilian lives in a children's playground, a residential settlement, and a filled soccer stadium, most observers joined the Bosnian government in affixing blame on the Bosnian Serbs. Over the following four days the EU passed a resolution calling for the lifting of the siege, while NATO issued an ultimatum to the VRS to withdraw all artillery beyond a twenty-kilometer-wide "total exclusion zone" or face air strikes. Despite their reluctance to cede their advantage in firepower against the numerically superior Bosnian government defenders, the besiegers complied within ten days.[33] Eighteen months later, a strike at the Habsburg-era city market barely 100 yards west of the Markale (28 August 1995) killed an additional thirty-seven people, prompting a Bosnia-wide NATO air campaign that brought an end to the war.

Given the immediate and telling consequences of each event, it is not surprising that the Bosnian Serbs and their apologists have steadfastly denied responsibility, something that they did not deem necessary following the even bloodier mortar attack in the Tuzla. In all three cases they have accused government forces of killing their own civilians, either by mortar fire or by detonating powerful explosives at the scene. UN Commander Lewis MacKenzie (1992–1993) lent credence to the claim by noting the efficiency with which the government had blocked off the site of the 1992 breadline massacre before the explosion and brought in journalists immediately afterward, while suggesting that most of the victims were actually "tame Serbs" whose ethnicity rendered them suitable for sacrifice.[34] The charge becomes more plausible in the light of two documented incidents of "friendly" sniper and mortar fire recorded by UNPROFOR personnel and subsequent claims by an American general that the Bosnians shot and shelled their own civilians during the siege.[35] Although both cases involved minimal loss of human life, the willingness of at least some ARBiH soldiers to engage in any such activity raises the question of whether they could have committed such an act in order to shame the international community into intervening militarily.[36]

On the other hand, the only "evidence" of ARBiH culpability in the three attacks comes from Bosnian Serb sources. Thus Belgrade's state-controlled media initially reported that a remotely detonated land mine had caused the breadline explosion because it left no crater and the victim's injuries were below the waist. The charge was, however, easily refuted by UN photographs showing the impact craters and by hospital records documenting an ample number of head and other upper body wounds.[37] A concurrent assertion that the speedy arrival of media on the scene pointed to a preplanned explosion ignored the fact that journalists had been filming an unrelated story just blocks away when the mortar shell hit.[38] After the first Markale explosion, Bosnian Serb President Radovan Karadžić asserted that media vans equipped with satellite dishes and ambulances were already parked at the marketplace, a claim repudiated by international officials who were at the scene moments before and after the explosion.[39] Nor does there appear any corroboration for Karadžić's claim that several of the Markale dead were refrigerated corpses trucked in from the morgue with ice still clinging to their ears. Whereas such counterclaims have failed to stand up under scrutiny, the ready resort to them certainly undermines Karadžić and other apologists as a source of credible evidence.

Unfortunately, UNPROFOR did not begin forensic examinations until after the controversy from the breadline attack. Nor could its investigation of the first Markale explosion prove conclusively that one side or the other had fired the shell, the trajectory of which was apparently skewed when it bounced off the corrugated roof of a market stall before exploding. A detailed forensics report for the second Markale explosion presented at General Milošević's ICTY trial appears to establish that the shell came from a VRS position, a judgment that has always been disputed by Russian UNPROFOR Colonel Andrei Demurenko, who was initially reprimanded by his superiors and dismissed from the ICTY trials of Generals Galić and Milošević after he admitted to knowingly misrepresenting the existence and substance of the report, as well as the scientific credentials and procedures employed by the Russian team investigating the incident.[40] Nonetheless, the origin of the fatal shell continues to be disputed privately by several military and intelligence officials from NATO countries previously interviewed by Cees Wiebes.[41]

Whereas it is difficult to dispute VRS culpability in the breadline attack, the inconclusiveness of the forensic evidence in the first Markale explosion and the insistence of unnamed—and, therefore, unaccountable—Western intelligence officers in the second are likely to sustain those voices that insist that the ARBiH fired the shells. Perhaps the most plausible reason for presuming VRS responsibility is that their prolific and indiscriminate shelling of Sarajevo—which totaled over a half million shells during the three-year siege and seven hundred rounds counted by UN observers on 5 February 1994—rendered moot any dispute over the origin of a particular salvo that took such a deadly toll. This was the justification that UN General Rupert Smith gave for blaming the Bosnian Serbs for the second Markale explosion, telling a lieutenant that their having fired all of the other salvoes that day had earned them the credit for the one that now triggered NATO strikes, even before a fuller investigation had been completed.[42] There had, in fact, been numerous other attacks during the seven months prior to the first Markale explosion—including modified air bombs introduced by VRS General Milošević—that UN observers had ascertained could only have been fired by the VRS; the attacks had killed 42 civilians, while wounding over 250.[43] Indeed, the aggregate record of the VRS besiegers—particularly the massive resort to indiscriminate shelling and snipers' specific targeting of individual civilians—renders moot the debate over any one incident because it leaves uncontested the premise for international intervention.

B. Goražde and Bihać

Much as the second Markale explosion helped end the war, the first one shifted the fighting elsewhere, partly because the creation of a total exclusion zone around Sarajevo prompted the VRS to relocate its artillery to Goražde and Bihać. And with the explosions began a new round of fighting and controversy. At the end of March 1994, the VRS launched a major offensive against Goražde. Not surprisingly, the international media claimed that the attack was unprovoked, whereas the Bosnian Serbs (and a U.S. House staffer) pointed to a 20 March sally by Bosnian government forces. This time NATO responded with air strikes, during which VRS gunners downed a British Harrier jet, then briefly seized 200 UN and civilian hostages. By mid-April the offensive had sharply reduced the Goražde safe area, during which shelling killed twenty civilians at the city's hospital. By 22 April NATO had created a new, twenty-kilometer exclusion zone for Goražde, which they quickly extended to the remaining four safe areas amid plans for an aggressive air campaign to end once and for all the shelling of civilians.[44]

Like Goražde, Bihać experienced a sharp increase in shelling following the February 1994 imposition of a total exclusion zone in Sarajevo. Like Sarajevo and the Drina Valley towns of Goražde, Srebrenica, and Žepa, Bihać was strategically significant because it sat astride the only rail link between Belgrade and the RSK capital of Knin. Yet, in virtually every other respect, the situation in Bihać was quite different from the other safe areas. Although completely encircled by the combined Bosnian- and Croatian-Serb military, the city's defenders controlled a 2,000-square-kilometer area with 250,000 inhabitants, 90 percent of whom were Muslim. Thus, although the town itself had been declared a safe area, the much larger Bihać pocket was not in immediate danger of falling, both because of its greater strategic depth and because the Bosnian Serbs were likely less eager to incorporate or expel its formidable Bosniak population. Another distinguishing characteristic was the presence of multiple military forces, including an independent Bosniak force headed by Fikret Abdić, who was allied with the Bosnian Serbs against the Izetbegović regime, and a Bosnian Croat (HVO) unit that collaborated with the ARBiH against Bosnian Serb and Croatian Serb forces. At one point or another, no fewer than seven military formations operated in and around the Pocket, including JNA units and a modest UNPROFOR garrison caught in the middle. Finally, the 7,000–10,000 Bosnian government troops of Atif Dudaković's Fifth Corps were fully capable of engaging and defeating any one of their many enemies—and of purportedly engaging in at least some ethnic cleansing operations of their own.[45] That summer Dudaković crushed Abdić's army and defeated a subsequent VRS offensive before launching a sustained counteroffensive at the end of October that seized the strategic Grabez Heights southeast of Bihać and over 250 square kilometers of additional territory. As in other cases, the use of a safe area for offensive operations exercised the Bosnian Serb leadership. Karadžić ordered a coordinated counterattack against the over-extended Fifth Corps that was spearheaded by VRS forces led by Mladić himself but assisted by Croatian Serbs, the remnants of Abdić's army, and even 500 army and militarized special police forces from rump Yugoslavia. The counteroffensive was not only launched "regardless of the safe areas" but in violation of the UN-imposed no-fly zone as warplanes from the RSK airfield at Udbina employed a full array of weapons, including rockets, napalm, and cluster bombs.[46] In less than a fortnight, the allies had not only recovered all of their losses but had entered the Bihać suburbs, seizing the city's water plant on a hill directly overlooking the town.

Despite the fury of the allied assault and the blatant violation of the no-fly zone, VRS operations do not appear to have targeted civilians or committed the kind of atrocities of which they were accused elsewhere. Nonetheless, the UN belatedly reacted to the threat by producing a map that, for the first time, actually defined the geographical extent of a safe area. At the same time UNSC Resolution 913 called on *both* sides to refrain from provocations that might endanger the city's noncombatants, while the secretary-general and Russian delegation tried to win approval for demilitarizing the entire pocket by disarming Bosnian government forces. British and French spokesmen went so far as to label Dudaković and the Fifth Corps the aggressors, whereas the U.S. government and media remained largely mute. Nevertheless, the employment of four converted SAM missiles and additional air strikes against targets in Bihać evoked pinprick NATO strikes against a SAM radar site and Udbina's runway. Although this fell far short of U.S. calls for punishing air strikes, it was more than enough for Mladić, who had been wounded in the fighting and now authorized the seizure of additional UN personnel.

Mladić's defiance elicited the predictable mix of international condemnation and empty threats. On 24 November UNPROFOR commander Sir Michael Rose publicly charged the Bosnian Serbs with violating the safe areas, while the NATO Council met in emergency session. One day later Rose ordered a retaliatory NATO air strike, although all ten aircraft returned to their bases without discharging any of their ordnance. The abortive sortie elicited a televised verbal assault from BiH Foreign Minister Haris Siladžić, who accused Rose of having the blood of thousands of Bosniaks on his hands. Equally anticlimactic was the NATO meeting, which featured yet another bold but futile call from the U.S., proposing the peaceful evacuation of the Fifth Army from a somewhat enlarged but demilitarized Bihać pocket, which would henceforth be protected from Bosnian Serb assault by the threat of punishing air strikes delivered across Bosnia. The French quickly rejected the plan, to which the U.S. would have only committed air support while leaving French and other UNPROFOR units exposed to attack and seizure. Instead, the council managed only to issue a declaration calling upon the two sides to negotiate a peace.[47]

C. Srebrenica and Žepa

In at least four respects, the confrontation over Bihać marked a turning point in the war. President Franjo Tudjman had already advised Mladić on 14 November that Croatia might intervene militarily to save the Bihać pocket from being over-run, a threat that he made public on 1 December.[48] Although the Clinton admin-istration was concerned about the ensuing preparations for intervention, it shared Tudjman's lack of confidence in the UN and in its own ability to overcome Anglo-French timidity to the extent that it offered one week later to deploy U.S. forces to assist UNPROFOR's withdrawal from Bosnia. The unspoken inference was that their removal would subsequently enable NATO air power to take action without fearing VRS retaliation against its member countries' ground contingents. The failure of the UN and NATO to deter or punish Mladić's forces also reinforced the Bosnian government's conviction that it should not place its hopes for what it regarded as a satisfactory peace in the hands of the international community. With the spring thaw, the ARBiH violated the ceasefire recently concluded by former U.S. President Jimmy Carter, launching a series of offensives around Travnik (March), Tuzla (May), and Goražde and Sarajevo (June).

But it was Mladić himself who may have derived the most important lesson from the IC's paralysis during the Bihać crisis. With the VRS outnumbered and overextended, he appreciated the need to consolidate his forces by eliminating one or more of the safe areas and the ARBiH garrisons within them. Although at-tacking them would violate the UN resolutions, he was equally confident that the British, French, and other contributing nations would not confront him so long as their UNPROFOR units were vulnerable to heavy casualties or hostage tak-ing. This was brought home in May 1995 when UNPROFOR Lieutenant General Rupert Smith authorized another pinprick NATO strike against an ammunition dump in the Bosnian Serb capital of Pale. His intention was to deter increased VRS shelling of Sarajevo and to compel Mladić to remove his heavy weapons from the total exclusion zone. Instead, on 25 May VRS forces began bombard-ing all six safe areas. A 130-mm shell from an M46 cannon landed in Tuzla's Kapija Square, killing 71 youths and wounding 124. When NATO aircraft retali-ated by bombing the ammunition dump a second time, Mladić authorized the sei-zure of nearly 400 UNPROFOR personnel, 27 of whom were surprised by VRS soldiers dressed in stolen French uniforms. Although the detainees were neither threatened nor physically abused, several were photographed while handcuffed to potential military targets. Whereas some legal scholars have argued that the seizure of the personnel might have been permissible under international law because other UNPROFOR units had engaged the VRS in hostilities, fettering them to military targets as human shields and photographing them in that condition clearly constituted yet another violation of international law.[49] But Mladić won his point, releasing the last hostages only after UN officials had renounced the use of force. New guidelines were issued stripping UNPROFOR General Smith of the authority to order air strikes, while making it clear that the execution of the UN's essentially humanitarian mandate in Bosnia was "secondary to the security of UN personnel."[50]

Having destroyed the credibility of UN deterrence in Bihać and Sarajevo, Mladić now turned to the three Drina Valley towns of Goražde, Srebrenica, and Žepa, whose seizure would release considerable forces for redeployment against the expected HV-ARBiH offensive in the west, while strengthening the Bosnian Serb claim to the entire Drina Valley in a future peace settlement. At first, he attempted to capture Goražde, which was the largest of the three enclaves and contained a key munitions factory. Yet here the UN stood firm as a handful of Royal Welsh fusiliers fought for several hours to hold onto the heights overlooking the town until they could be reinforced by ARBiH forces.[51] By contrast, Srebrenica and Žepa were the most militarily vulnerable safe areas. Yet another reason for targeting Srebrenica was the highly disruptive offensive thrusts that the ARBiH's Twenty-Eighth Division had launched from the town. Much of the credit for the division's successes lies with Naser Orić, a one-time member of the special forces of the Serbian Ministry of Internal Affairs (MUP) and bodyguard for Milošević who assumed command shortly after helping lead local Muslims in expelling Arkan's Tigers and other paramilitaries from the town in May 1992. By year's end his forces had created a sixty-kilometer-long enclave that snaked from Žepa in the south to Kamenica, just ten kilometers from the main ARBiH base in Tuzla. Orić attracted particular notice at the beginning of 1993, when his men were responsible for at least thirteen civilian dead among forty-three Serbs killed in the village of Kravica, which had been in the process of celebrating the Orthodox Christmas. Their temerity in shelling Yugoslav territory on the right bank of the Drina had also attracted attention. All told, Orić's men had razed scores of the one hundred villages and hamlets that had fallen into their hands, killing perhaps a thousand Serb soldiers and civilians. There is no question that some of them committed war crimes, which apparently included the immolation of civilians in their burning homes. Nonetheless, the ICTY could not establish that Orić himself exercised sufficient control over the raiders to justify convicting him of command responsibility for the atrocities, except for the mistreatment of some VRS prisoners detained in Srebrenica.[52]

Hence, Mladić's motivation may have included a mix of strategic and political considerations, together with a desire to retaliate for forays launched from within a safe area that the VRS itself had been prohibited from attacking. The

March 1993 counterattack brought immediate results, including the recapture of perhaps 80 percent of the territory once occupied by the Twenty-Eighth Division. Within just two weeks, Srebrenica's population swelled from 9,000 to 30,000, as refugees streamed in from the surrounding countryside.[53] But neither the VRS counterattack nor the town's subsequent designation as a UN safe area ended Orić's sallies, which persisted at a rate of three to four per week as his men foraged for food in the surrounding countryside. Both CanBat and the Dutch-Bat unit that replaced it at the beginning of 1994 routinely relayed the constant, heated complaints of VRS officers by warning of the possibility of Serb retaliation against Srebrenica's civilian population. By the beginning of 1995, Orić's raids had assumed a military posture as he implemented orders from ARBiH headquarters in Tuzla to reconnoiter, disrupt, divert, and demoralize VRS forces, which retaliated with counterstrikes of their own. Both sides were particularly active in the last two weeks of June, which featured an ambush of a VRS unit twenty kilometers northwest of the enclave. Within one twenty-four-hour period (23–24 June), DutchBat counted 1,815 rifle and machinegun shots and 253 artillery or mortar explosions.[54] Although Orić had already left the enclave for Tuzla, ARBiH headquarters there ordered another strike the very next evening (25–26 June), against the main Sarajevo-Zvornik road, employing 150 men, inflicting 40 VRS casualties and seizing weapons, radios, and livestock. A retaliatory artillery bombardment against Srebrenica elicited ARBiH protests that the VRS had once again violated a UN safe area. Meanwhile, the VRS also tried to exploit public outrage by citing an incidental firefight in the hamlet of Višnjica, where a Bosnian Serb woman was shot in the leg.

Even as the two sides fought for sympathy in the international press, Mladić was making the fateful decision to launch a full-scale assault on Srebrenica, most likely for the same reasons that informed the 1993 offensive.[55] Notwithstanding Mladić's earlier assurances to Lord Owen and others, there is evidence that Srebrenica's capture had always been part of his long-term strategy. In his ICTY testimony, VRS Intelligence Chief Momir Nikolić recounted how VRS forces were instructed to make life in Srebrenica unbearable in order to induce its civilian population to "leave *en masse* as soon as possible, realizing they cannot survive there." For this reason, Nikolić conceded that civilians were targeted and humanitarian aid blocked while fuel, food, and other supplies for the UN peacekeepers were halted so that "they could not be ready for combat." Yet preparations for a final assault did not commence until the end of May 1995, following the rebuff at Goražde.[56] Even then, the VRS does not appear to have anticipated a quick or easy conquest. Even with an estimated 2,000–3,000 reinforcements, including perhaps 200–300 Tigers and the somewhat smaller Greek Volunteer Guard, the VRS could count on no more than 4,000–5,000 men, of whom barely 2,000 actually took part in the decisive thrust against the safe area's southeastern corner.[57] Nor did the typically thorough Mladić begin making preparations for blocking—or even adequately monitoring—the flight of Bosnian soldiers or civilians, which he failed to anticipate in the event of a successful seizure of the safe area. In reality the Bosnian government had already forsaken Srebrenica in order to concentrate on an attempted breakout from Sarajevo. It was only after the attack had begun that the VRS command ascertained that ARBiH had psychologically placed their faith in the hands of the UN, which was itself unwilling to employ close air support, without which Srebrenica's 350 DutchBat personnel could not and, therefore, would not offer any resistance.[58]

This is not the place to recount the final, six-day assault on the city, which fell on 11 July 1995 to VRS forces, assisted by elements of the Yugoslav army (VJ) and assorted paramilitary formations, including the Greek Volunteer Guard.[59] Although the action—or inaction—of senior UN political and military officials and the DutchBat they directed has been the subject of considerable and often acrimonious debate within the international community, it is the aftermath of the city's fall that informs the salient controversy between the belligerents themselves. As in virtually every other combat zone in the Yugoslav wars, it is possible to speak of war crimes committed by both sides during the final hours of the Srebrenica safe area. After years of tense relations with UNPROFOR, ARBiH soldiers shot one Dutch soldier dead and took over a hundred others hostage in a desperate attempt to force them into defending the safe area's shrinking defense perimeter.[60] Their rationale was evident in the familiar taunt "30,000 for 300" signifying their fear that the UN was prepared to surrender 30,000 Bosnians to the Serbs in order to save the lives of its 300 DutchBat personnel. By contrast, it is not likely that his own men's survival was on Mladić's mind when he authorized the detention of twenty DutchBat soldiers in the first three days of the descent on Srebrenica. Rather, his readiness to seize additional hostages—and not release them all for twelve days, until after both Srebrenica and Žepa had fallen—suggests that he was once again using hostages to prevent NATO air support in defense of safe areas.[61]

A combination of eyewitness testimony, circumstantial evidence, and courtside confessions has answered many of the questions about what VRS forces did during that time. One fact that has never been in dispute is the distinction that VRS forces made between those males (roughly between the ages of fourteen and seventy) who either were or could be soldiers, and all remaining males and females. The latter were readily treated as noncombatant civilians and slated for expulsion, whereas men of military age were detained, ostensibly for interrogation. VRS personnel first turned their attention to the 3,000–4,000 Bosnians who had fled to the DutchBat headquarters at Potočari. Within three hours, all of the women and under- or overaged males at the compound were placed on buses for shipment to the front lines near Tuzla. Within thirty hours, a total of 23,000

people had been expelled in an operation that impressed DutchBat and other observers for its military efficiency.[62] The expulsions clearly constituted a violation
of IHL,[63] although the significance of the crime has been largely overshadowed
by the fate of the safe area's estimated 10,000–15,000 men and boys who were
deemed of military age. It is impossible to determine how many of this group had
actually served as soldiers at one point or another. Srebrenica's ARBiH Commander Sefer Halilović claimed that there were 12,000 among them who could
have fought to defend the enclave, although no more than 4,000 were armed.[64]
Given the ease with which men could shift between civilian and military status,
Mladić and his men confronted a difficult task in distinguishing between noncombatants and soldiers who could be legally detained as prisoners of war. All of
the considerable evidence available indicates that they never made any attempt to
do so. Beginning in Potočari, all men between fourteen and seventy were segregated, ostensibly for interrogation. In fact, several were killed on the spot, including fourteen executed in the proximity of DutchBat personnel. Meanwhile, the
great bulk of the male prisoners were trucked to Bratunac. DutchBat personnel
who attempted to follow them were seized, together with their UN vehicles and
some uniforms, weapons, and other equipment. Over the next few days DutchBat
hostages in Bratunac and elsewhere near Srebrenica witnessed additional executions, as well as boasts among VRS personnel about Bosnian women whom they
had raped and men whom they had killed.[65]

Whereas Mladić and his staff had expected the Twenty-Eighth Division to
regroup near Potočari, they learned only at midday on the twelfth that the great
bulk of Srebrenica's men had opted to break out of the pocket. One group of
700–900 fled east to Serbia, where at least 211 were interned and abused, but
not killed, by Yugoslav authorities before being released in April 1996. Another
body of 300–850 headed south to Žepa, just in time to be faced with a similar choice on the twenty-first.[66] By far the greatest number of 10,000–15,000,
including perhaps 6,000 soldiers (of whom 1,000–1,500 were armed), headed
north for Tuzla on the evening of 11–12 July.[67] There is no question that all three
columns were legitimate military targets, a status that was tacitly acknowledged
at the ICTY trial of VRS General Radislav Krstić. The VRS was, however, not
initially in the position to block or attack the main column as it commenced the
fifty-five-kilometer trek to Tuzla. By the time Mladić had redeployed his men, the
column's better-armed vanguard of roughly 3,000 soldiers had escaped to Tuzla.
The 9,000–12,000 who trailed behind were, however, successfully encircled by
a VRS cordon that attacked it with artillery, armor, and small arms fire. The relatively few who survived the experience have recounted how many of their panic-
stricken compatriots committed suicide, killed each other in the dark, or drowned
attempting to cross the Jadar River. It is likely that a considerably larger number
were killed by VRS fire. But by far the greatest portion of the main body sur-

rendered, some unwittingly to VRS soldiers equipped with stolen UN vehicles, helmets, and uniforms.

It was at this point that VRS forces committed far more egregious violations of international law by summarily executing many of their captives and trucking the majority to collection points where they were systematically killed. The evidence to support this conclusion is nothing short of overwhelming and has steadily grown over the past decade. The first eyewitness accounts came from a half dozen Bosnian escapees who gave precise, eyewitness accounts of a series of massacres. Among them was Hakija Huseinović, fifty-two, who described how several hundred captives were killed with grenades and small arms fire while trapped in an agricultural warehouse in Kravica, then scooped up for mass burial by tractors.[68] Nezad Avdić, seventeen, recounted shootings of prisoners who were taken off trucks at regular intervals and shot by the roadside while still handcuffed and blindfolded. Smail Hodžić identified a school complex at Karakaj, near Zvornik, from which groups of men were taken out for execution. Investigators were subsequently able to corroborate their testimony by visiting these sites. After their release, DutchBat hostages detained overnight near Nova Kasaba observed roughly 1,000 prisoners being held at a football pitch on the twelfth and approximately 600 bound and blindfolded corpses lying by the side of the road one day later. An array of reconnaissance photographs verified the presence of the prisoners and buses at the soccer field, together with piles of unburied corpses, bulldozers, and freshly turned earth at numerous sites nearby.[69] Other DutchBat personnel held in Bratunac testified to nightly executions of prisoners, some of whom had been collected in Potočari; they were held with captives from the main ARBiH column at a Bratunac soccer field before being transported to nearby execution sites. Some months later, a Bosnian-Croat serving with the VRS, Dražen Erdemović, recounted how he had participated in the execution of 1,200 prisoners at a state farm near Pilica. Acting on his testimony, UN officials located the site and buried corpses where Erdemović's unit had left them.[70] To date teams of investigators from the ICTY, Bosnia's Commission on Missing Persons, the International Commission for Missing Persons (ICMP), and the Tuzla cantonal prosecutor have recovered nearly 6,000 corpses—many still bound and/or blindfolded—from twenty-seven original burial sites and forty secondary ones to which most were relocated in an apparent attempt to hide the evidence. DNA testing by the ICMP has led to the positive identification of 5,653 individual victims (including eight women), with an estimated 2,400 persons still missing from the Srebrenica safe area.[71]

Over the past four years, this already considerable body of evidence has been supplemented by a series of ICTY trials, featuring confessions by several Bosnian Serb military high officials. While denying command responsibility for genocide and war crimes committed at Srebrenica, Drina Corps commander General Radoslav Krstić freely admitted during his August 2001 trial to the commission of mass executions by VRS forces. In October 2003, the chief of intelligence for the VRS Zvornik Brigade, Momir Nikolić, recounted the 12 July 1995 meeting in Bratunac, where General Mladić announced plans to kill all prisoners, after which Nikolić prepared for "the separation, detention and killings of the men." He approached Mladić individually the next day, after hearing him reassure several hundred prisoners detained in Konjević Polje that they had nothing to worry about, at which point the general reaffirmed with a sweeping gesture of his hand that they were all to be cut down. Nor did Nikolić's work cease there. After supervising four days of executions, Nikolić then directed the disinterment and reburial of many of the victims in order to frustrate the attempts of international officials to locate the bodies. According to Nikolić, Operation Krivaja 95 was common knowledge to all of the VRS officers present in Bratunac, including General Krstić.[72]

Nikolić's account of Mladić's 13 July speech to the prisoners at Konjević Polje corroborates the claims of survivors of the executions, much as his description of the reburials confirms the evidence presented by aerial reconnaissance photographs. It is also consistent with the October 2003 ICTY testimony of his immediate superior, Dragan Obrenović, chief of staff and deputy commander of the VRS Zvornik Brigade, who admitted reassigning some of his troops to assist in liquidating the prisoners detained in Bratunac. His rather detailed account of the operation also assigned direct responsibility to General Mladić, who attempted to conceal executions from the Red Cross and DutchBat personnel by ordering that the estimated 4,000 prisoners be shipped an additional fifteen kilometers from nearby Bratunac to Zvornik.[73] One month later, the testimony of Obrenović and Nikolić was complemented by one of Bratunac's municipal leaders, Miroslav Deronjić, who testified that Radovan Karadžić himself told him on 9 July 1995—two days before the fall of Srebrenica—that all of the prisoners "need to be killed—whatever [number] you can lay your hands on."[74]

The ongoing proceedings at The Hague will likely yield additional evidence and confessions by former VRS personnel.[75] A case in point is the revelation by Nataša Kandić of a videotape filmed by the Scorpions, a Croatian Serb paramilitary group, as they executed six Bosniak men after the town's capture. That said, the trials have been somewhat overshadowed by the public release in October 2004 of the final report of the Republika Srpska's Srebrenica Commission, which concluded its own extensive investigation by reaffirming that between 6,500 and 8,800 Bosnian men and boys were killed after the town's capture, their bodies distributed among thirty-two secret burial sites. While categorically confirming the massacre, RS Commission member Željko Vujadinović lamented that the executioners "should have buried the bodies deeper."[76] Nonetheless, RS President Dragan Čavić issued a public statement acknowledging the "staggering" scope of the crime detailed in the commission's report, terming the events of July 1995 "a black page in the history of the Serb people."[77]

With Srebrenica firmly in his hands, Mladić turned next to Žepa. To a great extent, the two towns' wartime experiences paralleled one another. Led by ARBiH Colonel Avdo Palić, Žepa's majority Bosniaks had defeated its small JNA garrison at the same time that Orić was expelling Serb paramilitaries from Srebrenica. Žepa's majority Bosniaks had cut off and defeated twenty-five JNA soldiers at a communications center in May 1992. When a relief column attempted to reach the garrison it was ambushed by Palić's men, with the loss of fifty-four Serbs killed, many of whom were from the Bosnian Serb capital of Pale.[78] The ambush infuriated the Serbs, who claimed that they had been promised safe conduct by the colonel. For much of the following twelve months Žepa shared Srebrenica's experiences as Naser Orić's Twenty-Eighth Division held and then lost the initiative in the face of the massive spring 1993 VRS counterattack. Because the May 1993 truce that Generals Morillon and Halilović concluded applied to both towns, Žepa experienced the same maddening stalemate among ARBiH forces that failed to surrender their weapons, VRS besiegers who continued to bombard the town, and UNPROFOR peacekeepers who had neither the mandate nor the numbers to enforce the compliance of either side. Not surprisingly, the Bosnian Serbs were willing to negotiate the peaceful evacuation of the town's estimated 7,000 civilians, whereas the Bosnian government resisted any agreement that would constitute another triumph for ethnic cleansing by ordering Palić to stand and fight.

As with Srebrenica, the VRS commenced operations by shelling the blocking force of UNPROFOR outposts on 8 July. Perhaps it was because of what had happened to DutchBat, that the much weaker 120-man Ukrainian contingent stood its ground, if only to buy what everyone realized was limited time before it would need to surrender. They readily acceded to Palić's request for the weapons that had been interned under the 8 May 1993 demilitarization agreement and after several tense confrontations eventually turned a blind eye to the seizure of some of their own ordnance by Palić's desperate men. Yet all hope ceased on 14 July, when the VRS launched Operation Stupčanica 95 in earnest against the Ukrainian and ARBiH defenders. Aside from some flyovers the UN military command ignored repeated pleas for air support. By the eighteenth, with four Ukrainian outposts taken and one of the remaining five surrounded and being openly threatened with annihilation, President Izetbegović and General Smith reached an agreement to evacuate Žepa's civilian population; as Izetbegović later told Carl Bildt, "ethnic cleansing is better than ethnic murder."[79]

Indeed, there would be no massacres in Žepa, largely because the Ukrainians still held the town and their weapons, while Mayor Mehmed Hajrić negotiated the evacuations directly with Mladić independently of ARBiH HQ and even

Colonel Palić.[80] By the nineteenth, roughly 5,000 civilians had been transported from Žepa, which was now systematically looted by VRS forces. Meanwhile, Palić's troops broke out of the enclave with perhaps 500 crossing the Drina into Serbia, where they were interned for the war's duration, and another 300 disappearing in the direction of Kladanj. These data do not account for the remainder of Palić's men. But we do know what happened to Palić, who stayed behind, was detained for a meeting with Mladić, and was executed the following day.[81]

III. Conclusion

States act in their own best interest, and where there is no interest, there is no action. This simple corollary of *raison d'état* explains the career of the safe areas from their creation to the fall of Srebrenica and Žepa. Ironically it was the resulting massacre at Srebrenica that finally shamed the great powers into addressing the humanitarian impulse to do something beyond posturing. The realization was particularly embarrassing for President Clinton, who was not only lambasted by Republican presidential candidate Robert Dole but by prominent Democrats like Senator Diane Feinstein, who confronted him with a photograph of a Bosnian girl who had hanged herself after being gang raped by Bosnian Serb soldiers following the fall of Srebrenica.[82] He now reluctantly confronted the inevitability of intervening militarily, either to send in ground troops to evacuate UNPROFOR garrisons that had become ready hostages for the VRS or to enforce heretofore empty UN resolutions and NATO threats by launching air strikes against the Bosnian Serbs. Some of the credit for this volte-face goes to the new French President Jacques Chirac, who readily characterized the Serbs as "unscrupulous people, terrorists" and now overruled his generals by demanding that the West undertake military action against the Serbs.[83] At the same time, the U.S. was eager to avoid the prospective fall of the much more populous Bihać pocket, which portended an even greater humanitarian catastrophe than had happened at Srebrenica.[84] As a result, the U.S. sanctioned the launching of Operation Storm (next chapter) and persuaded the NATO council to launch punishing air strikes against the VRS upon their next violation of *any* UN safe area.[85]

The launching of Operation Deliberate Force on the morrow of the second Markale mortar attack was swift and decisive in ending four years of war in Croatia and Bosnia.[86] What still remains to be resolved is the full extent of the crimes committed in and around the safe areas.

Despite the record of indiscriminate attacks against civilians and the weight of forensic evidence, it may never be possible to prove conclusively that Bosnian Serb forces were responsible for all three of Sarajevo's mortar massacres so long as there remain voices that continue to raise admittedly unsubstantiated claims that the ARBiH fired on its own people. Nonetheless, unanswered questions about the origin of any of these attacks cannot challenge the overwhelming amount of evidence that the VRS engaged in massive, indiscriminate shelling of civilians. More research also needs to be done to ascertain the extent of the crimes committed against the city's Serb population, particularly in the face of sweeping—but still undocumented—claims first made by RS Prime Minister Pero Bukejlović that the numbers may have been greater than those tallied in the Srebrenica massacres.[87] Although the ICTY has investigated crimes commit-ted by Bosniak gangs against Serb civilians, a thorough accounting will require the assistance of Bosnian Federation officials and civilians who have heretofore proven reluctant to look into them.[88]

Given the evidence, successive judgments by the ICTY and International Court of Justice (ICJ), the RS Srebrenica Commission report, and former RS President Čavić's "confrontation with the truth,"[89] there can be no doubt about the first legally recognized genocide in Europe since World War II. Nonetheless, there remain several subsidiary issues that merit additional research. It may never be possible to estimate accurately the relatively small number of the nearly eight thousand dead who were actually killed in action during the breakout rather than in cold blood by execution squads. On the other hand, interviews with former VRS commanders may enable us to determine whether Mladić intended all along to execute male prisoners or made the decision only after discovering that the bulk of the Twenty-Eighth Division had already escaped his grasp. Although there is considerable peripheral evidence that rump Yugoslavia's civilian and military leadership knew about the massacre and may have assisted in it, it could take years before access to the Serbian state archives will permit scholars to arrive at a definitive judgment. With the ICTY nearing the end of its mandate, it is impor-tant that the Bosnian government empower the projected Truth Commission for Sarajevo, so that it can establish the degree to which the city's Serb population was subjected to persecution and violence during the war.

Finally, more research needs to be undertaken concerning events in and around wartime Tuzla. Whereas VRS responsibility for the May 1995 mortar attack has never been disputed, other issues remain to be settled. Much as in Sarajevo and Žepa, Tuzla's JNA garrison was ambushed in May 1992 as it evacu-ated the city in violation of an agreement that it had concluded with Bosnian government civil and military authorities. Although the ICTY found no evidence of complicity by the signers, responsibility for the deaths of thirty-four JNA soldiers—and four members of the Bosnian authorities' security escort—merits closer attention. Belgrade's Serbian Documentation Center also claims evidence that the city's Serb minority was subject to violence, including rape and murder. In defense of its celebrated reputation for multiethnic coexistence, city authori-ties acknowledged, investigated, and punished seven wartime murders of Serb civilians by sentencing the perpetrators to prison terms averaging thirteen and one-half years.[90] Surely both sides in this and other remaining controversies deserve to learn together the extent to which such accusations are true or without foundation.

Notes

1 Jan Willem Honig and Norbert Both, *Srebrenica: Record of a War Crime* (London: Penguin, 1996), 136. Most recently, former UN civil and political officer David Harland, "UN Official Says Serbian Support Made Sarajevo Siege Possible," ICTY: Milošević Trial, 5 November 2003. Council for International Justice. www.cij.org (accessed 16 December 2003). Harland also characterized Sir Michael Rose's claim that the ARBiH fired a mortar from near Sarajevo's Koševo Hospital as "an accurate statement of what was going on."

2 Paul S. Shoup and Steven L. Burg, *The War in Bosnia-Herzegovina: Ethnic Conflict and International Intervention* (Armonk, NY: M. E. Sharpe, 1999), 141.

3 Honig and Both, *Srebrenica: Record of a War Crime*, 86, 91–92.

4 Ibid., 99; David Owen, *Balkan Odyssey* (New York: Harcourt Brace, 1995), 68.

5 Daniel Bethlehem and Mark Weller, eds., *The "Yugoslav" Crisis in International Law: General Issues,* Cambridge International Documents Series, 5 (Cambridge: Cambridge University Press, 1997), 35–36, 40–1.

6 Such as NATO's Atlantic Council (which authorized responses only to attacks on UN-PROFOR but not those on civilians); UNPROFOR General Michael Rose (who deemed *deter* insufficient to justify retaliation); and his successor, General Rupert Smith (who authorized retaliation for attacks on civilians as well as UN personnel).

7 Interview with former UNSC Ambassador Diego Arria by Charles Ingrao, January 2005.

8 Interview with former U.S. Deputy Chief of Mission Jack Zetkulic by Charles Ingrao, July 1997.

9 Interview with Diego Arria by Charles Ingrao, January 2005.

10 Thus the Turkish ambassador's judgment that "the 'joint action program' . . . appears to accept the *status quo* imposed by the use of force" and Diego Arria's characterization of Resolution 819 as a "total farce." Bethlehem and Weller, *The "Yugoslav" Crisis in International Law,* 284–293; Arria witness statement, ICTY 1 and 14 April, 22–25 September 2003.

11 Roy Gutman and David Rieff, *The Crimes of War: What the Public Should Know* (New York: W. W. Norton, 1999), 320. Although Sommaruga himself had assumed these conditions when first broaching the idea of safe zones, Austrian Foreign Minister Alois Mock had pushed for their implementation without requiring mutual agreement or disarmament. Honig and Both, *Srebrenica: Record of a War Crime*, 100–101, 104.

12 Although UNSCR 824 did call on "all parties" to respect UNPROFOR and other humanitarian agencies. Bethlehem and Weller, eds., *The "Yugoslav" Crisis in International Law,* 40–41.

13 Honig and Both, *Srebrenica,* 85, 89–90.

14 Nederlands Instituut voor Oorlogsdocumentatie, *Srebrenica: Reconstruction, Background, Consequences and Analyses of the Fall of a Safe Area* (CD, 2003), part II, chapter 3, section 3 (hereafter NIOD, II:3:3), also available at http://194.134.65.21/srebrenica/; Honig and Both, 105–106.

15 NIOD, II:3:5; Honig and Both, *Srebrenica,* 107–110.

16   Honig and Both, *Srebrenica*, 106; Owen *Balkan Odyssey*, 70–71. According to Lord Owen, VRS commander Ratko Mladić was content to tolerate the safe areas as a "dumping ground" for refugees if Bosnian government forces were allowed to keep their weapons. Owen, *Balkan Odyssey*, 82.

17   "The Serbs appeared not to want to physically take any of the so-called safe areas, even though they could have done so." Owen, *Balkan Odyssey*, 214.

18   Ibid., 178, 183, 190–192, 388–389.

19   UN Secretary-General Report S/1994/300, 16 March 1994.

20   Central Intelligence Agency, *Balkan Battlegrounds: A Military History of the Yugoslav Conflict, 1990–1995*, 1 (Washington: 2002), 186–187; Marko Attila Hoare, *How Bosnia Armed: From Milošević to Bin Laden* (London: Saqi Books, 2004).
     The number of Serb victims has been the subject of some dispute without any benefit of serious research. The Bosnian Serb Police Commission put the toll at 221 raped, 800 tortured, and 2,309 killed, with their bodies distributed among twenty-one locations within the besieged city. Both Republika Srpska's Office of Missing Persons and the Civil Security Center of Serb Sarajevo have placed the number at five thousand. On the other hand, team coleader Darko Gavrilović's attempts to document the center's claim that 200 Serb civilians were massacred and buried in a mass grave near the Restaurant Bazeni took on the character of a wild goose chase when Organization of Serbian War Prisoners Director Slavko Jovičić demanded $10,000 in exchange for the requested documentation; the RS government eventually withdrew the claim of a mass grave at the Bazeni. "Bosnian Serb PM Says Sarajevo Serbs Suffered More than Srebrenica Muslims," Agence France-Presse, 25 March 2005; "Swimming Pools Covered in Blood," *Glas srpski*, 29 October 2003, 5.
     Largely anecdotal evidence of murders committed across the city suggests that Čelo's and Caco's men were not alone, although other incidents involved random attacks against individuals or small groups of civilians. Mirko Pejanović, *Through Bosnian Eyes: The Political Memoirs of a Bosnian Serb* (West Lafayette, IN: Purdue University Press, 2004), 186; Faida Rahmanović, "Caco Wasn't the Only One," *Svijet*, 11 November 1997; Reuters, "Serbs Hunt for Bodies in Sarajevo Mountain Crevice," 1 June 2000.

21   Shoup and Burg, *War in Bosnia-Herzegovina,* 152–153.

22   This claim by UNPROFOR's controversial commander Sir Michael Rose has been corroborated by the ICTY testimony of UN Civil and Political Affairs official David Harland, even as he dismissed accusations that ARBiH forces fired on their own subjects. "UN Official Says Serbian Support Made Sarajevo Siege Possible," 5 November 2003, Coalition for International Justice (CIJ). http://www.cij.org (accessed 16 December 2003).

23   Although only two of the three judges concluded that Galić personally issued the orders, the evidence against Milošević elicited a unanimous judgment.

24   Robert Donia, *Sarajevo: A Biography* (Ann Arbor: University of Michigan Press, 2006), 298.

25   Gutman and Rieff, *Crimes of War*, 180, 338; Tom Gjelten, *Sarajevo Daily: A City and Its Newspaper under Siege* (New York: Harper Collins, 1995), 116.

26   "And let me tell you this right now, if the Military Hospital falls into the hands of the enemy, I am for the destruction of the Koševo hospital so that the enemy has nowhere to go for medical help." Transcript of Sixteenth Session of the Assembly of the Serbian People of BiH (12 May 1992), cited in *Prosecutor vs. Slobodan Milošević*, ICTY: IT-02-54, Exhibit 518, ERN 0190-8531–0190-8533.

226 ♦ CHARLES INGRAO

27   Interview with Dušan Bataković by Charles Ingrao, October 1998; András Riedlmayer,
     "*Convivencia* under Fire: Genocide and Book-Burning in Bosnia," in *The Holocaust
     and the Book: Destruction and Preservation*, ed. J. Rose (Amherst: University of Mas-
     sachusetts, 2001), 266–291.

28   VRS gunners openly admitted the attack to BBC reporter Kate Adie, apologizing pro-
     fusely for a stray shell that had struck the nearby Holiday Inn, where the international
     press corps was quartered. Michael Sells, *A Bridge Betrayed: Religion and Genocide in
     Bosnia* (Berkeley: University of California Press, 1996), 3.

29   *ICTY vs. Dragomir Milošević—Judgment*. www.un.org/icty/milosevic-d/trialc/judge-
     ment/ (accessed 16 February 2008).

30   Ibid., § 909, 927, 937. Moreover, the trams operated only during ceasefires. Ibid., §
     969.

31   Ibid., § 912–913; Gutman and Rieff, *Crimes of War,* 88.

32   Shoup and Burg, *War in Bosnia-Herzegovina*, 145; *ICTY vs. Dragomir Milošević—
     Judgment*, § 912–913.

33   CIA, *Balkan Battlegrounds*, 229–230.

34   Lewis MacKenzie, *Peacekeeper: The Road to Sarajevo* (New York: Harper Collins,
     1994), 293; Shoup and Burg, *War in Bosnia-Herzegovina*, 167–168.

35   Benjamin Rusek and Charles Ingrao, "The 'Mortar Massacres': A Controversy Re-
     visited," in *Resolving the Yugoslav Controversies: A Scholars' Initiative*, ed. Charles
     Ingrao and Thomas Emmert, special issue, *Nationalities Papers,* 32, no. 4 (2004), 845;
     Shoup and Burg, *War in Bosnia-Herzegovina*, 162, 165; Chuck Sudetic, *Blood and Ven-
     geance: One Family's Story of the War in Bosnia* (New York: W.W. Norton, 1998), 248;
     Charles G. Boyd, "Making Peace with the Guilty: The Truth about Bosnia, *Foreign
     Affairs* 74 (1995), 22–38.

36   For an analysis of the interplay of victimization and international intervention, see
     Alan J. Kuperman, "The Moral Hazard of Humanitarian Intervention: Lessons from the
     Balkans," *International Studies Quarterly* (forthcoming).

37   Tom Gjelten, "Blaming the Victim," *New Republic*, 29 December 1993, 14–16.

38   Rusek and Ingrao, "Mortar Massacres," 837.

39   Interview with former UNPROFOR Captain Ken Lindsay by Charles Ingrao 1997;
     UNPROFOR Investigation Report: Sarajevo Market Explosion, 5 February 1994, re-
     produced in *Serbian Studies* 17 (2003), 305.

40   "UN Officer Insists on Repeat Investigation of Markale Bombing," Russian Informa-
     tion Agency ITAR-TASS, 4 September 1995; "Russian Colonel's Conclusions Were
     Short," Sense News Agency, 6 July 2007; *ICTY vs. Dragomir Milošević—Judgment*, §
     703–713, 722–723.

41   Cees Wiebes, *Intelligence and the War in Bosnia* (Münster, London, and Hannover: Lit
     Verlag, 2003), 847.

42   Interview with former UNPROFOR Captain Ken Lindsay by Charles Ingrao, 1997.
     Indeed, General Smith's published account of the attack does not say a word about the
     evidence that led him to conclude VRS culpability. Rupert Smith, *The Utility of Force:
     The Art of War in the Modern World* (London: Knopf, 2005), 364–365.

43   Most notably the attack on the filled Dobrinja soccer stadium (1 June 1993; 12 dead,
     200 injured), but also attacks on a crowd in a residential community (12 July 1993; 12
     dead, 15 injured), on the Ciglane Market (6 December 1993; 4 dead, 13 injured), on
     a schoolyard (22 January 1994; 6 dead, 5 injured), and on a humanitarian aid line in
     Dobrinja (4 February 1994; 8 dead, 23 injured). These attacks and the three contested
     explosions are examined in greater detail in Rusek and Ingrao, "Mortar Massacres,"
     827–852.

44 Shoup and Burg, *War in Bosnia-Herzegovina*, 146–151.

45 For David Harland's acknowledgment of ethnic cleansing see ICTY, Milošević Trial, 5 Nov 2003; "UN Official Says Serbian Support Made Sarajevo Siege Possible." www. cij.org (accessed 16 December 2003).

46 CIA, *Balkan Battlegrounds*, 248–249.

47 Shoup and Burg, *War in Bosnia-Herzegovina*, 155–158.

48 Interview with former U.S. Ambassador Peter Galbraith by Charles Ingrao, 28 October 2002; CIA, *Balkan Battlegrounds*, 249.

49 Gutman and Rieff, *Crimes of War*, 177–178. Indeed, the incident made its way into the ICTY indictments against both Mladić and Karadžić. UN Press Spokesperson Alex Ivanko characterized the VRS leadership as a "terrorist organization," only to be threatened with "an accident" by an aide to Radovan Karadžić. Raphael Draschtak, *Endspiel* (Vienna: Braumüller, 2005), 87–89.

50 David Rohde, *Endgame: The Betrayal and Fall of Srebrenica, Europe's Worst Massacre since World War II* (New York: Farrar, Straus and Giroux, 1997), 27–28; Shoup and Burg, *War in Bosnia-Herzegovina*, 331.

51 James Gow, *The Serbian Project and Its Adversaries: A Strategy of War Crimes* (Montreal: McGill-Queen's University Press, 2003), 187, 270–271; Tim Ripley, *Operation Deliberate Force: The UN and NATO Campaign in Bosnia, 1995* (Lancaster, UK: CDISS, 1999), 114.

52 NIOD, II:2:4; Honig and Both, *Srebrenica*, 79–81; Rohde, *Endgame,* 44; CIA, *Balkan Battlegrounds*, 151; *ICTY vs. Naser Orić*, http://www.un.org/icty/oric/trialc/judgement/ ori-jud060630e.pdf (accessed 15 September 2008). Although Serbian sources claim 353 died at Kravica and up to 1,000 more elsewhere, the Office of the Prosecutor (OTP) dismissed these largely undocumented estimates in favor of captured internal VRS reports indicating that only 43 had been killed at Kravica, principally soldiers. http:// www.un.org/icty/briefing/2005/PB050706.htm (accessed 15 September 2008).

53 NIOD, II:3:1.

54 NIOD, III:5:8. That these raids constituted part of an overall strategy is reflected by an especially daring ARBiH raid from Goražde that overran a VRS position in Višegrad, inflicting forty-five casualties, including fourteen killed. Ibid., III:5:8.

55 For detailed discussion of Mladić's motives, see Wiebes, *Intelligence and the War in Bosnia*, 369.

56 Marlise Simons, "Officers Say Bosnian Massacre Was Deliberate," *New York Times,* 12 October 2003.

57 NIOD, III:5:8/11, IV:1:7.

58 Hoare, *How Bosnia Armed,* 118; Honig and Both, *Srebrenica*, 30, 34.

59 Ali M. Koknar, "The Kontraktniki: Russian mercenaries at war in the Balkans," *Bosnian Institute News*, 14 July 2003.

60 Rohde, *Endgame,* 35–36, 49, 65.

61 Honig and Both, *Srebrenica,* 45.

62 Ibid., 42, 45.

63 Gutman and Rieff, *Crimes of War,* 87.

64 NIOD, III:6:24.

65 Honig and Both, 37–38, 40.

66 NIOD, IV:1:1/7; CIJ, "Former Prisoner Testifies about Prison Camp in Serbia," Milošević Trial, Day 267, 10 December 2003.

67 Including top military and civil officials and their dependents. NIOD, IV:1:2/4.

68 Huseinović's testimony was confirmed in February 2003 by Bosnian Serb construction worker Krsto Simić, who recounted the painstaking process of loading and burying the

warehouse victims at one site, then returning several months later to excavate and move the bodies to a new location. "A Suspect Speaks Out," *Sence News Agency*, 24 February 2004.

69   Wiebes, *Intelligence,* 340–353. A combination of satellite, U-2, NATO fighter jets, and some UAV Predators was employed.

70   Honig and Both, *Srebrenica,* 52–62.

71   Karadžić Indictment, Attachment A, Article 28; "The Events in and around Srebrenica," RS Srebrenica Commission Report; "Number of DNA-Identified War Victims in Balkans Reaches 10,000," *Agence France-Presse,* 5 July 2006, and "More than 700 Skeletons Found so Far in Bosnian Mass Grave," *Agence France-Presse,* 27 July 2006; data updates through July 2008 courtesy of the ICMP. Remains are housed in a specially built structure for the Podrinje Identification Project (PIP) in Tuzla, Bosnia.

72   *ICTY vs. Momir Nikolić.* http://un.org/icty/cases-e/cis/nikolic/cis-mnikolic.pdf (accessed 15 September 2008). During his ICTY trial, Nikolić issued a statement apologizing "to the victims, their families and to the Bosniak people for my participation in the crime. I am aware I cannot bring back the dead, that I cannot mitigate the pain of families by my confession. But I wish to contribute to the full truth about Srebrenica."

73   Marlise Simons, "Officers Say Bosnian Massacre Was Deliberate," *New York Times,* 12 October 2003; "'I Am To Blame,' Srebrenica Defendant Tells Court." CIJ, 31 October 2003. During his trial Obrenović apologized to the victims' families, asserting that "I am guilty for what I did and did not do. . . . Thousands of innocent people were killed, only the graves remain. . . . Part of that is to be blamed on me."

74   Toby Sterling, "Appeal of Only Yugoslav Genocide Convict Begins at Hague War Crimes Tribunal," Associated Press, 21 November 2003.

75   Perhaps including Marko Boskić, whose August 2004 account of the executions corroborated the ICTY testimony of his fellow Bosnian-Croat Dražen Erdemović that all witnesses to the massacres, including bus drivers, were given the choice of shooting prisoners or being killed themselves. Shelley Murphy, "Written Account Says Boskić Confessed to 1995 Massacre," *Boston Globe,* 10 March 2005.

76   Interviews with Željko Vujadinović by Darko Gavrilović, October–November 2004.

77   Dragan Čavić, "Public Address on the Srebrenica Commission Report," 22 June 2004.

78   The attempted relief is covered in Slobodan Srdanović, *Pale: ratna hronika* (Belgrade: Edicija Dokumenti, 1998).

79   Carl Bildt, *Peace Journey: The Struggle for Peace in Bosnia* (London: Weidenfeld and Nicolson, 1998), 66.

80   Although Palić's chief of staff, Hamdija Torlak, participated in the agreement, ostensibly without the colonel's permission.

81   Palić's disappearance has spawned at least one story that he colluded with the Serbs to surrender Žepa in return for the peaceful withdrawal of its civilian and military personnel and another population, only to be executed afterward. Interviews with the former mayor of Pale, Savo Vasiljević, and the head of Žepa's Bosniak DP community, Alija Pavica, by Victor Bezruchenko, 1995.

82   Draschtak, *Endspiel,* 105–107.

83   Daniel Eisermann, *Der lange Weg nach Dayton: Die westliche Politik und der Krieg im ehemaligen Jugoslawien 1991 bis 1995* (Baden-Baden: Nomos, 2000), 309–310; Brendan Simms, *Unfinest Hour: Britain and the Destruction of Bosnia* (London: Allen Lane, 2001), 325–326; Brian Rathbun, *Partisan Interventions: European Party Politics and Peace Enforcement in the Balkans* (Ithaca: Cornell University Press, 2004), 141–145.

84   Interview with Ambassador Peter Galbraith by Charles Ingrao, January 2004.

85 The British went along only after an agreement in London that any attack on Goražde would elicit a massive NATO air assault to protect the beleaguered British garrison. Ivo Daalder, *Getting to Dayton: The Making of America's Bosnia Policy* (Washington: Brookings Institution, 2000), 68–79.

86 Charles Ingrao, "Western Intervention in Bosnia: Operation Deliberate Force," in *Naval Coalition Warfare: From the Napoleonic Wars to Operation Iraqi Freedom*, ed. Bruce Elleman and Sarah Paine (London: Routledge, 2007).

87 "Bosnian Serb PM says Sarajevo Serbs suffered more than Srebrenica Muslims," Agence France-Presse, 25 March 2005.

88 Pejanović, *Through Bosnian Eyes,* 142–143. The silence assumes more sinister dimensions in the face of charges by one Sarajevo journalist that certain newspaper editors "care more about the safety of their journalists" than ascertaining the extent of the crimes. Zlatko Dizdarević, "We Didn't Know," *Svijet,* 11 November 1997.

89 Čavić, "Public Address."

90 Dušica Borić, "The War in Bosnia, with a Description of Events in the Tuzla Region," *Serbian Studies* 17 (2003), 245–246, 251–259, and Sinan Alić, "Suffering of the Serbs in Tuzla: Reality or Deception?" *Serbian Studies* 17 (2003), 264–265, 268.

7

Mile Bjelajac, team leader
Ozren Žunec, team leader

Mieczyslaw Boduszynski   **Igor Graovac**   **Srdja Pavlović**
Raphael Draschtak   **Sally Kent**   **Jason Vuić**
                                 Rüdiger Malli

This chapter stems in large part from the close collaboration and co-authorship of team co-leaders Mile Bjelajac and Ozren Žunec. They were supported by grants from the National Endowment for Democracy to defray the costs of research, writing, translation, and travel between Zagreb and Belgrade. The chapter also benefited from extensive comment and criticism from team members and project-wide reviews conducted in February-March 2004, November-December 2005, and October-November 2006.

THE WAR IN CROATIA, 1991-1995

◆ Mile Bjelajac and Ozren Žunec ◆

Introductory Remarks

Methodology and Sources

Military organizations produce large quantities of documents covering all aspects of their activities, from strategic plans and decisions to reports on spending for small arms. When archives are open and documents accessible, it is relatively easy for military historians to reconstruct events in which the military participated. When it comes to the military actions of the units in the field, abundant documentation provides for very detailed accounts that sometimes even tend to be overly microscopic. But there are also military organizations, wars, and individual episodes that are more difficult to reconstruct. Sometimes reliable data are lacking or are inaccessible, or there may be a controversy regarding the meaning of events that no document can solve. Complicated political factors and the simple but basic shortcomings of human nature also provide challenges for any careful reconstruction.

The armed conflict in the former Yugoslavia has become the subject of a vast literature. This includes several memoirs or "documentary materials" written by both key figures and lesser participants in the conflict, ranging from international intermediaries and local politicians to soldiers, civilians, and journalists who were witnesses to events. Scholarly research is also expanding. However, many of the books and articles reflect the subjective perspectives of their authors. In the memoirs of participants who served in either the political or military apparatus, there is usually a strong apologetic effort to vindicate one's own assessments and actions. The publication of such works often provokes discussions in which former opponents or adversaries of the author push for their views. This rarely brings a balanced result; more frequently it just renews old disputes without opening new perspectives.

The war in Croatia from 1990 to 1995 is no exception to this. Beside obvious reasons why it is difficult to expect that a scholarly, nonpartisan, objective, and balanced historical account could be written only a decade after the end of the conflict, there are also many specific obstacles and impediments that make it hard to achieve such results. These obstacles continue to influence many current views among the public and in academic communities.

First, some of the most important developments in the war were never documented in the first place; many far-reaching and crucial actions were the results of deliberations that were made by decision makers and discussed in small circles without any written record. Given the nature of these decisions and the fact that many important power centers consisted essentially of nonstate actors without proper administrative infrastructure and culture, this poses very serious problems for historical reconstruction. Moreover, basic hard data—as, for example, the precise number, type, and structure of casualties, especially on the Serbian side— do not exist.

Second, many documents were simply lost or deliberately destroyed because of wartime circumstances or because authorities or individuals wanted to destroy the evidence of their activities and intentions.[1] Some participants, such as the wartime Croatian Serb civil and military authorities and organizations, vanished altogether in the war, and their documentation was only partially salvaged.

Third, the archives of former belligerents are for the most part still closed to scholars, and important documents are still inaccessible. On the other hand, many individuals for various reasons took possession of documents that would normally be part of the official archives (in Croatia, archivists estimate that at least the same number of original documents is in private hands as in the state archives). Access to the archives is still subject to the discretion of authorities who carefully weigh whom to admit; eligibility is not formally proscribed, but it is decided on an individual basis. Without being able to work systematically in archives, scholars will not be able to achieve precise insights into what happened and why.

Fourth, the war has left some smoldering fires. In the first place, there is the question of protracted prosecutions of war crimes. The International Criminal Tribunal for the Former Yugoslavia (ICTY), established by the UN in 1993, is still prosecuting violations of international humanitarian law. Extraditions of key inductees from their home countries to the ICTY were processes that took a very long time. Political elites feared that their regimes would be destabilized by the indictments or by the extraditions of persons considered to be national heroes in some circles, and heated political discussions ensued in all ethnic communities. On the other hand, many war participants were reluctant to write or talk about their war experiences, fearing that they also could end up in The Hague. All these circumstances create adverse conditions for free, unbiased, and independent research. Any published book or paper could be seen as additional evidence in the prosecutors' hands. The researcher is thus involved not only in the judicial process before the ICTY but also in domestic political struggles that surge almost every time the results of research are publicized. In addition to that, political development and even the current identities of the nations that participated in the war depend very much on an interpretation of recent history. Events and personalities tend to be seen in black and white. Every nation developed a corpus of "truths" that simply cannot be questioned and that have the status of sacred cows in both national ideology and politics. The "other" is always to be blamed. Direct victims of the war, or even entire populations for that matter, simply cannot accept that their fate was not only a consequence of the malevolent and criminal acts of the enemy but also due to the wrong assessments and blunders of their own leaders. Researchers themselves often feel an obligation not to rub salt into the wounds of their own nation; they tend to be biased without even knowing it.

Fifth, the conduct of the war in Croatia had many peculiarities that cannot be explained by the usual logic of history or social science. In this war there were many military operations that simply do not make sense in purely military terms; established motives, objective circumstances, and the known effects of certain actions sometimes simply do not match and do not present a coherent story. Perplexed by the impossibility of rational explanation, the general public and researchers alike consequently tend to give explanations based on various forms of conspiracy theories or on oversimplified historical explanations. Events that are complicated in themselves are explained by even more complicated interpretations. The reason for this is obvious. All wars are fought for political purposes, and military actions usually only translate political goals into practical military objectives. Sometimes military actions can be clearly understood as the logical means for accomplishing openly proclaimed ideological values and political goals (e.g., Nazi racist theory, the quest for *Lebensraum,* and the attack on the Soviet Union in 1941); but in other cases, when for different reasons political goals are not clearly articulated, military actions also become unintelligible and hard to understand. The political goals of many different actors in the war in Croatia often were not only badly defined, confused, and based on wrong presumptions, but they also changed radically over time. This means that military operations cannot be judged from a single perspective, valid for all situations and all times. There is also a general tendency for monocausal explanations that cannot bear fruit in complex historical situations.

Sixth, there is a general problem of sources for recent history. Working with data available in open sources brings also many dangers. Both media reporting and memoirist literature are often biased by the political opinions, affiliations, and agendas of their authors and editors. It is hard enough to find out what really happened, but many authors who played responsible roles and are aware of the portent of their actions choose sometimes to hide their real intentions and agendas. This often makes the research anything but an exercise in a logical ordering of things.

At the end of the day, one is left to one's own devices and cannot do much more than try to assess which interpretations seem most likely to be true based on available documentation and a reconstruction of the chronology. There are, of course, some honest and dependable accounts and collections, such as *Yugoslavia: Death of a Nation* by Laura Silber and Allan Little—certainly the most quoted work on the Yugoslav drama—and works by Tim Judah and Marcus Tanner.[2] The media as a source for the history of the recent conflicts do pose problems that concern many prominent scholars of Balkan and Yugoslav history. Some scholars have labeled all efforts to use media reports as sources as nothing more than attempts at "instant history." However, without media reports most research on the war would be impossible.

Inter- and Intraethnic Controversies

All these and other obstacles make research on the war in Croatia difficult and complicated. Even if facts are verified and both sides agree on their existence, their meaning could still be interpreted in contradictory ways for different communities. Everything depends on who is talking, and thus the academic work becomes a perfect example of how the social construction of reality works.[3]

The list of controversial issues in the war in Croatia is a long one. The divide runs between mainstream Croat and mainstream Serb interpretations that are usually mutually exclusive. There are also some interpretations by foreign researchers, by a small number of domestic researchers and, sometimes, even by government officials that differ from these widely accepted national narratives. Given the nature of war and different attitudes toward it in various social strata and groups, the war in Croatia has at least three main types of controversies: *Croat–Croat, Serb–Croat,* and *Serb–Serb.*[4]

This classification helps us to understand and evaluate different approaches in the scholarly literature. Sometimes these three controversies overlap. That is to say that some specific issues like ethnic cleansing, the engagement of the international community, or the role of the JNA, apply to each of these three types of controversy. Opposing views, such as those of the Croats and Serbs, can be considered as pictures of the past that emerged at one time and never ceased to exist. The historian or analyst should recognize this as a part of the mosaic of the past. No one can deny that the majority of the Croats saw the JNA as an aggressor against the Croatian homeland or state. On the other hand, Serbs in Croatia have insisted that their resistance was a form of legitimate self-defense against the violation of their constitutional rights and for the protection of their lives. In some aspects, neither Croats nor Serbs can come to terms among themselves.

The issues deal very much with national affiliations and identities.[5] In spite of this, controversies are often characterized by their similarities on both sides. The army generals quarreled among themselves on merits or failures and pointed out correct predictions or blindness. Controversies also emerge within each ethnic or other socially defined group when someone dares to reveal unpleasant facts, including those that challenge established truths.

Regarding interethnic disagreements, it should be noted that Serbian and Croatian views are a constituent part of the complex historical picture of the past (the war in this case) and should be taken as such. If cleared of obvious exaggerations, manipulations, and myths, these views have a certain legitimacy and should be taken seriously. Simple compromise among scholars cannot constitute the basic methodological principle in attaining definitive truth concerning the events in question. Future readers will not be best served by uncontroversial accounts of the events but will always have to deal with at least some discrepancies in the accounts and will then have to draw their own conclusions. A survey of controversies that existed and will probably exist in the future and the array of arguments concerning these controversies should not dim the picture but only help scholars find better interpretations.

Robert Hayden has summarized the problem of intellectual orthodoxy in dealing with conflicts involving living political communities. He warns:

> Protracted international conflicts often produce more partisans than scholars; if truth is the first journalistic casualty of war, objectivity is the first scholarly one. Academic debates on the former Yugoslavia are as polarized as those surrounding the creation of Israel or the partition of Cyprus, with criticism of a study often depending more on whether the work supports the commentator's predetermined position than on the coherence of its theory or the reliability and sufficiency of its arguments. When one side in such a conflict wins politically it usually also wins academically because analysis that indicates that a politics that won is, in fact, wrong tend to be discounted. Political hegemony establishes intellectual orthodoxy.[6]

Certainly political settlements cannot serve as a blueprint for scientific research. Scholars dealing with recent history or with social developments are not completely helpless in taking on their task. However, as already discussed, they are facing obvious limits.

Survey: Some Controversial Episodes and Issues

Causes of War

One of the biggest controversies of the whole conflict concerns the reasons for the Serb insurgency. A Croat interpretation of the causes of war includes a belief that the Serbs had an elaborate plan for establishing a Greater Serbia. This interpretation argues that Serbian Socialist Party (SPS) leader Slobodan Milošević encouraged the Croatian Serbs to rebel in order to take substantial parts of Croatia for Greater Serbia, while suggesting that the Serbs never had valid reasons for their armed insurgency. According to this school of thought, this plan originated in various nineteenth- and twentieth-century political theories and programs and was later accepted by Serbian intellectuals and Milošević. The main reason for the war was to proceed with the territorial expansion of Serbia. Among the evidence for this argument are some indisputable facts: (a) through various putschist policies Milošević abolished the autonomies of Kosovo and Vojvodina and thus abrogated the Yugoslav Constitution of 1974; (b) Milošević proclaimed that "All Serbs must live in one state," which neglected the fact that republics were states, thereby opening the way to a "rectification of borders"; (c) Croatian Serbs staged demonstrations and other activities in 1989, claiming, "This is Serbia." This was before any political developments had occurred in Croatia that could have been seen as dangerous for the existence and status of Serbs there.

The Serbian side claims routinely that the promulgation of the new Constitution of the Republic of Croatia in December 1990, created among the Serbs a fear that the suffering that the Serbs endured under the Ustasha regime of 1941–1945 would now be repeated. They were opposed to the wording in the constitution, which deprived the Croatian Serbs of their status of "constitutive people" and "reduced" them to the status of a "minority," and they were apprehensive of the extremist nationalistic politics of the new ruling party—The Croatian Democratic Union (HDZ).

The HDZ certainly did not show much sensitivity toward the Serbs in Croatia and did almost nothing to persuade the Serbs of their good intentions. Croats intended to leave Yugoslavia as part of their national and political liberation, but this legitimate goal was sometimes clouded with other political incentives that frightened Croatian Serbs. It is true that in some extreme right political circles there was a nostalgia for and a desire to resuscitate the Independent State of Croatia (NDH), a fascist puppet state during World War II.[7] It must be kept in mind, however, that in socialist Yugoslavia almost every voice for national rights, no matter how democratic its demands were, was branded as nationalistic and extremist. Thus Croatians were often labeled Ustashe by Serbs, although it is important to note that in 1990–1991 there was a certain amount of Ustashe revivalism in Croatia.[8] This not only generated fear among the Serbs but played right into the hands of the nationalistic program of Milošević. Some Serbs began to fear a repetition of 1941 and looked on socialist Yugoslavia as the guarantor of their personal and national security. Several Croatian historians have provided many documented details that corroborate the thesis that some Croat actions must have provoked the Serbs.[9]

The Serbs felt uneasy about developments that they deemed similar to the situation they faced in 1941–1945, when they were victims of persecutions and even genocide. However, their situation was not at all similar to what they had faced in World War II. To begin with, there was no plan to expel or execute members of Croatia's Serb minority. Moreover, the international community closely watched developments in Yugoslavia, so that even if the Croats had wanted to resuscitate the NDH they would have been unable to introduce the politics of terror, persecutions, and genocide against the Serbs. Although some representatives of the Serb people in Croatia—including Orthodox bishops—had warned that any repetition of 1941–1945 was highly unlikely and in fact impossible,[10] Serbian propaganda pounded its audience in Croatia with horrifying pictures from the past, stressing that Croats were genocidal killers by nature and that nothing could change that. Various propaganda tricks were employed to persuade Croatia's (and Bosnia's) Serbs that history was repeating itself, including reburying the victims of Ustashe persecution from World War II in elaborate rituals.

One can conclude that the Serbs in Croatia were exposed to various forms of discrimination[11] but that this discrimination was far from the persecution experienced in World War II. It is also important to remember that any killings or other forms of violent persecution directed at Serbs in Croatia in places like Gospić, Pakračka Poljana, Sisak, Osijek, and Paulin Dvor began only after the outbreak of full-scale armed conflict in the summer of 1991. Thus these crimes by Croats cannot serve as a justification for the rebellion because they happened after the insurgency and war were already in full swing.

The behavior of the Croats was partly a consequence of a growing fear that Milošević would use the JNA to launch an attack on Croatia immediately after the first multiparty elections, using local Serbs as pawns. After all, Belgrade had already been instrumental in mobilizing Croatia's Serbs and, later, in encouraging their armed insurgency in Croatia. Belgrade promoted various manifestations of the "antibureaucratic revolution," and it sent emissaries and helped to coordinate actions between various Serb nationalists in Serbia and in Croatia. The confiscation of the Croatian Territorial Defense weapons by the JNA in May 1990 ominously seemed to be paving the way for the attack.

Within Serbia itself a number of noted intellectuals, former prominent party or state leaders, generals and admirals, and NGO activists are more likely to agree with some of the standard Croatian claims about the causes of the war, notably the role of Serbian nationalism and the "Great Serbian Project." Few would deny the key roles played by Slobodan Milošević and by the army.

A number of Western analysts also consider the project for a Greater Serbia to be the primordial cause of Yugoslavia's collapse and the ensuing tragedy. These include such scholars as James Gow, Michael Libal, and Paul Garde.[12] On the other hand, some Western analysts argue as well that this plan for the establishment of Greater Serbia did not function in the later stages of the war. The evidence for this is that many declarations and plans for the unification of "Serb lands" (RSK, RS, Serbia proper, and Montenegro) were never realized; moreover, other Serb lands did not come to the aid of the RSK during the final Croatian operations in the war.

Some distinguished and influential foreign scholars have advanced the theory that the real and deeper cause of the war can be found in the disintegration of governmental authority and in the breakdown of a political and civil order. Susan Woodward argues, for example, that "the conflict is not a result of historical animosities and it is not a return to the pre-communist past; it is a result of the politics of transforming a socialist society to a market economy and democracy."[13] The situation was aggravated by declining social standards and an unfavorable international situation in which the former Yugoslavia was no longer of great importance.

Any resolution of the differences here should be found by taking into account all the facts on which these interpretations are based and discarding all the conclusions that do not follow from them. Beyond this it is necessary to take into account the dynamic aspect of wartime politics and changes in the policies of the main actors.

The Nature of War and Its Politico-Legal Character

Another controversy that directly stems from the first is connected with the political and legal character of the war. Ethnic Serbs in both countries claimed that the conflict was a classic instance of a noninternational or civil (internal) war. Serbs claimed that they were defending their very existence from the genocidal politics of a new Croatian regime. In this view, because the Croats had seceded from Yugoslavia the conflict was a clear case of two civil wars, neither of which had state actors on both sides (nonstate Croats against Yugoslavia, and nonstate local Serbs against Croats). The main argument for this claim is that the insurgent Serbs were citizens of Croatia who rebelled against Croatia's central government.

Conversely, Croats claimed, and were endorsed in these claims by much of the international community, that (a) Yugoslavia was simply in a "state of decomposition"; that (b) Croatia was proclaimed a sovereign state (25 June and 8 October 1991), which was duly recognized by dozens of countries (January 1992); and that (c) Milošević usurped federal Yugoslav institutions such as the JNA and rump presidency) thus effectively eliminating the federal state of Yugoslavia. According to this picture, Yugoslavia and Croatia were two separate countries, with Yugoslavia having its troops (JNA) on Croatian soil. Croatia insists that the armed conflict in Croatia was an international war, with Yugoslavia (Serbia and Montenegro) and the JNA as the aggressors as defined in international law.

It is evident that both claims are designed to achieve a more favorable status of victim for the respective claimants (Croatia as victim of external aggression, Croatian Serbs as victims of the Croatian government). This could in turn ameliorate their overall status and attract sympathy.

Both of these claims, although they look irreconcilable, are founded in facts and in law. There is no doubt that the resistance of local Serbs against the Croatian central government was not an international armed conflict, but it is also evident that rump Yugoslavia led an international war and was the aggressor between October 1991, at the latest, and the withdrawal of Yugoslav troops from Croatia in June–October 1992. The claim of local Serbs that they could not be aggressors or occupiers in their own country is correct, but it is equally correct to say that by leading an armed insurgency they abetted the foreign aggression committed by rump Yugoslavia and its institutions. In order to provide a legal framework for the conflict, the ICTY chose to consider the war in Croatia after 8 October 1991 as an international armed conflict.[14]

Establishment of Croatian Armed Forces

As already mentioned, Croatian Serbs felt threatened by the Croatian government's actions. In the second part of 1990 there were instances of discrimination against Serbs, who were dismissed in large numbers from their jobs, especially in the security sector (i.e., police, Territorial Defense [TO], etc.). The Serb minority in Croatia—581,663 people according to the 1991 census, or 12.2 percent of the republic's population of 4.8 million—was overrepresented within both the Communist Party membership (22.6 percent in 1984) and the political elite (17.7 percent of appointed officials in Croatia were Serbs)[15] and especially in the Ministry of the Interior (MUP), including the police (28–31 percent). Serbs were also overrepresented in federal institutions, especially in the JNA, where 57.1 percent of officers were Serbs. Contrast this with the fact that only 36.3 percent of the population of Yugoslavia was Serbs.[16] It must be noted, however, that the representation of Serbs in the republican police decreased in the late 1980s to a level of 17–18 percent,[17] but this was too late to change the long-existing perception of Serbs as guardians of the Communist regime—a regime that was eventually usurped by Milošević. Croats were afraid of Milošević's project of "All

Serbs in One State." Because they lived in an environment where the concept of the independent citizen was virtually unknown and where people existed only as members of a group, it was easy to equate *all* Serbs with Serb nationalistic politics. The Serbs' overrepresentation in critical services and institutions (police, military, party) was seen as a threat that had to be remedied if Croatia wanted to gain independence. Discrimination in the republican police was thus more the consequence of perceptions and mistrust between ethnic communities than it was a political program.

A CIA report clearly identified the personnel questions in the police force as one of the central issues in events that would eventually lead to the war:

> The crux of the dispute centered on Croatian efforts to alter the size and character of the republic's police force by building additional Croat-majority police stations and reducing the number of ethnic Serbs in the existing force. By bringing additional ethnic Croats into the regular force, the Croatian Government clearly hoped to decrease both absolute and percentage terms, as well as to move Croatian personnel into police stations in Serb territory. But the Croats' heavy-handed efforts to dominate the police force poured salt on an open wound and enraged ethnic Serbs everywhere.[18]

The Croatian police actually provided the only legal avenue to establish a military force in Croatia. According to General Anton Tus the Croatian government used the framework of the Ministry of the Interior after 30 May 1990, rather than that of the Territorial Defense (as was the case in Slovenia), to create the new Croatian army.[19] By buying weapons for the police, the Croats circumvented the ban on republican paramilitaries imposed by the federal presidency and managed to compensate for their losses when the TO arsenals were taken over by the JNA in May 1990.

The expansion of the Croatian police forces went hand in hand with growing unrest. On 17 August 1990 militant Serbs in Krajina closed all communications in northern Dalmatia, and the police in Knin, led by Milan Martić, future president of the Republic of Srpska Krajina (RSK), proclaimed that Serb police would not obey directives from Zagreb. By January 1991 the original force of 10,000 Croatian police had been nearly doubled. The centerpiece of the MUP's efforts to develop a military force, however, was the expansion of its special antiterrorist unit into "special police" battalions organized along military lines. By January 1991 the program created several battalion-size military units with 3,000 members.

To back up these regular forces, the MUP also began an expansion of its regional reserve formations estimated to number 10,000 personnel organized in sixteen battalions. In May 1991 the MUP's special police forces and reserve formations were transformed into the Croatian National Guard Corps (ZNG) and subordinated to the Ministry of Defense. Foreign monitors concluded that Croatia

> was going to have to go to war without the robust command and control structure necessary to direct combat operations in the field. In particular, the lack of strong regional commands to control Zagreb's often ill-disciplined and inadequately trained troops, combined with poor coordination between the MUP and the ZNG.[20]

Croatia's efforts to create its own armed forces, along with its political moves to separate from Yugoslavia, were closely watched by the JNA, which saw itself as the only federal institution still able and willing to thwart Croatia's secessionist intentions. Having dealt with the potential Croatian military threat, the JNA turned its attention to the political threat, drafting plans to remove the Croatian (as well as Slovenian) government. The JNA leaders intended to allow Croatia and Slovenia to proceed with their announced steps toward independence so that the JNA's planned military action could be amply justified. Although the JNA successfully confiscated Croatian Territorial Defense armaments in May 1990, it failed to foil the Croats' armament acquisition program from late 1990 to early 1991. In the fall of 1990, the JNA discovered those activities but could not get adequate support from the divided presidency for Operation Shield, designed to disarm the Croatian military organization and put its leaders on trial. In January 1991 the presidency ordered the Croats to hand over their arms, but the whole action failed. Nor could the JNA's effort in mid-March 1991 to impose a state of emergency garner support in the presidency. Although Milošević's ally Borisav Jović attempted to create a power vacuum by resigning as president of the presidency, the JNA was unable to exploit the opportunity.

First Incidents and the Outbreak of War

The inability of senior politicians to achieve a solution to the crisis and the unwillingness of the JNA to act ensured that the rising tensions within Croatia would eventually lead to open clashes between armed Croatian Serbs and Croatian government forces. The brief clashes that erupted at the town of Pakrac (3 March 1991), at Plitvice Lakes (31 March), and at the village of Borovo Selo (2 May, where at least twelve police died) were the first shots in the war that would consume Croatia for the rest of 1991. Both Serbs and Croats realized that all-out war was likely, and emotions reached the boiling point. Their fights and threats drew the JNA's Croatian garrisons into the role of peacekeepers, a role that did not fully satisfy either the Croatian Serbs, who wanted the JNA to defend them, or the Croats, who believed that the JNA was explicitly or tactically backing the rebellious Serbs.

After the Borovo Selo incident, internecine clashes spread like plague. Many outbreaks of violence appeared to be unplanned, undirected, and incoherent. This inchoate violence would serve to mask strategic military actions by the Croatian Serb leadership that aimed to expand its control over Serb areas in Croatia. President Tudjman resisted pressure from hardliners who wanted him to retaliate for Croatian Serb victories by attacking the JNA, which they viewed as pro-Serb. Tudjman continued to look to the international community for action to halt the fighting. His initial aim was to internationalize the conflict in Croatia rather than fight back with military force, hoping that the EC and the U.S. would recognize Croatian independence and put pressure on Belgrade to halt its operations against Croatia. Meanwhile, the JNA tried to keep the peace by acting as a buffer force until midsummer but failed utterly.

Throughout the summer major fighting occurred in the Banija region south of Zagreb, where Serb TO and police units tried to gain control over the towns of Glina and Kostajnica by seizing Croatian police stations in the region. Nevertheless, the Croats remained in control of Kostajnica until mid-September. The largest Serb operation in eastern Slavonia was the successful campaign to seize control of Baranja in late August. There were also clashes around the suburbs of Vukovar, Vinkovci, and Osijek in which each side attempted to expand its control. Much of the fighting throughout the summer consisted of intense, daily exchanges of fire between Croatian and Serb villages without any attempts by either side to capture territory. Farther south in northern Dalmatia (Knin), in contrast to other regions, the driving factor was the JNA. Although at first acting in a peacekeeping role as directed by the JNA high command, the JNA Ninth Corps (Knin) during August became more and more prone to initiating clashes with Croatian forces or defending Serb-held territory. This culminated in the capture—in cooperation with SAO Krajina troops—of the key Croatian-held village of Kijevo (26 August) and the seizure of the strategic Maslenica Bridge linking the Dalmatian coast to northern Croatia (11 September). To some extent these operations around Kijevo may have stemmed from JNA perceptions that it was being attacked, blocked, or threatened by Croatian troops.

Under pressure from the European Community, on 7 July all sides in the Yugoslav conflict accepted a three-month moratorium on any declaration of secession by Slovenia and Croatia with the goal of bringing about a peaceful negotiation concerning Yugoslavia's future. However, it was clear that all sides had other plans. Croat President Tudjman made the decision to go to war with the JNA in mid-September, launching a strategic offensive on 14 September to neutralize and capture its installations throughout Croatia. This added a new dimension to the defensive military strategy that Croatia had pursued throughout its conflict with local Serb forces during the summer. Zagreb intended to continue on the defensive at the front while attacking the JNA in the rear. The assault on the JNA barracks was the key element in the Croatian efforts to expand the ZNG. The weapons that the Croats seized in the barracks were used to arm dozens of newly mobilized active duty and reserve brigades. These weapons either replaced or were the same ones that the JNA had confiscated from the republican TO in May 1990.

The American ambassador in Yugoslavia, Warren Zimmermann, indicated that he was informed well in advanced about these plans:

> In late August Tudjman told me of his plans to launch a "war option"—an all-out offensive against the JNA and "Četnik separatists." I agreed with him that the JNA was not acting in a neutral fashion but asked him how he could possibly hope to take it on with his neophyte army. "Oh," he said offhand-edly, "your country will come to my rescue with military force." I told him there wasn't a speck of credibility in his assertion and urged him not to base any military calculations on an American bailout. I failed to puncture Tudj-man's serenity. "Perhaps I know more about your country than you do, Mr. Ambassador," he said with a smile.
>
> Shaking my head about his informants on American politics, I tried another tack. "Why don't you try to end the Serbian resistance by offering them au-tonomy within Croatia? In effect they have it anyway, protected by the JNA. A magnanimous gesture on your part might help provide the missing element of trust, and it would be popular in the West." Tudjman showed no interest in the idea. Nor did he want to discuss a proposal that his own ministers had been peddling—an "association of Yugoslav states." The proposal, in which the U.S. government had shown some interest, limited the central govern-ment to token powers; defense and foreign policy would be the province of the individual states. Thus the "association" would look more like the twelve-state European Community than Switzerland—not, in other words, a big concession for Croatia to make. Tudjman's only reference to it was his parting shot: "If this war goes on, don't mention any Yugoslav association to me."[21]

These intentions also could not be kept secret from the army and the rest of the Yugoslav presidency and thus provoked suspicions on the other side and countermeasures. On 14 August 1991 General Veljko Kadijević gathered the most trusted in his cabinet (General Blagoje Adžić, S. Milošević, M. Bulatović, B. Kostić, and B. Jović) and informed them:

> According to information from different sources—and the Greek one is defi-nitely reliable—the Croats have decided to escalate the conflict with the JNA expecting that the greater scale of combats will provoke military intervention from abroad. The current situation does not help them. They have support from the Vatican and the Federal Republic of Germany as well as the good will of the Americans.[22]

However, the Croatian decision to wage the war could be seen as a face-saving action at a time when the JNA and Serb insurgents had already launched their offensives and controlled much of the national territory. There was not much choice: the Croatian government could either yield to Milošević, the JNA, and Serb insurgents, or it could try to defend what was left. In the summer of 1991 its ramshackle forces could not do much more than try to defend its positions, occasionally attacking blocked JNA garrisons in towns. Tudjman later publicly stated that Croatia had "chosen" the war, but this was not much more than his usual boasting.[23]

It remains unclear why the rump presidency, with Branko Kostić as acting president, made moves that diminished the JNA's capacity for resistance. For example, on 1 September the presidency issued the order to discharge from active service the complete September 1990 class of conscripts, which was the most numerous and the best-trained contingent in the JNA. Further, a 26 August JNA directive actually allowed officers to go on summer vacations.[24]

On 14 September Croatian ZNG and MUP forces surrounded and blockaded every JNA installation (barracks and depots) in Croatian-held territory and shut off all utilities serving them (military hospitals included). Some smaller isolated posts or depots were quickly overrun, some after clashes. Through this rapid series of strategic actions, the Croats came into possession of a large amount of heavy weaponry and most of what the JNA had taken away from the TO in May 1990. The whole armory of the Thirty-Second Corps fell into Croat hands, only lightly damaged.[25]

JNA's Performance and Its Serbianization

In October, the JNA launched a full-scale strategic offensive to defeat the Croatian militarily and force them to capitulation. The general staff's strategic offensive plan—probably drafted in the spring of 1991 and actually launched in September—called for slicing up Croatia and defeating it militarily to compel the surrender of the Croatian political leadership and the renegotiation of a Yugoslav confederation. A key objective added in September was to relieve all the JNA barracks blockaded by the Croatians. This plan conflicted with Milošević's war aim of a rump Serbian-led Yugoslavia.

The JNA's plan consisted of five corps-level campaigns, for which mobilization and preparation would occur in two phases: a preliminary mobilization and deployment (which occurred in July) and a follow-up mobilization (ordered in September). The preliminary mobilization was meant to put increased pressure on the Croatians without launching an actual offensive. It also permitted the JNA to preposition key formations in their staging areas in case war actually followed.

Full mobilization was necessary to enable the JNA to carry out the full-scale plan that General Kadijević envisioned:

> Impose a full air and sea blockade on Croatia. Link the attack routes of the main JNA forces as directly as possible in order to liberate the Serb regions in Croatia and the JNA garrisons deep inside Croatian territory. To that end, intersect Croatia along the lines Gradiška–Virovitica, Bihać–Karlovac–Zagreb, Knin–Zadar and Mostar–Split. Liberate eastern Slavonia using the strongest grouping of armored-mechanized forces, and then quickly continue operations westward, hooking up with forces in eastern Slavonia and continuing on toward Zagreb and Varaždin. At the same time impose a land blockade on Dubrovnik with strong forces from the Herceg Novi-Trebinje region and penetrate the Neretva valley, thus working together with the forces moving along the Mostar–Split line. After achieving specific objectives, secure and hold the border of Serb Krajina in Croatia, withdraw the remaining parts of the JNA from Slovenia, and then withdraw the JNA from Croatia.[26]

Somehow the JNA deterred Croatia—or at least President Tudjman — from siding with Slovenia in late June and July. However, the JNA failed to frighten the Croats with its posture and had to respond to their attacks against its barracks with a partial mobilization on 15 September. Yet the wholesale refusal of many reservists to respond, the desertion of many others, and a distinct lack of enthusiasm among the Serbs who did respond left many of the formations earmarked for the offensive significantly undermanned. The mobilization disaster so severely undercut operational plans that some operations had to be abandoned. Even in the vital sector of eastern Slavonia where the JNA had planned its major effort, not nearly enough infantry would arrive, crippling the entire offensive. The chaos caused by the country's breakup, combined with the colossal failure of their plans, ultimately melted the confidence in the JNA and its high command. That led the JNA to ask the combined rump federal and Serbian presidency to authorize general mobilization, but there was no response. According to Jović, Kadijević abandoned his pro-Yugoslav stance at the end of September and advocated the "protection of Serb lands," thus embracing Milošević's policy of "All Serbs in One State."[27]

The eastern Slavonian operation began on 20 September. The JNA had initiated a small-scale operation on the fourteenth to relieve the Vukovar barracks, but unplanned and presumably unintended by the JNA, this small-scale operation became its main effort and would consume it for the next two months. The army lost its timing and resources, but the most significant losses were its combat morale and credibility in the eyes of personnel and public alike. The Fifth Corps from Banja Luka crossed the Sava River and took part in actions in western Slavonia. Farther west, it supported Serbian TO forces in Banija and Kordun, helping them consolidate their control over the territory around Karlovac and relieve the blocked garrison there. There were other important operations in Kostajnica, Petrinja, and Slunj. The Ninth (Knin) Corps launched operations around Zadar on 16 September, two days after the garrison was attacked. Because of mobilization problems and difficulties in Hercegovina, Operation Mostar–Split never materialized. The Dubrovnik suboperation began on 1 October, following mobilization of the Montenegro-based JNA forces and the Montenegro TO.

The newly formed Croatian general staff organized the expansion of the ZNG during October with captured weapons. Beginning in September, ZNG and MUP forces proved able to stop the advancement of the JNA, and field-unit commanders began to urge the general staff to authorize counteroffensives. The new offensives, however, were to have only mixed success. Beginning in late October, Croatian forces in western Slavonia went on the attack, continuing their relatively successful operations until the end of the conflict in January. The Croats also attempted two unsuccessful operations to relieve the siege of Vukovar in October and November. Attacks in the Banija area near Sisak and Petrinja were only partially successful. Great success was achieved in western Slavonia, where the Croats gained control over large parts of formerly Serb-held territory. Elsewhere they remained on the defensive, while maintaining their blockades of the barracks. Indeed, the barracks remained surrounded until the agreement with the JNA for the withdrawal of their garrisons in December 1991 as part of the negotiations that led to the Vance Plan.[28]

The military performance of the JNA in the opening stages of the war is usually rated as very poor. This is evident in the colossal fiasco in Slovenia (June 1991) and in the JNA's inability to conduct successful mobilization in Serbia proper and other locations. These deficiencies had critical operational consequences in conducting unfocused operations that were either unsuccessful (although opposed by much weaker forces) or stopped before attaining the objectives that were already at hand. The JNA conducted operations contrary to all military logic (i.e., the unnecessary siege of Vukovar) and, most importantly, was unable to fulfill its role of protecting the population against violence or assisting in a peaceful solution of the Yugoslav crisis in 1990–1991.

Some have argued that the JNA had already prepared in 1985 for an internal armed conflict and for the loss of Slovenia and those parts of Croatia where Serbs were not a majority. In that year it created a new organizational format with three theaters of war instead of five or six army districts that were more or less identical with the republican boundaries. It is evident that in 1991 the JNA tried to delineate new boundaries through the use of force, and thus, the reorganization of the late 1980s could be a part of the plan for the territorial expansion of Serbia; on the other hand, the JNA's very strong Yugoslav sentiment prior to the debacle in Slovenia suggests a contrary conclusion. In this context, the Rampart-91 Plan (RAM) should be thoroughly investigated.

Recognition of Croatia as a Precipitant to the War

The recognition of Croatia in December 1991–January 1992 by the international community, especially the EC, has sometimes been characterized as a powerful precipitant to the war and its eventual expansion to Bosnia-Hercegovina. This view is held especially by Serbs but also by various international scholars and politicians.[29]

The highest German and French officials of the time held completely opposite views on Germany's role in pushing for the recognition of Slovenian and Croatian independence. The French thought that the Germans were pushing for recognition for domestic political reasons and that the action would not help to stop the conflict. The chief of François Mitterand's cabinet (and future French foreign minister) Hubert Vedrine wrote that Paris was fully aware of Germany's actions and did not condone them.[30] On the other hand, Michael Libal, former chief of the Southeast Europe Department in the German Foreign Ministry (1991–1995), dismisses any German responsibility for the war's continuation and spread. According to Libal, Germany did determine its policy much differently than the rest of the EC and the U.S. He advocates the view that the EC failed to acknowledge in a timely manner the basic threat to the unity and stability of Yugoslavia that Milošević's policy posed.[31] Like Warren Zimmermann, the last U.S. ambassador to prewar Yugoslavia, Libal believes that the problems started in 1987, the year Milošević came to power in Serbia.

Borovo Selo Incident

Many individual events and episodes in the war in Croatia in 1990–1991 are either not fully documented or sustain contradictory accounts. In mentioning only a few of them we do not pretend to give either a complete list of such events or the most important of them. The interpretation of these and other similar events cannot change the overall meaning of the war, but it can aid in our understanding.

One of the episodes that opened the way to an escalation of the conflict is the controversial Borovo Selo incident. On 1 May, following two weeks of incidents and heightened tension, residents of the predominately Serb village of Borovo Selo hoisted Yugoslav flags, carrying the five-pointed Communist star, presumably to commemorate the traditional workers' day. Upon learning this, four Croatian policemen from Osijek drove into the village determined to replace one of the flags that stood in the center of Borovo Selo with the Croatian flag, which bore the red and white checkerboard shield, or *Šahovnica,* that was hated by the Serbs. The policemen ran into a hail of gunfire. Although two of the officers escaped, the other two were captured.[32] The next day a Croatian police convoy entered the village in order to liberate the prisoners. Instead, it ran into an ambush laid by Serb militiamen that killed twelve policemen and wounded more than twenty others. The JNA intervened with an armored unit and rescued the Croatian police detachment trapped in the center of the village, taking them to safety outside of the village.[33] The Serbs claimed that the real reason for the Croatian police attack was to instigate fighting and eventually provoke an all-out war. Some of the Serb participants in the incident have alleged that more than one hundred Croatian police were killed,[34] which is absurd and probably meant to serve as an argument that the Croats wanted to conquer the village and start a full-scale war.

Directly connected with this incident is a story that appears only in Silber and Little's book. During a tour in eastern Slavonia by widely regarded HDZ hawks Defense Minister Gojko Šušak, Deputy Interior Minister Vice Vukojević, and their aides, someone in their party fired three shoulder-launched Ambrust missiles on Borovo Selo. The chief of the Osijek police department, Josip Reihl-Kir, who was accompanying Šušak's party, later expressed disgust over this obvious provocation by high-ranking Croatian officials and the ensuing deterioration in interethnic relations.[35] The story served to illustrate that HDZ extremists wanted the war and tried to provoke it. The story cannot be verified in other sources[36] and appears rather incredible because top politicians have other means to provoke conflicts and do not have to walk around and fire rockets to do so. Nevertheless, it circulated widely, probably because of its rather sensational nature. Significantly, Reihl-Kir, who was committed to peaceful solutions, was killed by Croatian extremists soon thereafter. Clearly some circles did want to escalate the conflict.

The Siege of Vukovar

In August 1991, the JNA, local Serbian TO, and paramilitary units from Serbia attacked this eastern Croatian town situated just south of Borovo Selo. After three months of siege, they entered the devastated town at the end of November, giving way to the most horrible atrocities of the entire war. Why was Vukovar put under prolonged siege when military logic would dictate that the town be left isolated and attacks continue on towns and other objectives farther west? In this siege the JNA used armor and infantry in separate attacks, contrary to all principles of the art of war, and suffered thousands of casualties and the loss of more than 400 pieces of armor. Norman Cigar notes that Vukovar became a symbol of Serbia's determination to promote the cause of Croatia's Serbs. For the Croats, Vukovar became a symbol for the defense of its independence and territorial integrity.

Most importantly the battle of Vukovar went a long way toward swinging inter-national opinion in Croatia's favor.[37]

According to the Croatian census of 1991, the ethnic composition of the mu-nicipality of Vukovar was mixed and almost balanced among two major groups: 31,445 (37.35 percent) Serbs and 36,910 (43.8 percent) Croats. In the central area of the city the numbers were 47 percent Croat and 32.3 percent Serb. It is worth mentioning that according to the census 35 percent of the marriages were mixed.[38] Before major operations took place in September 1991, some 8,000 Cro-ats, including 6,000 children, were evacuated to the Adriatic Coast, while some 14,000 Serbs went to Serb-held territory.[39] When the JNA and Serb paramilitar-ies finally took control of the town, the entire population was evacuated. People could choose to go to Serbia or to Croatia. According to one source, in the fall of 1994 some 29,000 Serb refugees from western Slavonia and the Croat-held ter-ritories found shelter in the municipality of Vukovar.[40]

General Anton Tus, then chief of the Croatian general staff, maintains that the Croatian army fulfilled its task. It embarrassed the JNA, which had intended to crush Croatia within twenty days in a full-scale operation. The Twelfth (Novi Sad) and Seventeenth (Tuzla) JNA Corps, along with a guard brigade from Bel-grade, suffered so many casualties that the offensive came to a halt. That enabled the Croats to undertake a successful counteroffensive against the Serbs in west-ern Slavonia. Tus estimates that in the siege of Vukovar alone the JNA and Serb paramilitary units lost 5,000 killed; 600 tanks, armored personnel carriers, and combat vehicles; and 20 aircraft, against 4,000 Croatian dead.[41] In his memoirs, Tus's adversary General Kadijević boasts that the battle of Vukovar was a victory over the main forces of the Croatian army, totaling at least 6,000–8,000 soldiers, although the city was actually defended by fewer than 2,000 men.[42]

The Serbian (Yugoslav) side acknowledges that at the Ovčara farmhouse local TO forces executed some 200 wounded and sick prisoners of war taken from the municipal hospital after the city was sacked. In its indictments against Milošević, Hadžić, and others, the ICTY counts 260 victims in the Ovčara kill-ings. Seven guards who actually did the killing were charged and sentenced for war crimes by a special court for war crimes in Belgrade. The precise number of all who were killed after the fall of the city will probably never be known.

The Attack on Dubrovnik

Dubrovnik was surrounded and attacked by the JNA in October 1991 with no clear military justification. There were no JNA installations or Serb population to defend, while Croatian forces in the city were too weak to mount any signifi-cant attack against them. The consequence of this attack was a public relations catastrophe and the loss of all credibility that the JNA might still have had. As noted earlier, Kadijević's 1991 war plan contained a part dedicated to Dubrovnik that aimed "to impose a land blockade on Dubrovnik with strong forces from the Herceg Novi-Trebinje region and penetrate the Neretva Valley, thus working together with the forces moving along the Mostar–Split line."[43] He was resolute against the JNA's capturing the inner city area and opted for a blockade from a distance and well out of Croatian artillery range. The JNA had been interested in securing the strategic Dubrovnik–Trebinje route into eastern Hercegovina. But was Kadijević telling the whole truth?

More than eighty civilians were killed during the shelling of the city, which was not taken, although the occupied environs were subjected to wholesale looting and wanton destruction. JNA General Pavle Strugar and Admiral Miodrag Jokić, at the time in charge of the operations on the southern flank, were later indicted and sentenced for war crimes by the ICTY. The tribunal found that they bore command responsibility and did not prevent violations of war customs and laws. The Dubrovnik operation is still a very controversial issue. On the Croatian side, some politicians and academics have accused the Croatian government of letting Dubrovnik and its population fend for themselves.[44]

In the West, the JNA's siege of Dubrovnik was one of the war's most visible and inexplicable events. Why the JNA undertook the operation in the first place was difficult to discern, and the destruction of architecture and art in the historic city was impossible to justify. Of the two questions concerning why the JNA attacked and why the Dubrovnik area was subjected to looting and destruction, the first is easier to answer. The JNA's strategic plan to carve up Croatia called for one operation to sever southern Dalmatia from the rest of the country while blockading the port of Dubrovnik at its tip. There is no satisfactory answer to why the TO and volunteer troops and the JNA itself indulged in such gross looting and shelling of the region's nonmilitary areas. As in earlier ages of warfare, when such acts were more common, blame can perhaps be put on the recruiting of volunteers from the lower echelons of society and on the greed and envy of the conquerors left unchecked by proper discipline. Whatever the reasons, the international reaction toward the military operation and its associated looting and destruction greatly tarnished the reputation of the Serb nation and deepened the political isolation of the Belgrade government.

Srdja Pavlović writes that the case of Dubrovnik still provokes lengthy and passionate debates among historians and politicians, leaving many questions unanswered, while ordinary Montenegrins and Serbs are left to their own devices to cope with their feelings of uneasiness about the recent past. They struggle with many questions such as who initiated the process and who is to blame for its catastrophic results? Pavlović maintains that, during the early fall of 1991, Montenegro's political leaders and the JNA's military brass rationalized the attack on Dubrovnik as a necessary move not only to stop the so-called unconstitutional secession of Croatia but to protect the territorial integrity of Montenegro and Yugoslavia and to prevent a potential ethnic conflict.[45] Montenegrin Prime Minister Milo Djukanović raised the hopes of many nationalists in Montenegro when he stated that the "Croatian authorities want to have a war and they will have it. If Croatia wants to secede then the international borders must be revised."[46]

Some Serbian analysts have emphasized that Dubrovnik had been a demilitarized city for more than two decades but had been militarized by Croats once again in 1991. Yet the small Croatian garrison in Dubrovnik and its limited capacity for military action hardly justifies the attack. General Kadijević did invite President Tudjman to demilitarize the city under EC control, offering at the same time to allow foreign military attachés to visit the area. The JNA was convinced that such visits would change the mostly negative opinion in the West toward the JNA. The visit took place at the end of October but backfired. The Dubrovnik operation became the biggest public relations disaster for the JNA, Milošević, and the whole Serb bloc.

Operations Flash and Storm

The end of 1994 brought some prospects for a possible peace accord. In December, representatives of the Croatian government and the insurgent Serbs agreed on certain confidence-building measures that included the opening of the Zagreb–Belgrade highway, an oil pipeline, electric power grids, and waterlines. At the end of January 1995, Western negotiators tried to promote a comprehensive peace settlement between the Croatian and the Krajina Serb governments. This so-called Z-4 Plan envisaged the return of all refugees and substantial autonomy for an area consisting of eleven small and economically undeveloped municipalities around Glina and Knin that comprised roughly a third of the territory controlled by the Republika Srpska Krajina.[47] Zagreb tentatively welcomed Z-4, but the Krajina Serbs refused to discuss it unless the Croatian regime renounced their intention to block renewal of the UNPROFOR mandate for Croatia. Negotiations were prolonged over the next two months. Under pressure Zagreb finally agreed that the UN would remain, albeit under the new name United Nations Confidence Restoration Operation UNCRO. Throughout these months HV Chief of Staff General Janko Bobetko stated repeatedly that any closure of the Belgrade–Zagreb highway would bring a Croatian military response to reopen the road.[48]

The Croatian side made systematic preparations for a final showdown in case peace negotiations failed. In November 1994 the HV took Kupres, opening the way along the Dinara range. During the winter, HV engineer corps made roads through the area, and in the spring of 1995, the HV gained tactical control over the key Knin–Grahovo pass and other positions suitable for putting the Krajina Serb artillery positions under fire. Meanwhile, in UNPA Sector West, or western Slavonia, traffic along the Zagreb–Belgrade highway went smoothly until April, when RSK President Milan Martić ordered a one-day closure of the highway to protest Croatian customs procedures. At the end of the month there were violent incidents involving civilians, which resulted in several deaths on both sides and the highway's closure. On 30 April Tudjman ordered that the highway would be opened on 1 May at five o'clock in the morning. The HV main staff had, in fact, finished its campaign plan for the recapture of western Slavonia in December 1994, which envisioned a breakout to the Sava River. The idea of the two-pronged attack was to advance along the highway from both Nova Gradiška and Novska, meet at Okučani, and cut off Serb forces. The Croatian order of battle comprised some 15,000 troops with armor, artillery, infantry, and air force units. The Krajina Serb Eighteenth Corps had three undermanned brigades with a total of 2,000 troops on active duty and 4,000–5,000 reserves.

The Croatian attack, code-named Operation Flash, began on 1 May 1995 with almost no warning, leaving the Serbs minimal time to call up reservists or even deploy formations into appropriate defense positions. The HV attack struck the Eighteenth Corps artillery with both artillery and air strikes, creating chaos and panic in the rear flank of the Army of the Serbian Krajina (SVK). This left a withdrawal route to Bosnia open via the Bosanska Gradiška Bridge. In the early afternoon of 2 May, the HV took Okučani and proceeded to clean out pockets of resistance in the Mount Psunj foothills. Artillery and rocket fire was used to flush SVK troops from their hiding places and into a cordon of HV and MUP units surrounding the area. The tactics were instantly effective and, by the end of 4 May, some 1,500 had surrendered.[49]

The Eighteenth Corps of the SVK suffered one of the swiftest and most humiliating defeats of the whole war. The corps commander left his command post immediately after the Croatian attack began, thus leaving his troops without leadership. The Serb resistance was disorganized, weak, and short-lived. Military units, along with civilians, fled to Bosnia before Croat military and police even arrived. At least half of western Slavonia's Serb population is estimated to have left their homes. On their way to the bridge over the Sava River, mixed columns of troops and civilians came under fire, leaving casualties. Unable to stop the Croatian offensive, President Martić ordered retaliatory rocket attacks on Zagreb on 2–3 May that killed seven and wounded more than two hundred. Although the UN initially accused the HV of war crimes, it appears that Croatian forces did not commit many violations of humanitarian law during Operation Flash. The UN subsequently withdrew the accusations.[50]

The rapid collapse of the SVK defenses in western Slavonia provoked heated discussions among the political elite of the insurgent Serbs. The politicians and soldiers blamed each other. The rocket attack on Zagreb that was part of the Serb strategy of deterrence backfired, with Martić being promptly indicted before the

ICTY in July 1995.[51] Although everything indicated that the whole insurgency had reached a dead end, nothing was done to improve the situation, except for Milošević's dispatching General Mile Mrkšić from Belgrade to serve as the new SVK commander. Nor did the RSK leadership offer anything new to the Croatian regime to find a peaceful political solution to the conflict.

Operation Storm: Context

After the success in *Operation Flash* and with no peace initiatives on the table, the Croatian government continued with preparations to crush the insurgency. The reaction of Bosnian and Croatian Serbs toward the HV advance along the Dinara was weak, with the Bosnian-Serb Army of the Republika Srpska (VRS) losing one position after another. Meanwhile, the VRS launched substantial operations elsewhere in Bosnia in order both to achieve territorial advantages before the final settlement and to free up troops to face the coming HV offensive. In the first half of July, the VRS overran the Muslim enclave and the UN safe area of Srebrenica, killing thousands of prisoners; two weeks later the VRS swept into Žepa, another safe area in eastern Bosnia, expelling the whole population from the town (see chapter 6, "Safe Areas"). At the same time, the VRS and the SVK mounted another attack on the Bihać enclave in northwestern Bosnia. The international community, already humiliated by its inability to prevent the Srebrenica massacre, now feared that the fall and sack of Bihać might end in an even greater slaughter. The UN, NATO, and individual countries warned the Bosnian Serbs against repeating the horror of Srebrenica in Bihać and asked that the attack be immediately cancelled. In the last days of July the Serbian attack was, however, still in progress.

Why the Croatian Serbs took part in the attack on Bihać in the summer of 1995 is still incomprehensible. On the one hand, there were serious military reasons not to participate in the VRS offensive in northwestern Bosnia. The SVK was undermanned and low on morale; the advance of the HV along the Dinara and Livno Valleys should have made the defense of the approaches to Knin their first priority. Instead of defending the key towns of Grahovo and Glamoč, the SVK deployed most of its troops around Bihać. On the other hand, the concerns of the international community should have offered serious political reasons for not participating in the Bihać campaign. It was obvious that the project of uniting all the "Serb Lands" was no longer feasible and that Milošević and the Serb bloc had already radically reduced their war plans. Furthermore, there was nothing to expect from the VRS if the HV attack took place; the Bosnian Serbs had not come to the rescue of the SVK's Eighteenth Corps during Operation Flash. In July the ICTY indictments arrived against Karadžić and Mladić for genocide in Bosnia and against Martić for the rocket attack on Zagreb two months before. It was clear that the international community did not consider these people political leaders but rather criminals with whom it would not negotiate.

Moreover, on 22 July 1995 Tudjman and Izetbegović worked out an agreement in Split for mutual defense, making it possible for Croatian troops to operate in Bosnia-Hercegovina. In Resolution 43/49, The Situation in the Occupied Territories of Croatia, the UN General Assembly expressed the view that the Serb-controlled territories were under occupation, clearly showing that it did not consider the insurgent Serbs primarily as fighters for freedom and national liberation. All these signs should have led the Croatian Serbs to change radically their hitherto intransigent politics of secession from Croatia and unification with "All Serb Lands." The obvious and only rational course of action for the Croatian Serbs should have been to disentangle immediately from the Bosnian Serbs' attack on Bihać and to negotiate for a political solution with Zagreb. But no efforts were made in this direction and, when Grahovo and Glamoč fell in the last days of July, many inhabitants of the RSK, including government officials and their families, started to pack for Serbia.

Aside from Srebrenica and Žepa, the Serb offensives in Bosnia that summer were failures. On 5 May 1995 the VRS started Operation Flame-95 (*Plamen-95*) to wipe out the Croat Orašje pocket south of the Sava River in northern Bosnia, but on 10 June the action was called off. Soon after, the more energetic General Mrkšić, freshly sent from Belgrade, assumed command over the SVK. Plans were made for operations against the HV/HVO in the mountains above the Dinara and Livno Valleys, which were the most immediate threat to the RSK. However, on Belgrade's advice, the plan was changed, and the attack on the Bosnian Army's Fifth Corps at Bihać was given priority. The plan optimistically anticipated the quick collapse of the Bosnian forces, which were not only well led but numbered some 17,000 men. In fact, the final attack (Operation Sword-95) on 17 July deployed only a slightly larger force that included 5,000 assault troops, 9,000 garrison units, and 4,000 men provided by the renegade Muslim leader Fikret Abdić. The offensive not only failed to eliminate the Fifth Corps but left the initiative to the HV, which did not miss the chance to improve its own position by defeating weak Serbian defenses on 28–29 July and entering Grahovo and Glamoč.[52] Although the VRS and the SVK now halted their attack on Bihać, it was simply too late to regroup to face the impending HV attack.

The HV preparations for Operation Storm were completed in July. The plan envisaged attacks on UN Sectors North and South, which constituted all of what was left of the RSK except for Sector East (eastern Slavonia). The taking of Knin from newly acquired positions a few miles above the town was a top HV priority, given the symbolic and political meaning of the town as the seat of the insurgency. The general idea was to undertake a fast-paced operation, attacking first command and communication posts and then troops on the ground. As shown by a transcript of a meeting of Tudjman and his top military brass held at Brioni on 31 July, it was predicted that the Serb population would leave soon after the HV attack began, as had been observed already during Operation Flash. This was considered to be a critical factor for lowering the morale of the VSK troops and, thus, was an expedient for the swiftness of the operation.

It was a high priority that the operation be conducted and finished very quickly. In his testimony at the Milošević trial before the ICTY, the then U.S. ambassador to Croatia, Peter Galbraith, attested to the desperation of the international community. Having failed to stop the Serbian offensive against Bihać, it was very apprehensive over the offensive's impact. Tudjman had already assured Galbraith that his forces were ready and willing to relieve Bihać while crushing the Serbian insurgency in the process. According to Galbraith's testimony and Tudjman's words to his generals, there was a mutually beneficial understanding that Tudjman would save Bihać and the international community would leave him to restore order in his own Krajina backyard. The only conditions were that the operation be swift and that no crimes against the civilian population be committed.[53] When the UN special envoy Yasushi Akashi reached an agreement with Martić and other insurgent leaders to disengage the SVK from Bihać (30 July), Galbraith set in motion another peace initiative with the aim of preventing the Croatian attack. He met with Babić, who hesitantly agreed to negotiate with the Croats on the basis of Z-4, but Martić refused, and Milošević declined to receive the negotiators. Tudjman made his final decision no later than 31 July and agreed on negotiations with RSK representatives in Geneva on 3 August only to conceal his real intentions. The negotiations broke down and, at five o'clock in the morning of 2 August 1995, Operation Storm ensued.

The attack managed to break the Serb defenses everywhere, and in a day or two the HV attained all its main objectives. The Croatian advance and the collapse of the Serbian lines were facilitated by Martić's controversial order for the evacuation of the civil population, issued on the evening of 4 August immediately before Martić himself left Knin. Except for the situation around Petrinja, where poor leadership delayed the HV for a day, the situation on all fronts was the same: the SVK fled in disorder, as did almost the entire civilian population, leaving behind only those who were unable to move. Knin fell around noon on 5 August after an artillery barrage and without any resistance from the SVK infantry and armored units that were supposed to defend the town. The Serb military and political institution collapsed so quickly that even the Croatians were surprised by their successes and the low intensity of resistance they encountered after entering Serb-held territories. The Serbs everywhere fled, carrying all the belongings they could take with them. Only in Kordun were the escape routes closed, leaving the SVK's Twenty-First Corps and civilian masses with no way out. In order to avoid further casualties, the HV and local Serb commanders agreed on the surrender of the Twenty-First Corps. The military personnel and civilians were free to go wherever they wanted, which meant Bosnia and Serbia. After five years' existence, the insurgency was crushed militarily in only four days. The Serb military experienced one of the most bitter and most humiliating defeats in history.

Final Operations: Croat–Croat Controversies

In the aftermath of operations Flash and, especially, Storm there were public celebrations in Croatia marking them among the most important events in the nation's history. The day Knin fell was inaugurated as a public holiday, the Day of Homeland Thanksgiving (*Dan domovinske zahvalnosti*, 5 August). The ruling Croat Democratic Union (HDZ) tried to enforce its own legitimacy by virtually creating a myth around these achievements. Military commanders who led the troops in the offensives wanted their share, too. Both the HDZ and the army encouraged the public to celebrate the fact that the HV had become "a regional power."

The Croatian chief of military intelligence at the time of Operation Storm, Admiral Davor Domazet, abetted the view that the HV had proven itself as a regional power after these two anti-insurgent actions and that Operation Storm was in scale and military performance comparable only to the original Desert Storm in 1991. Indeed, Operation Storm was an example of the air-land battle that had been developed by the U.S. military for fighting the Warsaw Pact and had been applied so successfully in the Arabian Desert. These claims made no sense at all and should be seen for what they were: exaggerations with political or propaganda aims.[54] In addition to this, Croatia's success can only be evaluated by remembering as well the political-military situation of the insurgent Serbs. Their troops were demoralized, as was the civilian population; the whole Serb project was doomed and had no real future, either politically or militarily. This made it possible for the Croatian troops to record a great and important victory even when some of those troops—especially the reserve component—were poorly equipped and trained. The adversary simply evaporated before them.

Nor was there any public evaluation of the role of the Fifth Corps of the Army of Bosnia-Hercegovina (ARBiH) in Operation Storm. Moreover, except for a few texts, the Croats say nothing about the largely accidental support by NATO aircraft against Serb antiaircraft positions. These aircraft were on a routine patrol and opened fire on some SVK integrated antiaircraft positions after they had sensed Serbian radar. After this they quickly withdrew. Although this did not influence the outcome of the overall operation, it did encourage the impression that NATO was assisting the Croats. In repeated interviews with the Croatian weeklies and dailies in 1997–1998, Galbraith underlined the decisive role that the U.S. had played in the reintegration of Croatia and the victories in 1995. The

U.S. did not condone Operation Flash, but to Storm it at least turned a blind eye.[55] Croatia would have encountered more problems in crushing the insurgency if there had been no economic sanctions imposed upon Serbia and if there had not been a NATO–U.S. military threat to Serbia, as U.S. Secretary of State Madeleine Albright once reminded President Tudjman. In addition the U.S. turned a blind eye to the arms trafficking going into Croatia and Bosnia-Hercegovina. Ambassador Galbraith said that he knew about the plans for launching *Operation Storm* two weeks before it took place and advised his government to do nothing about it.[56]

Before Galbraith's interviews and testimony, American officials were reluctant to acknowledge U.S. involvement. The analysts however concluded that

> US officials did not turn a blind eye, they assisted the Croatian army's *Operation Storm*. Retired US military consultants provided tactical training and operational planning under the guise of "democracy training"—with the blessing of the Clinton administration. Indeed, there is evidence that U.S. assistance . . . may have included air strikes and psychological warfare operations.[57]

One could ask why it took Croatia so long to undertake these operations to gain control over its territories. Certainly they needed time to prepare the available military resources, and they were waiting for the strategic situation to improve, which it started to do in late 1994 when they took Kupres and advanced along the Dinara Mountains. Perhaps Croatia was awaiting the denouement in Bosnia, where it previously had broad ambitions. Another possibility is that Croatia waited for the best timing of its final operations in order to have backup from the international community. The siege of Bihać proved to be a perfect moment, and Croatia used it. There was also an opportunity in 1994 when the ARBiH Fifth Corps advanced from Bihać into Serb-held Bosnian Krajina. But besides the operational support that the Fifth Corps could provide at that time, the other two prerequisites for success—battle-ready troops and international support—were simply not in place.

Perhaps more interesting than questions concerning the performance of the Croatian war machine are the events in the aftermath of Operation Storm, when the Croatian authorities tried to resume control over the liberated territory. It is a well-documented fact that after the military part of the operation was over, the chaos of wholesale looting started, and several hundred Serbs, the majority of them elderly, were murdered. Some, including government officials and institutions, claim that this was the work of criminals who acted on their own, whereas various journalists, scholars, political and nongovernmental activists, along with the Office of the Prosecutor of the ICTY, think that it was a premeditated and organized operation.

The events after Storm became perhaps the most controversial issue surrounding the war in Croatia. In October 2001 a small Croat company presented a documentary film on Croatian television titled Storm over Krajina, that showed how much of the Krajina was looted and burned to the ground. The movie caught many by surprise, and the reactions were intense. Each of the prominent Croatian dailies commented on it, and even the Croatian parliament put it on its agenda. The prime minister gave his public announcement; local radio stations received opinions by e-mail; Web discussions centered on the film; and the leaders of most political parties commented on it as well. Organizations like the Croatian Helsinki Committee welcomed the film, and opinion polls showed that the majority was in favor of broadcasting it.[58] Was the documentary anti-Croat Serb propaganda? Was it a first step in the revision of the homeland war? Certainly some felt this way, especially some of those who participated in the war and some who believed that the film offended their patriotic sentiments.

What really happened after Storm, and why did not the Croatian authorities assume control and responsibility over Krajina, leaving it instead in the hands of looters and murderers? These are still unanswered questions. To close the area and deny access to civilians was a relatively easy task, but it was not done. Perhaps the Croatian authorities did not think that far in advance. Obsessed with the operation and with crushing the Serb insurgency, they forgot to think about what might happen next. It is, however, interesting to note that the Croatian police were given the task of protecting all of the Orthodox churches in Krajina—only a small percentage of which was desecrated or destroyed. Why did authorities fail to protect other public facilities, such as schools, medical facilities, factories, railroad infrastructure, and other valuable assets of Croatia's national wealth? And why did they not care to protect some 8,000 Serbs who were left behind? All this remains a mystery. Surely Operation Storm was a genuine success and a great Croatian victory; what followed was an equally great and totally unnecessary mistake.

Final Operations: Croat–Serb Controversies

The main controversy between Croats and Serbs concerning the events in 1995 is whether what happened was the liberation of occupied territories (Croatian view) or the occupation of the Republic of Srpska Krajina by Croats who willingly provoked the exodus of almost the entire population (Serb view). No less an important controversy involves the character of the exodus. On the Croat side some say that the Serbs fled willingly in spite of invitations made by President Tudjman to remain. Others claim that the Serbs fled out of fear of revenge, or "because they know what they have done to us [Croats]." Serbs, on the other hand, claim that, given their experience in Gospić (1991), Medak (1993), and western Slavonia (1995), they could not simply wait for the same destiny.

In his recently published contribution on this issue, Nikica Barić endorses what can be considered the standard "moderate" Croat view, a rational explanation that comes closest to what happened.[59] He offers selected arguments in support of the basic thesis that the Serbs, because they had sided with Milošević's policy, did not want to live with Croats at any price and opted to flee rather than to stay and live with the Croats. He further argues that they feared revenge for their expulsion of Croats in the first stage of the war. He also points out the important difference between the Croat attitude in their liberated areas and the Serbian attitude in the Srebrenica region in the summer of 1995.[60] Although not excusing the crimes committed in the aftermath of Storm, American historian Elinor M. Despalatović contextualizes them by emphasizing that they came only at the end of a war that had been started by Serbs and by their acceptance of the aggressive policy of Slobodan Milošević.[61]

Why did the Croatia leadership opt for a military solution despite a suitable opportunity for a political resolution of the crisis? The CIA's analysts note that the UN worked frantically to avert a Croatian offensive against its renegade minority, trying to bring the two sides together in Geneva on 3 August. Prime Minister Milan Babić—the same Babić who had led the Serbs out of the Croatian state in 1990–1991—made a last-ditch peace offer, pledging his acceptance of a modified Z-4 Plan. His efforts failed, however, despite their endorsement by the U.S. and Galbraith.[62] Why, then, did Croatia choose war instead of a peaceful political solution for which the Serbian side, including Babić and a few others (though not Martić), was allegedly ready. Some say that this was because Tudjman knew that a military operation was the only means to "get rid" of a substantial part of Croatia's Serb minority, a result he could never expect from a political solution. Arrayed against such an interpretation, however, is the fact that Croatia accepted the Z-4 Plan and was prepared for a political solution. It was actually the Serb side that refused to discuss it. But the Croats could not wait forever, and at the end of July, they prepared a military operation. Part of the Serb elite—namely Babić—did indeed accept the negotiations, but it was obviously too late and too unconvincing. It came only hours before the operation was scheduled to start, and it looked like the Serbs were only trying to buy more time but were not sincere in their efforts. It should not be forgotten that as late as the end of July the RSK assembly was discussing unification of the RSK with the RS, which was certainly not an action that would contribute to productive talks with Zagreb.

There is no doubt that the deliberate Croatian attack was the reason why almost the entire population of the western RSK fled. The exodus is certainly one of the greatest tragedies in the history of the Serbian people, but Croats cannot be blamed for this outcome. At the first phase of the war Croats living in areas held or attacked by Serbs were expelled or had to flee. As of 1 December 1991 there were half a million refugees in Croatia, almost all of them non-Serbs, who had had to leave their homes. The few Croats who remained in Serb-held areas were subjected to persecution and terror; from 1992 to 1995 several hundred of them were killed.[63] As Barić has shown, the very essence of the Serb insurgents' political project was a perpetual separation from the Croats and a refusal to live alongside other ethnic groups. This was achieved by taking parts of Croatia and was followed by the expulsion of Croats and other non-Serbs from the RSK. It was, then, natural to expect that Serbs would leave if the Croats eventually came back, especially in the event of a military action. On the other hand, the insurgency posed real problems for Croatia, making the situation unbearable. The country's main road and rail communications were blocked or cut off for five years. A large chunk of Croatia was not included in the national legal system and infrastructure. There were still hundreds of thousands of refugees waiting to go back to their homes, and the cities near the front line were occasionally subjected to SVK artillery attacks. Something had to be done, and if the Serbs were unwilling to make a political deal, then military action was the only possible course of action. Thus, given the situation, there were only two ways the exodus of the Serbs could have been avoided: either the Serbs would have had to reconcile with the Croats, which was impossible given the very essence of their political program, or the Croats would have had not to launch a military operation, which was also impossible given the staggering fiscal and economic costs that the armed insurgency imposed on Croatia. Military operation and exodus were thus consequences of the insurgency itself and could not be prevented.

Some authors, such as Svetozar Livada, claim that the Serbs were right when they chose to flee; what happened to those who stayed behind is proof that they would have been killed or otherwise persecuted. But this argument is based on the assumption that Croats are by their very nature Serb killers and that Croats will use every opportunity to harm Serbs. The peaceful reintegration of Serbs into Croatian society in eastern Slavonia between 1995 and 1998 showed that reintegration really was possible when done gradually and within the framework of a political agreement.

Other authors suggest that, from the onset, Tudjman hoped that the number of Serbs living in Croatia would be reduced in the course of the war or that the ultimate political goal of Croat extremists—Tudjman, and the HDZ included—was the wholesale expulsion of the Serb population. Jovan Mirić, a professor at Zagreb University and a bitter critic of Serb nationalistic politics, analyzed publicly available materials and sources and came to the conclusion that the expulsion was indeed the basic idea of the politics of the HDZ and of some of the other Croatian right-wing political parties.[64] Some other scholars, notably Nikica Barić, reject this and other arguments that Mirić makes as absurd. Croatian President Mesić, giving his testimony at the ICTY in the Milošević trial, testified that Tudjman told him that he *supposed* that the number of Serbs by the end of the war would be diminished to 5 percent of the population, down from a little more than 12 percent in 1991.[65] But his testimony does not imply that this was Tudjman's plan, only that it was what he expected would happen. It was easy to come to that conclusion. In 1995, well before Operation Storm, one of the authors of this present chapter predicted that the number of Serbs would be significantly diminished.[66]

Invited to comment on the ICTY indictment of the Croatian generals for "joint criminal enterprise," Nikola Visković, professor at the School of Law, University of Split, expressed his view that it is not correct to link ethnic cleansing with Operation Storm alone. Visković emphasized that such action started in the beginning of the 1990s. According to him, the diehard nationalists always saw the Serbs as a permanent cause of instability and obstruction, or a threat, for Croatian statehood. All the plans for diminishing that historical threat were encouraged. So the Serbs were exposed to harassment, plundering, or even killings (Sisak, Osijek, Pakrac, Zagreb), from which they could not expect any substantial legal protection. The region of Istria was the only exception to that practice.[67]

Some foreign observers in Croatia have also remarked bitterly about Tudjman's attitudes toward the Serbian minority after 1990. The last American ambassador in the SFRY, Zimmermann has left the notes on his talks with Tudjman and on his failed attempts to convince the president to reverse the HDZ's confrontational policy toward the Croatian Serbs by calming their fears.[68] The former American ambassador to Croatia, Peter Galbraith described Tudjman as a "nationalist, in some ways fascist." Tudjman subscribed to Samuel Huntington's thesis about an inevitable clash of civilizations and often compared Bosnia's Muslims to the point of an Islamic dagger aimed at Europe. Although he took pride in the presence of some Croatian minorities, including Italians and Jews, he was an advocate of ethnic homogeneity who "believed that Croatia's 12 percent Serb minority was too much. He may not have a plan to expel the Serbs, but once they left he did not want them to come back."[69]

Final Operations: Serb–Serb Controversies

The defeat of the insurgency, which was far more than a military defeat, has provoked a reexamination of the recent past among the Serbs themselves. Serbs from Krajina are likely to put the blame on the worthless promises made by Milošević, the JNA, and the international community. They use catchy slogans to describe what happened, like "Treason," "Krajina Betrayed," and "Milošević sold Krajina." They ask about the real mission of successive SVK Commanders-in-Chief General Milan Čeleketić and his post-Flash replacement General Mrkšić, who lost Krajina militarily in such humiliating fashion. In addition, Serbs question the agenda and role of RSK Prime Minister Borislav Mikelić (April 1994–May 1995), who had been closely allied with Milošević since the late 1980s.[70]

Politicians in Belgrade also accused the Krajina Serbs of deliberately fleeing their country instead of putting up a stout defense. In this view, if the Krajina Serbs had held on for at least a week, the international community might have intervened to halt the Croatian offensive and revive negotiations. Some accused them of stubbornness in their talks with Zagreb and the international community. According to Momir Bulatović, the Yugoslav Supreme Council of Defense on which he was then serving convened a special session at 5:00 p.m. on 4 August 1995 at the command post in Dobanovci, near Belgrade. He noted that the Supreme Council sent a cable to General Mrkšić encouraging him to organize firm resistance for at least two more days. After that Yugoslavia would be able to help him with all possible assistance.[71]

Some former military leaders have examined the deeper roots of the military defeat and found them in the SVK itself. They draw attention to factors that ruined morale, pointing out that Krajina was left alone to be retaken by Croatia, that its people were given false promises that both Republika Srpska and Serbia would come to their aid, and that the region suffered greatly from corruption, poverty, and pervasive uncertainty. They also blame the lack of discipline and the SVK's modest military capabilities. The region lacked men, qualified officers, and modern equipment. It adhered firmly to the former TO doctrine instead of adopting more mobile tactics, whereas the eccentric shape of Krajina's territory tended to obstruct maneuvers. These analysts also emphasize the unfavorable strategic situation that resulted from the joint HV–HVO–ARBiH strike from Velika Kladuša and Bihać into the rear of the Serbian front.

As mentioned before, it was Martić, acting in his capacity as the president of the republic, who ordered the evacuation of the civilian population. It is a fact that since 1993 the RSK authorities had made plans for a temporary evacuation of the population into shelters or, in the case of a major emergency, further to Bosnia. However, this is regular procedure in any military planning in order to avoid casualties among civilians and to leave the military's hands free for in-theater military operations. In that regard the Serbs were not unique, but the experience after Operation Flash called for serious reassessment of the plans for the protection of civilians.

It is also possible to interpret Martić's order for evacuation as pertaining only to Sector South (northern Dalmatia and Lika) and not to the whole territory of the RSK under attack. It is unclear whether Martić's order reached anyone beyond Knin because radio and TV ceased to operate and could not transmit orders and information. As part of psychological operations, the Croats distributed thousands of fake leaflets in which the RSK military authorities ordered that the civilians be evacuated.[72] Yet these leaflets could have had only limited effect, for the evacuation began not because the authorities ordered it in the first place but because people decided to leave for various other reasons.

Epilogue

It is hard to expect that a scholarly, nonpartisan, and balanced historical account can be produced less than a decade after the end of this conflict. This is because there are many specific obstacles and impediments that make it difficult to complete such an account.

Yet some facts can be established and some controversies can be resolved. We have offered here a survey of some of the more salient controversies and a narrative based on known facts. Having in mind not only the acts, but also the thoughts, mindsets, fears, perceptions, and emotions of all the actors who participated in the war in any capacity—including the international community—we have tried to give the most objective picture possible of these past events. We believe these to be the most plausible explanations and interpretations of Croat–Croat, Croat–Serb, and Serb–Serb controversies; every issue concerning the war in Croatia is echoed in all three sets. The controversies that will continue to cause discussions and dissent are the causes of the war in 1991 and the fate of the Serb population in Croatia. Was a peaceful solution possible at all?

The war cannot be forgotten, but societies and individuals must live on. The criminal prosecution of war crimes, be it before the ICTY or before national courts, can achieve many positive things in this respect. Trials will make entire ethnic communities face their past and can have cathartic effects. Even trials before national courts can have a positive impact on the process of reconciliation. This has been confirmed by the trial of the Ovčara murderers in Belgrade, where relatives of the Croat victims expressed their satisfaction with the fact that the Serbian side wanted to give satisfaction to the victims and to condemn the perpetrators. The trials also produced many documents of great importance that will have a profound effect on continuing research.

With its 22,000 dead on both sides (15,000 Croats and 7,000 Serbs), the war was detrimental not only for the country's Croats but also for its Serbs and other minorities. Croats were expelled from their homes and killed in summary or individual executions by their neighbors who tried to make "the westernmost Serbian land" ethnically pure. The Serbs also suffered. Their numbers and their role in Croatian society were drastically diminished as a consequence of what was an absurd political project. Researchers have a responsibility and a kind of moral obligation to show how such a thing could happen, in the hope that it may not be repeated here or anywhere else. We trust that our contribution has helped to achieve this goal as well.

Notes

1   Misplaced or destroyed war-related documents played a significant role in the legal proceedings against war criminals even a decade after the end of the war. The International Criminal Court for the Former Yugoslavia (ICTY) asked governments to produce thousands of documents. They usually obliged, although sometimes even the subpoena orders were not honored. A most recent example of this involves the medical files of General Ratko Mladić. Wishing to locate this indictee, the ICTY issued an order that these files, covering the period after 1995, be handed over to the prosecution. The Military Medical Academy (VMA, central military hospital) in Belgrade, where Mladić was treated after the war, reported that the hospital did not have these files. *Danas*, 12 January 2005).

2   Laura Silber and Allan Little *Yugoslavia: Death of a Nation* (New York: TV Books, 1996); Tim Judah, *The Serbs: History, Myth, and the Destruction of Yugoslavia*, 2nd ed. (New Haven and London: Yale University Press, 2000); and Marcus Tanner, *Croatia: A Nation Forged in War* (New Haven and London: Yale University Press, 1997). The semiofficial CIA report on the war in former Yugoslavia, *Balkan Battlegrounds: A Military History of Yugoslav Conflict, 1990–1995* (Darby, PA: Diane Publishing Company, 2003), also depended very much on Silber and Little but did not surpass the accuracy of its source.

3   Among many examples of how a single fact can be differently interpreted, we will mention only one that illustrates vividly how social meaning takes precedence over every other characteristic. It is well known that the Yugoslav Peoples' Army (JNA) built many military installations in Croatia—barracks, dump yards, firing ranges, etc. The Croats objected that these installations were situated in Serb populated areas and that in this way the JNA showed its Serb character and mistrust toward the Croats. Mile Dakić, one of the ideologues and a chronographer of the Serb rebellion in Croatia, acknowledged that—"without a single exception"—installations were really situated in Serb populated areas, but he expressed the opinion that this was a part of the genocide against Serbs in Yugoslavia. Serbs, he explained, were forced to free their land for military installations (and were remunerated), but no Croat had to yield his or her lot, and so Serbs ceased to live on their ancestral lands. Mile Dakić, *Srpska Krajina: Istorijski temelji i nastanak* (Knin: Iskra, 1994), 43–44.

4   J. B. Allcock's insights and comments are very useful for the development of the ideas presented in this section. He observed that extremely vigorous disagreements exist in relation to most if not all of the areas of controversy with which we are dealing. The authors wish to note that it is not their purpose to arbitrate between various interpretations defined in this way or to judge who is responsible for the war or who has a particular historical right. Our aims are modest—first to indicate the existing controversies and their advocates in the public and in literature and scholarship, second to contribute to a better understanding of how those views were established. We would also like to offer

our conclusions and insights concerning the intentions, events, military operations, and consequences of the war in Croatia, based on broader research that cannot be reproduced here in detail. Our contribution is based on recently available sources, literature, and the personal views in memoirs and diaries of both prominent actors and ordinary people.

5   In the case of Serb–Serb controversies it is important to remember that the Serbs in (from) Croatia held different views than the Serbs in Serbia proper from the very beginning of the Yugoslav crisis, throughout the war, and after.

6   Robert Hayden, *Blueprints for a House Divided* (Ann Arbor, MI: University of Michigan Press, 1999), 18–19.

7   The Croat historian Ivo Goldstein gave a list of profascist attitudes in the opening of the democratization period in the early 1990s: "The great majority of Croats greeted joyfully the fall of Communism and the establishment of a new government with national remit. Mass meetings and various celebrations were organized in Zagreb and throughout Croatia. A large number of Partisan war memorials placed by the Communist authorities were demolished and there was a new emphasis on Croatian national symbols. Streets named after notable Serbs or towns with Serbian names were quickly given new names with a Croatian symbolism. The Victims of Fascism Square in Zagreb become the Square of Great Croats. A number of political exiles immediately returned to Croatia from the Diaspora, including some who were pro-Ustasha, bringing back with them their old extremist ideas which they were not afraid to express in public. Tuđman proclaimed a policy of 'reconciliation of all the Croats,' which meant tolerance for extreme nationalism. Many members of the new government were drunk with success and behaved as if they had forgotten, or perhaps only underestimated, the fact that Croatia was still in Yugoslavia with over half a million Serbian citizens who relied on Yugoslavia and were being increasingly manipulated from Serbia." Goldstein, *Croatia: A History* (London: McGill-Queen's University Press, 2000), 211–212. Goldstein emphasizes that in such a climate the free press began to address previously taboo subjects, and he notes attempts to rehabilitate the NDH or at least to improve its historic image.

8   Tudjman's first minister of defense, General Martin Špegelj, acknowledged later that the JNA's complaints concerning the revival of Ustashism in Croatia were well grounded: "The propaganda by the military top brass as well as from Serbia emphasized the emergence of Ustashism in Croatia, like in 1941. Unfortunately, that was partly accurate. This Ustashism was brought from the outside, by the return of extremist emigrants in Croatia. They were not ranking officers of the former NDH, but simply those who thought that the heritage of Ustashism would be a good foundation for the creation of new power in Croatia and for the obtainment of personal profit. Indeed, they won power and personal profit; however, their presence in politics caused big problems which exist even today. This fact, together with the attacks on Serb houses in the spring of 1991, caused worse damage to Croatia's defense than the whole JNA aggression. We have suffered the consequences ever since and have witnessed the emergence of different sorts of neo-fascism." Martin Špegelj, *Sjećanja vojnika*, 2nd ed. (Zagreb: Znanje, 2001), 55–56.

9   See for example Dušan Bilandžić *Hrvatska moderna povijest* (Zagreb: Golden Marketing, 1999), and Goldstein, *Croatia*.

10   Bishop Simeon Zloković of Upper Karlovci in June 1990 pointed out the historical difference of the two situations: "It is not Hitler or Mussolini who are on the borders of Yugoslavia today, but Europe. . . . Tuđman and all his followers, even the extrem-

ists among them, have to know that." Radmila Radić, "Crkva i 'srpsko pitanje," in *The Road to War in Serbia: Trauma and Catharsis*, ed. Nebojša Popov (Budapest, 2002), 1:320. Militant Serb nationalists Vojin S. Dabić and Ksenija M. Lukić in their book on Serbian victims in eastern Slavonia concluded that in spite of alleged Ustashi ideology, the HDZ could not revive Ustashi politics: "The HDZ leadership could not repeat the Ustashi practice of mass liquidations of the Serbs. The international community would not allow it." Vojin S. Dabić and Ksenija M. Lukić, *Crimes without Punishment: Crimes Committed by Croatian Armed Troops against the Serb in Eastern Slavonia and Western Sirmium in 1991* (Vukovar: Serbian Unity Congress, 1997), 14.

11 See Momčilo Mitrović, "Etničko čišćenje Srba iz Zagreba 1992–1994," *Tokovi istorije* 3–4 (2003), 89–99; Tanner, *Croatia*; Silber and Little, *Yugoslavia*; Svetozar Livada, *Etničko čišćenje—zločin stoljeća* (Zagreb: Prosvjeta, 1997); Jovan Mirić, *Demokracija i ekskomunikacija* (Zagreb: Srpsko kulturno drustvo Prosvjeta, 1999).

12 James Gow, *The Serbian Project and Its Adversaries: A Strategy of War Crimes* (Montreal, Kingston, and Ithaca: McGill-Queen's University Press, 2003); Michael Libal, *Njemačka politika i jugoslavenska kriza 1991–1992* (Zagreb: Golden Marketing, 2004), translated as *Limits of Persuasion: Germany and Yugoslav Crisis, 1991–1992* (Westport, CT: Greenwood Publishing Group, 1997); Paul Garde, *Vie et mort de la Yougoslavie* (Paris: Fayard, 1992).

13 Susan Woodward, *Balkan Tragedy: Chaos and Dissolution after the Cold War* (Washington, DC: The Brookings Institution, 1995).

14 See, for example, the amended indictment against Pavle Strugar et al.: "At all times relevant to this second amended indictment, a state of international armed conflict and partial occupation existed in Croatia. On 25 June 1991, Croatia declared its independence from the Socialist Federal Republic of Yugoslavia ('SFRY') and became independent on 8 October 1991. Up to and including 7 October 1991, this armed conflict was internal in nature. From 8 October 1991 an international armed conflict and partial occupation existed in Croatia." http://www.un.org/icty/indictment/english/str-2ai031017e.htm (accessed 13 October 2008).

15 Drago Roksandić, *Srbi u Hrvatskoj od 15. stoljeća do naših dana* (Zagreb: Biblioteka Vjesnik vremena, 1991), 158.

16 Official JNA data presented by Dragan Nikolić, *Kadrovi i kadrovska politika* (Beograd, 1989), 15.

17 In the administration of the Ministry of Interior the Serbs' share, according to official data, was 28.6 percent in 1985; in the next five years it dropped by 10 percent. In 20 out of 114 municipalities in Croatia, a Serb was the head of police. In 1985 Serbs held 27.5 percent of the ruling posts in the ministry proper; this dropped to 16 percent in March 1990 (well before the HDZ came to power). See Ratko Bubalo, "Jesu li Srbi stvarno vladali Hrvatskom," *Arkzin* (Zagreb) 19/20, 5 August 1994, 7.

18 Central Intelligence Agency, *Balkan Battlegrounds: A Military History of the Yugoslav Conflict, 1990–1995* (Washington: CIA Office of Public Affairs, 2002), 83.

19 Anton Tus, "Rat u Sloveniji i Hrvatskoj do Sarajevskog primirja," in *Rat u Hrvatskoj i Bosni i Hercegovini 1991–1995*, ed. Branka Magaš and Ivo Žanić (Sarajevo and Zagreb: Jesenski i Turk, 1999), 72–77.

20 CIA, *Balkan Battlegrounds*, 86.

21 Warren Zimmermann, *Origins of a Catastrophe: Yugoslavia and Its Destroyer: America's Last Ambassador Tells What Happened and Why* (New York and Toronto: Times Books, 1996), 154–155.

22 Borisav Jović, *Poslednji dani SFRJ, izvodi iz dnevnika* (Beograd: Politika, 1995), 371.

23 In May 1992, speaking on Jelačić Square in Zagreb on the occasion of the first anniversary of the Croatian referendum for an independence, Tudjman said that there wouldn't be a war unless Croatia wanted it. In his words Croatia had perceived a war as the only tool to achieve independence (quoted in Mihaljo M. Vučinić, *Gradjanski rat u Hrvatskoj 1991-1995 (Belgrade, 2004)*, 6; Duško Vilić and Boško Todorović, *Razbijanje Jugoslavije 1990-1992* (Beograd: DIK Književne novine—Enciklopedija, 1995), 25.

24 The order for the dismissal of the September class was issued after Croatia declared mobilization. Even the commandant of the Thirty-Second Army Corps (Varaždin) was supposed to go on vacation on 7 September, but he asked to remain in office. Instead, his deputy went on vacation. See *Slučaj generala Trifunovića* (Beograd: Demokratski centar, 1995), 9. Dr. Branko Kostić tried to explain the decision, saying that he believed that the dismissed class would be easily replaced by reservists. Nikola Čubra, *Vojska i razbijanje Jugoslavije* (Beograd, 1997), 215; Branko Kostić, *1991: Da se ne zaboravi* (Beograd, 1996).

25 Tus, "Rat u Sloveniji i Hrvatskoj," 78, gives details on the arsenal that fell into the hands of Croats: 200 tanks, 150 armored personnel carriers, 400 heavy artillery pieces, some 180,000 small arms, and 18 naval ships of various types.

26 Veljko Kadijević, *Moje viđenje raspada* (Beograd: Politika, 1993), 135. Some analysts (i.e., CIA, *Balkan Battlegrounds,* 112n45) expressed the suspicion that Kadijević probably modified his memoirs in order to reflect a more pro-Serbian line rather than the pro-Yugoslav line he followed in 1991. The other possibility is that the 1991 planning did include options for pulling out of Croatia, but Kadijević's presentation or ideas were so muddled at the time that even Jović was unable to understand them. Another possibility is that the plan did not initially call for a withdrawal from Croatia, but after evacuating Slovenia, a further JNA withdrawal from Croatia could be added without modifying any of the planned campaigns.

27 Jović, *Poslednji dani SFRJ*, 387–388; this view is supported by the CIA, *Balkan Battlegrounds*, 92.

28 The Vance Plan, which had been unveiled during the last few weeks of 1991, called for setting up four sectors (east, west, north, and south) to be known as United Nations Protected Areas (UNPAs). These would coincide roughly with three chunks of territory held by Serb and/or JNA forces. Upward of 10,000 UN troops would be deployed in the UNPAs for the protection of the people there. In return, the JNA would withdraw entirely from Croatia, and the Serb paramilitaries would be disbanded and disarmed, surrendering their weapons either to the JNA before withdrawal or, if they preferred, to the UN forces, who would store them intact at locations inside the UNPAs. The UN would form the blue line of separation.

29 Noam Čomski, *Novi militaristicki humanizam* (Belgrade: Plato, 2000), 36. Originally published as *The New Military Humanism: Lessons from Kosovo* (London: Pluto Press, 1999).

30 Hubert Vedrine, *Les Mondes de François Mitterrand* (Paris: Fayard, 1996), 641–643. The views of top French politicians expressed after the conflict in the Balkans had turned into war are summarized in the words of François Mitterand on 23 February 1993: "All that was a sequence of errors: German action, American ignorance, hesitation of the Italians because of the intervention of the Vatican that paralyzed them. In

fact, Germany considers itself as a legitimate inheritor of the former Austrian Empire, and thus takes for itself all of that ancient Austrian spirit of revenge against the Serbs." Ibid., 625.

31   Libal, *Njemačka politika.*

32   L. Silber, *Yugoslavia,* 141–142.

33   Davor Marjan, *Bitka za Vukovar* (Zagreb and Slavonski Brod: Hrvatski institut za povijest, 2004), 52–54. Marjan showed that the Croatian Information and News Agency (HINA) incorrectly informed the public that the JNA had taken action against the police forces on this occasion.

34   See Jelena Guskova, *Istorija jugoslovenske krize 1990–2000* (Beograd: IGAM, 2003), 1–2. In 1994, Guskova interviewed some of the participants from the Serbian side in 1994 (Milan Milanović, Časlav Nikšić, and Slavko Dokmanović) and some Croats from Osijek. Dokmanović mentioned some 150 dead, 13 of that number in the center of the village.

35   Laura Silber and Allan Little, *Yugoslavia: Death of a Nation,* 140–141.

36   Marjan, *Bitka za Vukovar,* 50, writes that he was not able to verify the story on missiles and the involvement of Šušak.

37   Norman Cigar, "The Serbo-Croatian War, 1991: Political and Military Dimensions," *The Journal of Strategic Studies* 16 (1993), 297–338.

38   Guskova, *Istorija jugoslovenske krize,* 1:266. In 1931 the municipality had 46,100 dwellers, 19,300 (41.9 percent) Serbs, 12,200 (26.5 percent) Croats, and 7,500 (16.3 percent) Germans. In 1981 the proportions were 31 percent Serbs, 37.14 percent Croats, and 22 percent Yugoslavs.

39   D. Marjan, *Vukovar,* 96; J. Guskova, *Istorija jugoslovenske krize,* 1:269.

40   J. Guskova, *Istorija jugoslovenske krize,* 1:259. Interview with Borisav Mikelić, RSK prime minister, 26 September 1994.

41   Tus, "Rat u Sloveniji i Hrvatskoj," 85. Goldstein, *Croatia,* 235, gives similar casualty data: 5,000–8,000 JNA killed and 600 tanks and other armored vehicles lost, against 2,500 Croatian dead.

42   Guskova, *Istorija jugoslovenske krize,* 1:270.

43   Kadijević, *Moje viđenje raspada,* 135.

44   See Petar Kriste, *Iznevjereni grad: Dubrovnik 1991* (Zagreb: Golden Marketing, 2000).

45   Srđa Pavlović, "Reckoning: The 1991 Siege of Dubrovnik and the Consequences of the 'War for Peace,'" *Spaces of Identity* 1, no. 5 (April 2005), 1–47.

46   *Pobjeda,* Podgorica, 5 September 1991, 1.

47   Slobodan Jarčević, "Suština plana Z-4," in *Republika Srpska krajina deset godina posle,* ed. Veljko Mišina Djurić (Beograd, 2005), 177–184. Jarčević was the RSK's minister of foreign affairs.

48   Janko Bobetko, *Sve moje bitke* (Zagreb: J. Bobetko, 1996).

49   CIA, *Balkan Battlegrounds,* 297–298.

50   What really happened to the Serbian civilians and captured soldiers? Some authors, like Guskova, claim that, according to UNCRO data, Croatian authorities would not let them or any other foreign observers into the area around Okučani and Pakrac before 5 May. Even Yasushi Akashi, special UN envoy was denied admission into Daruvar to look after the refugees. Experts among UNCRO doubted that security was the real reason for the ban and suspected that the HV was hiding or had eliminated evidence of numerous civilian deaths. Some UN officers, such as Swedish policeman Hans Anders

Jarvestam were witnesses to these acts and horrible scenes. The Croatian ambassador repeated the official position that no crimes had been committed against civilians during what it characterized as a police operation conducted on a small scale in order to open the highway. Guskova, *Istorija jugoslovenske krize*, 2:233–239. Dr. Guskova was at the time in the UNPROFOR's headquarters in Zagreb, and she moved frequently around the areas in question. Her estimate of 12,000 refugees is very similar to what scholars determined at a later date.

51   Martić was convicted in June 2007 and is presently serving thirty-five years in prison for various crimes, including the rocket attack on Zagreb.

52   Milisav Sekulić, *Knin je pao u Beogradu* (Bad Vilbel: Nidda Verlag, 2000), 158–166.

53   See http://www.b92.net/doc/brijuni/index.php (accessed 15 October 2008). ICTY 2003a.

54   See detailed analyses and comparisons of these operations and concepts in Ozren Žunec, "Operacije Bljesak i Oluja," in Magaš and Žanić, 93–110.

55   In an interview given on 11 May 1995, when the consequences of military action in western Slavonia were already known, Galbraith said that neither he nor the U.S. administration gave the green light for the operation: "We warned the Government of Croatia against any military action in Western Slavonia. We warned that it would have the consequences that it in fact had, which included these attacks on Zagreb. We feel that it was a very unwise decision and that it was a violation of the Copenhagen Agreement and we made that very clear. There certainly was no green light of any kind. In fact, there was a red light. We are very concerned at the departure of the Serbs from Western Slavonia. We are not interested in supporting the process of reintegration in Croatia if the end result of that process is an ethnically pure country. So we believe that all steps should be taken to try to make the Serbian community in Western Slavonia feel that Croatia is their home and, further, to encourage those Serbs who left in 1995, as well as those who left in 1991, to return home. That is one reason why we believe that the continued presence of UNCRO is essential. Of course, it is a fundamental human right to be able to travel freely if the Serbs do wish to leave, and that is their free choice. We would urge them to stay."

56   Mirić, *Demokracija i ekskomunikacija*, 138–139.

57   James George Jatras, "NATO's Myths and Bogus Justifications for Intervention," in *NATO's Empty Victory: A Postmortem on the Balkan War*, ed. T. G. Carpenter (Washington, DC: CATO Institute, 2000), 26–27. See also "Four Navy Jets Bomb Serb Missile Sites," *Navy Times*, 21 August 1995, 2; Chris Black, "U.S. Veterans' Aid to Croatia Elicits Queries," *Boston Globe*, 13 August 1995, 12; Charlotte Eager, "Invisible United States Army Defeats Serbs," *Observer* (UK), 5 November 1995, 25; Yves Goulet, "MPRI: Washington's Freelance Advisors," *Jane's Intelligence Review*, 1 July 1998, 38; Raymond Bonner, "War Crimes Panel Finds Croat Troops 'Cleansed' the Serbs," *New York Times*, 21 March 1999, A1.

58   Boris Raseta, ed., *Storm over Croatia* (Belgrade: Samizdat B92, 2003). The book is completely documentary with records from parliament discussions, TV panels, Web discussion, and press clippings.

59   Nikica Barić, "Je li 1995. godine Hrvatska počinila 'etničko čišćenje' Srba?" *Časopis za suvremenu povijest* 36, br. 2 (Zagreb, 2004).

60   The scenes in *Storm over Croatia* show that the Serbs had good reason to flee at least temporarily. In the report of the Croatian Helsinki Committee for Human Rights, presented in April 1999, in just one UN sector, South, preliminary investigation showed

that 435 persons were killed during or immediately after Operation Storm (see HHO [Hrvatski helsinski odbor za ljudska prava] Izvještaj: vojna operacija "Oluja" i poslije, part 1 in *Srbi u Hrvatskoj i njihova sudbina*, ed. G. Babić (Beograd: Adeona, 2000), supplements 37–232.

61   E. M. Despalatović, "Koreni rata u Hrvatskoj," in *Susedi u ratu, Jugoslovenski etnicitet, kultura i istorija iz ugla antropologa*, ed. Joel M. Halpern and David Kideckel, (Beograd: Samizdat B92, 2002), 132–133 (after N. Barić, *Pobuna Srba u Hrvatskoj*, 564).

62   CIA, *Balkan Battlegrounds*, 367. They quoted Reuters, 3 August: "US says no reason for Croatia War after Serbian Pact." But this statement is questionable in the light of later available evidence. Mate Granić asserted on 6 August that Croatia had received advice from the U.S. on how to carry out mass assault on the Serbs in Krajina. See Stanko Nišević, *Hrvatska Oluja i srpske seobe* (Beograd, 2002), 195.

63   See for example Marko Vrcelj, *Rat za Srpsku Krajinu 1991–1995* (Beograd: Srpska kulturna društva "Zora," 2002), who gives a detailed firsthand account of terror experienced by Croats living in RSK. Vrcelj was an SVK colonel.

64   Jovan Mirić, *Demokracija i ekskomunikacija* (Zagreb: Srpsko kulturno drustvo Prosvjeta, 1999).

65   ICTY 2002:10656.

66   Ozren Žunec, "Okučanski zaključci," *Erasmus* 3/12 (1995), 7–20.

67   See an interview with Nikola Visković, "Zločinački pothvat počeo je još 1991," *Feral Tribune*, 27 July 2005, 10–12.

68   Zimmermann, *Origins of a Catastrophe*.

69   Peter Galbraith, interview by Charles Ingrao, January 2004.

70   See Milisav Sekulić, *Jugoslaviju niko nije branio a Vrhovna komanda je izdala* (Bad Vilbel: Nidda Verlag, 1997).

71   Momir Bulatović, *Pravila ćutanja: istiniti politički triler sa poznatim završetkom* (Beograd: Narodna knjiga Alfa, 2004), 181–182.

72   Facsimile in HHO (Hrvatski helsinski odbor za ljudska prava) Izvještaj: vojna operacija "Oluja" i poslije, part 1 (1998), 8.

8

Valentina Duka, team leader
Dusan Janjić, team leader

Elez Biberaj	**Ylber Hysa**	**Mariella Pandolfi**
Slobodan Bošković	**Ana Lalaj**	Nicholas Pano
Janusz Bugajski	Remzi Lani	**Besnik Pula**
Bejtullah Destani	Shkelzën Maliqi	**Blerim Reka**
Ferit Duka	**Ines Murzaku**	Predrag Simić
Bernd Fischer	Aurora Ndrio	**Rumen Stefanov**
Enver Hasani		Stefan Troebst

Principal author Dušan Janjić completed an initial draft of this chapter in December 2005 that ultimately incorporated substantial sections written by Ana Lalaj and Besnik Pula, passages of which were drawn from "The Emergence of the Kosovo 'Parallel State,' 1988–1992," *Nationalities Papers* 32/4 (December 2004), subsequently republished in Thomas Emmert and Charles Ingrao, eds., *Conflict in Southeastern Europe at the End of the Twentieth Century: A Scholars' Initiative* (New York & London: Routledge, 2006). Elez Biberaj, Blerim Reka and Rumen Stefanov also contributed text. A half-dozen team members received research stipends from the National Endowment for Democracy (Dušan Janjić, Besnik Pula, Blerim Reka), the Institute for Historical Justice and Reconciliation (Ana Lalaj, Rumen Stefanov), and the National Council for Eurasian and East European Research (Slobodan Bošković).

The text incorporates substantial material collected during a series of interviews with former public officials, most notably with Belgrade publicist Milenko Marković, who held a senior leadership position in the Serbian League of Communists and was in charge of Kosovo affairs prior to being removed from that position by Slobodan Milošević. Project-wide reviews in January-February 2006 and August-September 2007 elicited extensive comment and criticism from project participants, most notably James Gow, Marko Attila Hoare, James Lyon, Leon Malazogu, Stan Markotich, and Sabrina Ramet.

KOSOVO UNDER THE MILOŠEVIĆ REGIME

◆ Dusan Janjić, with Anna Lalaj and Besnik Pula ◆

Slobodan Milošević's rule over Kosovo (1989–1999) was marked by intense political conflict that led to open rebellion followed by international military intervention. By invoking the so-called ethnic principle, the government he led tried to establish a state in which Serb interests and aspirations would not be threatened by other ethnic groups, particularly by Albanians in Kosovo, but also across the territory of the former Yugoslavia. In Kosovo and elsewhere a premium was placed on "historic rights" and the sanctity of state sovereignty. Albanian leaders responded by building "parallel state" institutions and eventually proclaiming their own independent republic. Both sides justified their agendas in historic terms with nationalist Serbs claiming to preserve Kosovo as Serbia's cradle of statehood and nationalist Albanians endeavoring to reverse the division of Albanian lands by the Great Powers in 1913. This conflict has a long history. Yet the particular course that the conflict took at the end of the eighties was largely determined by the institutional framework inherited from the socialist era and by the particular political dynamics that precipitated and followed Yugoslavia's dissolution.

Kosovo as a Catalyst for Milošević's Rise to Power

As late as the 1980s, most of the Serbian political establishment preferred an authoritarian government in which a leading autocrat decided what is best for the people. The choice fell on Slobodan Milošević, who was strongly supported by Serbs in the highest ranks of the military. His open ambition for absolute power inspired the military leadership with the hope that he would be able to provide it with the budgetary support needed to maintain control over the Yugoslav federation. Apart from that, they also shared with him the same ideology and a common desire to maintain state socialism. In order to meet these goals, Milošević proposed constitutional changes within Serbia, intending to resolve the state issue by activating Serb nationalism.[1] Hiding behind the idea of protecting Yugoslavia,

Milošević pursued a policy of homogenization and ethnic mobilization of the masses aiming at a thorough "reorganization of Serbia and Yugoslavia."[2]

The first step toward dominating Yugoslavia was to subjugate Kosovo. Existing tensions between Serbs and Albanians served Milošević's strategy of reinforcing ethnic distance and distrust. It endeavored to make Serbs feel threatened and promote new institutions based on ethnic principles that would inevitably marginalize and frustrate Kosovo's Albanian majority. Massive rallies were frequently organized in Serbia around one leader, Slobodan Milošević. This atmosphere of ethnocentric superiority promoted the feeling of belonging to the nation and the need for a "firm hand." For example, the media delivered the message that "Serbs are brave, honest and civilized; others are cunning and mean and we will not let them rule over us." Dissatisfaction was intentionally turned into an aggressive large-scale national movement that fostered a spirit of revenge and retaliation.[3]

The Serbian public was exposed to the "psychology of the wounded lion," based on the belief of Milošević's supporters that the broad autonomy of Vojvodina and Kosovo had weakened Serbia.[4] The number and influence of those who shared this conviction helped intensify and escalate the crisis through fear that the dissolution of Yugoslavia would unite the Serbs' rivals while leaving them divided among several states.[5] Survival necessitated "quick and sharp solutions," efficiently administered by the traditional resort to centralism and Serbian nationalism. Many journalists, academics, and politicians who supported Milošević viewed any decentralization or federalization of Serbia as capitulation to the slogan "Weak Serbia—Strong Yugoslavia" dating from the time of Stalin's Cominterm that would lend "support to Albanian and other minority separatism" and Serbia's fragmentation.[6]

Serbian nationalist awareness of Kosovo was dominated by the conviction that "Old Serbia" had been "Albanicized" by a colonizing Albanian population. The possibility that Kosovo would separate from Serbia and turn it into an "ethnically clean" region was viewed as a direct threat to Serbian national identity. Kosovo was linked with the vital national interests of the Serbs, giving it a special role in Serbian history and ideology. Therefore, appeals to end Albanian repression against Kosovo's Serb minority were widely accepted by the Serbian public.

They were reinforced in 1986, by the Communist leadership in Kosovo Polje, which demanded the removal of officials in Kosovo, Serbia, and elsewhere in Yugoslavia who did not have sufficient sympathy for their plight. Their campaign fed an explosive mix of official nationalism, demagoguery, and populism that served the republic's bureaucratic and political establishment. Milošević's party packaged what was an essentially antireform agenda as an "antibureaucratic revolution" and "people's initiative."[7] The organizational nucleus of this movement inspired conflicts within the Communist bureaucracy both within and between the republics. The culminating event of this process was the Eighth Session of the Central Committee of the League of Communists of Serbia (23–24 September 1987), during which nationalism became the official policy of the Serbian political leadership. Pro-Yugoslav, antinationalist, and reform elements led by Serbian President Ivan Stambolić were removed or hounded from office. The beleaguered president's policy of preserving Yugoslavia, coexisting, and negotiating with Kosovo's Albanians while building a joint frontline against Serb and Albanian nationalism was branded as opportunistic and contrary to the interests of the Serb people. It was easily trumped by Milošević's promises to end the Albanian "terror" against the Kosovo Serbs and to solve the "Serb issue" by uniting all Serbs in one state. By 1987–1988, all preconditions were in place for reviving the Kosovo myth to mobilize the Serbs, first for political purposes, then for war against Yugoslavia's other nations.[8]

By raising the Kosovo issue and escalating political conflicts, the federal government hoped to recentralize power, perhaps in anticipation of Yugoslavia's future entry into the EC. On 11 February 1987, the regime presented its Proposal of the Presidency of Yugoslavia for Constitutional Changes, which foresaw a reduction in Kosovo's autonomy.[9] The federal, republican, and provincial parliaments duly gave their consent one month later, after which began debate about the federal project, including amendments to the constitution. Apart from the request for a strong federation, Milošević initiated an intense propaganda campaign against the "powers of secession and counterrevolution." In April he interrupted a meeting with Serbian officials in Priština who had many complaints about difficult living conditions for Serbs in Kosovo by going outside to join crowds of Kosovo Serbs who were quarreling with the police. He approached them by saying, "Nobody will beat you anymore. You must stay here. This is your land, your gardens, your valleys, your memories. . . . Otherwise you will disgrace your predecessors and disappoint your descendants. . . ." The very stridency of these words greatly influenced the future developments in Kosovo. Milošević presented himself very successfully as someone who cared about Serbs and their human rights. His attitude displayed a lot of aggressiveness, bitterness, disappointment, and regret that was shared by many intellectuals in Serbia, particularly in Belgrade. He now established close cooperation with them, spreading one-sided and inflammatory nationalist rhetoric in framing what they represented to be the Serb national interest in Kosovo. He thereby forged what came to be seen as a unified, well-organized, and focused alliance.

Stambolić recognized Milošević as the executor of the program whose real creator was a group of high-ranking Serb nationalist intellectuals in the Communist Party of Serbia, JNA, Serbian Orthodox Church, and various cultural and scientific institutions, such as the Serbian Academy of Sciences and Arts (SANU).[10]

A leading figure among them, often referred to as the father of the nation, was the writer Dobrica Ćosić, whose speech to the Central Committee of the Serbian Communist Party on 16 September 1966 became a blueprint for resolving the Kosovo problem.[11] The group's activities promoted aggressive tactics that they represented as necessary for the Serbs' survival. Their first public act was a memorandum signed by 216 prominent intellectuals in January 1986 and addressed to the federal parliament. The so-called SANU Memorandum claimed that Kosovo's Serb minority was being subjected to genocide. They cited the case of Djordje Martinović, whose brutal violation by a broken bottle they applied to the whole Serb nation.[12] The nationalists would later seize on the 3 September 1987 murder-suicide committed by Aziz Kelemendi, a mentally unbalanced Kosovar Albanian soldier who killed four other soldiers in their JNA military barracks in Paraćin in central Serbia. Although Kelmendi's victims included two Muslims, a Slovene, and only one Serb, Milošević and his allies quickly characterized it as part of an anti-Serb conspiracy, a judgment that was readily embraced by most of the Serbian public.[13] Many Kosovo Albanians interpreted the incident and its misrepresentation in official circles and media as part of a conspiracy to justify their repression.[14] They were, however, hardly in a position to buck the trend being set in Belgrade and trumpeted by the media. The nationalists soon organized a series of "meetings of truth and solidarity with the Serbs and Montenegrins in Kosovo" that lasted throughout 1988 and was reciprocated by a "Council for organizing protest meetings" by Serbs and Montenegrins from Kosovo Polje, which made appeals for "ending the Holocaust of the Serbs" and "defending Serb honor" with slogans like "Serbia is a winner in war and a loser in peace" and "We want weapons in Kosovo."

The Albanians' only recourse was to schedule meetings of their own that elicited some sympathy from the other republics but had little impact within Serbia proper. By then, however, Milošević had won the media war, both with the leaders of the other FRY republics and with Serbian Communists such as Stambolić, whose Titoist vision of a supranational state went down with them. Faithful mouthpieces like *Politika* and Belgrade TV replaced "brotherhood and unity" with crude stereotypes of Albanians, Slovenes, and Croats, thereby preparing the public for broad interethnic conflict.

Much of Milošević's support rested on long-simmering resentment of the federation. Many Serbs believed that SFRY had been imposed on the Serbs, with devastating material, spiritual, and cultural consequences under both Tito and his immediate successors. The implication was that the anti-Serb, Cominterm policy expressed by the slogan "Weak Serbia—Strong Yugoslavia" had survived Tito's death. According to this nationalist belief, Communist Yugoslavia saw an enemy in each Serb, an antipathy that promoted the cleansing of Serbs from Kosovo, Croatia's abolition of the Cyrillic alphabet, the disappearance of Serb cultural and national institutions from Bosnia-Hercegovina, the unchecked autonomist spirit in Vojvodina, and separatism in Montenegro.[15] One grievance that united Serbian officials, academics, media, and the public behind Milošević was the 1974 constitution, which had ceded essential state functions from Serbia to the two autonomous provinces of Kosovo and Vojvodina, thereby undermining its sovereignty and turning it into a "semistate." Therefore, Serbs in Kosovo and throughout Yugoslavia shared with Milošević the belief that only constitutional changes that recentered power in Belgrade would enable Serbia to govern effectively.[16] Certainly this would reduce the space for "Albanian separatism." So would the unification of all Serbs (possibly including those living in Bosnia and Croatia) in one state—a policy hidden behind their rationalization of the "struggle for preserving Yugoslavia."[17] Indeed, by representing their agenda as the struggle for preserving Yugoslavia they hoped to elicit support from nonnationalists and ensure for Serbia and its allies a claim to leadership within the federation.

But whereas Milošević's rhetoric incited resentment of Yugoslavia's other constituent peoples, it instilled a genuine fear of the Albanians. The Serbian public believed that Kosovo already enjoyed all basic rights and a high level of autonomy, interpreting Albanian calls for a republic as an intolerable sign of disloyalty that undermined the state unity of both Serbia and Yugoslavia. The quest for republican status was, therefore, seen as a precursor to outright secession and independence, which would reduce Kosovo's Serbs to a minority in their own state. Albanian separatists already stood accused of pressuring Serbs to leave Kosovo, fueling a steady collective emigration of Serbs that the regime blamed on the ineffectiveness of the League of Communists (see chapter 2). Many Serbs perceived Albanians as a people who were fond of violence, whose riots, demonstrations, and rallies hurt both themselves and the development of Kosovo.[18] By contrast, Serbs viewed themselves as a true nation, whereas the Albanians were considered only a national minority that should not expect more than autonomy. Indeed, many people in Serbia still subscribed to the longstanding belief that the Albanians were simply not capable of modern, national development.[19]

As repression of the Albanians intensified, so did the revival of the Serbs' Kosovo myth that culminated on St. Vitus Day, 28 June 1989, the 600th anniversary of the battle of Kosovo. Milošević and other republican leaders joined the Serbian Orthodox Church at a large public commemoration in Kosovo Polje. The Serbian president's speech employed the Kosovo myth in justifying his political agenda: a lack of unity and betrayal had followed the Serbs ever since the battle, for which reason they now needed to pledge unity and courage in order to remain undefeated.[20] The rally crowned Milošević's triumph in the struggle for Kosovo. Now he simply had to impose constitutional reforms that eliminated the Albanian bureaucracy's hegemony within the province, thus affording the diminishing Serb minority the protection and support necessary "to stay in Kosovo forever."[21]

The Constitutional Changes

Having captivated Serbs everywhere, Milošević now pressed for a basket of measures that created the impression that he knew how to handle Kosovo and other problems that Serbia and Yugoslavia faced, so long as the federal and provincial bureaucracies of Kosovo and Vojvodina did not interfere. The true character of Milošević's regime in Kosovo surfaced in a series of directives delivered to a joint session of the federal and state presidency on 8 September 1988. Milošević announced that it would use "all political, administrative, and compulsory means" (i.e., state of emergency, police and army) in the fight against Albanian nationalism. Part of this policy included "ideological and political differentiation" in the party and other social and political organizations and state authorities, meaning that individual organs of the League of Communists and state authorities would become mono-ethnic in composition. Town and street names were changed, as were the contents of educational TV programs that heralded Kosovo's entry into an era of concrete change. Then, in November 1988, the province's Albanian Communist leader, Azem Vllasi, was removed from office. The Kosovo leadership responded with major demonstrations that included five days of rallies that drew 300,000–400,000 participants.[22] There were also a protest march by Trepča miners and a miners' hunger strike in January 1989.

Federal bodies responded by trying to settle the problem in Kosovo. However, this made the situation even more complicated by raising the question of whether Kosovo was the problem of Serbia or Yugoslavia, thereby pitting other republics like Slovenia and Croatia against the regime in Belgrade, which insisted that Kosovo was an internal, Serbian matter. In an attempt to control the situation, the presidency of Yugoslavia met on 26–27 February 1989 and decided to impose a partial state of emergency in Kosovo to be enforced by the military. Some 15,000 JNA and police personnel were deployed there with supporting armor.[23]

The show of force coincided with a series of special measures at the beginning of March that outlawed strikes and instituted a province-wide curfew, enforced by the special police of the Interior Ministry (MUP).[24] Then, on the twenty-third the Kosovo Assembly was convened to approve the reductions in autonomy that had already been worked out in Belgrade, including the assembly's right to block legislation adopted by the Serbian parliament. Before the ballot, each deputy was interrogated by security police, who made a show of force inside the building while tanks stood guard outside.[25] A week of sometimes violent demonstrations followed, in which twenty-two protestors and two policemen were killed, dozens more wounded, and hundreds arrested in fighting between the army and Albanian protestors.[26] The province's Albanian leadership promptly resigned in protest, but Belgrade refused to accept the resignations, although it did order the arrest of Azem Vllasi, together with thirteen leaders of the Trepča miners, including the chairman of its managing council, Azis Abrashi, plus the Stari Tërgu mine director Buhran Kavaja. The interior minister declared that they would be tried by the courts, although their sentences were vacated under pressure from the other republics and international community.

By the twenty-eighth the Serbian Parliament had proclaimed the abolition of autonomy and the establishment of a united Serbia.[27] Kosovo and Vojvodina had now been defederalized, losing the attributes of statehood that extended beyond the veto to the loss of legislative, administrative, and judicial power. When the Kosovo Assembly's MPs resisted the unilateral revision of the Serbian constitution, the republic dissolved it altogether and assumed its functions. In fact, a system of special laws for Kosovo was established, including the Law on the Action of Republican Agencies under Special Circumstances, the Law on Termination of Work of the Assembly of Kosovo and the Executive Council of the Assembly of Kosovo, the Law on Labor Relations under Special Circumstances, the University Law, the Primary Education Law, the Secondary Education Law, and the High School Law.[28]

Thus ended successfully the first phase of defining the Serb national interest and officially inaugurating the "unitary state." Yet the abolition of the constitutionally granted political and territorial autonomy of Kosovo and Vojvodina changed relations among the republics. The unitarist pacification of Kosovo rang an alarm in the other republics. Slovenia argued that breaking the Trepča miners' strike was tantamount to "overthrowing the Anti-Fascist Council of National Liberation of Yugoslavia." On 27 September 1989 it used the destruction of Yugoslavia's federal system and the specter of Serbian hegemony to justify its intention to become the first republic to "escape" from Yugoslavia. The proclamation of independence and secession by Slovenia was public confirmation that the Kosovo crisis and the Serb–Albanian question were not the only problems in the former Yugoslavia.

The constitutional changes further escalated the intensity and breadth of the Albanian resistance. Job actions became the chief weapon. By September 1989, 230 enterprises throughout Kosovo had experienced strikes or other work stoppages at a cost of nearly two million work hours. On 3 September the resistance called its first general strike, which included private shops and supermarkets, to protest the dismissal of 15,000 Albanian workers from their jobs. All work halted throughout Kosovo in a powerful show of solidarity. Yet far from yielding to pressure, the Serbian regime responded by firing 5,000 additional workers. Meanwhile, Belgrade was systematically changing the constitution and reorganizing power in the province by positioning selected cadres in the executive and judicial branches, as well as in public companies and enterprises.

By the end of 1989 Albanian opposition had spread well beyond union workers to embrace virtually every segment of Albanian society, including students, children, politicians, and farmers. Previously illegal Stalinist-oriented groups now surfaced, growing into mass organizations. Most prominent among them was the Democratic League of Kosovo (LDK), which was established in December 1989. Inspired by a group of writers and intellectuals led by Ibrahim Rugova, the LDK rapidly became Kosovo's largest political organization and, with the introduction of political pluralism throughout Yugoslavia, its first non-Communist political party. Within a year its membership had exploded, with its leaders claiming more than half a million members.[29] Kosovo's first human rights groups emerged, as did the prodemocracy United Yugoslav Democratic Initiative (UJDI), which established a branch in Kosovo in 1989. By 1990, labor opposition had coalesced in the Independent Trade Unions of Kosovo (BSPK), which broke with the old Yugoslav Federation of Trade Unions (FTU). There were also a large number of smaller Albanian political parties vying with the LDK, though united with it against the Milošević regime.

Although Belgrade characterized the Albanian opposition as counterrevolutionary, separatist, and irredentist, the large-scale student demonstrations that followed in Kosovo were merely protesting the violation of their constitutional rights. Yet this did not discourage Milošević, who pointed to the cooperation of loyal Albanians as proof that his Kosovo policy enjoyed popular support.[30] Instead, the regime had forfeited the allegiance of a majority of the Albanian population. Moreover, the mistrust that his policies had sown between Kosovo's Albanian and Serb communities had extended the official policy of differentiation beyond politics and government to all levels of social and commercial relations. Supported by officials and media, Serb villages even organized guard units and prepared for armed conflict with weapons provided from government stocks.[31] Meanwhile, during 1990 the regime took the precaution of removing Albanians from the province's police force.

Amid the swirl of events generated by Milošević's rise to power, it is possible to identify two major consequences for Kosovo. First, his policies had mobilized the Serbs for conflict with the Albanian majority and introduced some elements of democracy in the political life both there and in Serbia, including a multiparty system, but had failed to establish effective democratic control over Kosovo.[32] While pluralism was taking root in Kosovo, it had become extremely polarized along ethnic lines. The new local political organizations were exclusively Albanian, whereas Serbs and Montenegrins remained tied to the state apparatus, now coming under the direct control of Belgrade. Serbian parties that had emerged following the collapse of one-party rule in Serbia were primarily branches of Belgrade-based parties that expressed little opposition to Milošević's policies in Kosovo. Second, Kosovo and the Serb-Albanian conflict constituted a

formidable challenge to maintaining internal national and state stability throughout Serbia, with detentions, persecution, and terror against Kosovo's Albanian
population by a now exclusively Serbian police force driving a strong wedge
between the populations, resembling apartheid.[33]

Intensification of Conflicts

At the beginning of the 1990s, political and ethnic conflicts intensified. In March
1990, the state imposed large-scale repressive measures as more than seven thousand people (mostly Albanians) were arrested. This forced the Albanian leadership to minimize the risk of public protests. When the war broke out in Croatia
and Bosnia-Hercegovina, the Albanians became very cautious not to be dragged
into the conflict. Hence, the Albanian movement, which stood for one of the most
explosive movements in this part of Europe, changed into a nonaggressive one.

Kosovo's provincial assembly articulated this desire for sovereignty when it
convened 2 July 1990. When Milošević loyalists locked the doors to the assembly, the delegates proclaimed independence on the stairs in front of the building.
The move came as a surprise to Belgrade, which believed that it had secured
the loyalty of the provincial leadership in toeing its line. Up until this point, the
assembly still had no formal connection with opposition groups like the LDK,
whose leaders were largely unaware of its plans to declare independence. Yet this
act of defiance helped forge a link between itself and the Albanian opposition
groups led by the LDK, giving the Albanian demands a strong legal basis. Serbia
responded by altogether suspending the assembly and all of Kosovo's provincial
governing organs, thus establishing direct rule in the province, and it reinforced
its security presence with police reinforcements from Serbia. Undeterred, the assembly held a second, clandestine meeting in the southeastern Kosovo town of
Kačanik, with two thirds voting on 7 September 1990 to adopt a new constitution
for an independent republic of Kosovo. Yet both the "Staircase" and Kačanik
meetings reflected the Albanian political leaders' commitment to nonviolent resistance consisting principally of public demonstrations and strikes—although
some opposition elements occasionally launched isolated, hit-and-run attacks
against law enforcement personnel. In reality, the policy represented by the Albanian political leaders as a nonviolent resistance was a package of pragmatic
political decisions that ultimately led to radical political demands.

The shift ultimately affected the LDK. Upon holding its first congress in May
1991, the LDK's position was still that Kosovo should become a republic within
the Yugoslav confederation—a new loose federal order advocated at the time by
Slovenia and Croatia. However, the demand for republic status became untenable
only a month later, when Yugoslavia entered its first phase of disintegration with
Slovenia's and Croatia's departure. The LDK, which had virtually turned into a

coalition of a variety of political currents among Kosovo's Albanians, now faced two difficult challenges. First, more radical currents within the party called for radical action – the unification of all Yugoslav Albanians into a single republic, and their unification with Albania as the rectification of historical injustice. Team member Shkëlzen Maliqi has characterized this as a conflict between "legalists" and "anti-legalists" within the LDK, the former maintaining that the demand for independence should adhere to some legal basis in the former Yugoslavia constitutional order, and the latter viewing the conflict in stark historic terms that demanded radical solutions.[34] Second, the LDK had to strategize its actions based on the rapidly unfolding developments that followed Yugoslavia's disintegration, including the outbreak of fighting in Slovenia and Croatia and the diplomatic intervention of the European Community (EC) and the United States. During the summer of 1991, the LDK revised its platform to embrace independence, while other Albanian parties followed suit.[35]

The tense situation in Kosovo deteriorated after an incident involving the poisoning of some Albanian schoolchildren from Podujevo, Priština, Mitrovica, and Vučitrn. Around 200 parents of Albanian children petitioned for a school boycott. The Serbian Health Authority and Military Medical Academy stated officially that there were no signs of poisoning. On the other hand, Albanians claimed it had been organized by the Serbian secret service.[36] Although the details of this incident are still not clear, it served as a classic trigger that produced a massive emotional and political mobilization of Albanians, who now prepared to forsake Kosovo's schools and other institutions. This "boycott of institutions" facilitated Belgrade's takeover of Kosovo's police, health system, schools, economy, and media, which it justified by representing Albanians as "primitive and mean."[37] Republican authorities had already imposed emergency measures in 1989 and 1990. Although they had reported them to the UN secretary-general based on Article 4 of the International Convention on Civil and Political Rights, some of these measures were contrary to the Yugoslav constitution.[38] Meanwhile, the LDK and especially the Council for the Defense of Human Rights and Freedoms (CDHRF) in 1990 began intensifying human rights monitoring efforts throughout Kosovo, producing daily and monthly reports of incidents of police violence, brutal treatment of Albanians while in custody, and other cases of ethnically driven maltreatment and violence perpetrated by the authorities.[39]

For its part, the Serbian authorities represented their actions as a Program for Peace, Freedom, Equality, and Prosperity for Kosovo Province, which the Serbian Assembly adopted on 22 March 1990. The state pledged to employ "all legal means" to guarantee (1) the security of people and property of the Serb, Montenegrin, and all other "nations and nationalities whose rights are violated" in Kosovo; (2) "national equality and respect for national traditions, religious freedoms, and all civilization accomplishments" of the Albanian citizenry; (3)

the human rights of all citizens of Kosovo; (4) "remedy for injustices done to displaced Serbs and Montenegrins and the creation of conditions for their return, and good environment for everybody who wants to live and work in Kosovo"; (5) establishment of a directorate for improvement of economic and social development of Kosovo, from the republic's resources (a euphemism for taking over one of the federal functions), and (6) the establishment of an efficient "legal state," which empowered the Serbian Assembly to abolish those laws and decisions of the Kosovo assembly, which violated the constitution and the principles of the program itself.

The program was supported by the Operational Plan for the Implementation of Program Tasks for the Establishment of Peace, Equality, Democracy, and Prosperity in the Province of Kosovo.[40] Numerous laws were also adopted in order to implement Milošević's policies, including the Law on Republic Authorities in Extraordinary Circumstances,[41] Article 2, Item 4 of which allowed for the imposition of temporary compulsory measures. The implementation of this law and the introduction of these constraints was authorized by the Decision on Defining Extraordinary Circumstances on the Territory of Kosovo Province that was adopted by the Assembly of Serbia and published the same day (26 June 1990). The temporary compulsory measures were enforced on an *ad hoc* basis, unlike the emergency compulsory measures, which applied to all vital functions and all life in Kosovo. The temporary compulsory measures meant taking over the executive functions of administration, economy, health, education, and justice. According to the Serb narrative, "mass dismissal" of Kosovo Albanians from state institutions during 1990–1991 was not the result of a Serbian government decision; but rather, according to Serbian narratives, Kosovo Albanians were ordered by their political leaders to leave their jobs as a sign of protest against the revocation of Kosovo's status in 1989. [42] In many cases, Serbs and Montenegrins were hired instead of Albanians, who were dismissed from their positions. The assembly, the executive council, and the presidency of Kosovo were all abolished.[43] Their abolition was followed by the closing of schools, dismissal of Albanian teachers, restrictions on Albanian children's right to enroll in Albanian schools, and suspension of financing for schools that did not adhere to Serbia's "integrated educational program."[44] Another "discriminatory law" was the Law on Special Requirements for the Sale of Property of 1991, which was originally adopted in 1989 as the Law on Restriction of Sale of Property.[45]

Following the abolition of Kosovo's Academy of Sciences, Ibrahim Rugova led representatives of eleven Albanian political parties in signing a declaration (17 October) offering three options for the solution of the "Albanian issue in Yugoslavia."[46] Four days after the Kačanik Assembly had adopted a Resolution on Independence and Sovereignty of Kosovo, an independence referendum was secretly organized for 26–30 September 1991.[47] The referendum won overwhelming support, with 89 percent of registered voters participating and 99 percent of the slightly more than one million balloters endorsing independence. When it next met on 19 October, the Kačanik Assembly proclaimed the independence of Kosovo and duly amended the September 1990 constitution to reflect the popular vote for independence. From this point on, the common goal of the Albanian movement—affirmed by "popular will"—became independence. After the referendum, any alternative platform or support for compromises over this issue became tantamount to treason.

Five days later, Albania recognized Kosovo's independence. On 13 December the conflict reached the floor of the federal parliament after sixteen Albanian MPs petitioned the UN secretary-general, accusing Serbian authorities and Yugoslav military of the armed massacre of Albanians and demanding the introduction of UN peacekeepers in Kosovo. Ten days later the Republic of Kosovo asked the EU for recognition.[48] In an attempt to stop the escalation of the Albanian nationalist movement, the government of Serbia removed from office Riza Sapunxhia, the representative of Kosovo in the presidency of SFRY on 18 March and three days later appointed a "loyal Albanian" Sejdo Bajramoviq, who according to many Albanians was a Roma from Montenegro and not an Albanian.

By 1992, Kosovo had developed two irreconcilable political blocs: the regime, which reintroduced a Serbian nationalizing project and was bent on breaking the political will of Albanians at all costs, and a popular Albanian secessionist movement that maintained its position that Kosovo was occupied and viewed the Serbian takeover as completely illegitimate and the Serbian regime as a colonial authority engaged in brutal repression. These stark differences not only manifested themselves across Kosovo's political institutions but pervaded all social life, thus forming the basis for the segregated, parallel political and social frameworks that Albanians and Serbs maintained in Kosovo for most of the 1990s.

By 1992, nearly all of these types of public protest either had ended, had been suppressed, or in the case of guerrilla attacks, had become marginal. By 1992, the parallel state had assumed its institutional shape, with the LDK leadership claiming ultimate authority in all matters political. The Albanian movement came to be known both locally and internationally as a nonviolent resistance movement—with Rugova gaining the mantle of an "Albanian Gandhi"—that defied Serbian authority by maintaining a set of parallel institutions. Meanwhile, the marginalization of guerrilla attacks greatly reduced the risk of armed conflict's being provoked by the Albanian side.[49]

Disagreements arose between the LDK, on one hand, and the Youth Parliament and other groups, on the other, concerning the organization of nonviolent protests. Borrowing from symbolic protests in eastern Europe under authoritarian regimes, the Youth Parliament, supported by the Association of Sociologists and Philosophers, organized a series of nonviolent protest events such as the Petition for Democracy, Against Violence, symbolic demonstrations where protestors carried empty caskets to symbolically bury the violence, and protests against curfews by knocking on pots and pans and shaking keys during curfew hours. The LDK's objections to such events resulted in the stifling of initiatives such as these, soon after which public demonstrations subsided.

Kosovo-Left off the International Agenda

Although the international community endorsed the nonviolent course charted by Rugova, it focused wholly on the dissolution of Yugoslavia, the status of the former republics, and the ensuing wars in Slovenia, Croatia, and Bosnia-Hercegovina. The EC Arbitration (Badinter) Commission expressed the consensus in its first opinion of 29 November 1991 that the SFRY was "in the process of its dissolution"[50] and in its opinion of April 1992 that the process had "come to its end" because SFRY did "not exist as a state any more."[51] Yet, despite intense lobbying in Switzerland, Germany, and Scandinavia by Kosovo's government in exile and the Albanian diaspora there and in the U.S., the Kosovo Albanians failed to get the international community to include the Kosovo crisis in its Yugoslav deliberations. The EC and the U.S. refused to support the Kosovo Albanians' contention that the former federal unit be recognized as an independent state like Bosnia, Croatia, and Slovenia, insisting instead that a high level of autonomy within Serbia and the FRY was the only solution.

The government of the Republic of Kosovo that formed right after Kačanik also sought international recognition of its independence on the basis of the principle of self-determination. The request was addressed to the EC on 23 December 1991. Yet the EC Arbitration Commission for the former SFRY did not apply this principle in the case of Kosovo and Vojvodina, basing its decision instead on the Helsinki Principles concerning the inviolability of European borders. According to the EC Declaration on the Recognition of New States, the Council of Ministers agreed to extend recognition by 15 January 1992 only to those republics that met the conditions of recognition.[52] On 15 January 1992, the EC internationally recognized Slovenia and Croatia but not Kosovo. More than one year later on 27 April 1992, the FR Yugoslavia, through the federal assembly, issued a Declaration on the Formation of the Federal Republic of Yugoslavia, known as Žablak's Yugoslavia.[53] The issue of the "direct succession" of the former Yugoslavia was a central feature of Milošević's policy interpreted narrowly in Serbia's interest. But it had opened a question of the succession of the dissolved federal state. The important issue was the date of succession, at which point the seceding state replaced the predecessor state. According to the opinion of the EC Arbitrage Commission, the dissolution process itself extended from 29 November 1991 to 4 July 1992.

Kosovo's failure to achieve international recognition as a sovereign Yugoslav successor state created many new problems for the Albanian leadership. Clearly they had to do much more if they wanted to be placed on the international agenda. They were helped in part by the Milošević regime's violations of human and civil rights, which they diligently reported to the international community as evidence that their nation stood in jeopardy. Moreover, as the number of Milošević's opponents increased, they found new allies in the common struggle.

Creating Parallel Institutions[54]

In the summer of 1992, the Serb and Albanian communities in Kosovo lived in apartheid and open hostility and without true communication. At the same time, the Kosovo Albanians tried to consolidate their parallel state and to present their Republic of Kosovo before the international public and the international community as a "strong and united mini-state."[55] Indeed, the Albanian resistance was chiefly organized through newly established parallel bodies that its organizers argued were Kosovo's only legitimate institutions. One of the most visible was the school system, which was established when Albanian teachers refused to abide by a new curriculum promulgated in 1990 by the Serbian Ministry of Education. Led by the Alliance of Albanian Teachers (LASH) and the Independent Teachers Union (SBASHK), instructors continued to use the old curriculum set by the now defunct provincial authorities.[56] Primary education was less targeted than secondary education. Out of 441 primary schools, 41 functioned in alternative premises, and 60 out of 66 secondary schools operated outside of their original facilities.[57] That same year the Mother Teresa Association (MTA) was established as the first large-scale organization to offer free medical services. It became truly indispensable at the end of 1992, following the mass dismissal and expulsion of Albanians from Kosovo's public and social life, which deprived around 750,000 of their social insurance and free medical care in the state and private clinics. Although the fledgling parallel state had neither the proper organization nor resources to respond to this challenge, the MTA was assisted by international humanitarian organizations and by 1998 was providing medical care to 350,000 people.[58]

Albanian residents and police learned to coexist and by 1993 had achieved a modus vivendi that permitted Albanians to patronize parallel institutions and conduct private economic activity so long as they deferred to police authority. The situation was less tenable in rural areas. After the removal of autonomy, MUP forces began a campaign of random house raids in villages throughout Kosovo, allegedly to search for hidden weapons. The raids, usually conducted at night, were intended to humiliate as much as to actually confiscate weapons. They included arrests, beatings, and even the killing of family members.[59] Peace activist Howard Clark describes one such incident, which occurred in December

1991 when the people of Prekaz in the traditionally unruly Drenica region fired shots at a police battalion marching into their village. The day after the incident, the village was immediately visited by LDK and CDHRF activists,[60] whose dual responsibility was to document the incident and urge restraint.

On 24 May 1992, the Albanian political parties organized parliamentary and presidential elections for the parallel state. Serbian authorities declared the elections illegal but only interfered in a few municipalities, where they impounded ballots and other election material and arrested some of the people in charge of the elections. The elections acquired a degree of legitimacy from the presence of eight observer teams from the United States and Europe—including U.S. congressional staff and reporters from more than one hundred foreign media organizations—who stated that the elections had been largely regular. Although Serbia called the elections illegal and dispersed the meeting of the new parliament a few days later, Milošević allowed it to proceed, apparently to avoid compounding Western condemnation of the violence in Bosnia-Hercegovina.

Many Albanian political parties participated in the elections, which filled one hundred seats by direct election, and allocated thirty more proportionally by party. The LDK won ninety-six mandates and the Muslim Slavs five, with the remaining twenty-nine being divided among other parties and independent candidates. An additional fourteen seats had been reserved for Serbs and Montenegrins, who refused to fill them by boycotting the election. Meanwhile, LDK presidential candidate Ibrahim Rugova ran unopposed, garnering 99.5 percent of the votes. The elections completed the process of establishing parallel institutional structures for Kosovo. Yet the parliament and government in Kosovo were never established as standing institutions.[61] Instead, President Rugova oversaw and coordinated the activities of groups of officials whose work gave the appearance of sovereignty.

Although the cultivation of relations with Albania's ruling Democratic Party representatives served this purpose, the parallel government was snubbed by the rest of the international community. When the British government and the United Nations organized an international conference in London to end the war in Bosnia-Hercegovina, the Kosovo Albanians were only permitted to observe the conference on TV monitors set up in a side room. Although the conference decided to send human rights observers to Kosovo, Vojvodina, and Sandžak and pledged to broker an agreement with Belgrade for normalizing Kosovo's educational system, the London conference was a significant humiliation for people who equated their suffering with Bosnia's Muslims.

Perhaps it was their relative isolation that gave the Kosovo Albanians an unrealistic perception of their importance on the international stage. Berisha, Rugova, and other Albanian leaders had accepted Washington's assurances that the Kosovo issue would be placed on the international agenda when, in most matters, it remained only a side issue. Meanwhile, the Albanian media paid much too much attention to Rugova's visits to Western countries, interpreting them as signs of international recognition of Kosovo's independence even though Rugova was received only as an NGO representative. Nor was anything achieved when Rugova and Milan Panić, the newly elected and reform-oriented Yugoslav federal prime minister, met at the London conference. Panić openly supported an improvement of conditions for Kosovo Albanians and the reopening of schools and hospitals, claiming at the same time that Kosovo was part of Yugoslavia. Although he believed in respecting the Kosovo Albanians' human rights, he expected them to participate in the political life of Yugoslavia and take part in the coming elections. However, according to LDK, there was almost no difference between Panić and Milošević, neither of whom was prepared to consider self-determination. Negotiations on the reopening of the schools and the university in the Albanian language started in 1992 in Belgrade between an Albanian delegation led by Fehmi Agani and the Serbian Minister of Education, Dr. Ivan Ivić. Although Belgrade accepted the Albanian request to talk about education at all levels, no agreement could be achieved due to the complexity of the Kosovo problem and the need for finding a political solution first. In fact, the status of Kosovo and education in the Albanian language were tied together.

Faced with growing desperation, the Serbs founded in Priština the Serb Block for Colonizing Kosovo with the goal of pushing the authorities in Belgrade to boost the number of Serbs in Kosovo. Belgrade responded by offering loans, construction of houses and apartments, and jobs to Serbs and Montenegrins who wanted to move there. By March 1992, fewer than 3,000 Serbs had accepted the offer, most of them Slav émigrés from neighboring Albania. Evidently the resort to "modern colonization" as applied by nationalist movements in the early twentieth century would not work overnight. Nonetheless, the Milošević regime did not waver, despite Serbia's obvious lack of financial and other resources to maintain its position in Kosovo. Although it is not possible to fix the precise cost of maintaining control in Kosovo, some assessments indicate that Serbia spent more than six billion dollars to maintain peace in Kosovo after 1989. Yet few Serbs were prepared to negotiate a settlement with the Albanian leaders, and no Albanian was willing to talk about anything but independence for Kosovo.

Instead the Kosovo Albanian leadership persisted in its policy of passive resistance amid the growing tensions, thereby avoiding the bloodshed that had enveloped Bosnia-Hercegovina. This was partly due the presence in Kosovo of Serb paramilitaries like the notorious "Tigers" led by Željko Raznjatović ("Arkan"), whose earlier depredations in Croatia and Bosnia had made him a key player in the Milošević regime's game of fear. The Albanians dreaded all-out war, just as the Serb minority dreaded an Albanian rebellion. The concept was to mobilize the Serbs by fear and to get their support for the program, with the goal of keeping the main industrial plants in northern Kosovo. There one found lead mines in Trepča and a ferronickel factory in Glogovac, all of which were in Serbian hands. Therefore, Milošević tolerated the situation but controlled his enforcer, Arkan, because he was aware of the international community's likely negative reaction if he played this game openly. The result was strong showings by the Serb ultranationalist parties in Kosovo during the Serbian parliamentary and presidential elections of December 1992, which only intensified fear among Kosovo's Albanians.[62]

Rugova's absolute commitment to passive resistance foreclosed the option of armed uprising. He recognized that he had no other realistic option, given the likely severity of reprisals by Serbian security forces. Nevertheless, Rugova's insistence on both nonviolence and independence created a status quo that was intolerable for a growing number of Albanian radicals.[63] In the spring of 1993, activists of the Kosovo Republic National Front disseminated leaflets calling for the removal of Albanian officials who abandoned the ultimate goal of unifying all Albanians in one country. The National Movement for the Liberation of Ko-sovo (LKCK) appealed to people to take up arms. In May, a group of armed Albanians killed two Serbian police officers in the village of Glogovac. With the 4 October arrest of several LKCK operatives in Dečani, the existence of an Albanian resistance organization could no longer be kept secret. Nonetheless, the LDK persistently denied the existence of any Albanian armed forces in Kosovo and rejected the statements that the parallel government led by Bujar Bukoshi controlled the Ministry of Defense and the Ministry of Internal Affairs. Such claims of Rugova's followers were refuted by reports from within the Albanian resistance that described Kosovo's liberation forces as a two-layered organization made up of military and special forces. The Kosovo army units were originally organized into four regiments and deployed in Kačanik, Prizren, Priština, and Podujevo. They were financed by entrepreneurs through smuggling, the sale of drugs, and money provided by Albanians living abroad. Arms were purchased from the black market and in the open international market, while recruits were trained both in the mountains and in nearby Albania.[64]

In January 1994, the Albanians boycotted the FRY elections, which not only enabled Milošević to remain in power but also made it possible for the extreme Serb nationalist Arkan to be elected MP in Kosovo.[65] Otherwise, Kosovo's Alba-nian majority likely would have taken control of twenty-four of the province's twenty-nine municipalities, a minimum of twenty-four seats in the Serbian As-sembly, and twelve more in the federal Parliament—all at the expense of the ma-jor Serbian parties, thereby significantly affecting the balance of political power. Yet the LDK had no intention of contributing to the democratization process in Serbia by abandoning its territorial agenda. At the same time, there was a wide-spread feeling that the situation in Kosovo would explode without a relaxation of the repression. The feeling spread that Rugova's policy of peaceful resistance and parallel institutions was enabling Serbian authorities to employ all means, including violence, to control Kosovo and force the Albanians there to emigrate. The situation became especially sensitive in August 1995 when 200,000 Croatian Serbs fled to Serbia following the Krajina's forced reintegration into Croatia. Although thousands of refugees were sent to Kosovo, most of the young men promptly returned to Serbia proper, leaving only women, children, and the elderly in Kosovo.[66] The Belgrade regime's justification for transferring the refugees to Kosovo was that they would bring balance to the national structure in Kosovo at a time when Serbs were believed to constitute as little as 6 percent of the population.

The Kosovo Albanians persistently tried to raise the problem posed by Serb refugee-colonists from Croatia on the international level but did not fully succeed. Despite some initial support, the international community continued to reject unilateral secession from Serbia and Yugoslavia, which would extend the conflict, first to Macedonia and then to other neighboring countries. Bearing this in mind, Milošević during his visit to Kosovo in 1995 spoke of it as a region of mutual trust, cooperation, and coexistence. At a meeting in Mitrovica, he openly showed his intention to divide Kosovo's Albanians from their political leadership by advocating a policy of "national equality" that would make "all citizens equal to each other." He asked the Albanians to reject their political leaders and support the Serbian administration. Yet during the same visit, it became clear that he and his Socialist Party were not prepared to negotiate with the Albanians and that an agreement between Rugova and Milošević was not possible.

The conclusion of peace in Bosnia and Croatia at the Dayton conference left Milošević with two options: either guarantee the Albanians' rights inside Serbia and FRY or follow the Bosnian example by splitting Kosovo in two along ethnic lines. Despite the Bosnian precedent, it was unlikely that Kosovo could be divided without serious local and regional conflict. Yet Milošević could not risk weakening Serbia and the federation by granting the province either full autonomy or outright independence. Any solution would have a high political price. Dayton confronted Kosovo's Albanians with equally stark choices. Despite their wishes and efforts, the Dayton Accords had wholly ignored Kosovo, let alone the question of independence. Thus the most important lesson they drew from Dayton was that the international community had rewarded the armed struggle of Bosnian Serbs by recognizing Republika Srpska. In other words, the international community understood only armed conflict, not nonviolence.[67]

As a result, two parallel processes began after Dayton. First, official public discussions on Kosovo's status, which had been frozen until then, started independently of, or rather against the will of, the government and political leadership. These were led by domestic and foreign NGOs, including the Forum for

Ethnic Relations (FER). The government, political leaders, and parties (SPS and LDK), both hard-liners and moderates, joined the discussions later. Second, there was a radicalization of the Albanian movement and political life and intensification of political conflicts among the Albanians themselves. By 1996, there was a growing tendency, particularly among younger Albanians, to reject the non-violent policy of Ibrahim Rugova. This hardening of anti-Serbian attitudes culminated in a series of "test attacks" by LKCK and the Kosovo Liberation Army (KLA), which began on 22 April 1996 and grew into full-scale armed insurrection in 1998 and 1999.[68] Throughout this period, the KLA attacked and killed not only Serbian police officers but also ethnic Albanians whom it perceived to be "collaborators" or "the people of the Serbian regime." It also kidnapped and murdered many ethnic Serbs and ethnically cleansed some areas where there were insignificant numbers of Serbs.

Rather than emulate Dayton's promise of peace, both the Albanian and Serbian political leadership continued their sparring while cynically affecting a willingness to negotiate. Their lack of responsibility abetted the radicalization of the political situation. Thus official LDK sources still denied the existence of the KLA and the LKCK by blaming extreme Serb nationalists for frequent armed attacks on authorities and local Serbs, whom they alleged wanted to goad the Albanians from passive resistance and give them an excuse for military intervention.[69] On the other side, the government in Belgrade and its media marginalized the complexity of the situation in Kosovo, believing that the problem could be resolved simply by amending the constitution and granting the Albanians genuine autonomy. As late as 1998, Belgrade's authorities and media also downplayed the KLA's influence and threat of armed resistance. For example, all newspapers and journalists who failed to use the word *alleged* before the acronym KLA were penalized. Instead, the authorities insisted through the media that, whereas all politically active Kosovo Albanians qualified as terrorists, their attempts to destabilize Kosovo were being orchestrated from abroad, assisted by senior diplomats in the Albanian Embassy in Belgrade under the direct control of President Sali Berisha.[70]

Meanwhile, the international community continued to press Serbs and Albanians to find a middle way that would ensure both the territorial integrity of Yugoslavia and self-determination for the Albanians. As late as 1996 some Albanians were still publicly proposing a solution inside the framework of Yugoslavia. Adem Demaçi advocated the idea of Balkania, in which an "independent and sovereign Kosovo" would remain within the new federal Yugoslavia. Demaçi's plan envisaged the revival of the old concept of a Balkan federation, with Serbia, Montenegro, and Kosovo as the core states. Other former Yugoslav republics could join later. There were also different proposals from the Serb side. First, the Serbian Renewal Movement led by Vuk Drašković proposed a multistage autonomy; Vojislav Koštunica's Democratic Party of Serbia advocated limited local decentralization; and Zoran Djindjić's Democratic Party proposed regionalization.[71] Yet all of the opposition party proposals were focused more on blaming Milošević for failing to solve the Kosovo problem than on solving it themselves.

Nor were Milošević and Rugova any more sincere or hopeful in their own gestures toward a negotiated settlement. Through the intermediation of the Italian NGO St. Edigio, they briefly lifted spirits by signing an agreement on 2 September 1996 normalizing education for Albanian schoolchildren and students in Kosovo. The agreement foresaw reopening the schools and faculties in the 1996–1997 school year.[72] Yet neither side was serious about the agreement, which was never implemented. Their intention was, however, only to demonstrate to the international community a capacity for peacefully resolving problems, when what they really wanted was to buy more time in prolonging the status quo. Achieving a peaceful settlement was virtually impossible because the starting point of the middle way was for Kosovo to be treated as an integral part of Serbia, which was not acceptable to the Albanians, particularly following the intensifying mistrust and anger after the St. Egidio efforts failed. Thus neither side confronted the mounting frustration of Kosovo's youth, who had expected to return to school but who now filled endless protest rallies and, increasingly, the ranks of the KLA.

Radicalization and Rebellion

At the end of 1996, rejection of Rugova's policy escalated among the Albanians, especially among the youth. More and more young people listened to messages sent by Adem Demaçi and to long interviews by Rexhep Qosaj in *Intervista* magazine. Both of them clearly argued that Rugova's policy had not achieved anything in five years. The LDK leadership was accused of lacking flexibility and damaging Kosovo's future. Rugova's claims that the international community would solve the issue of Kosovo "with a firm hand," were branded as lies. At that time, the vast majority of the population was totally divided. Most of the Albanians, like most of the Serbs, left contact with the other community to their political leaders.[73]

In 1996, it became clear to many Serbs that the solution to the Kosovo problem would be a bitter loss for them, and it seemed clear to most Albanians that they would get less than they wanted. It created among Kosovo's Serbs a feeling of anxiety and intensified their dilemma of whether to leave or stay. This anxiety grew worse when the Kosovo Serbs saw the indifference expressed by Serbia when Serb refugees arrived from Croatia and Bosnia-Hercegovina and when they realized how much they yearned for their homes.[74] Yet Kosovo Serbs continued to sell their land and houses to Albanian buyers, thereby confirming that subjecting

Kosovo to Belgrade's direct control had not brought meaningful security and economic prosperity to the majority of Serbs. On the contrary the state sector as the main employer of Kosovo Serbs suffered tremendous damage from international sanctions and bad management, whereas the private sector, which was run by the Albanians, remained almost unchanged. Most of the Serbs in Kosovo sank into poverty, further complicating their problems. As the situation deteriorated and become more dangerous, the Serbs decided not to end up like the Serbs in Bosnia and Croatia and started to mobilize themselves in an effort to keep Kosovo inside the borders of Yugoslavia. At the same time, the Albanians in towns of southern Serbia asked for self-determination and unification with Kosovo.

Tensions in Kosovo increased in the middle of July 1996, after a statement by SANU President Aleksandar Despić that Albanian demographic superiority in Kosovo justified the "peaceful and civilized secession of that area from the Federation." The LDK welcomed this statement, which LDK Vice-President Fehmi Agani interpreted as a sign that Milošević's policies had failed. Nevertheless, Despić's speech disturbed Kosovo's Serbs, who feared that Belgrade was about to sell them out. Several thousand expressed their fear in a mass demonstration at Gračanica Monastery organized by the Serbian Renewal Movement, at which they demanded that all Serbs reach a consensus and clearly define the Serb national interest before making any proposal for resolving the Kosovo problem. After that, lack of any consensus in Kosovo became an issue of general political discussion in Serbia.

Meanwhile, time was running out. The chaotic March 1997 rebellion in Albania against the government of President Sali Berisha accelerated the military agenda of the KLA, whose training camps in northern Albania benefited from the pillaging of government arsenals by Albanian mobs. By intensifying its attacks on Serbian police and civil officials the KLA became the "movement worth joining," albeit at the expense of Rugova and the LDK. As it grew, the KLA began to emerge from the shadows as the prime mover in the Albanian drive for independence. It was formed in 1992, initially from Marxist-Leninist resistance groups that had been active during the previous decade. By 1994 it had established a general headquarters in Priština's Qendra district, camouflaged as a student home. There were other bases for meetings, including Kodra e diellit and Dardani in Priština and Prekaz in Drenica. In March 1998 the KLA moved its headquarters to Likoc (Drenica), by which time it had developed several departments for personnel, information, logistics, finance, policy, military, and civil relations, and others. The military arm was divided into seven operational zones (OZ), each with its own commander and various political and military structures similar to Kosovo's. The KLA had its own military anthem and emblem, featuring a double-headed black eagle on a red field, surrounded by the words *Ushtria Çlirimtare e Kosovës* (Kosova Liberation Army) and its UÇK acronym. Meanwhile, outside

Kosovo, the foundation Vendlindja thërret (Fatherland Calls) served as its main financial source, funded mostly by donations from Albanian emigrants abroad.

Although the KLA had a general headquarters, it had no sole commander. Some have assigned Azem Syla that role, while others mention Adem Jashari, who led the Drenica Operational Zone until his death. Nevertheless, we do know that the members of general headquarters who also served as OZ military commanders included Mujë Krasniqi, Rexhep Selimi, Sulejman Selimi, Shaban Shala, and Sami Lushtaku. The KLA's political representatives were Sokol Bashota, Xhavit Haliti, Jakup Krasniqi, Bardhyl Mahmuti, Faton Mehmetaj, and Hashim Thaçi, while Adem Demaçi was their principal representative at all important domestic and international meetings. The KLA had its propaganda organs such as Radio Kosova e Lirë (Radio Free Kosova) and the news agency Kosovapress situated in the Berisha Mountains.

For years its leaders employed pseudonyms when communicating with the international media to obscure their identity. Although the 22 April 1996 attack represented something of a watershed in the armed resistance movement, no KLA official actually appeared in public until 28 November 1997, when three of its fighters, Mujë Krasniqi, Daut Haradinaj, and Rexhep Selimi, attended the funeral for "martyred" teacher Halit Geci in Llaushë (Drenica) while dressed in military uniforms with the KLA crest on their arms and hats. Moreover, the KLA initially targeted only Serbian police and officials—as well as ethnic Albanians who were perceived to be collaborators or people of the Serbian regime. Full–scale operations required not only the funds being raised abroad by Fatherland Calls but the weapons to spend them on. This need was met in 1997 during the pyramid crisis in neighboring Albania, when army depots were emptied and much of their stock transported to Kosovo. From there, the three OZs bordering on Albania (2, 3, and 6) transshipped the looted armaments and munitions. They even helped establish training camps in northern Albania for KLA recruits who now flooded in not only from Kosovo but also from the Albanian diaspora, especially in Germany and Switzerland. Thus, whereas the chaos in neighboring Albania unnerved the LDK leadership, it strengthened the hand of the KLA and emboldened those calling for a more radical, violent solution. Thus, it was a combination of widespread public unrest, disappointment with the Dayton Accords, and the sudden availability of weapons that fueled the KLA's decision to launch full-scale military operations.

The uneasy coexistence of peace and sporadic violence ended on 28 February 1998, when demonstrators in Priština were severely beaten while protesting the killing of twenty-five Albanians in Drenica and Likoshan in retaliation for the deaths of four Serbian policemen. On 5–7 March thousands of police and soldiers surrounded the Jashari family compound in Prekaz. During the three-day battle that followed, OZ commander Adem Jashari, Shaban Jashari, Hamzë Jashari, and fifty-seven other family members were killed. The next major action took place on 29 May as an Albanian delegation composed of Ibrahim Rugova, Bujar Bukoshi, Fehmi Agani, and Veton Surroi was meeting with American President Bill Clinton in Washington. Serbian police equipped with heavy artillery attacked the KLA's Dukagjin OZ, killing dozens of people and wounding several hundred. Thousands more fled their homes, while the VJ set up a security cordon along the Djakova–Dečani–Peč road. In response, Albanian negotiators who had attended peace talks with Serbian officials on 22 May canceled a follow-up meeting that had been scheduled for 5 June. Now the only road open was war.

Notes

1   David Gompert, "How to Defeat Serbia," *Foreign Affairs* 73, no. 4 (1994), 44; Jean-Philippe Melchior, "Réflexion sur le crise Yougoslavie," *Les Temps Modernes* (Paris, 1989), 277–278.

2   Christopher Cviic, "An Awful Warning," in "The War in Ex-Yugoslavia," *Balkan Forum* 2 (1994), 33, 36.

3   Rudi Supek, "Social Prejudice: Psychological Considerations," *Radnicka stampa* (Beograd, 1993), 244–248.

4   Among Serb intellectuals, there was a high level of consensus that it is "illogical for Serbia to have three Constitutions" (Miroslav Živković, "Realistic Search for the Feasible," in "Contribution to the Public Debate on the Constitution," special issue, *Sociološki pregled*, 1–2 (1988), 152, and that the amendment of the constitution of 1974 was the "first political precondition" for "the revival of Yugoslavia" (Mirjana Todorović, "Prerequisites and Principles of Constitutional Changes," in "Contribution to the Public Debate on Constitution," special issue, *Sociološki pregled*, 1–2 (1988), 136. That was also witnessed by the constitutional model proposed on 28 March 1988 by the PEN Club of Serbia, the Sociological Society of Serbia, and the Philosophical Society of Serbia. Mirjana Todorović, "Prerequisites and Principles," 137-141. Serbia was claimed to be the one and only state in the world not executing its constitutional power. In order to be able to do so, regulation of rights, responsibilities, and organization of provinces would have to be internal matters of the Republic of Serbia. Until then, Serbia, compared to other republics, would be on an unequal footing. Miodrag Jovičić, "Bringing Back the Constitutional Power to Serbia," *Književna reč*, 25 October 1988, 330; Ratko Marković, "Division of Legislative Functions in SR Serbia, Changes of SFRY Constitution and SR Serbia Constitution, study material," School of Law of the Belgrade University, Institute for Legal and Social Sciences of the School of Law (Belgrade, 1988), 417; Gajo Petrović, interview in *Stav*, 29 December 1989, 36.

5   *Preventing War in Kosovo* (Lund: Transnational Foundation for Peace and Future Research, 1993), 4.

6   Eugenio Galluto, "Conflicts in the States of Former Yugoslavia and Regional Security," *Balkan Forum* 1, no. 4 (1993), 77–78.

7   Carl-Ulirk Schierup, "The Post-Communist Enigma: Ethnic Mobilization in Yugoslavia," *New Community* 122 (1992), 123.

8   Marco Dogo, *Kosovo: Albanesi e Serbi: le radici del conflitto* (Lungro di Cosenza: C. Marco editore, 1992), 10–13.

9   *Rilindja* (12 February1987). Point 22 of the proposal questioned several articles of the RSFY constitution of 1974, which expressed status of the provinces as constitutional elements (250, 254, 271, 281, 369, and 378).

296 ◆ DUSAN JANJIĆ, WITH ANNA LALAJ AND BESNIK PULA

10 Ivan Stambolić, Put u bespuće (Belgrade: Radio B92, 1995), 166.
11 Dobrica Ćosić, Kosovo (Belgrade: Novosti, 2004), 6–7.
12 Noel Malcolm, Kosovo: A Short History (New York: New York University Press, 1998), 340.
13 Ćosić, Kosovo, 63–66.
14 Jean-Arnault Derens, Kosovo: Année Zero (Paris: Mediterranée, 2006), 95–96.
15 Vuk Drašković, "The Storm is Over but the Umbrellas Are Still Open Up," Glas Crkve (Šabac) 1, (1988), 40; Vladeta Kosutić, "Byzantinism Shall Live," Glas Crkve 1 (1988), 58–62.
16 Radomir Lukić, "Exercising Functions of FR Serbia as a State," in Changes of SFRY Constitution and SR Serbia Constitution, study material, School of Law of the Belgrade University, Institute for Legal and Social Sciences of the School of Law (1988), 409.
17 Dijana Vukomanović, "The Serb National Interest," Gledišta 1–6, (1993), 147.
18 Preventing War in Kosovo, 17.
19 A perception that has already been used to justify the invasion of northern Albania early in the century. (Dimitrije Tucović, Srbija i Albanija. Kritika osvajačke politike srpske buržoaske klase (Belgrade: Socijalistička knjižara, 1914), 117–118.
20 Slobodan Naumović, "The use of Tradition: Political Transition and Change of Relationship towards the National Values in Serbia, 1987–1990," in M. Prosic-Dvornic, ed., Culture in Transition (Belgrade: Plato, 1994), 109.
21 Svetislav Spasojević interview with Momčilo Trajkovič, executive secretary of Local Board of the Serbian Communist League in Priština, NIN, March 1987.
22 Significantly, there were as yet no separatist slogans; the slogans dwelt instead on saving the Yugoslav Federation and autonomy status of Kosovo with cries of "Long live 1974 Yugoslav constitution," "Long live unity and brotherhood," "Tito-party," "Save the 1974 autonomy."
23 ATA, Foreign News, Prishtinë, 23 March 1989.
24 Hugh Poulton, The Balkans: Minorities and States in Conflict (London: Minority Rights Group, 1991), 67–68.
25 The media reported that only ten members voted against the legislation; a photograph taken at the time showed thirteen hands raised in opposition. See: Zekeria Cana, "Apeli 215 i intelektualëve shqiptarë" (Prishtinë: 2001) 266.
26 Esat Stavileci, On Defense of Independence of Kosova (Prishtinë: The Independent Association of Jurists of Kosova, 1995), 106.
27 Ibid., 106. Amendments: IX–XLIX to the Constitution of the SR Serbia, 1974, adopted in 1989. Official Gazette of the SR Serbia 11 (1989).
28 Official Gazette of the SR Serbia, nos. 5, 30 33, 40 (1990) and no. 50 (1992)
29 Others included the Social Democratic Party of Kosovo, Parliament of the Youth of Kosovo, Peasant Party of Kosovo, Independent Trade Union of Kosovo, and Committee for the Truth about Kosovo.
30 This was illustrated by positioning Rahman Morina as the president of the Communist League of Kosovo; he had been the chief of internal affairs during the 1980s.
31 Fond za humanitarno pravo, Suđenje Slobodanu Miloševiću: Transkripti (Belgrade: Fond za humanitarno pravo, 2006). The Humanitarian Law Center published twenty-six volumes containing transcripts from the trial of Slobodan Milošević in BCS languages. Publications present a detailed insight into the indictment brought against Slobodan Milošević and the evidence that the ICTY Office of the Prosecutor presented to the chamber, as well as the evidence presented by Milošević himself. More evidence will be available after the publication of the transcripts of the ICTY trial of Milan Milutinović,

Nikola Šainović, Dragoljub Ojdanić, Vladimir Lazarević, Nebojša Pavković, and Sreten Lukić, all of whom stand accused of war crimes committed in Kosovo in 1999.

32 Milošević's success in the nationalist policy was possible thanks to the fact that he, in an utmost radical way, raised the painful issue of equality, namely of the position of the Serbs in the federation, which led to the raising of the Serbian national issue. Nevertheless, Milošević did not succeed in solving those issues but only intensified them. He understood them as state rather than democratic issues. Micheline de Félice, "La Yougoslavie en question," *Les Temps Modernes,* 519 (1989), 106.

33 Derens, *Kosovo,* 99–102.

34 Compare the "legalist" argument for independence in Gazmend Zajmi, *Vepra I* (Prishtinë: Akademia e Shkencave dhe e Arteve e Kosove, 1997), 143–144, and the "antilegalist" approach in Rexhep Qosja, *Çёeshtja shqiptare: historia dhe politika* (Tirana: Toena, 1998), 287–316. Although neither Zajmi nor Qosja were members of the LDK, their arguments represent both schools of thought.

35 Denisa Kostovicova, *Parallel Worlds: Response of Kosovo Albanians to Loss of Autonomy in Serbia, 1986–1996* (Keele: European Research Centre, 1979), 40.

36 Derens, *Kosovo,* 100–101.

37 As it was by the withdrawal of the Croatian, Slovenian, and Macedonian MUP contingents heretofore stationed in Kosovo. The intensifying conflict within federal institutions also led to the release of Azem Vllasi and his fourteen fellow prisoners, as well as the amnesty of Adem Demaçi, who had been imprisoned for twenty-eight years because of his commitment to Albanian separatism and Greater Albania. Poulton, *Balkans,* 68–69.

38 For example, the right of authorities to restrict the freedom of movement of persons suspected of being capable of jeopardizing public law and order, by placing them under house arrest or forcing them to reside in other places, most typically in jail. Such a possibility existed under the then applicable republic and provincial laws on internal affairs; however, in 1989, this was only applicable in the provisions of Articles 53 and 54 of the Provincial Act on Internal Affairs in Kosovo. *Official Gazette of SAP Kosovo* 46 (1987). It was yet another example of disrespect for Albanian rights, but also of the extremely low standards for collective minority rights as a whole. Vojin Dimitrijević, "Ethnicity and Minorities in the Yugoslav Federation," in *Open Problems of Ethnicity in Yugoslavia* (Novi Sad: Pravo i Univerza v Mariboru, Evropski center za proučavanje medetnisnih odnosev in regionalizma, 1991), 56–57.

39 Ibrahim Rugova, M. F. Allain, and X. Galmiche, *La question du Kosovo* (Paris: Fayard, 1994).

40 The plan's ninety-five articles established the republic's control over judicial, military, police, and other functions, applied its regulations in science, culture, education, media, welfare, healthcare, etc., and opened employment to Serbian citizens from outside Kosovo. *Official Gazette of the SR Serbia* 15 (1990).

41 *Official Gazette of the SR Serbia* 30 (1990). This act was based on the Act on Termination of Particular Acts and other Regulations. *Official Gazette of the SR Serbia* 18 (1993), Article 1, Item 7. Particularly interesting is Article 2, disestablishing Kosovo's assembly, executive council, and presidency which would be reconstituted following new "direct and secret elections under the provisions of the Constitution and provisional statutory decision to be made by the National Assembly"—which never took place. *Official Gazette of the SR Serbia* issue nos. 33 (1990) and 15 (1991).

42 See the testimony of ICTY indictee Fatmir Limaj in *ICTY vs. Fatmir Limaj, Haradin Bala and Isak Musliu.*

43 The Constitutional Act on Amendments of and Supplements to the Constitutional Act for the Implementation of the Constitution of the Republic of Serbia also abrogates all remaining laws and other acts of the provincial authorities. *Official Gazette of the Republic of Serbia* 20 (1993).

44 As a result, approximately 250,000 students were unable to continue their regular education. By 1991 only 28.8 percent of students were allowed to enroll in secondary schools. Numerous elementary and secondary schools were closed, and segregation on a national basis was introduced. *Vreme*, Belgrade, 3 June 1991; *Borba*, Belgrade, 31 May and 26 June 1991; *Republika*, Belgrade, July 1991, 12.

45 *Official Gazette of the Republic of Serbia* 22 (1991). This law restricted property transactions within the area covering the territory of Serbia without Vojvodina for a period of ten years. Article 3 determined that the Ministry of Finance would approve any property transaction so long it "does not cause a change in the national structure of the population or the emigration of members of a certain nation or nationality." The law's official rationale was to "prevent the emigration of Serbs and Montenegrins from Kosovo, by restricting property transactions between Serbs and Montenegrins on the one hand, and the Albanians, on the other hand."

46 The three options were: (1) if SFRY'S external and internal borders remained unchanged, Kosovo would become a sovereign and independent state with the right of association in a new union of sovereign Yugoslav states in which Albanians in central Serbia, Macedonia, and Montenegro would enjoy the status of a nation and would not be a national minority; (2) if only SFRY's internal borders were changed, but not the external ones as well, an Albanian republic would be established to include Kosovo and Albanian-populated territories in central Serbia, Macedonia, and Montenegro; (3) if SFRY's external borders changed, the Albanians would by referendum unite in one, inseparable Albanian state with ethnic borders proclaimed by the First Prizren League in 1878. Predrag Simić, *The Problem of Kosovo and Metohija, and Regional Security in the Balkans* (Belgrade: Institute of International Politics and Economics, 1996), 13.

47 Kosovo Information Center, *Albanian Democratic Movement in Yugoslavia: Documents 1990-1993*, (Priština: Kosovo Information Center, 1993). According to the official Albanian interpretation, Kosovo would not be integrated with other Albanian regions. Nevertheless, documents from Albanian organizations outside Kosovo have shown that the unification of all those regions into one state had been prepared for quite some time and that such regions would be united with Albania, specifically within the ethnic boundaries claimed by the Albanian movement in 1913. Rexep Ismajli, *Kosovo and the Albanians in Former Yugoslavia* (Prishtinë: Kosovo Information Center, 1993). After all, the desire for unification was common for all Albanian groups and parties, which in the course of 1990 integrated the political activities of Albanians in Kosovo and in western Macedonia. So, for example, as early as 1 February, around 2,000 Albanians demanded that this part of Macedonia with a majority Albanian population be guaranteed independence. On that occasion, the protestors in Tetovo shouted, "We want Great Albania!" As regards the issue of language (June 1990), even more massive rallies were organized (in Struga, around 11,000 Albanians took part); later the rallies spread to Kumanovo and Tetovo, and on 25 August 1990, the Party of Democratic Prosperity of Macedonia (PDP) was founded with Nevzet Hallili as its leader. Despite the fact that this party carried a nonethnic name, the goal of the party was to unite all the Albanians into one state. Consequently, in Macedonia, basic political conflict occurred between the Albanian block—PDP—and the National Democratic Party, on the one hand, and their political Macedonian counterpart—VMRO–DPMNE—on the other. In achieving this goal, not even the municipalities in the south of Serbia were forgotten

(Bujanovac and Preševo), where the Albanians represented the majority. B. Kosumi and S. Vinca, "Kjo eshte Kosovo lindore i Ky esthe vullneti i populit," *Zeri*, 29 February 1992, 14–15. In March 1993 Rexhep Qosja, who was the most determined public advocate of pan-Albanian unification, wrote Albanian Prime Minister Sali Berisha an open letter appealing for unification of "all the territories populated by Albanians," reminding him that unification is their "prime national interest" and calling Berisha a traitor for betraying this interest. *Borba,* 19 March 1993, 11.

48   "Ninety-One: The Year of War," *Borba*, 3 January 1992, special pages.

49   Although guerrilla groups had existed in Kosovo in the early 1980s, these had virtually disintegrated due to weak organization, lack of weapons, or the killing or imprisonment of the militants. By 1987, organizations such as the Popular Movement for the Republic of Kosovo (LPRK) staged guerrilla attacks and various acts of sabotage. "Ne vitin 1985 nis levizja guerile e Kosoves," *Zeri*, 5 February 2001, 5.

50   Opinion No. 1 of 29 November 1991, point 3.

51   Opinion No. 8, of 4 April 1992, point 4. The dissolution of Yugoslavia was also confirmed by UN Security Council Resolutions No. 747 of 30 May 1992 and No. 777 of 19 September 1992. Blerim Reka, *The Right for Self-Determination: The International Dimensions of Kosovo's Problem* (Skopje: Interdiscont, 1994).

52   International Crisis Group, "The Current Status of the FRY, and of Serbia and Montenegro," *Balkans Report,* 19 September 2000, 6.

53   According to the village of Montenegro where the new Constitution for FRY was drafted.

54   Parts of this section were contributed by Besnik Pula and have appeared in "The Emergence of the Kosovo 'Parallel State,' 1988–1992," in *Conflict in Southeastern Europe at the End of the Twentieth Century: A Scholars' Initiative*, ed. Thomas Emmert and Charles Ingrao, *Nationalities Papers* 32, no. 4, December 2004.

55   Toward that end in March 1992 Prime Minister Bujar Bukoshi visited Copenhagen, Vienna, and Helsinki, and Deputy Prime Minister Nick Geloshi went to the Vatican. Neither achieved anything beyond lukewarm congratulations for the peaceful approach of the Kosovo Albanians and a promise that "Kosovo shall not be forgotten."

56   Prior to 1990, curricula were adopted by the provincial secretariat for education. See Pajazit Nushi, "Shkaterrimi i arsimit, i shkences e i kultures shqiptare dhe i sistemit institucional te tyre nga sunduesi serbomadh," in *Reenimi i autonomise se Kosoves*, ed. Bardhyl Caushi (Prishtina: Shoqata e Pavarur e Juristeve te Kosoves, 1992), 73–74.

57   The failure to close all Albanian primary schools was undoubtedly influenced by the fact that they enrolled 300,000 students, which would have made their closure an overwhelming task. Denisa Kostovicova, *Kosovo: The Politics of Identity and Space* (London: Routledge, 2005), 130.

58   At the time, there were an estimated 166 such centers or clinics in Kosovo, with volunteer Albanian medical workers who had been dismissed from their former positions. A majority of the centers was not suitable for medical work, lacking sufficient medicines, medical supplies, and equipment and entirely without sanitary equipment and, in some cases, running water. Serbian authorities occasionally closed the clinics and arrested staff.

59   For example, in 1995, more than 2,324 households had been searched for weapons. Kostovicova, *Kosovo*, 53.

60   For the LDK version of the incident, see "Barbaret ne Prekaz," *Illyria*, 4 January 1992), 2. Rifat Jashari, brother of Adem and Hamze Jashari, witnessed the police raid and confirmed in an interview that the LDK's and CDHRF's mediation helped avoid bloodshed. See "Rrethimi i trete," *Illyria*, 22 February 1992, 4.

61 See interviews with Rugova in "Ne kemi legjitimitet per zgjedhje te lira ne Kosove," *Illyria*, 16 May 1992, 12, and "Bota e di cka do te thote okupim," *Illyria*, 27 May 1992, 12. The government continued to function in exile and wielded no real authority in Kosovo.

62 Milošević's Socialist Party won forty-seven seats in the federal parliament, whereas thirty-three seats went to the Serbian Radical Party led by Vojislav Šešelj, the extreme nationalist leader who in the course of the electoral campaign advocated expelling all Albanians from Kosovo. DEPOS, the main opposition coalition, won only twenty-one seats. Kosovo Albanians boycotted the elections, despite the international community's appeals to them to vote for Milan Panić, who promised to restore human rights and to negotiate some form of autonomy for Kosovo. The LDK condemned as traitors those Kosovo Albanians who advocated participating. Although one million Albanian votes could have toppled Milošević, Kosovo Albanian leaders freely admitted that they did not want him to be removed from power because his regime was creating a framework for the final success of the Albanian national project.

63 One such group from Peć, led by Reshat Nurboj, demanded "more active resistance measures," whereas Adem Demaçi began a hunger strike to protest the closing of *Rilindija* and other Albanian-language media, promising that "I will die for freedom of speech," and the LDK news bulletins declared that "Demaçi must not die!" *Bulletin* 109, 31 May 1993; *Bulletin* 110, 4 June 1993.

64 Henry H. Perritt Jr., *Kosovo Liberation Army: The Inside Story of an Insurgency* (Urbana and Chicago: University of Illinois Press, 2008), 102–103; A. Vasović, "Kosovo: Tensed and Unprepared for the Conflict," *IWPR*, January 1993, 19.

65 Of twenty-four representatives elected from Kosovo, twenty-one were from Milošević's Socialist Party, two from the Serbian Radical Party, and only one from DEPOS, the democratic opposition. Those MPs represented the choice of the Serbs because the Albanians boycotted the elections, as did the Party of Democratic Action (PDA) representing Serbia's 60,000 Muslim Slavs and the Turkish National Party, which spoke for the republic's 12,000 Turks.

66 The perhaps 6,000–7,000 "new" refugees from Krajina joined about 4,000 registered Serb refugees who had arrived earlier from Bosnia. Previously, 700 Serbs had settled in Kosovo during the summer of 1992, occupying cabins in the weekend cottage settlement Pishat e Decan near Dečani. Apart from the refugees, the main users of the confiscated Albanian land and houses were the Serbian soldiers. Vast areas were confiscated in Globočica (a part of Kačanik close to the Macedonian border), especially in Xhemajl Zeka, where the army started to build military facilities in Ponosec, close to the Albanian border, occupied by the reservists of the Serbian army. See *Dismissals and ethnic cleansing in Kosovo*, Report by the International Confederation of Free Trade Unions, Brussels (October 1995), 6.

67 Ger Duizings, Dušan Janjić, and Maliqi Shkëlzen, eds., *Kosovo: Confrontation or Co-Existence* (Nijmegen: Peace Research Centre, 1997), 70-72. Adem Demaçi, at that time the leader of the Parliamentary Party of Kosovo (PPK), the main rival of LDK, and the president of the Council for the Defense of Human Rights and Freedoms in Priština, summarily dismissed the international community's refusal to tolerate any change of borders: "I think that the borders have been changed. The fact that borders are discussed at this time is absurd, since Yugoslavia does not exist any longer. All of its borders have been nullified and one cannot apply different criteria according to which some borders may and some may not be changed" (D. Gorani, *IWPR*, May 1996).

68 For more about KLA activities, see Perritt, *Kosovo Liberation Army* and Derens, *Kosovo*, 111–118, 120–126.

69   Perritt, *Kosovo Liberation Army*, 15.

70   Belgrade claimed that there were two main goals behind this new campaign of Albanian violence: (1) to play the nationalist card harder on the eve of Berisha's election campaign, and (2) to secure in advance a strong negotiating position for future debates on the status of Kosovo; this sounded more convincing.

71   For useful contemporary discussion of possible solutions, see Alberto l'Abbate, *Kosovo: Una guerra annunciata* (Firenze: Dipartimento di Studi Sociali - Universita degli Studi di Firenze,1996).

72   The agreement was signed and transmitted via facsimile by Milošević in Belgrade and Rugova in Priština, but the texts differed. It manifested itself through contradictory reactions. According to *Tanjug*, "this Agreement commits the Albanians to accept the curriculum applied in schools throughout Serbia." Abdul Rhama, the spokesman for Kosovo Albanians' educational issues stated: "In this stage, the Albanian party agreed not to negotiate the manner of financing of the educational system in Kosovo," whereas Fehmi Agani, the vice-president of DSK, pointed out that the agreement does not mean that the Albanians will rejoin the educational system of Serbia but only that they will continue their education in proper school buildings: "We will keep our own system," said Agani. Bujar Bukoshi's reaction to the agreement was cautious: "This agreement should be welcomed as a gesture of the good will of the Albanians and their hope that this represents an opportunity for re-opening of their schools. It is wrong, however, to play on uncontrolled and naïve enthusiasm, but very cautious optimism may be considered. The experience with the agreements signed by Serbia has taught us that Serbia signs them easily, and does not respect them even more easily, even with the mediation of the UN Security Council." Ministry of Information of the Republic of Kosovo, *Bulletin* 277, 9 September 1996.

73   Julie Mertus, "A Wall of Silence Divides Serbian and Albanian Opinion on Kosovo," *Transition*, 22 March 1996, 49.

74   M. Karan, "Facing Reality," *IWPR*, May 1996.

9

James Gow, team leader
Miroslav Hadžić, team leader

Milan Andrejevich   Dušan Djordjevich   Michael Rip
Fotini Bellou   James Hasik   Brendan Simms
David Chandler   **James Lyon**   Vatroslav Vekarić
Svetlana Djurdjević-Lukić   Mariella Pandolfi   **Ivan Zverzhanovski**

Principal author James Gow initially circulated among team members a disparate collection of very lengthy scholarly papers and articles that he and co–leader Miroslav Hadžić had written for their comment and discussion at the July 2002 SI conference in Sarajevo, which was chaired in their absence by Fotini Bellou. Following that meeting, Gow prepared a single common draft for team review, to which Prof. Hadžić submitted a highly detailed 6,000-word critique on 6 January 2004. Prof. Gow then rewrote the team paper to address each of Prof. Hadžić's questions and concerns, as well as to integrate additional contributions from NED-funded research by team members Svetlana Djurdjević-Lukić and Ivan Zverzhanoski. The ensuing draft was submitted for project-wide review in January-February 2005.

Although the present study is based principally on documentation and interview material in the public domain, it is also informed by privileged official sources. This is very strongly supplemented by use of direct quotation from "the horses' mouths" of the participants in this process, available in *The Fall of Yugoslavia*, a three-part documentary film involving screen interviews with those participants, produced by Norma Percy at Brook Lapping Productions and directed by Dai Richards. Production materials for the films are housed in the Liddell Hart Centre for Military Archives at King's College London.

THE WAR IN KOSOVO, 1998-1999

◆ James Gow ◆

With the outbreak of hostilities in the spring of 1998, the Kosovo conflict quickly evolved from a cold war between the Democratic League of Kosovo (LDK) and the Milošević regime into a full-scale insurrection that pitted the Kosovo Liberation Army (KLA) against the combined forces of the Yugoslav Army (VJ), Serbian Interior Ministry special police (MUP) and, eventually, an assortment of paramilitary units. Within months the Western powers would intervene to end hostilities, prevent ethnic cleansing and encourage a settlement whether by diplomacy or by military action. Each of the three sides had its own set of problems and objectives that were distinct from those that they had pursued during the decade-long standoff that had followed the elimination of Kosovo's autonomy. Over the next year, their motives, intentions, and actions would create a new set of controversies that will be the subject of this chapter.

Certainly Belgrade and the Kosovo Albanians pursued their antagonistic objectives with unequal forces and means and employed them using divergent, asymmetrical tactics and strategy. The degree to which each conflicted or cooperated with the Western powers depended on the degree to which its objectives coincided with this third party to the conflict.[1] In addition to this, they may be judged to have had different relationships to time—the ways in which it is measured, spent, or available—historic, astronomic, operational. Different inputs necessarily produce different results. Accordingly, the resulting correlation of chosen objectives and the means applied within a limited time frame is also unequal.[2]

The Kosovo Albanians: Between Belgrade and Western Intervention

By 1988-89, the Kosovo Albanians were now united behind the quest for independence. Although the LDK's persistent advocacy of passive resistance had fuelled the KLA's rise as a militant alternative, the intensifying violence solidified support for both groups as the Albanian public embraced one or both in the common struggle against Serbia. Popular support was, however, no substitute for political power and military might. Unlike Slovenia, Croatia, and Bosnia-Hercegovina, Kosovo had no international status, let alone an army capable of standing up to the VJ and the MUP. The KLA's necessary resort to guerrilla tactics informs one of the first controversies to arise out of the war in Kosovo, namely, whether the KLA were criminals and terrorists or freedom fighters.

The KLA's approach was somewhere at the boundaries of terrorism and insurgency. It was a force of limited capabilities, lacking overall integrated organization, coherence and command structures. It was formed of different groups, but primarily of two types, all a reaction to the civilian resistance model long espoused by the Kosovo leadership of Ibrahim Rugova and the LDK. The actual label "Kosova Liberation Army" was coined by a clandestine group of only a few hundred members, organized outside Kosovo itself, from around 1995 onwards, which began terrorist attacks in 1996. The other element involved clans from certain parts of Kosovo starting to harass and attack Serbian police forces in the province.[3] Initially, terrorism dominated—the irregular use of violent means by a small, clandestine, and unlawful group to promote a political cause by focusing media attention, mobilizing support on one side, and intimidating and wearing down government and civilian opponents on the other. This approach underpinned the KLA's being labeled as a terrorist organization at times by Western figures, most notably U.S. special envoy Robert Gelbard. In this mode, KLA attacks focused primarily on Serbian policemen and positions but also included murdering ethnic Albanians deemed by the KLA to be collaborators, which also served to discipline others.[4] By March 1998, coincidental with the start of the first main insurgent phase, one estimate put the number of KLA victims at five policemen and sixteen civilians, including five ethnic Serbs.[5] In addition, the KLA destroyed homes intended for ethnic Serbs displaced from Croatia and Bosnia, who were effectively colonists; the KLA also occasionally kidnapped Serb civilians, typically holding them several days before releasing them unharmed. And perhaps most damagingly for their cause, the KLA fired at the orange vehicles of the Organization for Security and Cooperation in Europe (OSCE) Kosovo Verification Mission (KVM) following their deployment at the end of 1998.[6] In the course of 1997 and, especially, 1998, the KLA took more of an insurgent form, involving larger force sizes in more open engagements, albeit as an ill-organized (or, at least, decentralized) coalition of different elements.[7] In these operations the VJ/MUP juggernaut easily defeated KLA units, inflicting significantly higher casualties on them and their civilian sympathizers, forcing them to flee or surrender.[8] Yet the KLA had no illusions about winning victories on the battlefield, only the objective of goading their Serbian adversary into committing the kinds of atrocities that they had already employed in Croatia and Bosnia. They hoped to provide the West with sufficient evidence, or to be perceived as an innocent victim in need of help, which help, it was assumed, would come.[9] After all, the accelerated internationalization of the conflict represented the most realistic chance of achieving independence. Both the KLA and the LDK also enjoyed the significant advantage of almost unlimited time. Whereas Serbia was bleeding from years of sanctions and war expenditures against a host of adversaries, Kosovo's Albanians held a huge demographic edge that had not been blunted by colonization and could only accelerate with a continuous stream of Serbs leaving rump Yugoslavia for abroad.

Belgrade: Motivations and Perceptions Prior to Rambouillet

The Serbian oligarchic elite, under the control and leadership of Slobodan Milošević, had closed its Kosovo circle with the removal of autonomy. As in 1991 it again reached for the use of force, convinced as it was that it had a sovereign right to do so in the name of myth and historical, national, territorial, and constitutional right. The regime was satisfied that it had already given and guaranteed Kosovo's non-Serbs both minority and civil rights according to international standards. In any event, Kosovo was exclusively an internal affair that a 23 April national referendum had confirmed should not accommodate foreign interference.[10] The Yugoslav/Serbian state was therefore free—and its military constitutionally obliged—to use all means to fight KLA terrorism, as well as to preserve its territorial integrity against the Kosovo Albanians' separatism. The government already disposed of sufficient military and police forces to crush finally separatism and destroy Albanian terrorism by applying necessary but proportionate force. Nonetheless, the quest to defend Kosovo's "holy Serbian ground" would unite all patriotic Serbs under arms, while the rifle would find the others in accordance with the constitution and law. In recognizing the inviolability of external borders and sharing in the condemnation of terrorism, the Western powers were obliged to support Belgrade in its struggle against Albanian separatism.

It was with this mindset that Milošević picked up the gauntlet thrown down by the KLA, first creating a no-man's land along the Albanian frontier by expelling its civilian population, then meeting a KLA summer offensive head on. Although KLA spokesmen initially claimed to have seized control of over 40 percent of the province, the counterattack by 23,000 VJ/MUP devastated their motley forces, reducing the ranks of most operational-zone commanders to a few dozen men. For the next several months KLA units were compelled to "watch more or less helplessly" from a distance as Yugoslav army and Serbian special police torched whole towns, sending their residents into the countryside.[11]

Notwithstanding this tactical success, the regime faced several insurmountable obstacles that informed the Albanians' confidence. The use of force could

only temporarily subjugate Kosovo's huge Albanian majority but could not induce it to accept Serbian/FRY domination. Meanwhile the U.S. and its European
allies began to contemplate intervening as they had three years earlier in Bosnia,
basing their actions on international law and collective security in order to forestall what it expected to be Serbian forces' latest resort to excessive force and the
commission of gross human rights abuses.[12] Perhaps most sobering was the regime's own unwillingness to reform itself or change its policies, thereby making
its own behavior its greatest liability in dealing with the international community.
Indeed, the key internal obstacle to the protection of Serbian national interests
in Kosovo was the regime itself, which wanted to remain in power and still had
enough might to do so. It did not dare to start reforms, for these would have deprived it of all sources of strength. In addition, in Serbia there were no alternative
political or social forces powerful enough to force Milošević to change course or
step down from power.[13]

Such limitations informed the regime's lack of readiness to face the new
Kosovo reality. They also uncovered its fear of accepting the ultimate consequences of the governmental use of force. The regime's inconsistency was directly exposed in the official treatment of the armed conflict. Defining the KLA
as a terrorist organization, the regime at the beginning justified the systematic use
of the police force. However, as the conflict grew, the territorial spread and rapid
growth of the KLA blurred Belgrade's characterization of the enemy as terrorists.
When the VJ was introduced into the conflict, the official reason was the widening of the frontier belt and the protection of military assets, thereby finessing
the need to redefine the nature of the resistance. The regime found itself in an
insoluble contradiction. The allegedly minor terrorist KLA had to be confronted
with ever-growing military-police forces. The army and police would surely prevent a mass armed uprising by the Albanians and the development of the KLA
as a growing insurgent armed force, but they could not significantly weaken the
ethnic bastions and political positions of the separatist movement. By mistaking
consequence for cause, the regime was hiding both from itself and the public the
real causes and scope of Kosovo Albanian dissatisfaction.

The Western Powers: From Engagement to Confrontation

Whereas Belgrade's scorched-earth tactics fit the definition of "ethnic cleansing"
formerly pursued in Croatia and Bosnia, it is equally undeniable that Serbia and
the FRY had the right to take action to uphold order and suppress the insurgency—
notwithstanding the contribution that its own policies had made in generating it
in the first place.[14] The question was whether Belgrade was merely trying to deal
with the armed insurgency. If so, were its methods legitimate? Or was Milošević
seeking to use the armed insurgency as a pretext for an historic settlement of a

different kind where ethnic cleansing would permanently resolve the tension between the Albanian demographic tide and Serbia's claim to Kosovo?

These were questions that the Western powers had to consider as they contemplated intensifying their engagement in the Kosovo conflict. Given their disparate resources and distinctive agendas, it is not surprising that the U.S. and its NATO allies were not uniformly disposed toward the KLA or the greater cause of Albanian independence. There were also divisions within the six-country Contact Group,[15] with only the U.S. and United Kingdom seriously considering armed intervention, whereas France, Germany, and Italy initially rejected using force, and Russia steadfastly opposed any action against Belgrade.[16] Nevertheless, shared values and perceptions ultimately led the NATO allies to articulate a single vision that could be promoted with relative unity.

It was the Western leaders' perception of the Serbian leader's agenda that pushed them to address the Kosovo issue. The imperative to take action was driven by three factors: the long-term record of Milošević's regime, particularly in Bosnia; the short-term pattern of activity by Serbian and FRY security forces in Kosovo since the emergence of the KLA; and growing awareness and information, as Western leaders understood it, that Belgrade would again resort to ethnic cleansing.

With the emergence of the KLA and the Serbian response to it, as well as the long-term record of what the West regarded as political and human rights abuses by the Belgrade regime,[17] Western leaders had the history of Bosnia in the 1990s firmly in mind. According to UK Foreign Secretary Robin Cook: "It looked just like the ethnic cleansing in Bosnia."[18] There was a sense of trying to prevent history's repeating itself and taking responsible action where their predecessors had been judged to have failed. U.S. President Bill Clinton's view was that "We couldn't have another Bosnia where the international community and Europe and NATO in particular kind of fiddled around for two and half years."[19] The sense of history and avoiding the same outcome as in Bosnia also impelled U.S. Secretary of State Madeleine Albright, who was one of the strongest advocates of action, even from the early stages of the Serbian campaign in Kosovo. She addressed a meeting of the Contact Group at Lancaster House in London in the following terms: "Gentleman, remember that history is watching us and our predecessors sat in this room and watched Bosnia burn."[20] Thus, the image of Bosnia and the ethnic cleansing there weighed heavily in Western motivations.

Albright's comment was made in the wake of the reports of what quickly became known as the Drenica massacre of 28 February 1998, after which Kosovo Albanians took photos of each of the twenty men killed and then set up a Web site to show the world.[21] This was a significant propaganda victory for the KLA and ensured that there was international attention, including the calling of the Contact Group meeting that Albright addressed. Between that point and the onset of

NATO armed action on 24 March 1999, there was ever more intensive monitoring of the situation in Kosovo by international actors, including the Kosovo Diplomatic Observer Mission sponsored by the U.S. State Department, which was succeeded by the OSCE's Kosovo Verification Mission, as well as by individual governments and a variety of NGOs.[22]

Action by Belgrade's forces continued to draw international attention and criticism, with reports of massacres and, through the middle of 1998, massive refugee flows. The United Nations high commissioner for refugees (UNHCR) reported that 100,000 ethnic Albanians had been "forced" from their homes in July, accompanied by atrocities.[23] The pattern continued and the scale rose. Another 100,000 followed in August, with further atrocities reported, including the 29 September massacre at Gornji Obrinje of twenty-one women, children, and old people, including a seven-month-pregnant woman whose stomach had been slit open.[24] Toward the end of 1998, figures for refugees and displaced persons were in flux, though generally high, reaching an estimated 300,000.[25] Both the flux and this peak were evident in mid-October, when the UNHCR reported 200,000 displaced persons in Kosovo, plus approximately 92,500 refugees and displaced persons in neighboring areas.[26] At the same time, however, 50,000 people were estimated to have returned to their original villages during the second half of October following a ceasefire agreement on 8 October.[27] By 24 November, the figure for returnees had risen to 75,000—with returns registered at 70–100 percent where the KVM was present, although in a survey of 285 villages, 210 of which had been involved in the conflict directly, only 40 percent of homes remained habitable.[28] At the same time, 175,000 displaced persons remained at large, and confirming the flux, the estimated number of refugees in Albania had risen to 24,000.[29] By December, the UNHCR was reporting 100,000 returnees—even tentatively to some of the most "sensitive" locations, but was also reporting 200,000 displaced in Kosovo, higher than the November figure.[30] At the start of 1999, the estimated total number of returnees by then was 110,000, while the number displaced at that stage was reported as 180,000, with another 80,000 displaced, or refugees elsewhere.[31] Although the actual numbers fluctuated and there were extensive returns at times where conditions were suitable, what is clear is that the number of displaced persons and refugees during this period was never less than 100,000 and was mostly in excess of 200,000. This created a significant burden on the region and on the international community. It also created a clear context, where many in Western governments were deeply concerned at the prospect of further massive forcible expulsions—ethnic cleansing—especially in light of the pattern of events in Croatia and Bosnia-Hercegovina earlier in the decade and, crucially, reporting from the various international agencies in Kosovo about atrocities committed on a significant scale by Serbian forces.

From Račak to Rambouillet

Between February and October 1998 the Serbian and Albanian actors tested each other. Each of them, of course, weighed available assets. The testing started with the KLA offensive, continued with retaliatory operations by the Serbian police and the army, and was suspended with the agreement between Milošević and Ambassador Richard Holbrooke in October 1998 under the apparent threat of NATO air assaults if Serbian forces did not desist and draw down to pre-July force levels inside Kosovo.[32] This provided for a pause during which the different actors could assess their situations and how to proceed. That pause would include the talks at Rambouillet and Paris, which lie at the center of this study. Yet before anyone arrived at Rambouillet, Serbian forces began once more to test the KLA, international preparedness, and crucially, civilians in Kosovo. During this period, Ambassador William Walker, the American diplomat in charge of the OSCE KVM reported that, typically

> A village that had one KLA member would be subject to being surrounded by artillery, being surrounded by the army, being surrounded by the police, being bombarded for hours; the police units would then go in, separate the men and the boys, take them off and essentially pillage and loot and burn in the village.[33]

Although Serbian forces were withdrawn to comply with the October ultimatum, gradually as Christmas approached, ethnic cleansing operations resumed at low thresholds and some of those forces were reinserted.[34]

Serbian testing of limits culminated with the major incident at Račak on 15 January 1999, which proved a vital, final spur to international action. Račak was a contested moment. The testimony of then Colonel Jovan Radosavljević gave the Serbian perspective:

> We got reports that a family in Račak had killed three policemen. Then we received the order to prepare an action and destroy the terrorists there. We set out at 2 A.M. It was very cold. It was dark. We knew that if a single dog barked it could spoil the whole action. Fortunately, the few dogs still in the village must have been sleeping in the heat. We moved through the woods and reached the trenches. We managed to kill the men guarding the trenches. By then it was dawn and the battle began.[35]

Radosavljević's forces were said to have found fifteen bodies in the village. However, the position overnight is less clear in his testimony because Radosavljević left a small contingent to guard the village: "During the night the unit left their posts. We heard they came under fire and were frightened." If this is taken at face value, it means that those troops would not be responsible for what was subsequently discovered.[36]

The next morning the OSCE KVM became involved, with Ambassador Walker visiting the site, after receiving disturbing reports, first thing in the morning. According to him,

> I was told "If you want to see what happened yesterday, you go up this ravine." We came on the first body and there was a little rug over the head and as I walked up to it, there was no head on this body, just a napkin. As we walked up the ravine, we kept finding one body after another. We then came on a pile of bodies, 10–15 bodies all piled on top of each other.[37]

In total, the KVM reported forty-five bodies found, of which three were women, at least one a child, and several elderly. Eleven of the dead were found in houses, twenty-three up the ravine behind the village, which Walker mentioned, and the remainder at other sites around it.[38] Other analysts, based on witness interviews, have concluded that the twenty-three taken to the ravine were subject to extrajudicial execution.[39]

The official position was that the dead were KLA soldiers who had been killed in the previous day's engagements but that other KLA personnel had removed their uniforms and dressed them in peasant clothes to look like civilians for propaganda effect. Walker, who had gained relevant experience monitoring and investigating political killings in Latin America, saw it differently: "I noticed blood-stained clothes where the bullet had entered and the blood stains were around the wound. I found it impossible to believe that the blood stains had somehow been put in just the right place." He clearly stated his conclusion at a press conference that day: "From what I personally saw, I do not hesitate to describe the event as a massacre, a crime, very much obviously, against humanity." He later confirmed the conclusion that "I felt that what I had seen was a horror and that it was in fact perpetrated by the security forces from Belgrade." Walker's view seemed hard to reject and was generally supported by observers and concerned leaders in the international community, even as it was officially defiantly rejected by Serbian President Milan Milutinović, who called Walker's visit and statements "an act calculated to mislead the world public."[40]

Forensic evidence that could have given clearer confirmation of the circumstances of the deaths was muddled. On 25 January 1999, the head of Priština's Institute of Forensic Medicine, Slaviša Dobričanin reported that twenty-one autopsies had been conducted and that none of the bodies bore the signs of a massacre, a position in stark contrast to Walker's experienced eyewitness testimony. Dobričanin also stated that OSCE personnel had been present for some of the postmortem examinations, though the OSCE mission made no statement regarding its participation or judgment. Subsequently, an EU forensic report team of Finnish pathologists participated in the autopsies and was reported to have formally "distanced itself from Dobričanin's statements," saying that it was concerned that there had been tampering with the evidence.[41] This was, however, a partial misinterpretation according to the head of the Finnish team, who later reported that no "indication of tampering or fabrication of evidence was detected" and that the apparent distancing was a methodological issue, with the Finns unprepared to sign a document that Serbian and Belorussian pathologists had produced because, despite an agreed upon common approach, Finnish practice was not to comment until the whole process had been completed.[42]

Despite this, the head of the team also made perfectly clear that, technically, although the term *massacre* could not be used on the basis of the medical evidence gained in the postmortem procedures, the reason for this was that such evidence alone could not be enough to form such a conclusion. Rather, drawing such a conclusion required a comprehensive approach, including forensic investigation of the crime scene, as well as complementary investigation by others. Reading her report, the implication seems clear that the understanding of a massacre is likely to be right but that the evidence with which she and her team dealt was insufficient to make this inference. She certainly does not exclude the possibility of a massacre, saying that "the use of this term is better suited to be used by organs conducting criminal investigations for the purpose of initiating criminal proceedings."[43] The more comprehensive picture required was significantly inhibited, however, by the failure of the Serbian authorities. The UN secretary-general reported that the FRY authorities had "failed to respond to the plea of the Head of a Finnish forensic team to postpone examinations until the arrival of Finnish experts" and that by the time they arrived, sixteen autopsies had already been completed. He also concluded that "investigative and forensic efforts in the wake of the massacre have been willfully obstructed by the lack of cooperation by the authorities of the Federal Republic of Yugoslavia."[44] He later reinforced these judgments. On what could be inferred from the EU autopsy team, he commented that the "Finnish team stressed, during its two-week stay in the Federal Republic of Yugoslavia, that it was not carrying out an investigation into events at Račak, but an examination of the bodies moved from the place of death." Moreover, he noted that, after the events at Račak, "the scene was not isolated; the circumstances of evidence-gathering and the chain of custody of evidence remain unclear." And on the attitude of the Belgrade authorities, he confirmed that there was "no indication at this time of action by the authorities of the Federal Republic of Yugoslavia to bring the perpetrators to justice."[45] Thus the international community and Washington in particular concluded that Račak had provided firm evidence of Belgrade's suspected plans to carry out large-scale ethnic cleansing in Kosovo.

The third strand of evidence that shaped Western perceptions was secret information indicating that the Belgrade regime was planning extensive ethnic cleansing. Already in October, as Milošević was agreeing to the terms negotiated with Holbrooke, his chief of staff, General Momčilo Perišić, had somewhat obliquely expressed concern about what would happen to his NATO counterparts in negotiations—Supreme Allied Commander, Europe (SACEUR) U.S. General Wesley Clark and Chairman of the NATO Military Committee German General Klaus Naumann—while Milošević had made his intentions explicit.[46] Over the subsequent months, it became ever more clear and likely that Milošević would go beyond testing the limits of international tolerance, as shown in MUP and VJ action during December 1998 and January 1999, and move against the Kosovo Albanians. In this context, evidence of what would later be reported as Operation Horseshoe circulated among Western governments.[47] Moreover, as this scenario developed with MUP and VJ units evidently preparing for action (protesting, as had the JNA at the beginning of the decade, that they were merely conducting normal exercises), Western governments understood clearly that there was a deadline for any action to counter Belgrade's campaign on or around 24 March.

The long-term record in Bosnia, the short-term record in Kosovo, and emerging secret information persuaded the West that action was required. Precisely what action remained to be settled. Why did the talks at Rambouillet, with an attached threat to bomb Serbia and the FRY if Belgrade did not reach agreement, emerge as the Western policy option? Was the point of the talks, as some have suggested, no more than a pretext for bombing, in Western thinking? Or, was the intention in holding the talks in France to gain an agreement and avoid the hostile use of force? These questions can only be answered fully in light of the later sections on the conduct of military operations and what happened at Rambouillet. However, evidence of Western thinking and motivation can be considered here.

For the Americans, Račak had perhaps already been the final straw. It certainly appears to have been decisive. In the words of Madeleine Albright: "It is terrible to think that something like a massacre can actually galvanize people to action, but the truth is something terrible happened and the question then was what to do next."[48] Her special envoy formed a similar conclusion, though adding that others in the international community were not quite as inclined to use armed force: "I made it clear that I thought this justified immediate military response. Now the Europeans were not ready to do this."[49] However, according to U.S. Assistant Secretary of State James Rubin, who was present at Albright's meeting with her Russian counterpart Igor Ivanov, even Moscow had concluded that the Milošević regime had been a nuisance too often and that a threat or use of force would be required to alter the situation: "Ivanov made clear that he was tired of dealing with the consequences of Milošević's aggression, he was tired of having Russia appear always to defend Milošević, that he agreed that if anything was ever going to work it was going to require the use of force, but he told her quite candidly he could never say that publicly."[50]

Yet while all of them probably accepted that at least the threat of force might be needed, the Europeans were more sympathetic to Anglo-French advocacy of an alternative strategy: France's President Jacques Chirac reported telling UK Prime Minister Tony Blair that "we must make one more attempt to negotiate a political solution. We Europeans must take responsibility for Europe."[51] Blair also backed the move for negotiations: "The consequence of these threats was so serious in terms of the military action, for goodness sake let's give it another try with the political process, let's stick all the people together, get all the pressure we can on both sides to come round the table and sort it out."[52] Much of Western thinking, however, was still influenced by the understanding that at least the threat of force was needed, with a clear model and precedent in the pattern of events—NATO bombing and the Dayton peace talks—that had brought the Bosnian phase of war to an end. According to UK Foreign Secretary Robin Cook: "We took the view that if we could get both sides together, as had happened at Dayton, and make sure that they were obliged to confront each other and to confront these difficult issues we might achieve the breakthrough."[53] The outcome was that on 6 February talks began at the Chateau of Rambouillet, thirty miles from Paris, although, unlike at Dayton, Milošević himself was not there. This was a crucial difference, given that he and his regime were at the heart of Western motivation and aims.

Two possible options for using Western armed forces were discussed. One was to use air power, and the other was to seek a permissive environment in which a NATO-led international peace support force could be deployed. The former became the fallback plan as the latter was pursued. However, both were predicated on consideration and dismissal of a third option, the possible insertion of a ground force into Kosovo with a hostile mission. Getting a NATO ground force was judged to be essential. The only question was the route for getting it there. As both a practical and policy preferential step, using ground forces in combat mode was excluded.[54] In addition to practical factors, it was hardly likely diplomatically, for example, that Moscow or Beijing could have been reassured of the necessity and benign Western intent in such a situation, as evidence from the period of armed hostilities during 1999 confirmed.[55] But NATO-led implementation of any agreement was vital both to ensuring that the agreement was honored and to establishing a serious, physical-military impediment to the use of Serbian armed forces. Milošević would not be able to move on Kosovo with a major international force in place. But the permissive arrangements for deployment would make all the difference: there would be less need for major logistical backup and reinforcement to insert the force into a hostile environment, meaning that a smaller force and a lesser level of protection would be needed. The problems of deployment would still be significant, but they would be manageable—all the more so if the significantly better option of force transit through Serbia were a part of that package (this is discussed below in the context of the Rambouillet talks).

The effective impossibility of mounting a ground operation in a nonpermissive environment tallied with the political preferences of the leaders, especially those in Washington, DC, who had little taste for putting ground forces in harm's way, lest there should be difficulties that translated into negative domestic political opinion. On the other hand, those leaders were relatively comfortable authorizing what was seen as a largely risk-free use of air power—especially if it involved the use of standoff weapons. This was particularly the case because Western leaders, after years of dealing with Milošević in a variety of ways, had concluded that he would only accept an agreement if there were a credible threat of force—as had been most recently demonstrated by his accepting the October agreement with Holbrooke.

The aim of the Western actors was to get agreement and deployment before the Serbian campaign that they believed was to be launched in late March. Time was of the essence, and a strict timetable was put in place. International diplomatic agreement would provide the political mission for military implementation—and a NATO-led international military force on the ground would make the Serbian campaign of ethnic cleansing impossible. There was little desire to use destructive armed force if it could be avoided. Therefore, Western political leaders tried to persuade Milošević to accept terms. For example, German Foreign Minister Joschka Fischer tried personally: "We met alone and I said he must see that this would end in war. I told him it was crazy for Yugoslavia and Serbia to fight the USA. I said that Germany had fought the USA twice—and it was a disaster. He should learn from history." However, in Fischer's view, "It was clear he wasn't taking the West seriously."[56] It was Milošević who was the real problem in Western eyes. According to Rubin, Madeleine Albright banged the table at one meeting and said that getting rid of Milošević was her number one aim; he had to go before she did.[57] And when President Boris Yeltsin of Russia said that Moscow and Washington risked losing what they had developed over the preceding years, U.S. President Bill Clinton made clear that the Belgrade leader was the real problem, not U.S.–Russian relations: "I argued to him that we actually took a lot of heat off of Russia by having NATO do this. I went through all the steps: the warnings Milošević had been given, the opportunities that we had that were missed to avoid any kind of a conflict in Kosovo months before it materialized."[58] However, Milošević claimed that "We are defending ourselves. I think we are defending the right to be free and independent, and the right to live in peace."[59] This was a powerful line in the domestic context and among some parts of international public opinion. However, it was out of line with events. Both the course and outcome of the talks at Rambouillet and conduct on the ground in Kosovo offered evidence, as is discussed in the following sections, that the Serbian leader's protestation was nothing other than disingenuous.

Conduct and Outcomes

The conduct of both the NATO and Belgrade operations in Kosovo can inform understanding of the motivations of each set of actors prior to the Rambouillet talks and of their positions in those talks. To what extent do the conduct of operations and the outcome of armed hostilities shed light on our understanding of the intentions and perceptions of the actors? Was the West right to believe that large-scale ethnic cleansing was possible and likely? To what extent do events suggest that NATO was determined to use destructive armed force, whatever happened? What would have happened in Kosovo without NATO intervention? Did NATO violate international law? What was the extent of war crimes committed by the Yugoslav military/Serbian special police/paramilitaries? Did anyone flee NATO bombs? The answers to these questions posed by the Scholars' Initiative emerge in consideration of the conduct of operations.

There are two pairs of issues to be covered in the assessment of conduct and outcomes. The first is the conduct of Belgrade forces on the one hand and NATO's on the other. The second concerns international law. Legality constituted a significant motif in the debate over both Belgrade and NATO operations. The ethical and legal propriety both in launching operations and in carrying them out—*jus ad bellum* and *jus in bello*—is an important aspect of our overall understanding.[60]

Although the interactive context of statement and counterstatement, action and both countercomment and counteraction cannot be forgotten, the first important feature of Belgrade's armed action is that it had two dimensions and directions. One was against the Kosovo Albanians; the other was against NATO. In considering Serbian operations, it is necessary to consider both sets of action. This is because both affected NATO conduct and action—as noted already, NATO was motivated by concern at Belgrade's action against Kosovo Albanians, yet once the Alliance launched armed action it obviously had to take into account Belgrade's response to aerial attack.

Following this, the other important thing to note is that Belgrade operations began before NATO action. From the first moments of the Serbian campaign on 20 March, villages were shelled or directly razed while the strike units of persecution entered the villages and murdered, raped, and tortured. The campaign was a fluent combination of forces. The security service's (SDB) special operations shock troops (JSO) and the paramilitaries moving rapidly from one location to another in armored vehicles were at the sharp end of a joint operation supported by MUP and VJ infantry, including VJ special forces in places (such as Srbica and Suva Reka, as well as Djakovica, Priština, and Peć), and crucially by VJ artillery and tanks, with the latter, in particular, demonstrating the fruits of reflection over the preceding years, with emphasis on the capacity of armor and mechanized units to provide surprise and dynamism through fire and movement in local operations.[61] This integration was a product of careful preparation—which had also covered significant nonmilitary aspects.[62] The military leadership's view was that it had "to neutralise the Albanian terrorist forces quickly to prevent a massive armed rebellion."[63] However, as the record showed, in Western eyes, the means to achieve that legitimate end were hard-edged and involved extensive and gross human rights abuses—as had been witnessed in Croatia and Bosnia-Hercegovina earlier in the 1990s, as well as in Kosovo itself in the preceding year.

As the Serbian campaign got going, the stories and the pictures were familiar—destroyed and burned out property, dead and mutilated bodies, massive flows of displaced people and refugees who sought escape in the mountains of Kosovo and in neighboring countries—put at over 660,000 and over 700,000 respectively,[64] perhaps two-thirds to three-quarters of Kosovo's population. One of the early assaults was on Mališevo. This also gave rise to particular evidence— film recorded in the immediate aftermath by one of the survivors, Bali Thaci, who had fled the village as Serbian forces approached and then returned: "When I reached the spot where I had left my family, there was not a soul to be seen and everything was burning." He found his camera intact in the ruins and began to film. His film depicts his own burned out house and the dead bodies in and around it.[65] The footage is of mutilated corpses—thirty-six bodies, among them his uncle, whom he did not recognize at the time and who is shown in closeup with his throat cut. Thaci failed to recognize him because he was so mutilated. It also depicts the moment when a friend finds his brother's body. This captures the real, human experience at the receiving end of ethnic cleansing. The nature of his survivor's evidence is compelling: "Once the camera started rolling, I didn't stop. I did that so that no one could accuse me of faking the footage or adding to it." The straightforward, unedited images are testimony to actions that can only be consistent with the allegations against Serbian forces by the International Criminal Tribunal for the former Yugoslavia of crimes against humanity and war crimes.[66]

Thaci's wife, Elmije, had also left Mališevo as Serbian forces carried out operations—but as a part of those operations. As was the case with so many others, Elmije and the female members of her family were herded onto buses and removed. Elmije and her mother-in-law "waded through blood. We trod in pools of blood" as they were moved. Once removed, the future was bleak and the scene behind them grim: "We looked back to where we had left Bali. The place had been set on fire—cars, tractors, everything. The children were screaming 'We've left Daddy back there!'" Even the forced eviction, surrounded by murder, mutilation, and arson, was incomplete. Once removed and driven toward the border, the ethnic Albanians from Mališevo, as happened to hundreds of thousands of others, were abandoned, pointed toward the border and left to complete their experience of ethnic cleansing on foot—although their initial fears were that murder awaited them in the near future:

> They dropped us a long way from the border, then they shoved us out. We had no food. We hadn't eaten for four days. We had to rest. My feet had swollen. I couldn't walk. The others went on. I had never seen so many Serb police. We were sure they would kill us there and then. We kept stepping on spent cartridges. You couldn't see anything, it was dark and raining. We were really frightened they would kill us all. [67]

Some among the Serbian forces even confirmed the mistreatment of Kosovo Albanians. They reacted against what was happening and, in some cases, deserted rather than continue to be part of such a force. One of these was Dragoslav Bogičević, a member of the VJ: "I saw women on the roads with babies in their arms. I felt terrible. I was crying and saying: 'Serbs should not be doing this. The army never did such things. This is a disgrace for us.'"[68] There can be little doubt that Belgrade forces in Kosovo committed crimes against humanity and war crimes. This is confirmed, above all, by the evidence introduced by the prosecution at the ICTY—even where specific accusations against particular individuals are not sustained.[69] That evidence also includes evidence of attempts to cover up the crimes committed by dumping lorries full of dead Kosovo Albanians into the River Danube outside Belgrade.[70]

The Belgrade strategy, as in other cases, was ethnic cleansing—the removal of population groups that might be a reservoir of support for insurgent or terrorist military-political violence against Serbian rule. Belgrade's aim was to remove all, or most, of the Kosovo Albanians, as Serbian Radical Party leader—and both security service "friend" and paramilitary volunteer force organizer—Vojislav Šešelj made clear in a speech in the run-up to NATO action: "If NATO bombs us, we Serbs will suffer casualties. But no Albanians will remain in Kosovo."[71] Although this statement could be seen as being conditional on NATO action, the conduct of Serbian forces in Croatia, Bosnia-Hercegovina, and Kosovo in the preceding years suggested that the conditional aspect was a contingency of the situation—that is, it was an opportunity, as events seemed to support, to undertake large-scale, rapid ethnic cleansing and to imply that NATO, not Belgrade, was the cause of it.

Thus, when there were hundreds of thousands of Kosovo Albanians in the mountains and on the road who had been forced out of their homes physically or driven to flight by the fear of what might happen physically, Belgrade could blame everything on NATO. Milošević addressed an interviewer who raised the issue of the pitiful hordes on the road thus: "You are right, there are lots of refugees, but they are the result of bombing. And they are not only Albanians, everybody is running away because of bombing, Serbs, Turks, Gypsies, Muslims, Deers [sic] are running, birds are running because of bombing, bees are running." This caused problems for the alliance, as UK Prime Minister Tony Blair acknowledged: "A lot of people who were opposed to any action in Kosovo and against Serbia were saying 'You guys have caused this'—so we were getting huge pressure on that." Milošević was, of course, not averse to uttering words intended to exploit that sense of pressure: "When our soldiers are dying they know why they are dying. They are dying for the homeland, for their fatherland. And for what will die your soldiers 5,000 miles from home, killing children until they sleep, killing women and girls, and peaceful citizens, and ruining what we were building through the decades after the Second World War?"[72] The propaganda element was salient, as the success of the NATO mission appeared to be in question.

In this context, it is instructive to note that for most of the period of armed hostilities Western journalists were confined to Belgrade and had limited scope. There can be little doubt that the reason for this was to avoid further reports of the Belgrade forces' actions alleging yet more crimes. However, when there was an opportunity to show NATO in a bad light, both internationally and to a domestic audience (which could be all the more persuasively influenced by reports that included material filtered back through international sources), then the journalists were quickly rushed to the scene to report directly and firsthand about alleged NATO atrocities, especially against Albanian refugees. For example, when NATO planes hit a column of displaced persons near Djakovica, on the road between Prizren and Priština, Milenko Momčilović, the Serbian investigating judge, complained that "NATO fascists have bombed a column of refugees. Nineteen people have been killed." This happened three weeks into operations, and the final figure of dead was more than seventy.[73] Foreign journalists previously restricted to Belgrade were taken collectively to the site in Kosovo. The horrifying images of dead bodies laid out in a field spread around the world. This served the purpose of questioning NATO's role and undermining its legitimacy, while helping to reinforce legitimacy in Serbia. The aspiration here was, presumably, to undermine cohesion and morale in the alliance, both among its members and between each of the governments and their people.

Incidents such as the refugee column (others included attacking a train on a bridge)[74] and stray bombs on residential buildings in Niš (discussed further below) and Aleksinac,[75] for example, were not only damaging as signs of NATO's frustrations, thereby affecting support for the mission in the international public sphere, but they were also the material for accusations of NATO war crimes. This aspect of international law compounded concerns in some quarters that the

NATO action as a whole was unlawful. Thus, there was a legal-political nexus at the core of discussion about the NATO campaign.

The differences within NATO over the legal grounds for action vied with concerns over how force might be applied, as the alliance approached the prospect of action over Kosovo. NATO Secretary-General Javier Solana played an important role in reaching a position where the alliance could agree that its action would be lawful. On one level, he spoke to political leaders themselves. He asked U.S. President Clinton directly: "If it comes to it, do you have a legal basis to act against him [Milošević]?" Clinton replied without doubt: "I said to him 'yes' and when I authorized the use of force I said emphatically 'yes.'"[76] However, the issue was not quite as straightforward as Clinton's response suggested. There were accusations from Belgrade and elsewhere that NATO action would be an unlawful act of aggression.

At the same time, there had been serious differences within the alliance over the legal basis for action. Some countries were concerned that a further UN Security Council resolution was required explicitly to authorize action. Although a string of resolutions had defined the situation in Kosovo as a threat to international peace and security—the watchword for authorizing mandatory enforcement action in international law that overrides all other elements of international law under Chapter VII of the UN Charter—and intimated that consequences would follow, none of them had used any formulation of words that could clearly be interpreted as authorizing a use of force (for example, "all necessary means").[77] Others at NATO thought the duty to prevent genocide, under the Genocide Convention should be a legal basis.[78] Still others took the view that principles of natural law permitted a right to humanitarian intervention.[79] After the conflict, some preferred to view NATO's engagement as a justified breach of the law, given the overriding humanitarian situation.[80] However, there was no single interpretation throughout the alliance, but with each country having its own legal interpretation authorizing action, the NAC authorized action. However, the lack of a single stated legal interpretation must itself be taken as a sign of the legal uncertainty surrounding the conflict.[81] NATO's legal position has been seen as being strengthened by three other factors. The first of these is that an attempt to obtain a Security Council resolution condemning the action was lost by twelve votes to three, casting reflected and implicit legal legitimacy on the action, if not formal Security Council explicit authority.[82] To a limited extent, this might be seen as being reinforced by a twelve vote to four rejection of Belgrade's petition to the International Court of Justice, aimed effectively at declaring NATO operations unlawful—although the basis for this was the lack of prima facie jurisdiction to address the petition.[83] The second is that the action could be interpreted as being endorsed ex post facto by the UN Security Council's decision to pass Resolution 1244 on the outcome of the NATO engagement and endorsing NATO's role in implementing that resolution and the agreement, which informed it. The final element was the commitment of various Western countries to seek clarification and consolidation of the right to humanitarian intervention and the terms for it in international law through a UN commission—this gave rise to the notion of the "responsibility to protect."[84]

The lack of absolute, agreed, and generalizable legal certainty (qualified by a variety of confident understandings held by those carrying out the action) regarding the *jus ad bellum* on NATO's side only helped to accentuate problems regarding the *jus in bello*, with Belgrade and critics charging the alliance with war crimes. Given the extent of NATO's operations, involving some 38,004 sorties, of which 10,484 were strike missions, over 78 days,[85] it was quite remarkable only to register so few serious errors. Human Rights Watch produced a list of around eighty incidents in this context.[86] Most of these could not be questioned as even potential material for war crimes charges, but even if all of them were to be accepted as seriously meriting investigation, this would amount to a 0.8 percent rate of mistake—by almost any standards, a notable and near perfect record. However, the number of incidents really worthy of anything approaching serious consideration was perhaps a quarter of this figure. For example, the prosecutor at the ICTY conducted a preliminary investigation into allegations of war crimes against NATO, including a list with twenty-two entries on it.[87]

In terms of the conduct of those operations, a main focus for allegations of NATO war crimes was a report by Human Rights Watch in the course of operations, which was supplanted later by an extensive report on its view of the circumstances surrounding the deaths of more than 500 civilians as a result of NATO aerial action.[88] However, of the incidents cited by Human Rights Watch and other international NGOs, which were noted, a report for the prosecutor at the ICTY concluded that on the basis of the available evidence there was not a prima facie case to bring against anyone involved at whatever level in the NATO operations regarding allegations made.[89] To some extent this was to be expected because the alliance and its members took particular measures to ensure the lawfulness of action and to protect against accusations of intent to commit war crimes. The Allies imposed significant legal restraints on operations, with every single mission legally vetted at the national level[90]—although this also included air support missions where the specific targets could not be preapproved, only the nature of the action. At the strategic level, a legal advisor at the U.S. European Command Headquarters in Stuttgart participated in General Clark's video teleconferences with his U.S. commanders in his capacity as U.S. CINCEUR,[91] when final targeting decisions were made prior to the political approval process. Before approving each target, General Clark weighed its military value against the likely extent of civilian casualties. On occasion there were disagreements among the senior officers over whether a target was justified.[92] But, overall, there was a clear intention to act within the laws of armed conflict. That intention, of course, did not necessarily mean that every single action was beyond charge, or even potential conviction in court, but it did confirm that care was taken to try not to contravene the law. However, some cases would always stir attention. Among the most notable and controversial cases, the prosecutor's study concluded that in slightly different circumstances the bombing of the Chinese Embassy in Belgrade might have been susceptible to prosecution, but in the given case, it was not.[93] Close attention was paid to the bombing of Radio Television Serbia (RTS) in Serbia. However, although it was noted that had that attack been based purely on seeking to impede Serbian propaganda its legality might have been doubtful, the evidence suggested that NATO attacked RTS clearly because it formed part of Belgrade's military command and control communications network. The prosecutor, however, did not look in detail at one of the most contentious, and potentially strongest allegations, concerning cluster munitions. Although the legal authority of the Tribunal has to be acknowledged on this issue, it is worth further attention.

The focus here on cluster munitions seems warranted by a number of factors that suggest more of a prima facie case than the prosecutor's report admitted. The prosecutor did not look at specific incidents involving cluster bombs, including the case of Niš, which is described below. Instead, it treated cluster munitions as a general issue, thereby dismissing consideration of potential specific charges. The report noted that there might be cases involving the use of cluster munitions, although there was no specific treaty provision that precluded their use. It did so citing one case, a Rule 61 hearing decision at the Tribunal regarding Republika Srpska Krajina commander Milan Martić, where an Orkan rocket with a cluster warhead had been used in such a manner as to warrant criminal charges. This was based on three main elements: there was intention deliberately to attack civilians, the weapon was inaccurate, and it struck an area with no military objectives.[94] The inference in the report was that these circumstances did not apply to NATO action over Kosovo. Although no intention deliberately to attack civilians and the reasonable presumption that there were military targets, albeit mixed ones, in areas hit can be accepted, this is not sufficient. The weapon is indiscriminate by definition—that is its purpose: around two hundred separate explosive devices of different kinds can be held within one warhead. Thus, one of the three elements has to apply. Beyond this, *Additional Protocol 1 to the Geneva Conventions of 1949*, Article 52, indicates that there are two conditions to be satisfied regarding the legitimacy of a particular attack where a military objective has a dual character or is mixed with nonmilitary entities: that the purpose or use should make an effective contribution to military action and that destruction caused should give definite military advantage.[95] The detailed ins and outs in cases in Kosovo cannot reasonably be handled here. But it can be noted that the prosecutor's team, while considering these issues in a reasonably lengthy and balanced treatment of the

RTS tower, did not consider them at either a general level, or regarding specific cases in the one paragraph assessment regarding cluster bombs. This indicates that, at a minimum, other questions could have been and might be posed.

Cluster munitions, as noted, have perhaps two hundred separate missiles within one warhead. They are effective for battlefield use against concentrations of troops, tanks, or artillery, for example, dispersing multiple destructive devices over a widespread area. Similarly, they are useful against airfields, which was the intended mission in Niš. However, they are inaccurate pieces of weaponry. In addition, they have a relatively high rate of redundancy—out of 200 devices, it is recognized by military personnel that around 5 percent fail at any time.[96] This means that for every cluster device, there will be around ten unexploded bombs in the dispersal zone. This caused problems for the NATO-led ground forces of KFOR because they undertook their implementation mission in Kosovo, noting that both experienced soldiers and civilians were liable to maiming if they accidentally detonated one—which, for example, stepping on it could cause. This potential for civilian harm, with any military effect dislocated in time, is compounded by the potential for damage to civilian objects at the time of use if, as in the case of Niš, where the air base is located within the town, cluster bombs are used in an urban, civilian populated area.

In human terms, the effects of using cluster bombs against Niš were stark. Notwithstanding the visual fireworks, the strike was politically maladroit considering that the city's political leaders were among the most pro-Western in Serbia. But it was most devastating in its human impact. Pregnant schoolteacher Liljana Spasić was one of many injured left lying amid pools of blood and body parts. Her mother-in-law, who later described how they had been hit by "little bombs,"[97] was taken to the hospital to have her leg amputated, not knowing that her daughter-in-law and unborn grandchild had been killed where both she and Liljana had stood. The city's mayor (and later Serbian prime minister) Zoran Živković described the awful scenes, commenting ironically, as an anti-Milošević activist and friend-in-waiting of the West: "Their 'humanitarian' intervention killed fifteen people in a day."[98]

Although the deaths were clearly unintentional, this was not entirely evident until after the prosecutor's report had studied the incident for possible charges of military negligence. The prima facie case—using a weapons system known to be inaccurate and indiscriminate against an airfield in a civilian residential area without a compelling military objective—may well have influenced the U.S. decision to discontinue using cluster munitions soon afterward, particularly in view of a report by Human Rights Watch questioning their legality.[99] It seems reasonable to suggest (without prejudice) that the report's assertion that cluster bombs "should not have been used in attacks in populated areas, let alone urban targets, given the risks" might have been better tested by the prosecutor.

Incidents where war crimes were alleged (whether or not the allegations were well founded) clearly put additional pressure on the alliance, with Western journalists posing awkward questions at the daily NATO briefing to Jamie Shea, the official spokesperson. Shea was asked aggressively by an American journalist, "Do you deny that NATO was responsible for the incident, or incidents, which have been shown on Serbian television and to which Western correspondents were invited to go and look at those bodies and so on that appeared to have occurred on the road between Djakovica and Prizren?" Shea was unable to respond in any positive way for want of information. He could only say, "I have no indication at the present time that NATO was responsible," which under insistent pressure, did not sound reassuring.[100] As pressure grew, UK Prime Minister Blair phoned U.S. President Clinton and told him, "Look, we're losing this, we're losing the propaganda battle, I mean we're losing it big time. This is like, you and I are familiar with this, it's like winning an election. You've got to have a proper press war room, war propaganda room, where you are putting out the correct information, you're correcting the lines of your opponents, you're setting the agenda."[101] NATO was under pressure at this point because operations were not going according to plan. Indeed, from the outset, they had not been, as the plan was for no bombing or, at worst, up to one week of air operations, as noted below. In this context, the nature of the operation and the issue of ground forces became an important part of the debate on NATO's action.

There was intense discussion within the alliance on moving to a commitment to use ground forces, which involved crucial discussions between UK Prime Minister Tony Blair and NATO SACEUR Wesley Clark.[102] However, while debate, discussion, and virtual discussion occurred, in some sense, the KLA had begun to provide a very limited ground complement for the NATO air action, at least in the area close to the border around Mount Pastrik. The KLA role in this context has led some to suggest that the KLA was a proxy ground force for the alliance's airmen.[103] This would significantly exaggerate both the role and the capability of the KLA. Although there was a good deal of harassment, especially close to the borders with Albania, it did not amount to operations that could threaten Belgrade's forces directly. Absent NATO air power, the KLA stood no chance operationally against the VJ, as had been demonstrated many times during the previous year. On every occasion, VJ and MUP operations had rolled back the KLA insurgency. Aside from the convenience to the NATO air campaign, there is no suggestion that the "revitalized" KLA operations in May were in any way substantial. They were not directly threatening to Serbian forces. Despite the losses incurred by NATO's bombing of troops drawn into the open, the VJ was finding no problem in rebuffing KLA action. Thus, although some recognition has to be given to the fact that the KLA was present and that its raids played a limited role in making Belgrade forces more vulnerable to air attack, it is hard to make the jump to an inference that the KLA was NATO's proxy ground force in any but a limited sense. That limited sense was that in the last weeks of the conflict some KLA operations, especially around Mount Pastrik, were coordinated with the help of Albanian military intelligence intermediaries, according to Clark, with a view to flushing VJ personnel and targets out into the open, where NATO aircraft could strike them.[104] Not all NATO's successes were in the KLA area of operations close to the border with Albania. The only thing that could be said regarding the KLA action in those areas is that it provided a small-scale catalyst to what would have happened anyway once NATO had taken the decision politically to accept the deliberate killing of Belgrade troops if necessary to the pursuit of the military objective—which it did in mid-May.[105] At the same time, in terms of the ground conflict in Kosovo, it should be noted that KLA operations in some cases gave rise to suspicion of committing war crimes and crimes against humanity, which resulted in indictments against KLA personnel by the ICTY.[106]

Although examination of motivations in the previous section offered some evidence that U.S. Secretary of State Albright appeared keen to bomb, the weight of evidence also suggested that the U.S. and NATO as a whole were certainly not intent on bombing, and considered the possibility gravely. Gaining agreement at Rambouillet was a primary objective but the key aim was to ensure deployment of ground forces so as to prevent the possibility of Belgrade's conducting anything like ethnic cleansing operations. The threat of aerial bombardment was intended to coerce Belgrade—which meant Milošević—into agreement. There was intent behind NATO's threat to give it credibility—experience over the years had led to the conclusion that Milošević would only desist from actions if he felt there was a serious threat. The evidence from NATO's actual air campaign indicates that the alliance, while prepared to use force, was not intent on doing so.

The crucial evidence on this is that, in terms of actual conduct, there were plans for only very limited operations over perhaps only three days, certainly no more than one week. The hope at NATO was clearly that bombing could be avoided. This was clear when U.S. Envoy Holbrooke reported to Secretary-General Solana that he had not persuaded Milošević to accept terms: "The news from Dick was bad. The NATO Council prepared for the worst."[107] NATO governments had strongly hoped to avoid the resort to air power. And, as far as they had recognized that it might be possible, everything was predicated on a short campaign. One U.S. airman's account confirms that a campaign of less than a week was foreseen, all being well: "Everyone was talking three days. And all the pilots were telling me 'you gotta get me in, you gotta get me in cos I need to go, I want to go and bomb before the war is over.'"[108] There was a similar expectation, it seems on the Serbian side: "When the bombing began, I thought it would be over in one night. Then life would go back to normal. I thought it could not last 24 hours. Three days was unimaginable."[109] However, the campaign, as noted, ended up taking nearly three months.

Already, it was evident that the campaign could be a long haul. Bad weather meant that many operations could not be carried out, and NATO was unable to get around Belgrade's highly successful and ingenious asymmetric strategy of not seeking significantly to use its air defense capability,[110] especially after a couple of planes had been lost to NATO attack aircraft less than a week in. Within a week, NATO's campaign was stalling: "All the targets that were given had been hit. So there weren't any approved targets to hit anymore unless we went out there and hit the same targets again, which is what we did."[111] As the NATO SACEUR, U.S. General Wesley Clark, noted, "It was fairly clear by Monday that we were not going to get a knock-out blow."[112] Thus, it became obvious that succeeding would require more than initially thought, both conceptually and practically. That generated new problems for the alliance. The debate surrounding how to solve these problems revealed much about the West's real intentions at Rambouillet. This could be seen in discussion on using ground forces in a nonpermissive environment and in discussion regarding the nature of the operations themselves—how to use air power and what the purpose was.

The military wanted more extensive target sets, although even within the military command of NATO and the U.S. there were fierce differences. U.S. Air Chief General Mike Short bluntly and bullishly wanted simply to bomb his way down a conventional list of targets and destroy them, whereas General Clark saw the need for a more sophisticated campaign, a more "effects"-based approach calibrated to the strategic objective of forcing Milošević to end the ethnic cleansing campaign in Kosovo (the aim was not, therefore, directly to stop the ethnic cleansing on the ground as it happened).[113] According to Solana, "Wes Clark insisted we bomb targets with symbolic or psychological impact on Milošević. That way we could break his spirit," and the operations eventually undertaken, "were very specific operations, directed at symbolic buildings, targets connected with Milošević." However, although Clark was the relative sophisticate and insightful strategist vis-à-vis Short, his view was not acceptable to NATO political leaders. Bridges over the Danube were a particular point of contention. In Clark's view, "We had to strike at the Serb means of transportation, including their highway network, their rail network, their tunnels and so forth, and especially the highly significant bridges over the Danube River." This was unacceptable to French President Chirac: "General Clark wanted to destroy all the bridges in Belgrade. This was absurd and totally unnecessary given the mission that we had."[114] Indeed, all agreed that NATO's mission "was not to wage war in the traditional sense. Our aim was to neutralize Milošević's command capability."[115] For the most part, the bridges were not touched, but other sensitive dual-use targets were, notably the RTV building. This shows that the West, far from having a lust to bomb, had great reservations about using force despite judging it necessary to take such action in the end. It also shows that what made the West judge action to be necessary was the determination to stop the Milošević regime by denuding its forces and changing its policy.

Rambouillet, Paris, and Beyond

At Rambouillet, the Western intention was to secure an agreement that would provide broad-ranging and effective self-government for the province of Kosovo—short of its gaining independent international personality—secure the withdrawal of most Serbian and FRY forces, and also facilitate the deployment of an international armed force under NATO leadership, command, and control, which would ensure that there was no possibility of Belgrade's being able to initiate ethnic cleansing operations against the predominantly ethnic Albanian population in the province. The primary objective was deployment of an armed force that could block Serbian action. It was desirable that such an agreement should be broadly international and have the backing of the UN Security Council. With this is mind, and given the role of the international Contact Group dealing with the breakup of the old Yugoslavia, there was a great desire to ensure Russia's involvement.[116] However, there was a fine line to be walked between the desire for a truly international character to the agreement and the imperative of blocking, if at all possible, what Western leaders believed to be an imminent Serbian campaign of ethnic cleansing. For those focused on Western interests—including the viability of the NATO-led operation in Bosnia-Hercegovina and the credibility of the Alliance itself—an effective response to the problem posed by Belgrade was more important than securing broader international support, if that decision had to be made.[117]

The French and British, on behalf of the Contact Group, formally, and the EU, politically, led the negotiations at Rambouillet, with their respective foreign ministers as cochairs.[118] However, the talks were reinforced by the continuing presence of a NATO threat to use force against Belgrade if it did not cooperate in the talks.[119] Although these were technically separate tracks of international involvement, the reality was that London and Paris were prominent in both cases and that the U.S. was very close to each process. In a strong sense, the two tracks were part of the same Western approach, broadly: the aim was to avert the Belgrade campaign against the KLA and the ethnic Albanian population in Kosovo, including extensive ethnic cleansing, that Western leaders believed was imminent. Although there was no doubt that success in this would count on the use of Western armed forces, the issue of how best to use the military was not straightforward, as noted above. This made an agreement that allowed for the deployment of an international force highly desirable from the Western perspective.

Deployment of an international force was a key question that became part of the proposed agreement because most of the political questions appeared to be capable of interim agreement.[120] In February, Belgrade decided to send a delegation backed by a parliamentary vote. But that vote explicitly instructed the delegation to block any attempt to part Kosovo from Serbia or to impose an international presence that was greater than the KVM's already in place.[121] Despite this, political progress was made. The interim document tabled was developed from the "Hill plan"—that is, the draft arrangements for Kosovo that U.S. Special Envoy Christopher Hill had been quietly seeking to negotiate over several months.[122] There were additions to the Hill plan, but ostensibly these were less favorable to the Kosovo Albanians than to Serbia. One was that arrangements would only be interim and that a process to find a final status would begin only after three years. Another was that the KLA would have to disband completely—an element of the scheme not shown to the Kosovo Albanian delegation until two days before the second deadline in the talks—and one that clearly generated friction between the West and the Kosovo Albanians at the talks.[123]

Indeed, the key political difficulty appeared to rest with the Kosovo Albanians rather than Belgrade. The crucial issue for the Kosovo Albanian delegation was inclusion of a referendum on independence. Although the interim agreement offered a process that would lead to final status arrangements for Kosovo, it made no mention of a referendum. One commander of the KLA, known as Remi, admitted: "We phoned each delegate and warned them: Don't you dare sign!"[124] Head of delegation Hashim Thaci, a KLA leader, added that Remi had said that "to sign would be treason." However, the foreign ministers chairing the meeting excluded that possibility, knowing that it would not be acceptable to the Belgrade delegation, whereas there could be hope that something would change, one way or the other, after three years and whatever process would follow that period. The Kosovo Albanian position was a matter of immense frustration to the Western political leaders. Thaci was well aware that, "the time had come to say Yes or No to the document. It was an impossible choice. . . . The document ruled out independence. A referendum wasn't mentioned. Many men had died fighting for this. My response was, 'I will sign the document, but it must include a referendum.' . . . I knew that if we said no to the document we would lose all international support. The Kosovo question would be swept aside like the Kurds."[125]

Albright typified Western frustration: "When he wouldn't say yes, I remember taking off my earphones, just putting them down on the table in pure exasperation." In her mind, the "question was basically 'Do you agree with the framework—Yes or No?' And we were expecting a Yes, or I was." As the conference session was suspended, Albright held a private meeting with Thaci and said, "Look, I don't understand what just happened in there. You have let us down. It is an impossible situation now. How could you do this? We expected you to be a leader."[126] This much was completely in line with her colleagues from other Western countries, such as France, the UK, Italy, and Germany. However, her position in the discussion perhaps went beyond that which was clearly in common and revealed an inclination on her part, certainly, and possibly on that of the U.S., that seemed equally or more intent on isolating Serbia so that it would either have to agree, or as seemed more likely, face NATO's bombs. According to Thaci: "Mrs. Albright said: 'If you sign and the Serbs don't, we will bomb. NATO will activate. If you don't sign, our hands are tied.'" From her perspective, Albright "could see that he was just shocked. I mean he looked like a high school student that I had just dressed down." The Kosovo Albanians, according to Thaci, were pressed ever harder to accept the document, "with no referendum."[127]

In the end, there was no referendum, but only because the Kosovo Albanian delegation, working with American negotiators, came up with a side measure. In the words of one delegation member, Vetton Surroi, the highly respected publisher, journalist, and liberal political leader: "We had been negotiating for three weeks. We'd had ten years of conflict with Milošević. If we refused to sign, we would be throwing it all away. Three seconds could ruin everything. All we had to do was to find the right form of words. . . . So we left the door open for a referendum, but we told the international community we would stop trying to change the document." Their solution was a letter to Albright confirming the understanding that the wording "will of the people" in the interim agreement implied a referendum. Although Thaci wanted time and translations before he was sure, the Americans, eager to grasp this means of agreement, rushed to make it public and cement what would therefore mean Kosovo Albanian agreement. Before announcing it, Albright's spokesman, Assistant Secretary Rubin, hesitated a moment: "I thought that I'd better first check with the Secretary of State and I snuck in to the conference room and whispered in her ear what had happened, and she said 'go out and announce it.'" This is what Albright and her team wanted—as Rubin concluded: "The Albanians had chosen peace and deferred independence, and the Serbs had not. And now there was clarity that the world needed in deciding whose side they should be on."[128]

Although this seems indicative of an American urgency to put Serbia in a corner and possibly to frame air attacks, the latter did not necessarily follow from the former. At this point, had there been Serbian agreement, the subsequent aerial assault on the country would have been avoided. That seemed possible, given that political agreement was so close. It is also consistent with the instructions given to the Serbian negotiators at Rambouillet by Milošević, where the emphasis appeared to be on achieving some kind of solution that would avert NATO action.

The testimony of Zoran Andjeljković, minister for Kosovo, makes this clear: "It was late, Milošević was at home, he told us that we had to prevent NATO aggression. We had little room to manoeuvre. We faced the bombing of Yugoslavia. We had to make one last try. So Serbian President Milutin Milutinović would go to Rambouillet."[129] Although they seemed to have limited real authority initially, once Milutinović had been dispatched this was no longer so clearly the case, and negotiations offered the prospect of success in the eyes of some, such as Hill, as noted already.

Even though political agreement was close, in the end it slipped far away during a two-week gap in which the Kosovo Albanian delegation was allowed time to return to Kosovo and explain to the KLA commanders there what they had really agreed to at Rambouillet, the U.S. position, and the importance of either forcing Serbia to come to terms and accept interim and implementation arrangements or to be isolated and face NATO action. They could also explain how either of these outcomes would suit KLA purposes. However, when the parties returned, Belgrade tabled a new proposal,[130] which for the most part in both its terminology (consistent use of *Kosmet* rather than *Kosovo* beginning with the title and continuing throughout) and content (critically, for example, the promise of self-government was compromised by the statement that "federal organs and organs of the republic of Serbia shall also exercise their powers and rights in Kosmet"[131]), was a very long way in many respects from the document that had been close to political agreement a fortnight earlier.

Although the Belgrade proposal dealt with issues of autonomy, these clearly entailed less real self-government for the majority Albanians. Explicitly reducing them to equal status with a variety of other small "national communities," it effectively rejected the substantive autonomy envisaged in the Rambouillet document. Ironically, Milošević suggested that "What was tried to be imposed in Rambouillet was not autonomy at all but independence. And I really don't believe that if you can show it to any honest American that there is one single honest American who will tell you that if they were in the place of our delegation they would sign it."[132] Although there could be no doubt that the interim accord left Belgrade with no significant political role in the province—and enough to hint at future independence in the right circumstances for the Kosovo Albanians—the reality was that it left both a very real Serbian and FRY presence and responsibilities in Kosovo. This was despite what Milošević alleged to the contrary, appealing to those both in Serbia and outside the country, who were not aware of the detail and the real picture. That Rambouillet left Belgrade with a real presence in Kosovo can be understood through consideration of the military implementation provisions of the agreement.

The question of deploying troops through Serbia or, if this could not be achieved through agreement, then NATO bombing became the main point of contention in both public and political discussion. This was true at the time and subsequently. The real intention was not to gain the chance to bomb. As noted in the previous section, although ready to bomb, the alliance was not ready for a sustained campaign, believing that this would not be needed and that troops would be deployed. This was also confirmed by the reality that some European NATO countries, with the UK notably in the lead, had begun to deploy troops to Macedonia in February in anticipation of an agreement whose implementation would require immediate readiness—these forces would join with those already deployed there under NATO auspices as an extraction force for the OSCE mission in Kosovo. What the draft planning and the appendix envisaged, first of all, was an agreement under which (according to chapter 7 of the interim agreement[133]— the Rambouillet document) the parties would invite NATO "to constitute and lead a military force to help ensure compliance" with the provisions of the agreement and that affirmed the "sovereignty and territorial integrity" of the FRY.[134]

The version of KFOR proposed at that stage (primarily embodied in chapter 7 of the agreement), was considerably more limited than the version eventually deployed after armed hostilities ended in June 1999. Whereas the latter gave KFOR a wide-ranging security remit in the province, under the Rambouillet terms the mission would have been limited to supervising demilitarization and then ensuring that there was no retreat on that position and no armed hostilities[135]—and it would not have had the role it took, in the end, regarding Kosovo's borders with Albania and Macedonia, because Rambouillet would have permitted a continuing VJ presence of 1,500 troops for border monitoring, backed by up to 1,000 further troops to perform command and support functions,[136] as well as a small number of border police,[137] 2,500 ordinary MUP for public security purposes[138] (although these were expected to draw down and to be transformed), and 3,000 local police,[139] whereas the eventual deployment of KFOR saw the complete removal of all Serbian forces.[140] Belgrade would clearly have been better off in terms of its connection to Kosovo under Rambouillet than it proved to be afterward. However, in the end, after seventy-eight days of air action, Belgrade agreed to terms in which no Serbian or FRY forces remained in the province.

This change in the Western position emerged in the course of the conflict and was the subject of discussions between the Americans and the Russians in late May while framing a joint initiative. The Russian envoy, former Prime Minister Viktor Chernomyrdin still favored letting Belgrade police operate in Kosovo, whereas the Americans were insisting that NATO was needed for this and that Serbian forces should leave. As U.S. envoy Strobe Talbott made clear: "At the end of the day, the disagreement between us was going to come down to one three letter word, all—A-L-L, which also happens to be a three letter word in Russian, v-s-e. So, the only way to create what was called a secure environment in Kosovo is to get all of the Serbs out. That meant all of the Serb armed forces, all of the paramilitary, all of the Special Police, all of them, every one."[141] Thus, by rejecting the terms at Rambouillet, where the West had been prepared to allow, and work with, the presence of Serbian and FRY security forces, Belgrade had ended with no presence whatsoever in the province, de facto losing any effective authority over it—although formal rights over the status of borders remained.

Appendix B of the draft agreement was to become notorious and the centerpiece of criticism and conspiracy theories (noted above) depicting NATO as a provocative bully, delivering ultimatums that contained terms that were alleged to have been designed to be unacceptable and, therefore, to do no more than serve as the pretext for an armed air campaign that the alliance was determined to initiate. Milošević characterized it this way: "UN troops would be free to use all roads, harbours and airports on our territory. It would be occupation."[142] Appendix B was the basis of this notion.[143]

In terms of the appendix itself, however, it was a more-or-less off-the-shelf status-of-forces agreement. This can be seen in the wording, which in all but small details was a copy of that which had been used by NATO in Bosnia-Hercegovina, by reference to the most contentious elements of the appendix. The focus of contention was paragraph 8 of appendix B. Paragraph 8 stipulated freedom of movement throughout the FRY for the force—something simply transferred from the Bosnian model without particular thought. The wording of paragraph 8, however, is exactly the same as that of the start of the equivalent paragraph 9 in the Status of Forces Agreement for IFOR, the NATO-led multinational implementation force deployed to Bosnia-Hercegovina in November 1995:

> NATO personnel shall enjoy, together with their vehicles, vessels, aircraft and equipment, free and unrestricted passage and unimpeded access throughout the FRY, including associated airspace and territorial waters. This shall include, but not be limited to, the right of bivouac, maneuver, billet, and utilization of any areas or facilities as required for support, training and operations.[144]

However, despite being copied from the Bosnia SoFA in the first place, once thought about, the proposal carried significant logistical and transit advantages, given the physical difficulties of relying on Albania and Macedonia for deploying forces into Kosovo.[145] Alleged by Belgrade to be a mandate for an occupation force, this was, from the NATO perspective, a mixture of lazy borrowing from an existing template and the realization of greater practicality in using access from Bosnia-Hercegovina and, particularly, from Hungary, to transit through the rest of Serbia into Kosovo. However, whereas the authority to move freely throughout Bosnia-Hercegovina was not seriously contested, the identical provision regarding the FRY was seen by critics and willfully by Belgrade as contentious and unacceptable. Rather than being a device designed to be unacceptable, as critics suggested, it was something normal and sensible in military planners' terms.

The paramount fallacy in what Alex Bellamy has called the "orthodoxy" over the military appendix is the charge that it was nonnegotiable.[146] In fact, it was Milošević who refused to contemplate discussion over the annex. With perhaps seven points still to be agreed on the political part of the plan, Milošević told Ambassador Hill that the military implementation arrangements were wholly unacceptable—that not a country in the world could accept such terms (ignoring, as discussed above, that these were the same terms to which Bosnia-Hercegovina had agreed, in large part because of him). Hill said that the Serbian leader should make suggestions about what would be acceptable and that he would see what he could do. He offered Milošević his pen to mark the text. Milošević, however, sat with his arms firmly folded and what can only be imagined as a childish stubborn sulk on his face and did not speak again.[147] Hill's efforts were not the only ones. Secretary of State Madeleine Albright, in what must have been an uncomfortable act of personal concession, also secretly called Milošević, by arrangement, to make it clear that the U.S. (and, therefore, it could be presumed, its allies and partners) was prepared to negotiate the terms of the military annex, even proposing a meeting in Geneva, which the Serbian leader rejected.[148] Albright testified as follows: "I placed a call to Milošević and I explained to him what the stakes were and once again I did 'we're at a fork in the road and you have an option to come back and be part of Europe, this is a very serious time, you need to consider what's been offered here.'"[149] However, despite these offers, the Serbian leader would not even begin to discuss the possibility.

By now, Milošević appears clearly to have made up his mind and to have set course for conflict, expecting NATO air action and waiting to exploit it. This judgment is borne out by the political counterproposal at the Paris follow-up meeting to Rambouillet, which was so different from the near agreement two weeks before; by Milošević's clear refusal to contemplate offers to investigate changing the document on military implementation; and by the ultimate acceptance of terms far worse than anything on the table in France regarding Belgrade's presence and role in Kosovo—something that cannot rationally be explained as a function of the seventy-eight-day campaign of aerial force by NATO, given that if the stakes were genuine and high enough to warrant walking into such a campaign, the decision abruptly to capitulate in late May 1999 and accept far worse terms would not be tenable.

Even until the very last moment, there was an option to avert bombing and keep Belgrade forces in Kosovo while conceding the deployment of an international military force with a limited mission—one far more limited than that of the force eventually deployed. On 23 March 1999, Holbrooke was dispatched one last time. His mission was to convince Milošević to change course, freeing both him and the West of the prospect of armed conflict—except, as the conduct of both sides in the actual armed conflict indicated, as already seen, NATO was not really prepared for armed hostilities, assuming that coercive threat would produce agreement, whereas Milošević seemed both prepared for and intent on calling NATO's bluff and then exploiting NATO action to carry out ethnic cleansing operations while his forces showed themselves ready to face NATO and even outwit the alliance. In Holbrooke's words: "I was asked to go back and to give Milošević a very clear message that if he didn't accept the Rambouillet agreements, we would bomb."[150] While Milutinović confirmed that Holbrooke "told Milošević that their missiles were so precise they could hit his table," Hill observed that "Milošević looked almost disinterested in it, sort of moving his head to the side and shaking it in disgust." He told Holbrooke, "well there's nothing I can do. I'm not going to sign," and the American team left, with Milutinović saying goodbye to them and, "tell us when it's starting so we can hide." The Serbian parliament subsequently backed rejection of the Rambouillet terms.[151]

According to France's President Chirac, Belgrade's rejection took away any potential blurring around the issue: "Plainly, it was Milošević who had refused. So the die was cast."[152] It was Milošević who actively prevented any possibility of peace. More than this, the proposal was something about which there could have been discussion, had Belgrade shown even a smithereen of interest in engaging in negotiation. When the NATO Kosovo campaign came, it was by no means because NATO had sought to provoke it—as the conduct of that campaign confirmed. The Rambouillet and Paris talks were an opportunity for all concerned to avoid the use of destructive armed force—especially the West, which hoped that NATO threats would push Belgrade into agreement—rather than a pretext for NATO bombing. Although the talks had clear objectives from the Western perspective, political agreement with Belgrade had been close and the terms for military implementation were open to negotiation. Belgrade refused even to try to negotiate. Milošević had seemingly decided that he would use the Rambouillet document as a cover for using force and pushing NATO into using force too.

Conclusions

In keeping with the SI's focus on salient controversies, we offer some indicative conclusions.

What motivated the U.S. and its NATO Allies? The West was motivated by the experience of Bosnia, the direct evidence of Serbian action in Kosovo during 1998 and the first months of 1999, as well as a clear belief that Belgrade intended an extensive campaign of ethnic cleansing in its southern province. The West therefore sought to prevent what it believed to be an intended Serbian campaign. Eventually, it sought to do this through armed air action, which aimed to denude the Belgrade security forces' capability strategically and ultimately persuade Milošević to change his policy—Milošević and his regime were seen as the source of the problem and constituted the main target, politically. The West tried to avoid resorting to the use of air power while preventing the Serbian campaign of ethnic cleansing that it believed had previously begun and was due to start over in accelerated form by gaining agreement through negotiations that would permit a ground force, led by NATO, to be deployed without any use of force and blocking any use of force by others.

What would have happened in Kosovo without NATO intervention? NATO believed that extensive ethnic cleansing by Belgrade forces was imminent. Belgrade's record during the 1990s in Croatia, Bosnia, and Kosovo (where up to 300,000 people were displaced in the months preceding NATO's initiative) appeared to support this view. So, even more, did the onset of operations in March 1999, as the attempt to find a negotiated outcome in Paris failed and the Serbian campaign started, four or five days before NATO action began. To this extent, it seems reasonable to conclude that ethnic cleansing would have occurred. It also seems reasonable to conclude that without the NATO intervention the KLA would not have made significant progress, as the record of both 1998 prior to and even 1999 during the NATO engagement indicates that it was weak, relatively unformed, and incapable of mounting sustained operations, whereas Belgrade forces had shown themselves to have the measure of the KLA—notwithstanding the strategy of atrocity that accompanied the majority of their actions—and to be able to beat the KLA comfortably in direct combat. However, given the nature of the KLA and its political agenda, supported by the majority of the Kosovo Albanians, it seems unlikely that repeated military defeats would have wiped out the movement. Thus, the asymmetric struggle would have continued for many years, despite the extensive ethnic cleansing by Belgrade's forces.

Did NATO violate international law? There are two aspects to the issue of international law and the NATO engagement. The first concerns the lawfulness of NATO's intervention. The evidence is not absolutely clear. In an evolving area of international humanitarian law, there are different interpretations that support the lawfulness of the action, including interpretations that rely on compounding the various different elements. The record is that each member of the alliance assessed the action to be justified and had its own legal interpretation. However, that record is also that there was not one single interpretation on which the allies agreed. Thus, although there was a clear belief that the action was legal, this was not clear-cut, even among those carrying out the action. This gave strength to those who criticized the NATO action, whether in Belgrade or elsewhere, asserting that it was an unlawful campaign. However, the decision by three prominent states, which charged that the action was illegal, to propose a Security Council resolution to condemn the action and declare it to be unlawful backfired, for the vote on it was held and lost twelve votes to three. This gave backhanded legitimacy to NATO intervention in international law, reinforcing claims to legality by NATO states.

The second aspect of legality concerns the conduct of NATO operations and the issues of war crimes. This issue is given added relief by the lack of an absolute position on the legality of undertaking the action. However, although questions were raised regarding suspected war crimes, most of these were addressed and dismissed with appropriate care by the prosecutor at the ICTY. However, in one area, that of cluster munitions, the evidence was not thoroughly weighed by the prosecutor, either in general or in detail. The general basis on which potential charges relating to cluster munitions were dismissed does not appear to be comprehensive. In addition, there were elements in NATO's use of cluster bombs, particularly relating to the attack on Niš, that might suggest a prima facie case to investigate, in terms of specifics. This is not to prejudge the outcome of such an investigation, merely to indicate that perhaps not all the questions that might have been posed in this respect appear to have been addressed.

What was the extent of war crimes committed by the Yugoslav military/Serbian special police/paramilitaries? Did anyone flee NATO bombs? There can be no doubt that at some points some people were seeking shelter from NATO bombs in Kosovo and elsewhere in Serbia—this is both inevitable and human nature. It is also clear that some Kosovo Serb civilians fled KLA action, some of which warranted war crimes and crimes against humanities charges against their personnel. Nonetheless, the central, undeniable fact in this narrative remains the expulsion of over 700,000 Kosovo Albanians by Belgrade's forces through a systematic campaign of ethnic cleansing marked by diverse atrocities that led to indictments against a host of its military and civilian leaders, including Slobodan Milošević.

Was the Rambouillet diktat justified? . . . and was it a diktat? Although the term itself is both pointed and prejudicial in tone, there can be little doubt that the West issued an ultimatum to Belgrade. This was predicated on agreement by the Kosovo Albanians that proved much more difficult than Western actors had assumed prior to the Rambouillet negotiations. Once that agreement was reached, it then became clear that Belgrade was isolated and faced a clear choice between negotiating in good faith, including meaningfully accepting key aspects of the proposed agreement, or facing coercive NATO aerial bombardment. The value of the approach taken in this study, where motivations are considered first, then conduct, and finally, the negotiations themselves, is that evidence of Western motivations is confirmed by subsequent conduct, including inadequate preparation for sustained military operations and both political and strategic differences over how to prosecute the campaign successfully once it had begun.

Although there can never be any assurance that military plans will remain relevant once a campaign begins, the evidence is that NATO's bluff was called by Belgrade and that the desire to avoid, or if this were not possible, to limit action, indicates that the real aim was to get a ground force deployed to make ethnic cleansing impossible but to accomplish this via agreement. This can be taken to confirm that the West's intention at Rambouillet was to secure an agreement rather than to create a pretext for air bombardment, no matter what. In this context, it is vital to note two things. First, political agreement had nearly been achieved at Rambouillet; the much-discussed military annex was never a stumbling block because Western representatives desperate to avoid air strikes had made clear to Milošević personally that it was open to revision and tried to get him to engage in shaping its final form. Second, despite NATO's potentially humiliating eleventh-hour efforts to bring Milošević around, the Belgrade delegation returned to the negotiations with a counterproposal that was far different from the terms to which it had appeared ready to agree just two weeks before. This seems to have been not a gesture at gaining some form of reconciliation but another willful provocation aimed at calling the West's bluff. Although the interactive construction of any situation requires two participants, the shape of events prior to NATO's action, as well as the evidence of motivations in the West and Belgrade, the conduct of both in their military operations, and their approaches to the talks in France suggest that the NATO ultimatum was more justified than not.

Notes

1   This was the case, particularly when dealing with the U.S., which as a single actor often had a firmer and more tightly defined agenda than the composite of Western powers.

2   Miroslav Hadžić, *Security Ranges of NATO Intervention in Kosovo*, draft paper for the Copenhagen Research Institute, 2000. The analysis of motivations and perceptions in this chapter draws heavily on Hadžić's earlier work.

3   James Gow, *The Serbian Project and its Adversaries: A Strategy of War Crimes* (Montreal, McGill-Queen's University Press, 2003), 258-61; Judah, *Kosovo: War and Revenge* (New Haven: Yale University Press, 2000), 103-20

4   Ibid., 261; Henry H. Perritt Jr., *Kosovo Liberation Army: The Inside Story of an Insurgency* (Urbana and Chicago: University of Illinois Press, 2008), 73.

5   These figures, gathered by the International Crisis Group, as well as Gelbard's refer-
      ence, are reported by Judah, *Kosovo*, 116–117, 130–131, 137–138.

6   Gow, *Serbian Project*, 260.

7   Ibid.; Perritt, *Kosovo Liberation Army*, 81–87.

8   For example, thirty-one Kosovo Albanians were killed in just one incident resulting
      from KLA attacks near Prizren on 14 December 1998. See "Report of the Secretary-
      General Prepared Pursuant to Security Council Resolutions 1160 (1998), 1199 (1998),
      and 1203 (1998)," UN doc. S/1998/1221, 24 December 1998, Annex 1, para. 4. Opera-
      tional Zone leader Ramush Haradinah later observed that when his fighters "saw that a
      battle was not going so well . . . they just sought the safest place. They would run for a
      half day until they got there." Quoted in Perritt, *Kosovo Liberation Army,* 79.

9   Alan J. Kuperman, "The Moral Hazard of Humanitarian Intervention: Lessons from the
      Balkans," *International Studies Quarterly* 52 (2008), 64–71; Perritt, *Kosovo Liberation
      Army,* 55, 67.

10   For the referendum, see Robert Thomas, *Serbia Under Milošević* (London: Hurst and
      Co., 1999), xiv.

11   Perritt, *Kosovo Liberation Army,* 56–57, 70, 76, 79–80 OZ. Commander Ramush Ha-
      radinaj calculated that his forces fell over the summer from 8,000–10,000 effectives to
      56 by October, most of them family members.

12   See UN Security Council Resolution 1203, S/RES/1203, 24 October 1998.

13   On the ways in which the Milošević regime managed to survive by ensuring social
      fragmentation, see Eric D. Gordy, *The Culture of Power in Serbia: Nationalism and
      the Destruction of Alternatives* (University Park: Pennsylvania State University Press,
      1999).

14   Leaving aside normal considerations of domestic jurisdiction and the rights pertaining
      to statehood to address security challenges on a state's territory (underpinned by article
      2, paragraphs (iv) and most of paragraph (vii), a well-publicized statement by U.S.
      President Bill Clinton's special envoy to the Balkans at that stage appeared to reinforce
      the rightfulness of Belgrade's position—though not necessarily its methods—by con-
      demning "very strongly terrorist actions in Kosovo" and adding for clarity that the KLA
      was "without any questions, a terrorist group." Quoted in William G. O'Neill, *Kosovo:
      An Unfinished Peace* (Boulder: Lynne Rienner for the International Peace Academy,
      2002), 24. On Serbian policy and practice in the decade or so preceding NATO ac-
      tion, see Judah, *Kosovo*, chapter 2; Sabrina Ramet *Balkan Babel: The Disintegration of
      Yugoslavia from the Death of Tito to the Fall of Milošević* (Boulder: Westview, 2002),
      316–323; Independent International Commission on Kosovo, *The Kosovo Report: Con-
      flict, International Response, Lessons Learned*, chapter 1 (Oxford: Oxford University
      Press, 2000), and for a broader based approach to the emerging conditions see Julie
      Mertus, *Kosovo: How Myths and Truths Started a War* (Berkeley: University of Cali-
      fornia Press, 1999).

15   The Contact Group had been formed during the war in Bosnia and originally involved
      the U.S., the UK, France, Germany, and Russia, with Italy later joining. The original
      membership was based on countries representing particular international organizations.
      After pressure from Italy, the representation became that of the influential countries di-
      rectly. See Gow, *Triumph of the Lack of Will: International Diplomacy and the Yugoslav
      War* (New York: Columbia University Press, 1997), 260–261; David Owen, *Balkan
      Odyssey* (London: Victor Gollancz, 1995), 276.

16 Interview with Jack Zetkulic, DCM, U.S. Embassy–Belgrade by Charles Ingrao, February 1998.

17 The UN Commission on Human Rights, for example, issued a number of reports on the situation in the former Yugoslavia generally and Kosovo specifically, largely criticizing the Belgrade authorities in the years after 1989, when the formal autonomy of Kosovo as a province in Serbia was revoked. A selection of material relating to Kosovo appears in Heike Krieger, ed., *The Kosovo Conflict and International Law: An Analytical Documentation, 1974-9* (Cambridge: Cambridge University Press, 2001), 2.1.2.

18 *The Fall of Milošević*, Dir. Dai Richards, Brook Lapping for the BBC (3 Parts), 2003, Part.1. This invaluable documentary features a plethora of "talking-head" film interviews with the protagonists themselves, giving direct testimony on what happened and their parts in it.

19 *Fall*, part 2.

20 *Fall*, part 1.

21 *Fall*, part 1.

22 James Gow, "Kosovo after the Holbrooke–Milošević Agreement: What Now?" *International Spectator* 33, no. 4; Alex Bellamy, *Kosovo and International Society* (London: Palgrave, 2002), 96–101.

23 "Report of the Secretary-General Prepared Pursuant to Security Council Resolution 1160 (1998)," UN doc. S/1998/712, 5 August 1998, para. 12.

24 Reported by Ivo Daalder and Michael O'Hanlon, *Winning Ugly: NATO's Kosovo War* (Washington DC: Brookings Institution, 2000), 40–41, 43.

25 "Report of the Secretary-General Prepared Pursuant to Security Council Resolutions 1160 (1998), 1199 (1998), and 1203 (1998)," UN doc. S/1998/1068, 12 November 1998, annex I, para. 7.

26 42,000 in Montenegro, 20,500 in Albania, 3,000 in Macedonia, 10,000 in Bosnia-Hercegovina, and 20,000 within Serbia. In addition, 80–90 percent of the 28,000 internationally registered asylum seekers from the FRY were from Kosovo. "Report of the Secretary-General Prepared Pursuant to Security Council Resolutions 1160 (1998), 1199 (1998), and 1203 (1998)," UN doc. S/1998/1068, 12 November 1998, para. 20.

27 "Report of the Secretary-General Prepared Pursuant to Security Council Resolutions 1160 (1998), 1199 (1998), and 1203 (1998)," UN doc. S/1998/1068, 12 November 1998, para. 21.

28 "Report of the Secretary-General Prepared Pursuant to Security Council Resolutions 1160 (1998), 1199 (1998), and 1203 (1998)," UN doc. S/1998/1147, 4 December 1998, paras. 18 and 21.

29 "Report of the Secretary-General Prepared Pursuant to Security Council Resolutions 1160 (1998), 1199 (1998), and 1203 (1998)," UN doc. S/1998/1147, 4 December 1998, paras. 8–10.

30 "Report of the Secretary-General Prepared Pursuant to Security Council Resolutions 1160 (1998), 1199 (1998), and 1203 (1998)," UN doc. S/1998/1221, 24 December 1998, paras. 7–8, 10.

31 "Report of the Secretary-General Prepared Pursuant to Security Council Resolutions 1160 (1998), 1199 (1998), and 1203 (1998)," UN doc. S/1999/99, 30 January 1999, paras. 29–30.

32 Gow, *Serbian Project,*; Bellamy, *Kosovo*, 96–101. The NATO threat was apparent in that the governing political body of NATO, the North Atlantic Council, had authorized an activation order, which meant that in appropriate circumstances military command-

ers were now authorized to use force, but it was not yet clear that action would actually be taken. To reinforce its threat in what might well still have been a bluff predicated on achieving agreement to deploy the KVM, the U.S. made a major point of forward deploying bombers to bolster the credibility of its threats and making sure that these planes were clearly seen on television. As Ambassador Richard Holbrooke noted, "we made sure that the world saw this." *Fall*, part 1.

33 *Fall,* part 1.

34 Events in December and January are noted in "Report of the Secretary-General Prepared Pursuant to Security Council Resolution 1160 (1998), 1199 (1998), and 1203 (1998)," UN doc. S/1999/99, 30 January 1999, paras. 3–21.

35 *Fall,* part 1.

36 It should be noted that the NGO Human Rights Watch concluded that the twenty-three were killed at around 1500 on 15 January. Human Rights Watch, *Report on the Massacre in Račak, January 1999,* reproduced in Krieger, *Kosovo Conflict,* 193.

37 *Fall,* part 1.

38 "Report of the Secretary General," S/1999/99, 30 January 1999, para. 11.

39 Human Rights Watch, *Massacre in Račak,* 193.

40 "FRY Statement by the President of the Republic of Serbia, Milan Milutinović," 17 January 1999, reprinted in Krieger, *Kosovo Conflict,* 193–194.

41 Human Rights Watch, *Massacre in Račak,* 193.

42 "Report of the EU Forensic Team on the Račak Incident," 17 March 1999, reprinted in Krieger, *Kosovo Conflict,* 198.

43 "Report of the EU Forensic Team," 198.

44 "Report of the Secretary-General," S/1999/99, 30 January 1999, para. 12.

45 "Report of the Secretary-General Prepared Pursuant to Security Council Resolution 1160 (1998), 1199 (1998) and 1203 (1998)," UN Doc. S/1999/293, 17 March 1999, para. 16.

46 Daalder and O'Hanlon, *Winning Ugly,* 292nn137 and 138; General Wesley Clark, *Waging Modern War* (New York: Public Affairs, 2001), 148. Naumann's evidence to the UK House of Commons Defence Committee is cited fully by Bellamy, *Kosovo,* 121–122.

47 For more on Operation Horseshoe, including what, if anything, it was and its relationship to the actual Serbian campaign in Kosovo, see Gow, *The Serbian Project,* 207–209.

48 *Fall,* part 1.

49 *Fall,* part 1.

50 *Fall,* part 1.

51 *Fall,* part 1.

52 *Fall,* part 1.

53 *Fall,* part 1.

54 This is discussed more extensively in Gow, *Serbian Project,* 280–283, 294.

55 Moscow and Beijing, along with New Delhi, sponsored a draft resolution at the UN Security Council on 26 March 1999 to condemn the NATO action and declare it to be a breach of the UN Charter. However, the resolution was defeated twelve votes to three in a vote of the council's fifteen members. Ironically, the attempt to condemn NATO action had rather the reverse effect of legitimizing it with Security Council authority, while not giving formal and explicit Chapter VII authority for the action. See Nicholas J. Wheeler, *Saving Strangers* (Oxford: Oxford University Press, 2000), 279–281.

56 *Fall,* part 1.

57   *Fall*, part 1.
58   *Fall*, part 2.
59   *Fall*, part 2.
60   One of the classic discussions of just-war theory is Michael Walzer, *Just and Unjust Wars: A Moral Argument with Historical Illustrations* (London: Allen Lane, 1978).
61   Colonel Milinko Stišović, "Iskustva iz Lokalnih Ratova o Pripremi i Angažovanju Oklopnih and Mehanizovanih Jedninica," *Vojno Delo* 49, no. 1 (1997).
62   Among the ways in which the campaign had already been well prepared was the collection and removal of public documentation and records from many towns. The same was true of valuable cultural artifacts, including important pieces of religious heritage, presumably taken away for safekeeping.
63   General Nebojša Pavković, chief of staff of the VJ, *Fall*, part 2.
64   "Kosovo: Action by the European Commission," IP/99/319, European Commission, Brussels, 11 May 1999, reprinted in Krieger, *Kosovo Conflict*, 478; in the wake of the conflict, the UN secretary-general reported that there had been 800,000 refugees in Albania, Macedonia, and Montenegro, and at least 500,000 had been displaced inside the province, making a total of 1.3 million. "Report of the Secretary-General on the United Nations Interim Administration Mission in Kosovo," UN Doc.. S/1999/779, 12 July 1999, para. 8. Alberto R. Coll, "Kosovo and the Moral Burdens of Power," in *War over Kosovo: Politics and Strategy in a Global Age*, ed. Andrew J. Bacevich and Elliot A. Cohen (New York: Columbia University Press, 2001), 131, sets the number at 1 million expelled from Kosovo plus another 300,000–500,000 internally displaced.
65   See *Fall*, part 2.
66   *Prosecutor vs. Slobodan Milošević*, IT-02-54.
67   *Fall*, part 2.
68   *Fall*, part 2.
69   *Prosecutor vs. Slobodan Milošević*, IT-02-54, for example, has ample evidence of the crimes committed.
70   Marlise Simons, "Witness Links Milošević to a Plan to Cover Up Crimes in Kosovo," *New York Times*, 24 July 2002.
71   *Fall*, part 2. Although the filmmaker's translation is used here, to be consistent, it is notable that in the original, Šešelj follows the reference to NATO bombing with the words "if there is American aggression."
72   *Fall*, part 2.
73   *Fall*, part 2; *Final Report to the Prosecutor by the Committee Established to Review the NATO Bombing Campaign Against the FRY,* ICTY PR/PIS'510-E, 13 June 2000, III9.
74   The Korisa Bridge incident on 13 May 1999 resulted in from forty-eight to eighty-seven deaths. *Final Report to the Prosecutor*, III9; Human Rights Watch, *Civilian Deaths in the NATO Air Campaign* (Washington, DC: Human Rights Watch, 2000) and www.hrw. org/reports/2000/nato/; appendix A contains a list of all incidents identified by Human Rights Watch.
75   *Final Report to the Prosecutor*, III9 and 13.
76   *Fall*, Part 1.
77   James Gow, *Defending the West* (Cambridge: Polity, 2005), 55–58; nonetheless, reflecting the diversity of views within the alliance, the Kingdom of Belgium argued at the International Court of Justice that the Security Council resolutions provided "an unchallengeable basis for the armed intervention." "Belgium Oral Pleading in the Case

'Legality of the Use of Force,' CR 99/15 (translation)," 10 May 1999, reprinted in Krieger, *Kosovo Conflict*, 308, 504–505.

78 *Convention on the Prevention and Punishment of the Crime of Genocide* (1948), reprinted with discussion in *Documents on the Laws of War*, ed. Adam Roberts and Richard Guelff, 2nd ed. (Oxford: Clarendon Press, 1982), 157–168; this view was expressed in an interview by Gow with a German national working at NATO, December 1998.

79 "Belgium Oral Pleading in the Case 'Legality of the Use of Force,' CR 99/15 (translation)," 10 May 1999, reprinted in Krieger, *Kosovo Conflict*, 308, 504-5; for further discussion, see Wheeler, *Saving Strangers*, chapter 8.

80 This was the personal view expressed privately by a two official senior legal authorities from different NATO countries to James Gow.

81 This uncertainty and different views on it were discussed in expert testimony to the UK House of Commons Foreign Affairs Committee. The committee concluded that, in the circumstances, "the NATO allies did all that they could to make the military intervention in Kosovo as compliant with the tenets of international law as possible." *House of Commons Foreign Affairs Committee, Fourth Report on Kosovo*, London: HMSO, 7 June 2000, para. 133.

82 "Draft Resolution Submitted by Belarus, the Russian Federation, and India," S/1998[sic]/328, 26 March 1999, reprinted in Krieger, *Kosovo Conflict*, 432; for further discussion, see also Wheeler, *Saving Strangers*, 279–281.

83 "ICJ Case Concerning the Legality of Use of Force, Request for the Indication of Provisional Measures, Order," 2 June 1999, reprinted in Krieger, *Kosovo Conflict*, 309, 508–514.

84 "*A More Secure World: Our Shared Responsibility": Report of the High-Level Panel on Threat Challenges and Change*, UN Doc. DPI/2367, December 2004.

85 William M. Arkin, "Operation Allied Force: 'The Most Precise Application of Air Power in History,'" in Bacevich and Cohen, *War over Kosovo*, 1–37, which provides extremely detailed figures on the air operations. It also offers an excellent and detailed account of the operational campaign from the U.S. military perspective in Washington, DC—in any case, the hub of the air campaign, clearly based on extensive interaction with many of those involved. Other contributions to the volume, especially the one by Elliot Cohen, offer particularly engaging and informative essays on the strategic implications of the Kosovo conflict, while Michael G. Vickers' contribution is an especially useful source of further detail on operations in the former Yugoslav region.

86 Human Rights Watch, *Civilian Deaths*

87 *Final Report to the Prosecutor,* III.9.

88 Human Rights Watch, *Civilian Deaths*.

89 *Final Report to the Prosecutor*, III.9.

90 Interview with British officers engaged in targeting decisions and operational command by James Gow, December 2004 and May 2005.

91 Commander-in-chief, U.S. European Command, overall commander of U.S. forces in Europe (General Clark's U.S. hat in addition to his NATO hat as supreme allied commander Europe).

92 Interview with a senior Supreme Headquarters Allied Powers Europe, staff member present at the videoteleconferences by Charles Ingrao, 10 May 2000.

93 *Final Report to the Prosecutor*, IV.B.iv.80–85.

94 *Final Report to the Prosecutor*, IV.A.iii.27.

95 *1977 Geneva Protocol I Additional to the Geneva Conventions of 12 August 1949, and Relating to the Protection of Victims in International Armed Conflict,* article 52, reproduced with discussion in Roberts and Guelff, *Documents,* 416–417.

96 The present section is based on current research by James Gow and colleagues from the War Crimes Research Group, King's College London, carried out on a confidential basis among military personnel from different countries, some of whom had served with NATO countries in some part of the Kosovo engagement.

97 *Fall,* part 2.

98 *Fall,* part 2.

99 Human Rights Watch, *Civilian Deaths;* although the U.S. stopped using cluster munitions, the UK continued to deploy them but legally vetted all missions prior to launch to ensure their lawfulness.

100 *Fall,* part 2.

101 *Fall,* part 2.

102 *Fall,* part 2; Clark, *Waging Modern War,* 299–303.

103 The following draws on Gow, *Serbian Project,* 291–292.

104 Clark, *Waging Modern War,* 328–329.

105 Prior to this point, the alliance had sought to avoid inflicting either civilian or military deaths or casualties. The second half of May produced the majority of the Serbian MUP–VJ 525 dead, approximately 1,400 wounded, and 28 missing in action (of which forensic remains of four appear to have been identified at Košare, close to the border with Albania). Gow, *Serbian Project,* 298, quotes the slightly higher official figure of 576 dead, while suggesting that the real figure might run into thousands. However, although there were efforts to suppress the number of wounded at the time, it seems unlikely that so many more deaths could have been covered up so long after the fall of Milošević, when the identities, details, and biographies of all the dead had been published. This point and the accurate figures are thanks to Colonel Branislav Mitrović, operations officer in the Third Army command at the time of the Kosovo conflict, who was responsible for collating information and ensuring operational readiness. Interview by James Gow, 8 September 2005.

106 *Prosecutor vs. Ramush Haradninaj et al.,* IT-04-84, 24 February 2005.

107 *Fall,* Part 2.

108 Major James Hardin, U.S. Air Force, *Fall,* part 2.

109 Mira Marković (Milošević's wife), *Fall,* part 2; in the original, she actually adds that three days would be "really a lot."

110 Gow, *Serbian Project,* 215–223.

111 General Michael Short, *Fall,* part 2.

112 *Fall,* part 2.

113 Clark, *Waging Modern War,* 243–249, 298; Daalder, and O'Hanlon, *Winning Ugly,* 198.

114 *Fall,* part 2.

115 *Fall,* part 2.

116 U.S. Secretary of State Madeleine Albright, for example, made a special visit to Moscow in January 1999, reflecting a general Western sense that Moscow had to be engaged. *Fall,* part 1. See also "U.S. Secretary of State, Albright, and Russian Foreign Minister Ivanov, Joint Statement," Moscow, 26 January 1999, reprinted in Krieger, *Kosovo Conflict,* 253–254.

117 This is borne out by events, where NATO, in the absence of new and explicit UN Security Council authority, undertook the use of destructive armed force.

118 "Contact Group, Chairman's Conclusions," London, 29 January 1999, reproduced in Krieger, *Kosovo Conflict*, 255.

119 "Statement by the Secretary-General on Behalf of the North Atlantic Council," press release (99)020, 19 February 1999.

120 Ambassador Christopher Hill discussion with James Gow, December 1999.

121 *Tanjug*, 6 February 1999.

122 See, for example, "Final Hill Proposal," 27 January 1999, reprinted in Krieger, *Kosovo Conflict*, 176–185.

123 Alex Bellamy, "Reconsidering Rambouillet," *Contemporary Security Policy* 22, no.1 (2001), 130.

124 *Fall*, part 1.

125 *Fall*, part 1.

126 *Fall*, part 1.

127 *Fall*, part 1.

128 *Fall*, part 1.

129 *Fall*, part 1.

130 "Agreement for Self-Government in Kosmet," Paris, 18 March 1999, reprinted in Krieger, *Kosovo Conflict*, 280–286.

131 "Agreement for Self-Government," article 1, para. 2.

132 *Fall*, part 1.

133 "Interim Agreement for Peace and Self-Government in Kosovo," Rambouillet, 23 February 1999, reprinted in Krieger, *Kosovo Conflict*, 261–278.

134 For considerably fuller discussion of these issues and the fallacies of the critics, see Alex Bellamy's excellent "Reconsidering Rambouillet," 31–56.

135 "Interim Agreement," chapters 2 and 7, and appendix A.

136 "Interim Agreement," chapter 7, article IV, para. 2a.

137 "Interim Agreement," chapter 2, article VI, para. 2(a)(i).

138 "Interim Agreement," chapter 7, article VI, para. 2d, and appendix A, para. 4.

139 "Interim Agreement," chapter 2, article II, para. 2.

140 UN Security Council Resolution 1244 /S/RES/1244, 10 June 1999; "Military-Technical Agreement between the International Security Force (KFOR) and the Governments of the FRY and the Republic of Serbia, 9 June 1999," UN Doc. S/1999/682, annex, 15 June 1999.

141 *Fall*, part 2.

142 *Fall*, part 1.

143 "Interim Agreement," appendix B, reprinted in Krieger, *Kosovo Conflict*, 276–278.

144 "Interim Agreement," appendix B, para. 8; "General Framework Agreement," appendix B to annex 1A, para. 9.

145 Gow, *Serbian Project*, 284–285; Bellamy, *Kosovo*, 138.

146 Bellamy, "Reconsidering Rambouillet," 31-56.

147 Ambassador Christopher Hill discussion with James Gow, December 1999.

148 Jamie Rubin, "Countdown to a Very Personal War," features section, *Financial Times*, 30 September 2000. Albright's own account offers detail on a telephone conversation with Milošević from Washington, DC, after two weeks of negotiations at Rambouillet. It makes no reference to proposing a meeting in Geneva and has a generally hostile

tone, although it concludes with preparedness to "negotiate on specific concerns" once Milošević had met, as Albright proposed, with Special Envoy Hill. It seems highly likely that this has to be the same secret telephone conversation, although Rubin's crucial detail must be accurate, despite Albright's not including it—perhaps a sign of her sensitivity. Madeleine Albright, *Madam Secretary: A Memoir* (New York: Hyperion, 2003), 509–510.

149 *Fall*, part 1.
150 *Fall*, part 1.
151 Bellamy, *Kosovo*, 151.
152 *Fall*, part 1.

10

Vojin Dimitrijević, team leader
Julie Mertus, team leader

John B. Allcock	**James Gow**	**Richard M. Oloffson**
Edina Bećirević	Dejan Guzina	Diane Orentlicher
Mikloš Biro	**Olja Hočevar van Wely**	**Nenad Popović**
John Cerone	Constantin Iordachi	Blerim Reka
Ana Dević	**Selma Leydesdorff**	Ruth Wedgwood
Ranka Gašić	Vuk Maksimović	Paul Williams
Eric D. Gordy	**Lara Nettelfield**	**Maryanne Yerkes**

This chapter was revised and edited by John Allcock from previously discrete contributions written by him, Mikloš Biro, Vojin Dimitrijević, Eric Gordy, Julie Mertus and Richard Oloffson. Selma Leydesdorff provided material from Dutch-language sources. Other team members made additional, though less extensive contributions. The process of editing, summarizing and condensing the penultimate 33,000-word draft has necessarily merged formerly separate contributions to the point of making individual acknowledgment impracticable.

The National Endowment for Democracy funded an analysis of Serbian media by Mikloš Biro, as well as a series of statistical surveys conducted by Vojin Dimitrijević and Igor Bandević in Serbia, and by Julie Mertus and Olja Hočevar van Wely in Bosnia, Croatia and Kosovo. Field work by Maryanne Yerkes appeared separately as "Facing the Violent Past: Discussions with Serbia's Youth" in *Nationalities Papers* 32/4 (December 2004), subsequently republished in Thomas Emmert and Charles Ingrao, eds., *Conflict in Southeastern Europe at the End of the Twentieth Century: A Scholars' Initiative* (New York & London: Routledge, 2006).

The chapter benefited from extensive comment and criticism during three lengthy project-wide reviews in March-April 2004, July-August 2005, and December 2005-January 2006.

THE INTERNATIONAL CRIMINAL TRIBUNAL FOR THE FORMER YUGOSLAVIA

◆ John B. Allcock, Editor ◆

New Questions for Old

The Prospectus of the Scholars' Initiative (SI) summarizes the concerns of Group 10 in three questions. "To what extent is the ICTY [International Criminal Tribunal for the Former Yugoslavia] a political body? To what extent is it impartial? To what extent is it anti-Serb?" In the course of our research we have moved away from the attempt to answer them either in simple negative or affirmative terms and have arrived at the conclusion that it is more useful to investigate *the sense in which it might be said* that the Tribunal is political and *the gap between intention and effect* with respect to its impartiality. Perhaps more significantly, we believe that it is important to challenge the framing of partiality or impartiality in terms of the specific position of many Serbs.

The project sets out to challenge accounts of the Yugoslav experience embedded in the lay understanding of history, particularly in the region itself. These accounts often need to be challenged, not because the presumed "facts" upon which they are based are false but because the very intellectual framework within which they belong is distorted.

To What Extent Is the ICTY a Political Body?

The question contains the rhetorical implication that the ICTY should somehow not be a political body and that to reveal its political character is to expose its fundamental illegitimacy. This language is encountered frequently in press and public discussion of the Tribunal within the region, but no social scientist would ever entertain it seriously. *All* courts are political bodies: they are essentially embedded within the state. The fact that the ICTY is an *international* tribunal cannot be expected to elevate it above the world of politics into some Platonic realm of ideal justice. The properly social-scientific answer to the original question is an explanation of *the specific manner in which international justice takes on a political aspect.*[1]

To What Extent Is the ICTY Impartial?

Because courts are embedded within a political matrix they are *never* completely impartial—although their effectiveness and legitimacy rest upon the *belief* in their impartiality. A striking feature of the work of the ICTY, however, is the gap that has grown up between the international perception of its legitimacy (based substantially upon a belief in its impartiality) and local doubts on this score. Understanding of the importance of the Tribunal as an experiment in international justice is best advanced by rephrasing the original question in order to explore the origins and significance of that gap in perception.

Is the Tribunal Anti-Serb?

This certainly has been a widespread perception within Serbia. To tackle this question without further qualification would not be very helpful. The result would be to frame the SI irrecoverably as either pro- or anti-Serb. In fact, when one investigates the reception of the ICTY within the region, it is remarkable that different ethnic groups—and not only the Serbs—have come to perceive The Hague as at best indifferent to their own interests, if not hostile to them. Investigation of the reasons why that should be the case tells us interesting things about the Tribunal and about the differing characteristics of political cultures and processes within the post-Yugoslav states.

A central aim of the SI has been to provide "an attempt by scholars to bridge the gap that separates their knowledge of the tragic events of the period 1986–2000 from the proprietary interpretations that nationalist politicians and media have impressed upon mass culture."[2] Our account is offered in the belief that the best way to undermine these "proprietary myths" is to challenge their central questions rather than to attempt to answer them. To do so without challenge would be only to confirm their legitimacy. While avoiding the Scylla of extreme nationalism, however, it is equally important to avoid the Charybdis of implicit Orientalism.[3] While endeavoring to lay to rest some of the evidently mythological images of the ICTY that have become current in the Balkans, we are equally ready to point out that this experiment in international justice is open to critical scrutiny. Neither the process of demythologization nor that of independent critique will be completed on this occasion—but we hope that they both will have been given a significant impetus.

Our report did not set out to be—and cannot be—an encyclopedic work of reference on either the ICTY or the Yugoslav wars. Suggestions that it ought to have encompassed a comprehensive survey of the press of the region, a detailed analysis of court transcripts, an examination of the role of expert witnesses, a critique of the rules of evidence and procedure adopted by the Tribunal, or that it should engage with the problematic relationship between justice and reconciliation, all fall well outside the possibilities of a project that has been mounted here without the benefit of large research grants or permanent personnel.[4]

The Problem of Bias

The research goal that was originally given to Group 10 was to investigate the allegations of bias that had been laid against the ICTY. The task seemed, at first sight, to be fairly straightforward, but as members of the team began to explore the problem this originally defined exercise appeared to be pointless. Participants in the meeting that took place in Sarajevo in July 2002 were aware of no evidence of deliberate partiality on the part of the Tribunal, although allegations of bias were rife within the Yugoslav region. The question was how to reconcile these disparate, and apparently directly contradictory, observations.

At that time there was little scholarly investigation of the ICTY in any discipline.[5] There was extensive discussion within the legal community at the time regarding the implications of the creation of the ICTY for law and jurisprudence.[6] Within the legal literature critical discussion of the ICTY centered upon a number of procedural and conceptual issues, but the question of whether or not it was substantially biased in its practice was not addressed.

At the time when we conceived our project, we were aware of no significant attempt in English-, French-, or German-language literatures to expose bias in the working of the ICTY. The prevailing tone of discussion was to welcome its creation as a significant advance in the development of international humanitarian law, and the work of Aryeh Neier (president of the Open Society Institute and a figure who had been especially active in agitating for the creation of the Tribunal) was particularly important in setting the tone of discussion.[7] It is perhaps significant that the first chief prosecutor of the ICTY, Justice Richard Goldstone, in his own writing about the Tribunal did not regard it as necessary to defend it against accusations of bias.[8]

In 2002, the social-scientific literature devoted to the Yugoslav wars had little to say at all about the interest of any aspect of the ICTY.[9] Given the undoubted familiarity of the generality of specialists with conditions in the "Yugoslav space," it is reasonable to assume that, had the issue of the bias of the ICTY been one that was deemed worthy of attention, there would have been rather more evidence of this in the scholarly literature.

This lack of interest in the issue of bias on the part of foreign scholars of different disciplines contrasted sharply, however, with widespread popular perceptions of The Hague within the former Yugoslavia, where the citizenry (the purported constituents of the Tribunal) remained either ignorant or largely skeptical.

Following the Sarajevo conference, members of the group contributed a variety of types of input to the report, ranging from "desk research" synthesizing aspects of the literature; detailed scholarship addressing specific aspects of the Tribunal's work; a survey of the public opinion research available in the Yugoslav region; interviews with a small number of key actors; reflection on their own experience as participants in one aspect or another of the work of the ICTY and as researchers in the region; and a small, specially commissioned focus-group investigation to explore attitudes to its work.[10]

The present summary of our work substantially condenses and reorganizes the findings of the original report.[11] Section I presents a historical survey of the development of international humanitarian law before the creation of the ICTY. Section II examines the international context of its foundation and considers the contrasting stances of the principal international actors in relation to the ICTY. Section III provides a brief account of the circumstances surrounding the creation of the Tribunal. These three sections place the Tribunal within its historical context, explaining it in terms of a complex process, the outcome of which does not reflect directly the intentions of any one of the parties involved. Section IV turns its attention to the work of the ICTY itself, its structure and operation, taking in turn each of the major components of the organization. Section V offers a brief comparative study of the reception of the ICTY in Croatia, Serbia, and Bosnia-Hercegovina, attempting to probe the nature and sources of local perceptions of the Tribunal and to understand these within their political context. Section VI, finally, draws together and summarizes our conclusions, which provide a more nuanced view of the problems experienced by the Tribunal, and the reasons for the lack of a sympathetic response to it within the former Yugoslavia.

I. A Historical Survey

i. The Origins of International Humanitarian Law

Those who might be tempted to see in the creation of the International Criminal Tribunal for the former Yugoslavia a device directed specifically against one or another of the peoples or states of the former Yugoslavia should pause in order to place this event in its historical context. Historical accounts of the laws of war typically begin with the implications of the Peace of Westphalia, which concluded the Dutch–Spanish War and the Thirty Years War in 1648. The rapid expansion of international trade during the nineteenth century resulted in a number of international agreements, although war continued to provide the primary stimulus to the emergence of international law. The International Committee of the Red Cross was founded in 1863. A factor that promoted this enhanced awareness of the need to control the suffering occasioned by war was the growing activity of the press in reporting it. In both the Crimean War (1854–1856) and the American Civil War (1861–1865) the action was followed by war correspondents representing the principal newspapers. Increasing exposure of the public to the experience of war through the media of mass communication has played a major part in the "moralization of international relations."[12] Particularly important moments in this process were The Hague Convention with Respect to the Laws and Customs of War of 1899 and the 1907 convention, to which can be traced the idea of "crimes against humanity."[13]

A significant stimulus to the development of international law was given by the formation of the League of Nations in 1919, following World War I. The Permanent Court of International Justice (PCIJ) was founded in 1921 under the auspices of the League.[14] It is clear from the experience of the League of Nations, however, that international legal opinion (and that of leading political figures) was deeply divided with respect to the idea of international criminal responsibility. Despite the creation of the PCIJ, a project proposed in 1937 by the International Association for Penal Law, that this should incorporate a permanent chamber of criminal law, was never realized.[15]

ii. Nuremberg and After

The modern framework of international criminal law dates from the overthrow of the fascist regimes in Germany and Japan after World War II.[16] The Nuremberg and Tokyo Tribunals have been criticized frequently in subsequent years because of their ad hoc status and because they represented "victors' justice." Most significantly, the 1945 tribunals were specifically military courts, whereas the ICTY has a purely civilian status. Trials under similar circumstances could no longer claim legitimacy, and the ICTY was created with meticulous care to avoid this label. Moreover, the war was still underway when the ICTY was established, making it relatively easy to avoid the charge of victors' justice.

It would be a mistake to limit evaluation of the post-1945 Tribunals to this negative aspect of their work. The London Agreement of 8 August 1945, drawn up by the victorious Allied powers, ushered in three important new principles.[17] The first of these was the acceptance in international law of individual criminal responsibility for crimes against peace, war crimes, and crimes against humanity.[18] Secondly the notion of crimes against humanity was clarified. These have been described by Richard Goldstone as "crimes of such magnitude that they injured not only the immediate victims and not only people in the country or the continent where they were committed but also all of humankind."[19] Thirdly, and precisely because of their intrinsic nature, crimes against humanity were recognized as falling under "universal jurisdiction."[20]

The positive side of the story undoubtedly includes the impressive deployment of documentary evidence as the basis for the cases advanced by the prosecutor. In this respect they can be regarded as having set acceptable standards for subsequent endeavors. In 1946 the General Assembly of the UN reaffirmed unanimously the principles enshrined in the Nuremberg charter.

In the wake of World War II, between 1948 and 1954, the foundations were laid for the modern system of international criminal law. Although these measures are often referred to as relating to war crimes, it is significant that the first postwar treaty, the Genocide Convention of 1948, expressly acknowledged that the "odious scourge" of genocide is outlawed "whether committed in time of peace or in time of war."[21]

The International Court of Justice (successor to the PCIJ) was set up under the auspices of the UN in 1946. Although this court was created solely in order to adjudicate disputes between states, there was extensive debate at the time about the possibility of adding an additional chamber to the court for the purpose of trying cases involving individual criminal responsibility. For a variety of reasons these discussions came to nothing. It is evident, even so, that responding to the Nuremberg and Tokyo Trials, and in the context of the passage of the Genocide Convention, the possible need for an international penal court was already under widespread consideration.

The four Red Cross (Geneva) Conventions followed in 1949. These covered the treatment of the wounded and sick in time of war, the treatment of prisoners of war, and the protection of civilians during armed conflicts. To these were added in 1954 The Hague Convention and The Hague Protocol dealing with "the protection of cultural property in the event of armed conflict." Taken together (along with the 1977 additional protocols, noted below), these instruments can be regarded as providing the spine of contemporary humanitarian protection law.

The International Covenant on Civil and Political Rights was promulgated in 1966. After this the necessity for international intervention is defined in terms of the need to protect human rights, and conflict is addressed less in the form of situations in which the interests of states must be adjusted and more typically as primary threats to the rights of all.[22]

The changing climate of thinking in this area was reflected and confirmed in 1977 with the passage of two protocols supplementary to the Geneva Conventions. Article I of the first protocol included in its coverage "armed conflicts in which peoples are fighting against colonial domination and alien occupation and against racist regimes in the exercise of their self-determination." Clearly, in encompassing what had hitherto been regarded generally as civil wars, the old understanding of the laws of war as regulating only armed conflict between states had been substantially attenuated.

By the time of the creation of the ICTY in 1993, the boundaries between "war" and "not war" and between "armed forces" and "civilians" had been eroded from the point of view of the status of the actors and with respect to space and time. The older concept of laws of war had by then evolved into a wider understanding of international humanitarian law. The paradoxical fact arising from this series of measures, however, is that whereas international criminal law had become a reality, the enforcement of the law was left in the hands of separate contracting states. There was no international criminal court responsible for the trial and punishment of offenders, no group of experienced professionals to work in this area, no established body of procedure governing the activity of such a court, and no legal culture within which it could be embedded. Nevertheless, it is clear that the Tribunal's creation belongs consistently within the process of the development of international humanitarian law described here.

II. The ICTY in Its International Context

The fact that the Tribunal in The Hague is titled the International Criminal Tribunal *for the Former Yugoslavia*, marks its ad hoc status and implies that its existence requires some kind of special explanation. It is often assumed that its formation reveals the hostility of the major states toward one or another of the Yugoslav peoples or constituent republics. This assumption is questionable. An exhaustive survey of the international scene at the time of the breakup of the Yugoslav federation is unnecessary in the context of the other chapters of this book. Nevertheless, some features of that context merit special emphasis in relation to the attempt to understand the creation, form, and character of the Tribunal.

i. Genesis: The End of the Cold War

The principal feature of the configuration of political circumstances that surrounded the collapse of the former Yugoslavia was the ending of the cold war.[23] Following the collapse of Soviet hegemony in Eastern Europe, symbolized by the breaching of the Berlin Wall in 1989, the NATO states were deeply preoccupied with the reconfiguration of patterns of security as the Soviet threat receded, the possibility of a "peace dividend," and the future role of the alliance. Nor was this debate confined to the North Atlantic area. There was widespread—indeed, global—discussion of the hypothetical emergence of a New World Order (NWO) that might come to replace the centuries-old Westphalian paradigm of interstate relations, but it remained unclear just what were the normative or institutional components of this order—or, where these appeared already to be in existence, the degree of their effectiveness.[24] The beginnings of this NWO might be said to date from the founding of the Conference for Security and Cooperation in Europe (CSCE) in August 1975.[25] Following the end of the cold war, the adoption of the Charter of Paris on 21 November 1990 initiated the transformation of a primarily political forum for the discussion of a range of European issues into a set of institutions (the Organization for Security and Cooperation in Europe, OSCE) intended to manage conflict and ensure coordination in the face of common problems. When the Yugoslav crisis broke, however, these arrangements were entirely untested and embodied collective aspiration but without experience. What is more, as a British Foreign Office memorandum of November 1991 observed, "the consensus principle means that the CSCE's intervention can only be effective if, and in so far as, it is welcome to the government concerned."[26] In the circumstances of the breakup of Yugoslavia that consensus was not forthcoming—neither was it clear from whom it might be obtained.

ii. The Preference for Mediation and Negotiation

The strength of these predispositions and the apparent existence of appropriate European structures provided grounds upon which the U.S. could base its own preferences to allow European governments to respond to the Yugoslav crisis.[27]

In December 1991 the European Community (EC) had just redesignated itself as the European Union (EU) with the signing of the Maastricht Treaty, and the possible expansion of concerted political and diplomatic action by Europe was on the agenda. The leaders of the Union took the state of affairs in Yugoslavia as an opening to explore opportunities in this direction.[28] Both the EU and the OSCE held out great expectations with respect to the possibilities for responding to a major conflict in Europe. Neither organization had experience of how its potential might be translated into action, however, and the reality of the Yugoslav crisis did not match the scenarios that had served as templates in the process of devising these institutions. Crucially, neither body had at its disposal military forces other than those of their constituent states. Consequently, within Europe, the international response to war in Yugoslavia was heavily biased from the beginning toward negotiation or mediation rather than military intervention. With hindsight it is clear that the Community, in adopting a policy of mediation between the local parties to conflict, was committed in advance to limiting itself to diplomatic and humanitarian intervention and that by this stage without the backing of armed force it stood little chance of realizing its aims. [29]

iii. Explaining the Yugoslav Crisis

International responses to the Yugoslav crisis in 1991 were founded upon two main misunderstandings of the nature of the problem. The first of these anticipated that conflict in the Balkans would recapitulate aspects of World War II, in which (it was widely believed) Tito's partisan forces had succeeded in tying down a large number of German divisions. The impossibility of fighting a war in the Balkans without inordinate cost, based upon accounts of World War II, was taken for granted.

The second narrative was the myth of ancient hatreds fostered by publicists such as Robert Kaplan.[30] This view made the conflict in Yugoslavia essentially incomprehensible to the outsider, rooted as it was presumed to be in chronic mental states or cultural predispositions.

The arms embargo imposed by UNSC Resolution 713 of 25 September 1991 was clearly a reflection of such perceptions. Its justification was often framed in terms of the need to avoid pouring oil on the flames—in other words to avoid making worse a situation in which the locals were naturally combustible! The metaphor of the Balkan tinderbox was frequently deployed.[31]

Furthermore, approached by politicians or the communications media with requests for explanation, it was not uncommon for academic commentators to justify their own claims to expertise by insisting on the remarkable complexity of the Balkan situation. Academic insistence upon the complexity and intractability of this revived "Eastern Question" hardly provided assurance to politicians that effective international military involvement was possible.

It came to be believed that the best that the international community could do was to mediate and provide humanitarian support. By the time the war had spread into Bosnia-Hercegovina, the major international actors were already trapped in a framework of policy options that severely limited their capacity for action in Yugoslavia, and they were committed to the long round of fruitless negotiations, culminating in the failure of the Vance–Owen initiatives in the summer of 1993. It is against this background that, as we shall see in the next section, the proposal for a war crimes tribunal emerged as a favored response to the crisis.

iv. The Variability of Policy toward Yugoslavia

One of the most obvious features of the international context of the Balkans since 1992 has been the variability of several major international actors' stances toward the region's problems. Each of the major states involved experienced internal political conflict over the utility and character of the Tribunal. Power has as often been used in order to prevent developments as to accelerate them. The result has been notable for the way in which the unintended consequences of action by international actors have been as significant as their intentions.[32]

During the initial period of the Yugoslav crisis the attention of the administration of President George H. W. Bush was concentrated primarily upon the Middle East—particularly following the Iraqi invasion of Kuwait in 1990 and the subsequent Gulf War. The U.S. perceived no immediate threat in the Balkans to its own interests, and while taking the general view that a redrawing of the map was undesirable, the administration felt itself to be under no pressure to engage directly with the problems of Yugoslavia. The large-scale involvement of European countries in the region in the form of trade and investment (outweighing that of the U.S.) was expected to give the Europeans a superior economic leverage on the parties to the Yugoslav conflict. The policy of the administration of the U.S. toward the Tribunal shifted substantially at the point when Madeleine Albright took over as ambassador to the UN.

British attitudes under Conservative and Labour governments were far from identical, and the stances of the Mitterrand and Chirac presidencies in France were notably different. The Russian impact on events was relatively marginal in this area. As Richard Ullman has observed, "in its involvement with Yugoslavia, Russia has behaved less like a state seeking primacy than one which wants to be seen to be consulted, a member of the innermost circle."[33]

The UN itself was a significant component of the international political context of the creation of the Tribunal. As Thierry Tardy has pointed out, the new climate of cooperation between formerly opposed superpowers after 1989 created a situation in which it was possible for the UN to act in a much more interventionist spirit in general. Between its founding in 1945 and 1988, the UN authorized thirteen major peacekeeping and similar operations: thirty-three were undertaken after that date.[34] Whereas only five such missions had been in operation in 1985, no fewer than seventeen were current in December 1995. In understanding the ICTY, therefore, it is perhaps important to place it within an international climate that over time became more favorable to international intervention and that accorded to the UN an influence that in other times it might not have possessed.

The context during which the ICTY was conceived was unique, and the result of a number of coinciding factors. The end of the cold war, the election of the Clinton administration, the appointment of Madeleine Albright as the United States' envoy, and the culture of legalism within the leadership of the UN all laid the foundation for a possible international war crimes tribunal, whether its jurisdiction be Bosnia, Rwanda, or elsewhere. Had this conflict erupted even five years earlier, it is doubtful whether the UN Security Council would have done anything about it.

The timing of the birth of the ICTY suggests that it was not a long-standing conspiracy created as a means of debasing the Croats, Serbs, or Bosniaks before the international community, as some nationalists have claimed. No serious action was taken until after the flames of war had fanned from Slovenia and Croatia into Bosnia and the European stance of reliance upon negotiation and mediation had demonstrated its ineffectiveness.

v. Elite Inaction and Public Outrage

The pressure to break the international deadlock came, as Gary Bass notes, very emphatically from nonstate actors—especially from the press. Three stories were particularly important in focusing popular attention on the Balkan situation—the siege of Vukovar, which fell to Serb forces after a three-month siege in November 1991; the attack on Dubrovnik in December; and the U.S. publication of an interview by John Burns with the self-confessed war criminal Borislav Herak.[35]

The tide of public indifference really turned, however, with the reports in July and August of 1992 of detention camps filed by journalists (in the English-speaking world) such as Roy Gutman, Penny Marshall, Ed Vuillamy, John Burns, and Maggie O'Kane and (for Francophone audiences) Jean Hatzfeld and Yves Heller.[36]

A further impetus to the redefinition of the Yugoslav situation came in August 1992 with the publication of several reports on the war in Bosnia by significant nongovernmental and international organizations. The first of these was the Human Rights Watch report.[37] The first report of Tadeusz Mazowiecki, the UN special commissioner for human rights, was presented in August 1992.[38] (His reports were a significant factor in ensuring that governments could not remain in ignorance of the problems.) This was followed in September by publication of a report on the situation in Bosnia commissioned by the CSCE.[39]

On 26 and 27 August the London Conference was convened—involving representatives of more than twenty states, together with the leaders of the former Yugoslav republics and autonomous provinces. This took place partly because of the obvious gap between the rising international public concern about the situation and the conspicuous failure of the European-led Carrington mission. At the London Conference, responsibility for future negotiations was formally handed over jointly to Lord David Owen (acting for the EU) and Cyrus Vance (special representative of the UN secretary-general). Their efforts to negotiate a settlement of the conflict resulted in the Vance–Owen Peace Plan for Bosnia-Herce-govina, which was presented in Geneva on 2–4 January 1993. Although this was soon endorsed both by representatives of the secessionist Bosnian Croats and the Bosnian government, it became clear rapidly that the plan would founder on the opposition of the Bosnian Serbs; by the end of March it was a dead letter. Radovan Karadžić, the political leader of the Bosnian Serbs, was put under enormous pressure to accept the plan, and at the Athens meeting of 1–2 May even put his signature to it. He made it clear that effective endorsement was conditional upon its ratification in a referendum, which was to take place on 15–16 May. To the surprise of very few this was not forthcoming.

By the early autumn of 1992 it is possible to speak, without exaggeration, of public outrage in response to the reporting of events in Yugoslavia, and it was clear that in the face of enormous public concern a new approach was required. It is within this context that the formation of the ICTY needs to be understood.

III. The Formation of the ICTY

The Yugoslav crisis came before the General Assembly of the UN on 23 September, when the possibility of a tribunal was proposed by Germany's Klaus Kinkel. On 6 October, Resolution 780 was passed in the Security Council, establishing a Commission of Experts in order to explore the feasibility of a war crimes tribunal.[40]

That commission had before it not only the material already published but the results of investigative missions that it conducted, including the exhumation of mass graves.[41] In October, Amnesty International added its voice to the growing volume of well-documented protests about the scale and seriousness of "grave violations" of the Geneva and Hague Conventions in the region.[42]

In the context of the accusations that have been made regarding the political pressures that shaped the creation of the ICTY, it is important to acknowledge several features of the commission and its work.[43] Its original chair, the Dutch professor of international law Frits Kalshoven, has complained publicly about the difficulties faced by the commission, attributing some of them to deliberate obstruction (blaming Britain, France, Germany, and Italy). Several secret services were accused of refusing to pass on relevant information they were believed to possess. Kalshoven resigned his post (on medical grounds) before the commission had completed its task, handing over responsibility to Cherif Bassiouni (president of the International Human Rights Law Institute at DePaul University in the U.S.). A great deal of its eventual success was owed to Bassiouni's personal dedication and hard work in overcoming problems posed by the inadequacy of the resources placed at its disposal and the lack of cooperation from relevant parties. Bassiouni also believed that British diplomacy was hostile to the investigation, although both his own published account and the interviews given by Kalshoven make it clear that many of their difficulties were rooted in the bureaucratic culture of the UN itself. The members of the commission were nominated for their individual expertise in relevant areas and not as representatives of particular states.[44]

On 22 February 1993 the Security Council of the UN decided by a unanimous vote that "an international tribunal shall be established for the prosecution of persons responsible for serious violations of international humanitarian law committed in the territory of the former Yugoslavia since 1991."[45] Resolution 808 directed the secretary-general to submit to the UNSC a specific proposal to this effect. Accordingly, on 3 May 1993 the secretary-general submitted his report, which was approved by the council on 25 May, again by a unanimous vote (UNSCR 827) creating the International Criminal Tribunal for the Former Yugoslavia.

The experience of the Commission of Experts underlines several important general points in relation to the events that led to the creation of the ICTY. It was set up in response to widespread public concern rather than as an expression of the determination of the major international actors. Indeed, to some extent its existence seems to have been regarded as an embarrassment because the possibility that key players in the events were identified as possible war criminals was interpreted as potentially prejudicing the outcome of concurrent peace negotiations.[46]

Throughout the period of its operation, funding for the commission remained irregular and insecure, dependent initially in large measure upon contributions to a voluntary trust fund. Roughly a third of its direct financial support appears to have come from the U.S. Other backing in money, in services, and in personnel was contributed by a wide range of governmental and nongovernmental sources. Bassiouni attributes the persisting problem of serious underfunding that afflicted the commission primarily to the bureaucratic character of the UN and to inefficiency rather than to any systematic attempt to subvert its work.[47]

The commission's work was suddenly terminated in July 1994. Because the ICTY had already been established, the UN did not believe that it was necessary to keep the commission going. It is undoubtedly the case, however, that this did have one consequence of enormous importance. It prevented the government of Yugoslavia from making any formal presentation of its own evidence. That information was, therefore, not available in time for the commission to make its final report. This did lend credence to the idea that the ICTY, from its inception, was designed principally as an instrument to punish the Serbs and their allies. In this respect, it has been very damaging.

IV. The Structure and Operation of the Tribunal

The structure of the ICTY and its terms of reference are set out in its statute, first enacted as an annex to Resolution 827 of the UN Security Council.[48] The Tribunal was expressly set up in order to apply existing international law and not to create it. For this reason, Articles 2–5 of the statute confine its jurisdiction to international crimes already well established before its creation and, indeed, accepted by the government of the former Yugoslav federation. Any law becomes a reality, however, only when it is interpreted and tested in court. This has been particularly the case in relation to the Genocide Convention, which had not previously been tested in any court. The legal relevance of the distinction between international armed conflict and civil war had been taken for granted in popular parlance but never securely established in international law.[49] A particularly important element of judicial innovation was undertaken by the Tribunal in its determination of the status of the law relating to rape.[50]

There have been several legal challenges to the determinations reached by the Trial Chambers in The Hague, notably in its early years those relating to the concept of civil war and the possible immunity to prosecution of a former head of state. The appropriateness of the use of Chapter VII of the UN Charter as the mechanism for the creation of the Tribunal has also been called into question. Whereas these points of challenge have to do with the interpretation of international law, they have rested upon a general acceptance of the validity of the legal conventions themselves. Our report did not, therefore, explore legal issues of that kind, which for our purposes were taken as settled. The manner in which the operation of the ICTY has acquired political relevance has been shaped closely by its own structure and mode of operation. In examining its political relevance, therefore, it will be both logical and helpful to organize that discussion in terms of its several components.

i. The Trial Chambers

The Trial Chambers constitute the core of the Court. The judges are elected by the General Assembly of the United Nations for a term of four years. At the time of writing, the members of Chambers were drawn from twenty-two different countries. The president and vice president are elected by and from among the judges.

The judges are divided between three Trial Chambers, each of which elects a presiding judge, and the Appeals Chamber. Each trial is heard by a panel of three judges, of whom at least one must be selected from among the permanent judges. The Appeals Chamber is in common with the International Criminal Tribunal for Rwanda (ICTR). The judges in Chambers are collectively responsible, under Article 15 of the statute, for the determination of their own rules of procedure and evidence.

The permanent judges have important regulatory functions in relation to the work of the Tribunal, exercising collegiate responsibility under the president. They draft and adopt the legal instruments regulating the functioning of the ICTY, such as the rules of procedure and evidence.[51] Care is taken to ensure that judges do not sit on cases in which they might be expected to have an interested position. The sense of the independence of the Tribunal is maintained strenuously.

The Chambers can be said to operate as a kind of hermetically sealed element in relation to the rest of the Tribunal's work. This is an important factor in supporting its legitimacy; at the same time, however, it has resulted in some of the most serious public misunderstandings about the nature of the Tribunal. Because the members of Chambers are drawn systematically from so many states, the question of patronage has not been identified as a persisting and systematic political issue, although during the first rounds of voting great concern was expressed as to the adequacy or otherwise of the representation of Muslim countries.[52] Generally speaking, any controversy concerning the composition of the Chambers has involved the practical competence of candidates and not their partiality.

The task of synthesizing a coherent and workable practice from these diverse elements has been far from easy. In the event, a large part of the practice of the Tribunal has been adopted from common law (as opposed to civil law) systems. A key difference here is between the adversarial confrontation between prosecution and defense counsel before the judge(s) and jury, characteristic of the former, and the primacy of the investigating magistrate(s) charged with the independent pursuit of the truth, typical of the latter. The adversarial system permitted public debate of the issues, the open interrogation of witnesses, and the dissection of argument. Nevertheless, the status of the Chambers as a hermetically sealed element has meant that they have been slow to realize the importance of explaining clearly to the outside world the nature and significance of their modus operandi.

The concept of an indictment, for example, which is familiar within the American system, is not necessarily generally understood—particularly the difference between indicting somebody for an offense (which takes place before the trial) and actually finding them guilty after the evidence has been heard and weighed.

An important point upon which the Chambers have found themselves exciting wider political controversy has been Rule 61. Article 21:4(d) of the Tribunal's statute confirms the right of the accused "to be tried in his presence, and to defend himself in person or through legal assistance of his own choosing." Trials in absentia are thereby expressly forbidden. Rule 61 provides, however, for a revision of the indictment in the event of a prolonged failure to produce the accused in court following the original indictment. Whereas the purpose of this measure is clear—placing states under pressure not to conceal or protect those accused of serious crimes—Rule 61 has been interpreted not only as providing for trials in absentia but as aligning the judges with the work of the prosecutor, from whose office they are supposed to be clearly independent. These procedural devices are open to lay interpretation as the determination of guilt before a trial has taken place.

The penalties that the court may exact are limited (Article 24 of the statute) to imprisonment, and paragraph 1 specifies that "the Trial Chambers shall have recourse to the general practice regarding prison sentences in the courts of the former Yugoslavia." This leaves room for considerable interpretation, however, and judges from different countries have brought to their task quite different standards of appropriateness. Western European interpretations of a life sentence can appear astonishingly lenient in relation to American and Yugoslav practice. The multinational composition of the Trial Chambers has resulted in difficulties in ensuring consistency and comparability between sentences, not all of which have been settled on appeal.[53]

One of the most contentious areas of the practice of the Trial Chambers has been questions relating to plea bargaining. This practice is well established in the U.S. but regarded with mixed feelings elsewhere. The decision to (perhaps) set aside some counts on the original indictment in return for cooperation on the part of those indicted is often misunderstood.[54] The indictments are usually long and complex and often issued at an early stage of investigation. It can be in the interests of both sides to proceed to trial on a highly simplified indictment. In all of these areas it has been noteworthy that the Tribunal has suffered from its own failure to explain adequately to the outside world aspects of its practice.[55]

Rachel Kerr defends strongly the record of political independence of the Chambers. "Whilst politics permeates every other aspect of the Tribunal, including its very existence, it does not enter the courtroom and impinge upon due process of law."[56] While accepting this judgment, it is worth remarking that the most significant political consequence of the actions of the judges can be seen to flow unintentionally precisely from their determined depoliticization and their refusal to take into account extralegal considerations.

ii. The Registry

The Registry is responsible for the administration and judicial support services of the Tribunal, including the translation of documents, the interpretation of court proceedings, and the maintenance of records of evidence and material that is potentially available as evidence. Its judicial responsibilities cover the organization of the hearings, the legal files and archives, the operation of the legal aid program for indigent defendants, the provision of assistance and protection to witnesses, the management of the Tribunal's own detention unit at Scheveningen, and the provision of internal security.

To the registrar falls a good deal of the diplomatic work of the Tribunal; but whereas the president is largely concerned with the specifically judicial aspects of its work, the registrar is responsible for a good deal of the sensitive negotiation required in order to secure its budget. The Registry serves the needs of all other major elements of the Tribunal—the Trial Chambers, the prosecutor's office, and defense counsel.

The silence of commentators on the ICTY regarding the work of the Registry might well be taken as an indication of its politically uncontroversial status with respect to the outside world, but there is at least one area in which the conduct of the Registry can be seen as having significant political consequences. This has to do with the belatedness and limited nature of its provision for communication with the outside world.

The Outreach Section of the Tribunal was not created until the end of 1999. Before then there was a very small press office, the activities of which were confined largely to The Hague. Official communication had also been limited to the English and French languages, and the Press Office waited for enquirers to come to it in search of information. Having been established, the Outreach Section initially saw its task as directed primarily to improving the information available to the legal profession and to journalists. As a result, its effort tended to address public opinion only very indirectly and through institutions that either had an interest in the issues or that had already formed their views within a specific institutional/political context—often hostile to the ICTY. The video presentation of the work of the Tribunal, *Justice at Work,* which provides an overview of the Tribunal's structure and operations, was not produced until 2001.[57] Facilities for regular television coverage were only introduced with the Milošević trial in February 2002. Other efforts to familiarize people in the region with the statute, procedures, and operations of the ICTY have been produced mostly by outside researchers rather than by Tribunal staff.[58] It is still the case that the source most heavily relied upon by journalists covering the affairs of the Tribunal is the *Tribunal Update*, produced regularly by an independent charity, the Institute for War and Peace Reporting.[59]

A significant illustration of the failure of the Outreach program can be seen in the controversy surrounding the transfer of former Yugoslav President Slobodan Milošević to The Hague. Serbian President Vojislav Koštunica alleged that this was illegal on the ground that Yugoslavia had no treaty of extradition with The Hague. The transfer of Milošević took place under Article 29 of the ICTY's own statute, however, and did not require a separate treaty of extradition. A clear public rebuttal of Koštunica might have gone some way toward mollifying certain sections of Serbian public opinion.

Until very recently, the Tribunal has been very slow in appreciating the fact that it had a job to do in explaining the basics of its intentions and operations. The result of this is that, whereas the Registry has been far from political in the sense of its pursuing either its own goals or those of powerful others in the Yugoslav region, its very indifference to the outside world has given to the Tribunal a blank facade upon which it has been possible for others to project assumed purposes, uncorrected by the institution itself.

iii. The Office of the Prosecutor

The allegations that the ICTY is a political body and, in particular, that it is biased have related mostly to the work of the Office of the Prosecutor (OTP). Its members are experienced police officers, crime experts, analysts, lawyers, and trial attorneys. The prosecutor's office conducts investigations (by collecting evidence, identifying witnesses, exhuming mass graves), prepares indictments, and presents prosecutions before the judges of the Tribunal.

As with the Trial Chambers, lawyers within the OTP come from different traditions and take significantly different approaches (especially across the civil–common law divide). There are differences in the level of competence of those involved, and there may be differences of point of view between professional groups. Three areas of its activity have become the focus of allegations of bias: the supposed link between the financing of the Tribunal and the political compliance of the OTP; the pattern of detentions; and (most controversially) various aspects of policy relating to indictment.

Finance has always been a sore point in relation to the Tribunal. In the early days of its existence it operated on a shoestring—in the first year of its operation its budget was only $276,000. Financial provision subsequently has become both more generous and more secure. Its budget for 2005–2006 was $278,500,000—a tenfold increase. The severity of early budgetary constraints has left a legacy of suspicion that he who pays the piper must be in a position to call the tune. The U.S. has always provided a substantial proportion of the total financial resources of the ICTY, which laid it open to claims that there might be a link between its financial viability and the policy of prosecution. No clear evidence has emerged, however, that substantiates the view that specific prosecutions have been politically motivated by virtue of the Tribunal's financial dependence upon influential states.

An area of controversy relating to the Tribunal's finances has arisen in connection to the costs of defense. The statute of the ICTY provides that the accused shall be entitled to facilities for the preparation of their defense, to counsel of their own choosing, and to legal aid to ensure that defendants are adequately represented and that witnesses and evidence can support their cases. Not all defendants have taken advantage of these provisions. During the period of office of Croatian President Franjo Tudjman, defendants of Croatian national identity were supported by the Croatian state. Conspicuously also, former Yugoslav President Slobodan Milošević initially declined to recognize the court and prepared and conducted his own defense. Actions of this kind are, of course, profoundly political in their intention and are expected to create and reinforce the impression that defendants are themselves victims of the judicial system who either require support from their friends or who courageously stand alone in defiance of it. Clearly it is the case that if the ICTY is open to accusations of political manipulation in connection with its financing it is not only the OTP itself that merits scrutiny.

The Tribunal has been criticized repeatedly in relation to the detention (or failure to detain) of those who have been indicted by the OTP. To a large extent these criticisms have been misplaced, particularly in that the Tribunal itself does not have any agency that could be responsible for the detention of suspects under its control. It is entirely dependent in this respect upon the services of military or police forces that are either attached to specific states or part of the international forces operating within the region.[60]

Patterns of detainment are believed to be the objects of political pressure from one state or another. There have been significant differences in the pattern of detainment between different zones of control within Bosnia, which to some extent might support the notion that detainments take place as a reflection of policy and not by chance. There have been radically divergent interpretations of the rules of engagement by local commanders even working within the same national contingents, as a consequence of which suspicions of complicity have flourished. Detainment has been a highly controversial matter; but this fact should not be taken as supporting in one way or another the notion that the prosecutor's office itself is biased.[61]

Detainments have become one of the most regularly contentious aspects of the activities of successive chief prosecutors because they have attempted to use international pressure to ensure transfers to The Hague, linking these to the promise of diplomatic support or the availability of aid. Although this kind of pressure upon local governments to undertake detainments or to persuade those indicted to surrender themselves is valued by the international agencies themselves as a useful lever by means of which compliance with their own terms can be enforced in the region, its use is determined by these agencies. Its use is likely to be welcomed by the Office of the Prosecutor, but it cannot be used as evidence that the OTP itself adopts a position of systematic bias against any state that is on its receiving end, particularly because all of the post-Yugoslav states have been (from time to time and to varying degrees) the subjects of this type of leverage.

Ever since the Tribunal began its work, the pattern of indictments issued by the OTP has been the object of critical scrutiny, particularly in relation to their ethnic balance. The majority of indictments (more than two-thirds) have been issued against ethnic Serbs.[62] There have been counterallegations, however, that, given the pattern of crimes and the level of their seriousness, the balance ought to have been more weighted in that direction.

The emphasis upon command responsibility is one of the most problematic aspects of the indictment policy of the OTP. Whereas this idea is rooted in Article 7(3) of the Tribunal's statute, so that prosecution under this head is in accordance with the law, the effect of overreliance upon it is possibly counterproductive. The

Documentation Center in Sarajevo, responsible for a detailed audit of the casualties in Bosnia-Hercegovina during the Yugoslav wars, has definitely identified more than 93,000 deaths.[63] In light of the fact that it is practically impossible to ever ensure that individuals are brought to account for more than a fraction of these, it has been necessary for the OTP to adopt a principle of selection. Whereas the policy of "ascending the ladder of responsibility" may indeed help to ensure that the architects of ethnic cleansing or the directors of mass murder are brought to trial, it is still the case that many thousands of small fish responsible for specific acts of barbarity are left to return to open public life, often in the communities they formerly terrorized. It is hardly surprising under these circumstances that the Tribunal is seen as falling short of local expectations of justice.[64] It is important to point out, however, that the Tribunal's expectation is that responsibility for the prosecution of these minor cases increasingly will be taken over by municipal courts as institutions of justice become more securely established in the post-Yugoslav states and greater trust can be placed in their political independence, as well as their competence.

A further, and more dangerous, consequence of the policy of prosecuting on the basis of command responsibility is that it can be perceived as undermining the essential principle enshrined in the Tribunal's own statute that only individuals are to be held responsible for crimes. Michael Humphrey has argued that the prosecution of leading military and political figures may bring with it a special danger.[65] In an important sense leaders stand for the community, and it becomes hard to avoid turning "prosecutions into politically and symbolically managed events" in which the community itself is on trial. While setting out to challenge popular discourse about atrocity in terms of collective guilt and insisting upon individual responsibility, the judicial process implicitly places the collectivity in the dock.[66]

The most controversial area of this discussion relates to the possibility of the issue of indictments against NATO personnel for offenses alleged to have been committed during the air campaign against Serbia. Two aspects of this campaign have been claimed to constitute violations of the laws or customs of war. Article 3(a) of the Tribunal's statute prohibits "employment of poisonous weapons or other weapons calculated to cause unnecessary suffering," and paragraph (b) prohibits "wanton destruction of cities, towns or villages, or devastation not justified by military necessity." The deployment of munitions incorporating depleted uranium has been held to constitute an infraction of the first of these, and several features of the selection of targets, infractions of the second.[67] Given the fact that Article 1 of the statute gives to the ICTY "the power to prosecute persons responsible for serious violations of international humanitarian law committed in the territory of the former Yugoslavia since 1991," this possibility would seem not to be excluded from its competence, though not positively indicated.

The Tribunal took very seriously the need to confront this issue, which was the subject of a detailed internal report, following which it was decided not to proceed with action against NATO personnel.[68] This decision, whether soundly based in law or a triumph of prudence over principle, has had enormous political consequences, not only by reinforcing the idea that the ICTY is inherently anti-Serb and a creature of the U.S., but also in entrenching U.S. opposition to the International Criminal Court.

Finally, it is necessary to enquire to what extent a strategic error has been made in relation to public acceptance of the ICTY by allowing for all intents and purposes the public face of the court to be the OTP and not the president. The express function of the prosecutor is to prosecute, whereas the Trial Chambers (headed by the president) are charged with determining the truth in the light of evidence and argument submitted by both the prosecution and the defense. It is a vital question (although hypothetical and speculative) just what difference might have been made to the frame within which the Tribunal came to be defined had its most prominent public representative been seen as more obviously neutral in relation to the task of issuing indictments and prosecuting the accused.

V. Bias and the Perception of Bias: The ICTY in the "Yugoslav Space"

Questions relating to the bias in the ICTY's operations have been so persistent and so strongly sustained that they deserve additional consideration. These questions are patterned in such a way as to relate systematically to features of the political cultures of the different states that emerged from the former Yugoslavia. To dismiss this phenomenon as simple error would be to pass up an opportunity to investigate how the ICTY articulated with the politics of these states and learn something about the nature of the post-Yugoslav states. It is to this task that we now turn.[69]

The blankness of the facade that the ICTY presented to the region permitted the projection onto it of images that had little to do with its originating purposes and that bore little relation to the manner in which it actually functioned, either as a court of law or as an element of the international political environment. Not surprisingly, under these conditions, nationalist politicians who had succeeded in occupying the larger part of the ideological space in the ex-Yugoslav states found the opportunity to write their own narratives on this blank facade as elaborations of their own proprietary myths of recent history.

Although the ICTY itself has defined its work in terms of legal questions, domestic audiences within the Yugoslav region focus instead on political issues, such as the funding and operation of the ICTY, and on ethical questions related to the legitimacy and conduct of the wars of succession in the former Yugoslavia and on the political responsibility for war of the successor states. In contrast with the legalistic focus of international and professional actors on the punishment of crimes, local expectations often are based upon reporting that portrays the court and the accused as politically and morally controversial but has little to say about the crimes.[70]

The reception of the ICTY across the region has not been uniform. If we are to understand how these differing (and largely inconsistent) accounts of bias have flourished, we need to go beyond resorting to the Machiavellian intentions of local politicians and consider a wider range of significant features of the political institutions and cultures of the former Yugoslav states.

In the successor states of Yugoslavia, national identities came to be defined dialectically in relation to one another—a process that contributed to the dissolution of the federal state and arguably determined some of the most violent aspects of the way this dissolution took place. The ICTY has come to play the role of a medium through which the relationships between national identities are played out. Issues such as the commensurability of guilt and the question of responsibility for the war remain important in the postwar period. It is still the case that relations between the states and regions of the former Yugoslavia are being defined to some extent through competing discourses about war crimes. To this end, we now examine briefly the reception of the Tribunal in Croatia, Serbia, and Bosnia-Hercegovina.

i. Croatia and the ICTY

"No issue has polarized the post-authoritarian Croatian political scene as much as the issue of cooperation with the International Criminal Tribunal for the Former Yugoslavia," write Victor Peskin and Mieczysław Boduszyński.[71] There was always an element of suspicion in Croatia toward the ICTY, reflected initially in the almost complete silence of the press regarding its foundation. The first indictments, however, were all against ethnic Serbs: up until November 1995 only one indictment was issued by the Tribunal against an ethnic Croat. That picture changed dramatically when, on 10 November, the first of twenty-one indictments were issued in connection with events in west-central Bosnia—all against ethnic Croats. In fact by March 1996 roughly a third of the indictments issued were against Croats. This was hardly consistent with the official Croatian view that the war had been a matter of Serb aggression against innocent parties whose actions were invariably defensive in character.

At the heart of President Franjo Tudjman's anxiety about the ICTY was the issue of Bosnia-Hercegovina, at least parts of which he believed should belong by rights to Croatia.[72] The international settlement at Dayton, however, presumed the permanence of a Bosnian state—and hence its permanent alienation from

Croatia. For as long as Tudjman was at the helm there were powerful ideological reasons for noncooperation with the Tribunal.

In the cases against Tihomir Blaskić and Dario Kordić it became evident that the policy of prosecuting on the basis of command responsibility might eventually implicate President Tudjman himself and his minister of defense, Gojko Sušak.[73] It seems unsurprising, therefore, that there should have been tension between the ICTY and the Zagreb government, deteriorating from 1997 onward. Under constant international pressure, culminating in the postponement of an agreement with the International Monetary Fund (IMF), the government did pass a law on cooperation with the ICTY, and in October 1997 ten Croats indicted for war crimes were transferred to The Hague by the Croatian authorities.[74]

Following a January 1999 speech in which President Tudjman had criticized the ICTY, Chief Prosecutor Louise Arbour expressed her dissatisfaction with the Croatian government's record of cooperation with the Tribunal, which had been limited so far to gestures. In early March of the same year, a U.S. State Department report presented to the Organization for Co-operation and Development (OECD) criticized Croatia's human rights record and singled out for comment Croatia's noncooperation with the ICTY.

During the summer of 1999, in the case of Vinko Martinović-Stela and Mladen Naletilić-Tuta, the Tudjman government cooperated with reluctance with the ICTY, although eventually complying with its requests. Circumscribed by a high degree of legal formalism and responding to the leverage of possible international sanctions, Zagreb was finally persuaded to transfer both men to The Hague.

With the passing of Tudjman it became clear that the new government would take a different position with respect to the ICTY. In his inauguration speech to the Sabor on 18 February 2000, President Stipe Mesić reiterated his desire to accelerate the country's admission into international organizations and ultimately the European Union. This by implication meant accepting Croatia's obligations toward the Tribunal.[75] Large quantities of documentation were surrendered to The Hague, and in April the government acceded to a request to examine a reported mass grave outside Gospić. Accordingly, Croatia was accepted officially into the Partnership for Peace program on 25 May.

The new direction in policy created an opportunity for various nationalist groups to attack the policy of cooperation with the Tribunal. Matters were brought to a head on 28 August by the murder in Gospić of Milan Levar. Levar had served as a witness to the Tribunal in 1997 concerning reports of mass executions of Serbs in his hometown—a Croat testifying against other Croats. The government was compelled to act, and initiated a wave of arrests of those accused of war crimes, including a number of military officers.

The result was public uproar led by sections of the Croatian Democratic Union (HDZ) and veterans' organizations offended by accusations directed against men who were considered to be war heroes. The governing coalition found its cohesion under threat, for a rift appeared to open also between Prime Minister Ivo Račan and President Mesić on this issue. A group of senior military officers sent an open letter of protest to the press agency HINA, claiming that the arrests were part of a politically motivated attempt to discredit the 1991–1995 Homeland War. On 28 September Mesić dismissed the seven generals who had led the protest, insisting that the army should be depoliticized. Although sometimes dismissed as originating with extreme nationalists, these views do seem to have resonated with the public generally.

Three events in particular presented a challenge to the new government's position, against which it has found it difficult to defend itself—the indictments against Generals Mirko Norac, Ante Gotovina and Rahim Ademi, and Janko Bobetko.

On 8 February 2001 a warrant was issued for the arrest of General Mirko Norac, whose name was linked to the disappearance of Serb civilians from the Gospić area. Norac went into hiding, and the announcement was followed by further demonstrations led by nationalist groups and organizations of veterans. Having received assurances that he would be tried in Croatia and not handed over to the ICTY, Norac surrendered to the police, and on 5 March was formally indicted in Rijeka, at which point Mirko Kondić, head of the largest of the veterans' organizations, condemned the charges as "shameful and humiliating," and demanded an amnesty for all Croatian veterans.[76]

The cases of Gotovina and Ademi were in some respects even more controversial. Initially the government had resisted the invitation to transfer them. Following a visit to Zagreb by Carla del Ponte, at a meeting on 7 July 2001 the cabinet agreed that the two should go to The Hague, upon which Dražen Budiša, leader of the HSLS, and three ministerial colleagues resigned from the coalition government, and Račan faced a motion of no confidence in the Sabor. He survived and on 17 July successfully piloted a statement of the government's general policy toward the ICTY through the Chamber.

Ademi surrendered himself to The Hague; Gotovina went into hiding. The outrage expressed by some sections of the public and among certain professional soldiers and politicians was directed principally against the indictment of Gotovina. The events cited in the indictment against Gotovina concerned the conduct of Operation Storm, which had resulted in the successful recapture of the secessionist Serb Krajina in August 1995. The very existence of the Krajina compromised Croatian statehood. So important was this that almost any action could be regarded (by some sections of public and official opinion) as justifiable if it led to the confirmation of Croatian statehood in this area. For nationalistic Croats the supreme importance of the end justified any means employed in its realization. To contemplate prosecuting Croatia's military heroes for war crimes was a direct challenge both to the legitimacy of the Homeland War and the dignity of the state itself.[77]

A potentially greater embarrassment for the government attended the issue of an indictment against the former Croatian chief of staff, the architect of Croatia's military strength, General Janko Bobetko, in September 2002. The continuing economic difficulties of the Račan government and the fragility of its coalition rendered it ever more sensitive to controversy. Opinion polls indicated the steady recovery of the popularity of the conservative nationalist HDZ.[78] Accordingly, a policy of temporizing was adopted, beginning with a challenge to the indictment in the Appeals Chamber of the ICTY itself. Britain and the Netherlands cancelled their ratification of the Stabilization and Association Agreement between the EU and Croatia, and it became clear that the prospect of entry to the EU was under threat.[79] An apparently irreconcilable confrontation between the ICTY and the Croatian government was averted by the failing health of the eighty-three-year-old general, who died in April 2003.

The Social-Democratic government under Račan was defeated in the elections of November 2003, and an alliance headed by the HDZ returned to power under Ivo Sanader. During its period in opposition the HDZ underwent a radical change of ideological orientation, accepting the necessity of confronting the war crimes issue and the importance of cooperating with the Tribunal. The subsequent normalization of relations between Zagreb and The Hague has been recognized to some extent by the willingness of the international agency to support the prosecution of some war crimes cases in Croatian courts. The war crimes issue has remained one of the central areas of debate within Croatian political life and during June 2005 negotiations over entry to the EU featured as one of the principal points of conditionality.

The acceptance of Croatian candidacy was followed on 7 December by the arrest of Gotovina in Spain and his subsequent transfer to The Hague.[80] The relative quiet with which this news was received in Croatia, even by nationalist parties, suggests that the consolidation of the secure status of the Croatian state and its growing integration into the framework of European states has reduced the sense of anxiety that formerly hung over challenges to the sanctity of the Homeland War and the threat these might be felt to pose to Croatian identity.

ii. Serbia and the ICTY

The initial response of the international community to the breakup of Yugoslavia—insisting upon the integrity of international boundaries—encouraged the Serbian leader Slobodan Milošević to believe that his attempt to ensure the integrity of Yugoslavia by military means would be supported. It was not difficult for the Yugoslav press to shrug off the formation of the ICTY in 1993 as an irrelevance. This situation had changed dramatically by 1995, however, when in August Operation Storm ejected Serb forces from the Krajina and triggered in Bosnia a joint Croat–Muslim offensive that was eventually to threaten Banja Luka. International ineffectiveness and inaction was transformed dramatically into effective military intervention in the form of NATO's Operation Deliberate Force in September. By the end of the year Milošević had been maneuvered into pressuring the Bosnian Serb leadership into reluctant acceptance of the Dayton settlement.

The Tribunal took its place, not surprisingly, in the picture of hostile international encirclement that the Serbian leadership created, partly in order to explain this military and political collapse. This depiction of the ICTY as deliberately and unremittingly anti-Serb has persisted and was intensified by the events of the Kosovo crisis (following the Serbian rejection of the Rambouillet Plan, and the NATO bombing campaign that ended in June 1999) and the ensuing transfer to The Hague of Slobodan Milošević in October 2000.

Resistance to the ICTY has had less to do in Serbia with defense of the state (as in Croatia), and a great deal to do with defense of the regime. Delegitimation of the tribunal in The Hague through manipulative news management became for the leadership of the Socialist Party of Serbia (SPS) both an urgent practical objective, as well as a central ideological one.

The state manipulation of imagery of the war in general, and of the role of the ICTY in particular, was easier to sustain in Serbia because war remained at a distance from the majority of the population. It was not until NATO intervention over Kosovo that, for the most part, the population of Serbia itself had any direct experience of the war. The insistent demands of the Office of the Prosecutor for cooperation, together with the continuing succession of indictments, trials, and sentences of ethnic Serbs, facilitated the diffusion of an atmosphere of paranoia through the state-controlled media of communication.[81] This approach to an explanation of Serb attitudes toward the ICTY, however, cannot be reduced to this single dimension.

With the ousting of Milošević on 5–6 October 2000, international opinion anticipated a marked change of stance by the new leadership of the Democratic Opposition of Serbia (DOS). It rapidly became clear, however, that this was not a revolution but a putsch replacing one set of leaders by another. The new ruling coalition was marked by extreme internal divisions. Vojislav Koštunica and Zoran Djindjić had little more in common than their desire to depose the SPS leadership. As in Croatia, therefore, the Serbian response to the ICTY became an internal political issue, although in a very different way.

The war in Serbia produced a mafia-style elite entrenched in a war economy.[82] The new economic bosses were bound up closely with the old political bosses to an extent not matched in Croatia. The new leadership inherited not only an assembly still dominated initially by the SPS but also an unchanged military leadership and a firmly entrenched stratum who occupied the top echelons of the economy, state administration, the judiciary, and to a lesser extent the communications media.[83] This stratum was, in many respects, resistant to the kind of transition that Serbia was expected to make, and elite resistance was intimately bound up with the ways in which war criminality was intertwined with a range of other features of Serbian society, including the military and the "informal economy." As a result of this internal resistance, compliance with the demands of the Tribunal generally has been secured only by the strenuous exercise of international diplomatic and economic leverage.

A spate of arrests and self-surrenders to the Tribunal followed a period of intensive diplomacy by the EU emissary, Javier Solana, beginning in November 2001. His central concern was the prospect of the further disintegration of Yugoslavia in the form of the secession of Montenegro. A deal was signed on 14 March 2002, following which a new basis for a confederal structure was agreed upon. International efforts to moderate Montenegrin demands for a fundamental restructuring of the union had been secured at a price—cooperation with the ICTY. Coincident with this constitutional agreement, the U.S. government named 31 March as the deadline for Serbian compliance with the ICTY indictments, threatening the loss of 150 million dollars in aid.[84]

Relations between the Serbian and federal governments in Yugoslavia, already seriously tested by the arrest and extradition of Milošević, were placed under enormous strain. Having been defeated twice in the federal assembly (in June 2001 and March 2002), a law was finally adopted making provision for the surrender of citizens to the ICTY.[85]

The situation changed following the assassination of Prime Minister Djindjić on 12 March 2003. It is generally accepted that Djindjić's willingness to cooperate with the ICTY was one of the reasons behind his murder by agents acting for one of the large criminal organizations. Djindjić's successor, Zoran Živković, set in motion an energetic campaign to clean out the Augean stable of Serbian political life. A large number of arrests were made, not only in direct connection with the assassination; a reform of the judiciary was announced; and measures were undertaken to hand over several high-profile indictees to The Hague. Under these circumstances, the persistent pressures from the international community to cooperate with the ICTY, might even sometimes have been counterproductive.[86]

The end of the Milošević era in Serbia has not seen the rapid advance of public acceptance of the ICTY, however, and the persistence of skepticism and even hostility toward the Tribunal clearly cannot be reduced to a matter of elite (and, in particular, media) manipulation. The persistent demands of the international community for compliance produced a response on the part of many Serbs at two levels. At the time of his extradition to The Hague, Milošević had been indicted already by Serbian courts on charges relating to his alleged economic misdemeanors. In light of the decade of economic hardship that ordinary Serbs suffered while he was in power, the intervention of The Hague was perceived not as the supervenience of a higher justice but as the setting aside of their proper grievances in favor of some distant interest and more abstract ideal.

Serb perceptions that their needs for justice were marginalized in this process resonate at a deeper level. Croats see Europe as playing an important part in their ideological self-definition. For Serbs, however, Europe does not play this positive role, and whereas at one level Serbian culture is profoundly European, the relationship to Europe is shot through with an ambivalence that mingles xenophobia and resentment.[87]

Although public opinion in Serbia gradually has come to accept that there are issues relating to war crimes that need to be addressed, Serbs often feel themselves encircled by an unsympathetic and even hostile environment. Bearing in mind the enormous psychological shock of the NATO bombing campaign of 1999, it is possible to understand how it is that the ICTY took its place as one element in this picture of national isolation and exclusion. This rather paranoid image of the world cannot be reduced to the factor of elite manipulation alone but can be seen to be rooted also in far older and more complex strata of identity formation.

iii. Bosnia-Hercegovina

The experience of war in Bosnia-Hercegovina was markedly different from that of the other republics of the former Yugoslavia in two respects. Fighting touched directly the greater part of its population and territory, and the commission of war crimes was, to a greater or lesser extent, a key component of the strategy of contending forces rather than a set of incidental occurrences.

Not until the Kosovo campaign did the war directly affect the inhabitants of Serbia. Similarly, military action did not spread across the entirety of Croatia, although roughly a third of its territory was the subject of the attempted secession by its ethnic Serb population. Armed conflict was contained and stabilized with the acceptance of the Vance Plan, and the arrival of UNPROFOR in early 1992. In Bosnia-Hercegovina, on the other hand, there can have been very little of the territory and very few of its inhabitants upon whom the war did not directly impinge in one way or another. There were ethnic minorities present in every municipality of Bosnia-Hercegovina, so that at the very least, however relatively homogeneous their populations, they became the sites of ethnic cleansing.

An equally important characteristic of Bosnian experience is the fact that war crimes were not incidental to the action but intrinsic to and definitive of it. The commission of war crimes became in Bosnia-Hercegovina a primary aim of war and one of the principal means of achieving that aim. Only in this republic did one find created a network of detention camps designed as instruments for the relocation of populations, which became the sites for the commission of a succession of barbarities against those detained there.[88] For these reasons the character of the responses of the people of the region to the war crimes process in The Hague has also been different.

In general, the communications media in Bosnia have devoted greater attention than elsewhere to war crimes issues, and Bosnians have had more information about the ICTY and its operation available to them than have the citizens of other post-Yugoslav states. Nevertheless, it is probably true to say that within Bosnia opinion about the value and significance of the Tribunal is more sharply divided than elsewhere, particularly with respect to the difference between the federation and the Republika Srpska.[89]

An additional factor that has defined the nature of both the war and the following peace from Bosnia's point of view has been the role of international actors. In particular, it is necessary to appreciate the character and significance of the Dayton Agreements, which brought fighting in the republic to an end in November–December 1995. These provided an internationally sanctioned framework backed by military force, which has been upheld vigorously by all international actors involved in the region in the face of every indication that their role can be at best a temporary one and anticipating the construction of a more permanent constitution.

Reading the agreements, it becomes clear that the pursuit and punishment of war criminals was not a central concern of those who drafted and signed them. The General Framework Agreement does commit the parties (in Article IX) to "cooperate in the investigation and prosecution of war crimes and other violations of international humanitarian law." Similarly, Annex 6 (the Agreement on Human Rights) commits the parties to respect the measures in international law listed in the appendix, which covers comprehensively the legal foundation of the work of the ICTY. Article XIII, paragraph 4, of Annex 6 also records that "All competent authorities in Bosnia and Herzegovina shall cooperate with and provide unrestricted access to the organizations established in this Agreement," citing explicitly among these the ICTY. The Dayton settlement is almost entirely lacking, however, in providing for the enforcement of these provisions.

The key to the operation of the Dayton constitution in Bosnia is the position of the high representative (HR), whose powers and functions are detailed in Annex 10. The office of the HR is mandated to "monitor the implementation of the peace settlement" in general and to coordinate the activities of the various agencies set up under the agreements. Article II (9), however, notes that "The High Representative shall have no authority over the IFOR and shall not in any way interfere in the conduct of military operations." Although the International Police Task Force is directly responsible to the HR for its operation, it is not expressly mandated to undertake the pursuit and arrest of indicted war crimes suspects.

As a consequence of the imposition of the Dayton settlement by external agents, and the fact that questions continue to hang over both its durability and its legitimacy, the essential character of Bosnian society and a Bosnian state are permanently in question. Because of the acute sensitivity of any challenge to it, however, and the difficulty of finding a route toward an acceptable alternative, it is impossible to advocate any major constitutional change in Bosnia with any chance of success. To challenge accounts of what has happened in the past and attempt a dispassionate scrutiny of the route by which things came to be as they are, it is necessary to ask awkward questions about the role of powerful international agents and by implication to suggest that the Dayton settlement might have been contingent rather than necessary. Consequently, as Zlatko Hadžidedić expresses it graphically, "Bosnia now = no future/no past."[90] The Bosnia created by Dayton is founded upon the "ethnoterritorialization" of the republic—its division into entities and cantons based upon "the idea of an ethnic group's 'ownership' over an entire territory and its resources."[91] All questions about the past and the future of Bosnia, therefore, come to be refracted through the prism of definitions derived from this pattern of ethnic ownership of territories. By creating a rigid structure of oligarchic ethnocracy, the legacy of Dayton has been the blockage of the process of the normalization of Bosnian society in the postwar period.

Despite the fact that the Tribunal in The Hague is often justified in terms of its potential for enabling people to come to terms with their past, and thereby to move unburdened by it into their future, in Bosnia the ICTY is inescapably implicated in patterns and processes that encumber any consideration of the past or future with ideology and frustrate the possibility of recreating normal society.

Because so much of the fabric of life in the republic is bound up with an order imposed by the international community, there has emerged a tendency to see all forms of external intervention in Bosnian life as parts of a single tissue. The sense of stasis, blockage, and artificiality that has come to infuse all aspects of public life, emanating from the Dayton institutions, is diffused subjectively to all international agents. As a result, perceptions of the ICTY cannot be insulated from the prevailing mood of resignation and cynicism reflected in the responses of many in our focus group study.

These aspects of Bosnian life are clearly reflected in the pattern of cooperation or noncooperation between different local groups and organizations and the

ICTY. Although the government of Bosnia-Hercegovina recognized and agreed to cooperate with the Tribunal from the outset, the authorities within the two entities have not been distinguished by their eagerness to support its work. This has been the case particularly with the Republika Srpska, where it has not been difficult for the former leader of the Serbian Democratic Party, Radovan Karadžić, to continue to evade attempts to find and detain him. The RS has come to be regarded as a safe haven for ethnic Serbs under indictment, and Bosnian Serb politicians continue to maintain a public facade of denial. Ethnic Croats tend to be divided in their attitudes, with the uniformly Croat areas of western Hercegovina adjacent to the border with Croatia adhering to strongly separatist views and deeply suspicious of the Tribunal, and the more dispersed and ethnically mixed communities of central Bosnia and the Posavina inclined to favor the perpetuation of an ethnically diverse Bosnia and to view the ICTY with greater sympathy. In contrast, the Bošnjak parties and other groups committed to the integrity of a united Bosnia, such as the Social Democrats, have broadly given their support to the ICTY.

The situation is complicated, to some extent, by the power of the Office of the High Representative (OHR). Because the HR needs to consider the efficacy of his intervention across the entire range of issues that concern him, he is naturally likely to optimize the use of the resources available.[92] In other words, he is not able to secure simultaneously all of the outcomes that might appear to be desirable at any one time. Refraining from putting his entire weight behind the investigations of the ICTY under these circumstances can appear to be rational where doing so might allow room for maneuver in pursuit of other political goals.

Military commanders also can, and do, point out that their duties extend well beyond support for the ICTY and that they are operating with limited resources. What is more, it is appropriate for them to consider the circumstances under which they are prepared to expose their personnel to danger, and several arrests have involved the exchange of gunfire with those they have pursued. There has been confusion over the interpretation of the responsibilities of military commanders and, hence, lack of consistency in their conduct.

A good deal of the cynicism with which many Bosnians regard the ICTY has to do with the frequency with which individuals known to have been implicated in war crimes remain free to live their lives with impunity within Bosnia—either because the Tribunal has determined that their actions were not of sufficient seriousness to merit indictment or because the evidence does not appear to be sufficiently strong. Alternatively, the actions they committed may have fallen short of the level of seriousness that could expose them to retribution through the ICTY. Justifiably and understandably or not, there are gaps between indictments issued and arrests achieved and between perceptions of responsibility or guilt and liability for punishment. These perceived discrepancies between what might have been expected of the international presence in Bosnia and its actions are commonly seen as contributing to the prevailing cynicism about the international community and work together to reinforce the sense of disillusionment with which the Tribunal is generally regarded.

It is important to separate questions relating to legal (or moral) responsibility for the outbreak of war (*jus ad bellum*) from those relating to responsibility for conduct during war (*jus in bello*). The Tribunal in The Hague is mandated to deal with questions of the latter kind but not of the former. In the minds of many people in the Balkans, especially in Bosnia and particularly when viewed from a moral as well as a legal point of view, these two types of questions tend to merge. Because of the nature of the circumstances surrounding the extension of war into Bosnia there is a powerful sense of the extent to which the international community must be held to account for its share of responsibility for war, even if not for its conduct. These two types of questions, though separated in legal thinking in this area, are fused in popular understanding.

VI. Summary and Conclusions

This report has inevitably drawn attention to points on which the International Criminal Tribunal for the former Yugoslavia might be regarded as open to criticism. It would be a mistake to conclude without recognizing that the Tribunal has much to its credit. The team would not wish the critical points made here to distract from its positive achievements in bringing justice to the region and a measure of truth to the understanding of its recent past.

The wider importance of the Tribunal has yet to be determined, but it will certainly find an important place in the overall narrative of the development of international humanitarian law. We noted in our account of the foundation of the ICTY that international concerns with security and stability were in the forefront of the minds of international actors. Peace ranked as the primary goal, whereas justice was perceived as generally secondary and instrumental. Kerr asks whether it might be the case that the ICTY has actually succeeded "to elevate the status of justice in relation to order," and not simply within its original Balkan context.[93]

The conclusion to which our group has come is that there is no evidence of systematic bias—certainly not of deliberate bias—on the part of the ICTY against any of the ethnic groups in the former Yugoslavia. This is hardly a surprising conclusion because the scholarly literature available at the time of the launch of our project did not lead us to expect that we would find such evidence. We have confirmed, nevertheless, that the perception of bias is both persistent and widespread (although diminishing over time, to be replaced in some cases by cynicism and indifference), and we believe that this perception needs to be taken seriously. In the course of our investigation several things have become clear that help to make intelligible that apparent contradiction.

First of all, the absence of deliberate partiality on the part of the Tribunal does not mean that it is free from faults that are conducive to the attribution of one-sidedness. It was created primarily to promote peace and stability in the Balkans and to implement a body of international law. These requirements were principally for internationally recognizable professional standards and mutually acceptable compromises between different judicial traditions. None of these factors took account centrally of the perceptions of, and needs for, justice held by people in the ex-Yugoslav states.

The pursuit of justice through the Tribunal had to be framed in relation to specific constraints of resources, time, and political will. Resort to the Tribunal became a sanction that could be deployed in order to further ends other than justice. Since its creation, the Tribunal has added to its original purposes an ever-growing range of expectations that no court of justice could ever be expected to meet. It has been burdened with the tasks of creating a historical record of events; "healing the wounds of war"; "lifting the burden of collective guilt"; paving the way to reconciliation; and deterring future violators. The primary goals of the institution, however, have been the search for justice and for truth.

Despite the fact that those of the team (and others) who have had direct contact with the ICTY have paid tribute to the hard work, dedication, and professionalism of its staff, the constraints under which they have been recruited, as well as the conditions under which they work, do reveal differences in their degree of competence. Errors of judgment, however, do not equate to deliberate bias, even if they might contribute to perceptions of unfairness.

These critical remarks certainly do not identify the ICTY as a failure or seriously challenge its legitimacy. It has constituted an important development in the field of international justice and one that has probably made a significant contribution to transitional justice, as well as to its original purpose of furthering peace and stability in the region. Nevertheless, the orientation that it has adopted toward global actors and the global criteria of its success have resulted in its presenting, to some extent, a blank facade toward the very region that might have been presumed to be its most important constituency—the peoples of the former Yugoslavia. In retrospect, perhaps, it can even be said to have been seriously negligent in its failure to address this audience.

On this condition of blankness and relative unintelligibility, it has been possible to project a variety of different interpretations of its character and purposes.

These have varied among the states emergent in the Yugoslav space, dependent upon their different political processes and culture. The ICTY has come to be inserted in contrasting ways into local political processes, meeting responses that in many ways were quite dissimilar and following divergent trajectories. In Croatia, although the ICTY was at first experienced as a direct threat to Croatia's newly realized independent statehood, the growing security of its situation worked together with the sustained pressure of international agents to promote a fairly general acceptance of the importance of the work of the Tribunal—especially among its political elite. In Serbia, on the other hand, the manner in which political and military elites became enmeshed with a culture of violence and criminality worked together with aspects of the country's economic deprivation and its historical culture to deepen the widespread conviction that the ICTY was only one component of an international environment that was hostile to Serbs and Serbia. Public opinion studies show that the modification of these antagonistic perceptions of the Tribunal there has been far slower and is more incomplete. In Bosnia-Hercegovina the structure of ethnic oligarchies created by war has been sustained by the action of international agents, with which the ICTY is grouped in public perceptions. Here attitudes toward The Hague are inseparable from the general sense of alienation that pervades other aspects of Bosnian political culture.

Despite these differences, it has been possible to identify some uniformities in local responses to the ICTY. Aspirations that it might provide anything like a complete account of the experience of war have not been met—and for pragmatic reasons, cannot be. The hope that it might promote reconciliation between the peoples of the region does not appear to have been realized. Reconciliation, if it is to be achieved, is an immense task that will clearly require more than judicial intervention and will extend well beyond the lifetime of the ICTY. The demand that the Tribunal should furnish a reckoning of the moral responsibility for the war has been deliberately set aside. It is not because the ICTY has been a bad court of law that it has failed to deliver a sense of realized justice in these areas—it is precisely because it is a court of law and for that very reason is unable to address these questions.

Caution should be exercised, however, in the extent to which criticism of the ICTY should be reduced to the status of the proprietary myths of nationalist politicians and thereby dismissed. There is a danger that a desire to support the legitimacy of the Tribunal could lapse into a kind of orientalism. In North America, and in a Europe intent upon expansion of the Union, there is a tendency to disparage all concerns over national identity as irredeemably nonmodern. Such negativity is frequently implicit in the judgment of nationalism. The search for national identities and an understanding of their significance is an understandable element of cultural development throughout the Balkan region (as elsewhere). It is not always easy to judge which aspects of this process might be malevolent and to what extent.

The penetration into the Yugoslav space of global judicial institutions (which in any case are of relatively recent creation, and poorly understood anywhere) is naturally and necessarily problematic. If the Scholars' Initiative has a role to play in relation to these events, it must go beyond an aspiration merely to debunk local mythologies and embrace the task of furthering a more objective general understanding of changes that affect us all.

Notes

1   For a fuller recognition of the issues, see appendix 1 of the original report.
2   Scholars' Initiative, Prospectus, 3.
3   *Orientalism* here is used in the sense developed by Edward Said in his book of that title. Edward Said, *Orientalism* (London: Routledge and Kegan Paul, 1978).
4   The need for brevity also dictates a minimal use of footnotes on this occasion. Only works directly cited in the text, or centrally relevant to it, are singled out for mention here. A comprehensive bibliography on the ICTY would already require a text at least as long as this chapter.
5   Michael J. Scharf, *Balkan Justice: The Story Behind the First International War Crimes Trial since Nuremberg* (Durham, NC: Carolina Academic Press, 1997). The verdict on Tadić had only been delivered in May of the year of publication, and the role of this book was primarily to acquaint the public with how the ICTY worked rather than to provide a critical analysis or evaluation. See also Virginia Morris and Michael P. Scharf, *An Insider's Guide to the ICTY* (Irvington on Hudson, NY: Transnational Publishers, 1995). Also available at that time was Roger S. Clark and Madeleine Sann, eds., *The Prosecution of International Crimes: A Critical Study of the International Criminal Tribunal for the Former Yugoslavia* (New Brunswick and London: Transaction Publishers, 1996). Gary J. Bass, *Stay the Hand of Vengeance: The Politics of War Crimes Tribunals* (Princeton, NJ: Princeton University Press, 2000). In French, Pierre Hazan, *La justice face à la guerre: de Nuremberg à La Haye* (Paris: Stock, 2000); Jean-Paul Bazelaire and Thierry Cretin, *La justice pénale internationale* (Paris: Presses Universitaires de France, 2000). See also Karine Lescure, *Le Tribunal pénal international pour L'Ex-Yougoslavie* (Paris: Monchrestien, Centre de Droit International de Paris I, No. 6, 1994). In the German scholarly literature, see Herwig Roggemann, *Der Internationale Strafgerichtshof der UN von 1993 und der Krieg auf dem Balkan* (Berlin: Arno Spitz 1994). The Krstić trial had been treated in a collection of documents edited by Caroline Fetscher and Julija Bogojeva, *Srebrenica: eine Prozess* (Frankfurt am Main: Suhrkamp Verlag, 2002).
6   A flavor of this extensive literature can be gained from Belinda Cooper, ed., *War Crimes: The Legacy of Nuremberg* (New York: TV Books, 1999); Timothy D. Mak, "The Case against the International War Crimes Tribunal for the Former Yugoslavia," *International Peacekeeping* 2, no. 4 (Winter 1995), 536–563. Other influential voices were those of Geoffrey Robertson, *Crimes against Humanity: The Struggle for Global*

Justice (London: Penguin Books, 1999), and Payam Akhavan, "Justice in The Hague: Peace in the Former Yugoslavia," *Human Rights Quarterly* 20 (737–816), 1998. Representing contrasting approaches and points of view see Aleksandar Jokić, ed., *War Crimes and Collective Wrongdoing: A Reader* (Oxford: Blackwell, 2001); Mark J. Osiel, "Why Prosecute? Critics of Punishment for Mass Atrocity," *Human Rights Quarterly* 22 (2000), 118–147; Antonia Cassese and Mireille Delmas-Marty, eds., *Crimes internationaux et juridictions internationaies* (Paris: Presses Universitaires de France, 2002). The question of bias was not actively pursued despite recognition that it is possible to examine the political dimension of the Tribunal's creation and functioning. See Y. Beigbeder, *Judging War Criminals: The Politics of International Justice* (London and New York: Macmillan, 1999).

7 Aryeh Neier, *War Crimes: Brutality, Genocide, Terror, and the Struggle for Justice* (New York: Times Books, 1998).

8 R. Goldstone, *Prosecuting War Criminals* (London: David Davies Memorial Institute of International Studies, no. 21, 1996); Richard Goldstone, *For Humanity: Reflections of a War Crimes Investigator* (New Haven, CT, and London: Yale University Press, 2000).

9 The following specialists, whose work would have been available to those attending the Sarajevo meeting of the Scholars' Initiative in 2002, at least mention the work of the ICTY in passing. Susan Woodward, *Balkan Tragedy: Chaos and Dissolution after the Cold War* (Washington, DC: Brookings Institution, 1995), 322–323; Carole Rogel, *The Breakup of Yugoslavia and the War in Bosnia* (Westport, CT, and London: Greenwood Press, 1998), 65, 72–73; John B. Allcock, *Explaining Yugoslavia* (London: Hurst, 2000), 440; Aleksandar Pavković, *The Fragmentation of Yugoslavia: Nationalism and War in the Balkans* (London: Macmillan, 2000), 172–173, 180. It is remarkable how many experienced commentators on the region at that time made no mention at all of the Tribunal and its work. Particularly noteworthy in this respect, in view of its explicit concern with issues relating to international intervention in Yugoslavia, is Richard H. Ullman, *The World and Yugoslavia's Wars* (New York: Council on Foreign Relations, 1996).

10 Regrettably, Rachel Kerr's extensive study of the Tribunal has come to hand too late for her work to be considered in our report. Rachel Kerr, *The International Criminal Tribunal for the former Yugoslavia: A Study in Law, Politics, and Diplomacy* (Oxford: Oxford University Press, 2004).

11 The original 147-page report included five main sections and seven appendices. Radical abbreviation has been necessary in the preparation of this summary.

12 Pascal Boniface, ed., *Morale et relations internationales* (Paris: Institut de relations internationals et stratégique, and Presses Universitaires de France, 2000).

13 M. Cherif Bassiouni, "The Normative Framework of International Humanitarian Law," in Michael N. Schmidt, ed. *International Law Across the Spectrum of Conflict. Essays in Honour of Prof. L.C. Green on the Occasion of his Eightieth Birthday* (Newport, RI: Naval War College, 2000), 1–55, esp. 3.

14 The League of Nations also took the first steps toward the international protection of refugees with the creation of the office of Commissioner for Refugees in 1921. This became the Intergovernmental Committee on Refugees in 1938.

15 The interwar period also saw the adoption of The Hague Rules on Aerial Warfare in 1923 and the Geneva Protocol prohibiting the use of poisonous gas and bacteriological agents in 1925. In 1927 the Kellogg–Briand Pact between the U.S. and France was ad-

opted by the Assembly of the League of Nations and subsequently ratified by forty-two states. This may be taken as an early effort to identify a crime of aggression, which still evades international consensus.

16   A useful general review of these developments for the reader who is not a legal specialist is provided by Robertson, *Crimes against Humanity*, esp. chapters 5, 6, and 7. Detailed discussions of the work of the Nuremberg and Tokyo Tribunals are provided in chapters 2 and 3 of Beigbeder, *Judging War Criminals*.

17   For a broad assessment of the significance of the Nuremberg Tribunal, see Cooper, *War Crimes*.

18   Malcolm N. Shaw, *International Law* (Cambridge: Cambridge University Press, 1997*)*, 185. The statutes of the Nuremberg and Tokyo Tribunals are reprinted in Bazelaire and Cretin, *La Justice*, appendices 2 and 3.

19   Goldstone, *For Humanity,* 75.

20   Robertson, *Crimes against Humanity*, 237–242.

21   Convention on the Prevention and Punishment of the Crime of Genocide, Article I. See Adam Roberts and Richard Guelff, eds., *Documents of the Laws of War*, 3rd ed. (Oxford: Clarendon Press, 2000).

22   Martti Koskenniemi argues that such was the magnitude of the shift in its character at this time that it is possible to speak of the "fall of international law" (following its "rise" in the last quarter of the nineteenth century). See, Martti Koskenniemi, *The Gentle Civilizer of Nations: The Rise and Fall of International Law, 1870–1960* (Cambridge: Cambridge University Press, 2002), especially his discussion of the work of Hans Morgenthau.

23   Diane F. Orentlicher, "Internationalizing Civil War," in Cooper, *War Crimes*, 107–112. See also Peter Maguire, "Nuremberg: A Cold War Conflict of Interest," in Cooper, *War Crimes*, (67–86); Jörg Friedrich, "Nuremberg and the Germans" in Cooper, *War Crimes*, (87–106); and Thierry Tardy, *La France et la gestion des conflits yougoslaves (1991–1995). Enjeux et leçons d'une operation de maintien de la paix de l'ONU* (Bruxelles: Bruylant, 1999), xxi–xxii. The wider significance of this context is also stressed by Renéo Lukic, *L'Agonie Yougoslave (1986-2003). Les États-Unis et l'Europe face aux guerres balkaniques*, chapter 1 (Quebec: Les Presses de l'Université Laval, 2003).

24   See the discussion of these issues in Steve Terrett, *The Dissolution of Yugoslavia and the Badinter Arbitration Commission*, chapter 3 (Dartmouth, MA: Ashgate, 2000). Perhaps it is not surprising that in this context attention should have been focused with respect to matters of international law upon questions having to do with secession and the recognition of states as members of that order.

25   See Terrett, *Dissolution of Yugoslavia*, chapter 4.

26   Foreign Affairs Committee of the House of Commons, *Central and Eastern Europe: Problems of the Post-Communist Era*, vol. 2 (London: HMSO, February 1992)*,* 18.

27   David Binder has remarked that the phrase "United States policy towards Yugoslavia" at this time was "a widely noted oxymoron." David Binder, "Thoughts on United States Policy Towards Yugoslavia," *South Slav Journal* 16, no. 3–4 (1995), 1.

28   The foreign minister of Luxembourg proclaimed it "the hour of Europe." Quoted by David C. Gompert, "The United States and Yugoslavia's Wars," in *The World and Yugoslavia's Wars*, ed. Richard H. Ullman (New York: Council on Foreign Relations, 1996), 127.

29 This abbreviated summary of events might be supplemented by a reader of the rather fuller coverage provided by chapters 1, "The Dissolution of Yugoslavia," and 5, "The International Community and the FRY Belligerents, 1989–1997" of this volume.

30 Kaplan's book is widely credited as a major baneful influence in popularizing this view. See Robert Kaplan, *Balkan Ghosts* (New York: St. Martin's Press, 1993). It should be recognized, however, that these ideas were both in circulation well before the appearance of his book and, if anything, held in a more extreme form by others. In particular, several books by Stjepan G. Meštrović, in which he set out to revive and popularize the ideas of Dinko Tomasić, examining the consequences of the existence of supposedly antithetical character types among the Balkan peoples, attracted wide attention. Even a historian as respectable as Mark Wheeler referred (in 1992) to events in the Balkans at this time as "tribal madness"! Foreign Affairs Committee, *Central and Eastern Europe*, vol. 2, 77. In France, the venerable Marxist historian Étienne Balibar delivered himself of the following extraordinary opinion (also in 1992). "'Croates,' 'Serbes' et 'Mussulmans' ne sont, à coup sûr, ni des nations ni des religions. Pour leur malheur ils sont beaucoup plus: des incarnations volontaires ou involontaires de civilisations 'inconciliables,' et ils sont beaucoup moins: de simples solidarities claniques, resurgissant comme l'ultime recours contre le ravage des identités politiques de la "modernité.' En réalité, je ne vois qu'*un seul nom* qui leur convienne exactement, *ce sont des races* (entendons par là des racisms réciproques)." Cited in Lukic, *L'Agonie Yougoslave*, 18. Presumably their status as specific "races" called into question their relation to the human race.

31 Foreign Affairs Committee, *Central and Eastern Europe*, vol. 2, 98–99. The phrase is also used (apparently without irony) by Richard Ullman, *The World and Yugoslavia's Wars*, 20–22.

32 The original report considered these issues to be of such significance that, in addition to discussion in the main body of the text, a special appendix written by Richard Oloffson considered them further.

33 Ullman, *The World and Yugoslavia's Wars*, 30. This section of our report relies heavily upon Ullman's discussion, 27–31.

34 Tardy, *La France et la gestion des conflits yougoslave*, 39–41.

35 Aryeh Neier, *War Crimes: Brutality, Genocide, Terror, and the Struggle for Justice* (New York: Times Books, 1998), 126. See also Antoine Garapon, *Des Crimes qu'on ne peut ni punir ni pardoner: pour une justice internationale* (Paris: Odile Jacob, 2002), 30.

36 Lukic, *L'Agonie Yougoslave*, 7; M. Cherif Bassiouni, *The Commission of Experts Established Pursuant to Security Council Resolution 780: Investigating Violations of International Humanitarian Law in the Former Yugoslavia* (Chicago: International Human Rights Law Institute of De Paul University), Occasional Paper 2 (1996). *The Commission of Experts*, 29.

37 Helsinki Watch, *War Crimes in Bosnia-Hercegovina* (New York and London: Human Rights Watch, 1992). On the significance of this report, see Neier, *War Crimes*, 120–123. Neier was the founder, and at that time the director, of Human Rights Watch. A crucial factor motivating the organization to take up the Yugoslav question was the possibility of putting to the test legislation relating to genocide. An earlier report published in June by a Bosnian NGO was perhaps significant in drawing attention to the problem, although it had less public impact than did the Helsinki report. See Le Nouvel

Observateur et Raporter sans frontiers, *Le Livre Noir de l'Ex-Yougoslavie* (Paris: Arléa, 1993), 1–25. (Bass also deals with this, as does Hazan.)

38 *Livre Noir*, 181–197.

39 *Livre Noir*, 199–233.

40 A detailed account of the creation and operation of the commission is given by M. Cherif Bassiouni, *Commission of Experts.* See also Hazan, *La Justice face à la guerre*, 48–49. There are some minor discrepancies between these two accounts. We have relied heavily upon Bassiouni (a former chair of the commission) in this section. The idea of a tribunal was first aired by Mirko Klarin in an article in *Borba* (16 January 1991). See also the interview with Klarin by Zlatko Dizdarević, "Mirko Klarin, novinar koji je inicirao Nürnberg," *Arhiv Dani,* (1 December 2000), 183.

41 *Livre Noir*, 285–295, 261–302. See also, Beigbeder, *Judging War Criminals*, 147–148.

42 *Livre Noir*, 235–278. Resigning from his position as head of UNPROFOR in August 1992, General Lewis MacKenzie returned to Canada. It has been suggested that his pressure upon the Canadian government (and the publication of his memoirs) was an important factor in promoting Canadian support for the creation of the ICTY at this time. See James Gow, *The Triumph of the Lack of Will: International Diplomacy and the Yugoslav War* (London: Hurst & Co., 1997), 96.

43 We are grateful to Selma Leydesdorff for providing an English summary of Cees Banning and Petra de Koning, *Balkan aan de Noordzee, Over het Joegoslavie-tibunaal, over recht en onrecht* (Amsterdam: Prometheus-NRC Handelsblad, 2005), which has been useful in the preparation of this section of the report.

44 Bassiouni, *Commission of Experts*, 4–7; also Garapon, *Des Crimes qu'on ne peut ni punir ni pardoner*, 31.

45 All resolutions of the Security Council can be seen on the UN Web site, www.un.org.

46 Bassiouni, *Commission of Experts*, 7–8. For a wider consideration of the possible incompatibility between the diplomatic pursuit of peace and a concern for justice, see Jean E. Manas, "The Impossible Trade-Off: 'Peace' versus 'Justice' in Settling Yugoslavia's Wars," in Ullman, *World and Yugoslavia's Wars*, 42–58. The tension over this issue is also noted by Richard Holbrooke in his memoirs. Richard Holbrooke, *To End a War* (New York: The Modern Library, 1999), 107–108 and 332–333.

47 Bassiouni, *Commission of Experts*, 8–11, esp. fn25.

48 The following information draws heavily upon the ICTY Web site, www.un.org/icty, although the statute of the Tribunal has been widely reprinted.

49 See Diane F. Orentlicher, "Internationalizing Civil War," in Cooper, *War Crimes*, 154–158.

50 Julie Mertus dealt with this issue extensively in appendix 6 of our original report. See also, Patricia Viseur-Sellars, "Rape under International Law," in Cooper, *War Crimes*, 159–167.

51 Statute of the ICTY, Article 15. The rules of procedure and evidence are also available on the ICTY Web site, although they are not examined here.

52 See Scharf, *Balkan Justice*, 64–65. Although Cherif Bassiouni had been responsible for a great deal of the preparatory work in setting up the ICTY, he was not accepted as its first prosecutor, and the grounds for that appear to have included his Egyptian origins, which were assumed by some to make him partial to the Muslim cause. See Edina Bećirević, *International Criminal Court: Between Ideals and Reality* (Sarajevo: Arka Press, 2003), 175–177.

53 It is clear from the film *Justice Unseen* that sentencing issues are highly contentious not only among lay observers of The Hague but also among its legal personnel. The experienced Tribunal journalist Emir Suljagić comments that "sentencing policy does not exist."

54 JudgeWolfgang Schomburg, interviewed for *Justice Unseen*, remarks that: "Truth can't be found in a plea agreement." Former Chief Prosecutor Louise Arbour also comments in the same film on the contentious nature of plea bargaining.

55 See the discussion of the outreach program below for further treatment of this issue. Note that the agreement of the accused to cooperate with the Tribunal has resulted in release from custody pending trial but not in a reduction of sentence from those offenses for which a guilty verdict is subsequently returned. This issue was especially controversial in the case of Biljana Plavšić.

56 Rachel Kerr, "International Judicial Intervention: The International Criminal Tribunal for the Former Yugoslavia," *International Relations*, 15 (2) 2000, 24.

57 The film was produced by ICTY for publicity purposes and is available for viewing online at http://www.un.org/icty/bhs/outreach/outreach_info.htm. It is available in all of the languages of the Tribunal. A good deal of the comment in this section draws also upon interviews for *Justice Unseen*. See also, Vojin Dimitrijević, "The 'Public Relations' Problems of International Criminal Courts," unpublished typescript.

58 The most important early efforts to provide an authoritative and balanced treatment of ICTY include Vladan Vasiljević, *Medjunarodni krivični tribunal* (Belgrade: Biblioteka prava čoveka, 1996), and Edina Bećirević, *Medjunarodni krivični sud: Izmedju ideala i stvarnosti* (Sarajevo: Arka, 2003). Refik Hodžić, who directed *Justice Unseen*, formerly worked for the Outreach Department.

59 Its Web site can be consulted at www.iwpr.net.

60 Article 29 of the Tribunal's statute enjoins all states to cooperate with it in arrests or detentions. Whether or not they do so, and the circumstances under which they comply with the terms of Article 29, are not under the control of the prosecutor.

61 The group has been assisted in this area by Majbrit Lyck, a doctoral candidate at the University of Bradford.

62 Slightly over half of the remainder have been against ethnic Croats, with the remainder divided between Kosovar Albanians, Bošnjaci, and Macedonians. These figures should be treated with considerable caution for several reasons. The ICTY documents carefully refrain from identifying the ethnicity of those indicted, and it cannot be guaranteed that this is always evident from the context. Some individuals have been acquitted when brought to trial, and some indictments have been abandoned on revision. It might well be possible to produce more refined figures after very careful cross-checking, but at the time of writing we have not been able to undertake this. Because broad comparisons are sufficient to make the point in this context, however, and little would be added by an attempt at refined statistical analysis, it seems to be acceptable to leave the matter at this stage.

63 Information from Mirsad Tokača, director of the center. His estimate is that the final total will approach 100,000, including both military and civilian casualties.

64 Hugh Griffiths, "Bosnia: War Crimes Lottery," *Balkan Crisis Report* 544 (March 2005), 4. Somewhere in the region of 9,000 criminal acts that could possibly be prosecuted under the terms of the ICTY's statute have been identified during the war in Bosnia alone. *Justice Unseen*. This issue features prominently in the film.

65   Michael Humphrey, "The International Prosecution of Atrocity and National Reconciliation: The ICTY and ICTR Compared," paper presented to the conference *Law and Justice under Fire: The Legal Lessons of the Yugoslav Wars*, Inter-University Center, Dubrovnik, June 2001, 7–8.

66   General problems that attach to the notion of command responsibility cannot be addressed here. See Ilias Banketas, "The Contemporary Law of Superior Responsibility," *American Journal of International Law* 93, no. 3 (July 1999), 573–595..

67   For some insight into the substantial controversy that raged over the use of depleted uranium munitions see *The Health Hazards of Depleted Uranium Munitions*, 2 parts (London: The Royal Society, 2001 and 2002). Also the *Regional Environmental Report of the EC*, Center for Central and Eastern Europe, July 1999.

68   Information at this point has been supplied in interviews and correspondence with current and former ICTY personnel.

69   Because of the importance of these issues the greater part of the original report was devoted to them. Three preliminary papers were written in this area, and in addition to a lengthy section of the main report, two appendices (by Mikloš Biro and Eric Gordy) examined aspects of public opinion in the region toward the ICTY. We also commissioned a small focus group study (summarized by Julie Mertus) in order to probe further some patterns that seemed to emerge. Because of the extensive nature of this material it has certainly undergone the most radical compression in the preparation of this overview of our work.

70   For a discussion of rejectionist approaches to crimes and legal rules, see Vojin Dimitrijević, "Two Assumptions of the Rejection of Responsibility: Denial of the Act and Denial of the Rule," *SSRC Global Security and Cooperation Quarterly*, no. 8 (Spring 2003). The article is available online at http://www.ssrc.org/programs/gsc/gsc_quarterly/newsletter8/.

71   Victor Peskin and Mieczysław P. Boduszyński, "International Justice and Domestic Politics: Post-Tudjman Croatia and the International Criminal Tribunal for the Former Yugoslavia," *Europe-Asia Studies* 55, no. 7 (2003), 1117–1142. See esp. 1117. The analysis offered in the following section is complemented in many respects by that of Peskin and Boduszyński (although this research was completed before the publication of their paper).

72   The discussions between Tudjman and Milošević at Karadjordjevo on the subject of the partition of Bosnia and subsequent negotiations in Graz have been well documented and are no longer regarded as contentious. What is still a matter of dispute, however, is the extent of the aspirations of the HDZ in this direction, particularly in the early days of the war.

73   The Blaskić trial ran from 24 June 1997, ending on 30 July 1999, and the Kordić trial from 12 April 1999, ending in February 2001. Details of all indictments, trials and other relevant documents can be obtained from the ICTY official Web site: http://www.un.org/icty/.

74   "Croatia: Facing Up to War Crimes," International Crisis Group, *Balkan Briefing*, Zagreb/Brussels, 16 October 2001, 2.

75   Stipe Mesić has backed his words with actions by appearing himself as a witness at the ICTY.

76   The trial has turned out to be an important test of the international acceptability of the Croatian judicial system. See Tihana Tomičić, "Croatian Courts on Trial," *IWPR Tribunal Update*, no. 266, 13–18 May 2002. Norac was convicted of war crimes charges

in March 2003 and sentenced to twelve years imprisonment. For further detail on the Norac case, see Peskin and Boduszyński, "Croatia and the ICTY," 1126–1128.

77 For additional material relating to the Gotovina case, see Peskin and Boduszyński, "Croatia and the ICTY," 1128–1131. On the centrality of statehood to the question of Croat identity, see Alex J. Bellamy, *The Formation of Croatian National Identity: A Centuries-Old Dream?* (Manchester and New York: Manchester University Press, 2003).

78 For further detail of the Bobetko affair, see Peskin and Boduszyński, "Croatia and the ICTY," 1131–1135. They report that an opinion poll conducted in September 2002 indicated that "84% of Croatian citizens opposed sending Bobetko to The Hague; 71% retained the same attitude even under threat of economic sanctions" (1133).

79 "Croatia Faces Sanctions over Bobetko," *Balkan Crisis Report*, 375, 21 October 2002.

80 Helen Warrell, "Fugitive General to Be Tried for Role in Operation Storm," *IWPR Tribunal Update* 433, 8 December 2005. Prosecutor Carla del Ponte, thanking the Croatian government, commented that they were now cooperating fully. Tim Judah, Dragana Nikolić Solomon, and Dragutin Hedl, "Top Croatian War Crimes Suspect in Custody," Balkan Investigative Reporting Network, *Balkan Insight* 13, 8 December 2005. The fact that Gotovina was arrested in Spain does suggest accusations that the Croatian government was actively complicit in concealing him may well have been unfounded.

81 The news media alone cannot be held responsible for the dissemination of a predominantly negative view of The Hague. Kosta Čavoški, an influential member of the Serbian Academy, also wrote a direct attack on the Tribunal—*Hag protiv pravde* (The Hague against Justice) (unpublished typescript, University of Belgrade, 1998). A number of established jurists in Serbia added their voices to the campaign.

82 See, for example, Nir Rosen, "Mafia Fuels Balkan Crisis," *IWPR Balkan Crisis Report*, no. 333, 26 April 2002, 7–9. "Serbia after Djindjić," *Balkans Report,* no. 141, Belgrade/Brussels, 18 March 2003; see esp. 2–5.

83 See, for example, Bojan Dimitrijević, "Serbia: Culture of Secrecy Persists," *IWPR Tribunal Update*, no. 264, 15 May 2002, 4–6. It is largely for these reasons that the relatively rapid movement toward ICTY support for the holding of war crimes trials in Croatia has not been evident in Serbia, where the competence of the judiciary is still not respected by the international community. See Slobodan Beljanski, "Could Serbia Hold War Crimes Trials?" *IWPR Tribunal Update*, no. 238, 11 October 2001, 3–4.

84 "Serbia: Djindjić Under Pressure to Begin Extraditions," *IWPR Balkan Crisis Report*, no. 327, 28 March 2002, 5–7. Washington linked this demand also to the release of Albanian prisoners held in Serbian prisons.

85 The passage of this measure was strictly cosmetic in relation to international law, where the detention and transfer of suspects to the ICTY was already provided for, independently of any extradition treaties.

86 Jasna Dragović-Soso, "Western Policies and the Milošević Regime," in *International Intervention in the Balkans since 1995*, ed. Peter Siani-Davies (London: Routledge, 2003), 120–135; see esp. 129.

87 The view suggested here is based in part upon the work of Ivan Čolović. See his *The Politics of Symbol in Serbia: Essays in Political Anthropology* (London: Hurst, 2002).

88 The extent and character of war crimes in Bosnia was recognized as early as 1992, in a Helsinki Watch report. Helsinki Watch, *War Crimes in Bosnia-Hercegovina* (New York: Human Rights Watch, 1992).

89 There is also a big difference, in Bosnia as elsewhere, between the level of information available to urban and rural populations. The fact that Republika Srpska is significantly less urbanized than the federation contributes to the relative lack of public knowledge there.

90 Zlatko Hadžidedić, "Bosnia Now = No Future/No Past," *Variant*, no. 18, October 2003. www.variant.randomstate.org/18texts/18bosnia.

91 Hadžidedić, "Bosnia Now," 1.

92 Consistent use of the masculine pronoun appears to be appropriate here: all of the incumbents of this position have been male. In an interview with Wolfgang Petritsch, who held the post of HR between August 1999 and May 2002, it became clear that the issue of war crimes in fact has a high degree of salience. He did acknowledge, however, that he had negotiated directly with Radovan Karadžić during his term of office. The need to persuade him to step down from any political office was construed as a more important step than his immediate arrest. Interview by John Allcock, 6 May 2004. It may well be relevant to note that occupants of the post before the appointment of Paddy Ashdown tended to be drawn from diplomatic backgrounds and possibly were inclined to interpret their role primarily in terms of negotiation rather than enforcement.

93 Kerr, "International Judicial Intervention," 20–21.

11

Marina Blagojević, team leader
David Bruce MacDonald, team leader

Neven Andjelić	Jelena Milojković-Djurić	Dragan Popadić
Elazar Barkan	Julie Mostov	Branka Prpa
Mikloš Biro	Ines A Murzaku	Iwan Sokolowsky
Tone Bringa	**Richard Oloffson**	**Cynthia Simmons**
Joe Burton	Aleksandar Pavković	**Margaret Smith**
John Cox	**Tatjana Perić**	**Rumen Stefanov**
	Falk Pingel	

The text combines major textual contributions by Mikloš Biro, Marina Blagojević, David MacDonald, Tatjana Perić, Falk Pingel, Cynthia Simmons and Margaret Smith. It also benefited from comment and criticism from other team members.

Although the team was not part of the original project, it was added at the suggestion of Marina Blagojević, during the June 2002 SI meeting in Sarajevo – by which time NED research funds had already been apportioned among the previously established ten teams. Nonetheless, David Bruce MacDonald organized the team in 2004, which was inspired by Blagojević's work on "positive history". The research and writing was apportioned among the seven authors, each of whom contributed to an initial 35,800-word draft that was then reviewed by all SI participants in September-October 2007, after which Prof. MacDonald revised and abridged it for publication.

LIVING TOGETHER OR HATING EACH OTHER?

◆ David MacDonald, Editor ◆

Introduction

After years of research by the Scholars' Initiative, much of the history has already been documented and discussed by the other teams. Team 10 has argued that "if the Scholars' Initiative has a role to play . . . it must go beyond an aspiration merely to debunk local mythologies, and embrace the task of furthering a more objective general understanding of changes that affect us all." We take this role seriously and aim to promote efforts to dispel negative myths about the past while exploring ways of gaining an objective or at least more neutral understanding of the 1990s and before.

Whereas the first ten chapters examine the events that led from dissolution to a decade of armed conflict, we conclude this volume by revisiting a central justification of the nationalists: that the peoples of former Yugoslavia could not live together in a single state—at least not in a democratic setting. Certainly the events of the 1990s and the current cultural landscape would appear to bear out this stark judgment. Yet we propose to challenge this fatalism by reexamining the state of interethnic relations on the eve of Yugoslavia's demise. We also intend to consider the feasibility of strengthening confidence in the viability of multiethnic coexistence within the newly formed successor states after one decade of "socio-cide"[1] and another decade of nation-state building by advancing a more balanced representation of the past that affords equal space to the positive experiences of life in a multiethnic society.

Living Together

The efficacy of multiethnic coexistence is supported by scholarship across the historical and social sciences. Western scholarship has led the way, examining for

almost a century the unfortunate and oftentimes catastrophic effects of the post–
World War I world of nation-states. This has been especially true of the plethora
of postmortems of the multiethnic Habsburg monarchy, where a dozen national
groups coexisted—and arguably prospered—under the umbrella of constitutional government, parliamentary institutions, and the rule of law, which were
applied with equity by a professional judiciary and bureaucracy. Of course, many
multiethnic societies coexist today, both worldwide and within the narrower
geographical space of central Europe, including new EU members Bulgaria, Romania, Slovakia, and the Baltic states, which host significant national minorities.
In virtually every instance, there exist below the surface fissures among socioeconomic groups, including finite levels of separation and discrimination that
can occasionally manifest themselves in violence. It is no different outside the
Balkans, whether in the U.S., Canada, or France, although in most settings conditions rarely reach levels of mass violence like that experienced until recently in
Northern Ireland.

For whatever reason, outside of the literature tailored to the study of multiculturalism,[2] we rarely speak or write about the success stories of peoples living
together in harmony, if only because their experiences are not deemed newswor-
thy. There is often a disconnect between what people experience and what they
are all-too-often told by journalists, politicians, and even academics like ourselves, who prefer to focus on national awakenings, riots, and revolutions rather
than on the unremarkable chronology of everyday life.

This can certainly be said of life in Yugoslavia prior to 1987. Arguably, the
history of Communist Yugoslavia was marked by cooperation and ethnic and
religious tolerance. By the 1970s, discrimination against minority ethnic groups
in each of the republics was a relatively rare phenomenon. Data from the 1981
census demonstrate that almost nowhere in Yugoslavia did individual upward
mobility depend on ethnic origin.[3] For the majority of the population, regardless of ethnic origin, there was a high probability that until the end of the 1980s
individuals born after 1945 could live their lives without experiencing ethnic
or religious discrimination. This was especially true in urban settings, of which
Sarajevo was a prime example.

Moreover, former Yugoslavs shared common assumptions propagated by
the state of successful Partisan resistance, of "brotherhood and unity," of Yugoslavia's leadership role in the nonalignment movement, and finally, of the country's
unique socialist self-management economic system. Compared to the dangers
of wartime, and compared to the situation faced by peoples in other Communist
countries, cold war-era Yugoslavia appeared relatively tolerant, free, and prosper-
ous. Until the mid-1980s ethnic distance was stable, low, and even decreasing.[4]
A further study in 1990 showed that nationalistic value orientation in Serbia was
manifested by less than 30 percent of the population, whereas extreme national-

istic attitudes were exhibited by about 15 percent.[5] Yugoslav society of the 1980s could hardly have been called a "nationalistic time bomb."

Ethnic distance is obviously much higher now, as recent studies from 1997 to 2003 suggest. To the question, "Would you accept a member of 'x' nationality to be your son- or daughter-in-law?" only 21 percent of Croats from Croatia would accept such a relationship with Serbs, only 23 percent with Bosnian Muslims.[6] Conversely, only 20.5 percent of Bosnian Muslims would accept such a relationship with Serbs, 25.1 percent with Croats.[7] This willingness is somewhat higher among Serbs in Serbia: 49 percent would accept such relationships with Croats, 36 percent with Bosnian Muslims,[8] but among Bosnian Serbs, only 13.9 percent would accept this relationship with Bosnian Muslims, and only 15.9 percent with Croats.[9] Such views vary according to education level and age. A young age and low education level seems to produce higher ethnic distance, perhaps because young people grew up during the conflict and were educated in a spirit of mistrust, even hatred.[10] Clearly there is much work to be done to attain prewar levels of interethnic relationships.

Hating Each Other?

Nonetheless, in contrast to the other SI teams that have studied the history of what went wrong, we wish to explore potential solutions for many of the negative legacies of the 1990s. To some extent this relies on addressing unresolved trauma and anger from the 1940s. We argue that war developed for two primary reasons. The first reason was a result of manipulation of the population by political, intellectual, and media elites, facilitated by the lack of institutional power to stop conflict. Elites fed the collective consciousness with explanations and justifications for the "necessity" and "inevitability" of war; the weaker the "real" reasons for war, the stronger the propaganda. The media played a key role in this process. Without this mobilization of propaganda, ethnic conflict simply made no sense for most of the social actors, who were and remain the main losers. The process of manufacturing war began first with the deconstruction of the commonalities among peoples, the promotion of divisive ethnic cultures, and the demarcation of nonnegotiable differences that required physical separation. Demands were made that "something must be done" to justify concrete political acts and military actions.[11]

The second contributing factor to conflict was unresolved trauma from the past, which helped create an emotional climate where negative myths could be promoted and readily believed. Older people in the former Yugoslavia continued to remember the atrocities of World War II. As their memories of suffering were suppressed by the state, traumatic experiences were passed from generation to generation and remained unresolved. Fear and anger made the escalation of violence substantially easier. While a process of truth telling and positive history will be a crucial step in promoting healing and reconciliation, acknowledgement of past trauma and the ability to promote collective mourning will also play a key role in this process.

In a climate of economic and political instability, a power vacuum at the center allowed nationalism to rise to the surface. Economic crisis during the 1980s and 1990s helped heighten a sense of ethnic and religious difference, giving rise to the search for scapegoats to explain social and economic problems. The authoritarian legacies of the Communist era, coupled with earlier traditions of patriarchy, permitted thinking and acting only in accordance with the official ideology. Former Communist leaders changed into neonationalistic clothes and, by controlling the media, abundantly took advantage of people's readiness to obey authority uncritically.

A key conclusion of our team is that, although "nations" can be seen to have committed atrocities against other "nations" in the Yugoslav conflict, both perpetrator guilt and the suffering of victims are primarily individual experiences. Justice for perpetrators and victims may involve decoupling ethnicity from the crimes and citing the importance of victimization at an individual level. As Karl Jaspers observed decades ago, "there is no such thing as a national character extending to every single member of a nation. . . . A people cannot perish heroically, cannot be a criminal, cannot act morally or immorally; only its individuals can do so."[12] Realistically, any sort of healing or progress can only come about when a shared understanding of individual traumatic experiences cuts across national and ethnic boundaries.

Another important consideration is the ideal of "rehumanizing the other." As Halpern and Weinstein argue, "The dehumanization of specific groups through concomitant stereotyping does not stop when conflicts end. The inability to see former enemies as real people impedes reconciliation. While much attention has been paid to the reconstruction of infrastructure and the establishment of rule of law, little thought has been given to what is required at the day to day level in order to restore a sense of interpersonal security." Reflecting these authors, we strive for a "process of rehumanization."[13] Precisely how this is to take place is not easy to say. Contributors suggest that a potential (if not partial) solution could be in challenging the exclusiveness of dominant negative national narratives by introducing more positive experiences of living together through a positive history approach. This could be done by depolarizing education systems, promoting tolerance and reconciliation by religious communities and churches, and privileging other voices (women's groups for example). It is also important to support stronger independent media, truth and reconciliation commissions, and mourning. These and other initiatives can be interpreted as steps forward, even if some seem overly optimistic or even utopian at this stage in history.

We hope to show how reconciliation and healing, at least over the long term, may be possible. However, this report is but a first step—an exploration of what went wrong with some of the solutions attempted to date. More time, funding, and energy on the part of the academic community, civil society, and church and political leaders, will be required before any long-term solution can take root. Working together with other members of the Scholars' Initiative, this report lays out some of the major themes and ideas involved in promoting a positive history approach in the interpretation of a shared past and arguing for the future of living together and the necessity of healing. The concluding section features a series of recommendations for further discussion.

Toward a Balanced Narrative[14]

The basis of this report lies in engendering forms of what might be termed "positive history"—a narrative of cooperation and tolerance that cuts across ethnic and religious divisions, stressing the commonalities of people during the existence of the former Yugoslavia and their shared experiences of hardship, powerlessness, and victimization during the succession wars of the 1990s. Such a narrative would not replace or cancel the heretofore dominant narrative of national consciousness, competition, and conflict but deserves to be placed alongside it in any recounting or analysis. Its presence alone challenges the notion that these conflicts were logical and inevitable simply because they occurred. This is achieved by stressing the undeniable periods of cooperation and association among the peoples of the former Yugoslavia and the resistance to the wars by many, which, due to various limiting factors, was insufficient to actually prevent the conflicts. This chapter highlights two aspects:

> 1. Prewar practices and experiences of living together in multicultural, functional, and functioning communities; intergroup mixing in everyday life practices; and building supranational identities as a part of belonging to the former Yugoslavia (from 1945 until the 1980s)

> 2. Open resistance to the succession wars of the 1990s, resistance and opposition to different expressions of hatred toward others, including positive actions such as mutual help, sacrifice, and sharing

Central to this approach is the questioning of the idea that war was a natural and inevitable outcome of life in the former Yugoslavia.[15] Hence our focus is on those admittedly weaker parties in the wars who were not powerful enough to stop it. Their weakness, however, did not stem from objective factors, such as small numbers, unwillingness to intervene, or "eternal hatreds." Instead, weakness was a consequence of the paradox that wars could not have been prevented *because they were not expected*, with the result that no strong internal or external structures had been established to empower peaceful solutions.[16] On the other hand, there existed powerful agents (local political elites, arms producers and smugglers, journalists and intellectuals) who brought about a negative spiral of destruction. The fact that the weaker, peace-loving side did not stop the wars and did not prevail does not prove that the wars were objectively inevitable. It only proves that those agents who produced the wars were stronger and that Yugoslavia's chaotic environment and the international community lacked adequate mechanisms to prevent the escalation of violence.

Ethically, the presentation of a more balanced narrative that accommodates more positive evidence helps create knowledge that will support healing and reconstruction because it avoids assigning collective guilt and imposing ethnicized interpretations. It also emphasizes the relevance of agency and free choice on both sides: those producing the wars and those resisting. By revealing and documenting numerous practices and discourses opposing the wars, we can reaffirm that history is always a choice, although not for all social agents in the same way and to the same extent. Responsibility largely depends on social positioning; responsibility and power are interconnected. At another level, positive history reconnects pieces of former Yugoslav society through a narrative that might be widely shared by most of the ordinary people from all sides who perceive themselves as victims. This could be a ground for new solidarity and healing beyond the boundaries of newly formed states and ethnic affiliations. By countering narratives of civilizational and other forms of conflict, images of living together can offer evidence of equally (if not more) important practices—examples of cooperation and tolerance across ethnic, religious, or any other divisions among human groups.

New Narratives and Negative History[17]

Although we recognize the role that a more positive, balanced narrative can and should play in promoting healing and reconciliation, the prevailing pattern of negative history is not easy to overcome. Although accounts based on myths of persecution and victimization may have been manipulated by cynical elites for their own purposes, they play an identity-defining role for many individuals, and they do rely on strong evidence for support. However, the problem is not with the evidence, which exists and should be always taken into account, as much as with an overall interpretation that tends to mythologize and sustain the victimization narrative. In the long run, it will take more than the work of critical historians to defuse the power of national myths and falsified memories. This is not simply because politicians recognize the capital to be made by spreading myths but, more fundamentally, because individuals become dependent upon them. Myths, by their very nature, are deeply rooted in the psyches of individuals and groups.

We generally think of history as a repository of information about the past and a source of explanations about the present. But history and memory serve a variety of functions in a society. History and its interpretation is critical to the development of ethnic groups and nations, given that shared past experience, or the perception of shared past experience, is the strongest rationale for the existence of the group. History texts, monuments, museums, and other forms of public commemoration provide a sense of stability and tradition that assist the legitimation of the existing regime.

Prevailing history interpretations and the instititionalization of negative memories supply the facts of injustice and grievance, both of which can be powerfully mobilized by political leaders. The capacity of historical memories to coalesce politicized groups cannot be understood fully without recognizing that, at the same time, historical memories play several critical roles in the lives of individuals. The prevailing historical tradition is a way of recording and remembering the traumatic events of past generations that have an emotional or physiological impact, and possibly a material impact, on their descendants. Because of the individual's dependence on the group that supports him or her, the individual will often identify with the group in order to receive what is offered to group members, absorbing cultural elements and a shared sense of the past. Introducing a different historical narrative means challenging psychological and sociological patterns that are often of long duration and that are perpetuated by institutional design and the existing power structures.

Psychoanalysts argue that group experiences of catastrophe are carried psychologically from one generation to the next and, whereas memory of that event is likely to be maintained in the public arena through rhetorical history, the personal effect can be understood as separate and profound.[18] Vamik Volkan's "chosen trauma" describes the collective memory of a calamity. Chosen traumas reflect an unconscious decision to define identity through transgenerational transmission.[19] A group's interpretation of a trauma goes through various transformations. As the years pass, legends develop. Rituals reinforce particular aspects of the event. A group's chosen trauma can lie dormant for a time, in which case a political leader may play a role in igniting the dormant group memory.[20] The overall process may distort the group's perception, causing new enemies to appear as old enemies. Mobilization by elites can recharge historical memories, but this is only possible because some imprint from the past is already in place.[21]

This process however is not inevitable, nor is it irreversible. As Biro and Milin have shown, the presence of trauma or post-traumatic stress disorder (PTSD) does not necessarily prevent people from seeking reconciliation.[22] Their 2004 study of refugees from Croatia and Bosnia-Hercegovina living in Serbia demonstrates that the presence of PTSD as such did not impede "readiness for reconciliation."[23] However, the greatest obstacle to reconciliation was the presence of nationalistic/xenophobic and ethnocentric attitudes, with negative stereotypes of the opposing nation. Crucially, the experience of being discriminated against by the other nation (while feeling that the discrimination was ongoing) was the biggest problem.[24]

Postwar psychological studies thus demonstrate that traumatic experience as such is not a serious hindrance to the reconciliation process at an individual level. This certainly does not mean war crimes and material destruction should go unpunished or that apologies from national leaders are not important. Indeed, punishment of perpetrators will have great significance for guilt individualization, whereas apologies will help change the perceptions of victimized groups. At the individual level, the biggest obstacle to the reconciliation process is value orientation, not the experienced war trauma per se.

Based on their findings, Biro and Milin argue that friendly relations with members of other ethnic groups represent one of the major predictors of readiness for reconciliation. Media acknowledgement of the positive aspects of Yugoslavia's history, especially interaction between members of conflicting nations, can significantly contribute to changing views of formerly enemy ethnic groups. This will be facilitated by the fact that all three warring groups speak essentially the same language. As Hewstone and Brown suggest, intergroup contact can help reverse the cycle of negative generalizations and stereotypes and help promote positive attitudes.[25] Citing examples of neighbors of different nationalities helping each other during the war could help decrease prejudice and negative stereotypes about other nationalities. Institutionalizing such an approach by educational systems would broaden the effects and ensure the sustainability of reconciliation efforts.

Rewriting history, therefore, entails bringing truth into the open. Telling the truth, first of all, means acknowledging painful and controversial events. But a society grounded in truth telling gains for other reasons. When freedom of speech is limited and political ideologies encounter minimal criticism, leaders can expand their mythologizing to employ lies or gross exaggerations. A society that fails to challenge the lies of its leaders will soon experience other kinds of oppression.[26] Our most essential contribution to the post conflict countries of the Balkans must be to model a professional methodology of truth seeking. At the same time it would be a mistake to dub such accounts of the wars an achievement and thereby overlook the fact that this history will be contested immediately and continually. The point is that a higher standard of scholarship and collaboration is being set for future debates.

Everyday Resistance to the Dissolution of Yugoslavia[27]

In everyday life, people faced a number of limitations in trying to resist the politics of war. There was a lack of institutional channels to express attitudes against war. Too many people had the overwhelming feeling that it was not "we" who wanted the war, but "they"; therefore, we could not do anything except defend ourselves. Limited material resources severely curtailed the activities of those who were trying to oppose the wars, and for many the very effort to survive during the wars exhausted all of their human resources. Nevertheless, there is much evidence of both political resistance and mutual help across ethnic lines during the wars. Even in the chaos of the war, there are many cases where individuals acted with bravery and tolerance in dangerous situations to counteract animosity, hatred, and destruction. Individual testimonies collected by Svetlana Broz, for example, disclose many cases where ordinary people helped each other in life-threatening situations. For participants, war was actually perceived as some kind of natural catastrophe over the heads of normal people, causing spontaneous solidarity. Broz demonstrates that the war situation was extremely chaotic on the ground, exactly because the texture of society was so interwoven, so interconnected.[28]

Building a more positive, balanced narrative will require acknowledging that, even if largely invisible, there were numerous initiatives, actions, organizations, and individuals who attempted to speak out against the wars. These included peace and antiwar organizations, autonomous women's groups, organizations for the protection of human rights, and a number of outstanding intellectuals and artists. In the beginning of the 1990s in Serbia, the term *Other Serbia* was coined by the Belgrade Circle, an antiwar organization that gathered some of the intellectual elite of Belgrade to demonstrate that "Another Serbia" strongly opposed the wars. However, even before the wars there were different political initiatives that aimed to promote the democratic transformation of Yugoslav society and to prevent its violent dissolution.

Some of the most important initiatives included Yugoslav-wide political parties committed to a peaceful transition to democracy and the peaceful resolution of hostilities. A prime example was the Association for a Yugoslav Democratic Initiative (a coalition of thirty civic-oriented parties, movements, and associations), founded in Zagreb in 1989. It was both a party and a movement, combining the idea of Yugoslavism with democracy.[29] Among its initiatives, the UJDI insisted on the nonviolent resolution of the Kosovo dispute.[30] Its members proposed that the federal assembly pass an amendment to elect a constitutional convention that would determine the fate of Yugoslavia. UJDI also created a roundtable of government representatives and members of the opposition. This met six times in 1991–1992 and culminated in a peace proposal that was not implemented.[31]

Another example of positive mobilization for peace was the formation in the summer of 1990 of the all-Yugoslav party—the Alliance of Reformist Forces of Yugoslavia (SRST). This party was defined as a "nucleus for the growing pan-Yugoslav movement for reform." The Reformists proposed a program of economic and political reforms that included democracy, economic recovery and the overhaul of the banking system, and a market economy and unfettered competition based on knowledge and ability. They wanted to abandon the practices of classical political parties and to strengthen individual initiative."[32] In 1991 UJDI and SRST together published a program of political and economic reforms.

Other groups included the European Movement in Yugoslavia (EPJ), which was founded in March 1991 as a recognized member of the European movement,[33] and the Civic Alliance (GS), which was formed in the summer of 1992. In July 1991, the Center for Anti-War Action was founded immediately after the outbreak of hostilities in Slovenia and comprised the UJDI, Women's Parliament, the Women's Party, the Helsinki Assembly of Yugoslavia, and the Helsinki Citizens' Parliament. The center's major premise was that everybody has the right to life and civil disobedience. The center initiated several peace activities and demonstrations, such as the Walks for Peace. In September 1991, the Helsinki Citizen's Parliament organized a Caravan of Citizens of Europe, which traveled throughout the former Yugoslavia and started the *Yugofax* publication.

After the bombardment of Sarajevo several antiwar groups organized the citizens of Belgrade in a procession that carried a 1,300-meter-long black ribbon. The column stretched from the Albanija Building in the city's central Terazije Square to Slavija Square, with up to 50,000 people participating. Early in 1994 activists from various alternative groups came together in support of a group project called Living in Sarajevo. Other groups included the Civic Resistance Movement, launched at the beginning of the war, and the 1992 Fund for Humanitarian Law.

To these initiatives we can add a variety of women's groups dedicated to peace and tolerance.[34] Women were particularly targeted during the wars. Gender identities in public discourses in times of conflict were mostly constructed to fit to the oppositional model of identity formation, where the Other, being an ethnic or gender Other, was seen as an enemy. Gender difference was also ethnicized, a notable example being Serbia. In the Serbian public discourse of the 1990s, for example, women were seen as Westernized Others, whereas Serbian ethnic identity and Serbian male identity were tied together and essentialized. Misogyny, which exploded in the 1990s, was an ideological answer to the "implosion of patriarchy" at the everyday level.[35]

The Belgrade Women's Lobby was founded in 1990 with the aim of organizing pressure against the regime, the institutions of the system, and the political parties "so that women's experiences and women's demands would no longer remain below the threshold of social visibility and sensibilities." There was even an initiative by some women to create a women's parliament because so few women were elected to the National Parliament of Serbia. In 1991, Women in Black was founded during the armed hostilities against Dubrovnik. They gathered every Wednesday to express their opposition to the war. Dressed in black, their slogan was "Let us banish war from history and from our lives." They called for the establishment of an international court for war crimes. Also in 1991, a women's party was created in Belgrade with an antiwar program and policies advocating regional restructuring of the federal state. The idea was that regions as smaller units of republics would enable peaceful democratic transformation, contrary to the strengthening of the nation-states.[36]

Why Did these Initiatives Not Work?

Despite the best efforts of their participants, these and other initiatives failed to prevent the successor wars. A number of reasons account for their failure. First, these initiatives did not have sufficient institutional, financial, or human resources to play an important role, especially not in comparison to the war machinery they were opposing. There was no widespread support from the international community, and antiwar activists and peacemakers were initially isolated. Later, the appeal of being isolated and ghettoized was used as a means of seeking outside funding, so many NGOs became more outwardly than inwardly oriented. This also weakened their position on the local political scene.

Moreover, peace activists were not homogeneous—they had different backgrounds, political views, expectations, and explanations of what was happening. Most peace initiatives were not democratically organized but often had strong, even authoritarian leaders, whose international promotion became the most important raison d'etre. As the conflict progressed, outside support increased the competition among leaders, contributing to the impossibility of defining a necessary metanarrative that would be acceptable for all opponents of the wars. The problems associated with antiwar activism also led to a high degree of burnout because many found themselves in very difficult conditions and without adequate organizational infrastructure. And finally, the actual number of people involved in antiwar and peace activism was very small. Many activists circulated between different initiatives, thus creating an illusion of much more activity and larger numbers than was really the case.

However, it would be wrong to judge the success of these initiatives by the fact that they did not stop the wars. Another, more adequate gauge of their effectiveness was the buildup of antiwar feeling among the general public. Resistance to war gradually gave rise to a coherent civil society and the spread of civil initiatives. For example, in Serbia, civil resistance was taught, developed, and disseminated through the protests against Milošević. But methods, communication models, and organizational know-how used in small antiwar and feminist groups were quite successfully transported and extended to new political movements.[37]

In producing a more positive narrative, a key goal must be to offer a focus on those who did resist the spiral of ethnic hatred and who did demonstrate against the rise of ethnic conflict, either openly or more clandestinely. This metanarrative remains underexplored in contemporary literature on the Yugoslav conflict, yet it is necessary in order to deconstruct nationalistic mythologized narratives and pave the way for reconciliation.

Media, Ethnic Conflict, and the Resolution of Conflict[38]

In Serbia and Croatia the media became an active participant in the escalation of nationalist violence. At times it became a mouthpiece of the government. At other times it promoted more radical interpretations of the nationalist message, spurring national leaders to greater excesses. At first, much of this did not seem to have much to do with everyday life. As Slavenka Drakulić described this early period: "Long before the real war, we had a media war, Serbian and Croatian journalists attacking the political leaders from the opposite republic as well as each other as if in some kind of dress rehearsal. So I could see a spiral of hatred descending on us, but until the first bloodshed it seemed to operate on the level of a power struggle that had nothing to do with the common people."[39] Fortunately, in both Serbia and Croatia some excellent media acted as critics of the regimes under which they operated. They included the weeklies *Borba*, *Vreme*, *Republika*, and *Feral Tribune*; television stations NTV and Studio B; and Radio B92.

This section evaluates the role of the media in escalating the level of fear in the former Yugoslavia, with an emphasis on both Croatia and Serbia. Communist Yugoslavia consciously differentiated itself from the Soviet Union by promoting open media, although they were hardly free. Promoting the official party line was important throughout the Communist era. The period until the 1974 constitution was largely marked by central control of the media from Belgrade. Thereafter it devolved to the capitals of individual republics. Eventually, "Media outlets accustomed to one-man, one-party rule merely followed a new, local man and party in Serbia, Croatia, and Bosnia."[40] As such the media continued the centralization that characterized the Communist period, but the mission changed from selling "brotherhood and unity" to manufacturing hatred for one's neighbors.[41]

In both Serbia and Croatia control of the media was crucial to underpinning support for the nationalist regimes of Milošević and Tudjman. In Serbia, new provisions under the Serbian penal code made it an offense to criticize the government or cast doubt on the country's leaders. Government ministries of information and the interior now had a mandate to censor, delete, or change any aspect of reporting found to be at odds with official government accounts.[42] The government-controlled Serbian Radio-Television (RTS) soon gained a broadcasting monopoly. The Milošević regime also did its best to limit if not destroy independent print media by imposing high taxes while cutting supplies of newsprint and fuel.[43]

Media control was stricter in Croatia. Within two months of the 1990 elections, the Croatian Radio-Television Act was rushed through Parliament, changing the name of Radio-Televizija Zagreb to Hrvatska Radio-Televizija (HRT), while submitting it to government control.[44] Print media were a favored target. HDZ faithful replaced journalists and editorial staff at HINA (formerly Tanjug). Independent papers, such as the Vjesnik Group, were slowly taken over by the government. Magazines owned by this group were often scuttled if they ran stories contrary to government interests.[45] The satirical weekly *Feral Tribune* was also harshly treated, with a 50 percent sales tax in 1994 and constant defamation in the government press, while its editors were drafted into the army after criticizing Tudjman.[46]

Certainly the media's role in the promotion and escalation of conflict was crucial. There were, however, differences in the two countries. The Croatian government had a hands-on approach to the media and brooked little dissent.[47] Things seem to have been slightly less controlled in Serbia, perhaps because Milošević was more interested in promoting the *idea* of media freedom. The media were also more assertive and creative in avoiding the government. When Milošević took B92 Radio off the air during the 1999 NATO bombing of Yugoslavia, the station defiantly made use of the Internet to cover the effects of the bombing. In other cases, Belgrade's Studio B asserted its independence by aligning itself with opposition leader Vuk Drašković. In Serbia, independent media outlets helped erode Milošević's popularity, especially B92 and members of the Association of Independent Electronic Media (ANEM). After the elections in September 2000, coverage of official vote fraud by the independent media brought outraged citizens to the streets, eventually bringing down the regime.[48]

Yet after Milošević and Tudjman, the legacies of violent nationalism continued. For example, there is an almost complete lack of remorse among individual nations for their own group's actions in precipitating the violent dismemberment of Yugoslavia. In the Serbian case, the media aligned themselves with Koštunica with almost dazzling speed, suggesting that rather than abandoning their tendency to follow the leader, they had merely switched leaders. In Bosnia, forms of "media apartheid" continued, with a wide variety of exclusivist nationalist-oriented media outlets giving a very narrow perspective on current and historical events.[49] Serbs continue to see themselves as victims. Even now, the Serbian Ministry of Information promotes Serbia as the victim of history rather than an aggressor. Its online encyclopedia perpetuates the claims that the 1974 constitution was at the root of the 1990s conflict and that the bloodshed was the fault of Slovenia and Croatia's illegal separation from the federation.[50]

Despite the ICTY and massive media coverage of the events in Yugoslavia, the Serbian public remains ignorant of Serbia's role in the conflict. Public opinion polls conducted in 2001 revealed that over 52 percent of respondents "could not name a single war crime committed by Serb forces in Bosnia, Croatia, or Kosovo. Nearly half, however, could name at least three crimes committed against Serb civilians by other forces." Furthermore, Karadžić and Mladić continued to be heralded as the two "greatest defenders of the Serb nation."[51] The 2003 elections demonstrated clearly the memory problems still present in Serbia, as have more recent elections.

Currently, the media have become a vehicle for promoting the transformation of the nation into something more palatable for the West. However, neither Serbia nor Croatia has fully engaged with the history of atrocities in the 1990s. Few media institutions feel inclined or empowered to explore national guilt too far. Nevertheless, outside assistance in promoting media objectivity can help. For example, B92 was able to continue its activities thanks to support from the Media Development Loan Fund, which helps fund independent media in emerging democracies.[52] This is in line with Jack Snyder's work that suggests that outside funding must target media with cross-national appeal, which resists the allure of exclusivist nationalism. NGOs must strive to "attract a politically and ethnically diverse audience, invite the expressions of various viewpoints, and hold news stories to rigorous standards of objectivity."[53] Such media sources are not always easy to find but are necessary if any sense of identity that cuts across ethnic boundaries is to be found.

NGOs like the International Press Institute in Vienna help train journalists from newly democratized countries and help with the costs of equipment, newsprint, and logistical support.[54] The Institute for War and Peace Reporting (IWPR) sets high journalistic standards while providing training for journalists in media objectivity. IWPR places emphasis on collaboration between international and local journalists. Integral to the role of IWPR is its desire "to break down rather than reinforce grievances across ethnic, national, tribal or other conflict lines . . . to build cross-community confidence, support collaborative projects and develop regional and international information sharing."[55] IWPR works to develop collaborative projects throughout the region, including investigative reporting, and publishes articles in the *Balkan Crisis Report* that focus on issues of human rights and democratization.[56]

The International Federation of Journalists' organization Media for Democracy in South-Eastern Europe covers Bosnia-Hercegovina, Croatia, Serbia, Slovenia, and FYROM. Its work has involved such activities as building trade unions and journalist associations, offering legal assistance to defend media freedom, and promoting public-service broadcasting. They also encourage the professionalization of journalistic standards when reporting on conflict and human rights abuses, and they promote basic safety standards for journalists.[57]

The situation will certainly be improved in the states of the former Yugoslavia as the region becomes more affluent and is able to access alternative media such as the Internet.[58] As this medium of communication spreads, there is reason to hope that the situation will continue to improve, although Internet access does not guarantee more informed opinions. It can sometimes simply lead one to search for nationalist-oriented sites that buttress one's own viewpoint. Accepting the official line was easy during the successor wars. The challenge now is to give people the opportunity to access and appreciate alternative media sources that may tend to criticize as much as praise the government. NGOs willing to play a constructive role in promoting journalistic objectivity can make a difference. We, therefore, recommend that efforts to promote media objectivity, the training of journalists, and the promotion of cross-ethnic reporting be further encouraged and funded.

Finally, both Serbs and Croats need to be receptive to critical viewpoints that may raise unwelcome questions about their national pasts. A change in attitudes will slowly evolve, but the space for an independent media depends not only on government acquiescence but also public support. Although after 2000 the main Serbian state TV station started broadcasting a serial on Serbian crimes in Srebrenica, "great pressure from the public" stopped this broadcast after the first episode. Similarly, after the broadcast of the popular talk show "Latinica" on Croatian TV, which treated the subject of Croatian war crimes, there was so much public reaction that after a few days Croatian TV broadcast a short film on Serbian war crimes in Croatia in order to establish "balance."[59] Ultimately improving the media will help reshape civil society, but the public must also be persuaded that open and objective media serve their individual and collective interests. This process will take time and will need to be underwritten by other initiatives.

Religious Reconciliation[60]

Although the role of religion during the collapse of Yugoslavia was sometimes divisive, the evolving political climate after 2000 provided a more conducive environment for the development of relations among religious communities and their congregations. This section reviews recent efforts to promote religious reconciliation, while offering some tentative conclusions.

The postnationalist era has arguably seen some effort toward bridging religious and national divides. The depth and strength of this cooperation vary from case to case. Ecumenical efforts appear to be present in the work of the Roman Catholic Church in Serbia. Ecumenical cooperation on all levels was backed by strong support from its authorities and was a matter of regular discussion in the local Roman Catholic press in both Croatian and Hungarian languages.[61] There have been frequent visits by Roman Catholic dignitaries to their counterparts in the Serbian Orthodox Church. In May 2002, Cardinal Walter Kasper, president of the Pontifical Council on Christian Unity, met with Patriarch Pavle of the Serbian Orthodox Church and extended the Vatican's invitation for a visit to the Holy Synod.[62] In his later meetings with representatives of the Serbian state, Cardinal Kasper also expressed the Vatican's support for the integration of Serbia into European institutions.[63] Additionally, representatives of the Serbian Orthodox Church took part in a number of conferences and meetings with the Roman Catholic Church outside Serbia.[64]

The general attitude toward Muslims in Serbia has admittedly improved, at least on the part of formal authorities.[65] However, there remains considerable work to be done. Widespread intolerance toward Muslims remains firmly present in Serbia. According to research conducted in late 2001, Islam tops the list of "dangerous religions" in the minds of 15 percent of Serbs and 17 percent of Montenegrins.[66] NGO sources have pointed to evidence of harassment of Muslims by Serbian police in Novi Sad in 2002,[67] the use of hate speech, and registered cases of torture of persons of Muslim origin.[68] Members of the Islamic community in Vojvodina face the additional hardship of having no place of worship because there are no mosques in the entire region.[69] The situation in Serbia is closely intertwined with that of Republika Srpska, where violent attacks against Muslims continue.[70]

Other religious communities in Serbia are also not immune to intolerance. The Jewish community in Serbia was subject to public verbal attacks from Žarko Gavrilović, a retired priest of the Serbian Orthodox Church and the spiritual leader of *Obraz*, an ultranationalist association of university students.[71] After his words drew protests from Israel and the Yugoslav minister for foreign affairs, the Serbian Orthodox Church issued a public statement in which it clearly disassociated itself from Gavrilović's remarks.[72]

On the positive side, a draft for a law on religious liberties was crafted in April 2002; it proposed that there would be no state religion and that all religious communities would be equal. Furthermore, the draft law guaranteed freedom of belief and introduced noticeably shortened procedures for the registration of new religious groups. Beyond these legislative changes envisaged for the future, the government has done little to improve the situation of smaller religious communities.

At the other end of the spectrum are instances of interreligious dialogue, though these are rare and almost by definition initiated by NGOs. Examples of such initiatives are the Novi Sad School of Journalism, with its series of seminars open to the public on topics related to religion and society, and the research projects of Women's Studies and Research, also based in Novi Sad.[73] Exceptionally, there are initiatives such as that of the Novi Sad-based Ecumenical Humanitarian Organization, the only interchurch charity in Serbia. Additionally, the Interreligious Center of Yugoslavia, founded in Belgrade in March 2000, includes, inter alia, the members of authorities of the local Roman Catholic Church, the Islamic community, and the Jewish community.[74] Together with the Belgrade branch of the Konrad Adenauer Foundation, the center organized a conference on religion and conflict in May 2002.[75] Such initiatives remain isolated. Generally religious communities can reach a much higher level of cooperation when they are not addressing issues related to their relations with one another but rather the relations of all religious communities toward the state.

Of course, it is important to ask where the power to effect change actually lies. That is, how much actual power do religious leaders have over their (real or alleged) congregations? Estimates vary, but a public poll of April 2002 clearly indicated that the Serbian people have a very high level of trust in the Serbian Orthodox Church, with as much as 79 percent of those interviewed stating that the church is where they would turn for truth.[76] Nevertheless, the power of influence of religious leadership is often disputed when compared with other, perceivably stronger centers of power, principally political.

Human rights, rarely mentioned by the church in the Serbian context and then mostly in a negative sense, are quickly raised when the rights of Serbs are at issue. At its session in May 2002, for example, the Holy Synod noted the "essential necessity of the protection and improvement of human and religious rights and freedoms." It emphasized the necessity of acting so that "the voice of the Church is heard in international organizations which deal with the protection of human rights." However, the synod clarified that this referred particularly to the rights of Serbs in Kosovo, displaced Serbs, and Serbian refugees from all parts of the former Yugoslavia.[77] It is most unfortunate that the Serbian Orthodox Church did not use this opportunity to address and call for the respect of the human rights of others as well.

The Serbian Orthodox Church participated in two major interreligious initiatives in December 2001, both of which ended with detailed joint public statements. After the first initiative, participants concluded their joint declaration with a note on the "firm belief that, in a long-term perspective, only those churches and religious communities in SEE [Southeastern Europe] will be affirmed, which respect freedoms of people in a pluralistic society and deepen the spirit of reconciliation, co-operation and stability of their followers and other citizens."[78]

The second interfaith conference, on the topic of Peace of God in the World, was held in Brussels in December and sponsored by the EU. It was attended by Patriarch Pavle and other representatives of the Serbian Orthodox Church and also by the highest representatives of the Islamic and Jewish communities in Serbia. The concluding declaration addressed the responsibility of religions and religious leaders in conflict: "It is the responsibility of religious leaders to prevent religious fervor from being used for purposes that are alien to its role." It affirmed the constructive and instructive role of religions in the dialogue between civilizations, rejected all forms of discrimination, and supported the foundations of mutual respect, human rights, religious liberties, peaceful coexistence, and interreligious cooperation. The declaration ended with a set of recommendations for religious communities in their peace-building work.[79]

The role of religious communities remains problematic. Issues of truth and reconciliation do not often make the agenda. In fact, religious communities in the main deny their responsibility for wrongdoing during the recent wars or have only accused each other of contributing to war efforts. Interreligious relations have witnessed some improvement on a formal level; however, there is still intolerance of and attacks against non-Serb religious communities, particularly Muslims, Jews, and members of small religious communities. Some contend that the actual influence of religious communities is not so great after all, but this runs contrary to popular opinion: citizens of Serbia have considerable trust in their religious institutions. Through their own improved cooperation, the religious communities could serve as a coexistence model for the rest of Serbian society, especially given their apparently respected role. We feel that religious institutions can and should take more initiative in promoting dialogue and peace-building initiatives. This is, of course, a long-term objective.

In the interim, special emphasis internationally should be placed on supporting the work of faith-based NGOs (such as Relief Services, World Vision, the United Methodist Committee on Relief, and the Center for Strategic and International Studies' Center for Religious Dialogue), which have and continue to play a crucial role in promoting interfaith dialogue and reconciliation. Local initiatives like Bosnia's Interreligious Council should also be encouraged. In 2004 at the behest of the U.S. Institute of Peace, Branka Peuraca concluded a fifteen-month study of Protestant, Catholic, Orthodox Christian, Muslim, and Jewish NGOs operating in Bosnia. She found their work was largely positive in promoting dialogue and forms of reconciliation.[80]

Although some Muslim organizations were suspected of having links with terrorist organizations, most NGOs have played a positive role and should be encouraged in their efforts. As such, "enlightened action by faith-based NGOs can contribute to inter-religious reconciliation in places where religion is a source of conflict. These NGOs can bridge religious divisions, diminish the level of animosity, and focus attention on the shared responsibility to rebuild society."[81] We can be heartened by the USIP's Religion and Peacemaking program launched in July 2000; it promotes faith-based NGOs as a key to building peace.[82] Another avenue is for the European Union to strongly encourage religious organizations in Croatia and Serbia to take an active role in the reconciliation process and even in accession negotiations. The EU's Representative for the Common Foreign and Security Policy Javier Solana began this process in 2003 when meeting with religious leaders in the Serbian, Croatian, Slovenian, and Bosnian capitals.[83] In promoting religious reconciliation, outside intervention and encouragement will prove invaluable in the medium term as civil society develops anew.

Textbook Revision in the Former Yugoslavia[84]

Education is crucial to the development of a more tolerant and cooperative society. However, it can also be used in the wrong hands to perpetuate stereotypes, intolerance, and even violent ethnic chauvinism. In general there are positive and negative examples from the Yugoslav region. In Slovenia, the government had been decentralizing its school system, albeit cautiously, since the 1980s. It also consulted extensively with Western European institutions when reworking school curricula and textbooks.[85]

After the war, Croatia also made progress in the textbook sector. The curriculum did stress the continuity of a Croatian-Catholic national history from the Middle Ages onward. Yet textbook revision also spurred historical and political debate. Although nationalists and conservatives wanted to force schools to follow their interpretations, multiperspectival, even critical interpretations were also integrated into textbooks, with crucial input from experts at the University of Zagreb. The Croatian case indicates that if scientific and academic circles offer no encouragement and support for new approaches, the initiatives and endeavors of schoolbook authors will rarely come to fruition. The fact that the history faculties in Bosnia-Hercegovina, Albania, and Macedonia are virtually isolated from more recent international research is one of the main reasons why schoolbook reform in these countries has not gathered speed.

State-controlled revision of schoolbooks in Bosnia is concerned with subjects that deal with the concept of nation, or nationhood, namely language and literature, history, geography, the environment, and society, as well as religion, and to some extent music. These subjects have a special status because, in contrast to other disciplines, they concentrate much more on the traditions and specific cultural features of each of the three "constituent ethnic groupings." The need for a revision of schoolbooks resulted from the war of 1992–1995 and the subsequent peace agreements, which established the sovereign state of Bosnia but at the same time organized education on a federal principle. The war not only destroyed the political structures of a united Yugoslavia but also disrupted the relatively uniform education system that had previously existed.

The Serb-dominated regions forming the Republika Srpska orientated their curricula on books that came from Serbia, whereas the areas with a predominantly Croat population were mainly Catholic and influenced by the curricula and schoolbooks from Croatia. The Bosniaks were the major political factor in the movement toward unity. Because the government in Sarajevo had no direct links with another nation or state, it had already decided during the war to produce schoolbooks that espoused the idea of a Bosnia that transcended ethnic differences and conflicts. After the war each of the three regions developed new curricula and teaching schemes with materials that it felt were appropriate. Unfortunately, these curricula served only to cement the differing cultural outlooks rather than to promote the idea of integration.[86]

Textbooks continue to perpetuate national rivalries over and above a sense of common regional identity. This problem is best exemplified by the rivalry between Croatia and Serbia. The two countries have initiated very few bilateral educational projects in the field of history and the social sciences. For this reason the European Association of History Educators (EURUCLIO) programs, which aim to produce teaching materials for use in both countries, are a highly welcome development. However, these will be additive rather than core materials, so their effect will be limited. Teachers and the relevant authorities agree that new textbooks can only be introduced after the curricula have been revised and, conversely, for revised curricula to be successful there is a need to develop new textbooks.

One obstacle in overcoming this dilemma lies in the fact that educational reform receives scant support from both the public and the teachers themselves because the social status and the remuneration of teaching staff are comparatively low. The dissolution of the socialist system saw a sharp decline in the respect that teachers had traditionally enjoyed. Many schools, especially those in a rural environment are poorly equipped to deal with the challenges of technology and the advances in modern communication.

Since 1998 various revision bodies have been engaged in "defusing" the content of textbooks to ensure that they contain no passages that could hurt the national and religious feelings of another ethnic community or incite pupils to hatred and violence. The subject that led to the most contention was history. However, the books of all three ethnic groups display a shameful and consistent attempt to justify the present divisions and social structures by tracing them back through history. Bosniak books tend to paint a rosy picture of a tolerant Ottoman Empire, failing to stress the manifold social and political hierarchies that granted only a lower status to the non-Muslim communities.[87] Experts from Serb and Croat regions insist on using *Islamic subjugation* to describe the process of forceful proselytizing under the Ottomans; the Bosnians, in turn, refuse to accept this term.

A common platform for the representation of the modern national movements is still beyond reach. Serb and Croat books either stress their own expansive nationalism or an exclusive ethnicity. In both cases they neglect a separate Bosniak identity, and the Bosniaks, as well as Bosnia as a whole, receive scant attention. On the other hand, Bosniak authors face problems whenever they stress that Bosnia-Hercegovina is a unified and sovereign state with its own identity. They are moderately pro-Ottoman and pro-Yugoslavian because both of these systems espoused the goal of a mixed Bosnian society. But this is the very reason why they seem to be unpatriotic and retrogressive from a Serb or Croat point of view. To compensate for this, Bosnian Muslim authors are now writing their own national history and see themselves as a distinct group striving for a multiethnic society with roots that go back centuries.

The interventions of the revision commissions have—more by chance than intention—ironed out many of the problems concerning content and visuals, as well as neutralizing the treatment of disputable issues. However, they have been unable to clear up or end fundamental differences. It seems quite impossible to harmonize the various interpretations. Proposed changes would first have to be incorporated in the common core curriculum before they could be implemented in all syllabuses throughout the country. Such a framework was formulated by the Conference of Education Ministers in August 2003. Working in parallel with the parliamentary consultation process, an interministerial committee compared all the existing syllabuses and filtered out what they had in common. In mathematics and the sciences, surprisingly, this amounted to 70–90 percent of the teaching content. In the "national subjects," the percentage was much lower, around 50 percent or less. The common core curriculum for history is almost exclusively limited to international developments and delegates the history of the different ethnic groups completely to the syllabuses of the cantons and the entities. In its present form it still fails to meet the requirements of the law, which states, firstly, that pupils must be offered a consistent education of a high quality, secondly, that changing from one school to another must become easier and, thirdly, that pupils must be encouraged to develop a positive relationship and commitment to Bosnia-Hercegovina. For this reason there is an urgent need to expand the common core curriculum.

Parallel to the inclusion of a comparative approach in the syllabuses, textbooks must also incorporate a perspective that takes the three ethnic groups into account. In 2004, on the basis of a proposal made by the OSCE, the education ministers established a new and independent commission of textbook experts for geography and history. Their task is to develop recommendations for future authors, to make possible a comparative representation that is balanced, multiperspectival, and based on different interpretations. Although there is much work ahead, some of it extremely challenging, the end goal of creating impartial curricula and textbooks needs to come about for any real healing to occur in the next generation.

In consultations at the Georg Eckert Institute, the education ministers somewhat unexpectedly proposed that the last decade of the twentieth century, and thus the war from 1992 to1995, should be covered in the classroom. However, under the prevailing circumstances this can hardly be achieved by subjecting pupils to a lecture, for example, on the siege of Sarajevo. Teachers must adopt a different approach to the topic, perhaps for instance modeled on an American organization, the Children's Movement to Creative Education (CMCE).[88] The CMCE brings together pupils from the three constituent ethnic groups living in Sarajevo and its surroundings and offers them various possibilities to express their own experiences of the war or to talk about the stories that they have heard in their own families. These can be expressed through artwork or drama, both of which play an important role. In a second phase these experiences undergo an objective analysis through the introduction of documents and reports from external sources, with the result that a new narrative is constructed by combining subjective experience with objective information. The aim of such a project is to enable the pupils to communicate about the war and not to teach an "authorized and exclusively valid" version.

As far as schools are concerned, teaching correct or sanitized history will not be enough. School textbooks and teacher training, while significant, are only one part of the task. Children, and older students and adults, will have to be helped to confront the narratives that have taken hold within themselves. Some ways this could be done are by getting students to undertake research of their own on debated topics; by discussing, and thus raising awareness about, ways that historical ideas are used in the present; or by putting students in safe but also challenging situations where they can discuss contested histories with others of differing points of view. The truly creative educators of the future will find many more approaches, and as they pursue them, they will join with many others in becoming the midwives of the new narrative.

Overall Solutions: A Truth and Reconciliation Commission?[89]

Truth and reconciliation may be helped by the creation of public commissions bringing together government, churches, NGOs, and other institutions of civil society to come to terms with the crimes of the 1990s, promoting memory, justice, and healing. The following section details the highs and lows of the truth and reconciliation commission (TRC) process in Serbia and Bosnia-Hercegovina.

In Serbia, the first key conference dealing with truth and reconciliation was organized in March 2000 by B92 and the Fund for an Open Society. Here, conference participants had an opportunity to meet with and learn about firsthand experiences of former members of truth commissions from Argentina, Chile, and

South Africa.[90] It was followed by another conference organized a month later by the Association for Independent Media (ANEM).[91] In October 2000, Koštunica became the first president of a new democratic Yugoslavia. At least nominally, the change of administration removed restrictions on public debate on the issues banned from the agenda during the Milošević regime, including the responsibility for war crimes committed in armed conflicts in neighboring countries and in Kosovo.

The only formal response in Serbia to the calls for truth and reconciliation was the establishment of the governmental nineteen-member Commission for Truth and Reconciliation in March 2001. The commission was not empowered to grant amnesties,[92] nor did it have power to subpoena witnesses.[93] It met very different responses from the start. There were claims that it was founded only under strong pressure from the West because ongoing foreign aid had been made conditional on progress in this area. Another view held that the commission might be an attempt to avoid responsibility for war crimes.[94] There was also public criticism of the decree-like manner in which Koštunica formed it.[95] A further problem was the fact that the commission was mandated to address events outside Serbia that were the results of actions by the Serbian people but it did not have members from outside Serbia.

One of the methods in which the commission was supposed to gather information was through public hearings with regard to the most significant events from the armed conflicts in Bosnia, Croatia, and Kosovo. The first hearing, focusing on Srebrenica, was initially scheduled for May 2002, then postponed for the fall of that year. The reason stated for the postponement was that the commission did not consider that there was enough trust on behalf of the Bosnian Muslim war victims' associations to come and testify in Serbia.[96] Eventually, Bosnian Muslim witnesses definitively refused to testify when they heard that Serb victims from the Srebrenica region would be invited to testify as well. The Srebrenica hearings— or any other hearings—never took place.[97] Some commissioners considered that state sponsorship of the commission rendered the independence of the institution questionable.[98] There was also a concern that the "state sponsored Truth Commission's reconciliation domains would not provide for the inter-ethnic reconciliation."[99] Scholars warned that the commission was monopolized, becoming "a political tool of only one political party and person (President Koštunica and his party)."[100] On the other hand, "legal, moral and material" support from the state was necessary to protect witnesses and make the process viable.[101]

A better form of dealing with the past came with a conference on truth and reconciliation titled "In Search of Truth and Responsibility: Towards a Democratic Future." This was organized by B92 in Belgrade on 18–20 May 2001 and gathered an impressive group of participants, including the presidents of Serbia and Yugoslavia. However, there were no participants from Kosovo or from Montenegro.[102] The conference ended with a set of recommendations for the TRC, including the extension of the commission to involve a higher number of representatives of minorities and religious communities.[103]

A TRC for Bosnia-Hercegovina

Following the Dayton Peace Agreement, the formation of a Bosnian TRC seemed moot.[104] This idea was not followed up by either the former Yugoslav authorities or any of the external powers involved. The first actual discussion on forming a TRC dates from July 1997 and was the outcome of the Roundtable on Justice and Reconciliation in Bosnia-Hercegovina.[105] Among other conclusions, participants agreed that the three existing separate commissions investigating war crimes might result in three conflicting versions of history and that a single, joint Bosnian truth commission should be formed. However, by 2000, little had been accomplished. In that year, around 100 participants, mainly from local NGOs, gathered at a roundtable on truth and reconciliation in Sarajevo to discuss how a commission should work.[106] This roundtable was followed by a similar conference in Banja Luka. Although both events were criticized for the lack of young people and women in the discussion, the Sarajevo roundtable resulted in the birth of the nongovernmental organization association Truth and Reconciliation.[107] More than a year after the association was founded, a draft law on the Truth and Reconciliation Commission in Bosnia-Hercegovina was prepared,[108] and it was expected that it would be submitted for adoption to the Parliamentary Assembly of Bosnia-Hercegovina in June 2001.[109] Although this did not come to pass, the principles of the draft law are sound and could lay the future basis for an effective TRC.

As envisaged in the draft law, the commission would examine events in Bosnia-Hercegovina and the former Yugoslavia from November 1990 to December 1995. It would examine inter alia the circumstances that produced ethnic mistrust and lack of understanding that resulted in unprecedented human rights violations; the political and moral responsibility of individuals, organizations, and institutions for the abuse of human rights; the role of the media, political parties, religious communities, international nongovernmental actors and other relevant sectors as determined by the TRC; and acts of individuals who refused to take part in the abuse of their neighbors.[110]

The commission would also attempt to establish the numbers "killed, wounded, missing, tortured, raped, imprisoned without a just cause, and forcefully displaced"; the numbers of religious objects destroyed or attacked; and the location of mass graves.[111] Unlike the majority of truth commissions so far, the Bosnian commission would not need to discover any hidden truths because the war in Bosnia was carefully followed by the media, nongovernmental organizations, and international institutions around the world. Instead, it would need to dispel the "multiple truths, each with a distinct ethnic coloration," where each ethnic group portrayed itself as a victim and denied any abuse committed by its own ranks.[112]

Special groups of victims required particular attention. One such group was the Women of Bosnia. Sexual violence was used as a weapon to punish the victim's entire ethnic group, and the extent of the gravity of that abuse is reflected in the ICTY judgment defining mass rape as genocide.[113] Abuses against Roma, who were also victimized during the wars, were also to be investigated.[114] The participation of minorities in the process would not merely pay lip service to political correctness but rather would pave the way to real state-building in Bosnia-Hercegovina.[115]

At the time of this writing, the TRC has yet to be created. Scholars have argued that, because the war in Bosnia-Hercegovina was resolved by outside military intervention and not by Bosnians themselves, it will be much more difficult for the people of this country to make a clean break with the past, which is a prerequisite for a successful TRC.[116] Much mistrust among Bosnia's different ethnic groups remains, and nationalist parties are still strong. Research has shown that there is no general agreement on whether or not it is a good time to launch an inquiry into the abuses of the recent past.[117] In that case, should not sooner be better than later? Team 11 recommends that the draft law be implemented to allow a TRC to be created in Bosnia-Hercegovina.

Further we recommend the continuation and extension of NGO efforts to document and come to terms with crimes committed in Bosnia-Hercegovina. The Association of Truth and Reconciliation continues to coordinate efforts to establish a truth commission. Outside organizations like the USIP have been assisting. At the same time the International Center for Transitional Justice has convened discussions with representatives from Bosnia-Hercegovina, Serbia, Montenegro, and Croatia to discuss further the development of truth commissions.

We also advocate increased cooperation with the ITCY. The Hague Tribunal is set to continue until 2008 with appeals allowed until 2010. Thereafter, the ICTY will hand over the remaining cases to domestic courts, which are currently unable to handle even routine matters, let alone war crimes trials.[118] So far cooperation has fallen short of the ideal, and as Team 10 has cogently outlined, the ICTY has not promoted reconciliation. The Tribunal is seen in most quarters as favoring the "other side" rather than one's own nation. Although Radovan Karadžić has recently been handed over for trial, it is our belief that continued pressure must be put on Serbia, Croatia, and Bosnia-Hercegovina to cooperate fully with the ICTY. Pressure is clearly producing results. Nevertheless, suspects like Ratko Mladić still remain at large. Organizations like NATO, the Office of the UN High Representative, as well as the OSCE can all play a more constructive role in rounding up suspected war criminals and obliging EU aspirants to cooperate more fully with the Tribunal.[119]

The Role of Mourning[120]

If justice is the outward means of addressing the ills of the past, mourning is its internal counterpart. The lingering memory of trauma suffered by individuals or groups does not fade with time. It can place burdens on individuals and become the chief source of meaning-making in groups. Collective responses to harms and injustices of the past are a frequent underlying contributor to the next battle or war. A society that wishes to move beyond its past must seek ways to lay that past to rest. Trauma psychologists advise against repeated discussions of the traumatizing event with recent victims of trauma.[121]

Although postconflict societies may be capable of addressing some aspects of their immediate past, timing is crucial. It seems clear that time has to pass before these societies will be able to talk about what happened and thus to begin to mourn in public as a group. It may not be possible to discuss the past until new political realities are in place. However, those who have been involved in a conflict have a need to talk about it, and people on all sides must find a way of listening to each other. Talking and listening are needed even if the traumatic event occurred several generations previously.[122]

What is being described here is a mourning process.[123] Mourning is a necessary reaction to loss and change. A group's inability to mourn can have political outcomes. If mourning can occur, the next generation creates a new version of the event, strengthening the group's self-esteem and moving into the future without having to carry the burden of the past.[124] Beyond talking about the past, societies can mourn their past by building monuments or museums, creating days of remembrance, or using music, art, theater, literature, or film creatively and collectively to remember.

Many argue that joint mourning processes are an essential prerequisite for effective peace negotiations. Montville speaks of an act of "letting go" that is needed on both sides, where victimizers accept responsibility for their acts, recognize injustices done, and ask forgiveness. Likewise, victims may also have been victimizers and may have to recognize their own acts of injustice.[125] Mourning is better understood as a continuing experience that extends well into the postconflict period. Thus, in addition to recommending the promotion of a more positive, balanced narrative; the reform of media and educational institutions; and the promotion of religious reconciliation, we conclude by also encouraging collective and individual mourning as a crucial alternative to resentment, hatred, and the desire for revenge.

Proposals[126]

Based on the sections presented in this report, we advance a series of recommendations extracted from the themes elaborated herein that can form the basis for further debate and discussion:

1. Narrate a new history with the following elements:

• Encourage a more positive balanced history of the pre-1990s wartime era, focused on experiences of cooperation, exchange, tolerance, and diversity.

• Encourage a narrative centered on the experiences of the common people during the 1990s conflict. This can deal with forms of victimization that are shared by groups not bound by ethnicity—for example, residents of a particular community, such as Sarajevo.

• Emphasize the history and struggles of peace movements and opposition parties and NGOs working for peace during the conflict and against the rise of nationalist extremism.

• Stress the victimization of women across ethnic boundaries and their special suffering, as well as their role in promoting peace and countering violence.

• Highlight the role of ordinary people and communities who stood up against violence and hatred and saved lives, not unlike Yad Vashem's commemoration of the "righteous" who saved Jews during the Holocaust. These and not the belligerents should be seen as the heroes of the successor wars.

• Signal the duplicity (where appropriate) of national governments, journalists, intellectuals, nationalist leaders, novelists and other cultural figures, as well as religious leaders. However, equally important will be signaling the contributions of some leaders who spoke out courageously against nationalist extremism and violence.

2. Promote more international support for and training of independent non-nationalist oriented media, media committed to fostering pluralism and a diversity of opinions. Such media must have the mandate to critically examine the past and present actions of their own governments. Part of the process of creating a freer and better informed civil society must also include support for alternative media like the Internet.

3. Encourage efforts of international and domestic religious leaders from all faiths to work toward reconciliation. This not only must include striving for cooperation and peace but must also involve exploration by religious leaders of what people of one's own nation have endured, both as victims and as perpetrators. The current political climate may not be favorable for such initiatives, but one can hope that in the future it will be. In the interim, special emphasis internationally should be placed on supporting the work of faith-based NGOs, which have played and continue to play a crucial role in promoting interfaith dialogue and reconciliation. Local initiatives like Bosnia's Interreligious Council should also be encouraged.

4. Continue the revision of school textbooks, with an effort to unify the curriculum across ethnic divides. New education can and should include the privileging of individual stories and experiences to which students can relate. As much as possible, history should be taught in an impartial and objective way. This will not be easy, but it must be an end goal of current efforts.

5. Continue international support for a Truth and Reconciliation Commission for Bosnia-Hercegovina and for similar TRCs in Serbia, Croatia, and the other warring republics. This can be a crucial step in allowing victims and perpetrators to speak publicly of their experiences. Information gathered in the process of such trials can create a crucial body of information for historians and the general public to draw upon. Further support from the UN, NATO, the EU, and the OSCE is crucial in rounding up war crimes suspects.

6. Emphasize the role of mourning for individual victims and families but recognize that this cannot be hurried.

7. Encourage international support for increased trade with the former republics of Yugoslavia, with a view to securing their entry as members into the European Union. This is well beyond the scope of this report, yet having a positive end goal in sight may help embittered individuals and communities to set aside their enmities and focus on a brighter future. It was to some degree instrumental in Hungary's, Poland's, and the Czech and Slovak republics' efforts in embracing a peaceful approach to post-Communist transition. As a precondition for entry into the EU, state governments must be obliged to issue apologies for the crimes committed in their name and to attempt to publicly engage with the legacies of the 1990s. This means stopping the propagation of myths of righteous victimization. It also means a concerted campaign in conjunction with media and educational institutions to investigate and lay the facts of the government's complicity in mass murder before the population.

Notes

1   As articulated by Keith Doubt, *Sociology after Bosnia and Kosovo: Recovering Justice* (New York: Rowman and Littlefield, 2000).

2   See for example Will Kimlicka, *Multicultural Citizenship: A Liberal Theory of Minority Rights* (Oxford: Oxford University Press, 1995); Andre Liebich, "Ethnic Minorities and Long-Term Implications of EU Enlargement," European University Institute Working Paper RSC No. 98/49 (December 1998).

3   Marina Blagojević, "Društvene karakateristike etničkih grupa: Kako meriti diskriminaciju?" in *Položaj manjina u Sveznoj Republici Jugoslaviji* (Belgrade: SANU, 1996), 653–666.

4   Z. Golubović, B. Kuzmanović, and M. Vasović, *Društveni karakter i društvene promene u svetlu nacionalnih sukoba* (Belgrade: Filip Višnjić, 1995), 192.

5   "Political Values and Needs of the Serbian Voters," unpublished study for the Democratic Party in Serbia.

6   I. Šiber, "War and the Changes in Social Distance toward the Ethnic Minorities in the Republic of Croatia," *Politička Misao* 5 (1997), 3–26.

7   S. Puhalo, *Etnička distanca građana Republike srpske i Federacije BiH prema narodima bivše SFRJ* (Banja Luka: Friedrich Ebert Stiftung, 2000).

8   M. Biro, V. Mihić, P. Milin, and S. Logar, "Did Socio-Political Changes in Serbia Change the Level of Authoritarianism and Ethnocentrism of Citizens? *Psihologija* 35 (2002), 37–47; M. Biro and H. M. Weinstein, "Societal Values, Beliefs, and Reconciliation in the Post-War Communities of Former Yugoslavia," Materials for the International Conference on Post-War Communities (Charlottesville: University of Virginia Press, 2002).

9   Puhalo, *Etnička distanca građana Republike srpske i Federacije BiH.*

10   M. Biro, S. Logar-Đurić, and S. Bogosavljević, "Politički uticaj državnih i nezavisnih televizija u Srbiji," *Nova srpska politička misao* 1–2 (2002), 227–242; M. Biro et al., "Did Socio-Political Changes in Serbia Change the Level of Authoritarianism and Ethnocentrism of Citizens?" 37–47.

11   Marina Blagojević, "Prebrojavanje mrtvih tela: viktimizacija kao samoostvarujuće proročanstvo," *Temida* 2 (2000), 5–10, and Marina Blagojević, "Conflict, Gender, and Identity: Conflict and Continuity in Serbia," in *Gender, Identitaet und kriegerischer Konflikt. Das Beispiel des ehemaligen Jugoslawien*, ed. R. Seifert (Münster: Lit-Verlag, 2004), 68–88.

12   Laurel E. Fletcher. "Violence and Social Repair: Rethinking the Contribution of Justice to Reconciliation," *Human Rights Quarterly* 24, no. 3 (August 2002), 604.

13   Jodi Halpern and Harvey Weinstein, "Rehumanizing the Other: Empathy and Reconciliation," *Human Rights Quarterly* 26, no. 3 (August 2004), 651.

14   Primary contributor: Marina Blagojević.

15   M. Blagojević, "War in Kosovo: A Victory for the Media?" in *Understanding the War in Kosovo*, ed. Florian Bieber and Z. Daskalovski (London: Frank Cass, 2003), 166–184.

16   M. Blagojević, "Even Better than the Real Thing," *Fightnight*, 357 (1997), 17–20.

17   Primary contributors: Margaret Smith and Mikloš Biro, with Petar Milin.

18   Vamik Volkan, "Bosnia-Herzegovina: Ancient Fuel of Modern Inferno," *Mind and Human Interaction* 7 (1996), 110. Volkan uses the term *enveloping* for this process of bundling and externalizing.

19   Ibid. The term *chosen trauma* is Volkan's.

20   Some new genetic research has proven that there might be something like genetically inherited trauma passed from mother to child. These types of discoveries are creating new challenges for social scientists.

21   John Mack, "The Psychodynamics of Victimization," in *The Psychodynamics of International Relationships*, ed. Vamik Volkan, Demetrios Julius, and Joseph Montville, vol. 1 (Lexington, MA: Lexington Books, 1991), 125.

22   M. Zotović, "Faktori rizika za pojavu mentalnog poremećaja kod dece i adolescenata nakon NATO bombardovanja" (doctoral dissertation, University of Novi Sad 2002).

23   This consisted of three criteria: (1) readiness to reconcile with the conflicted nationalities, (2) readiness to accept interstate cooperation, and (3) readiness to accept the presence of members of the opposing nationalities in eight different situations (in stores, parks, sporting events, sports teams, concerts, parties, schools/offices, and nongovernmental organizations).

24   L. Cherfas, Explaining Variation in Aversion to Germans and German Related Activities among Holocaust Survivors (bachelor's thesis, University of Pennsylvania, 2003).

25   M. Hewstone and R. J. Brown, "Contact Is Not Enough: An Intergroup Perspective on the 'Contact Hypothesis,'" in *Contact and Conflict in Intergroup Encounters*, ed. M. Hewstone and R. J. Brown (Oxford: Blackwell, 1986).

26   Leonard Thompson, *The Political Mythology of Apartheid* (New Haven: Yale University Press, 1985), 2.

27   Primary contributor: Marina Blagojević.

28   Svetlana Broz, *Good People in an Evil Time* (New York: Other Press, 2004).

29   Bojana Šušak, "An Alternative to War," in *The Road to War in Serbia: Trauma and Catharsis*, ed. Nebojša Popov (Budapest: CEU Press, 2000), 479–508; Marina Blagojević, "Belgrade's Protests, 1996–1997: From Women in the Movement to Women's Movement?" in *Women and Citizenship in Central and East Europe*, ed. J. Lukić, J.Regulska, and D. Zavirsek (London: Ashgate, 2006), 161–178.

30   *Kosovski čvor: drešiti ili seći?* (Belgrade: Geca Kon, 1990).

31   Šušak, "An Alternative to War," 481–485.

32   Ibid., 481.

33   Ibid., 482–483.

34   M. Blagojević, ed., *Ka vidljivoj ženskoj istoriji: ženski pokret u Beogradu 90-ih* (Belgrade: Centar za ženske studije, 1998).

35   Marina Blagojević, "Svakodnevica iz ženske perspektive: samožrtvovanje i beg u privatnost" (Everyday Life from Women's Perspective: Self-Sacrifice and Escape to Privacy), in *Drustvene promene i svakodnevica: Srbija početkom 90-ih*, ed. Silvano Bolčić (Belgrade: Institute for Sociological Research of Faculty of Philosophy), 1995; Marina Blagojević, *Fertilitet i roditeljstvo, Srbija 90-ih* (Belgrade: Institute for Sociological Research of Faculty of Philosophy, 1997), 211.

36   Blagojević, *Ka vidljivoj ženskoj istoriji: ženski pokret u Beogradu 90-ih Centar za ženske studije*.

37   Blagojević, "Belgrade's Protests, 1996–1997," 161–178.

38   Primary contributor: David MacDonald

39   Quoted in Jonathan Glover, *Humanity: A Moral History of the Twentieth Century* (London: Cape, 1999), 130.

40   Philip W. Lyon, "Words of War: Journalism in the Former Yugoslavia," *SAIS Review* 23, no. 2 (Summer–Fall 2003), 222–223.

41 Kemal Kurspahić, *Prime Time Crime: Balkan Media in War and Peace* (Washington, DC: United States Institute of Peace Press, 2003), 26–27.

42 Mark Thompson, *Forging War: The Media in Serbia, Croatia, Bosnia, and Hercegovina* (Luton, England: University of Luton Press, 2003), 59–60.

43 Ibid., 146, 152.

44 Vesna Pusić, "A Country by Any Other Name: Transition and Stability in Croatia and Yugoslavia," *East European Politics and Society* 6, no. 3 (1992), 138–142, 176, 177, 259.

45 Pusić, "A Country by Any Other Name.

46 Ivančić, "Dossier."

47 Suzana Jasić, "Monitoring the Vote in Croatia," *Journal of Democracy* 11, no. 4 (October 2000), 160.

48 Lyon, "Words of War," 223.

49 Ibid., 224.

50 See http://www.serbia-info.com/enc/history/breakup.html and http://www.serbia-info.com/enc/history/worldwar.html (accessed 7 November 2006).

51 Dević, "War Guilt and Responsibility: The Case of Serbia," http://programs.ssrc.org/gsc/gsc_quarterly/newsletter8/content/devic (accessed 7 November 2006).

52 http://www.b92.net/english (accessed 7 November 2006).

53 Jack Snyder, *From Voting to Violence* (New York: Norton, 2000), 336.

54 Ibid., 226.

55 IWPR, "The Role of the Institute for War and Peace Reporting," http://www.iwpr.net/index.pl?development/resources/training_editorialpolicyandprocess.html (accessed 7 November 2006).

56 http://www.iwpr.net/index.pl?archive/bcr3/bcr3_200504_hr_2_eng.txt (accessed 7 November 2006). Joe Burton contributed this paragraph to the chapter.

57 "Media for Democracy in South-Eastern Europe," *IFJ*, 21 March 2003. http://www.ifj.org/default.asp?index=283&Language=EN (accessed 7 November 2006).

58 "Serbian Propaganda: A Closer Look," Media Diversity Institute, http://www.media-diversity.org/articles_publications/Serbian%20Propaganda%20A%20Closer%20Look.htm (accessed 7 November 2006).

59 M. Biro, A. Logar-Djurić, S. Bogosavljević, "Politički uticaj državnih i nezavisnih televizija u Srbiji," *Nova srpska politička misao* 1–2 (2000), 227–242.

60 Primary contributors: Tanja Perić and Richard Oloffson.

61 Dubravka Valić-Nedeljković, "Verski mediji i verski sadržaji u laičkim medijima," Drugi međunarodni skup saradnja između zemalja naslednica bivše Jugoslavije u oblastima društvenih nauka i culture kao činilac izgradnje civilnog društva (Subotica, 10–12 May 2002).

62 "Patrijarh Pavle primio kardinala Kaspera," Radio Station B92, Belgrade, 12 May 2002.

63 "Patrijarh u uzvratnu posetu primio Franca Rodea, nadbiskupa ljubljanskog," Informative Service of the Serbian Orthodox Church, Belgrade, 22 November 2000.

64 "Nadbiskup Hočevar osveštao kamen temeljac crkve u Smederevu," Radio Station B92, Belgrade, 7 April 2002.

65 "Djindjić čestitao Kurban-Bajram" and "Djukanović čestitao Kurban-Bajram," Radio Station B92, Belgrade, 21 February 2002.

66 Novak A. Popović, *Da li smo tolerantni: anketno istraživanje o pitanjima problema tolerancije u Srbiji i Crnoj Gori* (Belgrade, 2001).

67 See "Criminal Complaint for Ethnically Motivated Abuse," Humanitarian Law Center, Belgrade, 17 April 2002. http://www.hlc.org.yu/english/minorities/mminorities3.htm (accessed 7 November 2006).

68 See "Victim of Police Abuse Awarded Only 15,000 Dinars," Humanitarian Law Center, Belgrade, 27 August 2002. http://www.hlc.org.yu/english/torture/torture2.htm (accessed 7 November 2006).

69 Fadil Murati, chief imam of the Islamic community in Vojvodina, interview by Tatjana Perić, Novi Sad, 18 July 2002.

70 "Protection, Promotion and Monitoring of Human Rights in the Republic of Srpska, Period: 1 April–30 June 2002," Helsinki Committee for Human Rights in Republika Srpska, Bijeljina, July 2002. Similarly, a newly built mosque in the village of Ključ near Gacko was dynamited on 22 September 2002. "Srušena džamija u Ključu kod Gacka" and "Osuda rušenja džamije," Radio Station B92, Belgrade, 22 September 2002.

71 "Serbian Orthodox Church Condemns Anti-Semitic Comments by Retired Priest," Radio Free Europe/Radio Liberty, Prague, 6 February 2002.

72 The Holy Synod of the Serbian Orthodox Church, Belgrade, 5 February 2002.

73 According to Professor Milan Vukomanović in a seminar on religion and tolerance organized by the Novi Sad School of Journalism, Novi Sad, 29 May 2002.

74 "Predstavnici Medjureligijskog centra kod Patrijarha," Informative Service of the Serbian Orthodox Church, Belgrade, 16 December 2000.

75 More information on this conference is available at the foundation's Web site: http://www.kas-bg.org (7 November 2006) "Ministar napustio skup," *Blic*; "Oštar verbalni obračun," *Danas*; "Kovačević-Vučo oterala saveznog sekretara vera," *Nacional*; "Žestoko o toleranciji," *Politika*; "Šijaković napustio skup," *Politika Ekspres*; "Varnice oko veronauke," *Večernje novosti*, all published in Belgrade, 28 February 2002.

76 "Stanovnici Srbije najviše veruju VJ, SPC i Koštunici," Radio Station B92, Belgrade, 30 April 2002.

77 Informative Service of the Serbian Orthodox Church, Communiqué from the regular session of the Holy Assembly of Bishops of the Serbian Orthodox Church held in Belgrade from 23 May to 31 May 2002, Belgrade, 1 June 2002.

78 Belgrade Declaration. http://www.yahoo.com/group/balkans/message/1788 (accessed 7 November 2006).

79 Brussels Declaration (in Serbian). http://www.spc.org.yu/Vesti/12/31-12-01_c1.htm (accessed 7 November 2006).

80 David Smock, "Divine Intervention: Regional Reconciliation through Faith," *Religion* 25, no. 4 (Winter 2004). http://hir.harvard.edu/articles/1190/ (accessed 7 November 2006).

81 Ibid.

82 Religion and Peacemaking (USIP). http://www.usip.org/religionpeace/about.html (accessed 7 November 2006).

83 Nicole Lindstrom, "European Integration and Ethnic Reconciliation in Croatia and Serbia," Wilson Center (December 2003). http://www.wilsoncenter.org/topics/pubs/MR295Lindstrom.doc (accessed 7 November 2006).

84 Primary contributor: Falk Pingel.

85 Miha Kovac and Mojca Kovac Sebart, "Textbooks at War: A Few Notes on Textbook Publishing in Former Yugoslavia and Other Communist Countries," *Paradigm* 2, no. 6 (2002), 30–34.

86   Branislava Baranović, *Education for Peace: A Conflict Resolution Initiative for Post-War Bosnia.* See http://www.osservatoriobalcani.org/article/articleview/156/1/42/ (accessed 17 October 2008).

87   Ibid., 1999; Heike Karge, "Geschichtsbilder im postjugoslawischen Raum: Konzeptionen in Geschichtslehrbüchern am Beispiel von Selbst- und Nachbarschaftswahrnehmung," *Internationale Schulbuchforschung* 21, no. 4 (1999), 315–337.

88   www.childrensmovement.org (accessed November 2006).

89   Primary contributors: Tanja Perić and David MacDonald.

90   Biljana Vasić and Tamara Skroza, "Povodom ideje da se formira Komisija za istinu: Drmanje tihe većine," *Vreme*, 23 November 2000.

91   Ibid.

92   Alex Boraine, "Reconciliation in the Balkans?" *New York Times*, 22 April 2001.

93   "O komisiji za istinu i pomirenje," Radio Station B92, 28 March 2001.

94   Jelena Stanić, "Istina, odgovornost i krivica," *Republika* 262 (2001).

95   "Svrha i dometi Komisije za istinu i pomirenje," *Dani*, 19 May 2001.

96   "Organizovaćemo javna svedočenja o zločinima," *Blic*, 22 April 2002.

97   "Komisija za istinu i pomirenje: Iluzija ili stvarnost," Radio Station B92, 18 February 2003.

98   "Krivi i huškači," Radio Station B92, 12 April 2001.

99   Nebojša Bjelaković, "Reconciliation, Truth, and Justice in the Post-Yugoslav States," *Southeast European Politics* 3 (2002), 166.

100 Vesna Nikolić-Ristanović, "Truth, Reconciliation, and Victims in Serbia: The Process So Far," lecture given at the Ninth International Symposium on Victimology, Stellenbosch, South Africa, 13–18 July 2003.

101 Veran Matić, "Odbacivanje istine," *Reč*, 8 June 2001.

102 Jelena Stanić, "Istina, odgovornost i krivica," *Republika* 262, (2001).

103 The full text of recommendations in Serbian can be accessed at http://www.b92.net/trr/2001/preporuke.html (accessed November 2006).

104 http://www.b92.net/trr/2001/preporuke.html (accessed November 2006).

105 "Cooperation Agreements in Bosnia," USIP, August 1997.

106 Alan L. Heil Jr., "A Truth and Reconciliation Commission for Bosnia and Herzegovina?" *Washington Report on Middle East Affairs,* June 2000. See http://www.wrmea.com/archives/June_2000/0006026.html (accessed 17 October 2008).

107 Tanja Topić, "Kako do pomirenja?" *AIM*, 24 (July 2000). Information available on the association's Web site, http://www.angelfire.com/bc2/kip (accessed 17 October 2008).

108 H. Arifagić, "Istina i pomirenje u BiH: Došlo vrijeme da se ne lažemo," *Oslobodjenje*, 12 May 2001.

109 Neil J. Kritz and Jakob Finci, "Bosnia Needs a Truth Commission," Institute for War and Peace Reporting, 21–26 May 2001.

110 Draft law, Article 6, The Mandate of the TRC.

111 Ibid.

112 Neil J. Kritz and Jakob Finci, "A Truth and Reconciliation Commission in Bosnia and Herzegovina: An Idea Whose Time Has Come," Preconference Internet Forum on Strategies for Resolving Inter-Ethnic Conflicts in the South Eastern Europe (26 January 2001). Available at http://www2.arnes.si/~ljinv16/pakt/inputs/004.htm. (accessed 7 November 2006).

113 See Judgment: The Prosecutor v. Mućić et al., IT-96-21, 8 April 2003. http://www.un.org/icty/Supplement/supp41-e/mucic.htm (accessed 7 November 2006).

114 For more information on the sufferings of Roma in this conflict, see http://www.errc. org/cikk.php?cikk=112 (accessed 7 November 2006).

115 Rusmir Mahmutćehajić, *The Denial of Bosnia* (University Park, PA: Pennsylvania State University Press, 2000), 87.

116 Gregory Gisvold, "A Truth Commission for Bosnia and Herzegovina? Anticipating the Debate," in *Post-War Protection of Human Rights in Bosnia and Herzegovina*, ed. Michael O'Flaherty and Gregory Gisvold (The Hague: Martinus Nijhoff Publishers, 1998), 241–261.

117 Damir Huremović, ed., "Suočavanje s prošlošću; Nacionalni izvještaj za Bosnu i Hercegovinu," *Quaker Peace and Social Witness*, July–August 2003.

118 K. Zoglin, "The Future of War Crimes Prosecutions in the Former Yugoslavia: Accountability or Junk Justice?" *Human Rights Quarterly* 27, no. 1 (2005), 41.

119 "War Criminals in Bosnia's Republika Srpska: Who Are the People in Your Neighbourhood?" *Europe Report*, 103 (2 November 2000). http://www.crisisgroup.org/home/ index.cfm?l=1&id=1518 (accessed 7 November 2006).

120 Primary contributor: Margaret Smith.

121 For a discussion of the way reminders of traumatic experience may bring back the traumatization, see M. J. Horowitz, *Stress Response Syndromes* (New York: Jason Aronson, 1976).

122 John Mack, "The Psychodynamics of Victimization," in *The Psychodynamics of International Relationships*, ed. Vamik Volkan, Demetrios Julius, and Joseph Montville, vol. 1 (Lexington, MA: Lexington Books, 1991), 126.

123 Vamik Volkan, "Psychoanalytic Aspects of Ethnic Conflicts," in *Conflict and Peacemaking in Multiethnic Societies*, ed. Joseph Montville (New York: Lexington Books, 1991) 89.

124 Ibid., 89–90.

125 Joseph Montville, "Epilogue: The Human Factor Revisited," in Montville, *Conflict and Peacemaking in Multiethnic Societies*, 538–540.

126 Primary contributor: David MacDonald.

ROSTERS

The following roster identifies all scholars who joined the SI over the past decade and provided a valid email address through which they could monitor and contribute to all project correspondence. Affiliation afforded them the right to participate at any stage of the process of organizing, researching, writing, critiquing and revising each of the eleven team reports. Nearly half of the scholars listed here (and a dozen others who provided no email address) chose not to participate in this process. Hence, this comprehensive roster represents *access* to project deliberations, without implying participation or interaction.

For the sake of clarity, the list employs **boldface** to identify those scholars who contributed materially to the preparation of the volume, whether by (1) participating in a team or plenary meeting, (2) conducting interviews or other research, (3) contributing text to any of the successive drafts or to other SI-commissioned publications, or (4) offering substantive comment/criticism at any stage of the process. Neither access nor active participation implies that individual scholars endorse the findings of those research teams to which they did not belong.

The roster also specifies the year during which each scholar joined and, in some cases, left the project, whether through the interruption of reliable email access, resignation, or death. Team leaders are identified with an asterisk (*). Country designations reflect solely the preferences expressed by each individual scholar and do not necessarily represent their political views or those of the directors, administrative staff, or project as a whole.

ALBANIA
Elez Biberaj 03-
Ferit Duka 03-
Valentina Duka* 03-
Piro Misha 01-03

Ana Lalaj 07-
Remzi Lani 01-

AUSTRALIA
Aleksandar Pavković 04-08

AUSTRIA
Raphael Draschtak 02-
Horst Haselsteiner 01-
Georg Kastner 03-
Paul Leifer 04-
Rüdiger Malli 01-
Josef Marko 04-
Wolfgang Petritsch 03-
Ernest Plivac 04-
Iwan Sokolowsky 02-
Branislava Stankov 01-08†
Arnold Suppan 01-

BOSNIA
Vlado Azinović 01-
Edina Bećirević 02-
Boro Bronza 04-
Nejra Čengić 02-
Ismet Dizdarević 03-
Vjekoslav Domljan 06-
Sead Fetahagić 06-
Sačir Filandra 04-
Darko Gavrilović* 03-
Ilijas Hadžibegović 04-
Edin Hajdarpašić 01-04
Olja Hočevar 03-
Dževad Juzbašić 04-
Husnija Kamberović 02-
Suada Kapić 04-
Dubravko Lovrenović 01-
Rusmir Mahmutćehajić 03-
Davor Marko 06-
Nedjo Miličević 01-02
Asim Mujkić 02-
Marko Oršolić 07-
Sabina Pstrocki 06-
Edin Radušić 04-
Ermin Sarajlija 02
Dzemal Sokolović 03-07
Mirsad Tokača 04-
Bisera Turković 02-
Edin Veladžić 04-
Ugo Vlaisavljević 03-
Željko Vukadinović 05-
Miodrag Živanović 05-

BULGARIA
Rumen Stefanov 07-

CANADA
Mark Biondich 03-
Lenard Cohen 01-04
Dejan Guzina 03-
Renéo Lukić 02-
David MacDonald* 04-
Stan Markotich 02-
Dalibor Mišina 03-
Wayne Nelles 02-07
Mariella Pandolfi 01-
Nancy Partner 06-

CROATIA
Nikica Barić 03-05
Albert Bing 02-
Branka Boban 03-05
Dunja Bonacci 03-
Mirjana Domini 03-
Hrvoje Glavać 03-
Ivo Goldstein 08-
Igor Graovac 02-
Vesna Ivanović 03-
Tvrtko Jakovina 02-
Vjeran Katunarić 02-
Davorka Matić 02-
Maja Miljković 03-05
Zoran Oklopčić 03-
Drago Roksandić* 01-
Tonći Šitin 03-
Robert Skenderović 03-05
Dubravka Ugrešić 02-
Radovan Vukadinović 02-
Ozren Žunec* 02-

DENMARK
Ana Dević 01-

EGYPT
Ivan Iveković 02-

ESTONIA
Kristiina Lilleorg 07-

FRANCE
Catherine Horel 02-
Rada Iveković 02-
Jacques Semelin 05-

GERMANY
Wolf Behschnitt 03-
Thomas Bremer 01-
Marie-Janine Calic* 04-
Sabine Meijvogel-Volk 02-
Dunja Melčić 03-
Falk Pingel 05-
S. Schwandner-Sievers 02-
Ludwig Steindorff 04-08
Stefan Troebst 01-
Tobias Vogel 02-

GREECE
Fotini Bellou 02-

HUNGARY
Gábor Hamza 04-
Martha Fazekas 04-
Georg Schöpflin 02-

ISRAEL
Orli Fridman 03-

ITALY
Stefano Bianchini 01-
Daniele Conversi 03-
Anna DiLellio 02-07
Egidio Ivetić 03-
Francesco Privitera 01-
Helena Zdravković 06-

KOSOVO
Ylber Bajraktari 03-
Ylli Bajraktari 06-
Anton Berisha 03-
Isuf Berisha 02-
Isa Blumi 02
Bejtullah Destani 03-
Enver Hasani 02-
Enver Hoxhaj 02-03
Ylber Hysa 03-

Leon Malazogu 02-
Shkëlzen Maliqi 03-
Luigj Ndou 04-
Besnik Pula 02-
Blerim Reka 03-

LUXEMBOURG
Florian Bieber 02-

MACEDONIA
Dalibor Jovanovski 07-
Dimitar Mirčev 04-
Aurora Ndrio 04-
Vladimir Ortakovski 01-
Boban Petrovski 01-

MONTENEGRO
Srdja Pavlović 01-
Šerbo Rastoder 02-
Srdjan Vukadinović 02-

NETHERLANDS
Robert De Graaff 02-
Ger Duijzings 01-05
Ernst Jan Hogendoorn 06-
Jan Willem Honig 01-
Selma Leydesdorff 04-
Cees Wiebes 02-

NEW ZEALAND
Joe Burton 05-

NORWAY
Mats Berdal 01-
Tone Bringa 03-
Gorana Ognjenović 04-
Sabrina Ramet 02-08

ROMANIA
Constantin Iordachi 03-

SERBIA
Igor Bandović 03-
Mile Bjelajac* 01-
Mikloš Biro 01-
Marina Blagojević* 02-

Silvano Bolčić 01-
Judit Deli 04-
Ljubiša Despotović 07-
Vojin Dimitrijević* 02-
Svetlana Djurdjević-Lukić 03-
Aleksandar Fira 05-
Ranka Gašić 02-
Dinko Gruhonjić 06-
Miroslav Hadžić* 02-
Dušan Janjić* 03-
Djokica Jovanović 02-
Emil Kerenji 02-
Ranko Končar 01-
Miloš Ković 03-
Todor Kuljić 03-
Milenko Marković 05-
Predrag Marković 01-
Jelena Milojković-Djurić 06-
Gojko Mišković 00-
Andrej Mitrović 01-02
Momčilo Mitrović* 02-
Momčilo Pavlović* 01-
Tatjana Perić 04-
Latinka Perović* 01-
Toni Petković 03-
Aleksandra Petrović 03-
Vladimir Petrović 04-
Milan Podunavac 02-04
Dragan Popadić 04-
Milenko Popović 02-06
Nenad Popovič 02-
Olga Popović-Obradović 02-07†
Branka Prpa 01-
Milan Ristović 01-
Petar Rokai 01-
Nikola Samardžić 02-
Obrad Savić 02-
Bogoljub Savin 01-
Milan Simić 07-
Predrag Simić 04-
Ana Trbovich 06-
Ljubinka Trgovčević 01-
Tanja Tubić 04-
Vatroslav Vekarić 02-
Lazar Vrkatić 01-07†
Radina Vučetić 02-

Sretan Vujović 02-
Ivan Zverzhanovski 02-

SLOVAKIA
Denisa Kostovicova 02-05

SLOVENIA
Anton Bebler 02-
Danica Fink-Hafner 04-
Matjaž Klemenčič* 01-
Vladimir Klemenčič 02-
Miran Komac 03-
Kristof Jacek Kozac 03-
Oto Luthar 03-
Tomaz Mastnak 04-
Mitja Žagar 01-
Jernej Zupančič 04-

SWEDEN
Tomislav Dulić 06-

SWITZERLAND
Urs Altermatt 01-
Goran Jovanović 01-03

UKRAINE
Victor Bezruchenko 02-
Valentin Yakushik 06-

UNITED KINGDOM
Kathleen Adams 07-
John Allcock 01-
Neven Andjelić 07-
Christopher Bennett 01-
Sumantra Bose 01-
Wendy Bracewell 01-
Cathie Carmichael 02-
Gemma Colantes Celador 02-
David Chandler 02-
Dejan Djokić 02-
Jasna Dragović-Soso 01-04
Mark Etherington 03-
James Gow* 01-
Vidan Hadži-Vidanović 07-
Zlatko Hadžidedić 03-06
Marko Attila Hoare 03-

Dejan Jović 01-
Michael Palairet 03-
Vanessa Pupavac 02-06
Anna Sheftel 06-
Brendan Simms 03-
Nebojša Vladisavljević 02-

UNITED STATES
Milan Andrejevich 02-
Robert Austin 02-05
Karl Bahm 05-
Elazar Barkan 05-
Doris Bergen 03-
Mietek Boduszynski 02-05
Melissa Bokovoy* 01-
Keith Brown 01-
Audrey Helfant Budding 01-
Janusz Bugajski 05-
Steven Burg 01-05
John Cerone 03-
Norman Cigar 01-02
Rory Conces 04-
John Cox 03-
István Deak 01-
Dušan Djordjevich 01-05
Robert Donia 01-
Keith Doubt 02-
Thomas Emmert 00-
Theodore Fiedler 08-
Jozef Figa 04-
John Fine 01-
Bernd Fischer 01-
Jennifer Foray 06-
Francine Friedman 01-
Chip Gagnon 02-
Eric Gordy 01-
Michael Haltzel 05-
James Hasik 02-
Kimberley Harris 06-
Elissa Helms 02-
Brian Hodson 03-06†
Charles Ingrao* 97-
A. Ross Johnson 01-
Sally Kent 02-
Tijana Krstić 05-
Alan Kuperman 07-

James Lyon 01-
Vladimir Matić 02-
Julie Mertus* 01-
Sasha Miličević 04-
Nicholas Miller 01-
Alexander Mirescu 04-
Julie Mostov 02-
Ines Murzaku 04-
Norman Naimark 02-
Lara Nettelfield 03-
Lana Obradović 06-
Richard Oloffson 04-06
Steven Oluic 07-
Diane Orentlicher 02-
David Ost 04-
Nicholas Pano 04-
Nancy Partner 06-
Vjeran Pavlaković 05-
Lisa Penn 06-
Trudy Peterson 06-
Paula Pickering 02-
Michael Rip 02-
Karl Roider 01-
Benjamin Rusek 03-
Dennison Rusinow 01-04†
Mary Rusinow 01-
James Sadkovich 02-05
Marija Sajkas 07-
Louis Sell 01-
Paul Shoup 01-
Cynthia Simmons 02-
Margaret Smith 03-
Tammy Ann Smith 02-
Gale Stokes 98-
John Treadway 01-
Frances Trix 04-
Milan Vego 02-
Jason Vuić 02-
Andrew Wachtel* 01-
Ruth Wedgwood 02-
Mark Wheeler 01-
Paul Williams 02-
Nancy Wingfield 05-
Maryanne Yerkes 01-
Kathleen Young 05-

ADMINISTRATIVE STAFF
(2001-2007)

Advisory Board: Mile Bjelajac, Matjaž Klemenčič, Drago Roksandić, Gale Stokes

Regional Liaisons: Gojko Mišković (2001-05) / Milan Djukić (2006-07)

Regional Staff:	Academic Liaisons	Media Liaisons
Banja Luka:	Darko Gavrilović	Miloš Šolaja / Nenad Novaković
Belgrade:	Dušan Janjić	Svetlana Djurdjević-Lukić / Danica Vučenić
Ljubljana:	Matjaz Klemenčič	Stanislav Kočutar
Novi Sad:		Dinko Gruhonjić
Podgorica:		Srdjan Darmanović
Priština:	Ylber Hysa	Ylber Hysa
Sarajevo:	Mirsad Tokača	Nidžara Ahmetašević
Skopje:		Sašo Ordanoski
Zagreb:	Drago Roksandić	Stojan Obradović

Graduate Assistants: Ron Geier, Lisa Penn, Lana Obradović, Richard Oloffson, Christopher Snively

CONFERENCES-SPONSORS

September 2001: Morović, Serbia – University of Novi Sad
co-organizers: Ministry of Science, Republic of Serbia
Vojvodina Assembly

July 2002: Sarajevo, Bosnia – United Nations Mission in Bosnia & Hercegovina (UNMiBH)
co-organizers: Citizens' Pact for Southeastern Europe (Novi Sad)
Open Society Institute (Belgrade & Priština, FRY)
Konrad-Adenauer-Stiftung

September 2003: Edmonton, Canada – Canadian Centre for Austrian & Central European Studies

December 2004: Budapest, Hungary – Andrássy University
Skopje, Macedonia – Center for Interethnic Tolerance & Refugees
co-organizers: U.S. Institute of Peace
Vojvodina Assembly

April 2005: Washington, DC – U.S. Institute of Peace
co-organizer: National Endowment for Democracy
January 2006: Philadelphia – American Historical Association

June 2007: Salzburg – Salzburg Global Seminar/Institute for Historical Justice & Reconciliation

INDEX